THOMAS CHALMERS

GIFT OF
SCOTTISH ARTS COUNCIL

GIFT OF
SCOTTISH ARTS COUNCIL

Thomas Chalmers and the Godly Commonwealth in Scotland

CF
85.241
092
CHA

STEWART J. BROWN

WITHDRAWN
from
STIRLING UNIVERSITY LIBRARY

OXFORD UNIVERSITY PRESS

1982

31059694

194

Oxford University Press, Walton Street, Oxford OX2 6DP

London Glasgow New York Toronto
Delhi Bombay Calcutta Madras Karachi
Kuala Lumpur Singapore Hong Kong Tokyo
Nairobi Dar es Salaam Cape Town
Melbourne Auckland
and associates in
Beirut Berlin Ibadan Mexico City Nicosia

Published in the United States by
Oxford University Press, New York

© Stewart J. Brown 1982

The publisher acknowledges the financial assistance of the Scottish
Arts Council in the publication of this volume.

All rights reserved. No part of this publication may be reproduced,
stored in a retrieval system, or transmitted, in any form or by any means,
electronic, mechanical, photocopying, recording, or otherwise, without
the prior permission of Oxford University Press

British Library Cataloguing in Publication Data
Brown, Stewart J.
  Thomas Chalmers and the godly commonwealth in
  Scotland.
  1. Chalmers, Thomas   2. Free Church of
  Scotland-Biography
  I. Title
  285'.2'0924   BX9225.C4
  ISBN 0-19-213114-1

Library of Congress Cataloging in Publication Data
Brown, Stewart J. (Stewart Jay), 1951-
  Thomas Chalmers and the godly commonwealth in
  Scotland.

  Bibliography: p.
  Includes index.
  1. Chalmers, Thomas, 1780-1847.   2. Free Church
  of Scotland--Clergy--Biography.   3. Clergy--Scot-
  land--Biography.   4. Social reformers--Scotland--
  Biography.   I. Title.
  BX9225. C4B78 1983   285'.23 [B]   82-8219
  ISBN 0-19-213114-1

Typeset by DMB (Typesetting), Oxford
and printed in Great Britain
at the University Press, Oxford
by Eric Buckley
Printer to the University

TO
TERI

ACKNOWLEDGEMENTS

I have incurred many debts in preparing this work, of which I can unfortunately name but a small portion. The bulk of my research was supported by a two-year Fulbright-Hays grant awarded by the United States-United Kingdom Educational Commission, and the final stages of writing were supported by a grant from the Giles-Whiting Foundation for the Humanities. Both the author and the publisher also gratefully acknowledge the Scottish Arts Council for their generous financial assistance in the publication of this volume.

I wish to express my appreciation to Professors William H. McNeill, Jerald C. Brauer, and Martin E. Marty of the University of Chicago, and to Professors Thomas William Heyck and Garry Wills of Northwestern University, who read the whole of the book in typescript and were generous with their advice and suggestions. The Revd Professor A. C. Cheyne of Edinburgh University was a most gracious friend and adviser during my two years of affiliation with that University, which I number among the happiest of my life.

Mr Peter J. Spicer and the Delegates and staff of Oxford University Press extended their confidence, their help, and their patience. I would also like to convey special thanks to Mr J. V. Howard and Mrs Margot Butt of New College Library at Edinburgh University, and to Mr Paul G. Anderson, the Revd Dr James Bulloch, Mrs. E. O. A. Checkland, and the Revd Eric Craig, Mr Iain F. Maciver, the Revd Ian Muirhead, the Revd Dr W. J. Roxborough, the Revd Friedhelm Voges, and Mr Donald J. Withrington. The Earl of Elgin and the Rt. Hon. Baron Moncrieff of Tuliebole kindly permitted me to view and cite from the private collections of family papers in their possession, and the Earl of Dalhousie allowed me to cite from his private papers located at the Scottish Records Office. The staffs of numerous research libraries in Scotland, England, and the United States were unfailing in their courtesy and assistance. The Scottish Church History Society permitted me to include portions of my article, 'The Disruption and Urban Poverty: Thomas Chalmers and the West Port Operation in Edinburgh', which previously appeared in their *Records*. Mrs Marion E. Brown generously typed the manuscript through its successive drafts and provided encouragement throughout the writing process.

I cannot adequately express my gratitude to my mentor, Professor Emmet Larkin of the University of Chicago, who first directed my attention to the Scottish national experience and its fundamental importance to an understanding of British history. An exacting critic, Professor Larkin has also been an inspiring teacher and generous friend.

Nor can I adequately express my appreciation to my wife, Teri Hopkins-Brown, who shared with me every stage in the preparation of this work, the frustrations perhaps more than the joys. Her confidence and commitment made this book possible.

Any errors, either of fact or interpretation, are of course my own.

The University of Georgia   STEWART J. BROWN

CONTENTS

LIST OF ILLUSTRATIONS

All illustrations are reproduced by courtesy of the New College Library, University of Edinburgh. Numbers 1 and 3-7 are reproductions from the series of calotype portraits made on the occasion of the Disruption of 1843 by David Octavius Hill (1802-70), the celebrated Scottish pioneer in photography. The author is especially indebted to Mr J. V. Howard and the New College Library staff for introducing him to their rare D. O. Hill collection, and for generously providing assistance in the production of the prints.

INTRODUCTION

I

Thomas Chalmers's vision and influence touched nearly every aspect of nineteenth-century Scottish society. As a parish minister, educator, and ecclesiastical reformer within the Established Church of Scotland, he developed innovative programmes for the parish ministry—in the areas of poor relief, popular education, and household visitations—which were designed to recover a sense of individual and communal responsibility, particularly in the impoverished working-class districts of the expanding cities. As an impassioned Evangelical preacher and orator, he created a personal ascendancy within the Church of Scotland during the turbulent 1830s, and led his Church in a national campaign to achieve his Christian social ideal. As an author of numerous works in social theory, he exercised immense influence upon the Established Churches of England and Ireland, as well as Scotland, and achieved an international reputation as an advocate of national religious Establishments as the most efficient, indeed the only sufficient, force for substantial social reform.

And yet in 1843, at the height of his influence, Chalmers broke up the Scottish Establishment. After a bitter struggle with the civil courts and the Westminster Parliament, he led more than a third of the clergy and nearly half the membership out of the Church of Scotland in protest against what he regarded as the British State's attempt to crush the Church's spiritual independence. He thus abandoned the Establishment, which he had devoted his lifetime to defending as the only hope for the elevation of Scottish society. The Disruption of the Church of Scotland ultimately marked the collapse of Chalmers's hopes for the realization of his Christian social ideal. It was the decisive event in the history of nineteenth-century Scotland, and his role in it remains a subject of controversy. Many honour him as the champion of the Church's spiritual independence, who had been willing to sacrifice his most cherished hopes and a lifetime of effort for the struggle to preserve the Church's fundamental integrity against the overbearing power of the British State. For others, he is the 'evil genius' of nineteenth-century Scotland, whose personal ambition and drive to create an ecclesiastical despotism destroyed the unity of the Church of Scotland, embittered Scottish religious life for nearly a century, and permanently eroded the social influence of Christianity in Scotland.

Both of these conflicting viewpoints fail either to provide a balanced interpretation or to focus upon the principal concerns of Chalmers's life and career, which were far more complex than has hitherto been recognized. The Disruption of 1843 was undoubtedly the most dramatic event of his career. His role in this upheaval, however, must be considered in the context of his larger campaign for comprehensive social reform and of his vision of the ideal society. Chalmers's life was one of astonishing achievement and bitter disappointment: neither has been adequately understood. 🍂

II

Within a few years of Chalmers's death in 1847, his son-in-law, William Hanna, produced the four-volume *Memoirs of Dr. Chalmers*, published between 1849 and 1852. A labour of love, the work represents one of the better Victorian religious biographies, written in often eloquent prose and preserving large quantities of material from Chalmers's correspondence and private papers. None the less, the work is also not without serious weaknesses. An Evangelical clergyman, who had left the Church of Scotland with Chalmers at the Disruption of 1843, Hanna had been an active participant in many of his father-in-law's most bitter controversies. These controversies were still heated when Hanna wrote the biography, and he not unnaturally wished to portray his father-in-law in the most favourable light. The *Memoirs*, then, were intended as both a warm defence of Chalmers's actions and a permanent monument to the memory of an illustrious representative of Hanna's family and Church. For this purpose, Hanna did not shrink from altering quotations, suppressing evidence, or omitting significant episodes from his narrative of Chalmers's life.

For over 130 years, Hanna's *Memoirs* have remained the standard biography of Chalmers. There have, to be sure, been several shorter, also highly laudatory biographies based upon Hanna's work, including the most recent, Professor Hugh Watt's *Thomas Chalmers and the Disruption*, published in 1943. On the whole, however, these biographers accepted Hanna's research and interpretations as definitive, and made no attempt to return to the original sources. Their works were essentially commentaries upon Hanna's *Memoirs* which shared Hanna's Evangelical perspective.

Fortunately, most of Chalmers's correspondence and private papers survive, in a massive collection which in 1940 was donated by his heirs to New College Library of Edinburgh University. In the early 1970s, aware of both the growing interest in Chalmers and the value of the collection for modern British historians, New College began a long-term project to organize and catalogue the Chalmers papers. The project was scheduled to near completion in 1980, the bicentenary of Chalmers's birth. These papers, together with recent research in Scottish social, religious, and political history, have made possible a new interpretation of this complex figure. It was my privilege to have access to the Chalmers papers during the final stages of the cataloguing process. I have written the first biography of Chalmers, since that of Hanna, based upon extensive research among the wealth of primary sources that are available for this period. The portrayal is less laudatory than the 'family portrait' produced by Hanna. I have tried to capture Chalmers's 'warts and roughnesses'—the youthful ambition, the drive for power and influence, the degree of callousness toward those he sought to help—as well as his very considerable strengths. My portrayal is that of a man, all too human, who burned with a rage against social injustice and human suffering—a man who, with a passionate religious faith, rose to greatness in his time.

The central thesis of this biography is that Chalmers's life and career must be understood in terms of his struggle to realize an ideal Christian society—a 'Godly commonwealth'—in response to the social dislocations of early nineteenth-century industrialization and urbanization. The biography focuses upon his conversion to the ideal of the godly commonwealth during his youth in rural northern Fife, his adaptation of this ideal to the new social conditions of Glasgow and of industrializing Britain, his campaign to reorganize Scottish society around this ideal through the extension of the Established Church, and, finally, the failure of his campaign with the Disruption of the Church of Scotland and its aftermath. The emphasis, then, is on his career as an Evangelical social reformer and ecclesiastical politician. I have not provided extensive analysis of his contributions as a theologian or moral philosopher. Though I have dealt with these writings when they have been pertinent to the narrative of his struggle for social and ecclesiastical reform, this biography is neither a work of intellectual history, nor an extended psychological interpretation of Chalmers's spirituality.

III

The fundamental concept, that of the godly commonwealth, is one which has had different meanings in the history of Western civilization. Its use in my study therefore requires some preliminary explanation. When Chalmers referred to the ideal of the godly commonwealth, he meant essentially the sixteenth- and seventeenth-century Calvinist social ideal, as it had been expressed in such basic documents of the early Reformed Church of Scotland as the First Book of Discipline (1560), the Second Book of Discipline (1578), the National Covenant (1638), and the Westminster Confession of Faith (1647). Sixteenth- and seventeenth-century Calvinism was a world-affirming and revolutionary faith, which sought to penetrate every aspect of social, political, and economic life. It was concerned to reform not only the

Church, but the whole of society; indeed, Calvinism recognized no clear separation of Church and State, or Church and society. Calvinism placed special emphasis upon the Old Testament concept of the covenant, the idea that a people, or nation, might be chosen for a special relationship with God. In such a covenanted, or elect, nation, Church and State would co-operate in the elevation of the whole society for the glory of God—the Church by disseminating the pure Word of God, the State by enforcing God's laws for man as discerned from Scripture. Under Christian discipline, people would learn to live in unison, sharing nature's bounty for the common welfare, suppressing usury and mandating a 'fair price' for goods and services, practising benevolence towards the sick and indigent poor, and cultivating their spiritual, moral, and intellectual natures in the service of God. Where the pure Word was preached, it was believed, there would be consensus upon the essential matters of faith, and society would not be divided by faction or dissent. In short, the commonwealth would represent the rule of God on earth. Many, indeed, viewed the godly commonwealth as the awaited millennium, or the thousand-year reign of Christ on earth which (in the 'pre-millennarian' tradition) would precede the Last Judgement and the end of the world.

The ideal of the godly commonwealth had a turbulent history in Scotland, inspiring intense commitment in the fifteenth and sixteenth centuries, but after that waning in social influence. With the beginning of the Scottish Reformation in the late 1550s, devout Calvinists had believed the achievement of a godly commonwealth in Scotland to be imminent. The Reformers had expected to take possession of the considerable wealth of the medieval Roman Catholic Church in Scotland, and use it to support a national system of parish churches, parish and burgh schools, universities, and parish poor relief—for the purpose of preparing the population for their communal responsibilities in the new social order. But the Reformers' hopes soon receded. In the political tumult of the 1560s, the Scottish landed aristocracy and gentry seized most of the medieval Church properties. The Stuart monarchs, moreover, proved unsupportive or hostile to the Reformed Church's social ideal and made no attempt to halt the expropriations. Thus, although the Reformation in Scotland achieved the creation of a Protestant national religious Establishment, with a loose presbyterian hierarchy of Church courts, this Establishment was crippled by poverty and its educational and social programmes were only partially fulfilled.

Calvinist hopes for the commonwealth ideal later revived in the 1630s, when the blunders of Charles I weakened the central State authority, creating an opportunity which the Reformed Church of Scotland tried to exploit. But the landed interest refused either to return the Church properties they had seized in the sixteenth century, or to co-operate with the Church's goal of social revolution. As a result, the turmoil of the seventeenth century—the Civil War, the Cromwellian conquest, the Restoration of 1660, and the Revolution of 1688—first raised, but ultimately brought an end to Scottish Calvinist hopes.

In 1707, Scotland relinquished its national Parliament and its national sovereignty and entered into the Act of Union with England. By the terms of this Act, Scotland retained an independent Calvinist and presbyterian national religious Establishment, although its social programmes remained constrained by poverty and by the rising power and influence of the landed interest. In other respects, however, the Union of 1707 proved a major boon to Scotland. With the help of British arms, the military power of the Scottish Highland clans was subdued and the rule of civil law was gradually imposed upon most of the country. With internal peace, there followed the development of communications and transportation, the expansion of Scottish trade and manufactures, and the improvement of agriculture. By 1750, Scotland had entered its 'age of improvement'. The landed interest prospered and dominated Scottish society politically, becoming increasingly Anglicized in social outlook and manners. In the larger towns, especially Edinburgh and Glasgow, increased security and economic growth created the atmosphere for a unique flowering of intellectual culture in the second half of the eighteenth century. The work of such Scottish intellectuals as Adam Smith and David Hume, William Robertson and Adam Fergusson, inspired the admiration of Europe and established the Scottish Enlightenment as a major force in Western intellectual history. There was new emphasis upon individualism and toleration, and greater appreciation for commercial capitalism as a force for beneficial social change. Among the late eighteenth-century Anglicized landed interest and the social élites of urban and commercial Scotland, the commonwealth ideal was increasingly viewed as an expression of a less tolerant, less civilized era, beyond which society had happily advanced.

Not all of Scotland, however, benefited from the social changes resulting from the Union and the eighteenth-century age of improvement. The Highlands suffered a systematic destruction of their traditional culture under the direction of the Government and Anglicized Highland landowners. On the east coast of Lowland Scotland, a number of once prosperous commercial burghs were unable to compete with English commercial interests for European markets or the British coastal trade, and declined into the backwaters of British civilization. In other Lowland rural districts, enclosures and the improvement of agricultural estates forced small tenants off their farms and into poverty. In such rural areas, the old ideal of the godly commonwealth did not die away. It was preserved by Calvinist preachers of the 'old orthodoxy' and by popular attachment to the communal traditions of rural Scotland. It survived as a deep-felt opposition to the Act of Union, to the growing influence of commercial capitalism, and to the declining social influence of Christianity. In particular, it remained as an often bitter antagonism to the landed interest, viewed as the betrayers of the godly commonwealth ideal, who had seized and employed for their private advancement the Church properties which should have been the common property of the nation.

It was in such a rural community that Thomas Chalmers embraced the ideal of the godly commonwealth, and reshaped it into a social ideal with which he struggled to reform the whole of Scottish, and indeed of British, society.

1

AMBITION AND COMMUNITY

I

Across the Firth of Forth from the Scottish provincial capital of Edinburgh lies the Lowland county of Fife, a district of gentle, rolling hills and some of the best arable land in Scotland. Along the eastern shore of Fife, facing out upon the North Sea, stand a number of small coastal towns, among them the town of Anstruther. In the closing decades of the eighteenth century, Anstruther was a closely-knit community of tradesmen and merchant sailors, with a primitive harbour, narrow winding streets, and closely-crowded stone dwellings. A moderately prosperous fishing community in the sixteenth and early seventeenth centuries, it had, like the surrounding eastern Fifeshire towns, declined in wealth and status from 1650 to 1750, largely as a result of decreased yields from surrounding fishing grounds. Only after 1770, with the development of a modest coal-mining industry, did the economic prospects of the district begin to improve.

The town of Anstruther was divided into two royal burghs, Anstruther Easter and Anstruther Wester, separated by the narrow waters of Dreel Burn. Each burgh was governed by a separate burgh council, a self-elected body of approximately a dozen members. In 1791, James Forrester, minister of Anstruther Wester, wrote a description of his burgh for the *Statistical Account of Scotland*. This description, combined with a short anonymous account of Anstruther Easter published in the *Statistical Account* in 1795, provides a view of the town in the last decade of the century. The population of Anstruther Wester was 370 and of Anstruther Easter 1,000. Among the labouring population of Anstruther Wester, Forrester found 34 per cent were engaged as sailors, 9 per cent as carpenters in a small ship-building concern, 14 per cent as weavers, 9 per cent as farmers or farm labourers, and the remainder scattered along a broad spectrum of trades, including millers, brewers, bakers, shoemakers, and tailors. In 1790, there were twenty ships attached to the port, thirteen involved in the coasting trade, six in foreign trade, and one in fishing. Coal transport was the principal business for Anstruther's shipping, although there was also a moderate industry in processing and transporting woollen goods.

Each burgh possessed a parish church, and the entire population, with the exception of only one or two families, were members of the Church of Scotland. In Anstruther Easter, there was a parish school under Church of Scotland supervision, providing primary education

for children in both burghs. The poor who required relief received
assistance from church-door collections, supplemented by private
charity, while the ship-owners and some of the trade guilds maintained
funds to provide for the widows and orphans of their employees and
members. Material living standards for Anstruther Wester labourers,
Forrester maintained, had improved in the last two decades. Wages
were rising, and 'thrice the quantity of butcher meat and white bread
are used now, than were twenty years ago in this parish.' The population was characterized by a respect for law and order. From 1732 to
1790, for instance, only one man from Anstruther Wester had been
tried in court for a criminal offence, and he had petitioned successfully
for banishment from the town. 'The people in general', Forrester concluded, 'are sober and industrious. They enjoy in a reasonable degree
the comforts and advantages of society, and are contented with their
situation.'[1]

In the last decades of the eighteenth century, the Anstruther district
was dominated by Sir John Anstruther, Bt. (1718-99). Sir John possessed large estates in eastern Fife and was an ardent agricultural
improver, with a particular interest in drill husbandry. He diversified
his wealth, moreover, by investments in salt-pans and coal-mines. In
1771, he was a principal founder of the Newark Coal Company, which
had proved a major boon to Anstruther's coastal shipping interests.
Although a chief contributor to the district's economic improvement,
however, Sir John was also unpopular, both for his arrogance and for
the ruthless manner in which he dispossessed tenants while enclosing
his estates. In 1760, for instance, he had removed the entire village of
Balclevie, reputedly at the whim of his wife, in order to improve the
amenities of Elie House, his family seat located five miles south of
Anstruther.[2]

Sir John owned nearly a third of the property in the Anstruther
burghs, and was the patron of both parish churches. He employed this
influence for political purposes. At the Parliamentary union of Scotland
and England in 1707, the two Anstruther burghs had been grouped
with three other small neighbouring coastal burghs for the purpose of
returning one representative to the Westminster Parliament. The
representative of the Anstruther Easter Burghs was elected indirectly,
each burgh council selecting one delegate who possessed a single vote.
The support of at least three burgh councils, then, was necessary for
the successful candidate, while the cost of a council's favour, in dinners
and drink alone, was often considerable. Indeed, the corruption displayed by the councils of the Anstruther Easter Burghs was among the
most blatant in Britain. Bribery, intimidation, and even kidnapping of
burgh councillors, however, constituted a political game which Sir
John Anstruther played well, and from 1766 until the early nineteenth

century, Sir John or one of his sons represented these burghs in Parliament, despite their unpopularity in the district. Ironically, for most of the 1780s Sir John and his family were firmly attached to the Whig political interest of Charles James Fox, the celebrated 'friend of liberty'. They strongly opposed the political ascendancy which Henry Dundas, the friend and adviser of Fox's political opponent William Pitt, created for himself in Scotland during the early 1780s. In 1788, however, Sir John finally bowed to the reality of Dundas's power, and entered into an agreement with him for sharing the patronage of the Anstruther Easter Burghs. Fear of democratic ideas and potential civil violence in Scotland following the outbreak of the French Revolution, moreover, drove Sir John into still closer alliance with the Pittite party.[3]

In 1736, James Chalmers (1718-88), the second son of a Fifeshire clergyman, settled in Anstruther Easter as a merchant in woollen goods. Through a single-minded devotion to business, he prospered in spite of the economic languor affecting the district in the mid-eighteenth century. In partnership with George Hall, a merchant in the neighbouring burgh of Crail, he became a commercial ship-owner and the proprietor of a dye and thread works, the largest manufacturing concern in Anstruther. When he retired in the mid-1770s, he left his eldest son, John Chalmers (1740-1818), a partnership in a flourishing business and a capital sum of £10,000.[4] John Chalmers, however, lacked his father's talent for commercial affairs; larger economic and political developments also combined against him, and under his management the family business gradually declined. The war which commenced between Britain and France in 1793 disrupted the Channel trade and diminished the profits from his commercial shipping operations. His thread and dye works could not compete with large-scale textile industries developing in Glasgow and the west of Scotland. He was, meanwhile, burdened with the expense of a large family, with thirteen children surviving to adulthood. In 1804, following a stroke which severely impaired both his sight and hearing, he finally closed his unprofitable thread and dye works and devoted his remaining years to a small retail woollen goods shop in Anstruther.[5]

Although unfortunate in business, John Chalmers was an affable man, who was warmly devoted to his family and community. In religion, he was a devout Calvinist, strict in religious observances, including a rigid keeping of the sabbath. He also possessed the finest library of devotional books in Anstruther. Unlike his father, who had strictly avoided burgh politics, Chalmers became a prominent magistrate in the burgh of Anstruther Easter, and served several terms as provost. His politics were simple, consisting in unremitting support for Sir John Anstruther, whose Parliamentary interest he managed in the Anstruther Easter burgh council during the politically troubled decades of the 1780s and 1790s.[6] As Sir John's man, Chalmers opposed attempts to introduce a popular voice into either burgh or national politics. He believed that public business should be left to those with the leisure to pursue these matters on a regular basis, and that popular meddling in politics all too often culminated in mob violence.[7] He saw nothing wrong with the political manoeuvres which enabled an unpopular Anstruther to be returned to Parliament at general election after general election with as little discussion as possible.[8] Although Chalmers received little personal benefit at the time for his political services, he doubtless believed that his efforts would eventually be rewarded, when his nine sons reached maturity. With his business declining, the Anstruthers' influence and patronage would be extremely important for settling his sons in professional situations.

In 1771, Chalmers had married Elizabeth Hall (1750-1827), the only daughter of his father's business partner. She was an energetic woman, graced with an Edinburgh education. Having been much indulged by wealthy parents, she found the management of a large family with dwindling financial resources to be a trial. None the less, although lacking her husband's strict religious views, she demonstrated a strong humanitarian concern for the poor of Anstruther, combined with a sense for the practical detail regarding their needs. She visited the homes of the poor on a regular basis with parcels of food and clothing, and her surviving letters abound with detail about wage levels and grain prices. During the dearth of 1812, she was active in founding a society in Anstruther in which members subscribed a shilling a week to a fund which was distributed to the poor by household visitors. At her death, she left provision in her will for several paupers whom she had assisted regularly for many years.[9]

Thomas, the sixth child and fourth son of John and Elizabeth Chalmers, was born in Anstruther on 17 March 1780. From the early age of three, he attended the parish school in Anstruther. His instruction there, by an aged and half-blind schoolmaster with authoritarian manners, was uninspiring. However, he was fortunate in having access to his family library, while his uncle Thomas Ballairdie, a retired naval captain and prominent burgh politician and philanthropist, instructed him in mathematics. He enjoyed a healthy and active childhood in Anstruther. Although his father's business was not thriving, the family was still relatively well-to-do. Of his three elder brothers, one entered a commercial firm in Liverpool, while the other two became ship's officers.[10]

In 1791, at the age of eleven, and in company with his elder brother William, Thomas matriculated at St. Andrews University, which was located on the east coast of Fife about eight miles north of Anstruther. The town of St. Andrews had decayed considerably since its period of medieval importance, when its bishopric, cathedral, and university had been at the centre of Scotland's religious and cultural life. The bishop's palace and cathedral were now ruins, and its university the smallest, and at this time probably the least distinguished for learning, in Scotland. The university comprised two colleges, the United College, offering an arts curriculum in Greek, the humanities, and natural philosophy, and St. Mary's College, forming the divinity college, the only professional training offered at St. Andrews. Late eighteenth-century enrolments were small. Thomas matriculated in the United College with an entering class of twenty-seven, while the university as a whole numbered less than two hundred students.[11] For all its weaknesses, however, St. Andrews offered two major advantages. It was near Anstruther, and the fees and lodging expenses were within the moderate means of the Chalmers family.[12]

In the last decade of the eighteenth century, St. Andrews University was dominated by George Hill (1750-1819), Professor of Divinity from 1772 to 1819 and Principal of St. Mary's College from 1791 to 1819. Hill was an accomplished scholar, and from the mid-1780s an acknowledged leader in the Church of Scotland. With the assistance of his uncle, Joseph McCormick, Principal of the United College from 1781 to 1799, Hill managed to settle a number of his relations in St. Andrews academic chairs. This family ascendancy in the university during the 1790s was reflected by the proverbial popularity of Psalm 121 in St. Andrews ('I will lift up mine eyes unto the hills, from whence cometh my help'). Conservative by political inclination, and closely connected to the political interest of Henry Dundas, Chancellor of St. Andrews University from 1788 to 1811, Hill and his family transformed the quiet provincial university into a stronghold of Dundas Toryism.[13]

Completion of the arts course in the United College required four sessions, with each session lasting from early November until early April. Chalmers was extremely young when he began university study, and his education in the Anstruther parish school had been poor, particularly in Latin, which entering students were supposed to have mastered. Wealthier families generally sent their sons to grammar schools in the larger towns for training in Latin and Greek before they entered university, but John Chalmers had apparently lacked the financial means. As a result of this weak preparation, Chalmers was a mediocre student during his first two sessions, which were devoted to instruction mainly in Greek and the humanities.[14] In his third session, however, his intellectual talents began to attract notice. Having completed his work in Greek, he now advanced to the course in mathematics. He had, it will be recalled, already received some instruction in this subject from his uncle. His poor Latin training, moreover, presented no obstacle to the grasp of mathematical concepts. In short, it was a study

which he began on at least an equal level with the other students, and
he zealously endeavoured to prove himself. With his friend James
Miller, he commenced a rivalry in the mathematics class taught by
James Brown, the assistant to Professor William Vilant. Their enthusiasm attracted Brown's attention, and they began to be invited on
a regular evening basis to Brown's room. Brown not only recognized
the gifted mind of the thirteen-year-old Chalmers, but endeavoured to
inspire him further with a love for mathematics and scientific enquiry.[15]

Like Chalmers, Brown had emerged from a relatively obscure background. Born a miller's son in the small Fifeshire village of Lochgelly
in 1760, Brown had been appointed assistant to Vilant in 1784, following a distinguished student career at St. Andrews. Brown was a man of
wide interests, with a vibrant imagination and gift for conversation.
A Foxite Whig, he opposed the ascendancy of the Hills and Dundas at
St. Andrews, a fact which in part accounted for his failure to advance
to a St. Andrews chair. When revolution erupted in France in 1789, he
applauded its principles of increased popular representation in government, while later, in 1793, he criticized the British Government for
waging war upon the infant French republic. His republican sympathies
were shared by several young intellectual friends, including John
Leslie, a brilliant mathematician and natural scientist, who like Brown
was at this time unable to obtain a university chair.[16] Chalmers's
companion James Miller later recalled the feeling of adventure at their
evening meetings in Brown's room. 'There we met', Miller informed
Chalmers's son-in-law and biographer, William Hanna, in 1847, 'with
the late Sir John Leslie and Mr. James Mylne, afterwards Professor
of Moral Philosophy in Glasgow, both of whom were considered in
those days, like Dr. Brown, as marked men—ultra Whigs, keen Reformers, and what would now be called Radicals.' 'The seeds of our
reforming notions', Miller added, 'were then sown in our minds, by
our conversation with these men.'[17]

During this third session, Chalmers also began to explore political
questions. Again, he demonstrated a precocious mind. In December
1793, shortly after the beginning of his third session, he entered the
student Political Society, a forum for papers and debate. His first discourse before the Political Society, 'That the Miser is more pernicious
to Society than the Prodigal', was delivered on 21 December 1793. It
revealed an understanding of the 'invisible hand' doctrine in Adam
Smith's *Wealth of Nations*, that by a self-interested pursuit and enjoyment of wealth, an individual stimulated the economy and thereby
unconsciously benefited society. Chalmers, however, rejected Smith's
argument, preferring the consciously benevolent man of 'liberal disposition' who with 'unbounded charity' contributed directly to 'the
relief of the poor and distressed'.[18] Brown, meanwhile, encouraged his

interest in political and economic thought. During the session of 1794-5, on Brown's suggestion, Chalmers read and became enamoured with William Godwin's *Enquiry Concerning Political Justice*, which had been published in 1793. In this reply to Edmund Burke's conservative *Reflections on the Revolution in France*, Godwin advocated a radical dimin-ution of the role of national government, with major governing authority to be vested instead in small communities, where the persuasive power of community opinion would replace statute law. Although Godwin's work was widely condemned throughout Britain as advocating revo-lution and anarchy, Chalmers praised the work to his companions. During his fourth arts session, again on Brown's suggestion, he taught himself French in order to read the works of the eighteenth-century *philosophes*.[19] By the end of his four-year arts session, he had begun to demonstrate a strong and original mind, capable of enthusiasm for scientific learning, and of serious consideration of larger questions of social organization. Under the influence of Brown and Leslie, his political thoughts had assumed an increasingly liberal direction.

In November 1795, having completed the arts course, Chalmers at the age of fifteen entered the divinity college of St. Andrews University. The Church's ministry represented a respectable profession, in which mathematical or scientific learning might also be pursued. His father, moreover, was willing to support a professional education for the ministry. But Chalmers was an indolent student during his first div-inity session, where he had to listen to the theological lectures of George Hill. Erudite and systematic, Hill's lectures, when posthumously published in 1821, provided perhaps the most comprehensive exposition of scholastic Calvinism in the English language. Although tolerant of other religious creeds, Hill personally adhered strictly to the standards of the Westminster Confession of Faith which he defended with force and eloquence.[20] Chalmers, however, was not impressed. As he con-fided to his college friend William Burns, he could not accept Hill's expositions, because he questioned Hill's sincerity. 'He had got the idea strongly into his mind', Burns later related to Hanna, 'that the orthodoxy of the lectures of Geo. Hill was formed just in conformity to the [Westminster] Standards, rather than as the truth most surely believed.' 'You are a sincere Calvinist,' Burns further recalled Chal-mers stating to him following one of Hill's lectures, 'there is none in St. Andrews that I know. Come down to Anstruther with me on a Saturday, and see my father and Mr. Hodges.... They all agree with you.'[21] Calvinism, as Chalmers had experienced it, was a practical faith which flourished in villages and small towns, like Anstruther, where a communal culture survived. There a common faith in the majesty and power of God served to bind the community together. In the academic society of St. Andrews, the systematic exposition of

Calvinism was to him sterile. He objected to Christianity being presented as a system to be accepted upon authority, rather than as a faith
to be nurtured through personal experience in an organic community.

During his second divinity session, apparently under pressure from
his father, he devoted more attention to his theological study. He prepared a discourse defending the Calvinist doctrine of predestination
which was highly acclaimed. He also joined the student Theological
Society, and assumed an active role in the debates.[22] Although he
embarked seriously on the study of theology, however, Chalmers did
not relinquish his interest in mathematics. His mentor, James Brown,
had left St. Andrews in the summer of 1796, to assume the Chair of
Natural Philosophy at the less politically conservative University of
Glasgow. Chalmers not only maintained a correspondence with Brown,
but he also began friendship with Robert Coutts, Brown's successor
as assistant to the Professor of Mathematics.

Nor did he leave off political concerns upon entering the Divinity
Hall. It was the practice at St. Andrews for the divinity students, in
turn, to deliver Sunday evening prayers to the assembled student body.
Chalmers's prayers, William Burns recalled to Hanna in 1847, often
focused with 'astonishing, *harrowing* delineations' upon the evils of war,
and included some implied criticism of Britain's war with republican
France.[23] This was a bold sentiment to express in a Scotland dominated
by the political interest of Henry Dundas, now Secretary for War in
Pitt's Government. Dundas regarded support for the war as a virtual
test of loyalty to the British constitution. On 12 January 1796, for
instance, Henry Erskine, the respected Whig Dean of the Faculty of
Advocates in Scotland, had been deprived of his office by the Dundas
interest in consequence of his having presided at a public meeting to
petition against the war.[24] When the population in several Scottish
districts rioted against the Militia Act of 1797, which gave the Government power to conscript men into the militia for home defence, the
Government treated the disturbances as a Jacobin-inspired revolutionary movement and brutally suppressed the riots.[25] In such an environment, it was not surprising that Chalmers's prayers elicited, as Burns
recalled, 'the wonderment and interest of the hearers' in Tory-dominated St. Andrews. During his years in the Divinity Hall, Burns further
related, 'he was full of heart, and bouyant of spirit—an ardent lover of
liberty. In these days of domineering Toryism, when Melville and
Braxfield held the reins in Scotland, we really thought our young companion in no little danger of being seized as one of the democrats and
sent to durance.'[26] Chalmers was not in fact a political democrat, nor
did he advocate resistance to the State. The Christian, he asserted in
a student sermon delivered on 12 November 1796, 'submits to the
wanton exercise of extensive authority with a becoming patience and

composure, and his love of order, harmony, and peace often prompts him to forgo the advantages which would result from resisting the encroachments of power.'[27] None the less, by his opposition to the war and by several of his student compositions, he demonstrated dissatisfaction with the Pitt and Dundas Government's 'wanton exercise of extensive authority'. He advocated not democracy, but pacificism and the diminution of oppressive government.

In the spring of 1798, following his third session in the Divinity Hall, his father arranged a position for him as tutor to the children of John Stevenson, a landed proprietor residing near Arbroath, twenty-five miles north of Anstruther. Tutorships were common among divinity students. In addition to providing room and board, and a small income, the tutorship enabled a future minister to imbibe the manners and morals of the wealthy propertied classes who dominated Scottish social life. John Chalmers's agreement with the Stevensons provided that Thomas would have a leave of absence in order to complete his fourth and final divinity session at St. Andrews. After that he could return to their employment until he was presented to a church living, which might require years to effect. This last consideration was important to his father, who was under increasing financial strain.

A few weeks after his arrival in the Stevenson household, however, Chalmers began complaining bitterly to both James Brown and his father of the 'intolerable arrogance' of the Stevensons and their fellow gentry, who treated him with what he regarded as 'contemptuous reserve'. They had, he explained, no respect for his education, and discouraged his conversation. The low esteem in which John Stevenson and his wife held the tutor's position encouraged, in turn, the children to rebel against his authority. When he attempted to discipline his charges, he was rebuked by their parents for over-extending his authority.[28] 'It was', he wrote his father on 19 July 1798, 'a great object of mine in entering Dr. Stevenson's family, and I believe you had it yourself in view, that I would have opportunities of seeing men, and manners, and wear off those habits I had contracted by excessive solitude.' The Stevensons' arrogance, however, had defeated this object, and he now wanted to return home. 'Be assured,' he continued, 'I have a lively feeling of the folly of Pride, and the fitness of Modesty. But I know there is a medium between expressing insolence, and a mean, unmanly subjection. ... Neither my own feelings, nor respect for my friends, will allow me to sit in silent submission under any glaring indignity.'[29] At his father's request, he persevered in the position for another four months, although he continued to plead for permission to resign. Finally, in November 1798, John Chalmers gave his reluctant consent, and Thomas returned to St. Andrews to complete his final session.

The Stevensons were probably no more arrogant than the other landed gentry of eastern Scotland. John Stevenson, in fact, was by reputation a kind and benevolent man. In part, Chalmers's complaints were those of an indulged young man, who although intellectually gifted was too emotionally immature to bear the responsibility of employment, despite the financial pressures on his family. He continually complained to his father, for instance, of the long hours he was expected to devote to his charges and the resulting lack of time for his own study. But his hostility to the Stevensons was also conditioned by ideas he had absorbed in the community of Anstruther, and which had been reinforced by his reading of William Godwin and by his conversations with Brown.

In student discourses written prior to his tutorship, Chalmers had repeatedly expressed disdain for the 'pride of external grandeur', which encouraged men of property to treat those without wealth as inferior. In a discourse delivered before the student Theological Society on 25 May 1796, for instance, he had described the social privileges of wealth, such as 'allotting a magnificent seat or a convenient situation in a church to any one man in preference to another', as 'artificial distinctions' which should be abolished.[30] A man's wealth, he had observed in a student sermon delivered on 12 November 1796, should 'have no tendency to exalt him in his own esteem'.[31] In view of these previous expressions, it was hardly surprising that he should resent being regarded a social inferior in the Stevenson household. 'It is impossible', he wrote his father regarding the Stevensons on 29 October 1798, 'to be upon a good understanding with people disposed to treat me in so inferior a light as they do.' 'I don't know', he added, 'what it is to act the part of an underling.'[32] On the contrary, he considered it his duty to oppose the Stevensons' pride with a haughtiness of his own, which antagonized the family and forced John Stevenson to attempt to remonstrate with him. 'There are', Chalmers replied to Stevenson's complaints, 'two kinds of pride, sir. There is that pride which lords it over inferiors; and there is that pride which rejoices in repressing the insolence of superiors. The first I have none of—the second I glory in.'[33] While at Arbroath, Chalmers joined the nearby St. Vigeans lodge of Free Masons. The secretive masons were at this time under suspicion by the Government for being possibly bent upon political subversion.[34] Although little is known regarding the St. Vigeans lodge, it is probable that political and social reform formed a major topic of discussion.

As a student, Chalmers had embraced the idea that a man's value was based on his contribution to the welfare of society: this in turn was a function, not of his wealth, but of his principles and his integrity. For him at this time, the fundamental social principle was benevolence. It

was through benevolence, he maintained, that men were bound together in harmonious communities, where they devoted their efforts 'to
the diffusion of knowledge, to the instruction of ignorance, to the benevolent superintendence of temporal concerns, not to the paltry objects
of private emolument and worldy distinction.' Such communities were
free of the 'artificial distinctions' of privilege. The wealthy did not
scorn the poor 'by a wanton display of superior power', nor endeavour
'to .acquire any advantage from their poverty and wretchedness'.
Rather, they sought to assist the poor in an unostentatious manner,
respecting the essential equality of men before God. Individual self-
interest and ambition were to be subordinated to the communal spirit.
'Nature is kind enough,' Chalmers observed in a student sermon on
18 January 1798,

if only we were kind to each other. But often, alas, do the dark designs of malice work
in our breasts; often do the silly emotions of pride and envy obstruct the enjoyments of
social intercourse. O that the principle of benevolence within us were powerful enough
to eradicate these passions from our hearts. O that we were sacrificing our absurd
notions of importance and dignity, our views of interest and ambition, to that great
object—the good of others.

In both his hatred for the 'artificial distinctions' of wealth and his
emphasis upon the role of benevolence in social organization, Chalmers
reflected the social traditions of pre-industrial Fifeshire in which he had
been raised. The social structure of early eighteenth-century Fifeshire,
like that of the whole of Scotland, had been characterized by a hierarchical arrangement of social ranks, with great landowners at the top
and landless labourers at the base. Between them was a gradation of
numerous occupational orders, representing what a recent historian of
the period has termed the 'classless hierarchy' of pre-industrial society.[35]
In Scotland, this hierarchy had been characterized by close, even intimate interrelationships. Landed proprietors and tenants, merchants
and tradesmen, had generally lived in proximity to one another, sharing a common culture. A major unifying factor in this culture had
been the social teachings of the Church of Scotland. Sunday worship
had assembled persons of all social ranks under a single roof. The
children of rich and poor had usually been educated together in the
Church-supervised parish school. In its exhortations, the Church had
emphasized each man's responsibility for his neighbour. This was
evidenced especially in the Church's supervision of poor relief. The
parish fund for poor relief was based primarily upon voluntary contributions accepted at the church door; parish relief allotments, moreover,
were supplemented by religiously-motivated private charity. In a
word, the religious duty of benevolence had in large part been the
cement binding the early eighteenth-century Scottish community.

By the late eighteenth century, however, this social cohesion was disintegrating. The improving spirit of the century, while it contributed to an increase in material living standards for most members of society, also contributed to a growing distance between social ranks. In the predominantly rural society of eastern Fife, economic improvement generally assumed the form of enclosures, with landed proprietors removing small tenants to increase the size and efficiency of farms on their estates. The fate of dispossessed tenants was an acute problem for the parish communities. The growing numbers of landless agricultural labourers and their families suffered seasonal unemployment and required poor relief during years of dearth. With their increased personal wealth, meanwhile, the Fifeshire gentry began emulating the manners and morals of their English counterparts. Non-resident landlords became more common, as landed families achieved the degree of opulence which enabled them to reside most of the year in Edinburgh or London. When they remained in the district, the gentry often signified their separation from the local community by surrounding their country houses with large private parks. Sir John Anstruther, it will be recalled, had levelled an entire village to ensure the privacy of Elie House, while criers marched through the streets of neighbouring Pittenweem commanding no one to approach the sea-coast near Elie House when Lady Anstruther intended to bathe.[36] The children of the gentry were removed from the parish schools, and either educated at home by tutors or sent to public schools in England. Among the gentry, there developed what the literary historian David Craig has termed a 'polite culture', élitist, Anglicized, and provincial—alien to the traditional communal culture of Scotland.[37] Many landed families, moreover, ceased attending the local parish church of the national Establishment. Church collections, therefore, declined at the same time that enclosures and the growing number of landless labourers were increasing the strain upon parish poor-relief funds.

In the small commercial town of Anstruther, the traditional communal culture had continued to flourish in the late eighteenth century. Comprising a wide spectrum of trades and occupations, Anstruther was a largely closed and self-sufficient community. The inhabitants were intimately acquainted with one anothers' characters and circumstances, and helped one another in adversity. The Church of Scotland remained an effective social force, and virtually the entire population were active church members. There was, moreover, a certain popular hostility to the 'great', as the Anstruther family and their fellow Anglicized and élitist gentry were derisively termed, which despite John Chalmers's management occasionally surfaced in vociferous outbreaks in the Anstruther burgh councils.[38] Even while he was a student at St. Andrews University, Chalmers resided with his family in Anstruther nearly seven months of the year. He knew and loved the Anstruther community, and it was not surprising that his thinking should reflect both the traditional communal values of pre-industrial Scotland and the local dissatisfaction with the gentry who, like the Anstruther family, were emphasizing their self-interest and separating themselves from the surrounding communal culture.

At the same time, however, Chalmers's own ambition, awakened by a successful university career, was beginning to pull him away from these communal roots. Early in December 1798, he returned to St. Andrews from the Arbroath tutorship, and although despondent over his experiences in the Stevenson household, he managed to complete his final divinity session.[39] In the Church of Scotland at this time a candidate for the ministry was required to be licensed as a preacher before he could be presented to a church living. For this, he had to perform satisfactorily in an oral examination in doctrine and in a series of trial sermons delivered before the presbytery under whose juris-diction he resided. The minimum age for licensing was twenty-one, and Chalmers was only nineteen. His father, however, was anxious to see his son settled quickly in a church living, which would help relieve financial pressures upon the family. He enlisted the assistance of his cousin and close friend, John Adamson, the Whig Professor of Civil History at St. Andrews, to obtain for Thomas a special dispensation 'as a lad o' pregnant pairts' from the St. Andrews presbytery. The Tory George Hill raised objections to this, from what Thomas regarded as 'political Reasons of his own'. Recognizing, however, that the dispen-sation was 'matter of *Favour* and not of Right', Thomas visited Hill several times with a humble demeanour, and Hill finally acquiesced. Chalmers completed his trials before the presbytery, and was licensed on 31 July 1799.[40]

But he was still without employment or immediate prospects. Late in October 1798, before he had resigned the Stevenson's employment, his father had arranged yet another tutorship with a landed family near Anstruther. Chalmers, however, had refused the position. If the family proved to be like the Stevensons, he had explained to his father on 6 November 1798, he would be obliged to leave their employment. 'This', he observed, 'will make people think I am unstable or turbu-lent, and so be hurtful to my character.' 'You yourself know best,' he continued candidly,

what influence you or your friends may have in procuring me a comfortable settlement in the Church. If the prospect of such a settlement is far distant, then the situation of a tutor is a necessary evil, which I must be submitted to. In that case, then it is my best plan to endeavour to get into such families as may be most agreeable at present, and have the greatest interest to promote my future views.

The family his father had arranged for him, he intimated, possessed no such influence.[41]

In November 1799, Chalmers was summoned to Edinburgh by the prospect of a tutorship to young Lord Rosehill, whose family did possess influence to 'promote his future views'. He arrived too late to obtain the position, however, and his father instructed him to return to eastern Fife where there was an opening for an assistant minister in the parish of Logie, near St. Andrews. But Chalmers ignored his father's instructions and determined to remain in Edinburgh.[42] The home of Scotland's highest secular and religious law courts, publishing trade, and major university, Edinburgh possessed attractions which he was not about to relinquish for a rural assistantship. He lodged with a cousin of his father, and was meagrely supported by his father and by occasional loans from James Brown, while he sought university students who might pay for part-time tutoring in mathematics.[43]

Chalmers remained two years in Edinburgh. Through Brown's influence, he was permitted to attend, gratis, the university lectures of Dugald Stewart, Professor of Moral Philosophy, and of John Robison, Professor of Natural Philosophy. Chalmers was not impressed with Stewart's lectures, feeling that he 'uniformly avoids every subject which involves any long or difficult discussion'.[44] Robison's lectures, however, had a profound impact, helping to focus his youthful search for an underlying meaning to his world, and inspiring him with a love for the scientific method and ambition for a career as a natural philosopher. To understand Robison's influence, a brief survey of Chalmers's intellectual development is necessary.

It will be recalled that he had not been impressed with George Hill's erudite presentation of scholastic Calvinism during his first year at the St. Andrews Divinity Hall. He had already developed doubts concerning systematic theology, through his reading of William Godwin and his conversations with James Brown and John Leslie, and he felt that Hill gave too much attention merely to describing a system of thought which students were expected to accept solely on the authority of the Church. Then, near the close of his first divinity session, Chalmers read Jonathon Edwards's celebrated treatise on the *Freedom of Will*, imbibing Calvinism in a new, more potent form. He was deeply impressed with Edwards's vision of the awesome omnipotence of God, a power which manifested itself in every aspect of the creation. Everything was determined by the inexorable will of the creator; every part of nature, every human action, was bound by regular laws—the divine decrees. Chalmers found security in this vision of a law-bound universe, as well as a stimulus for intellectual enquiry. To be sure, Edwards's adherence to a strict doctrine of predestination, the concept that every soul was predestined by eternal divine decree to either salvation or damnation, offered little consolation to the person tormented by doubt concerning his death and eternal fate. But the young Chalmers was full of life, with little concern about his death and its meaning. What he found profoundly moving in Edwards's exposition of Calvinism was the concept that man could come to understand much about the laws which defined the world. In a word, the world was comprehensible, if only man could discover a proper method of enquiry.

John Robison's lectures strengthened Chalmers's attachment to Edwards's Calvinist world-view by revealing just such a method of enquiry. Through Robison, Chalmers was introduced to the thought of the seventeenth-century English philosopher, Francis Bacon, and particularly to Bacon's idea of scientific method, or the idea that by beginning with simple hypotheses about the world, which can be tested by experiment, man can gradually advance to more complex hypotheses, and finally to clear and distinct ideas about the natural laws. Chalmers embraced the Baconian method: science confirmed for him Edwards's vision of an orderly, law-bound universe, and it offered a means to investigate and appreciate its harmonious structure. Robison, meanwhile, was also careful to point out that science could never reveal to man the whole of the divine plan, that there would always remain mysteries which the progress of intellect would never penetrate; and Chalmers respected this limit.[45] But he was now inspired by the prospects of scientific progress, and he nurtured an ambition for a career as a natural philosopher. In his second year in Edinburgh, he managed to pay the fee to attend the popular chemistry lectures of Thomas Charles Hope, and he began devising chemical experiments of his own and corresponding with others who shared his new interest.[46]

As a student at St. Andrews and Edinburgh, Chalmers was well liked by his fellow students. He was now a young man of middle height, with a stout build. He was good at athletic games, and enjoyed companionship and conversation, especially jocular banter. His dark hair was worn close-cropped, in the 'republican' fashion of the day; his face, scarred slightly by childhood smallpox, was not handsome, and his large eyes often appeared vacant. He was a moody young man, subject to prolonged periods of depression and brooding, as well as to periods of elation, and he had a tendency, even in the company of friends, to withdraw into silent meditation upon some abstract idea. 'His character, during all my acquaintance with him,' recalled his student friend, James Miller,

was that of the strictest integrity and the warmest affection. He was enthusiastic and persevering in every thing he undertook, giving his whole mind to it, and often pursuing some favourite and even foolish idea (as we thought) whilst we were talking around him, and perhaps laughing at his abstractions, or breaking in upon his cogitations, and pronouncing him the next thing to mad; and then he would goodnaturedly join in the merriment with his common affectionate expression, 'very well, my good lads'.[47]

In the urban environment of Edinburgh he was beginning to break away from the communal attitudes and values of eastern Fife which had defined so much of his development during his first twenty years. The intellectual world of the late eighteenth-century Enlightenment in Edinburgh presented him with new vistas, particularly in the natural sciences, and he now began to turn his ambition towards a university career in mathematics and natural philosophy. While he enjoyed the intellectual stimulation of Edinburgh, however, his father was working finally to obtain for him a presentation to a rural church living in Fife.

II

The Patronage Act of 1712 had established that the right of presenting a minister to a parish living in the Church of Scotland belonged to the legal patron of that parish. Church patronage was a property right, which, in theory at least, had been awarded to the family which had contributed the greater part of the building costs and endowment of the church; like other property, patronages could be inherited, bought, or sold. In 1780, the patronages of approximately a third of the 877 parish livings in the Church of Scotland were possessed by the Crown. The remainder were possessed by individual landed proprietors, or by municipal or university corporations—for instance, the Edinburgh Town Council or the United College of St. Andrews University. Church patronages continued to be bought and sold as private property, with their sale often advertised in the newspapers. Their value lay in the political influence they provided the patron, as well as in their usefulness for settling a friend or family member in a comfortable living. When a church within his gift fell vacant, the patron was allowed by law six months in which to present a licensed preacher of the Church of Scotland to the living. The early eighteenth-century Church had also required that there be a 'Call', or document signed by the majority of the heads of family in the parish signifying their approval of the presentation. But this requirement, representing a popular element in the Church, had fallen into abeyance after 1760.

Sir John Anstruther possessed six church patronages in eastern Fife, including those of four of the five burghs of the Anstruther Easter Burghs Parliamentary constituency.[48] By his patronage agreement of 1788 with Henry Dundas, moreover, Sir John also gained influence over the disposal of several more Fifeshire Crown patronages. John Chalmers, it will be recalled, expected that his years of service to Sir John's Parliamentary interest in the Anstruther Easter burgh council would be rewarded in part by a presentation for his son. In March 1798, John Chalmers had learned that James Forrester, minister of Anstruther Wester, was to be presented by Sir John to the more lucrative parish of Kilrenny. Since Anstruther Wester was also within Sir John's gift, Chalmers had requested Sir John to postpone Forrester's transfer until Thomas, who at that time still had his final divinity session to complete, was licensed as a preacher and could therefore receive the presentation to the Anstruther Wester vacancy.[49] Although this had proved impossible to manage within the six-month limit 're-quired by law, Sir John had apparently promised the next vacancy within his gift to Chalmers's son. Sir John Anstruther, however, died in July 1799, and John Chalmers was unfortunately not on close terms with either Sir John's widow or his sons. When in the summer of 1800, then, a parish within the Anstruther's influence fell vacant, Lady Anstruther awarded the presentation to another candidate.[50] Chalmers received only another promise that his son would eventually be pro-vided for. Thomas, who was in Edinburgh at the time, was enraged when he learned of Lady Anstruther's behaviour. It was, he believed, a further demonstration of intolerable gentry arrogance. 'I shall only say', he informed his father regarding the Anstruthers on 18 July 1800,

that if you allow yourself to be imposed upon by their most solemn assurances, I may renounce for ever all hope, and all dependence upon your political influence. You have too often experienced the shocking ingratitude of these people to be warranted in attaching any confidence to their most sacred professions. I confess that I feel galled, when I reflect on the abominable policy of the Ansters [Anstruthers]. They heap Insult upon Insult with Impunity—secure in this, that you are too good to resent it, that you are so confirmed in your attachment to the good old Family, you will receive with a quiet submission any Injury or any Neglect they may please to impose on you, that you will look on with a tame forbearance, see the best hopes of your family disappointed, see Sycophants preferred, who while they enjoy the fruits of your influence and Exer-tions, laugh at your simplicity, and triumph over your unsuspecting goodness.

The only language the Anstruthers understood, he continued, was that of political power. After their long dominance in Fifeshire the gentry no longer responded to appeals either to justice or to gratitude for past service from those they considered social inferiors. He therefore advised his father to change his political allegiance and lead the opposition in the burgh council—in short, to organize the local Whig opposition to the Dundas ascendancy, which the Anstruthers now represented in the Anstruther Easter Burghs Parliamentary seat. This opposition should be built up secretly, so that 'they may not take the alarm, and secure their Interests in the other Burghs' before the next general election. 'By supporting them', he continued,

you have only their gratitude to trust to—and this you have often found to be a miser-able dependence. By a firm, manly, decided opposition, you alarm their Interest, and compel them to a decent deportment. Far be it from me to think of temping that un-shaken Integrity which has ever marked your political conduct. I know that you would disdain to bargain your vote, and I feel proud at the Idea.... But though your honour does not allow you to enter into any previous bargaining, are you not entitled to expect the gratitude of those, you have obliged; and if you don't meet with such gratitude, what is there in reason, or in justice that forbids you to withdraw your support?[51]

A sensible man, John Chalmers did not follow his son's advice. Rather, he continued to rely upon the Anstruthers' expressed intention to assist his family. In November 1800, then, when George Gib, minister of the Fifeshire parish of Wemyss, became seriously ill, John Chalmers approached the Anstruthers for assistance in procuring the presentation for Thomas in the event of Gib's death. Although Wemyss was actually in the gift of the Edinburgh Town Council, the Council deferred to the wishes of Henry Dundas, while Dundas, in turn, generally consulted the opinion of his principal political supporters in the district. In this case, however, the Anstruthers informed John Chalmers that Dundas had a candidate of his own in mind, so they could render him no assistance. Thomas, meanwhile, made his own canvass of members of the Edinburgh Town Council, and became convinced that the Anstruthers had fabricated the story of Dundas having his own candidate. They were, he believed, actually working to thwart his opportunity for the Wemyss presentation. By keeping him unprovided for, he explained to his father on 19 November 1800, the Anstruthers believed they would keep his father dependent upon them. 'But I hope', he continued, 'you will never suffer yourself to be imposed upon by such despicable finesse.' In the actual event, Gib recovered from his illness.[52] Chalmers's hatred for the Anstruthers, however, continued to rankle in his heart, and he repeatedly pressed his father to desert their connection.[53] Thomas also succeeded in gaining his older brother James's support for his campaign against his father's connection with the Anstruthers. 'I am anxious to see him settled,' James wrote his father of Thomas in September 1801,

but I think if we depend only on the promises of the great, our hairs may all be grey before we see that accomplished. If he is to owe his advancement to any political influence you may have, I think you should be carefull in what way it is used, for if their gratitude is all you have to depend on you will most assuredly be disappointed and I think it would be advisable your securing his interest before you bestow your favours— If the Anst[r] family had been uncertain of your support Thomas would have been provided for long ago.

Frustrated by the refusal of the Anstruther family either to recognize his abilities, or to reward his father's services, Chalmers reacted with bitter expressions to his friends about the evils of the Fifeshire gentry as a body. Eastern Fife, he complained to a former St. Andrews University companion, William Berry Shaw, now assistant minister in the border parish of Cavers, in July 1801, 'bears about with it every symptom of decay—a languishing trade—an oppressed tenantry—a rapacious gentry.' The gentry were 'a set of insolent oppressors' who employed the national war effort as an excuse for 'crushing all attempts at even an innocent freedom of observation and thought' among the home population. 'It would be well', he continued, 'for the great to reflect on their critical and dependent situation—to abolish that putrid system of interest which threatens to extinguish all the ardours of generous and patriotic sentiment—to adopt a more just and liberal conduct to inferiors.' Political opposition to self-interested landed families like the Anstruthers, he informed his father on 23 December 1801, was a Christian duty, so long as the opposition was pursued through legal channels.[54]

Chalmers did not advocate major social or political reform to destroy the 'putrid system of interest' and create a more just social order in Scotland. Instead, he told Shaw in July 1801, the only effective path to social reform was 'an individual reformation through the different orders of society'. In short, he was neither a political democrat nor a radical social reformer. However, in his anger with the gentry for ignoring his abilities and refusing to acknowledge his family's proper status in the hierarchy of social orders, his thought was beginning to move in a radical direction. A precocious young man, he began to feel alienated from the larger social structure which he believed did not respond to his talent or needs. The gentry, as the dominant social element in that society, were singled out for particular blame: their corrupt manoeuvres formed a convenient explanation for his failure to achieve his goals. This is not to say that many of the gentry in eastern Fife did not in fact set their self-interest against the good of the surrounding community. None the less, Chalmers's sense of alienation and the radical direction of his thought were more a function of thwarted ambition than of any defined social ideal.

His prospects for employment, however, soon began to improve. In August 1801, James Wilson, Professor of Ecclesiastical History at St. Andrews, had died, and was succeeded by John Trotter, Professor of Oriental Languages at the university. George Hill's cousin, John Cook, minister of Kilmany, a rural parish nine miles north-west of St. Andrews, then received Trotter's Chair of Oriental Languages, but on the condition that he resign the Kilmany living. Learning of these arrangements, Chalmers hurried to St. Andrews in September to solicit the professors of the United College, who were the patrons of Kilmany, for the presentation.[55] His father wished to request the Anstruthers to use their influence with Dundas, the University Chancellor, but Chalmers pleaded strongly against such a step: 'You surely see', he wrote to his father on 21 September, 'that this would dispose the professors to renounce me for another candidate who would consider his gratitude as due them, and to them only.' Moreover, he assured his father on 23 December, he would rather lose the presentation than receive a favour from the Anstruthers. In the event, the presentation was secured for him through the management of his father's cousin, the Whig professor John Adamson.[56] The Kilmany living was a large 'plum' for a young man not related to the Hill family to receive—the endowment of the parish guaranteed an income of approximately £200 per annum for the minister, while the parish population was only about 800.[57]

In the quiet St. Andrews University community, the arrangements occasioned by Wilson's death required several months to complete. During this interim, Chalmers accepted the offer of a position as assistant minister in the prosperous border parish of Cavers, vacant since the incumbent, Chalmers's friend William Berry Shaw, had been ordained minister of a neighbouring parish. Chalmers commenced his Cavers assistantship in December 1801, and was soon gratified to discover, as he told his father on 23 December, that his duties were 'sufficiently easy'.[58]

Meanwhile, in Cavers, his attention was devoted less to the parish ministry than to preparation for a course of mathematics lectures. Since at least the winter of 1801 he had directed his hopes toward eventually securing a university position as a mathematics instructor.[59] Then in December 1801, while he was travelling to Cavers, he had learned that his friend Thomas Duncan, who since 1798 had been the assistant to William Vilant, Professor of Mathematics at St. Andrews, had resigned his assistantship to assume a teaching position at Dundee Academy. Although Chalmers had experienced some personal conflicts with Vilant, a staunch Tory, in the past, he none the less asked both Duncan and James Brown to recommend him to Vilant. To his surprise, Vilant proved receptive.[60] By May 1802, he had secured both the mathematics assistantship and the presentation to Kilmany. In September, he resigned the Cavers assistantship and returned to St. Andrews. He was formally presented to Kilmany by the professors of the United College on 2 November 1802. Since he had the legal right to postpone his actual ordination as minister of the parish for another six months, he did not commence his duties in Kilmany until the following spring. Late in October, meanwhile, he began teaching three classes of elementary mathematics at St. Andrews University.

Although he was an eloquent lecturer, Chalmers's mathematics assistantship proved less than successful. From surviving portions of his lectures, it is evident that he combined social commentary with his mathematics lessons, emphasizing in particular the impact of scientific enquiry upon social improvement. 'In fact,' David Duff, one of his students, recalled in 1847, 'the study of Math^{cs}, under his extraordinary manag^t, was felt to be hardly less a play of fancy than a labour of the intellect, the lessons of the day being beautifully interspersed with continual applications and illustrations of the most lively nature.' Although his students apparently enjoyed his lectures, they did not progress as rapidly through the basic material as had classes in previous years. Vilant soon developed doubts regarding Chalmers's competence, and interfered with his authority over his classes. Chalmers, in turn, attempted to revenge himself upon Vilant by staging an exhibition before the assembled faculty and students during the public examinations at the close of the session. Accusing Vilant of granting certificates to students for successful completion of his classes without consulting him, Chalmers launched into sarcastic personal invective against him, which finally had to be silenced by George Hill. Not surprisingly, Chalmers's mathematics assistantship was terminated after one session.[61]

In May 1803, shortly after his public attack upon Vilant, Chalmers was ordained minister of Kilmany. With two sisters and a younger brother, whose support he undertook from his financially hard-pressed father, he moved into the rural manse. Throughout the summer, however, he brooded over his dismissal from the mathematics assistantship. It was legal in the Church of Scotland for a minister to combine a university teaching position with a parish living, and he had intended to pursue both occupations. He had hoped, moreover, that the assistantship would in time have led to a university chair. He convinced himself that he had been unjustly dismissed. To vindicate his reputation, then, he decided to return to St. Andrews in the next session and offer private mathematics classes in direct competition to those of Vilant's new assistant. 'You may perhaps by this time', he wrote to his father on 18 October 1803,

have heard of my intention to open Mathematical classes next Winter. I believe the measure will be opposed by a certain party of the St. Andrews professors. But I am sure they will not be able to ruin the success of my intended proceedings except by having recourse to dishonourable artifices. These artifices I shall be obliged to expose for my own vindication.

His chief purpose in writing, he explained, was to reconcile his father to his non-residence in Kilmany during the university session. His father, it will be recalled, was devoutly religious, with strict ideas regarding the responsibility of a parish minister. Indeed, father and son had already battled over what John Chalmers considered his son's neglect of his spiritual office. Therefore, although Chalmers would reside in St. Andrews during the academic session, he now assured his father that he would ride to Kilmany every Sunday to deliver a sermon. Two neighbouring clergymen, moreover, had promised to attend to his clerical responsibilities during the week. 'Your apprehensions with regard to the dissatisfaction of the parish are I can assure you quite groundless. I feel the footing on which I stand with them, and am certain that no serious or permanent offense will ever be excited.'[62] In truth, his father was correct to have apprehensions. Church-door collections, which had averaged £40 per annum during the last years of Cook's ministry at Kilmany, fell to £23 in 1804 and £16 in 1805, indicating dissatisfaction with Chalmers's ministry at least among the gentry and wealthier farmers of the parish.[63]

In November 1803, he commenced his private lectures to a small class of students meeting in the St. Andrews town hall. 'My appearance in this place', he announced in his initial lecture, 'may be ascribed to the worst passions; some may be disposed to ascribe it to the violence of a revengeful temper—some to stigmatize me as a firebrand of turbulence and mischief. These motives I disclaim. I disclaim them with the pride of an indignant heart which feels its integrity.'[64] His private lectures were an unprecedented event in St. Andrews, and aroused considerable excitement. Although George Hill evidently remained aloof from the affair, a party of professors led by John Rotheram, Professor of Natural Philosophy and a staunch Tory, endeavoured to rid the town of the interloper. Rotheram now alleged that he had voted for Chalmers's presentation to Kilmany only because Chalmers had promised him that he would give up teaching mathematics after his ordination. He therefore insisted that Chalmers was in honour bound to relinquish one of his occupations.

This allegation elicited a violent response. On 14 November, Chalmers accosted Rotheram on the street, and calling Vilant, who was passing by, as a witness, he accused Rotheram of being an impudent liar. On Vilant's suggestion, the enraged Rotheram threatened a civil prosecution for the slander. While he did not carry out his threat, the incident none the less increased the antagonism toward Chalmers among the St. Andrews Tories.[65] The Whigs in the university, meanwhile, led by John Adamson, Professor of Civil History, John Hunter, Professor of Humanities, and James Playfair, now Principal of the United College, encouraged Chalmers's efforts, evidently enjoying the embarrassment he was causing Hill's Tory interest.[66] The general excitement increased the enrolment in Chalmers's mathematics class, despite Vilant's efforts to restrain university students from attending. Growing more self-confident, Chalmers began teaching an additional course in chemistry in December 1803, which also proved popular[67]— so much so, that Rotheram now promised to offer a chemistry course in the university in the following year to compete with that of his young enemy.[68]

A more immediate challenge to Chalmers's lectures, however, arose in the neighbourhood of Kilmany. The parish lay within the ecclesiastical jurisdiction of the presbytery of Cupar. Since the mid-1790s, the clergy of this presbytery had agitated to abolish the right of a university instructor to hold a parish living.[69] Although their efforts had so far been unsuccessful, they remained hostile to this right, which constituted the only plurality of office allowed within the Church of Scotland. Not surprisingly, then, on 8 May 1804, a motion was introduced in the presbytery that Chalmers must either relinquish his private classes in St. Andrews, or be censured for neglecting his parish responsibilities.

Forewarned of the motion, he was prepared with a lengthy written defence. His dismissal from the mathematics assistantship in the university, he informed the presbytery, had been the work of a self-interested group of professors, who feared competition from a zealous young scientist. 'They had', he continued, 'gained their object—a name expunged from the list of competition—no further disturbance from interlopers—no literary upstart to stimulate their delicious repose, or to outstrip them in public esteem.' Without powerful patronage to protect him, his only recourse to vindicate his reputation had been to appeal to 'the confidence of an enlightened public'. It was for this reason alone that he had offered his private lectures. Strip him of this recourse, he exclaimed with oratorical hyperbole, and death itself would be welcome—'It would withdraw me from the agitations of a life that has been persecuted by the injustice of enemies, and still more by the treachery of violated friendship.'

Further, he asserted with rising passion, it was not only his own reputation that was at stake, but rather justice itself in the ecclesiastical courts. He had violated no Church law. It was still legal for a minister to teach in the university or to offer private courses, so long as he did not neglect his parish—and no one could prove he had done this. The only way he could be censured, therefore, was for the presbytery to claim a 'discretionary power' to contravene Church law. The fomenters of the present censure motion, Chalmers further intimated, were in fact acting as the tools of a powerful party of St. Andrews professors. If the presbytery, then, admitted discretionary power in this case, it would nullify the protection which the law should offer to the weak against the strong. 'Admit discretionary power,' he exclaimed,

and you open a scene of the grossest injustice. Our courts will become the humble instruments of men who have power or influence to overrule their proceedings. They will lend the aid of their decision to the policy of the powerful. At one time they will resist the impressive appeal of the injured, and laugh at his indignation as the ravings of a frantic enthusiasm. At another, they will refuse him a hearing, because they wish nothing disagreeable to come out—nothing to the disgrace or prejudice of a respectable body. True, the individual may have been injured, but far better to let him suffer than expose the infirmities of those who are men of rank and consideration.[70]

The presbytery's debate on the censure motion was public, and attended by a numerous body of spectators. Chalmers's eloquence apparently gained the sympathy of most spectators. More important, his argument won over the majority of the presbytery. The presbytery of Cupar opposed pluralities largely because they viewed them as a device by which the Hill connection of St. Andrews were enabled to increase their wealth and influence at the expense of surrounding parish communities. St. Andrews professors with parish livings all too often neglected their parishioners' spiritual needs. By emphasizing the danger of discretionary power, then, Chalmers identified himself with the local popular interest against the Hills, despite the fact that he was defending his plurality. So long as pluralities were legal in the Church, he argued, they must be legal for a 'poor literary pedlar, who trudges on to his literary station with a bundle of manuscripts and old wares from the country', as well as for a wealthy relation of the Hills. On the evening of 8 May, Chalmers was able to inform Brown that the censure motion 'met with the fate it deserved—was quashed and reprobated'.[71] Although successful in his defence before the presbytery, however, he became more circumspect in his behaviour. In the winter of 1804-5, he taught only his popular chemistry course, which required only two days a week of residence in St. Andrews.[72]

At the same time, he began to seek with greater earnestness a university chair. On 6 November 1804, before he could offer his chemistry course in competition with Chalmers, John Rotheram died. Chalmers immediately offered himself as a candidate for Rotheram's vacant Chair of Natural Philosophy. Unfortunately for him, however, the vacancy was of keen interest to both Hill and Dundas. The competition for this chair, Hill wrote to Dundas on 26 November, was extremely important politically, since the Foxite Whigs under the leadership of Adamson, Playfair, and Hunter had already gained a majority among the faculty of the United College and were thus in position to challenge Hill's Tory ascendancy in the university as a whole. Among the Whig candidates, Hill continued, were James Brown, John Leslie, and 'Mr. Chalmers, an eccentric Mathematician, who comes in from his parish in the country to read Lectures on Chemistry in our Town-Hall'.[73] All three Whig candidates would have to be blocked. In the event, Hill succeeded, on 1 December 1804, in managing the election of his brother-in-law, James MacDonald, to the chair.[74] 'My contempt', Chalmers assured his father that same day, 'for the low, shuffling artifices of college politics supports and elevates my mind against the vexation of regret.'[75]

A few weeks later, however, a vacancy occurred in the Edinburgh University Mathematics chair, and he again submitted himself to the 'low, shuffling artifices'. He travelled to Edinburgh in early February

1805, in order to solicit members of the Town Council, who were the patrons of the university, for the presentation. His father attempted to restrain him, but when Thomas persisted, his father did what he could, asking his business contacts on the Edinburgh Town Council for their assistance. However, as John Chalmers told James in regard to the Edinburgh Mathematics chair competition on 28 February 1805, 'I am rather concerned about Thomas.... He is no doubt very Clever and I have no doubt of his fitness for that situation but then his youth opened to the greatest abilities, experience, and Interest in the Country makes me doubt of his success and disappointment rather crushes an Aspiring young man. I should feel more comfortable were he to cultivate his present Situation where in my Opinion every comfort and necessary might be obtained and enjoyed.'[76]

The competition for the Edinburgh Mathematics chair in 1805 was a major event in both the political and ecclesiastical history of early nineteenth-century Scotland.[77] This is not, however, the place to discuss the complex issues and political manœuvres involved in the affair. Suffice it to say that Dundas's Tory interest on the Town Council and their clerical allies in the Edinburgh presbytery supported Thomas MacKnight, an Edinburgh clergyman, while the Whigs on the Town Council and their clerical allies supported John Leslie, who had recently been awarded the prestigious Rumford Medal by the Royal Society of London for his work on the nature of heat, and who was undoubtedly the better-qualified candidate. Leslie's appointment to the chair, after a hard-fought contest, represented both the beginning of the recovery of the Scottish Whig party after their bleak years in the 1790s, and a major defeat for the Dundas interest. It is significant that the Whig success in the Leslie affair coincided with the Parliamentary impeachment of Dundas, now Viscount Melville, for corruption in his office as Lord of the Admiralty, in April 1805. A more liberal political climate was commencing for Scotland.

Chalmers, however, was far from elated with a Whig victory which left him still without academic preferment. 'As you expected,' John Chalmers wrote to James on 24 April, 'Thomas did not succeed in his attempt at the Mathematical Chair in Edin^r. He was too late in appearing and had a very powerfull Interest against him in the Aplications of the great in favour of another Candidate, th'o its alowed he was the best qualified for that office.'[78] His father's letter no doubt reflected Chalmers's own feelings about his failure. Unwilling to acknowledge Leslie's superior achievements, he again attributed his defeat to the effects of privilege. It made little difference to him that the 'great' who had triumphed in this case had been Whigs. Returning to Kilmany, he broke the monotony of what he described to his brother James as 'the dull and unvaried course of a Clergyman's life', by indulging his wounded pride in writing a pamphlet. During the Leslie affair, John Playfair, Edinburgh Professor of Natural Philosophy, had published a remark impugning the capacity of clergymen to achieve eminence in mathematics, because, Playfair alleged, the two occupations did not complement one another. Chalmers responded to Playfair's allegation with his *Observations on a Passage in Mr. Playfair's Letter to the Lord Provost of Edinburgh Relative to the Mathematical Pretensions of the Scottish Clergy*, which he published in Cupar in August 1805.

The pamphlet was a juvenile and irresponsible production, which he would later regret. He devoted much of the work, for instance, to the argument that a clergyman possessed sufficient leisure in which to pursue excellence in mathematics, because a minister's parochial duties required little time or intellectual effort. 'The author of this pamphlet', he wrote, 'can assert, from what is to him the highest of all authority, the authority of his own experience, that after the satisfactory discharge of his parish duties, a minister may enjoy five days in the week of uninterrupted leisure, for the prosecution of any science in which his taste may dispose him to engage.' Almost no mental effort, he insisted, was required to preach 'the simple and homebred lessons of piety'.[79] In fact, the minister desperately needed intellectual stimulation to avoid sinking into mental apathy amid the tedium of parish life. Such expressions, to be sure, did not reveal a very serious view of a clergyman's parochial responsibilities. In truth, Chalmers's neglect of his own parish was blatant—reflected in the declining church-door collections, declining church attendance, and hostility towards him among many Kilmany parishioners.

The reason, Chalmers further argued, why more clergy did not employ their abundant leisure for mathematical or scientific pursuits was a prejudice existing against them among the otherwise enlightened public. People believed that the clergy, because of their theological education and spiritual office, were incapacitated for scientific effort. As a result of this prejudice, the doors of academic preferment were closed to them.[80] Discouraged, the clergy withdrew from scientific pursuits altogether, and a great potential seed-bed for academic accomplishment was lost to the nation. A major agency behind this prejudice, he continued, was the monopoly over preferments in the five Scottish universities, maintained by a relatively small group of established academic families and their connections. By encouraging the anti-clerical prejudice, these academic élites effectively restricted competition for academic positions, and thus helped to sustain their monopoly. During the Leslie affair, Playfair had asserted that if Mac-Knight, a parish minister, received the appointment, there would be a danger of creating a clerical monopoly in the Scottish universities. But in fact, Chalmers argued, Playfair was striving to preserve a monopoly for his own 'literary junto'. 'I am', he continued,

ready to join with MR. PLAYFAIR in deprecating the domineering influence of church politics; and I hope he will be equally ready to join with me, in deprecating the haughty and unprincipled arrogance of a reigning school—a school that would arrogate to itself, and to a junto of interested friends, all the praises of philosophy—a school that would exclude the pretensions of obscure and unsupported genius—a school that would aspire to the unlimited direction of taste and science in the country—and would presume to erect an uncontrollable despotism in the republic of letters.[81]

Chalmers's 'monopoly' argument, when applied to Leslie's appointment, was hardly realistic. Leslie had travelled widely, and had published a number of translations and reviews in natural science and mathematics before being awarded the Rumford Medal. Further, Leslie had spent many years in the 'wilderness' of Scottish academic life, without the recognition or the university chair which his accomplishments had warranted, largely because of his attachment to liberal political principles. In a word, Leslie had paid his dues. Although his talents had earned the respect of leading academics like Playfair, his appointment was by no means the mere machination of an entrenched academic élite. Chalmers, on the other hand, had published nothing, while his teaching career at St. Andrews, including his private lectures, had not been impressive. There was no reason why he should have received the appointment over Leslie. For him to blame his failure in the competition on anti-clerical prejudice fomented by such an élite in fact revealed his lack of maturity—his inability to recognize his limitations and accept responsibility for his shortcomings. He had yet to learn that academic prestige required sacrifice and work as well as talent and ambition.

The pamphlet, however, was not totally without value. It contained, in particular, some eloquent passages extolling the ideal of equality of opportunity. He sincerely believed that his ambition had been thwarted by an established, self-seeking political interest—that the Anstruthers, the Hills at St. Andrews, and now the Whig academic establishment at Edinburgh had stifled his professional development at every turn. His fervent opposition to such privileged élites carried him still further towards the popular cause in the political divisions of early nineteenth-century Scotland. He was neither by conviction nor temperament a political democrat. What he now passionately espoused was the right of each individual, regardless of his place of birth in the hierarchy of social orders, to be allowed to advance himself up the social ladder by his merit alone, unhindered by established interests or corporate bodies. Given his birth and upbringing—without wealth, and largely (though not wholly) without influence to advance his career—it is not, perhaps,

surprising that he should envisage an open society in which men of
talent and initiative alone might rise through the social ranks. Free
competition in the learned professions was particularly important for
achieving this social ideal. He possessed little faith in political action
for establishing a more open society, placing his hope, rather, on the
moral reformation of individuals. For this, he looked to the educational
functions of the universities and the Church. In order to fulfil their
potential for national reform, however, these institutions would have
to be purged of 'the putrid system of interest', and opened to talent
from all social ranks.

Chalmers was also influenced towards these views by a group of
young Edinburgh Whigs. Mainly lawyers, whose politics made it
difficult for them to obtain briefs in a Tory-dominated legal system,
this group included Francis Jeffrey, Henry Brougham, Francis Horner,
and Sydney Smith. In October 1802 they had founded the *Edinburgh
Review*, with the aim of levelling entrenched academic and political
interests, in order to create a more open society of free competition.
In pursuing this goal, the reviewers struck, with animation and wit, at
the literary canons and social, political, and economic ideas which they
believed supported the privileges of entrenched interests[82]—that is, the
means they adopted were essentially educational. The immediate
success of the review indicated that there was indeed a large literate
public in Scotland weary of Dundas's repressive political ascendancy.
From its first appearance, Chalmers had been a regular and enthusiastic
reader, writing to Archibald Constable, the publisher of the review on
1 October 1803: 'In ability of discussing the variety of its ingenious and
original speculations, in its enlightened contempt for the insolence of
literary authority, I think it far outstrips any publication of the kind
that this country has to boast of.' 'May the young Philosophers of
Edin^r', he continued,

succeed in their manly and independent effort at literary distinction. May they learn to
rise though unfavoured by the patronage of the established characters. May they
succeed in overthrowing those vile monopolists of literature who arrogate all the praises
of Philosophy to themselves, and to the junto of interested friends, who exclude the
pretensions of obscure and indigent genius, who aspire to the unlimited direction of
Taste and Science in the country, and who would presume to erect an uncontractable
despotism in the republic of Letters.[83]

In a word, the *Edinburgh Review* encouraged Chalmers to define his
personal struggle against 'the putrid system of interest' in larger terms.
Instead of a merchant's son struggling for university preferment, he
elevated his ambition into a crusade for a more open and progressive
society.

There was indeed a new vision of social improvement developing among the young Whigs of Scotland in the first years of the century. The Foxite Whigs of the previous generation had conceived of social reform almost exclusively in terms of political action. In the 1780s, the Scottish Whigs had struggled to extend the narrow Parliamentary franchise, to reform the corrupt self-electing burgh councils by pro- viding a more popular election of councillors, and to abolish corruption in national government, largely through the abolition of sinecure offices. The movement for political reform, however, had been almost totally suppressed by the political reaction to the threat of revolution in the 1790s. The generation of Whigs coming of age in the 1790s, therefore, held little hope for social change through political means. Rather, they based their hopes on the education of the new generation of public opinion.[84] By destroying the ideological bases upon which the privileged interests rested, they believed those interests would in time fall, and the way be cleared for an improved social order. The emerging generation were more idealistic than their fathers, with a greater faith in the social effects of moral persuasion. They were not, however, unrealistic in their expectations. The press was growing rapidly in the early nine- teenth century, with a dramatic increase in the number of newspapers and reviews, and there was a real possibility of creating the foundation for eventual social and political reform through appeals to an enlightened public opinion.

III

In October 1801, the British Government entered into a peace agree- ment with Napoleonic France. For Scotland, the peace of Amiens sig- nalled a gradual easing of the political tensions of the 1790s. Fear of Jacobin revolution was decreasing, and men of all shades of political persuasion were growing weary of the bitter divisions of the previous decade. The changing political atmosphere was further reflected in the waning of Henry Dundas's Tory ascendancy. As early as 1797, Dundas had begun to lose control over the numerous personal connections which bound candidates and constituencies to his interest. By February 1801, with the resignation of Pitt's Government, Dundas was out of office. The reign of 'Harry the ninth', which had dominated Scottish life and kept the Scottish Whigs in the wilderness for nearly two dec- ades, was approaching its end.

The peace of Amiens, however, lasted only fourteen months. Neither Britain nor France trusted each other's desire for peace; neither fulfilled the treaty's terms regarding withdrawal of troops from key strategic areas. In May 1803, war was resumed and Napoleon massed an army near Boulogne, in preparation for the invasion of Britain. The threat of invasion in 1803 united the Scottish nation as the war effort had not done in the 1790s. Beginning in 1794, local regiments of volunteers had been formed throughout Scotland, ostensibly for defence against French invasion. In reality, the volunteers had been employed largely to maintain internal tranquillity by suppressing political reform meetings and bread riots. Although his father had commanded a volunteer unit in Anstruther during the 1790s, Chalmers, like most men of liberal sentiments, had deprecated the volunteer movement.[85] With the peace of Amiens, the volunteers had been disbanded, to the general relief of the Scottish Whigs. In 1803, however, they were reconstituted, and the threat of imminent invasion gave them a changed complexion. Whigs now enlisted with Tories in local volunteer units. Francis Jeffrey, for instance, the young Whig editor of the *Edinburgh Review*, envisaged for himself a heroic death at the end of a pike, while his fellow Whig reviewers, less pessimistically, enjoyed the cameraderie of manœuvres on the Portobello beach.[86] 'Napoleon's obvious progress toward military despotism', the Edinburgh Whig and volunteer Henry Cockburn later recalled, 'opened the eyes of those who used to see nothing but liberty in the French revolution, and the threat of invasion, while it combined all parties in defence of the country, raised the confidence of the people in those who trusted them with arms. ... Instead of Jacobinism, Invasion became the word.'[87]

The Government's proclamation of a national fast day on Sunday, 20 October 1803, received a warm response from most pulpits of the Church of Scotland. There was, however, probably no more enthusiastic a fast-day sermon than that of the young minister of Kilmany, who thrilled to a martial spirit which could now also be regarded as popular. With impassioned oratory, Chalmers summoned his congregation to the defence of their liberty and property. With Napoleon's 'cannibal banditti' poised across the channel, he explained, patriotism had become a popular cause, and every individual now possessed a fundamental interest in Britain's war effort. Were the French invaders to triumph, British communities would be rent asunder, property plundered, and the survivors enslaved. Each individual was therefore summoned to sacrifice in the national defence effort—for himself, his family, and his community. At issue was the survival of civilization in Britain.

His language reflected intense feeling. 'We are not called upon', he exclaimed, 'to defend any particular order of men. We are not called upon to defend the principles and views of any party. We are not called upon to defend the possessions of the wealthy, or the rank of the noble. It is to defend the country from massacre.' French invaders, he assured his congregation, would spare no one, rich or poor. 'Let it not be said that you have no interest in the defence of the nation. You may live in a straw-built shed, and have an equal interest with him who triumphs in all the magnificence of wealth, and is invested with the proudest honours of nobility.' To preach patriotism, then, was neither to defend the privileges of the few, nor to demand the submission of the people to unjust authority. 'I trust there is not a man among us who would not willingly renounce the smiles of the great and the patronage of power, rather than concur in supporting the measures of an arbitrary and oppressive government.' Rather, to preach patriotism was to proclaim man's Christian responsibility. For the protection of the national community, each man was called by sacred duty, even to the supreme sacrifice. 'May that day', he exclaimed, 'in which Buonaparte ascends the throne of Britain be the last of my existence; may I be the first to ascend the scaffold he erects to extinguish the wealth and spirit of the country; may my blood mingle with the blood of patriots; and may I die at the foot of that altar on which British independence is to be the victim.'[88]

Immediately after his fast-day sermon of October 1803, Chalmers enrolled in the St. Andrews volunteer corps, with a dual commission as lieutenant and chaplain. He was an enthusiastic volunteer. In the autumn of 1805, for instance, after the publication of his pamphlet against Playfair, he joined his volunteer corps for several weeks of active duty in Kirkcaldy, twenty miles south of Kilmany. He could have avoided active duty, which required another period of non-residence in his parish, but he revelled in the forms of military life. Indeed, he seriously considered a career in the regular army. While in Kirkcaldy, he made a lasting impression while preaching to his corps one afternoon in the church: warming in his patriotic discourse, he threw back his black clerical gown to reveal, with dramatic effect, the blue of his volunteer uniform.[89]

Chalmers now became preoccupied with the volunteer movement and the cause of national defence. For years, he had struggled to gain the patronage of the 'great' and the recognition of an 'enlightened public', in his pursuit of academic prestige and influence. Embittered by his failure to achieve academic preferment, he had reacted with bitter denunciations of social élites and the politics of interest. There was, in a word, a tension which had grown steadily during his youth between his personal ambition for enhanced social status, and his denunciations of those privileged élites, whether gentry like the Anstruthers or academics like the Hills of St. Andrews or Playfair of Edinburgh, who refused to patronize him.

The Scottish Enlightenment and the academic élite into which Chalmers had sought entry were essentially urban in nature. Late eighteenth- and early nineteenth-century Scottish intellectual life elevated individualism, entrepreneurship, competition, and the other values of urban commercial society. If each individual pursued his self-interest, Adam Smith had argued in his celebrated *Wealth of Nations*, the 'invisible hand' of God would ensure the welfare of society as a whole. The *Wealth of Nations*, in many respects, epitomized the ideology of the Scottish Enlightenment. There was, however, another Scotland, which for Chalmers was represented by the closed and largely self-sufficient community of Anstruther. During his youth there he had been nurtured within the essentially communal values of benevolence, interdependence, and co-operation. In Anstruther, the hand of God was not so hidden: the Church was explicit in its social teachings.

The threat of French invasion had provided a common national cause, in which internal political conflicts and the 'putrid system of interest' might be absorbed. The volunteer movement became for Chalmers the occasion for a return to the communal values of his Anstruther youth. The national interest, as Chalmers had defined it in his fast-day sermon of October 1803, meant essentially the interest of the small cottager in his 'straw-built shed' and of the small parish community. With his fast-day sermon, he passionately reaffirmed allegiance to the communitarian social ideal of Scotland's covenanting, pre-Enlightenment past. His ideological response to the threat of Napoleonic despotism was almost Spartan. The hierarchy of social orders and the various social interest groups would, he hoped, be re-united by a common benevolence, but, more important, by a shared willingness to sacrifice their wealth and lives in order to perpetuate the national community. The satanic barbarism of French military power would provide the occasion for the revival of Scotland's social traditions. Men would no longer be content to pursue their self-interest, while relying upon chance or the 'invisible hand' of God to protect the common interest. Rather, each member of the community would work, sacrifice, and assume conscious responsibility for a goal greater than the individual—that is, the preservation of the national community and the ideals of liberty, security, and benevolence which it represented. Through the volunteer movement, the Scottish people would covenant together, as of old, for the preservation of their civilization. This national community ideal, meanwhile, offered Chalmers an opportunity to resolve the tension between his individual ambition for admission into the ranks of the privileged élite, and his bitterness towards the élites who would not recognize his talents or grant him admission. With Napoleon poised for invasion, he believed, there was now only one interest, that of defence, and only one criterion for judgement of a man, that of his willingness to struggle and sacrifice for the national community.

Chalmers was not, however, destined to lead his volunteers in battle against French invaders. On 21 October 1805, Nelson incapacitated the combined French and Spanish fleets at Trafalgar, ending the

immediate threat of invasion. Both the British and French Govern-
ments now reverted to economic warfare. France attempted to close the
European Continent, which Napoleon largely controlled, to British
trade; Britain, in turn, attempted to blockade the French-controlled
Continental ports. The consequences of this interruption of British
commerce with the Continent were serious for British shipping and
manufactures. British exports fell dramatically, resulting in economic
depression, and alarm that economic warfare might soon force Britain
to sue for peace.

In April 1807, with the economic crisis approaching its most serious
stage, Chalmers left Kilmany for three months to make his first journey
to London. The trip was a major educational experience, and the detailed journal which he kept of his impressions indicates his readiness to
learn. On his southward journey, he remained a week with relatives in
Liverpool, where the effects of the interruption of trade were particularly acute. He visited the stock exchanges and the harbour facilities,
and requested information about the city's provision for the poor, who
were increasing in number as a result of the commercial depression.
From Liverpool, he travelled to Birmingham and other Midlands
industrial centres. Armed with letters of introduction from his Liverpool acquaintances, he was given tours of Midlands factories; soon his
journal abounded with detailed technical descriptions of the industrial
processes which were transforming English society.[90]
His scientific curiosity was aroused by the new marvels of English
ingenuity.

He arrived in London on 3 May and remained three weeks with his
brother James, now an accountant with a commercial firm in the City.[91]
He visited most of the sights of London, attended scientific lectures and
exhibitions, and met a few minor literary figures. On the whole, he was
not impressed with either the religious or intellectual life of the capital.
'Oh London,' he noted in his journal on 12 May, 'artful as a serpent in
the dark and tortuous paths of iniquity, but simple and credulous as a
child in the higher fields of intellect.'[92] Politics, however, were a different matter. The country was then in the midst of a general election,
and Chalmers spent long hours listening at the Westminster hustings,
where he delighted in the eloquence of the great Whig orator, Richard
Brinsley Sheridan. Having long admired Charles James Fox, the Whig
leader who had died in the previous year, Chalmers was now deeply
moved by 'a most eloquent eulogium on Fox' given by Sheridan at the
hustings. He also visited the House of Commons, where he 'looked
with veneration at Fox's seat'.[93] Immediately after the inspiration of
Sheridan's eulogy of Fox, Chalmers proceeded to the Covent Garden
theatre, where he thrilled to Mrs Siddons's performance in Shake-
speare's *Coriolanus*. 'I was electrified at the drawing out of the dagger,
"to die while Rome was free".' James, meanwhile, was amazed at the

scope of his brother's activity, informing their father that Thomas had seen more of London in three weeks than he had in as many years. But their father, anxious about his son's neglect of his parish, was not impressed, and urged James to hurry Thomas home.[94] In early July, Chalmers finally returned to Kilmany. The three month journey to London had been a significant exposure to the diversity of the British Kingdom. His reactions to this experience, as reflected in his journal, reveal an increasingly romantic and sentimental direction in his thought.

Although he had displayed curiosity regarding the technical aspects both of high finance in London and of the industrial processes in the Midlands, Chalmers had chafed against the social effects of English industrialization. Rather, his imagination had been drawn towards vistas of English glory, learning, and grandeur, which he also feared were fading before the new industrial order. At Blenheim, for instance, the home built by the British nation in the early eighteenth century to honour the military achievements of the Duke of Marlborough, his imagination was stirred to romantic reverie. 'The pleasure I felt,' he noted of his afternoon at Blenheim on 30 April,

was heightened by a variety of circumstances which supplied associations of grandeur. In addition to the stateliness of actual display, I had the recollection of its origin, the immortality of its first owner, the proud monument of national glory, the prospect not of a house, or scene, or a neighbourhood, but the memorial of those events which had figured on the high theatre of war and of politics, and given a turn to the history of the world.

He wandered about the park surrounding Blenheim, contemplating 'the prowess of the first of warriors', and wept with rapture. Romantic visions of past glory were further awakened by his visit to Oxford the following day. 'Amid the grossness of a mercantile age,' he observed, 'it is the delight of my spirit to recur to the quiet scenes of philosophy, and contemplate what our ancestors have done for learning, and the respect that they once paid to it.'[95]

On the whole, then, Chalmers's impressions of industrializing England had been disturbing. Just as Napoleonic power threatened the independence of the British nation, so, he believed, the 'grossness of a mercantile age' threatened the ideals of military glory and intellectual achievement which for him provided the chief *raison d'être* for the national community. English industrialization represented for him the social dangers of unrestrained materialism. As with his volunteer enthusiasm, so during his London tour he demonstrated his veneration for an ideal-ized past when, he believed, ideals were more valued than material production or wealth.

Excited by his experiences in England, he was in no mood to devote himself wholly to his clerical office in Kilmany. 'You hinted to me, when in London,' he wrote to James from Kilmany on 9 September 1807, 'the propriety of making some effort in the way of publication. I have accordingly been engaged in some discussions on the subject of the Public Revenue, which I think may excite the attention of politicians.'[96] By early December 1807, his first major work, the *Enquiry into the Extent and Stability of National Resources*, was substantially complete. Unable to contract with a publisher, he travelled to Edinburgh in February 1808, and personally supervised the printing of 500 copies at his own expense. The volume of 365 octavo pages appeared in Edinburgh on 28 March, and 200 copies were dispatched to the London booksellers, Longman and Rees—from whom he expected 'a very handsome allowance' from the English sale of the work.[97] He requested James to convey complimentary copies to leading Government ministers and a few other 'public men', including William Wilberforce, the Evangelical politician, and William Cobbett, the radical journalist. He also dispatched an abstract of the work, which James was to request Cobbett to print in his *Political Register*, the leading radical journal in London. 'Assure Cobbett,' he instructed James on 6 April, that 'the author is attached to no party, but has followed the logical train of his speculations to conclusions which may prove disagreeable to both parties.'[98] James and Thomas's friend David Wilkie, an artist born and raised in Fifeshire, but now residing in London, were further requested to ensure that the work was adequately advertised in the London press. 'The only thing wanted', he informed James on 20 April, 'is to impress the public with the idea, that it is by no means a fleeting or ephemeral performance—that it is a subject of permanent importance, and independently of all application to the present circumstances of the Country, that it offers some new and original doctrines to political science.'[99]

The *Enquiry* was, on one level, directed to the debate then occupying the public mind regarding the effect of Napoleon's Continental System upon Britain's capacity to continue the war. But Chalmers intended his work to be more than simply a polemical tract written in response to a particular set of circumstances at a particular time. It represented, he believed, an original contribution to the comparatively new science of political economy, and if properly heeded would provide the blueprint for a fundamental transformation of British society. The key to the work lay in its challenge to the prevailing commercial spirit in Britain. In the *Enquiry*, Chalmers rejected as erroneous the belief then predominant among Government ministers and economic writers that foreign commerce was essential to the survival of the nation. This error, he believed, lay at the foundation of what he viewed as Britain's present 'gross mercantile age'. In the past, British wealth and energy had been devoted to projects of national glory, represented, for instance, by

Blenheim, a monument to military power, and Oxford, a monument to learning. In the present 'mercantile age', however, wealth was squandered upon insignificant luxury consumption. But now, he hoped, Napoleon's Continental System would finally awaken the nation to the sufficiency of its natural resources to support its entire population in comfort, and to the importance of rechannelling the wealth and energy previously wasted upon commerce towards the more permanent good of national glory. The central argument of the book was that the diminution of foreign commerce would prove beneficial to the British nation.

The *Enquiry* represented the culmination of the early development of Chalmers's social ideal. First, the work reflected his experiences in the primarily agrarian society of eastern Fife. The economic ideal of the *Enquiry* was static and agrarian; his ideal society would produce sufficient food to sustain its entire population, and therefore would not be required to import foodstuffs. There would be only enough small factories or cottage-based trades to provide the population with basic clothing, housing, and a few simple comforts. Commerce would be limited to a coastal trade, like that which predominated in Anstruther. He possessed little appreciation for the dynamic forces of industrialization developing in the west of Scotland or the Midlands of England. Rather, he argued that the Government should curb industrial growth. Unrestrained industrial growth, he maintained, created what he termed a 'redundant population' of industrial labourers who could not be fed from Britain's own agricultural resources, and who therefore required the importation of foodstuffs in exchange for the export of industrial products. Should a foreign enemy interfere with Britain's commerce, this 'redundant population' would be threatened with starvation. By taxing the surplus agricultural wealth which he believed sustained the industrial sector, and by transferring the redundant industrial population to State service in the armed forces, the State would achieve national economic self-sufficiency. At the same time, moreover, the whole of British society would return in tastes and habits to 'the humble stile and simplicity of our grandfathers'—to a time when communal virtues such as benevolence and self-sacrifice were more highly valued than the material luxuries provided by commerce and industrialization.[100]

Secondly, the *Enquiry* reflected Chalmers's opposition to privileged social élites, who through wealth, or political influence purchased by wealth, were encouraged to pursue individual self-interest at the expense of other members of the community, particularly the lower social orders. Increased taxation, he believed, would prove an effective means for rechannelling the wealth which supported privilege, and thus for absorbing 'the putrid system of interest' in a general national cause. Chalmers did not advocate levelling the existing hierarchy of ranks in British society; rather, he advocated basing an individual's social rank upon his contribution to the cause of the nation, instead of upon the extent of his luxury consumption. For this purpose, he advocated an unprecedented rate of taxation—20 per cent of an individual's landed income above £50 per annum, (£50 per annum being in his view sufficient to maintain a family in 'the humble stile and simplicity of our grandfathers').[101] There was, he argued, only one pre-eminent national interest, and each individual's social value was a function of his service to this national cause.

Finally, in the *Enquiry* Chalmers expressed a desire to organize the kingdom for the pursuit of ideals which transcended the materialistic standards of the present 'gross mercantile age'. In this, he opposed in particular the emerging doctrine of utilitarianism. With increasing influence, the utilitarian school of economists were arguing that the greatest temporal pleasure for the greatest number of people was the supreme justification for social organization. This temporal pleasure, they further maintained, would be achieved through increased material consumption, which in turn would result from increased industrial production. Greater production, in turn, would come when each individual was allowed the maximum possible freedom to pursue his self-interest. Chalmers, however, rejected this view. Social happiness, he argued, would not be truly attained through increased material consumption. Rather, each individual had to be educated, through participation in the life of the national community, to direct his thoughts toward a higher, communal ideal. In the *Enquiry*, he elevated the independence and the military glory of the British nation to supreme importance as transcendent ideals around which individuals would be united into a national community. He did not question the importance of the individual. Rather, he argued that the individual would discover his real fulfilment by contributing to the achievement of national glory and thus helping to perpetuate British civilization through time. Napoleonic France, he added, had mobilized the resources of the entire nation behind the military effort which had subdued most of Europe. Britain, then, would also need to learn both to subordinate private interests to the national good and to practise the principles of Spartan self-denial, were she to transmit her civilization to future generations.[102]

His vision of social reform found few converts. 'It is not a little remarkable', the *Eclectic Review* noted in its review of the *Enquiry* in July 1808,

that a man should write a book for the rectification of human affairs, plausible enough, and not devoid of a certain kind of knowledge and ingenuity, yet should never, in the whole course of it, reflect upon the great spring of human movement and action; should propose a scheme of political arrangement, in express contradiction to it. ... Who knows not that the grand principle of all industry and improvement among mankind, is the desire and hope of bettering their condition.

Chalmers's scheme of national organization, 'formed on the principle of reducing the population to the bare necessaries of life', would 'destroy completely all industry'. Without the prospect of improving their material living standards, of enjoying certain 'luxuries', men would not exert themselves. Ideals like national glory, the *Eclectic* argued, were insufficient to sustain men in daily labour. Under Chalmers's communal plan of social organization, a general social languor would swiftly reduce British society to the same level of 'barbarism' which Chalmers feared from the extension of Napoleonic despotism.

Further, the *Eclectic* maintained, Chalmers's plan for empowering the British Government to tax away surplus agricultural wealth, to curb industrial growth, and to force a large portion of the industrial labouring population into the military, would in effect create a Napoleonic despotism in Britain. Indeed, Chalmers apparently desired to eliminate the 'redundant' population through unnecessary warfare in order to achieve his goals of national self-sufficiency and military glory. The country, according to the *Eclectic*, wanted neither goal at such a cost in human life.[103] Similar sentiments, meanwhile, were also expressed in the June issue of the *Farmers Magazine*, an Edinburgh agricultural journal. 'We cannot sufficiently admire', the *Farmers Magazine* observed, 'the coolness with which this rev. gentleman speaks of sweeping the redundant population from the face of the country. He absolutely rivals Richard III,

> "Off with his head!
> So much for Buckingham."'[104]

Aside from the reviews in the *Eclectic Review* and *Farmers Magazine*, Chalmers's *Enquiry* received little attention from the literary journals. His son-in-law and biographer, William Hanna, believed that this was a result of the public attention directed to William Spence's pamphlet, *Britain Independent of Commerce*, which had appeared late in 1807, shortly before the publication of the *Enquiry*.[105] Like Chalmers, Spence had argued that Napoleon's Continental System would prove healthy for Britain's economy, because foreign commerce only diminished national wealth. Spence's basic argument was that through foreign commerce, Britain exchanged durable and useful commodities, like clothing and machinery, for perishable luxury goods, like tea and wine. Although he lacked Chalmers's enthusiasm for military glory, Spence shared much of his social vision. Britain, Spence had asserted, should relinquish foreign commerce, which catered only to the luxuries of the upper social orders, and concentrate upon developing internal industries and a more equitable distribution of industrial products for the benefit of all social ranks.[106] Spence's arguments had been ably refuted by the utilitarian economist, James Mill (in a pamphlet entitled *Commerce Defended*), and by the English clergyman, T. R. Malthus (in two articles in the *Edinburgh Review*).[107] Both Mill and Malthus argued that commerce encouraged individual entrepreneurship, and along with it the development of manufacturing industries. Industrialization, in turn, provided increased employment and inexpensive consumer goods, which improved material living standards for all social orders. With Spence so competently disposed of, few journals were prepared to grant the *Enquiry* much attention.

Chalmers had anticipated initial opposition or even indifference to the *Enquiry*. When Spencer Perceval, the Chancellor of the Exchequer, did not acknowledge receipt of his complimentary copy, he was not discouraged. 'He may not have read it,' he told his brother James on 16 April 'and even if he has read it, he may not relish it, because he and his colleagues are all mercantile. Both parties and individuals may condemn it, not because they can refute its principles; but because they dislike them. All this may happen but I would not be discouraged by it. For throwing aside all regard to individuals and the opinions of individuals, my whole anxiety is to be fairly and speedily introduced to the notice of a London public.'[108] In a word, he looked to the public (that is, to the community as a whole) for the support denied his work by private individual or party interests. Once the public had been properly introduced to the work, he believed, private interest groups would be forced to yield to the general will. In order to educate the British public, however, Chalmers was convinced he must contract with a London publisher.

This, however, proved impossible to manage. In late April, the London bookselling firm of Longman and Rees turned down Chalmers's offer to contract with them for the publication of a second edition of 1,500 copies, and evidently showed disrespect to James in voicing their refusal. 'I received yours,' Chalmers informed James on 3 May, 'and am quite disgusted at the Longmans. I beg, you would expose yourself to no further indignities from that quarter. ... I hope the day may yet come when I shall have my revenge by lashing their Insolence in the Ear of the public.' He convinced himself that Longman and Rees were conspiring to repress the sale of the *Enquiry* in London from a personal dislike for Scotsmen, and he therefore instructed James to remove all unsold copies of the *Enquiry* from their hands.[109] On Chalmers's instructions, David Wilkie and James then attempted to sell the copyright to several other London publishing firms, but without success. In May, Chalmers decided to have the second edition published in

Edinburgh, but he could find no publisher there either. Nor could he afford, he confessed to James on 25 May, to print another edition in Edinburgh at his own expense. He now began to complain of ill health, and his letters to his brother reveal nervous irritation. He complained to James, for instance, of Wilkie's incompetence, alleging that he had 'blundered the affair' of locating a London publisher. In June, Chalmers decided to print a second edition at his own expense in Cupar, only to be informed by the Cupar printer that he had no time to assist with such a work. Growing desperate, on 28 June he instructed James to circulate a final offer among the London publishing firms. 'I surrender every consideration of Emolument, and offer it to them upon no terms, only that they take the risque and management, and proceed to the execution of it immediately.'[110] The London publishers, however, refused the work even upon 'no terms'.

Chalmers was deeply hurt by the failure. Nevertheless, he remained convinced that the *Enquiry* constituted a major contribution, promising to 'give a totally different aspect to the Science of Political Economy'. A well-advertised second edition, he believed, could not fail to win public opinion to his principles. In mid-July, then, despite poor health and straitened financial circumstances, he decided to travel to London. 'My great object in going to London', he told James on 23 July, 'is to get introduced into some of the literary circles, and if possible initiated into some of the mysteries of the *Trade*. ... What I at present think of doing is to throw my discussion into a more permanent shape, and bring it forward in a form that may render it applicable to all times and to all countries.'[111] In particular, he contemplated writing a major refutation of the arguments of Adam Smith regarding the social benefits of free trade and unrestrained economic individualism.

On the eve of his departure for London, however, he was summoned to Anstruther by the news that his sister Barbara had entered the later stages of consumption, and was approaching death. Five years older than Thomas, Barbara had been a close companion. She had accompanied him on journeys to Liverpool and the south of Scotland, and had shared his manse at Kilmany for several summers. Her death on 19 August, after a painful illness, was a severe blow, and in his grief he now postponed his intended London journey. In the autumn he visited his younger brother Patrick, a factor on a landed estate near Edinburgh. There he collapsed, with a severe illness no doubt aggravated by the emotional strain of the past several months. It confined him for several weeks in Patrick's cottage, and it was only in late November that he was able to return to northern Fife. His health remained poor, and rather than return to the manse at Kilmany, which during the past several years had been allowed, through his neglect, to decay to the point where it was uninhabitable, he rented a small house on the southern shore of the Firth of Tay, overlooking Dundee. On 17 January 1809, he informed James that he had decided to postpone indefinitely both the London journey and his proposed revision of the *Enquiry*.

The failure of Chalmers's *Enquiry* may be attributed in part to his lack of reputation as an author. More important, however, the book failed to gain significant public support because it criticized the existing social, economic, and political structures, and fundamentally offended against many of the most cherished values of early nineteenth-century Britain. In the *Enquiry*, Chalmers had envisaged a communal society characterized by unity and consensus of purpose, closely directed by a strong central government, and organized for military defence. Although he advocated preserving a hierarchical order of social ranks, he none the less maintained that each individual's rights within this hierarchy should be strictly subordinated to his duty to the communal welfare. Freedom, in Chalmers's conception, meant primarily the liberty of the community as a whole from foreign domination. For the individual, then, freedom meant not personal liberty from governmental restraint, but rather the opportunity to find personal fulfilment by contributing consciously to the independence of the national community. His was a closely-defined social system, Spartan in its demands upon the individual.

Such a social vision, however, bore little relation to the existing society of early nineteenth-century Britain. Following the civil and religious strife of the seventeenth century, British society had accorded increasing respect to individual rights, diversity, and toleration. Freedom, for most British citizens, meant the freedom of the individual from restraint by the State, and the opportunity of the individual for self-improvement and (to a certain extent) advancement through the hierarchy of social ranks. The national debating forum of Parliament functioned relatively effectively to represent the broad spectrum of diverse and often competing interests within the political nation. The dynamic behind the economic achievements of industrializing Britain, as the *Eclectic Review* had asserted in its critique of the *Enquiry*, was its relatively open society, which encouraged individual initiative and exertion. In order to preserve this open society, the power and the functions of central government were limited. In truth, the Spartan social ideal of the *Enquiry*, as both the *Eclectic Review* and the *Farmers Magazine* had observed, bore more resemblance to the social principles of Napoleonic France than to the tastes or inclinations of the British people. In early nineteenth-century Britain, the doctrines of Adam Smith's *Wealth of Nations* were increasingly becoming orthodox social and economic theory. The *Enquiry*, however, fundamentally opposed the emerging doctrines of economic individualism, free trade, pacificism, and limited government, which characterized both Smith's *Wealth of Nations* and British society during its nineteenth-century era of Classical Liberalism.

For Chalmers, the failure of the *Enquiry* was a crushing disappointment. It had represented an attempt, following his failure to attain university preferment, to subordinate personal ambition and self-interest to a general communal ideal. It had been intended in part as his personal resolution of the tension between his ambition to advance his own interest, and his bitter denunciations of the 'putrid system of interest' which he believed responsible for thwarting his ambition. In the *Enquiry* he had sought to inspire the entire nation with an enlarged version of the social ideal which he had known during his early years in Anstruther. It had reflected his yearning to rediscover a sense of social belonging, by reaffirming his communal origins. The failure of the work to receive public approbation was an especially painful rejection, which alienated him still further from his society. He had failed to establish for Britain a national cause, that of independence and military glory, under which the diversity of separate interests might be unified, and under which Britain might return to a simple, agrarian, and communal organization. He remained an unrecognized talent. Impulsive, even rash by temperament, his first thirty years had been characterized by almost continuous conflict, as he struggled to achieve academic preferment and reputation. He had little in the way of positive achievement to show for his effort, while his health was collapsing under the strain of repeated disappointment. In Kilmany, meanwhile, a decayed church, an uninhabitable manse, and declining church attendance bore testimony to his neglect of his professional responsibilities as a minister of the gospel.

CONVERSION AT KILMANY

I

Prior to the failure of his *Enquiry* of 1808, Chalmers had demonstrated neither a fervent religious faith nor an earnest search for religious certainty. His religious ideas had encompassed a loosely-defined natural theology, combined with a distaste for the rigid scholastic Calvinism of his father, and indeed for all forms of religious enthusiasm. However, in the last years of the eighteenth, and the early years of the nineteenth century, a movement was developing in Scotland which would ultimately have a greater impact upon society than the influence of either the French Revolution or the Napoleonic wars and which was to affect his life profoundly. Throughout Scotland, men began embracing a vital biblical Christianity, with emphasis upon the transitory nature of both the natural world and human society, and the necessity of individual salvation through divine grace. As a clergyman in the Church of Scotland, Chalmers could not, by 1809, fail to notice the increasing national influence of the Evangelical revival.

The Scottish Evangelical revival was a unique national expression of a larger European movement towards vital Christianity. To understand the revival, attention must be directed to the Scottish religious environment. Eighteenth- and early nineteenth-century Scottish religious life was dominated by the national Established Church of Scotland. In its structure, the Church of Scotland had three main characteristics. First, it was a territorial establishment. In the late eighteenth century, the country was divided into approximately 950 territorial parishes. Each parish possessed a church and a clerical living, endowed through taxation of property within the parish which had once belonged to the medieval Roman Catholic Church. Secondly, the Church of Scotland exercised authority over national education. It maintained a system of parish schools, and supervised instruction in the five Scottish universities (Edinburgh, Glasgow, St. Andrews, and Marischal College and King's College, Aberdeen).

Finally, the Church of Scotland was organized on the presbyterian model, with ecclesiastical law defined and enforced by a hierarchy of Church courts. At the base of the hierarchy was the parish kirk-session, made up of the minister and lay elders of the parish church. Above the kirk-session was the local presbytery, with territorial jurisdiction over several parishes, and including the minister and one or more representative lay-elders from each of the parishes. The next higher court was the provincial synod, which met twice a year, in April and October. Each synod exercised territorial jurisdiction over several presbyteries, and included the members of each presbytery within its district. At the peak of the hierarchy was the General Assembly, or supreme court of the Church of Scotland, which consisted in representative ministers and lay-elders selected by each presbytery, university, and royal burgh in the Country. A newly elected Assembly convened each May in Edinburgh for a two-week session. It reviewed cases of ecclesiastical discipline and considered 'overtures', or motions for new Church law, transmitted from the lower courts. At the close of its annual session, the Assembly appointed a Commission, or committee of the whole house, which met three times during the following year—in June, November, and March—to consider matters that could not be postponed until the next annual meeting.

Within the Church courts, two clerical factions, or parties, had developed in the latter half of the eighteenth century. Each party represented a distinct interpretation both of the Calvinist orthodoxy of the Westminster Confession of Faith and of proper ecclesiastical order within the Establishment. Party discipline, to be sure, was weak, and in 1800 only a minority of the Establishment's clergy regarded themselves as strict adherents to either one of the parties. None the less, the tension between the two parties, reflected in debates in the Church courts and in the public press, created a unique dynamic for Scottish religious life.

From 1766 to 1833, the Church of Scotland was dominated by the Moderate party. Reflecting the ethos of the Enlightenment, Moderate clergymen emphasized the themes of order, rationality, and social progress. The civil warfare of the seventeenth century, they maintained, had demonstrated the futility of men governing their affairs by the puritan 'fanaticism' of the Scottish covenanters. Through objective enquiries into the human mind, history, and the natural world, Moderates believed that men could discern the natural laws governing the world and ensure that social institutions reflected the wisdom of nature. By placing 'moderate and literary men' in church livings and university chairs, they sought to disseminate Enlightenment thought through the hierarchy of social orders, and thus to contribute to a general improvement in social manners and morals. The Moderate approach to religion was both man-centred and world-affirming. They endeavoured to restore a sense of balance to the Calvinist orthodoxy of the Westminster Confession of Faith, by emphasizing works as well as faith, reason as well as revelation, and charity as well as religious certainty. While not actually offending against the letter of the Westminster Confession, their theological focus upon practical expressions of Christian charity tended to soften harsher aspects of Calvinism.[1]

As a political party acting within the Church courts, Moderate policies centred upon support for lay patronage in the Church. A relic of the medieval Roman Catholic Church in Scotland, lay patronage survived into the nineteenth century largely as a result of the influence of the great landowners and the Crown, who between them possessed the vast majority of church patronages, and who employed this patronage to enhance their social influence and political power. The Moderate clergy's support for patronage was based primarily upon two considerations. First, patronage was part of the civil law of the land. Members of an established national Church had to submit to the civil law regulating Church affairs, including obedience to the patronage law. Without such submission, the Established presbyterian Church of Scotland would dissolve into congregational Independency, and the benefits of the State connection would be forfeited. Secondly, Moderate clergymen believed that patrons, whether landed gentry or Crown officials, presented a superior quality of clergymen to Scottish pulpits—men of refined tastes and accomplishments, who were independent of the 'vulgar' prejudices of most parishioners and could therefore exercise a civilizing influence upon the lower social orders. Basic to Moderate policies was a concept of 'enlightened élitism', or the belief in the subordination of social ranks with authority vested in educated members of the upper social orders.[2]

The years from 1766 to 1780 were the high tide of Moderatism in the Church of Scotland. Under the leadership of William Robertson, an Edinburgh clergyman who was Principal of Edinburgh University and a celebrated historian, the Moderate party secured the enforcement of the unpopular patronage law by the Church courts. A number of Moderate clergymen, moreover, achieved scientific and literary eminence. Indeed, through Moderate influence, the Church of Scotland assumed a leading role in the unique flowering of intellectual talent in late eighteenth-century Scotland. Close interaction between the Church and universities was fundamental to the Moderate programme for social improvement and leading Moderates often combined a parish living with a university chair. In 1789, the Moderate clergyman Alexander Carlyle could boast without much exaggeration that the clergy of the Moderate-dominated Church of Scotland had been responsible for a significant proportion of the eighteenth-century Enlightenment's most important intellectual achievements.[3]

By 1800, however, the Moderate tide was receding. The Enlightenment ideals of reason and natural harmony, which had inspired thinkers in the mid-eighteenth century, had now spent much of their force. The Romantic movement had commenced, emphasizing feeling as opposed to reason, and the power and versatility as opposed to the harmony of nature. In secular politics, movements after 1780 for an increased

popular voice in government challenged the Moderate ideal of 'enlightened elitism'. The Moderate party's response to their waning
influence was unfortunate. William Robertson had retired from leadership of the Moderate party in 1780. George Hill, a St. Andrews parish
minister and Professor of Divinity at St. Andrews University (whose
lectures, it will be recalled, Chalmers had found uninspiring), emerged
as leader in about 1785; however, he lacked Robertson's political
astuteness. Robertson had managed, despite his party's enforcement of
patronage, to preserve the independence of the Church of Scotland
from State control over her internal affairs. Hill, on the other hand,
reacted to the late eighteenth-century popular political agitation by
connecting the Moderate ascendancy in the Church firmly to the Tory
political paramountcy of Henry Dundas. When in the 1790s Dundas
adopted repressive policies against popular reform movements,
Moderate clergy joined the propertied classes in expressing enthusiastic
approval, often employing their pulpits for political sermons against
reform.[4] As a consequence, admitted one Moderate clergyman, James
Lapslie, in a discourse delivered to the synod of Glasgow and Ayr in
April 1791, the Moderate clergy had become stigmatized by many 'as
the servile flatterers of men in power, who have no regard to the
spiritual interests of their flock, but who court the priest's office, to
obtain a bit of bread'. In short, the Moderate ascendancy in the
Church, which under Robertson's leadership had been based upon
progressive ideals and the intellectual eminence of leading Moderate
clergy, by 1800 relied mainly upon the cement of Government and
landed patronage, and fear among the propertied orders of liberal ideas
in a revolutionary age.[5] To be sure, a number of clergymen with high
principles remained attached to the Moderate party. None the less,
the Moderate-dominated Church of Scotland was becoming less a
national Church, expressing the religious impulses of the nation as a
whole, and more a separate corporate interest, connected by bonds of
patronage to the dominant Tory party. Meanwhile, alienated by the
Moderate leadership, increasing numbers seceded from the Established
Church and swelled the membership of dissenting religious bodies in
Scotland.

   In the last decades of the eighteenth century, the rigid Moderate
ascendancy in the Church of Scotland was challenged by a vigorous
Evangelicalism. The Evangelical revival in Scotland had its origins in
the early eighteenth-century Orthodox party, or, as it was usually
called after 1750, the 'Popular party'. Strict Calvinists, Popular party
adherents believed in the total corruption of human nature and man's
absolute dependence upon God's grace for salvation. The question
foremost in their minds involved not the divinely-ordained harmony of
nature or the progress of society, but rather the eternal fate of the

individual soul. Although they viewed salvation as the free gift of God
to his elect, and not as a function of man's works, Popular party
adherents emphasized obedience to God's laws as revealed through
Scripture or defined by the Westminster Confession. It was, they
believed, God's will that preachers should act as vehicles for his grace,
conveying the Scriptural word to all men. Popular party preachers
generally delivered highly emotional sermons, intended to impress the
listener with the consciousness of his sin and probable damnation, until
he prayed for release from his torment through divine grace. The
Calvinist belief in predestination, or the idea that God, in his omnipotence and wisdom, had predetermined the salvation or damnation of
every soul from all time, led the devout to seek for 'evidence' of their
predestined salvation. Special emphasis was therefore placed on the
conversion experience, and Popular party Calvinists could often cite
the precise hour when they were 'plucked from the burning'. The
psychological tensions of strict Calvinist piety occasionally erupted in
mass revivals, such as the celebrated 'Cambuslang Wark' of 1741,
when thousands were drawn to a village church outside Glasgow for
several weeks of preaching and communal prayer, accompanied by the
writhings and moanings of suffering sinners.[6]

Popular party activity in the Church courts centred upon opposition
to patronage. There was, they argued, no justification either in the
Bible or in the practice of the early Church for entrusting the selection
of a parish minister to a single wealthy landed proprietor or Crown
official. Instead, the Popular party maintained, the minister should be
selected by representatives of the parish congregation—male heads of
families, or the kirk-session and all the landowners in the parish. But,
despite widespread opposition to patronage among Church members,
the Popular party were unable to secure its abolition. The Crown and
the landed interest continued to support patronage through their Moderate party allies. The Popular party, moreover, were slower than the
Moderates to accept the concept of party discipline in the Church
courts. For most eighteenth-century orthodox Calvinists, the existence
of 'factions' within God's Church was a curse. Rather than adapt to
the system of adversary politics in the Church and join the Popular
party, many leading orthodox clergy seceded to a Dissenting church in
Scotland, or emigrated to the 'New Jerusalem' across the Atlantic.[7]

By the late 1770's, however, this situation began to change. Under
the leadership of the Edinburgh clergymen John Erskine (1721-1805)
and Sir Henry Moncrieff Wellwood (1750-1827), an effective Popular
party organization was created. In the early 1780s, seizing upon the
opportunity provided by Robertson's retirement, the party agitated
with renewed strength to secure the abolition of patronage. In this campaign it received assistance from the Foxite Whigs in Scotland, who

were anxious to use the anti-patronage agitation in the Church to
further their own political campaign for Parliamentary and burgh
reform. Although the anti-patronage campaign had failed by 1785, the
Popular party continued their struggle to overthrow the Moderate
ascendancy by fastening upon a number of lesser issues in Church
government.[8] The Popular party-Whig alliance, meanwhile, remained
a significant factor in Church politics into the nineteenth century.[9]

In the last decades of the eighteenth century, moreover, the Popular
party in the Church of Scotland received powerful support from the
south. Under the leadership of William Wilberforce, John Venn,
Zachary Macaulay, and other lay and clerical adherents of the celebrated 'Clapham Sect', the English Evangelical movement, which had
been gathering strength since the 1730s, had culminated in a surge of
local and overseas missionary activity near the close of the century. In
this missionary fervour, English Evangelicals made effective use of the
press and the voluntary association, and the late eighteenth and early
nineteenth centuries witnessed a proliferation of Evangelical pamphlets,
tracts, and periodicals, intended to educate English public opinion.
Equally important was the formation of scores of Evangelical missionary
and benevolent societies, generally multi-denominational in membership and linked by overlapping memberships and regular correspondence. The orthodox Calvinists of the Scottish Popular party often
disagreed with English Evangelicals on specific questions of theology
and Church polity. Nevertheless, they respected English Evangelical
piety, with its emphasis on the conversion experience, regular Bible
study, and missionary activity; and after 1790, they borrowed English
Evangelical organizational methods. Three factors, then—the formation of an effective Popular party organization, the alliance with the
Scottish Whigs, and the influences from the English Evangelical movement—contributed to the Evangelical revival in the Church of Scotland.
After 1800, the Popular party was increasingly referred to as the Evangelical party, and their intense Calvinist piety as Scottish Evangelicalism.

In the first decade of the nineteenth century a group of young clergymen began to exercise influence within the Scottish Evangelical party.
They adhered to the traditions of the eighteenth-century Popular party.
Having been educated in the thought of the Scottish Enlightenment,
however, they endeavoured to combine Popular party Calvinism with
Enlightenment concepts of the harmony of nature and the progress of
society. In politics they were, like their Popular party forebears, Whigs,
and advocated Parliamentary and burgh reform. Like the young Whig
authors of the *Edinburgh Review*, they also believed that the most effective
means to level entrenched and corrupt élites was to educate the new
generation of public opinion by an intelligent criticism of the ideologi-

cal bases which supported those élites. In missionary, benevolent, and prayer societies, modelled after English Evangelical associations, the young Scottish Evangelicals established forums for discussion that were lacking for them in the Moderate-dominated Church courts. Under the leadership of Andrew Thomson (1778-1831), minister of the rural parish of Sprouston, 1802-8, of the East Parish, Perth, 1808-10, of New Greyfriar's parish, Edinburgh, 1810-14, and of the prestigious St. George's parish, Edinburgh, 1814-31, the young Evangelicals rapidly emerged to leadership of the Evangelical movement in the Church of Scotland.

II

Prior to the illness which followed the failure of his *Enquiry* in 1808, Chalmers had been essentially a Moderate in his religious views. In his sermons in rural Kilmany he condemned those religious 'enthusiasts', who claimed a 'mystical' knowledge of God's will and of the predestined fate of their souls which transcended both reason and Scriptural revelation. Systems of theological thought, including Calvinism, he believed, contradicted and confused the simple teachings of Scriptural Christianity. For him, the value of Christianity lay in its moral code, through which men might live together in harmony. As a mathematician and natural philosopher, moreover, he shared the Moderate interest in natural theology and the harmony of nature.

Along with antipathy to Calvinism and religious enthusiasm, however, Chalmers also lacked commitment to his clerical profession. In his pursuit of university preferment and literary reputation, he exhibited the most irresponsible aspects of early nineteenth-century Scottish Moderatism. He used his parish for his own support while he pursued a career in mathematics or political economy. He wrote his sermons hastily, and frequently left his parish for weeks or even months at a time. He neglected household visitations, the religious instruction of the young, and the other responsibilities of a parish minister. His neglect had not been without consequences. In 1804, he had been summoned before the presbytery of Cupar to answer charges of neglecting his parish, and again in 1805 his neglect of Kilmany had been condemned in a Cupar presbytery minute. With the preparation of his *Enquiry* of 1808, and with the illness which followed the failure of that work, his neglect of his parochial duties worsened.

Then, strangely, in early February 1811, Chalmers appeared upon the quiet, Moderate-dominated religious scene of northern Fife as an impassioned Evangelical preacher, proclaiming man's total depravity and alienation from God, and his absolute dependence upon divine grace for salvation. With powerful oratory, he now pleaded with men to embrace the Evangelical views which he had previously denounced. Many acquaintances believed that repeated disappointments and too much study in the solitude of Kilmany had mentally unhinged him. To the Evangelicals in northern Fife, however, Chalmers had experienced conversion. 'On the fast day', Janet Coutts, a young clergyman's widow residing in the Fifeshire village of Dairsie, informed her friend Jane Burns on 19 February 1811, 'we had a new miracle of Divine grace, in a Mr. Chalmers of Kilmany, a great philosopher, but once an enemy avowedly to the peculiar doctrines of the gospel. For a year back the Lord has been teaching him by the rod.... and now he comes forward to preach the faith which once he destroyed, and I trust we glorify God in him.' 'But', she concluded, 'you cannot enter into it as we do who know the man and his character.'[10] News of Chalmers's conversion spread rapidly throughout Fife, and crowds gathered in Kilmany to witness the 'new miracle'. Within several months, the hitherto neglected mathematician and political economist acquired a national reputation for his Evangelical preaching. For many, his conversion became a symbol of the Evangelical revival in Scotland.

Chalmers's Evangelical conversion was indeed a watershed, which gave new direction to his life. In one sense, as a religious conversion, it is inexplicable. Something undoubtedly happened to him between 1809 and 1811, which fundamentally changed the way he conceived of God and the world, so that he committed himself to the Evangelical movement which once he had despised. He adopted a new language, becoming, as he informed a friend on 2 May 1812, 'a serious man', who found his 'conclusion and repose in the peculiar doctrines of the gospel'.[11] Whatever his former acquaintances thought of the 'peculiar doctrines' of Evangelicalism, few doubted the genuineness of his personal transformation.

Although the actual event of his conversion is largely inexplicable, three stages to his transformation can be discerned. In the first, which began early in 1809, following the failure of the *Enquiry*, Chalmers was drawn into a relationship with the young Evangelicals in the Church of Scotland. In the second stage, a mounting series of personal crises, including serious illness and the unhappy end of a romantic affair with a young Fifeshire beauty, undermined the stabilizing factors in his life. Neither Enlightenment philosophy nor Moderate theology could help him. In the third stage, his conversion was consolidated, both through the support and encouragement of the Evangelical party in the Church of Scotland, and by the immense popularity of his Evangelical preaching. In Evangelical fellowship, he rediscovered the sense of communal belonging which he had known in Anstruther, but which he had lost during the years he spent in ambitious pursuit of personal academic distinction. Through fame as an Evangelical preacher, he achieved the influence over public opinion which he had so long sought in vain.

Chalmers's involvement with the young Evangelicals commenced about the time of the publication of the *Enquiry*. He was introduced into this group of Evangelical clergymen largely through his earlier connection with several young Whig intellectuals of Edinburgh, whom he had met during his period of study there between 1799 and 1801. In February 1808, David Brewster, the twenty-seven-year-old editor of a projected multi-volume *Edinburgh Encyclopedia*, invited Chalmers to contribute articles on scientific subjects to it.[12] Brewster was a natural philosopher, a Whig, a contributor to the *Edinburgh Review*, and a friend of Chalmers's mentor James Brown. Brewster was also the brother of one leading Evangelical clergyman, James Brewster, and the close friend of another, Andrew Thomson.

The *Edinburgh Encyclopedia* was the project of some thirty young Whig intellectuals and Evangelical clergymen.[13] Its purpose was not only to provide a compendium of knowledge, but also, like the *Edinburgh Review*, to criticize the ideological supports of the ruling Tory-Moderate connection in politics, the universities, and the Church. Chalmers, not surprisingly, accepted Brewster's invitation and decided upon an article on trigonometry for his first contribution.[14] Then in the autumn of 1808, Andrew Thomson, who had committed himself to write a large number of articles for the encyclopaedia, decided that he lacked the time to write the article on Christianity as he had promised. In his place, Thomson suggested to Brewster that Chalmers be requested to write it. Thomson had apparently recognized Chalmers as a possible recruit to the Evangelical party.[15] Although not Evangelical in his piety, Chalmers had demonstrated strong opposition to the Moderate concept of government by 'enlightened élites'. Chalmers for his part enthusiastically embraced the opportunity to write one of the more important articles in the encyclopaedia. He would, he promised Brewster, conduct a careful scientific enquiry into the historical evidence for the Christian revelation, and in February 1809 he began a serious study of the Bible and of the writings of the early Church Fathers. Brewster, in turn, was pleased that the subject would be undertaken by a man of Chalmers's scientific training and lively style. 'Christianity', he confided to Chalmers on 3 September 1810, 'I expect will, in your hands, become alluring to many who would otherwise be alarmed at the subject.'[16]

A few months later, in May 1809, Chalmers attended his first General Assembly, as a representative of the presbytery of Cupar. There he introduced a motion to reform the legal process pursued by individual clergymen for the periodical augmentation of their stipends to meet rising price levels. Although the issue was minor, his speech attracted attention for its lively attack upon the Moderate party's alliance with the landed interest. In the Church of Scotland, the stipends

of rural parish ministers were paid by the 'heritors' of the parish, or
those proprietors who either owned or held long-term leases on land
which had once belonged to the pre-Reformation Church. Under the
existing system, a parish minister was obliged to sue the heritors of his
parish for his augmentation in the civil court of teinds, or tithes. This
system, Chalmers argued, favoured the heritors, who were better able
than the minister to bear the expense of lengthy litigation. Indeed, the
system provided the heritors with 'a most powerful instrument for
inflicting upon their minister the most wanton and vexatious tyranny'.
The heritors were thus enabled to pay an inadequate stipend, and the
status and usefulness of many rural clergymen was undermined.
Obviously, he asserted, it was the Church's duty to petition Parliament
to provide legislative assistance for the rural clergyman in his uneven
struggle against 'the whole weight of the landed interest'. But this the
dominant Moderate party would not allow the Church to do, because it
might threaten their connection with the Tory Government and the
landed interest.[17]

The Moderates managed to quash Chalmers's motion on a legal
technicality. The young Whigs and Evangelicals, however, were encouraged by the speech, which effectively argued that the Moderate
party was sacrificing the rural parish clergy to maintain its ascendancy.
Andrew Thomson and David Brewster immediately pressed Chalmers
to publish his speech. 'You may have perhaps heard', Chalmers wrote
to his father on 30 May 1809, 'of my taking some little part in the
deliberations of the Assembly. ... I have been beset from all quarters
with solicitations to publish my speech—all of which I withstood, till
the booksellers came forward with the temptation of a handsome offer,
and overset my firmness.'[18]

By June 1809, then, Chalmers had begun co-operating with, and
receiving encouragement from, Andrew Thomson and the young
Church of Scotland Evangelicals. He appreciated them for many of the
same reasons he respected the young Whigs. The Evangelicals, he
believed, were a party with high ideals, opposed to a Moderate party
that existed mainly to further the self-interest of social élites. Moreover,
they offered opportunities to young men of talent, while the Moderate
party appeared more concerned with family and political connections.
Having failed to achieve university preferment as a natural philosopher
or political economist, Chalmers began to be attracted to the Evangelicals and the prospect they offered him for increased influence within
the Church. He was ready to settle down into a clerical career, and was
even, at this time, contemplating marriage to an Anstruther woman.
But at the same time, his dislike of Evangelical piety prohibited him
from becoming a real part of their party.

Serious illness, meanwhile, now prompted him to review his attitude towards Moderate theology. His health had not fully recovered from his physical collapse late in 1808, and his activity in the 1809 General Assembly proved too great an exertion. Returning from Edinburgh in early June 1809, he collapsed on the road with an illness, which forced him to relinquish a proposed visit to Anstruther and hurry directly to Kilmany. Throughout the summer, his condition steadily worsened. By October 1809, he was confined to his room with consumption. This was a disease particularly dreaded in the Chalmers family, of which it had already claimed two lives—his brother George in 1806, and his sister Barbara in 1808. For nearly four months during the winter of 1809 to 1810, he was completely bed-ridden. When his friend Thomas Duncan visited him that winter, he was shaken to discover that the formerly stout Chalmers had grown pale and emaciated. His face, Duncan later recalled, seemed that of an old man. Duncan left the sickroom convinced that were Chalmers to survive, he would remain an invalid for life.

Confined to a small cottage near Kilmany, with death apparently imminent, Chalmers reviewed his life in a new perspective. The months passed slowly in isolation. Few visitors arrived; few former friends wrote. 'My confinement', he confided to Andrew Carstairs, minister of Anstruther Wester, on 19 February 1810, 'has fixed on my heart a very strong impression of the insignificance of time—an impression which I trust will not abandon me though I again reach the heydey of health and vigour. ... Strip human life of its connection with a higher scene of existence, and it is the illusion of an instant, an unmeaning farce, a series of visions and projects, and convulsive efforts, which terminate in nothing.'[19] In February 1810, he began reading the *Pensées* of Blaise Pascal, and comparing himself to the celebrated French mathematician, who had ultimately relinquished mathematical studies and devoted his final years to cultivating his soul. Chalmers's mood grew increasingly introspective. On his thirtieth birthday, he began a private confessional journal. During the last fifteen years, he noted in the opening entry on 17 March 1810, his conduct had been 'dictated by the rambling impulse of the moment, without any direction from a sense of duty, or any reference to that eternity which should be the end and motive of all our actions'.[20] Through daily scrutiny of his thought and action, he now vowed to bring his life under 'the habitual regulation of principle'.

He recovered slowly from his illness. By April 1810, he was able to return to his family home in Anstruther to convalesce. With his returning strength, however, he now confronted a painful personal crisis. In the months prior to his illness, he had entered into an informal engagement with Anne Rankine, a spirited beauty who lived with her mother and sister in Anstruther. Although little is known of her, or their early relationship, they had probably been acquainted since childhood. Then, during his confinement, Chalmers had begun to torment himself with doubts about her fidelity. Although she had protested her innocence of any wrong-doing, he was not convinced, and with wounded pride he drew back from their relationship, probably expecting her to provide fresh proof of her devotion. Instead she responded by informing her friends that she had initiated the estrangement. Chalmers was enraged. To his friends, he bitterly denounced both Anne and her family. Privately, however, he asked his sister Jane to attempt to arrange a reconciliation. He now discovered the cost of his outbursts of temper. Anne informed Jane that she had been deeply hurt by Thomas's attacks upon her family, and that the break had in consequence become 'irreconcilable'. He was stung with regret as the permanence of the estrangement became evident. 'I feel', he confided to his diary on 22 June 1810, upon learning of Anne's words to Jane, 'tenderness and regret and anything, but resentment at all this. There is a solemnity in a final examination—and an overpowering pathos in the reflection, that two people who breathed at one time mutual tenderness cannot meet in confidence again till they meet in heaven.'

But he was unable to overcome his love for Anne. Although by June 1810 he had largely recovered from his illness, he avoided returning to Kilmany and his parish responsibilities, but rather remained in Anstruther, where he could at least be near her. Thoughts of her, he confessed in his diary on 28 June, tormented him even while he was in church. On 29 June, he stood for several hours outside her house, in the hope of catching a glimpse of the 'figure in white' as she passed by a window. He sought to overcome his pain through ocean-bathing and country rides, but without success. 'I was the victim of the predominant feeling,' he confided in his diary on 24 July, 'and my love for A. R. [Anne Rankine] recurred in all its soreness and with all the vexatious difficulties which have attended that unfortunate attachment. Under A.'s influence I lost all self-command and sought to relieve myself by gossiping with Mrs. Smith [a cousin of his father], when I dilated on Mrs. Rankine [Anne's mother] with my accustomed freedom and severity.' He reminded himself of the vow he had taken during his illness to cultivate a new spiritual life, and he admitted that in Anstruther, 'my proximity to the Rankines fills me with sentiments which only serve to harass and unhinge me'. But he was able to tear himself away. His parents, meanwhile, complained of his negligence of his parish of Kilmany and finally hinted that his continued presence in their home was no longer welcome. So in August 1810 he at last returned to Kilmany and began preaching again in the church after a year of absence from his parish duties. Thoughts of her continued to trouble him, but he now sought to discipline his affection through activity and literary discussions with neighbouring clergy. In early September, Anne fell seriously ill with a fever, and sent for him. It was the final hope for the relationship. In his pride, however, Chalmers fought the urge to go to her. It was over. Anne recovered from her fever, and eventually married another, only to die in childbirth, along with her infant, a few years later. With the end of their affair, Chalmers considered other marital prospects, but never felt again the same passion, the 'pleasureable delirium', he had known in her presence.[21]

While Chalmers struggled with the personal crises of his illness and the end of his engagement, the situation of his family had also been deteriorating. After 1804, his father suffered a series of strokes, which left him both blind and deaf. By 1810, his mind was also affected, and he began, Chalmers noted in his journal on 26 December 1810, 're-lapsing fast into imbecility'. His father, though often critical of his son's excesses, had also been a source of love and stability in Chalmers's life; it was agonizing now to watch him lose all awareness and interest in his surroundings. As the eldest surviving son still living in Fife, Chalmers was obliged to assume more and more responsibility for his family's financial affairs, which with his father's decline had grown almost desperate. In his own vulnerable and distracted state of mind, however, he was unable to cope with his family's problems. He quarrelled with his mother, who accused him of both neglecting his professional responsibilities and not contributing what he should to the financial support of the family. In truth, Chalmers was suffering serious financial difficulties of his own. Although he had continued to receive his stipend during his illness, old debts, combined with medical expenses and poor management of his personal finances during his confinement, had placed him under considerable pressure from his creditors.[22]

Then on 23 December 1810, the family suffered yet another blow when Thomas's older sister, Lucy, died of consumption. The following day, Thomas arrived in Anstruther to assist with the funeral arrangements. Lucy, who had never married, was a kind woman, who had cared for their parents and had nursed Thomas through much of his own struggle with consumption. Her death made the previously warm family home seem still more empty, and the December nights more long and cold. In order to escape from the unhappiness in his former home, Thomas spent most of his time there withdrawn in his room. In his solitude, he read William Wilberforce's *Practical View of the Prevailing Religious System of Professed Christians*. For the first time, he discovered an Evangelical piety in a form he could appreciate. Wilberforce's essay was directed towards those members of the educated upper and middle classes who, though nominally Christian, deprecated Evangelicalism as a type of antisocial fanaticism. To such persons, Wilberforce presented

the ideal of the Evangelical gentleman—an active man in the world
of politics, commerce, or literature, whose social contributions were
enhanced by a strict personal integrity, based upon a sincere desire
to obey God. For Wilberforce, Evangelicalism meant not a retreat
from the world, but an aggressive campaign to enter and to master
the world with Christian principles. The Evangelical gentleman
was not the pawn of worldly interests, but was strengthened by awareness of the eternal life of the soul and the promise of assistance from the
Holy Spirit. Chalmers had long admired Wilberforce's political activity
as an MP and hard-working advocate for the anti-slavery movement.
But reading the *Practical View* in the bleak December of 1810 exercised
a far more profound effect. It placed him, he later recalled, 'on the eve
of a great revolution in all my opinions about Christianity'. It offered
a bulwark against 'the vortex of earthly passions', and the prospect of
a new life.[23]

Chalmers returned to Kilmany in January 1811 eager to pursue
further the ideas introduced into his life with such force by Wilberforce's essay. He began seeking religious conversation and guidance
from neighbouring Evangelical clergy, including James Johnson,
minister of the Burgher Secession church at Rathillet, and Robert
MacCulloch, minister of the parish of Dairsie and son of the William M.
MacCulloch who had been minister at Cambuslang during the celebrated revival of 1741. In MacCulloch's pulpit at Dairsie, on the
national fast-day on 14 February 1811, Chalmers delivered his first
decidedly Evangelical sermon.[24] His description of the Christian as
a lonely exile in a world of sorrows profoundly moved the Dairsie
congregation. Among those present was MacCulloch's daughter Janet
Coutts, the young widow of Chalmers's former St. Andrews friend,
Robert Coutts. She was deeply affected by Chalmers's efforts to convey
the force of the Evangelical message. 'He does so, indeed,' she wrote
to a friend a few days after the sermon, 'like a babe lisping the language,
but most striking are his expressions, especially on our lost, helpless,
undone state. His humble, teachable disposition, and serious conversation in private, were equally delightful with his appearance in
public.'[25]

Support and encouragement from the Evangelical clergy and public
in Scotland helped to crystallize Chalmers's conversion. In the autumn
of 1810, Andrew Thomson and several young Evangelical clergymen
founded the *Edinburgh Christian Instructor*, a monthly Evangelical literary
review, modelled upon both the Whig *Edinburgh Review*, and the London
Christian Observer, the vehicle of Wilberforce's 'Clapham Sect'. On
Thomson's invitation, Chalmers became an occasional contributor to
the *Edinburgh Christian Instructor*, submitting review articles on political
as well as devotional themes.[26] In the first of these, published in May

1811, Chalmers advocated the creation of an Evangelical party in Parliament, which he hoped would attract members away from Tory and Radical party allegiances, and eventually subsume private secular interests in a single-party state, based upon Evangelical piety and moderate Whig ideals of toleration for Roman Catholics and Dissenters.[27] On 22 July 1811, Thomson confided to his friend Robert Lundie (with a slight trace of jealousy) that while he personally considered Chalmers's first contribution to be 'a meagre thing', he had to admit that it was 'much admired by many people'. Even the venerable Moderate clergyman Samuel Charters, though no admirer of the *Edinburgh Christian Instructor*, congratulated Chalmers on his first contribution, 'the only good article of late'.[28]

It was, however, as an Evangelical preacher that Chalmers achieved real fame. Almost immediately, his preaching began attracting large crowds to Kilmany. At his annual Communion service in Kilmany in 1810, 270 adults had received the sacrament. The following year, however—his first annual communion after his conversion—458 adults received the sacrament, many coming to Kilmany from neighbouring parishes.[29] Kilmany church-door collections increased appreciably in 1811 and 1812, reflecting the growing attendance at his sermons.[30] By the spring of 1812, his services as a visiting preacher were in high demand throughout Fife and even in the cities of Dundee and Edinburgh. He became almost an itinerant preacher, straining his health in order to respond to the many invitations from fellow Evangelical clergy. Between 22 March 1812 and 21 March 1813, for instance, Chalmers preached a total of sixty sermons, of which twenty-three, or over one-third, were preached outside Kilmany.[31] The crowds which gathered to hear him preach increased steadily. When on 30 October 1814, for example, he preached the funeral sermon for a college friend in rural Bendochy, in Perthshire, the crowd was so large that a window of the church had to be removed. Chalmers preached from the window-sill to the masses filling both church and churchyard.[32] His fame as a preacher soon became known in London, and in October 1813 he was invited to become minister of the London Wall Scottish presbyterian church in the capital. 'Burning and shining Lights', Robert Simpson, an elder in the London Wall congregation told Chalmers upon communicating the invitation on 28 October 1813, 'cannot be long concealed.'[33] Although he did not accept the London invitation, his ambition began to extend beyond the confines of rural Fife. Among the promising effects of his new religious life, he wrote in his journal on 13 January 1814, was 'an opening prospect of Edinb[r] preferment'.[34] By 1814, his preaching was indeed carrying him to a leading position in the Scottish Evangelical movement, which an appointment to an Edinburgh church would have further consolidated.

Chalmers's power as a preacher, then, was considerable. This power, however, even sympathetic observers found difficult to explain. He was, according to contemporary accounts, an unattractive man, with a dark complexion and drooping lower eyelids, which gave him a sleepy appearance. His clerical gown was usually dishevelled; his gestures in the pulpit were clumsy and contrived. Many observers, like J. G. Lockhart, the son-in-law and biographer of Sir Walter Scott, were taken aback at their first sight of him.[35] While most Evangelicals either memorized their sermons or spoke extempore, Chalmers always read his sermons, with one finger never leaving the line of manuscript. Even fellow Scots often had difficulty understanding his broad Fifeshire accent.

What, then, accounted for his unique impact?[36] Three factors might be suggested. First, as a preacher, Chalmers powerfully conveyed his absolute belief in the 'peculiar doctrines' of man's corruption, his duty to obey God's laws, and his salvation by grace alone. He might begin reading his sermons in a low voice, but as he progressed his pitch would heighten, his face would tauten, until with bulging eyes he hung over the pulpit, imploring each individual to recognize the power and accept the love of God. By this point, the congregation forgot his ungainly figure and abandoned itself to his will. Men of all social orders felt his sincere passion for their souls. For his part Chalmers usually left the pulpit in a state of complete exhaustion, which often incapacitated him for days.

Secondly, his preaching appealed to a growing Romantic spirit among the educated middle and upper classes. The story of his conversion appealed to the public imagination. Men attended his sermons in the expectation of witnessing something miraculous, which would transcend the rationalistic moralism which was the legacy of the eighteenth-century Enlightenment. In his presence, they more often than not found what they were looking for—a moment of intense emotion that seemed to defy rational explanation. 'In spite of the external disadvantages', the Whig lawyer Henry Cockburn later observed of Chalmers,

of a bad figure, voice, gesture, and look, and an unusual plainness of Scotch accent, he is a great orator; for *effect* indeed, at the moment of speaking, unapproached in our day. ... Neither devotional fervour, nor enlightened philosophy, nor vivid language, nor luminous exposition could produce the effect he does, without the aid of his manner. I have often hung upon his words with a beating heart and a tearful eye, without being brought to my senses till I read, next day, the very syllables which had moved me to such admiration, but which then seemed cold. The magic lies in the concentrated intensity which agitates every fibre of the man, and brings out his meaning by words and emphasis of sufficient force, and rolls magnificent periods clearly and irresistibly along, and kindles the whole composition with living fire.[37]

Finally, despite his Evangelical conviction and Romantic appeal, Chalmers did not forsake his education in the language and thought of the Scottish Enlightenment. He endeavoured to express Evangelical doctrine in what he termed the 'academic elegance of style', reflecting eighteenth-century standards for prose.[38] His sentences were long, and his language tended towards a certain grandiloquence. He flattered his congregations with illustrations from natural philosophy and political economy, and he bitterly resented the charges of ignorance or simple-mindedness which were often levelled against Evangelicals. In short, he was concerned to win the upper social orders from Moderatism.

This concern contributed to the success of his first major theological work, as well as to his triumphs as a preacher. In October 1812, after several interruptions, he finally completed his article on Christianity for Brewster's *Edinburgh Encyclopedia*. The article purported to prove, through a lengthy examination of historical evidence supporting the New Testament narrative, that Scripture was indeed divine revelation. This 'external evidence', he argued, if properly heeded, would awaken man to the mysteries of Christianity, and compel him to faith in that which was beyond human comprehension. The encyclopaedia volume containing the article was published in the summer of 1813. A few months later, in December 1813, he secured permission from the publishers of the *Edinburgh Encyclopedia* to bring the article out as a separate volume. The first edition of 1,500 copies of *The Evidence and Authority of the Christian Revelation* was published in Edinburgh in January 1814, and Chalmers received 100 guineas from an Edinburgh bookseller for the sale rights.[39]

The work received considerable attention both in Scotland and among the London Evangelical public. In February 1815, for instance, the London Evangelical *Christian Observer* reviewed the work with unqualified praise. For almost a century, the reviewer asserted, Scottish intellectual life had reflected either a puritanical and rigidly dogmatic Calvinism, which looked backward to the intolerance of the seventeenth century, or else Calvinism's antithesis, a worldly, humanistic, and admittedly brilliant Enlightenment philosophy. In Chalmers, however, the *Christian Observer* perceived a new synthesis, a thinker reflecting the brilliance of Scotland's eighteenth-century academic achievements, but employing Enlightenment language and analytical techniques to disseminate the teachings of Scriptural Christianity. Chalmers, the *Christian Observer* predicted, was destined to a leading role not only in the Scottish, but in a larger British Evangelical movement.[40]

Chalmers's thought was indeed a synthesis of the old Enlightenment ideals of rationality, harmony, and progress (which such eighteenth-century religious Moderates as William Robertson, Alexander Carlyle, and George Hill had sought to disseminate through the social teachings of the Church) and the new, more impassioned ethos of Scottish Evangelicalism. He agreed with the Evangelicals that there were mysteries which reason and the progress of science would never penetrate. Illness, suffering, and death mocked many of the cherished beliefs of natural theology, including the idea that natural and social harmony reflected clearly the benevolence of the deity. With the Evangelicals, he believed that the salvation of each individual soul was the central thrust of Christianity; and that the Christian must thirst for grace and burn with passion for the souls of others. However, he also felt uncomfortable with what he perceived as an anti-intellectual mood in some Evangelicals, a tendency to dismiss man's intellectual traditions and achievements as mere vanity, and to oppose revelation to reason, spiritual to worldly knowledge. Like many eighteenth-century Moderates, he sought a balance between reason and revelation, faith and works. He was uncomfortable with religious enthusiasts, whose intensely personal faith caused them to neglect the value of a nurturing national religious establishment. He was an Evangelical, but with strong ties to the Moderate traditions of the eighteenth-century Church.

Along with his increasing status as an Evangelical preacher and author, Chalmers achieved a degree of prosperity unusual among rural Scottish clergymen. In Scotland, the heritors of a parish were legally responsible for the repair of the parish church and manse, and the payment of the minister's stipend. In 1810, following a lengthy lawsuit in the civil court of teinds, Chalmers won a decision obliging the Kilmany heritors to rebuild his dilapidated manse. A more spacious structure was completed in the summer of 1811. His new manse was a showplace in the district, fitted with an innovative system of gas pipes of Chalmers's own design, and surrounded by an extensive garden in which he conducted minor botanical experiments. In January 1812, following another lengthy suit in the court of teinds, he secured a decision obliging the heritors to increase his stipend. Although not as large as he had desired, the award represented 'a very substantial addition to my independence and comfort', raising his annual stipend by about £60, or to between £260 and £300 per annum, depending upon grain prices.[41] Kilmany now became one of the more richly endowed rural livings in the Church of Scotland.

With improved financial circumstances, Chalmers again considered marriage, and in August 1812, following a brief courtship, he married Grace Pratt, the daughter of an army captain and the niece of one of the wealthiest Kilmany heritors. She was a very different woman from the beautiful and high-spirited Anne Rankine, and his feelings for her had none of the passion of the former tumultuous relationship. At twenty-one years of age, she was eleven years his junior, and had lived a secluded existence in her aged uncle's home for three years since her mother's death. She was, Chalmers confided to a friend in July 1812, neither a beauty nor an educated companion. Her chief assets consisted in being 'modest, tractable, acquiescing, and ... in actual wealth and future expectations enough to make me independent'. Her dowry of £1,000 indeed formed a welcome addition to his finances. Grace Pratt, however, also proved to be an intelligent woman, with a mind for practical detail regarding domestic and financial matters.[42] Elizabeth Chalmers wrote approvingly to her son James on 17 October 1812: 'she seems an agreeable Pleasant Woman, well looked but not a Beauty, above the Midle size, a good person but not Hansome, well accustomed to Houshold Maters having kept her Uncles House for three years.'[43] Although she evidently did not share all her husband's Evangelical enthusiasm, she had a warm heart, and demonstrated considerable kindness to Chalmers's parents. She also had a beneficial influence in tempering the more extravagent aspects of his own character.

With his conversion, he had found a new foundation for his life. From a rambling 'series of visions and projects, and convulsive efforts, which terminate in nothing', he had discovered a sense of purpose. He now employed his talents in the service of God, striving to awaken men to the truth that transcended 'the vortex of earthly passion'. His inspiring preaching, with its magnetic power, became for many a symbol of the Evangelical revival in Scotland. In the years immediately following his conversion, moreover, his life assumed a new stability, which complemented his rising status as a preacher and author. He became financially secure. In his marriage, which was blessed with a healthy daughter within a year, he began to experience once again the happiness and security of family life. As he overcame much of the emotional tumult of his early years he also returned to the questions of social organization that had so engrossed him prior to his illness in 1809. Evangelical commitment, however, now gave a new direction and impulse to his social thought.

III

Chalmers's Evangelical conversion coincided with Scotland's second wave of enthusiasm for overseas missions. The first had commenced in the early 1790s, with the formation of a number of local missionary societies in Scotland, which corresponded with and sent contributions to the London Missionary Society. The missionary societies, however, had encountered considerable opposition in Scotland. The Government and landed interest, fearful of Jacobin revolutionary activity, had discountenanced such corresponding societies. Missionary societies, they feared, might serve to develop a political consciousness among the lower social orders and instruct labourers and shopkeepers in the techniques of political organization. Many Moderate clergymen, moreover, considered overseas missions inexpedient at the present time. Heathen populations, they argued, had to be gradually 'civilized', through trade and intellectual contact with Europeans, before they could understand Protestant Christianity. To attempt to evangelize among non-Westernized peoples, they maintained, would only alienate them from all Western influences, and might precipitate revolts in the colonies at a time when war with France demanded all Britain's resources. When in the General Assembly of 1796 the Popular party had attempted to secure the Church's recommendation for a special parochial collection for overseas missions, the move was thwarted by the Moderates. Following this defeat, Scottish public support for overseas missions waned.[44]

The second wave of Scottish missionary enthusiasm commenced in 1809. The main impetus now came from the British and Foreign Bible Society, the most successful of the nineteenth-century voluntary religious associations. Founded in London in 1804 with the support of Wilberforce and the 'Clapham Sect', the Society's purpose was both simple and ambitious: it sought to provide every inhabitant of the world with access to a Bible, printed in his native language and without commentary or appendix. The Society's work of translation and distribution was financed by voluntary contributions and supervised by a London committee of management. By avoiding either commentary or appendices in its Bibles, the Society sought to enlist interdenominational support. For its first five years, meanwhile, the British and Foreign Bible Society gained little public support outside London. In 1809, however, national interest awakened, and auxiliary branch societies began to be formed in counties, towns, and parishes throughout Britain. These sent contributions to the London committee for support of the overseas distribution of Bibles, and in return were allowed to purchase Bibles at low prices from the Society for distribution among the poor in their home district.[45] The success of the movement after 1809, reflected both decreased political repression in Britain and increased public weariness with the war against France. The Bible Society movement provided an alternative cause to patriotism and the war, which many now embraced. In Scotland, Andrew Thomson and the young Evangelicals became enthusiastic supporters. By 1810, auxiliaries had been formed in Edinburgh and Glasgow, while Thomson's *Edinburgh Christian Instructor* helped to advertise the Scottish campaign.

Chalmers's interest in the British and Foreign Bible Society was awakened shortly after his conversion. The movement had at this time scarcely reached northern Fife, and was viewed with suspicion or hostility by most of his neighbours. The first efforts for the Society in his district were made by the Dissenter James Johnson, the Evangelical minister of the Burgher Secession church at Rathillet. Early in 1811, Johnson had attempted to form an auxiliary among his congregation. He met with little enthusiasm, however, and his efforts lagged.[46] Then in September 1811, inspired by the Society's published reports and by Johnson's example, Chalmers began to plan the formation of a Kilmany parish auxiliary. Further, he encouraged neighbouring Evangelical clergy to form auxiliaries in their parishes and to co-operate in combating the local prejudice against overseas missions.[47] His initial efforts, however, also met with little encouragement. The Kilmany gentry were hostile. Neighbouring Church of Scotland clergy, including the Evangelicals, declined to assist a Bible Society directed from London and including Dissenters.[48] Even Chalmers's close friends refused support. 'The same people', he was told by the Whig mathematician Thomas Duncan on 9 March 1812, in response to his request for a contribution, 'that subscribe so liberally for the propagation of the Gospel are equally forward in supporting schemes for the conquest of the most distant nations of the globe.[49] Duncan, a pacifist, probably intended an allusion to the militaristic tendencies of Chalmers's unsuccessful 1808 *Enquiry*. At any rate, he assured Chalmers that he would find no support for Bible societies among his academic friends.

But Chalmers persisted, and in early March 1812 he instituted the Kilmany Bible Society as a parish auxiliary of the British and Foreign Bible Society. Because of opposition from the local gentry, he turned to the lower social orders of his parish for his Society's main base of support. In order to raise contributions for the London committee, he adopted what he termed the 'penny-a-week' plan, by which the poor were welcomed to full society membership and encouraged to subscribe a small sum each week. Contributions of a penny or two each week, Chalmers believed, would not greatly affect a poor family's standard of living, and if enough labourers and servants subscribed a weekly penny, their many small contributions would in fact surpass the amount to be expected from a few wealthy landed patrons.[50] It proved an effective plan. Indeed, by 21 April 1812, Chalmers boasted of 160 subscribers from his parish population of 780.[51] This number included members of the nearby Rathillet Secession church, who after April 1812 joined the Kilmany Bible Society. Through penny-a-week subscriptions, Chalmers informed Samuel Charters, minister of the border parish of Wilton, on 18 November 1812, he anticipated that his Kilmany auxiliary would collect over £30 per annum for the London committee. 'Would it not be a fine spectacle', he continued, 'to see the parish system extended over Scotland, and a whole people combining their energies in a cause, the very supporting of which is an exercise of piety?' If a penny-a-week auxiliary were formed in every parish of Fife, he assured Charters, that county alone would raise over £3,000 per annum for the cause.[52]

In March 1812, shortly after forming his Kilmany society, Chalmers
began work towards establishing a county auxiliary Bible Society in
Fife, to supervise the formation and activity of parish auxiliaries.
Together with two young Fifeshire Evangelical clergymen who shared
his enthusiasm, he organized a meeting of forty clergymen on 15 April
1812, immediately prior to the April meeting of the synod of Fife, to
discuss the formation of a county auxiliary.[53] The next day, Chalmers
addressed the synod. The great value of the British and Foreign Bible
Society, he asserted, was its capacity to unite the entire British nation
for a shared world mission ideal. Its purpose transcended differences
between the Protestant denominations and the national groups within
the British state. Through its emphasis upon the pure word of Scripture,
moreover, it promised to convert even the Roman Catholics of Britain
and Ireland to Protestant Evangelicalism. The nation, he concluded,
would achieve a new consensus in the Bible Society's world mission,
while each citizen would be morally and spiritually elevated through
participation in 'one of the finest and most inspiring spectacles in the
moral history of the species'.[54]

Chalmers and his Evangelical associates succeeded in gaining clerical
support in the synod of Fife. A few months later, at a public meeting in
Cupar on 7 July 1812, the Fife and Kinross Bible Society was instituted
as a county auxiliary to the British and Foreign Bible Society. Chalmers
delivered one of the key speeches at the meeting. In his view, he
remarked, the purpose of the county society should not be to collect
money itself, but rather to supervise the formation and activity of
parish auxiliaries, which, he argued, would prove far more successful
than a county society in gaining the support of the lower social orders.
Indeed, the county society would need to take care that its existence did
not lull parish communities into complacency and discourage local
initiative. Emphasis sould be placed upon the penny-a-week scheme.[55]
In short, he advocated a popular movement, based in the local parish
community, with the larger county society acting solely as a supervisory
body on behalf of the London committee.

His interest soon extended to the overseas missions movement in
general. On 26 October 1812, at the invitation of the directors, he
delivered the annual fund-raising sermon for the Dundee Missionary
Society. Until now, his foreign mission enthusiasm has focused solely
upon the overseas distribution of Bibles. In this sermon, however, he
broadened his approach, asserting that the Holy Spirit worked through
the spoken as well as the written word and that it was just as important
for the Evangelical nation to send preaching missionaries overseas, as
to distribute Bibles. Support for missionary societies, moreover, need
not diminish support for Bible societies: the nation possessed a vast
surplus wealth, most of which was devoted to luxury consumption.

Bible and missionary societies should therefore co-operate to inspire the public with a missionary impulse, convincing men that they should sacrifice their luxuries for the support of the two-pronged overseas mission. Indeed, the overseas mission promised to provide a cause for which luxury consumption and selfish interests would be diminished. He contrasted this vision with the militaristic nationalism of Napoleonic France. 'I have only to look forward a few years,' he exclaimed, 'and I see *him* [Napoleon] in his sepulchre; and a few years more, and all the dynasties he has formed give way to some new change in the vain and restless politics of the world.' The missionary ideal, however, transcended the seething world of power politics, and promised a new world order.[56]

The success of Chalmers's Dundee sermon was phenomenal. 'Scarcely a copy of this sermon can be procured,' the *Edinburgh Christian Instructor* observed in its review in December 1813, 'though the London Missionary Society have republished the whole of it, and given it a very extended circulation, a circumstance we believe altogether unprecedented.' By 1817, the sermon had proceeded through four editions. Its impact in London was considerable. Visiting the capital in early 1813, Robert Burns, a young Scottish Evangelical, later recalled his astonishment at the praise lavished upon Chalmers's sermon by leading English Evangelicals.[57]

By late 1812, Chalmers had emerged as a leading advocate of voluntary missionary societies. In the overseas mission movement, and particularly in the British and Foreign Bible Society, he had developed a social expression for his Evangelical piety. In his 1808 *Enquiry*, it will be recalled, he had advocated the organization of the British nation on an authoritarian Napoleonic model. Through sacrifice for the Spartan ideals of independence and military glory, he had argued, individual citizens would be morally elevated, and private interests subordinated to the communal welfare. With his Evangelical conversion, he embraced a new social ideal, while retaining certain similarities to the old. In place of military glory, he now elevated the Christian conversion of the world. Britain was now to achieve glory as God's instrument for sending Bibles and missionaries overseas. Against the radical economic individualism of the now dominant *laissez-faire* political economy, Chalmers argued for a social purposiveness, based upon a national Evangelical ideal. For achieving this ideal, he looked to voluntary Bible and missionary societies, organized in a hierarchical structure, with county societies supervising parish societies, and a London committee co-ordinating the whole. This system of corresponding societies, he believed, would unite the entire British nation. Differences between the Protestant sects, like differences between private interests, would be subordinated to a missionary ideal which focused upon the common denominator of the Bible.

Although his Kilmany parish auxiliary had proved effective, however, Chalmers soon grew disillusioned with the progress of the Bible Society movement in Fife. The actual movement did not approach his increasing expectations. Despite his pleading for a popular movement of penny-a-week parish auxiliaries, for instance, few Fifeshire parishes adopted the plan. His initial reaction was to blame the county Bible Society which, he believed, had not followed his advice and encouraged such auxiliaries. 'Our county society', he complained to Samuel Charters on 18 November 1812, four months after its creation, 'is doing nothing, and, what is worst of all, it has suspended the far more efficient operation of districts and parishes.' He even contemplated disassociating his parish society entirely from the 'dull and inactive County Society'.[58]

Further study of the controversies surrounding the British and Foreign Bible Society, however, awakened him to a more fundamental cause for the lack of missionary enthusiasm. Many Christians believed it to be unwise to contribute to overseas missions while pressing social needs existed in Britain. Charity, they asserted, began at home. Money devoted to distant missionary adventures diminished the amount available to combat local poverty and irreligion. Opponents of the Bible Society maintained that this was particularly irresponsible in Scotland, where poor relief in most parishes was financed almost exclusively by voluntary church-door contributions. Even small subscriptions from poor families diminished the personal savings of the poor and rendered them less able to help themselves in old age or illness.[59] Poor harvests in Scotland in 1811 and 1812, meanwhile, added weight to these arguments. By late 1812, many poor families in northern Fife were on the verge of starvation, and communities were hard pressed to avert disaster.[60]

Chalmers realized that if left unchallenged such arguments would undermine progress towards his ideal of a popular Bible Society movement. The poor, Christ himself had proclaimed, would always be present. The existence of poverty at home, then, must not be admitted as a valid reason for postponing an overseas mission effort. In April 1813, Chalmers began a pamphlet defending his concept of penny-a-week parish auxiliaries.[61] When he finally published it in January 1814, *The Influence of Bible Societies on the Temporal Necessities of the Poor* not only recapitulated his arguments for a popular Bible Society movement, but also defined his developing Evangelical social ideal.

In this pamphlet, he argued that the improvement of the condition of the lower social orders and the extension of the overseas mission movement were not, in fact, mutually exclusive goals. Rather, parish Bible Societies actually contributed to the welfare of the poor, both by elevating their moral character and by increasing benevolence among their wealthier neighbours. First, Bible Society membership increased the self-respect and industry of the poor. As a penny-a-week subscriber, Chalmers asserted, a poor labourer became less apt to allow himself to become a pauper through idleness or carelessness. He stood 'on the high ground of being a dispenser of charity; and before he can submit to become a recipient of charity, he must let himself farther down than a poor man in ordinary circumstances.' Inspired by an ideal that transcended mere survival, he worked harder, and curtailed his consumption of such luxuries as tobacco or whisky, in order that he might give something to overseas missions. This increased dignity and industry among the poor would gradually serve to limit the number of paupers to only those cases of genuine and inevitable misfortune. No longer would public charities by assailed by 'unworthy poor', or those able-bodied persons who refused to work or who squandered their wages, rather than save a portion for their old age or periods of adversity.

Secondly, parish Bible Societies encouraged the benevolence of the wealthy. If the propertied classes curtailed their luxury consumption, he argued, their surplus wealth would prove sufficient both to support the overseas mission and to provide for the legitimate needs of the 'worthy poor' in their neighbourhood. For this sacrifice, Bible Societies educated the wealthy. Parish societies, he explained, brought all social orders in a community together in voluntary association for a shared ideal. 'In such associations the rich and the poor meet together. They share in one object, and are united by the sympathy of one feeling, and one interest.' The wealthy learned to respect the 'worthy poor' as their brothers in Christ. Witnessing the sacrifices of the poor for overseas missions, the wealthy were inspired to similar sacrifices. Further, they learned to recognize the legitimate needs of the 'worthy poor' and to assist them in a spirit of brotherly affection, rather than in the patronizing manner of a superior to an inferior.

At the foundation of Chalmers's argument was the concept of a Christian community, in which a shared missionary ideal strengthened both piety and benevolence. The parish community became united by the spontaneous spirit of charity, which improved the quality of life for all. He then proceeded to contrast this Christian communal ideal to the legal system of poor relief, particularly as it functioned in England. Poor laws, he argued, created an artificial system of contractual relationships, emphasizing a legal right to relief on the part of the poor. Under the legal system, he maintained, the wealthy gave no more than was required by law. Perhaps worse, the poor were encouraged to think more of their rights than of their responsibilities. As a result, they became morally degraded to a condition of 'pauperism', or a permanent legal dependence upon the labour or property of others, which compromised their real freedom, as well as making them less industrious.

The radical weakness of the English system of poor relief was that it functioned according to a low view of human nature. The wealthy, according to the supporters of the legal system, had to be coerced to charity by the power of the State, while the poor were credited with neither a sense of personal responsibility, nor any capacity to help themselves.

Communities organized for an outwardly-reaching Christian ideal, on the other hand, recognized man to be a free agent, formed in the image of God. Inspired by the overseas mission ideal, Chalmers believed, the poor would overcome their circumstances, and rise not only to independence, but to noble sacrifice for others. It was, he asserted, insulting to the poor when benevolent members of the upper social orders argued that they should not be encouraged to subscribe to penny-a-week parish Bible societies. 'Perhaps it does not occur to these friends of the poor, while they are sitting in judgement on their circumstances and feelings, how unjustly and unworthily they think of them. ... [The poor] may not be able to express their feelings on a suspicion so ungenerous, but I shall do it for them.' 'We have', he proclaimed on their behalf,

souls as well as you, and precious to our hearts is the Saviour who died for them. It is true, we have our distresses; but these have bound us more firmly to our Bibles, and it is the desire of our hearts, that a gift so precious should be sent to the poor of other countries. The word of God is our hope and rejoicing; we desire that it may be theirs also, that the wandering savage may know it and be glad, and the poor negro, under the lash of his master, may be told of a Master in heaven, who is full of pity and kindness. Do you think that sympathy for such as these is your peculiar attribute? Know, that our hearts are made of the same materials with your own; that we can feel as well as you; and out of the earnings of a hard and honest industry, we shall give an offering to the cause; nor shall we cease our exertions till the message of salvation be carried round the globe, and made known to the countless millions who live in guilt, and who die in darkness.

For Chalmers, poverty was essentially a moral disease. Its cure would be found in the ideal of the covenanted community, in which both industry and benevolence would be encouraged by a missionary ideal which transcended individual interests. This communal ideal had its origins in Scotland's seventeenth-century convenanting traditions, the memory of which remained alive among the lower social orders of many rural communities in northern Fife. His pamphlet, however, was directed in particular towards the gentry and commercial middle classes, who had lost touch with these traditions. As a result, he maintained, their benevolence had become misguided; they had adopted patronizing or legalistic attitudes towards poor relief, which insulted or degraded the lower social orders. The answer, then, was to revive Scotland's communal traditions among all social orders, through a transcendent ideal for which communities might once again covenant together. In his 1808 *Enquiry*, Chalmers had already endeavoured to gain public support for such a communal vision. His *Enquiry* had failed to win public approval, his critics had argued, because its central ideal of military glory was not worthy of sacrifice. The same, Chalmers believed, could not be said of the overseas mission: nothing, surely, was more worthy of sacrifice than the purpose of providing all men with Bibles for their salvation.

The Influence of Bible Societies marked a watershed in the development of Chalmers's Evangelical thought. In 1812, his primary concern had been the voluntary British and Foreign Bible Society and its overseas mission. By 1813, however, his focus returned to the communal ideal of his youth in Anstruther. Voluntary Bible Societies now became important mainly for providing a cause which would strengthen traditional communal sentiment. They were subordinated to a supportive role in the covenanted parish community.[62] Indeed, in the second edition of the pamphlet, published in 1817, he attached an appendix in which he asserted that parish Bible Societies should not send their collections exclusively to the British and Foreign Bible Society, but should divide their collection among a variety of overseas missionary societies and national benevolent societies. The important thing was that the parish community unite for some unselfish ideal, which in turn would increase local benevolence and industry and decrease the need for legal poor relief. This 1817 appendix alarmed at least one member of the London committee of the British and Foreign Bible Society, who feared that Chalmers's plan for parish societies would seriously diminish contributions to the Society. In a pamphlet published in 1819, Robert Steven, an 'old member' of the London committee, alleged that Chalmers advocated sacrificing the Bible Society's overseas mission to a backward-looking social ideal and misguided notions about the causes and cures of poverty.[63] In truth, by the time *The Influence of Bible Societies* was first published in January 1814, Chalmers's interest in the British and Foreign Society, and in all voluntary missionary societies, had waned. He had grown disillusioned with the whole concept of voluntary effort in religion. Voluntary missionary societies, he now believed, could accomplish their goals only as part of a general Christian nurturing process structured around the parochial institutions of a national religious establishment. He did not completely relinquish interest in the overseas mission, but he subordinated this effort to a new vision of improving the condition of the Scottish people through strengthening traditional communal sentiment in parishes.

'I understand', James Chalmers wrote to his brother from London on 18 April 1814, upon learning that Thomas had been invited by the

London Missionary Society to preach a fund-raising sermon in the capital, 'you are considered as a *great Gun* in the Religious world. I was lately informed that you was highly spoken of at a meeting of one of our Bible societies in the neighbourhood.'[64] Chalmers had indeed extended his national reputation through his activity on behalf of voluntary Bible and missionary societies. His voice now resounded in Evangelical circles even in London. Nevertheless, within the Church of Scotland, he, like his fellow Evangelicals, still lacked real power and influence, Scottish religious and social institutions remaining under the domination of the Tory-Moderate alliance. By 1813, however, he had realized that real reform would not be achieved solely through voluntary Evangelical associations. It would require more than the oratory of a 'great Gun' to effect his communal ideal in Scotland. Rather, he would need to discipline his energy to the pursuit of power within the established national Church of Scotland, both at the parish level and in the hierarchy of Church courts.

IV

The responsibility of the parish minister in the Church of Scotland encompassed both the temporal and spiritual welfare of the parish inhabitants. Along with regular Sabbath preaching, Church law required the parish minister to pursue his calling in three fields of endeavour. First, he was expected to supervise education in the parish. The Church did not recognize a separation of religious and secular learning; consequently, the minister was to supervise general instruction in the parish school, as well as to provide religious instruction to his parishioners. Secondly, he was expected to visit regularly each home in the parish, to encourage family devotional exercises, enforce moral discipline, and inform himself of the material needs of the poor. Thirdly, the parish minister, together with the kirk-session of elders and the parish heritors, was responsible for the collection and distribution of the parish poor-relief fund. In a word, the national established Church of Scotland claimed to exercise considerable authority over Scottish social welfare. In its ideal, the parish ministry focused upon fulfilling the needs of the whole 'natural' man—intellectual, moral, and physical —as well as upon providing vehicles of divine grace for the salvation of God's elect saints.

The effectiveness of social services in the parish depended largely upon the commitment of the individual parish minister. In the Moderate-dominated eighteenth-century Church of Scotland, however, the Church courts had all too often failed to discipline clergymen who neglected their parish responsibilities. As a result, the standard of the parish ministry declined. Many Moderate clergymen, like Chalmers prior to his conversion, regarded their parish as little more than a sinecure while they pursued eminence in other, academic, endeavours— secure in the knowledge that the Church courts would not deprive them of their legal 'right' to the living, provided they at least appeared in the pulpit on most Sundays, baptized infants, and served an annual Communion sacrament. Many Popular party Calvinists, in effect, also neglected their pastoral charge, by focusing their attention upon the spiritual development of those parishioners who demonstrated election, while neglecting the 'chaff'. With declining standards in both the Moderate and Popular clergy's parish ministry, the Church's authority over Scottish social welfare also diminished. Local civil courts assumed increased authority over education and poor relief. This, in turn, contributed to an increasing secularization of Scottish society.

In the early nineteenth century, however, in the wake of the Evangeleical revival, several Scottish clergymen began pursuing a more active and creative parish ministry, independently of any direction from the Church courts. This was by no means a general movement in the Church, and the individual efforts remained widely scattered. None the less, in the parish ministry of such Evangelical clergymen as Henry Duncan of rural Ruthwell or Stevenson Macgill of Glasgow, and of such Moderate clergymen as Samuel Charters of rural Wilton, there was evidence of a new mood in the Church, directed toward reviving the 'ideal parish system', as a means of strengthening religion and improving the quality of life for the Scottish people.[65] Evangelicals, perhaps unsurprisingly, tended to embrace this new mood more than did Moderates. Opinions varied as to the precise form the revived parish system should assume, but the new group of committed parish ministers agreed that the standard of the Establishment's parish ministry had declined and needed to be improved.

Two factors in particular accounted for their concern. First, there was fear within the Establishment of the growing strength of the Evangelical movement in the Scottish Dissenting churches, and especially in the Scottish Congregational movement begun by the Evangelical brothers James and Robert Haldane in the 1790s. Between 1790 and 1810, a considerable number of Evangelical clergymen seceded from the Church of Scotland to join one of the Dissenting denominations, alleging that the Establishment had become so corrupted by Moderatism, patronage, and governmental domination that it could no longer be regarded as a Church of God.[66] Evangelicals who remained in the Establishment now felt constrained to put their house in order, both to defend the character of their spiritual office within a true Church and to discourage further secessions.

Secondly, there was growing interest in the historical roots and traditions of the Reformed Church of Scotland. Eighteenth-century

Moderates, reflecting Enlightenment historiography, had tended to regard John Knox and the sixteenth-century Reformation fathers as semi-literate fanatics, whose influence upon religious life had been mainly negative. They had looked rather to the 'glorious revolution' of 1688 as the foundation of the Church of Scotland. In the second decade of the nineteenth century, however, several Evangelical writers began to revise this picture. In 1810, *A History of the Lives of the Protestant Reformers in Scotland*, by James Scott, minister of Perth, was privately published in Edinburgh with the financial assistance of Andrew Thomson and several Evangelicals, and favourably reviewed by Thomson in the *Edinburgh Christian Instructor*. In the following year Thomas M'Crie published his celebrated *Life of John Knox*, the product of years of meticulous research, which was reviewed at length by the Evangelical clergyman, David Dickson, in the *Edinburgh Christian Instructor*.[67] For these authors, the fathers of the Scottish Reformation had indeed been men who had considerable human failings and who had reflected in part the brutality of their times. Their achievements had, none the less, been substantial—probably the greatest achievement being the creation of a national system for the Christian instruction of the people through parish institutions. It was the responsibility of modern Churchmen to preserve this heritage. This involved, first, individual efforts for a more effective parish ministry and, secondly, a more concerted effort by the Evangelical clergy in the Church courts to ensure disciplinary action against clergymen who neglected the parish ministry: more particularly, this meant securing the abolition of pluralities, or the right in the Church of Scotland for a clergyman to combine a parish living with a university position. For many Evangelicals, pluralities became the main symbol of parish neglect.

By the early months of 1813, Chalmers's thought and activity had begun to reflect this new mood. Shortly before he began writing his pamphlet on *The Influence of Bible Societies*, he commenced a vigorous and innovative parish ministry in Kilmany. In part, he was influenced towards increased commitment to the parish ministry by his waning enthusiasm for the voluntary Bible Society movement. He was also inspired by the examples of such committed parish ministers as Samuel Charters, with whom he corresponded regularly after 1810 on social questions, and the English Evangelical Thomas Scott, whose *Force of Truth*, a treatise on pastoral theology, he had studied with keen interest. He grew increasingly convinced that he must pursue his ideal of the Evangelical community within the national Established Church, rather than within voluntary missionary associations. At the beginning of 1813, he began declining invitations to preach outside the parish and devoting more Sundays to the Kilmany pulpit. He now focused attention upon the three areas of the traditional Scottish parish ministry

—education, visitations, and poor relief. The parish ministry became the practical expression of his Evangelical communal vision.

In 1813, Kilmany was a stable agricultural community, typical of rural parishes throughout the Scottish Lowlands. It lay in gently rolling Fifeshire countryside three miles south of the Firth of Tay, and five miles north of Cupar, the nearest market town. From east to west, the parish was about six miles long; in width, it varied from between one and four miles. Its boundaries encompassed a portion of the valley of the Motray Water, a narrow stream flowing east from the Ochil Hills into the North Sea. Agriculture was almost the sole occupation in the parish, which included some of the finest arable land in Fife. Its 4,042 acres were owned by the United College of St. Andrews University, and divided into a number of estates. In 1813 there were fourteen such estates, varying in size from 54 to 700 acres each, and rented on nineteen-year leases to ten landed proprietors, or heritors. These had been enclosed and improved in the 1780s and 1790s, with marshes drained and ploughed, small tenant holdings consolidated into larger farms, and many tenants removed from the estates. One result of the improvements had been increased agricultural productivity, reflected in increased prosperity among the heritors. Spacious country houses, surrounded by woods and gardens, had been erected on several larger estates. Most heritors, moreover, had begun emulating the manners and morals of the English gentry, including both indifference and non-residency, which resulted in their withdrawal from the communal culture of the parish. Of the ten Kilmany heritors, for instance, only six resided in the parish, and only two demonstrated an active interest in parish affairs. Another result of the enclosures was a declining parish population. In 1797, the parish population was 869. By 1811, it had decreased to 787. The enclosures and removals, however, had been accomplished without violence, and the labouring orders remained politically quiescent.[68]

There were two small villages in the parish, Kilmany and Rathillet, inhabited by tradesmen and handloom weavers who provided most of the clothing and shelter required in the parish. The Motray Water powered a sawmill and two grain mills in the parish. The parish church stood in the village of Kilmany, atop a low hill at the eastern end of the parish. A mile to the west, in Rathillet, stood an Old Light Burgher Secession church, which had been established in the parish in 1762, as a result of a patronage dispute in the parish church.[69] In general, Chalmers did not regard members of the small Rathillet congregation as his responsibility and made no attempt to draw them back into the Established Church. He respected their Evangelical Calvinism and tolerated their dissent. Kilmany, then, was already a stable, largely self-sufficient agricultural community, with social tensions contained by a general respect for order, when in 1813 Chalmers commenced his parish educational, visitation, and poor-relief programmes.

First, he focused increased attention on popular education. A system of almost universal education through parish schools was probably the greatest legacy of the Scottish Reformation. In 1813, virtually every Scottish parish possessed a schoolhouse and employed a schoolmaster. Scottish parochial education was financially supported in part by the heritors of the parish, as a legal obligation upon their property, and in part by modest fees required from the pupils. In Kilmany, virtually all children attended the parish school for six years. In cases where a family could not afford the fees, the Church paid the fees for them from the parish relief fund. The curriculum at the Kilmany parish school, as in most parishes, consisted in reading, writing, Bible study, arithmetic, and geography.[70]

After 1813, Chalmers assumed a more active interest in the Kilmany parish school than hitherto. He began visiting the school on a regular monthly basis, assisting John Lees, the parish schoolmaster, with school administration and instruction. He also began regularly examining the children in matters of general learning, as well as in the Bible. Through this experience he became impressed with the fact that intellectual capacity was not a respecter of social origins, and that in parish schools, children of all social orders could be trained in basic skills which would enable them to grow steadily in knowledge and judgement. He became an enthusiastic believer in the importance of both parish education and a 'well-informed peasantry' for continued social improvement. This enthusiasm for parish education complemented his developing Evangelical communitarian vision. Parish education, he argued in a pamphlet based largely upon his Kilmany experience which he published a few years later, in 1819, was a communal endeavour and served a communal function. The presssure of community opinion in a well-organized parish ensured that all families sent their children to the parish school. There the children learned a common language and a common set of ideals, which in turn bound the community more tightly together.[71]

Chalmers also experimented with other educational programmes in Kilmany. In the autumn of 1813, influenced by the Sunday-school movement of the English Evangelicals, Chalmers commenced a Saturday Bible school for his parish children. He originally intended to teach his school on a monthly basis. So enthusiastic was the response, however, that after November 1813 he held the class every two weeks.[72] Chalmers loved children and devoted considerable time to his preparations. In 1814, for instance, he published an index of religious propositions and Scriptural proofs for use in his school. Within a year, the index was republished in Glasgow, and it soon became a standard text for Bible schools throughout Scotland.[73] Chalmers's school, meanwhile, attracted children of all social orders, including the daughters of David Gillespie of Mountquhannie, the wealthiest heritor in the parish and an Episcopalian. Chalmers later wrote to his sister Jane, on 13 October 1818: 'I met with a more satisfying evidence of good done by a school which I taught when at Kilmany, than by all I did there beside.'[74]

He also devoted attention to a series of popular lectures on the Bible, directed to the adult population of the parish. He had first begun delivering a Bible lecture on most Sunday afternoons in 1812. In May 1813 he increased this to two lectures—in the afternoon and in the evening. His lectures were essentially a commentary upon chapters of the Bible, employing illustrations familiar to his parishioners, and applying Scriptural concepts to community life. He delivered the lectures in series, progressing chapter by chapter through a book of Scripture. Afternoon lectures were generally devoted to the New Testament; evening lectures to the Old.[75] His lectures were not intended for publication; he avoided his usual 'academic eloquence of style' and directed his language to the understanding of all social orders. Years later, in 1838, he was finally persuaded to publish, virtually unrevised, his Kilmany lectures on Romans. The four-volume commentary possesses an attractive childlike simplicity of thought and expression, with emphasis upon Scripture as a guide for the practical Christian life.

Chalmers's educational programmes in Kilmany after 1813 complemented his regular Sunday preaching, and like his sermons, his Bible school and popular Bible lectures were well attended. In part, his interest in parish education reflected his earlier desire for an academic career, and his enthusiasm for education as a force for social reform. The parish of Kilmany now became his school, where he could pursue his educational ideal freely, without fear of being impeded by the influence of 'entrenched academic élites'. After 1813, however, there was also a significant change in his educational vision. In Kilmany, he did not place emphasis upon education as a 'ladder of opportunity', or encourage academic or professional ambition among children of the lower social orders. No longer did he feel the same enthusiasm for his earlier vision of an open society encouraging social mobility for the talented youth, regardless of his social background. He did not discount the existence of intellectual talent among the poor: the emphasis in Kilmany parish education, however, was upon educating men to subsume individual ambition in communal welfare, and to assume willingly the duties of their station within the hierarchy of social orders. Intellectual capacities were to be focused mainly upon growth in religious knowledge and faith within the confines of the parish.

The second focus of Chalmers's parish ministry was in the area of household visitations, commencing a systematic programme of them in February 1813. In his parish, the cottages of the labouring orders were arranged into twenty-two hamlets, including the small villages of Kilmany and Rathillet. He now made several formal visitations to each hamlet in the course of each year. His procedure was simple. During the day, he visited each household in the hamlet for informal discussion, often of a non-religious nature. This enabled him to establish a personal relationship with each family, and to discern their problems and needs. In the evening, he requested the inhabitants of the hamlet to congregate in one of the larger cottages, where he either delivered an informal sermon, or asked them questions from the Longer or Shorter Westminster Catechisms, or discussed the meaning of a Scriptural passage. During these evening meetings, he employed a familiar language and used illustrations from the common experience of the hamlet which he had gleaned during the day's household visits. At the close of each meeting, he invited those with special problems or unresolved religious doubts to arrange with him for further personal consultation. On days when he was not conducting a formal visitation at one of the hamlets, he visited the sick and dying, or the more remote outlying cottages. Because the heritors seldom attended the meetings at the hamlets with their tenants and labourers, he addressed their families separately. Indeed, recognizing the influence of the gentry in a rural community, he pressed his visits upon them with some aggression.[76]

The purpose of his visitation programme was threefold. First, he encouraged regular family Bible study and worship. Nightly religious exercises in each home would complement parish Bible Society meetings, Bible lectures, and Sunday services, and intensify the process of nurturing souls to the acceptance of grace. Secondly, he encouraged the reformation of moral character. During his visitations, he was confronted with occasional instances of wife-beating, drunkenness, and profanity. He not only admonished the offenders in terms of the authority of his spiritual office, but more important, he repeatedly visited offenders and recorded their improvements. He realized, in short, that moral improvement was a gradual process, which required his continued interest. His concern for morality involved more than interest in social harmony. Chalmers regarded moral reformation as a necessary first step towards the acceptance of grace and thus towards individual salvation. Despite the communal direction of his parish ministry, he also retained his Evangelical passion for individual souls. 'Their giving up what is plainly wrong', he informed Janet Coutts in regard to his parishioners on 27 January 1815, 'is a proof of earnestness; it is a putting of themselves into the attitude of seekers. ... Nay, what is sure, it may be the first evidence of a regard to the Saviour, and such an evidence as he may reward with his promised manifestation.'[77] Such views, to be sure, approached very close to Arminianism, or the belief that man contributed to his own salvation through his works. Indeed, his views on the role of moral instruction in the parish ministry were regarded as heretical by some strict Calvinists in the Scottish Evangelical movement, and were condemned in the December 1815 number of the *Edinburgh Christian Instructor*.[78] In any event, his modification of scholastic Calvinism, with his emphasis upon practical morality, strengthened his commitment to the visitation scheme.

Finally, Chalmers used his visitations to gain insight into the material needs of the poor, in order to assist them in an effective manner. He was not solely concerned with the spiritual and moral condition of his parishioners; he employed his influence to secure medical assistance, food, and clothing for the poor, in response to needs which he discovered during his visitations. He also personally donated substantial sums. On 21 February 1814, for instance, he noted in his diary his personal commitment to support two aged parishioners. On the same date, he vowed in the future to devote ten per cent of his annual income 'to the relief of the wants of others either spiritual or temporal'.[79]

On 18 April 1813, a few months after he began his visitation programme, Chalmers delivered a fund-raising sermon in Edinburgh on behalf of the Society for the Relief of the Destitute Sick, in which he defined his developing ideas on the relationship of visitations to the problem of poverty. In the sermon, he opposed a 'realistic' to a 'sentimental' benevolence. The interest of the poor would not be served, he asserted, by the 'refined' paternalism of 'visionary sons and daughters of poetry', influenced by the sentimental literature of the previous generation. Sickbed conversions or gentle deaths in the 'enchanting retirement' of pastoral cottages were fictional creations. In reality, hunger, sickness, and·death were cruel. Delicate sentiments, or even gratitude, were not to be expected from the victims of poverty. In order both to confront actual poverty on a regular basis and to earn the respect of the poor, visitors had to be persons of strong character, motivated not by humanitarian sentiment, but by commitment to serve God. In order to achieve real good, moreover, their Christian conviction had to be combined with sound judgement and a sense of practical detail concerning the poor. 'You must', he instructed the benevolent person, 'give your time and your attention. ... You must make yourself acquainted with the object of your benevolent exercises. Will he husband your charity with care, or will he squander it away in idleness and dissipation? ... What is his peculiar necessity?'

When needed, money should be given cheerfully. But money alone was not sufficient. The poor also had to be helped to help themselves; their rights and their independence had to be secured. 'You must go to the poor man's sick bed. You must lend your hand to the work of assistance. You must examine his accounts. You must try to recover those debts which are due to his family. You must try to recover those wages which are detained by the injustice or the rapacity of his master. You must employ your mediation with his superiors.' 'This', he concluded, 'is benevolence in its plain, and sober, and substantial reality; though eloquence may have withheld its imagery, and poetry may have denied its graces and its embellishments.'[80]

In his Kilmany visitations Chalmers did indeed demonstrate such a knowledge of practical matters concerning the poor. From his communal roots in Anstruther, and the example of his mother's philanthropic activity, he had had early acquaintance with rural poverty. He had learned to despise the élitist paternalism, which had been celebrated by eighteenth-century sentimental novels and which defined many of the current attitudes among the upper social orders regarding the poor.[81] For Chalmers, true philanthropy was directed to restoring the self-respect and, where possible, the independence of the poor.

This conviction was reflected in the third focus of Chalmers's parish ministry—that of parish poor relief. In Kilmany, as in most rural Scottish parishes at this time, no permanent legal assessment had been imposed upon property for poor relief. Rather, Kilmany poor relief was based upon the traditional parish funds for relief in rural Scotland— voluntary collections at services in the parish church, the rental of the parish mortcloth at funeral services, and the interest from a small capital (£209. 9s. 12d., to be exact) which had been donated to the Kilmany church by pious parishioners at their deaths. According to Scottish law, relief in rural parishes was distributed according to the joint decisions of the parish kirk-session and heritors, and was subject to review by local sheriff courts. Relief recipients were legally required to fulfil three criteria. First, they had to be of good moral character, as determined by the parish minister and kirk-session. Secondly, they had to be legal residents of the parish. Scottish residency laws were complex, but in general, residency was established either by birth or by three years of self-supporting residence in the parish. Thirdly, recipients had to be incapacitated for regular work by physical infirmity or old age. The exclusion of able-bodied poor from parish relief, however, was controversial in Scotland, and some parishes did grant assistance from the parish fund to the unemployed during periods of economic distress. In general, legal poor relief in rural Scotland was controlled by the landed interest: since 1750, the gentry-dominated sheriff courts had gradually withdrawn most real authority over local poor relief from the parish ministers and kirk-sessions, and had given it to the heritors, who, the courts reasoned, paid the bulk of financial support for poor relief.[82]

Recipients of relief were listed on parish rolls as either regular or occasional paupers. In Kilmany, regular paupers received money payments from the parish fund every two or three months; occasional paupers received payments only in times of exceptional need. Between 1808 and 1810, the Kilmany parish fund supported between six and eight regular paupers, each receiving between £2 and £3 per annum, and an equal number of occasional paupers, each receiving allotments of 5s. or 6s. two or three times a year. Total disbursements to regular and occasional paupers averaged £24 per annum.[83] This expenditure was extremely small, especially when Kilmany is compared to parishes of similar population in England or southern Scotland, where poor-relief disbursements sometimes exceeded £300 per annum. One reason for its low expenditure was the fact that Kilmany refused any parish relief to the able-bodied unemployed. Another reason was that in Kilmany, as in most rural parishes north of the Firth of Forth, parish relief was regarded as only a supplement to the pauper's income from other sources: even the maximum yearly allowance of £3 was not in itself sufficient to sustain a pauper's life and health.

In addition to the parish fund, according to Chalmers, four sources of relief existed to the Kilmany poor.[84] The first was the industry and foresight of the poor themselves. Kilmany labourers, he observed, tended to postpone marriage until they were in a position to support a family, and could save something for periods of agricultural distress, sickness, or old age. Even when incapacitated for regular work they managed to earn something from light chores, gardening, or weaving. Secondly, most Kilmany inhabitants recognized extended family relationships and regarded it a matter of honour to assist impoverished relatives. Thirdly, tenants and labourers recognized a communal duty to assist the poor in their hamlet with gifts of food, clothing, and fuel. Fourthly, heritors and other wealthy parishioners occasionally distributed private charity. As a result of these four factors, Chalmers argued, the Kilmany poor were in fact better off than the poor in those parishes which had imposed legal assessments upon property to support larger legal allowances to paupers.

After 1813, Chalmers endeavoured to strengthen the traditional communal factors that operated on behalf of the Kilmany poor, and sought to eliminate all legal poor relief. His plan was to replace legal parish relief with a communal spirit of benevolence, directed by the moral voice of the Church, rather than by the definitions and dictates of the civil courts. His activity in Kilmany moved in essentially two directions. First, through his parish Bible Society, and through sermons on the value of benevolence, he worked both to increase the self-respect of the poor and to strengthen communal sentiment in the parish, through purely moral persuasion.[85] Complementing this endeavour was his vision of the convenanted parish community, united for a religious cause, such as overseas missions, and growing in practical benevolence at home. Secondly, in early 1813, he began a social 'experiment' in Kilmany, intended to demonstrate a process by which parish pauper lists and legal definitions of eligibility for relief might be gradually eliminated, and replaced by anonymous private charity.

Late in 1812, Chalmers had been secretly given £15 for the Kilmany poor by John Anstruther Thomson of Charleton, a Kilmany heritor who was concerned over the poor harvest of that autumn. During his 1813 visitations, Chalmers began quietly distributing this fund in small amounts to needy persons, without listing the name of the recipient on the parish relief roll. He informed recipients that the gift was from an anonymous benefactor, separate from the parish fund, and that it was intended mainly to enable them to maintain their independence from parish relief. He distributed sums to able-bodied unemployed, who were not legally entitled to assistance from the parish fund, as well as to the disabled. His only requirements were genuine need and good moral character, as judged by him during his regular visitations.

In August 1814, he announced the result of his 'experiment'. Through small but timely gifts from Thomson's donation, he informed the Kilmany heritors and kirk-session on 12 August 1814, several individuals who had been on the verge of swallowing their pride and applying for parish relief had been enabled to sustain their self-respect and regain their independence..His anonymous distribution of Thomson's donation, Chalmers asserted, had thus spared the parish the expense of several additional paupers as a result of the agricultural distress of 1813. More important, it had rescued those individuals from the moral degradation of legal pauperism, and enabled them to become once again productive members of the community. He now requested the permission of the heritors and kirk-session to distribute part of the parish fund in the same anonymous manner during his visitations, without listing the names of recipients on the relief rolls, but simply crediting the amount 'to the deserving and industrious poor'.[86]

The heritors and kirk-session, however, refused their permission. Chalmers's request, if approved, would have enabled him to distribute parish relief without consideration for the laws regarding eligibility. For Chalmers, this would have represented a step towards eliminating the legal system of poor relief and restoring a Christian communal charity. Parish relief would have become an anonymous arrangement between the charitable, the visiting minister, and the needy, without interference from the secular law of the State. But his plan would also have been illegal, and might have subjected the parish to lawsuits on behalf of those poor individuals to whom Chalmers refused relief.[87] Noting, therefore, that Chalmers still possessed nearly £5 of Thomson's original donation, the heritors and kirk-session simply instructed him 'to go on in the same way as before', distributing the remainder of Thomson's gift anonymously, but respecting legal guidelines and preserving a full public record of all disbursements from the parish fund.[88] Though his attempt at poor-law reform in Kilmany was thwarted, Chalmers continued to distribute anonymously private donations from Thomson and from his own purse during his visitations. He continued also to advocate the abolition of legal poor relief, and its substitution by a Church-directed system of anonymous private charity.

It is difficult to evaluate Chalmers's poor-relief policies in Kilmany. He was not permitted to pursue them as he would have desired, and as a result total relief expenditures in Kilmany remained stable at about £24 per annum into the 1830s. His policies may well have been impracticable, even in the small agricultural community. His emphasis upon pauperism as a moral problem caused him to play down such economic factors as enclosures and unemployment resulting from agricultural improvements, over which the poor had no control, and which Christian benevolence could not overcome. The removal of any legal apparatus for pressuring the heritors to contribute something to poor relief might well have consigned the Kilmany poor to a precarious existence. What, moreover, would have become of the 'undeserving' poor? Chalmers's plan made no provision at all for them, for those individuals so victimized by the economic forces which created poverty as to lose all regard for the moral standards of the community. Unless reformed, the 'undeserving' would have been forced to leave the community, which means the problem would simply·have been exported.

None the less, three principles in his Kilmany poor-relief policies warrant particular notice. First, he endeavoured to combine the distribution of relief with regular visits to the homes of the poor. The Church of Scotland had long recognized in theory that visitations were essential to effective poor relief, but by the early nineteenth century the practice had ceased in most parishes, and Chalmers therefore performed a real service by reviving it in Kilmany. Secondly, he sought to preserve the anonymity of relief recipients, in the interest of preserving both the recipient's self-respect and social position within a Scottish society which widely regarded pauperism as a sign of moral infirmity. Thirdly, he attempted to strengthen communal sentiment in the parish. He realized that a viable community life was probably as important as institutional relief for improving the permanent condition of the poor.

After 1813, then, through educational programmes, visitations, and an innovative approach to poor relief, Chalmers cultivated his parish of Kilmany with a new sense of commitment. There were two dimensions to his parish ideal—communal and Evangelical. First, he saw the parish as a small, organic, largely self-sufficient community, with a stable agricultural economic base. To be sure, a hierarchy of social orders would exist in this community. Emphasis, however, would be placed upon each individual's duties, rather than his privileges or rights. Each individual, rich or poor, would be equally responsible to contribute to the communal welfare to the best of his abilities, and the entire community would be bound together by a spirit of mutual bene-volence.

Secondly, he believed that at its highest level, such a community could be created only through a shared commitment to God. The parish had to be a covenanted Christian community. Men, he believed, had to turn away from self, and towards the service of God, before they could practise true benevolence towards one another. A humanistic morality, such as that disseminated by eighteenth-century Enlighten-ment philosophy and sentimental literature, was not sufficient to over-come the natural selfishness in human nature. This, he argued, his own experience in the parish ministry had demonstrated. For the majority of his twelve years as minister of Kilmany, he asserted in *An Address to the Inhabitants of Kilmany* (a pamphlet he published in 1815), he had endeavoured to reform the character of his parishioners and the nature of parish life through appeals to the virtues of 'honour, and truth, and integrity'. Despite his efforts, he confessed, 'I am not sensible, that all the vehemence with which I urged the virtues and proprieties of social life, had the weight of a feather on the moral habits of my par-ishioners.' Then with his conversion, he explained, he had shifted his emphasis from values directed towards the preservation of society through time, to values directed towards the glorification of the com-munion of saints through eternity. To his surprise, he discovered that the social reforms for which he had long struggled in vain suddenly began to be effected. In Christ, he maintained, the parishioners began to achieve the communal stability, justice, and contentment, which had eluded politicians and political economists. In the grass roots of Kilmany, then, Chalmers believed he had witnessed the beginning of a revival of Christian communal spirit, destined to transform the nation. 'A sense of your heavenly Master's eye', he declared to his parishioners in the 1815 *Address*, 'has brought another influence to bear upon you, and while you are thus striving to adorn the doctrine of God your Saviour in all things, you may, poor as you are, reclaim the great ones of the land to the acknowledgement of the faith.' 'You have at least taught me,' he continued, 'that to preach Christ is the only effective way of preaching morality in all its branches; and out of your humble cottages have I gathered a lesson, which I pray God I may be enabled to carry with all its simplicity into a wider theatre.'[89]

It is difficult to determine the precise effect of Chalmers's ministry in Kilmany after 1813. To be sure, through his influence, and particularly his preaching, the parishioners seem to have grown in appreciation for Evangelical Christianity, and a few, including the Kilmany plough-man's son, Alexander Patterson, and the tenant's son, Robert Edie, experienced Evangelical conversions which altered the direction of their lives.[90] His Evangelical message, then, had considerable impact upon some individuals. With regard to his communal ideal, however, there is no evidence that his policies effected much real change in parish life. Most of the heritors remained aloof from this programmes, and continued to pursue their self-interest with little regard to the needs of their tenants and labourers. Poor-relief expenditures did not decrease as a result of his appeals to self-help and private charity. His innovative parish programmes, including his Bible Society, collapsed when he left the Kilmany ministry.

Setting aside the actual impact of his parish programmes, however, it is significant that Chalmers believed that he had accomplished, with God's help, a great change in the parish. For him it became a microcosm of the nation and a model for national development. The programmes he pursued for the communal organization of Kilmany, he believed, should be adopted in every parish in the nation. Basic to his parish policies was an Evangelical piety, emphasizing individual obedience to God's Scriptural laws as the initial step towards salvation through grace. This piety was not simply to be something superadded to the organic community, but rather was to inform every aspect of community life. His Kilmany experience strengthened him in his vision of Scotland, or rather Britain, as an Evangelical nation, a godly commonwealth of parish communities, in which individual parishioners joined together in pursuit of Christian ideals, under the direction of the national Established Church. Economic growth would be subordinated to Christian idealism, and individual self-interest to the communal welfare, in all temporal matters.

Chalmers had, to be sure, embraced the vision of a communal Britain prior to his Evangelical conversion, in his 1808 *Enquiry into the Extent and Stability of National Resources*. It had failed, however, to gain public support: The Napoleonic threat had not proven sufficient to draw the British nation away from the developing ethos of economic individualism. The failure, in turn, had contributed to his embracing a new direction of social thought after his Evangelical conversion of 1810-11. Initially, his conversion had been reflected in an intense preoccupation with death and the fate of his soul, which found expression in impassioned preaching. By 1814, however, Chalmers had redefined the communal ideal of his the *Enquiry* around his new Evangelical values. He now worked to transform Kilmany into a model Evangelical community, committed to a Christian mission (as represented in part by the parish Bible Society) and cultivating Christian knowledge, moral discipline, and communal benevolence. His Kilmany ministry after 1813 was in fact the fulfilment of his Evangelical conversion experience begun in 1810. From initial preoccupation with death and the individual soul, he had gradually developed greater appreciation for communal life. He had discovered a sense of belonging in the Kilmany community, while his enthusiasm for such crusades as the defeat of Napoleonic France, or even the overseas mission movement, had waned as he focused attention upon the parish community.

The key to his Christian communal ideal was the active Evangelical minister, committed to restoring man's faith in the Bible and the doctrines of man's total depravity and need for divine grace, and to reviving communal sentiment in parishes through visitations, educational programmes, and Christian poor relief. With committed Evangelical ministers labouring in every parish he believed a communal spirit would rise up to transform the nation. To achieve this purpose he turned to the Evangelical party in the Church of Scotland, and particularly to the Evangelical party's campaign against clerical pluralities. Prior to his Evangelical conversion, it will be recalled, Chalmers had been no enemy to pluralities, but in late 1813 he reversed his former position, and embraced the campaign against them which the Evangelical clergy of Fife had revived after a hiatus of several years.[91]

V

The immediate cause of the revival of anti-plurality agitation in Scotland was the case of William Ferrie. In April 1813, Ferrie, Professor of Civil History at St. Andrews University, was presented by the Earl of Balcarras to the parish of Kilconquhar, twelve miles south of St. Andrews. The Evangelicals in St. Andrews presbytery, however, immediately raised the objection that it would be impossible for Ferrie to fulfil his responsibility to the parish while teaching in St. Andrews. Ferrie's Moderate supporters, on the other hand, including his uncle and mentor, George Hill, replied that the union of a parish living and university chair was legal, that such unions strengthened the connection between religion and higher learning, and that Ferrie would be able to fulfil the duties of both positions. In the event, the presbytery accepted the Evangelicals' objection, and refused to ordain Ferrie unless he first resigned his professorship. But Ferrie refused to resign the professorship, and appealed for justice to the General Assembly. In May 1813, by a narrow majority of five, the General Assembly upheld Ferrie's right to both livings and instructed St. Andrews presbytery to ordain him.

St. Andrews presbytery, however, again refused to ordain. An irregularity in the form of Ferrie's presentation, they argued, had rendered the presentation illegal. Because the General Assembly would not meet again until May 1814, Ferrie now appealed to the synod of Fife, the intermediate court between St. Andrews presbytery and the

General Assembly, which was scheduled to meet in October 1813. At this point, Chalmers entered the agitation. Kilmany was not part of St. Andrews presbytery, so he had been merely an observer to the initial proceedings against Ferrie. But Kilmany was represented in the synod of Fife, and in the weeks preceding the October synod, Chalmers helped plan the Evangelical party's synod strategy. Further, he prepared a speech asserting the illegality in the form of Ferrie's presentation, which was evidently assigned by the party to open the debate for the Evangelical side.[92]

On 12 October 1813, however, the day of the synod debate on Ferrie's plurality, Chalmers's nerve failed. He was evidently intimidated by the presence in the synod of his former St. Andrews professor, George Hill, and other members of the St. Andrews faculty who supported Ferrie. Hill, as leader of the Moderate party in the Church of Scotland for nearly thirty years, was a master of ecclesiastical law and politics, and Chalmers probably feared appearing intellectually inadequate before his former university professors and colleagues. The presence of the university faculty may well have revived his former insecurities, connected with his dismissal from his mathematics assistantship and his failure to be seriously considered for a St. Andrews chair. He had evidently not entirely subordinated academic ambition to his Evangelical piety. At the assigned moment for his speech, he remained silent, throwing the Evangelical strategy into confusion. Hill and the Moderates now easily convinced the synod simply to instruct St. Andrews presbytery to correct the legal irregularity in Ferrie's presentation, and proceed to his ordination. The months of Evangelical agitation had apparently been in vain. Chalmers returned from what he termed his 'day of mortification' at the October synod, feeling 'weak, vain, timid, and capricious'. Severe mental depression brought on physical illness, which confined him to his manse for several days.

In his confinement, Chalmers entered in his diary the promise to subordinate his vanity and ambition more fully to the Evangelical movement. He also vowed to apply himself 'most strenuously to the acquirement of [ecclesiastical court] forms and Church law', in order to pursue a more effective role for the movement in the Church courts.[93] His opportunity soon appeared. At the April 1814 meeting of the synod of Fife, the Evangelicals renewed the agitation, and convinced the synod to request the 1814 General Assembly to reconsider the law regarding pluralities. Chalmers had meanwhile secured his election as a commissioner to the 1814 Assembly, and managed to convince the Evangelical party to allow him to repair his 'day of mortification', by delivering the first of two speeches introducing the synod's overture.

His speech, delivered in the Assembly on 26 May 1814, revealed careful preparation. He based his argument upon the idea that pluralities were an eighteenth-century innovation, with no basis in the law of the sixteenth-century Reformed Church of Scotland. It was true, he admitted, that some pluralities had existed in the early Reformed Church. This, however, had been intended only as a temporary response to a pressing shortage of ministers. The Reformation Fathers had clearly meant the parish ministry to be a full-time occupation, and had considered pluralities to be an evil. Pluralities, he continued, had only become accepted practice in the Church after 1760, with the triumph of the Moderate ascendancy, while the recent agitation against them reflected 'the awakening of a righteous spirit amongst us'. 'It is, indeed,' he asserted, 'a refreshing spectacle, and recalls to my imagination the zeal and purity of better days.' The abolition of pluralities would help restore the spirit of self-sacrifice and commitment to parish communities which had once characterized the whole body of Scottish clergy. There was no need for new legislation to eliminate the Moderate abuses regarding pluralities: rather, the Church had only to reassert, by a simple 'declaratory act', the existing Church law against pluralities. Chalmers's historical analysis, in fact, was both simplistic and erroneous. None the less, his argument appealed to the majority of commissioners, and the Assembly decided, by a vote of 81 to 61, to adopt his position. A 'declaratory act' was passed, prohibiting pluralities as an infraction against existing Church law.[94]

George Hill had not been a commissioner to the 1814 Assembly. His health had been weakened by a severe stroke in 1811, and he now delegated much of the management of the Church to younger Moderates. In late 1814, however, he responded to the Evangelical victory over pluralities with renewed vigour. The abolition of pluralities, he realized, fundamentally threatened the eighteenth-century Moderate policies of 'enlightened élitism', or the direction of social improvement from above by a professional élite of clergy and university professors, united by bonds of patronage to the landed interest. Pluralities enabled a relatively small group of Moderate leaders to dominate the positions of influence within both the Church and universities. Without them, then, Hill feared the Moderate party ascendancy would be undermined. Perhaps worse, without the leaven of pluralists, combining religion and higher learning, the clergy as a body would lose all sense of enlightened detachment from general society. As mere parish ministers, they would begin to mirror the popular prejudices and ignorance of the majority of their parishioners, and the Church would no longer represent a force for the rational improvement of society. Hill therefore employed his Tory political connections to raise the alarm against the 1814 Assembly's action, and in May 1815 he declared that he would introduce a motion in the 1816 Assembly to rescind the 1814 'declaratory act'. Among his arguments was the observation that there had in fact been no existing law against pluralities prior to 1814, and that therefore a simple 'declaratory act' asserting previous law was insufficient to abolish the practice.[95]

Chalmers secured his appointment as a member of the 1816 General Assembly. Public opinion, meanwhile, had been aroused by the plurality issue, and on 22 May, the day scheduled for Hill's motion, the public galleries were overcrowded with spectators. During the celebrated fourteen-hour debate, one of the longest in the history of the Assembly, Chalmers profoundly impressed the crowd with the power of his oratory. The real issue now before the Assembly, he realized, was the conflict between the Moderate concept of 'enlightened élitism', or the dissemination of religious knowledge from above by a socially detached clerical order, and the emerging Evangelical concept of a popular parish ministry, with the minister the focal point of the parish community. Although he briefly reiterated his position on the illegality of pluralities in the sixteenth-century Church, Chalmers did not allow himself to become entangled in the complexities of Church law, on which Hill was the expert. Following his brief legal summary, he declared: 'I would not again, upon this subject, plunge the Church into the fathomless obscurities of law, or commit the fruit of the battles she has already won to the ocean of a thousand uncertainties.' Rather, he focused upon the practical benefits the Church would gain from the abolition of pluralities. With pastoral hues he painted the portrait of a committed rural minister, devoting his life to the cultivation of piety and morality within the parish community. It was a picture calculated to stir the Romantic sensitivities of an early nineteenth-century, educated audience, newly awakened to the traditions of Scotland's past. The most effective appeal, however, was reserved for the conclusion, when he shifted the scene from rural pastures to the overcrowded parishes of the new industrial towns, Here, he asserted, the duties of a parish minister were already too pressing for even the most committed clergyman. Here, he exclaimed,

the minister may live out all his existence in the field that is assigned to him, and multiply his daily rounds through the peopled intricacies which abound in it, and listen to as many calls of duty as time and strength and the other elements of exertion make him able for, and ply his conscientious labours amongst the tenements of the sick and the destitute and the dying, and after many years spent in making his way through the throng of that countless and ever-shifting multitude by whom he is surrounded, be as little known to the vast majority of his people as if—separated from them by the whole diameter of the earth—he took his station at the antipodes.

'Give a professorship to such a man,' he concluded, 'and you multiply still farther this lamentable distance.' The message was clear. However corrupting pluralities may have been to piety and morality in the agrarian Scotland of the eighteenth century, they were an evil which absolutely could not be abided in the industrializing and urbanizing Scotland of the nineteenth century.[96]

Hill and the Moderates then managed to convince the Assembly that because no previous law against pluralities in fact existed, the 1814 'declaratory act' abolishing them was an illegal proceeding. Their victory, however, was hollow. For the Assembly immediately passed, by a vote of 118 to 94, an overture for a new act of Church law, which greatly limited pluralities. Sensing the new mood of the Assembly, and particularly of his younger Moderate supporters, Hill now felt constrained to give his support to the overture, which was at least less comprehensive in its condemnation of pluralities than the 1814 'declaratory act'. The overture was transmitted for approval to the presbyteries, and by June 1817 it became law. According to the new act, no university instructor could be admitted to a parish living outside the boundaries of the university town, and presbyteries were enjoined to the strict disciplining of ministers who neglected parish duties.

While not all they had desired, the 1817 act nevertheless represented a major victory for the Evangelical party—a victory manifested more in the results of the act than in the actual wording of the law. After 1816, the Church of Scotland increasingly regarded itself as a popular body and demonstrated growing concern for its parish ministry. With the plurality agitation, the Evangelical movement in the Church of Scotland came of age, and the Evangelicals in particular now achieved a greater influence within the Church courts. The eighteenth-century Moderate social ideal of 'enlightened élitism', in turn, declined in influence, and the Moderate party ascendancy in the Church continued to wane. Indeed, several years passed before the Moderates were prepared to defend a new union of a university chair and parish living even within the limits of the 1817 law. For George Hill, the plurality issue was the last major effort of his career. He now retired from active management in the Church, and two years after the passing of the 1817 act he died quietly in St. Andrews at the age of sixty-nine. Hill was the last of the great eighteenth-century Moderate ecclesiastical politicians, and his retirement left the Moderate party without effective leadership.

Along with the Evangelical party, Chalmers had come of age during the anti-plurality agitation. The plurality issue served as his apprenticeship in the art of ecclesiastical politics within the Church of Scotland. Following his 'mortification' in October 1813, he had studied the art of Church politics and rapidly demonstrated real ability in the Church courts. In the Assembly of 1816, he had proved an effective adversary even to George Hill. By shifting his emphasis from his 1814 legal argument against pluralities to an argument based upon their social inexpediency, particularly in an urbanizing society, he had rendered

Hill's legal knowledge largely irrelevant and employed his own gift for impassioned oratory to maximum effect, while his contrast of the rural ideal of the parish ministry and stable parish community with the growing urban challenge to social order had profoundly affected the Assembly and spectators. 'This topic', the *Glasgow Courier* noted of Chalmers's pluralities speech on 6 June 1816, 'was illustrated by the speaker in a torrent of eloquence which seemed to astonish the house, and which has, in the opinions of the best critics and judges, perhaps never been exceeded.'[97]

'I know not what it is,' Francis Jeffrey, the Whig editor of the *Edinburgh Review*, was reported to have remarked following Chalmers's 1816 Assembly speech, 'but there is something altogether remarkable about that man.'[98] Impulsive and passionate, and yet accepting the strict discipline of Evangelical piety; ambitious and eccentric in character, and yet preaching a communal ideal—Chalmers indeed embodied tensions which in turn expressed themselves in powerful oratory. This was both an asset and a liability. His gifts as an orator enabled him to rise rapidly to a position of influence within both the Evangelical party and the Church. At the same time, however, his rise had perhaps been too rapid, and his apprenticeship too short. He had not had sufficient time to master 'forms and Church law', or that unique blend of humility and the pursuit of power which is the mark of the ecclesiastical politician. His oratory alone, though it might 'astonish the house', did not necessarily resolve the tensions in his own thought and character. Perhaps what was worse, his rapid rise to influence within the Church courts caused him to place too much confidence in his passionate oratory, and to despise 'the fathomless obscurities of law', as well as to hold too readily in contempt the opinions of those who differed from him.

The most effective moment of his 1816 General Assembly speech had been his contrast of the urban to the rural challenge to religion and social order. By May 1816, Chalmers had come to realize that the urban environment of the rapidly growing towns and cities of Scotland was radically different from the agrarian community of Kilmany. The industrial and commercial expansion which he had vainly inveighed against in his 1808 *Enquiry* was rapidly creating a new social structure, and the Church was proving unable to contain the social change within any traditional social order. His new insight into the urban situation was, in fact, the fruit of nearly eleven months experience as minister of one of the most crowded urban parishes in Scotland. For he was no longer the minister of Kilmany at the time of his triumph in the 1816 General Assembly. Despite his idealization of the rural parish community and his new commitment to the 'common people' of Kilmany, increasing fame as an Evangelical preacher, author, and ecclesiastical politician had again stirred his ambition. It was, he believed, his duty to carry the communal message of Kilmany 'with all its simplicity into a wider theatre'. In late 1814, he received the offer of an urban parish in Scotland, with prospects of increased influence and prestige. He had, it will be recalled, hoped for an Edinburgh preferment. The home of Scotland's major university, General Assembly, civil Court of Session, and main publishing industry, the provincial capital had long represented an object for his ambition. But the offer had not come from staid Edinburgh. Rather, it was Glasgow, the centre and standard of a new industrial Scotland, which now called the minister of Kilmany. It was in Glasgow, then, that he discovered the 'countless and ever-shifting multitude', sunk in poverty, and rapidly sinking also into depravity and irreligion, which even the most conscientious labours of a parish minister seemed powerless to rescue. Here, indeed, would be the test of his communal ideal.

GLASGOW AND THE URBAN CHALLENGE

I

In September 1814, Stevenson Macgill, the Evangelical minister of the Tron parish in Glasgow, was appointed to the Chair of Theology at Glasgow University. A leading anti-pluralist, Macgill resigned his parish living, and several prominent Glasgow merchants, organized by the brothers John and Robert Tennent and Chalmers's cousins John and Walter Wood, decided upon Chalmers for the vacancy. The prospect did not appear promising. He was not well known in western Scotland, and there were rumours that his conversion was dubious. 'The cry today', John Tennent admitted to a friend in early September, 'is that Chalmers is mad!' None the less, the Tennents and Woods persisted, and in mid-September they convinced the venerable Robert Balfour, the leading Evangelical clergyman in Glasgow, to visit Kilmany to hear Chalmers preach. Balfour was impressed. He immediately informed Charles Parker, a leading member of the Glasgow Town Council, that although Chalmers was 'spoken against by many', Balfour was convinced that 'he is indeed converted'.[1] On 30 September, Chalmers gave his cousin John Wood permission to introduce him as a candidate for the Tron. But a few days later, on 6 October, he discreetly declined a suggestion from another supporter that he seek to create public pressure on the Glasgow Town Council, the legal patron of the Glasgow churches, by preaching in Glasgow. 'I am here', he explained of Kilmany, 'labouring in the field which Providence has assigned to me, and I wish to leave my call to another field purely and entirely to the same Providence.'[2] Instead of visiting Glasgow, he met with a deputation from the Tron congregation in late October in Perth. The deputation was won over; in mid-November, the majority of elders and heads of families in the Tron congregation submitted a petition to the Town Council for Chalmers's appointment.[3]

The Glasgow Moderate clergy, meanwhile, with the support of leading Glasgow Tories, had decided upon Duncan Macfarlane, the minister of rural Drymen, for the Tron. Many Tories were anxious to avert any Evangelical appointment, regarding Evangelicalism, with its impassioned sermons on the equal depravity of all souls, as a threat to the subordination of social ranks. Tory politicians in both Glasgow and Edinburgh, including Kirkman Finlay, the MP for Glasgow, Henry Monteith, the Glasgow Lord Provost, and Alexander Maconochie, the Lord Advocate of Scotland, employed their influence against Chalmers. William Taylor, minister of the Glasgow parish of St. Enoch's and Principal of Glasgow University, circulated rumours of Chalmers's 'madness'. There were also rumours of bribes being offered to Town Councillors to vote against Chalmers, including the alleged offer of a contract valued at £200 per annum from a West Indian commercial house to Chalmers's cousin John Wood, a cooper.[4]

On 25 November, the day of the election, the scene outside the Council Chambers was boisterous, with both parties mobilizing crowds to shout slogans at the Councillors as they entered the Chambers. Chalmers's chances for election appeared slim in the face of Tory influence, yet the Town Council elected him for presentation to the Tron, by a vote of 15 for Chalmers, 10 for Macfarlane, and 4 for James McLean, a compromise candidate. Thomas Snell Jones, a prominent Edinburgh Evangelical clergyman, wrote to Chalmers from Edinburgh on 26 November:

I have this instant received the accounts from Glasgow that the battle, the great battle, has been fought, and the victory won ... Heaven and earth, and all the principalities and powers in high places, have been moved; from the great officers of State at St. James, and the Court of alderman in King Street, and the Crown lawyers in Edinburgh, down to the little female sluts, who were taught to squal what they did not understand, 'No fanatics! No Balfourites! Rationalists for ever!' No small stir, I'll assure you, has been in that city, and no such stir has there been since the days of John Knox, it is said, about the choice of a minister.[5]

Chalmers was swept along with the feeling that something providential had occurred. 'I think', he confided to his mother on 30 November,

that considering the wonderful perseverence of my supporters, the wonderful difficulties they had to contend with, the many attempts that were employed to seduce them from the side they had taken, the petitions of the Glasgow congregation in my behalf signed by 140 heads of families, 70 individuals, and 8 out of a [kirk] session consisting of ten members, I say that taking all these circumstances together if ever there was such a thing as a Call of Providence ot a minister—this is that call.[6]

The Glasgow Evangelical public was also euphoric. The seats of the Glasgow churches at this time were rented by the Town Council, as a means of defraying the burgh's expense in maintaining the church buildings and paying the clergy's salaries. As soon as his election became known, the rush to rent vacant seats in the Tron was astounding. 'I got seats in the Tron church yesterday,' his wife's cousin Isabella Turpie informed Grace on 29 November, 'and had reason to account myself fortunate in getting a back seat in one of the Galleries. Some of the most genteel people in Glasgow have taken seats as far back as we are and [are] glad to get them.' 'The Beadle', she added, 'told me that since Saturday morning he could have let all the seats in the Church twice over and at any rent.'[7] On 2 January 1815, Chalmers signified to the Tron kirk-session his acceptance of the appointment. The date of admission was scheduled for July 1815, to allow him time for a gradual separation from Kilmany.

His final months in Kilmany were painful. It was here that he had been converted to the 'peculiar doctrines' of Evangelicalism, and had embraced the ideal of Christian community. A petition by his Kilmany parishioners begging him to remain raised inner doubts as to whether he had not in fact allowed ambition to delude him regarding the 'Call of Providence'. He was also anxious about his ability to fulfil the high expectations of the Glasgow Evangelicals. Not only were the Evangelical hopes for him perhaps 'too high and too sanguine'; there were also, he feared, powerful Moderates and Tories who wished to see these hopes disappointed.[8] There was yet a further risk to his career in the move to Glasgow. His influence as preacher and author was largely based on his origins among the 'common people' of rural Scotland, and on his character as a rustic figure, expressing a simple faith and traditional values. In this role, his provincial accent and clumsy mannerisms had contributed to his impact. But would these same characteristics be appreciated, or even tolerated, in the minister of a genteel urban congregation in a city renowned not only for its commerce, but also for its fine university? His brother James, who opposed his move to Glasgow, thought not. 'Kilmany', James wrote from London on 26 November 1814,

is the place where you began your career. The Rev. Mr. Chalmers of Kilmany is known; his fame is far spread, his character is respected, his reputation is established, and his abilities acknowledged and admired. But the Rev. Mr. Chalmers of Glasgow is another person; he has to begin the world afresh; and there is little doubt but he will be considered in the literary as well as religious world as a very different man from his reverence of Kilmany. Shining abilities are naturally looked for and expected to be met with at the seat of learning, and of course are not estimated so highly as when they proceed from humble life.

He would, James assured him, 'sacrifice his happiness for ever' among the crowds of Glasgow. Further, he would suffer a decline in standard of living. Glasgow ministers were not provided with a manse, but had to rent their own houses. Chalmers, therefore, would in fact be poorer on his £400 per annum stipend as a Glasgow minister than he had been in the well-endowed Kilmany living.[9]

Despite these discouragements, Chalmers left Kilmany, and on 21 July 1815 he was admitted to the Tron church: an event celebrated as a major triumph for the Evangelical movement in Scotland. The venerable Sir Henry Moncrieff Wellwood, minister of St. Cuthbert's parish in Edinburgh, and leader of the Evangelical party in the Church of Scotland, travelled to Glasgow to preach the sermon formally introducing Chalmers to his new congregation. A number of distinguished

Evangelicals attended, including Charles Simeon of Cambridge, regarded by many as the father of the Evangelical movement in England.
The crowd, Chalmers informed his wife, who remained behind in
Kilmany for several weeks supervising the moving of their belongings,
was 'immense'.[10] The Evangelicals had reason for celebration. They
had triumphed over the power of the Moderate-Tory alliance in Glasgow, and brought the man whose conversion was regarded by many as
a symbol of the Scottish Evangelical revival to the city that represented
the centre of a new industrializing Scotland.

Chalmers's initial impressions of Glasgow were not favourable.
'Were I to judge by my present feelings,' he observed of the city to
Charles Watson, minister of the Fifeshire parish of Leuchars, on 29 July 1815, 'I would say that I dislike it most violently. ... All around me
carries the aspect of desolation.' As the months passed, his dissatisfaction grew. Two matters in particular disturbed him. First, he became
convinced that the office of Glasgow parish minister had been degraded
by a burden of civic and ceremonial functions that left little time for
religious thought or composition. 'The peculiarity which bears hardest
on me', he complained to Watson of the Glasgow public on 27 October
1815, three months after beginning his Tron ministry, 'is the incessant
demand they have on all occasions for the personal attendance of the
ministers. ... [S]uch is the manifold officiality with which they are
covered that they must be paraded among all the meetings and all the
institutions.' 'I am like to be devoured', he complained to his mother
on 15 November 1815, 'by a clamorous demand for attentions from
every quarter.' As a result of this burden of civic functions, including
meetings on such subjects as drainage ditches or the type of soup served
to paupers in the Town Hospital, he believed the Glasgow clergy were
relinquishing their status as ministers of God, and being relegated to
the role of civic functionaries in the Glasgow government.[11]

Second, and more disturbing, was the effective collapse of the parish
system in Glasgow. The 'genteel' crowds who occupied their rented
seats in the Tron church each Sunday were a non-parochial congregation, drawn from throughout the city. Because they paid seat-rents,
many of them regarded Chalmers as their property, a salaried agent
responsible for preparing their individual souls, and those of their
families, for salvation. They 'devoured' him with visits and invitations,
leaving him no time for the labour of visiting parishioners, which
formed one of the main pastoral duties of the rural minister. The Tron
parish, meanwhile, with a population of over 10,000, was one of the
poorest in Glasgow, with pressing need for pastoral attention. In 1815,
he later recalled, only one out of every ninety-seven Tron parishioners
attended his sermons.[12] There was no sense of parish community.
Discouraged, he grew homesick for the his 'dear vale' of Kilmany. On

25 November 1815, four months after his arrival in Glasgow, he opened his heart to young Robert Edie, the farmer in Kilmany who had been one of his special converts. 'Oh! with what vivid remembrance', he confided to Edie,

can I wander in thought over all its farms and all its families, and dwell on the kind and simple affection of its people, till the contemplation becomes too bitter for my endurance—and contrast the days which now are with the days which once were, when I sat embosomed in tranquillity and Friendship, and could divide my whole time between the pursuits of sacred literature and the work of dealing out simple and spiritual teaching among my affectionate parishioners.

'This system', he observed of the parish ministry in Glasgow, 'is now, I grieve to say it, greatly broken up; and one must signalize himself by resisting every established practice, or spend a heartless, hard driving, distracting, and wearing out life among the bustle of unministerial work, and no less unministerial company.'[13] Chalmers had arrived in Glasgow committed to two themes based upon his Kilmany experience—an aggressive Evangelical pastoral ministry and the traditional parish community. Glasgow, it seemed appreciated neither.

In 1815 it was an energetic city. Its commercial interests extended throughout the world, its manufacturers had established large-scale iron foundries and chemical dye works, and were beginning to harness steam power to revolutionize textile production. Glasgow University, where Adam Smith had once instructed the sons of 'merchant princes' in moral philosophy, remained one of the finest in Europe, and John Gibson Lockhart's account of entering the city from the west in March 1815 and passing through the centre of the Tron parish, in *Peter's Letters to his Kinsfolk*, emphasizes its diversity and activity.[14]

The recent growth of the city had been phenomenal. In 1780, the population had been only about 40,000. By 1811, however, it had reached 100,749, and by 1815 it exceeded 120,000. Prior to the beginning of the American War in 1775, there had been little manufacturing in Glasgow, the city economy being based almost exclusively upon the tobacco trade. With the collapse of the American tobacco trade in 1775, however, emphasis shifted to manufactures. In 1815, cotton was king among Glasgow manufactures, the industry having grown from virtually nothing in 1775 to comprise 52 separate cotton mills, with 511,200 spindles, 2,800 power looms, and about 32,000 handloom weavers. There were also extensive dye works, printing works, iron foundries, and machine works in the city and suburbs. Glasgow, to be sure, suffered the effects of the general economic depression in Britain at the close of the Napoleonic wars: during the first three months of 1816, a series of bankruptcies, amounting to £2,000,000, shook the city's financial foundations. None the less, close co-operative

interrelationships among the city's leading commercial and manufacturing élites, cemented by cousinships and intermarriages, enabled
most to weather the post-war depression in much the same way as they
had survived the collapse of the American tobacco trade after 1775. They
extended credit to one another, recognizing the limitation of bankruptcies and the preservation of a sound financial system to be in the
interest of all. Despite the economic depression, then, the élite continued to exhibit confidence, enjoying their social clubs, dinners, and
country residences. They cut back production, reduced their labour
forces, and waited for the crisis to run its course.[15]

The situation was different for the poor. Conditions for the Glasgow
labouring orders had in fact been declining for a number of years prior
to the post-war distress—largely as a result of the rapid population
increase throughout Scotland in the late eighteenth-century. Until
about 1800, for instance, Glasgow handloom weavers, the largest single
occupational group in the city, had been relatively prosperous. After
the turn of the century, however, intense competition among the
growing number of weavers began driving wages down, until sixteen or
more hours a day at the loom were often insufficient to stave off ruin.
Equally tragic was the fate of many rural tenants and labourers, forced
off the land by enclosures and less labour-intensive agricultural methods.
With each day, more families pressed into Glasgow from the countryside seeking employment, many making their way across the narrow
channel from Ireland, half-starved or weakened by disease. The post-
war distress was a capstone to their misery; Glasgow was unable to
provide them with employment, adequate housing, or sanitary conditions. Behind the picturesque pillars, turrets, and spires of the main
thoroughfares were often tragic scenes of human suffering. Families
crowded into damp cellars and derelict tenements. Drainage was insufficient, and water supplies polluted. Garbage and faecal matter
rotted in stagnant pools in narrow closes. The air, like the buildings,
was darkened with coal soot. Corpses often lay for days in crowded
rooms because families lacked the money for burial. In late 1817, an
epidemic of typhus began its grim sweep through the Glasgow slums.[16]

There was, indeed, a growing distance between the 'two Glasgows'—
between the upper and middle classes, who managed to weather the
post-war depression, and the labouring poor, whose precarious living
standards of the past twenty years now suffered a devastating blow. In
eighteenth-century Glasgow, rich and poor had often lived in close
proximity to one another, sharing the same close or courtyard, or even
different floors of the same tenement. To a large degree, traditional
rural relationships of paternalism and deference had survived, miti-
gating the worst effects of poverty. But with the rapid population
growth in the late eighteenth and early nineteenth centuries, the

wealthy tended to move to the outskirts of the city. Increasingly, the poor were isolated within older, decaying sections of the inner city. Traditional social relationships broke down, and the labouring poor were left more and more vulnerable to the harsh forces of the post-war market economy. In desperation, many turned to mob violence—for the most part in the form of bread riots. In September 1815, for example, Kirkman Finlay, the Tory MP for the city and an advocate of high duties on imported grain, was accosted by a Glasgow mob and barely escaped injury. By December 1816, troops had to be quartered near the city to protect grain merchants from the mobs. Some labourers, however, particularly weavers, looked to more rational political action as the only means to improve conditions. In October 1816, an estimated 40,000 attended a political reform meeting at Thrushgrove, an estate on the outskirts of the city. By November 1816, secret societies were discovered by the authorities to be administering illegal oaths. The political élites, recalling only too vividly the excesses of the French Revolution, became anxious to stifle calls for even moderate reform.[17] Rich and poor, master and labourer, were becoming more and more polarized.

Reflecting the breakdown of traditional relationships between social orders was the virtual silence of the Church of Scotland in Glasgow about the social suffering and its divisiveness. For centuries, the Established Church had endeavoured to strengthen benevolence and co-operation among the social orders. Although its dissemination of the communal ideal had declined in vigour during the late eighteenth-century reign of Moderatism, the rural Church, at least, still regarded the parish community as the focus of its ministry. In Glasgow, however, the parish ministry was almost non-existent. Its breakdown was reflected in three areas. First, the Established Church in Glasgow had not sufficiently increased its church accommodation to provide for the needs of a rapidly growing population. In 1815, the parish churches in the city offered only 15,546 sittings.[18] In the previous fifty years, eight chapels-of-ease, churches without legal parish boundaries or representation in the Church courts, had been erected by special acts of the General Assembly to ease the burden of overcrowding in the parish churches. But even including these chapels-of-ease, the Established Church provided only 21,690 sittings for the population of 120,000.[19] High seat-rents, and such expectations as respectable Sunday clothing and church-door contributions, meanwhile, effectively excluded most of the labouring poor. The Church of Scotland in Glasgow became virtually a voluntary association for the upper social orders—a class-oriented Church, which none the less retained the privileges of the State connection.

Secondly, there was in Glasgow no system of Church-supervised

endowed parish schools, such as the system that provided inexpensive
and almost universal elementary education in rural parishes. Education
in Glasgow was left to the exertions of charitable foundations and
private enterprise. In 1815, the Church of Scotland educated about 450
children in endowed charity day-schools. Dissenting churches provided
charity day-school education for another 743 children.[20] The vast
majority of families, however, were obliged to send their children to
private day-schools, which were expensive and often of poor quality.[21]
Many families were either unwilling or unable to provide private
schooling for their children. In a nation that had long prided itself on its
system of inexpensive, almost universal education provided by local
parish schools, a large proportion of Glasgow's children remained
totally uneducated.

Finally, the Church of Scotland in Glasgow had relinquished most of
its authority over poor relief. The poor-relief system in urban Scotland
was in fact radically different from that in rural parishes. Although
church-door collections at the Glasgow parish churches were still
devoted to poor relief, this source had been largely superseded by two
other poor-relief sources. First, there was the Glasgow Town Hospital,
a civic institution founded in 1733, and supported by a legal assessment,
or tax, upon property in the city valued at £300 or more. The Town
Hospital employed the assessment to provide both indoor and outdoor
relief to paupers. Although it accepted most of its paupers on the
recommendation of the Church of Scotland, its Directors were accountable more to the Magistrates and Town Council than to the Church.[22]
Secondly, there were donations to the poor from charitable foundations
and voluntary philanthropic societies. Comparison of the contributions
from these three sources to the Glasgow poor reveals the extent to which
the Church of Scotland's role in poor relief had declined. In 1815, the
assessment-supported Town Hospital distributed about £10,000 in
poor relief, and the charitable foundations and voluntary societies
distributed over £20,000 in pensions, fuel, meal, and clothing. During
this same year the Church of Scotland in Glasgow distributed only
£2,000, or less than 7 per cent of the total poor relief in the city.[23]
Besides the diminishing role of its church-door collections in poor relief,
moreover, the Church of Scotland in Glasgow no longer employed the
parish as the main unit for its poor-relief management. Because of
disparities in wealth among the eight parishes within the burgh limits,
the Church had vested its poor-relief functions in an institution called
the General Session, a body composed of all the parish ministers and
parish elders in the burgh. All church-door collections from the eight
parishes were sent to the General Session, which in turn distributed the
combined collections to the sessional paupers on the Church rolls. The
General Session, rather than the individual parish kirk-sessions, pos-

sessed the final authority to decide which applicants should be refused relief, which should be accepted for sessional relief, and which should be referred to the Town Hospital for assessment relief.[24] As a result of this complex apparatus, bold and assertive (often fraudulent) claimants tended to receive relief, while many needy families sank beneath the purview of the Church.

One result of the decline of parish institutions in Glasgow was the increasing role of the voluntary association in social welfare matters. Dozens of voluntary charity societies sprang up in late eighteenth- and early nineteenth-century Glasgow. Indeed, by 1815, such societies as the 'Old Man's Friend Society', 'Old Ladies Visiting Society', or 'Female Society' were providing the majority of city charity.[25] Along with the rise of the voluntary society, there was a dramatic increase in religious Dissent. In 1815, Dissenting churches provided more than half of the total church sittings in Glasgow.[26] The city was religiously pluralistic. Dissenters, whose churches also functioned on the voluntary principle, assumed leading roles in voluntary societies for charitable purposes. For many, Churchmen and Dissenters alike, it seemed that voluntary associations, if properly patronized, and if assisted by the assessment-supported Town Hospital, would prove sufficient for Glasgow's social needs. In a word, they regarded the traditional parish communal ideal as irrelevant to Glasgow.

Surveying conditions in his parish in late 1815, however, Chalmers could not share this confidence in voluntary associations. Something was radically wrong in Glasgow, that such suffering should exist. The question for him became how to revive the pastoral ministry and parish institutions, so that the Glasgow labouring poor might experience the same sense of community that existed in the rural parish. Early in 1816, six months after his arrival in Glasgow, he commenced an 'experiment' in urban ministry, starting with a visitation of his parish. 'I was', he later explained, 'anxious to become acquainted with the habits of a city population.' Such a visitation was unusual for a Glasgow clergyman; it was also dangerous. The Tron parish included some of the poorest and most violent districts in the city. He conducted his Tron visitation on his Kilmany plan, dividing the parish into small districts, each of which might be covered in a day. He visited each household, including those of Dissenters and Roman Catholics. Generally, his household visits were brief, consisting in a few words of introduction, enquiries into Church attendance and the children's education, and words of encouragement to the sick and the aged. As he departed, he invited the family to attend, in their workclothes, a special week-night worship service which he conducted in a neighbouring private schoolroom or workshop for the benefit of their district.[27]

Shortly after beginning his visitation he found it necessary to separate his household visitations from any connection with the voluntary charity societies. 'My first entry', he later recalled of the initial day of his Tron visitation, 'was upon a close, reaching from the Saltmarket to the celebrated Molendinary Burn; and, to be sure, in that close there was to be found wretchedness and misery of every kind.' '[None the less],' he continued, 'I was struck with the great apparent interest and cordiality of my reception—so very unlike to what I had anticipated.... I was not prepared for it in Glasgow, and among such a wretched population. ... There was even a competition for me, each one wanting me in their own house. I could not understand it.' He soon discovered the reason for this unexpected welcome. 'I was thought to possess great influence in the city charities. I found that this was the subject they constantly broached whenever they got me into their houses.'[28]

He was not unaffected by the suffering he witnessed. Nevertheless, he refused to tolerate being regarded as an agent for the voluntary charity societies or the Town Hospital. He had come among them as their parish minister, and as such he demanded their respect. Prior to this date, he had, like most Glasgow parish clergy, involved himself in the management of voluntary charities. He had, for instance, been elected president of Millar's Charity, a foundation for clothing and educating pauper girls. But now he decided that the parish ministry and the voluntary association principle were fundamentally opposed. Shortly after his experience in the Saltmarket, he resigned the presidency of Millar's Charity, and severed his connection with all voluntary charity societies. 'The people', he explained of this action, 'were disabused of the imagination that I had an inexhaustible treasury to dispose of. If they would insist upon asking me, I could tell them that any thing I might do for them must be at my own expense, and I was not very rich.' As a result of this severance, he added, he was received 'more cordially than ever'.[29]

To Robert Edie, the Kilmany farmer, he wrote in early February 1816: 'I have commenced a very stupendous work lately—the visitation of my parish. ... A very great proportion of the people have no seats in any place of worship whatever, and a very deep and universal ignorance on the high matters of faith and eternity obtains over the whole extent of a mighty population.'[30] Throughout 1816, he pressed forward with the visitation, winding his way through narrow closes, conversing with the crowded inhabitants of cellars and attics. He possessed an ease with the labouring poor, many of whom were, like himself, recent arrivals from the countryside. He could banter in a broad country humour, as well as communicate with unaffected earnestness the gospel imperatives. Chalmers, in truth, liked the poor, and enjoyed their company. His genuine concern and his warm regard, moreover, were felt and reciprocated by his urban parishioners. 'I can say', he later observed of his 1816 visitation, 'that out of 10,000 individuals whom I visited, there were not six by whom I was rudely or disrespectfully treated.' He was deeply moved by the welcome he continued to receive, even after he severed his connection with the city charities. It taught him, he recalled, 'the greatest respect for the people—it showed me that the poor have a delicacy of feeling for which they get little credit'.[31]

Along with increasing attachment to his parishioners, however, grew also discouragement over the real effect of his visitation. It became evident that, with his other duties, he could not visit all his parishioners in less than a year, and this, he realized, would contribute little to improving their condition. 'I feel,' he observed of his parish in a Tron church sermon in December·1816,

as if it were a mighty and impenetrable mass, truly beyond the strength of one individual arm, and before which, after a few furtive and unavailing exertions, nothing remains but to sit down in the idleness of despair. It is a number, it is a magnitude, it is an endless succession of houses and families, it is an extent of field which puts at a distance all hope of a deep or universal impression—it is an utter impossibility, even with the most active process of visitation, to meet the ever pressing demands of the sick, and the desolate, and the dying.

He did not, however, relinquish his communal ideal. His response was rather 'to seek for relief in some wise and efficient system of deputation'—in short, to solicit lay assistance.[32] His first effort was to enlarge and revitalize the session of lay-elders in the Tron church. During his first year at the Tron, the session was composed of only eight elders— most of them older men, lacking the vigour for visiting. 'Some of the elders of the Tron', David Stow, a member of the congregation, later recalled, 'were excellent men, but ... their spiritual duties and exertions were but small, and almost exclusively confined to a few of the sick.' The Tron parish, like most urban parishes in Scotland at this time, was subdivided into twenty-five districts, or 'proportions', each of which was supposed to be supervised by an elder. In fact, the system of proportions had ceased to have much real meaning. In December 1816, however, Chalmers revived the proportion as a unit of organization, and ordained twelve younger, more vigorous men to the eldership, raising the number of Tron elders to twenty. He assigned to each the supervision of at least one proportion. His appointees were upper- and middle-class members of his Tron congregation, who shared his belief in the parochial system, and who possessed leisure and private resources to employ for benevolent activity among the poor.[33]

In his address at the ordination of his new elders on 20 December 1816, Chalmers spoke of the decline in house-to-house visitations by lay officers throughout the Established Church, and of the need to reform the Church from within by providing a positive example of a parish community in the urban environment. His charge to his elders was threefold. First, they were to communicate Christian knowledge and consolation to the inhabitants of their respective proportions through regular household visitations. Secondly, they were to help the poor in their proportions, by combining household visitations with invest-tigations to seek out the 'worthy poor' needing assistance, rather than waiting for them to apply for relief. As in his Kilmany poor-relief programme of 1813-14, he emphasized preserving the inde-pendence of the poor from the relief rolls. Whenever possible, his elders were to employ discreetly their private wealth and influence, or that of their friends, to help families through periods of temporary distress with small monetary gifts or employment. Only as a last resort would the needy be referred to the General Session for institutional relief. Finally, the elders were to encourage others, especially wealthy parishioners with leisure, private resources, and influence, to join them in the work of visiting and private benevolence, until the entire parish was permeated with regular communication and assistance between the social orders. 'I know of nothing', he asserted of such visiting, 'which would serve more powerfully to bring and to harmonize into one firm system of social order the various classes of our community.'[34]

At the same time as he revived the office of visiting elder, he also drew upon lay assistance for a parish educational programme. From the beginning of his Glasgow ministry, he was disturbed by the fact that, unlike rural districts, Glasgow lacked endowed parish schools, and that a large portion of Glasgow children, particularly in the poorest parishes, remained uneducated. Chalmers's interest was soon attracted to efforts to remedy this evil through sabbath schools; if not a complete solution, they might at least impart the rudiments of reading and biblical knowledge in a few hours of instruction each Sunday. Voluntary sabbath-school societies had first appeared in Glasgow in 1786. By 1815, they were providing instruction to 2,370 children, 600 in schools taught by members of the Established Church, and 1,770 in schools taught by Dissenters.[35] Even so, these societies were reaching only a small number in the city's poorest districts. During his 1816 visitation, for instance, Chalmers discovered that less than 100 children from his parish of 10,000 attended such a school.[36]

The reason for this ineffectiveness, he believed, was that the existing sabbath-school societies drew their pupils from throughout the city on a non-parochial basis, and relied too much upon a supposed demand for sabbath-school education. As a result, they attracted mainly middle-class children, who also attended day schools during the week, and who already had a strong religious family life. In the poorest districts of the city, however, few families appreciated the value of Christian education, and few, therefore, took advantage of the society schools.

Following discussions with two voluntary sabbath-school teachers who were operating independently in the Tron parish, Chalmers decided to establish a local parish sabbath-school society, functioning on what he termed the 'principle of aggression'. 'It instantly occurred to me', he later recalled, 'that if, instead of the boys being left to find out the Sabbath schools ... I instituted district schools over the parish, and got a principle of aggression to bear upon the families of the parish, then I should like to know the result.'

Early in December 1816, Chalmers instituted the first parish sabbath-school society in Glasgow. Unlike the existing societies, which accepted children from throughout the city, his parish society accepted no child from outside the Tron parish. Further, he subdivided the parish into smaller districts, assigning to each a teacher. 'I began', he recalled, 'with four Sabbath school teachers, and told them I did not want them to operate superficially over the whole 10,000 inhabitants of the parish. [Instead], I assigned to each of them thirty families [who] lived perhaps in one close, or at any rate in close juxtaposition with each other.' With modest fees collected from the pupils, the society rented a 'respectable dwelling' in each district for a few hours each Sunday. The teachers were instructed to visit 'aggressively' each family in their district during the week, both to encourage the children's attendance and to interest parents in their progress. Monthly society meetings, meanwhile, provided the teachers with a forum to discuss methods, and give one another encouragement.[37]

Under Chalmers's guidance, the Tron Parish Sabbath School Society flourished. By late 1818, the initial four teachers had increased to forty, and over 1,200 children were attending the society's schools. In Glasgow, largely through the influence of Chalmers's 'aggressive principle' on the other societies, the total number of children attending such schools nearly doubled between 1816 and 1819, increasing from 2,370 to 4,747. By 1821, local sabbath-school societies, modelled on Chalmers's 'aggressive principle', had also been established in Paisley and Edinburgh. David Stow, the noted Scottish educational reformer, and member of the Tron Sabbath School Society, later asserted: 'I consider [that] had Dr. Chalmers done nothing more than promote the principle of this local system of Sabbath-schools, he would not have lived in vain.'[38]

Chalmers had, in fact, accomplished far more than that. In revitalizing the Tron session of lay-elders and creating the Tron Parish Sabbath School Society, he had begun to inspire lay enthusiasm in Glasgow for his parish ideal. During his 1816 visitation, he had learned that the supervision of an urban parish of 10,000 was beyond his individual power. By subdividing his parish into elder's proportions and sabbath-school districts, and deputizing lay agents to visit 'aggressively' each home, he extended the reach of his parish ministry. In monthly meetings of the kirk-session and sabbath-school society, moreover, he began to educate the upper social orders of Glasgow with his Evangelical communal ideal. In short, he began to laicize the parish ministry, and to subsume the principle of voluntary association for social improvement under his ideal of the covenanted parish community. In place of what he regarded as an anarchic confusion of voluntary religious and philanthropic societies, competing with one another for public support and objects of charity, he began to impress the laity with a new sense of social purpose, based upon the old consensus of the traditional Christian community.

He achieved considerable success in educating his upper-class lay visitors to his social views, particularly to the importance of encouraging the poor to help themselves, rather than patronizing them with charity in the manner of a voluntary philanthropic society. On 10 December 1818, for instance, two years after Chalmers had begun to mobilize lay participation in the parish ministry, George Burns, one of his December 1816 appointees to the Tron eldership, reported to him his success with a persistently irreligious family. After repeated visits and much argument, Burns had finally persuaded them to send their children to sabbath school, but only after he had promised to pay half the children's fees. 'I cannot resist', Burns continued,

the pleasure of informing you of the additional triumph which I met with. I found that they had sent two of their children to school, and I accordingly offered to pay what I had promised, *but upon no account could I prevail upon them to accept of it*, and that *solely* as they said themselves because they could not think of allowing an *individual* to incur so much expense—that they would rather make a struggle and discharge the debt themselves, adding, and which is most important to take notice of, 'we cannot think of letting *you* give so much out of your own pocket—it is not like as if we were getting it from *a Society*'—this needs no comment.[39]

Chalmers must have been pleased with this report. It vindicated the role he advocated for his lay-visitors—to be regarded by parishioners not as representatives of voluntary societies, but as individual members of the same community, demonstrating their communal responsibility not by donating money, but by encouraging Christian morality and independence. His concept of the lay-visitor's role, to be sure, was paternalistic. Indeed, he hoped to revive a traditional rural ideal of landed paternalism among the wealthy business classes of Glasgow. But although paternalistic, his lay visitors were not to patronize the poor: they were not to use charity as a means of purchasing the loyalty of the poor in order to preserve their own social domination, or even as a salve for a troubled conscience. Rather, communal benevolence was their duty to God.

Chalmers had not commenced his parish programmes without opposition from a significant portion of his non-parochial congregation, who objected to his devoting so much time to the Tron parish population at the expense of ministering to congregational members. It was, after all, his congregation, and not the parishioners, who had petitioned the Town Council to bring him to Glasgow; it was, moreover, his congregation who, through their seat-rents, helped to pay his salary, and the upkeep of his church. The parish system, many insisted, had long been moribund in Glasgow, and it was incumbent on this new arrival from the countryside to accommodate his ministry to the different urban conditions. Chalmers's often brusque manner in refusing invitations from members of his congregation, and his forgetfulness in honouring those invitations he did accept, further increased tensions. In late October 1816, moreover, he preached two indiscreet sermons, instructing the congregation to cease troubling him with invitations or visits to the manse, and to leave him to pursue a more active pastoral ministry in the parish.[40]

The murmurings against him grew so pronounced that when in early November 1816 the Magistrates and Town Council of Stirling offered him a vacant parish in their town, he quietly encouraged them, particularly after they promised him full support in pursuing a vigorous parish ministry.[41] December 1816 saw the beginning of his revival in the Tron of a visiting eldership and organization of a parish sabbath-school society. Then, in January 1817, with congregational opposition to these programmes mounting, he let it be known that he was contemplating a move to Stirling. This disclosure called forth a demonstration of loyalty from his supporters. In mid-February they presented hin with two petitions, one signed by 136 men, and the other by 37 women, expressing their 'unqualified approbation of every part of his services as a Minister'. 'We not only wish', the petitioners assured him, 'to express our conviction of the decided Superiority of that better part you have chosen ... but we beg leave to assure you of our most willing and cordial co-operation to give extension and energy to those benevolent designs for promoting the temporal and Spiritual interests of your People.' At the same time, 129 members of his congregation subscribed to pay the salary of a permanent assistant minister.[42] Chalmers accepted this as a mandate for his pastoral ministry, and agreed to remain in the Tron.[43] Many of his congregational opponents now left the Tron for other Glasgow churches, leaving their seats to be taken by other supporters of Chalmers. He thus succeeded in creating a middle- and upper-class congregation willing to allow their interests to be subordinated to those of the parish population, in the interest of reviving a parish communal ideal among the labouring poor.

II

A major reason for Chalmers's victory over his opponents in the Tron congregation was the extraordinary impact of his Evangelical preaching in Glasgow. Between 1815 and 1817 he reached the height of his power and influence as a preacher, attaining an eminence perhaps unsurpassed in the history of the Scottish pulpit. Thirty-five years old in 1815, five years into his new life as an Evangelical convert, and now exposed to a dynamic, industrializing Glasgow, he reached the full maturity of his powers. His reputation grew rapidly with the increased public exposure of an urban pulpit. His brother James's fears regarding the acceptance of his preaching by the social élites of Glasgow, it seemed, had proved groundless. Chalmers's singular pulpit presence and flowing language mesmerized his urban listeners. Even former Tory and Moderate opponents of his Tron appointment were obliged to acknowledge his preaching gifts, and official recognition followed closely upon his arrival in Glasgow. On 21 February 1816, he was awarded the degree of Doctor of Divinity by the unanimous decision of the Glasgow University Senate. The degree signified that he was now recognized by the Church as possessing the power not only to preach, but to interpret Scripture. James informed their sister Jane that Chalmers 'was quite astonished, as he had no expectation of it, till one of the Professors called and told him that he had been created Doctor.'[44] The Senate's unanimous vote was indeed surprising, in view of the widespread opposition to his Tron appointment among the University faculty only a few months before.

May 1816 saw Chalmers's appointment as one of the Glasgow Presbytery's representatives to the General Assembly, where his great speech extolling the rural pastoral ministry contributed to victory on the plurality issue. Equally impressive was the effect of three sermons which he delivered in Edinburgh during the meeting of the Assembly. The high point was reached on 27 May, when by special invitation he preached before the Lord High Commissioner, the Crown representative to the Assembly, in the Edinburgh High Church. The crowd began gathering at nine for his eleven o'clock service. 'When the doors opened at half past ten,' the *Glasgow Courier* reported the following day, 'the rush into the church was so great that several persons, particularly females, were hurt, and many had their clothes torn. ... There never was such an immense audience in this church, and it was even with difficulty that the Commissioner, Judges, Magistrates, etc., could reach their seats.' 'His speeches last year in the General Assembly of the Scottish Church, and his sermons before the Lord High Commissioner and for the sons of the clergy,' *Blackwood's Edinburgh Magazine* recalled in April 1817, 'made known his merits to most of the eminent men in this part of the kingdom, and will be long remembered in this quarter as the most brilliant display of eloquence and of genius which we have ever had the good fortune to witness.'[45]

More than by any other achievement, however, his reputation as the foremost preacher in Scotland was established by a series of six discourses which he delivered in Glasgow between November 1815 and October 1816 on the relationship of revealed theology to astronomical science. It was the practice in Glasgow at the time of his arrival for one of the eight parish clergymen in the burgh to deliver a discourse on Thursday afternoon in the Tron church, mainly for the benefit of the business and professional classes who worked in the city centre. Each clergyman performed once every eight weeks, reserving the occasion for examples of his finest pulpit eloquence. Chalmers's decision to focus upon the single theme of religion and astronomy reflected his continued interest in natural philosophy. However, it was also intended to demonstrate to the cultured despisers of Evangelicalism among the Glasgow social élite that his was not the religion of the unlettered fanatic or demagogue.[46]

In his first two discourses, he presented a lucid survey of the Newtonian concept of the universe. True science, he concluded, did not claim to explain, but simply to describe the natural order. Sir Isaac Newton, who had been content to describe the law of gravity, without encroaching upon the domain of revealed theology, exemplified this 'modesty' of true science. To understand the will of the creator, the natural philosopher had to look beyond observable nature to God's self-revelation in Scripture. In the next three discourses, Chalmers presented the biblical account of sin and redemption in a new guise, which represented his attempt to reconcile this account with recent astronominal discoveries. Sin and redemption became a drama played against the vastness of the Newtonian universe. He suggested a multiplicity of populated planets, each with its history of sin, and each redeemed by the power of God incarnate in Christ. It was God's purpose to draw each back 'within the circle of heaven's pure and righteous family', until the universe reflected his sovereignty and glory.[47] Finally, in the sixth discourse, Chalmers returned to the theme of the 'modesty' of true science, and concluded by emphasizing the danger of man forsaking his Christian faith through his intellectual pride. Without biblical standards, he warned, scientific speculations would lead to what he termed 'mysticism', or a subjective faith by which each individual defined his own righteousness. Instead of advancing society, science would atomize it, inciting each man to become a law unto himself.

A bare outline does not do justice to the poetic imagination which informed the discourses. The language was grandiloquent, with flowing

sentences and strong imagery. 'If, by the sagacity of one infernal mind,'
he exclaimed in one passage,

a single planet has been called from its allegiances, and been brought under him who
is called in Scripture, 'the god of this world,' and if the errand on which our Redeemer
came, was to destroy the works of the devil—then let this planet have all the littleness
which astronomy has assigned to it—call it what it is, one of the smaller islets which
float on the sea of vacancy; it has become the theatre of such a competition, as may
have all the desires and all the energies of a divided universe embarked upon it ... It
stands linked with the supremacy of God.[48]

The Glasgow public was captivated. Enthusiastic crowds overflowed
the Tron church for his Thursday afternoon discourses. Commercial
houses and retail shops granted their clerks half-holidays. The Trongate
reading room, a meeting-place for prominent merchants and journalists,
was deserted during his performances.

Early in 1817, the discourses were introduced to the larger British
reading public. Until this date, volumes of sermons had seldom sold
well. Publication costs were therefore generally subsidized by subscriptions from the preacher's friends before a publisher would undertake the venture. When Chalmers requested the Glasgow publisher
John Smith to publish his discourses, Smith had recommended a subscription. But Chalmers had refused, regarding a subscription as demeaning, and Smith, a member of Chalmers's Tron congregation and
a personal friend, finally agreed to accept the full publication risk. *The
Discourses on the Christian Revelation, Viewed in Connection with Modern
Astronomy* were published as a slim volume in Glasgow on 28 January
1817. Its success was extraordinary. Within ten weeks, 6,000 copies
were sold, and Chalmers had realized £1,000 from the initial sales, or
one-and-a-half times his annual stipend as a Glasgow parish minister.
Within a year, nine editions, or nearly 20,000 copies were in circulation,
making it one of the best-selling volumes of sermons ever to appear
in Britain.[49] 'Those sermons', the English essayist William Hazlitt
later observed of the *Astronomical Discourses*, 'ran like wild-fire through
the country, were the darlings of watering-places, were laid in the
windows, of inns, and were to be met with in all places of public
resort.'[50]

Critics were quick to note the extravagant language and questionable theological positions. Despite Chalmers's claim to reconcile science
and the Bible, the Baptist essayist John Foster observed in the *Eclectic
Review* of November 1817 that his rhapsodies on the multiplicity of
populated worlds had no basis in Scripture. His vision of Christ re-
deeming other worlds reduced the significance of Calvary; his 'un-
pardonable license of strange phraseology' in extolling the sublime
majesty of the universe bordered on pantheism.[51] None the less, the

reading public embraced the work with enthusiasm. Many enjoyed the *Astronomical Discourses* simply as a romantic epic, an opportunity for escape. There was real demand for such literature, particularly among strict Evangelicals, whose piety would not permit them to read 'secular' novels or poetry, and yet whose tastes were not entirely satisfied by dry theological volumes or pious tracts. Others appreciated his boldness, as he struggled to master and synthesize the truth of both science and theology. 'The mind', Hazlitt observed of the author of the *Discourses*, 'is naturally pugnacious, cannot refuse a challenge of strength or skill, sturdily enters the lists and resolves to conquer, or to yield itself vanquished in the forms.'[52] This pugilistic Christianity appealed to readers with little time or taste for academic theology.

In the spring of 1817, Chalmers followed up the initial success of his *Astronomical Discourses* with a visit to London. The ostensible purpose of the journey was to preach a benefit sermon for the London Missionary Society. Another, more cogent purpose was to ensure that, unlike his 1808 *Enquiry into the Extent and Stability of National Resources*, the *Astronomical Discourses* were properly advertised and distributed in London. He left Glasgow on 14 April 1817, in the company of his publisher's son and business manager, John Smith junior, and making a leisurely journey southward, they arrived in London on 13 May. During the next two weeks, Chalmers created a sensation. The *Astronomical Discourses* had already made their appearance in the capital, and were selling well, whetting the public appetite to hear him preach. He delivered four benefit sermons in the city between 14 May and 25 May, to vast crowds, including Government ministers, peers of the realm, and MPs. London was profoundly moved by this voice from the north, which expressed traditional Christian communal ideals which still flourished on the Celtic fringe of Britain. Perhaps his deepest note was sounded in his sermon for the benefit of the Hibernian Society, a voluntary association for the distribution of Bibles and dissemination of education among the Irish poor. His praise of the Irish national character visibly affected the cool and dignified Anglo-Irish Viscount Castlereagh and reduced George Canning, the Parliamentary orator (who had an Irish mother), to tears.[53] 'The Tartan beats us all,' Canning exclaimed to friends following the sermon. Again, it was Hazlitt who probably best expressed the English response to Chalmers. 'He has,' Hazlitt observed,

neither airs nor graces at command; he thinks nothing of himself: he has nothing theoretical about him ... but you see a man in mortal throes and agony with doubts and difficulties, seizing stubborn knotty points with his teeth, tearing at them with his hands, and straining his eyeballs till they almost start from their sockets, in pursuit of a train of visionary reasoning, like a Highland seer with his second sight. The description of Balfour of Burley in his cave, with his Bible in one hand, and his sword in the other, contending with the imaginary enemy of mankind, gasping for breath, and with the cold moisture running down his face, gives a lively idea of Dr. Chalmers's prophetic fury in the pulpit.[54]

'All the world wild about Dr. Chalmers,' Wilberforce noted in his diary on 19 May. The *Morning Chronicle* reported of his two sermons on 25 May that thousands were turned away after even the aisles of the churches had been packed. Indeed, for his final London sermon, on the afternoon of that day, the crowd at the church door was so thick that he could not gain admittance, the Londoners refusing to believe that this squat and dishevelled figure was the great Dr. Chalmers. He had re- solved to leave the scene altogether, when friends inside the church learned of his plight and extended a plank from a window near the pulpit to an iron palisade outside, enabling him to climb in.[55] His pul- pit celebrity, meanwhile, brought other honours. On 15 May, he was entertained by the prestigious Royal Society of London for Improving Natural Knowledge. On 17 May, he was entertained in Cambridge by the university faculty. 'The agitation here on account of Dr. Chalmers', John Smith wrote their friends in Glasgow on 20 May, 'is quite un- precedented. The Chancellor of the Exchequer [Nicholas Vansittart], Lord Sidmouth [the Home Secretary], Lord Melville, and others, have desired to be introduced to him. At present he is off to the Chancellor, and we have just had a call from the Lord Mayor, telling us of his intention to call here to-day.'[56] Perhaps most important, however, was his introduction to leading members of the London Evangelical 'Clapham Sect', including William Wilberforce, Zachary Macaulay, Thomas Babington, and John William Cunningham, with whom he developed lasting friendships. Fresh from their political triumphs over the abolition of the British slave trade and the opening of India to Christian missionaries, the 'Clapham Sect' were now turning with their considerable public prestige and Parliamentary influence to matters of social reform and church extension in England. They were impressed not only with Chalmers's preaching, but also with his com- munal social ideal and parochial programmes in the Tron of Glasgow.

Chalmers left London on 26 May, and returned to Glasgow by a circuitous route which included visits to Bristol and Liverpool. In Bristol, he met Hannah More, the great advocate of the Evangelical Sunday-school movement, and John Foster, the celebrated Baptist essayist. In Liverpool, he spent three days in the home of John Glad- stone, the Scottish-born commercial magnate, and father of the future prime minister. Chalmers had received a letter of introduction to Gladstone from Zachary Macaulay, another Scottish-born Evangelical, who suspected that Chalmers would be interested in Gladstone's efforts to build additional churches in overcrowded Liverpool parishes.[57]

Gladstone's plan included the sale of interest-bearing shares in new churches to private subscribers, whose investment would gradually be redeemed from the seat-rents. Chamers was indeed impressed. He and Gladstone became friends, and later corresponded on the subject of church extension.[58]

Arriving in Glasgow in mid-June, Chalmers discovered that his influence in Scotland had also increased in the wake of his London success. He was now recognized as a great public figure—a man who, as John Gibson Lockhart observed in *Blackwood's Edinburgh Magazine* the following year, had 'taken a station in the eye of the country, above what is, or has lately been, occupied by any clergyman either of the English or of the Scottish church'.[59] He soon endeavoured to employ this influence in the cause of his Christian communal ideal. In October 1817, he began a second series of Thursday afternoon discourses, in which he shifted his concentration from astronomy to 'the application of Christianity to the commercial and ordinary affairs of life'.[60] His approach, based on the idea that Evangelical religion elevated an already harmonious natural moral order, represented a further movement away from the intensely personal Evangelical religion of his conversion period, towards the more Moderate-Enlightenment view of Christianity as contributing to social progress. First, following the ideas on man and society of such Scottish Enlightenment philosophers as Francis Hutcheson, Adam Ferguson, and Adam Smith, Chalmers argued that the impulse towards social life was an innate human characteristic. Social institutions, including the market economy, the division of labour, and the expanding cities, reflected man's natural moral constitution and social instincts. The harmony of the moral order, like that of the natural world, was divinely ordained; indeed, he argued, even if God had never revealed his law through Scripture, men would still, more often than not, have been industrious, honest in business, loyal to their families, and patriotic. Such values, he observed, had been venerated even in the classical pagan cultures of Greece and Rome.

What, then, was the social benefit of revealed religion? The answer, for Chalmers, lay in the concept of Christian freedom. The Christian embraced moral values not simply on the basis of social instinct, but on the basis of 'principle'. Made aware of God's will through Scripture, he consciously chose to contribute to the welfare of his community. This, for him, was the essence of freedom: it marked the distinction between man as a social animal responding merely to instinctual drives, and man as a mature being, fashioned in the image of God and consciously accepting social responsibility. Christian principle, he further argued, formed a firmer foundation for social improvement than mere social instinct. Natural man was too easily corrupted by false and narrow impressions of his self-interest; his intellect, if uninformed by Christian principle, tempted him to act contrary to his moral nature, and to place his self-interest against the community. The vital Christian, however, was strengthened against these temptations by his 'second sight' beyond death to eternity. It was the duty of Christians to seek to extend this realm of Christian principle, by striving to transform society into a godly commonwealth of Christian communities.[61]

As he developed the godly commonwealth theme within the new context of urban society, Chalmers became increasingly concerned with the 'problem' of religious diversity. His concept of the nurturing community, elevating man's moral constitution with Christian principle, demanded consensus upon the articles of faith. He perceived little real barrier to the eventual achievement of this consenus in the diversity of doctrine among the several Protestant denominations: their differences, as he had argued in the *Edinburgh Christian Instructor* as early as 1811, related mainly to externals, particularly to different concepts of ecclesiastical organization.[62] These differences, he believed, would gradually, but inevitably, be absorbed in a revived Evangelical faith within the Established Church, with emphasis shifted from the ecclesiastical court structures to small Christian communities informed by preaching and individual Bible study. But what of the Roman Catholics, who, he believed, did not share his Protestant emphasis upon individual Bible study? There had been no Roman Catholics in Anstruther or Kilmany, and his exposure to their faith had been negligible. In Glasgow, however, he confronted a sizeable, and growing, Roman Catholic population, mainly recent immigrants from Ireland. During his Tron visitations, he regularly entered Irish Catholic homes. In virtually all these visits he was warmly received, and some Irish Catholics even attended his week-night neighbourhood religious services.[63] He enjoyed Irish company—the bantering humour, the openness and unselfish hospitality. Indeed, he discovered within himself a deep-seated affection for the Irish, an affinity which perhaps stemmed from shared origins in a rural communitarian culture on the Celtic fringe of the British State. He became convinced that Roman Catholics too could be drawn into his communitarian ideal of a godly commonwealth, if only the historical prejudices separating Protestant and Catholic were overcome.

In December 1817, he employed the opportunity of a benefit sermon for the Edinburgh auxiliary branch of the Hibernian Society to appeal for an end to anti-Catholic prejudices and for a new era of religious and political toleration. Nearly 4,000 persons crowded the church.[64] He opened the sermon by asserting that most Protestant criticisms of Catholicism focused either upon long-neglected practices of the medieval Catholic Church, or upon popular distortions of Roman Catholic doctrine which had emerged among the illiterate Catholic peasantry. Such criticisms, he observed, were unfair and irrational, and merely masked another, more deep-seated reason for anti-Catholic prejudice.

To reach the real root of the prejudice, he continued, required an honest examination of the Scottish Protestant mind. Such an analysis, he maintained, would reveal that 'the radical mischief of the whole business' lay in the inner tension within the Scottish Calvinist, between first, his feeling of self-righteousness based upon his faith in the rigorous logic of Calvinist doctrine, and second, his own intense need for certain irrational expressions of piety. The Scottish Calvinist, he explained, in fact experienced guilt over his inability to sustain faith in the pure logic of the Calvinist doctrinal system. He sought release from this guilt by means of a self-righteous hatred of the Roman Catholic for sharing similar irrational expressions of piety. In a word, he hated the Catholic for being merely human like himself, for reflecting his own failings and falling short of the rigorous demands of rational Scriptural Christianity. The deep-seated psychological foundations of this historical animosity made it all the more difficult to root out. But there was hope in the extension of popular education. If, Chalmers asserted, Protestants would recognize their own failings, if they would co-operate with Catholics in such an educational venture as that represented by the Hibernian Society, in which Irish schools were taught by both Catholic and Protestant teachers, then together Protestants and Catholics might overcome the mystical element in their respective faiths, and find a common faith in a rational interpretation of Scripture.[65] British Protestants, he added, would receive additional benefit by opening their hearts to the Irish Catholic population—that is, exposure to the rich communal traditions of the Celtic Irish peasantry. 'I do think', he concluded, 'that I perceive something in the natural character of Ireland, which draws me more attractively to the love of its people, than any other picture of national manners has ever inspired.'[66]

The sermon went too far for many of his fellow Church of Scotland Evangelicals. Shortly after its delivery, the venerable Edinburgh Evangelical clergyman Thomas Randall Davidson wrote to Chalmers's friend Henry Grey, another Edinburgh minister, 'beseeching' Grey to 'beg' Chalmers not to allow the Hibernian Society to publish the sermon in accordance with their usual practice. 'It appeared to me,' Davidson explained, 'as it did so to every man with whom I have conversed, to be unguarded and injudicious—by representing Protestants in general, as no better than Papists in their Hearts—it will be perverted to have intended to shew, that it is of little importance, whether men are Catholics or Protestants.' Chalmers was, Davidson added, virtually encouraging Protestants 'to assist in building popish Chapels, or in promoting the cause of popery'.[67] Despite such warnings, Chalmers allowed the Hibernian Society to publish his sermon in early April 1818. Angry protests now swept the country. Andrew Thomson, although long an active proponent of Catholic emancipation, had not even waited for the sermon to be published before violently attacking the spoken version of it in the *Edinburgh Christian Instructor* of February 1818. But although Thomson questioned Chalmers's judgement regarding the failings of popular Scottish Calvinism, he did not challenge his Calvinist orthodoxy.[68] He evidently trusted that Chalmers would see his error, and retract his indiscreet statements.

Such forbearance, however, was not practised by Duncan Mearns, Professor of Divinity at King's College, Aberdeen. Convinced that no sincere Calvinist could preach such a sermon, Mearns turned to Chalmers's only major theologicial treatise, his 1814 *Evidence and Authority of the Christian Revelation*, for evidence of unorthodox doctrine. Mearns discovered that in this treatise Chalmers had discussed only the 'external evidences' of Christianity, particularly the testimony of the early Church regarding the authenticity of the New Testament narrative, while almost totally neglecting the 'internal evidences', or the signs of election in the predestined saints, which were at the heart of scholastic Calvinism. This emphasis upon the external testimony of the Church, and neglect of the internal testimony of the Holy Spirit, was, for Mearns, more Roman Catholic than Calvinist. Mearns brought his case before the Church courts, challenging Chalmers's qualification to preach in the Church of Scotland. 'The Aberdeen Synod met here on Tuesday,' Daniel Dewar, minister of the Aberdeen College Chapel, informed Chalmers on 17 April 1818, 'when a violent attack was made on your treatise on the *Evidences of the Christian Revelation*.' 'Its author,' Dewar warned of Mearns, 'is ... a man whose measures all go to bear down every thing like practical godliness, and who is a violent persecutor of all good men.' Immediately after his Aberdeen Synod speech, Mearns had published a lengthy attack upon the orthodoxy of Chalmers's *Evidence and Authority of the Christian Revelation*. The matter was serious, said Dewar and he advised Chalmers to hurry into print with a treatise on the 'internal evidences'.[69] Chalmers, however, remained silent. To have rushed out a treatise on the 'internal evidences' in reply to Mearns would have seemed a public admission of guilt. Dignified silence, as it turned out, was probably his best defence against Mearns, who failed to gain sufficient support to carry his case against Chalmers to the May 1818 General Assembly.

'It is,' the Whig *Scotsman* newspaper observed in an article entitled 'Dr. Chalmers and his Assailants' on 4 April 1818, 'hardly in human nature for men, nominally equal, to see any one of their brethren reach such an elevation, without feeling something of an emulous, and even envious spirit.' Although no friend of Chalmers, the *Scotsman* was disgusted by the mounting clerical attacks upon him, which, it suspected, had little to do with genuine concern about either the judiciousness of his Hibernian Society sermon or his Calvinism. A number of his clerical assailants, the *Scotsman* asserted, were 'obviously' motivated by 'the double purpose of lowering him, and elevating themselves'.[70] There was no doubt some truth in this judgement. His immense popularity as a preacher among the social élites of Scotland, and more especially of England, was stirring jealousy—not least among acknowledged leaders of the Evangelical party in the Church of Scotland. Many resented this newcomer, who only a few years back they had rescued from the obscurity of rural Kilmany, and who now not only rose above them in national stature, but refused to respect the party's strict Calvinist orthodoxy. Indeed, many suspected that his departures from Calvinist orthodoxy—his emphasis upon the natural 'goodness' of man's moral instincts and upon the 'external evidences'—were largely responsible for his influence among the more Arminian Evangelicals of the Church of England. If not calculated, Chalmers's theological liberalism had at least proved expedient to his rapid rise, which made it, in many eyes, all the more deplorable.

Chalmers's popularity as a preacher, however, remained high, despite the growing clerical jealousies. He continued to attract a wealthy congregation to his Sunday morning services. Late in June 1817, moreover, following his return from his London visit, he began preaching a second sermon in the Tron church on Sunday evenings, for the benefit of those who could not afford the seat-rents for the morning service. Attendance at his evening services was considerable; indeed, at an evening service in the spring of 1818, the heavy Tron vestry door was actually battered down by a crowd pressing for admittance to an already packed church.[71] He now grew almost to regret his popularity. 'I fear,' he confessed to his diary following a sermon on 10 March 1818, 'or rather I know and am sure, that personal distinction is one of my idols. O that I could bring it out, O Lord, and slay it before Thee.' 'Preached to the magistrates,' he again confided to his diary on 24 March 1818, 'Vanity, violent exertion prompted by vanity—a preaching of self—a want of singleness of aim after the glory of God.' 'Oh my Heavenly Father!' he prayed, 'sweep away these corruptions.'[72]

He regretted, too, his growing isolation from his clerical brethren. Despite his fame, or perhaps because of it, he was beginning to feel once again an outsider. He made frequent visits to Kilmany and Anstruther, perhaps seeking the feelings of communal belonging he had sacrificed for the fame of his Glasgow pulpit. His sense of alienation was deepened by the loss of one who had been a symbol of love and stability in his Fifeshire youth: late in July 1818, he was summoned to Anstruther to attend the last hours of his father, who died on 26 July, blind, deaf, and senile, and probably unaware of his son's national reputation. Chalmers wrote to his younger brother Patrick, a few hours after their father's death: 'The world is a cheat, and he whose affections are set upon it is living the delusion of idolatry. How fearfully, then, does the guilt of idolatry attach to us all!'[73] As a student, and as a young Kilmany minister, he had been largely insensitive to his father's constant anxieties for his success and happiness. Now that he had achieved success, however, premature senility and death had deprived him of his father's recognition.

Happiness, moreover, eluded him. By early 1818, he had begun to experience serious doubts about the real effects of his preaching upon the 'enlightened public', He had achieved considerable fame in the pulpit, but he now questioned whether this was in fact the fruit of the 'Call of Providence', or simply of his personal ambition. He was disturbed by his growing alienation from the Evangelical clergy. He questioned the value of his 'fashionable preaching', with its appeal to the upper and middle classes. There was still the other Glasgow—that of the labouring poor, suffering acutely the effects of the continuing post-war depression. Perhaps by renewed service to them, he could rediscover a sense of purpose, and of communal belonging. A few years earlier, he had begun seeking to alleviate their suffering by the revival of a traditional rural parish communal ideal. With his disillusionment with the pulpit, he intensified this effort.

III

'I consider you as my ablest and best ally', the English political economist and clergyman Thomas Robert Malthus wrote to Chalmers on 22 July 1822.[74] By early 1817, after a year of visiting in the Glasgow slums, Chalmers had yearned for a solution to the problem of urban poverty—a formula that would reduce the problem to manageable limits. Like many social thinkers in the bleak years of post-war distress, he found this formula in the Malthusian theory of population. After 1817, he embraced the Malthusian doctrine with the zeal of a convert. 'Parson Malthus and his pupil, the arch-Parson Thomas Chalmers'—so Karl Marx later described them in *Capital*.[75] If the rational Evangelicalism of Wilberforce represented Chalmers's main hope for the spiritual salvation of mankind, the moral teachings derived from the Malthusian population doctrine provided him with the hope for general improvement in man's material conditions.

Malthus had first published his theory of population in 1798, in a short essay which had challenged the vision of unlimited human progress presented by the English philosopher William Godwin. In 1804, Malthus extended his essay into a two-volume treatise, *The Principle of*

Population. He based his arguments on what he perceived as the natural tendency for population to grow beyond the limits of food production. Increasing pressure upon available food supply resulted in the progressive impoverishment of the labouring orders, and eventually climaxed in the 'natural' population checks of mass starvation, war, or revolution. His vision was grim. There was no natural progress for the human species—only a recurring cycle of population growth, increasing poverty, and disaster. But if nature offered no promise for human progress, there was, Malthus believed, some hope in man's moral and intellectual capacities. With these same capacities that separated man from lower animal forms, man could elevate his society above the natural population cycle. This could be achieved through what Malthus termed 'moral restraint', or the decision of society members to limit population through birth control—which in the early nineteenth century meant marrying at a later age, and thus reducing the number of child-bearing years. The great challenge for society was how to convince individuals to curb their natural instinct to satisfy sexual urges and to procreate. One possibility urged by Malthus was to extend popular education, teaching individuals, particularly among the labouring orders, the benefits of supporting smaller families on their incomes and of increasing their wages by decreasing the labour supply. Another, more radical, expedient was to abolish legal poor relief. A legal provision for indigence, Malthus maintained, discouraged 'moral restraint' by encouraging the poor to believe the State would assume responsibility for their families if they could not. Abolishing poor laws, he argued, would force the poor to adopt this 'moral restraint'. At the cost of some short-term suffering for existing paupers, society would be spared the greater misery of impoverished labouring orders and the 'natural' population checks—assuming, of course, that the poor would react rationally to poor law abolition, and voluntarily adopt family planning.[76]

Chalmers had first read Malthus in about 1807, and had cited his population theory briefly in his 1808 *Enquiry into the Extent and Stability of National Resources,* and again in his 1814 *Influence of Bible Societies on the Temporal Necessities of the Poor.*[77] But in rural northern Fife, where the population of most parishes, including Kilmany, was declining, the Malthusian spectre had seemed remote. In Glasgow, however, the question of overpopulation became urgent. He discovered an increasing misery among the urban poor that seemed beyond the cure of either a free market economy or Christian charity. Two phenomena in particular convinced him that Glasgow was suffering the effects of overpopulation. First, the size of the assessment necessary to support the poor-relief expenditure of the Town Hospital was increasing dramatically. In 1790, the assessment was £1,420. By 1800, however, it had grown to

£4,534, and by 1814, to £10,709—an increase far in excess of the cost of living.[78] Secondly, the increasing assessment did not appear to alleviate social misery. On the contrary, the number of paupers and the suffering of the poor seemed to grow in proportion to the increasing assessment. Viewing the situation through Malthusian eyes, Chalmers became convinced that the assessment in fact created pauperism, by discouraging industry, personal responsibility, and 'moral restraint'. This was, to be sure, a simplistic explanation for the complex problem of urban poverty in early industrial Britain. None the less, it was straightforward, with a certain logic. Further, unlike such explanations as the depopulation of the countryside through enclosures and more labour-efficient agricultural methods, the fluctuations of foreign markets for British manufactures, or the instability of early industrial capitalism, the Malthusian explanation offered a simple solution. Abolish the poor laws, extend popular education, and the disease of urban poverty would be cured.

A major problem for Malthus was how to abolish legal poor relief without starving those paupers already dependent upon that relief. During the post-war depresssion, he began to question the expediency of total abolition, whatever its long-term benefits. Decent men would be appalled, and the poor might be driven to rebel. 'I had almost despaired on the subject,' he later confided to Chalmers, on 23 August 1821, 'and almost began to think that in a highly manufacturing state where so large a portion of the population must be subject to the fluctuations of trade, and the consequent sudden variations of wages, it might not be possible entirely to give up a compulsory provision without the ['pressure' scratched out] sacrifice of too many individuals to the good of the whole.'[79] That is, Malthus continued, until Chalmers introduced his own plan for the abolition of legal poor relief in urban districts, which promised to affect the cure without sacrificing existing paupers.

Chalmers first described his plan in an anonymous article, 'The Connexion between the Extension of the Church and the Extinction of Pauperism', written at the conclusion of his first year of the Tron visitation, and published in the March 1817 number of the Whig *Edinburgh Review*.[80] After outlining the Malthusian doctrine, he described a three-part plan for the gradual abolition of assessment-supported legal relief in Glasgow, which, he maintained, could be applied in any large city in Britain. First, all extra-parochial agencies for poor-relief management, such as the Glasgow Town Hospital and General Session, were to be abolished. Each parish in the city would then assume the full and independent management of its own poor relief. Secondly, paupers already receiving relief from the assessment fund would continue to do so, but no additional paupers would be granted assessment relief. Instead, new paupers would receive relief only from the kirk-session fund, based upon the church-door collections of the parish where they had established their legal residence. Visiting elders would carefully investigate each new applicant for relief to ensure that only 'worthy poor' without other resources would be granted parish relief. At the same time, the elders would encourage private charity for the poor from their wealthier neighbours, in order to decrease the number of applicants for parish relief. Such activity by the elders, he maintained, would ensure that the cost of relieving new paupers would never exceed sessional income, even in crowded urban parishes. With no new paupers granted assessment relief, meanwhile, and with the 'old' assessment-supported paupers gradually dying off, a steadily increasing portion of the assessment fund would be freed for other purposes. But the portion thus freed was not to be returned to the ratepayers in the form of reduced rates. The wealthy should not benefit from the abolition of assessment relief. Instead, he demanded that the resulting surplus in the assessment fund be employed to build additional parish churches and schools. In Glasgow alone, he advocated the creation of thirty additional parishes, increasing the existing number from nine to almost forty, and thus decreasing the average parish population from about 10,000 to 3,000. Smaller parishes, combined with an aggressive Evangelicalism, would restore the urban population to the traditional Christian communal ideal of the rural parish.

It was perhaps well, Chalmers continued, that the evil of assessment-supported legal poor relief had proceeded so far. Increasing pauperism and social misery, social unrest, and political disaffection had made the necessity for a radical solution obvious. The moment for decisive action had come. Scotland could continue its misguided policy of legal assessments for poor relief, or it could embrace his plan, and in small, closely-knit Christian communities, under the supervision of a parish church and school, rediscover vital Christianity, industry, and benevolence. 'Out of the ruins of the present system,' he concluded,

we should see another system emerge, under which pauperism would be stifled in the infancy of its elements; and a reaching application be brought into effectual contact with the very root and principle of the disease; and another generation should not elapse, ere, by the vigorous effect of Christian education of the young, we should have to do with a race of men, who would spurn all its worthlessness and all its degradation away from them.[81]

Legal pauperism became for Chalmers the radical social evil, which morally degraded the whole of society. He was, however, careful to distinguish pauperism from poverty. The latter, Christ had taught, would always be with us. Disparities in wealth were part of the divine order; they obliged men to unite into communities on the basis of benevolence

and need. But pauperism, with its legal apparatus of rights and obligations, destroyed both individual responsibility and communal benevolence. It represented the extension of eighteenth-century interest
politics into the social realm, transforming rich and poor into opposing
interest groups seeking justice, not from God through his Church, but
from the secular State. It institutionalized social conflict, rather than
resolving it. The suffering already caused by over-population, Chalmers
believed, was a warning of greater misery still to come, if the nation did
not return to the social teachings of Christianity.

With the publication of his *Edinburgh Review* article, Chalmers began
a new career as political agitator. The abolition of legal poor relief was
a political issue, requiring support from the secular authorities. To
gain this support, he began a campaign directed towards the 'enlightened
public'. During his London visit of May 1817, he delivered a sermon
on the connection of church extension with the elevation of the labouring
poor, also discussing his social ideal privately with prominent politicians
and 'Clapham Sect' Evangelicals.[82] In December 1817, he published a
sermon in Glasgow attributing the increase of political disaffection
among the labouring poor to the weakening of the parish community
ideal, and outlining his plan for building additional Glasgow parish
churches.[83]

Francis Jeffrey, the editor of the Whig *Edinburgh Review*, meanwhile,
had placed the journal behind Chalmers's plan. 'What we have already
published', he assured Chalmers on 25 July 1817, 'has excited great
attention, and done, I am persuaded, much good.' If, Jeffrey continued, Chalmers would follow up his March 1817 article with one on
the same subject in the *Edinburgh Review* every three months, he was
convinced 'that by this means the great end might be pretty certainly
attained in the course of two or three years'.[84] On Jeffrey's invitation,
Chalmers published a second article in the issue of February 1818.
Based upon his observations of English poor relief during his 1817 tour,
his article advocated extending his communal reform plan to England
as well as Scotland, and called upon Parliament for legislative action.[85]

Chalmers's plan, like the radical social reform proposals of his 1808
Enquiry, generated considerable opposition. Many critics recalled his
earlier work, and compared his new plan for poor-law abolition with
his 1808 proposals to conscript the poor into the military—portraying
both as heartless expedients to achieve social stability through the elimination of the 'redundant population'. Thus, critics first condemned his
poor-law abolition proposals as inhumane. The poor were already suffering too much, and poor relief was the only real benefit society offered
them. 'To the poor,' the Whig *Glasgow Chronicle* observed on 21 October
1817, 'Government is little else than a vast system of punishments; and
the poor laws, for the relief of suffering industry, form the only general

attempt to employ the influence of reward in governing.'[86] An anonymous pamphlet published in Manchester in 1818 focused upon an
indiscreet argument that Chalmers had employed in his March 1817
Edinburgh Review article. Through luxury consumption, he had argued,
the wealthy provided employment. An assessment for poor relief,
therefore, which decreased luxury consumption, would increase
unemployment, and thus help to destroy the independent spirit of the
labouring orders. In a word, the Manchester pamphleteer caustically
observed, Chalmers encouraged the wealthy to indulge their taste for
luxuries as a Christian duty, while showing only benign neglect towards
the poor.[87] This was not entirely fair. Chalmers's social teachings
stressed the Christian duty of compassion and benevolence. None the
less, his use of such terms as 'worthless' and 'degraded' in reference to
paupers, and of such arguments as the importance of luxury consumption for employment, seem to betray middle-class prejudices,
including a certain callousness towards the poor, which had not been so
evident in his Kilmany writings on poverty. Evidently his status as a
respected Glasgow clergyman, as well as the influence of Malthus—with
his warnings of the grave social dangers to follow from 'indulging' the
poor—had not been without some effect on Chalmers's social views.

Secondly, critics condemned his plan as a subtle scheme both to
undermine religious Dissent and to enrich the Established Church. In
1818, James Haldane, the leading figure in the expanding Scottish
Congregational Church, published anonymously two pamphlets outlining the threat to Dissent in Chalmers's plan. By abolishing legal
poor relief and employing the assessment for the extension of the Established Church, the State would be directly taxing Dissenters for the
enlargement of a Church that they could not in conscience support.
With legal poor relief abolished, moreover, many Dissenting poor
would be made dependent upon parish sessional relief managed by the
Established Church. Unlike Established churches, Haldane explained,
which were endowed from the tithes, or a portion of the income from
the medieval Church lands, those of the Dissenters had to be built
and maintained by their congregations, and their clergy paid from
seat-rents and church-door collections alone. This meant that Dissenters could devote far less money to Church-supervised poor relief
than could the Establishment. It would, Haldane concluded, be all
too tempting for Establishment elders to employ sessional relief as
a means for punishing Dissenting poor.[88] The *Glasgow Chronicle* also
opposed the plan, maintaining that Chalmers meant to enrich the
Establishment clergy at the expense of the poor. 'The legal claims of
the poor', the *Chronicle* observed on 4 November 1817, 'he thinks ought
to be done away; but nevertheless the assessment ought not to be closed
up.' 'It is, no doubt,' the *Chronicle* continued, in a parody of Chalmers's

rhetoric, 'a pernicious fountain that spreads waters of bitterness over the land; but for all that, the clergy are quite ready to drink it up to the last drop.'

Finally, critics dismissed the plan as 'utopian'. Haldane compared Chalmers's parish community ideal to the 'parallelogram' communities of the Utopian socialist Robert Owen, who had developed a model community at his cotton mill at New Lanark, thirty miles south-east of Glasgow, and who was then, like Chalmers, beginning a national campaign for the extension of his communitarian ideal.[89] In truth, Chalmers was one of a number of early nineteenth-century com-munitarian theorists, reacting against eighteenth-century interest-politics and the social dislocations of early industrialization by seeking a new harmony in small communities based upon faith in human perfectibility within a properly structured social environment. For the Evangelical Haldane, however, Chalmers neglected the cardinal fact of man's natural depravity. Diversity and diffusion of power, Haldane argued, not uniformity and the concentration of power in the State and Established Church, represented society's best hope against the effects of human corruptibility. For the liberal *Glasgow Chronicle*, on the other hand, the greatest evil was that it was the poor who would be made to suffer for Chalmers's folly. It included him among the 'pitiless pro-jectors of experiments on mankind', who 'regard a nation of human beings, as a philosopher regards a frog in his air pump, with as little compassion for their sufferings, under the experimental process, and as little apprehension of their vengeance at the result of it.'[90]

Chalmers's *Edinburgh Review* social reform proposals might have suffered the same fate as the proposals of his 1808 *Enquiry*, had it not been for unexpected support from a leading figure in Glasgow's governing élite. James Ewing was a prosperous Glasgow merchant and iron manufacturer, a prominent member of the Town Council, and a 'Tory of the old school'. In 1817, he had been appointed by the Town Council to chair a committee to investigate the need for a new Town Hospital building. The investigation was soon extended to the broader questions of poor-relief policy. Ewing was also a moderate Malthusian, and like many among the city's élite was disturbed by the increasing assessment. Impressed with Chalmers's *Edinburgh Review* proposals, Ewing asked him to submit a brief outline of the plan to the committee. On 21 March 1818, Ewing's committee published its report, which included Chalmers's synopsis of his March 1817 *Edinburgh Review* article. The Ewing report concluded with a general recommendation that the Town Council consider providing Chalmers with an opportunity to demonstrate the viability of his plan.[91]

In fact, Chalmers and Ewing had something more definite in mind. Two years earlier, in 1816, the Town Council had approved a plan for building and endowing two additional parish churches in Glasgow, to be completed in 1819.[92] One of these parishes, St. John's, was to be created mainly out of the western portion of Chalmers's Tron parish. After private discussions during the spring of 1818, Chalmers and Ewing agreed upon a twofold plan. First, Ewing would employ his influence to convince the Town Council to transfer Chalmers to the new St. John's parish church, where he would conduct an 'experiment' designed to demonstrate the feasibility of abolishing assessment relief and restoring independent parochial poor-relief management in Glasgow. At the same time, Ewing would convince the Town Council to grant St. John's legal immunity from the existing civic poor-relief regulations, so that Chalmers would suffer no interference from what he termed 'the artificial and multiplied regulations of the present extended arrangement'.

Secondly, Ewing would seek to convince both the Town Council and Town Hospital no longer to recognize the authority of the General Session.[93] Under the existing system, it will be recalled, the General Session possessed authority over sessional relief in all the Glasgow parishes. It received all church-door collections from the parishes, and it decided which applicants would be accepted for relief. For Chalmers, however, the General Session's authority was 'artificial', and stifled parish communal sentiment. Abolishing the General Session's authority, then, would oblige each parish to accept full and independent authority over its sessional poor, and thus render parish ministers and kirk-sessions more receptive to the programmes he would be demonstrating in St. John's. 'It were well', Chalmers informed James Reddie, the presiding judge on the Glasgow burgh court, on 14 March 1818, 'for Glasgow to retrace its steps—to restore to its clergy the same unfettered and independent parishes that they have in the country, and to release them altogether from that multifarious control over their kirk-sessions which has in fact deprived your town of the forms of the Scottish ecclesiastical system as well as all its substantial benefits.'[94]

Ewing proved an effective ally. His committee's report on Glasgow poor relief was well received by the city's governing élite.[95] Ewing managed, moreover, to gain the support of Kirkman Finlay, a former Lord Provost of Glasgow, and the MP for the city. A staunch Tory, Finlay had opposed Chalmers's appointment to the Tron in 1814. Through Ewing's mediation, however, Finlay, who also had a keen interest in poor-law matters (and had testified on the failings of Scottish urban poor relief to a House of Lords committee the previous year), now became convinced of the merit in Chalmers's proposals.[96] In late March 1818, Ewing and Finlay convinced the Magistrates and Town Council to instruct the Town Hospital to cease accepting paupers for assessment relief on the recommendation of the General Session, and to accept paupers only by referral from an individual parish kirk-session. This weakened the poor-relief authority of the General Session, but did not abolish it—as the General Session retained control over all church-door collections. However, as Robert Findlay, a Glasgow merchant and member of the Town Council, assured Chalmers on 3 April, it was as far as the Town Council would now go toward strengthening the poor-relief authority of individual parishes, until it saw some substantial evidence from the proposed experiment.[97] In early June 1818, through Ewing's and Finlay's management, the Town Council elected Chalmers to St. John's. Before accepting, he demanded that his new parish be exempted from the requirement of sending its church-door collections to the General Session. The Town Council accepted his condition, and on 10 June he announced that he would move to St. John's as soon as the church was completed.[98]

With plans evidently determined regarding his St. John's experiment, however, Chalmers now confronted a new challenge from two leading Evangelical clergymen in the Church of Scotland. In November 1818, an article by Andrew Thomson appeared in the *Edinburgh Christian Instructor*, challenging the statistical evidence employed in arguments against assessment relief. Assessments, Thomson maintained, were not a heavy burden upon property, nor was there substantial evidence that they contributed either to over-population or to a decline in worker productivity.[99] A few months later, in early 1819, Stevenson Macgill, Chalmers's predecessor in the Tron and now Professor of Theology at Glasgow University, published an essay in defence of assessment-supported poor relief. Macgill also challenged Chalmers's plan for abolishing the General Session and making each parish responsible for its own poor relief. In Glasgow, Macgill observed, the rich and poor tended to reside in separate parishes—with the poorest inhabitants isolated in slum districts. To make each parish responsible for its own poor, then, would in effect leave the poor to bear the full burden of poor relief, while absolving inhabitants of wealthy parishes from any expense.[100]

In mid-June 1819, Thomson sought to reconcile the growing differences between Chalmers and the Evangelical leadership on the subject of poor relief through private discussion in Edinburgh, only to discover that they had no common ground. Thomson presented Chalmers with his evidence that assessments did not, in fact, increase pauperism; Chalmers replied that he now advocated the abolition not only of assessment relief, but also of all forms of institutional relief, including sessional relief based on church-door collections. Informing the Evangelical clergyman Robert Lundie of this discussion, on 14 June 1819, Thomson wrote: 'I have had a long set-to with Chalmers; but he is wilder than ever.'[101]

Late in July 1819, Chalmers terminated his ministry at the Tron and prepared for a September move to St. John's. He had already convinced twelve elders from the Tron kirk-session to accompany him to his new parish, and they now met regularly to discuss the proposed St. John's experiment. None the less, as the date for beginning the experiment approached, he grew anxious about the continued opposition to his plan, especially the recent opposition from the leading Evangelicals Thomson and Macgill. His nerve weakened. His fears were aggravated by the fact that he had heard little from either Ewing or Finlay since the previous summer. His old Anstruther insecurities regarding the duplicity and arrogance of the Tory 'great' began to revive. On 3 August 1819, he wrote to the Glasgow Lord Provost, asking that the Town Council reconfirm their promise of June 1818 that St. John's would be exempted from the requirement of having to send its church-door collections to the General Session. He received no reply, and became convinced that the Town Council intended to renege on their previous promise in the face of mounting clerical and public opposition.[102] On 7 August, believing that he had been betrayed by Ewing, Finlay, and the Town Council, and would now have no opportunity to vindicate his communal plan against his opponents, he suddenly departed alone from Glasgow, ostensibly for a visit to Anstruther.

In fact, he first went directly to Edinburgh. There he consulted privately with the Edinburgh Whigs, including both Andrew Thomson and his old friend David Brewster, of the *Edinburgh Encyclopedia*, about the possibility of his leaving the ministry to assume the Edinburgh Chair of Natural Philosophy, left vacant in late July by the death of the Whig John Playfair. The actual exchange between Chalmers and his Whig friends is unknown. It is, however, clear that Thomson sought an Evangelical candidate to thwart the appointment of Thomson's old enemy, John Leslie, who since the celebrated Leslie Affair of 1805 had occupied the Edinburgh Chair of Mathematics. Thomson may also have wished to rescue Chalmers from what he perceived as the folly of his proposed poor relief experiment. On 10 August, Chalmers left Edinburgh for Anstruther. That same day, Thomson announced Chalmers as the Whig-Evangelical candidate for the Natural Philosophy chair, informing the Edinburgh Town Council that he had received assurances from Chalmers that, if elected, he would accept the appointment.[103]

Thomson's announcement raised a public *furor*. For many, including the Whig *Scotsman* newspaper, Chalmers was either using the Edinburgh chair to put pressure on the Glasgow Town Council regarding his St. John's experiment, or else fleeing impending failure in Glasgow. No one, the *Scotsman* implied, could ever be certain what Chalmers intended—save that he would go to any length, however unscrupulous, to glut his ambition for wealth and position.[104] On 14 August Thomson informed Chalmers, who remained in Anstruther, that the Whig-Evangelicals had been obliged to withdraw Chalmers's name as candidate for the Edinburgh chair; the pretext given was that he had not given sufficient guarantee that he would accept if elected.[105] In fact, Thomson had not given Chalmers time to confirm his candidature, but had withdrawn his name in response to the public outcry.

In Glasgow, meanwhile, Chalmers's supporters, and especially the new St. John's session, were furious when they learned of Thomson's announcement. On 19 August, while still in Anstruther, Chalmers received a letter from his wife informing him that his St. John's elders threatened wholesale resignation. It appeared that he had lost both the Edinburgh chair and the Glasgow parish experiment, and he now began to contemplate 'being more happily and more usefully employed in some other walk of exertion'. Then, on 20 August, he received the news that the Glasgow Magistrates and Town Council had finally decided to reconfirm their previous promises regarding St. John's, and grant the parish exemption from the General Session. Quickly, he relinquished his plans for resigning from the Glasgow parish ministry. 'The only point now', he wrote to his wife that same day, 'is the zeal, and cordiality, and sound-heartedness of the agency [of elders], and I trust that the vile, and malignant, and ignorant gossip of the place will have no influence upon them.' He wrote to ask William Collins, the most trusted of his elders, to assure the St. John's session of his (Chalmers's) commitment to the experiment. All the same, he informed his wife on 23 August, if the session should insist upon resigning, 'I shall try and carry on the matter upon the strength of weavers, and the native population of the parish.' In the meantime, he remained secluded in Anstruther, composing a public defence of his conduct, and waiting for tempers to cool.[106]

Several days later, another crisis involving his plans developed in Glasgow, as the General Session reacted to the Town Council's decision favouring Chalmers. On 2 September, at their regular monthly meeting, the General session was about to consider the question of the St. John's exemption, when it was presented with instructions from the Magistrates and Council, stating that they had already granted Chalmers the exemption, and there was no need for further discussion. The General Session was furious. On 7 September, it submitted a protest to the Magistrates and Council. First, it challenged the wisdom of granting St. John's an exemption. To do so, it argued, would diminish the fund available for sessional relief in other parishes. Chalmers's preaching had attracted a large and wealthy congregation at the Tron, and had raised Tron church-door collections far above the average in the city. He would, it assumed, attract a similarly large and wealthy congregation at St. John's. At the same time, however, the number of sessional paupers residing in the area to be included in St. John's was smaller than in most parishes. 'In such a case of inequality', the General Session asserted, 'it appears reasonable and just, in such a city as this, where such a variety cannot be avoided, to unite all the collections in one [General Session] fund, and thence to allocate a proportion to each parish, according to the number of its poor.' For ninety years this had been the General Session's function. If St. John's were now granted exemption from the redistribution programme, it would not only decrease the General Session fund, but would also encourage other wealthy parish churches to demand the same exemption, until, as Stevenson Macgill had argued a few months before, the poorest parishes were left burdened with the full expense of sessional relief. This, in turn, would force the Town Hospital to increase the assessment, in order to make up the deficiency in sessional relief. In short, to give Chalmers an exemption would render the whole existing poor-relief system in Glasgow unworkable. Secondly, the General Session protested that it was by law an equal partner with the Magistrates and Council in determining Glasgow poor-relief policy, and that the Magistrates and Council had no authority unilaterally to grant St. John's an exemption.[107]

A committee of five, headed by Ewing and Finlay, drafted a reply to the General Session, which was approved by the Magistrates and Council on 28 September. The reply ignored the first part of the protest, and focused on the second; it asserted that the Magistrates and Council were the sole authority in poor-relief matters, with the power to instruct the General Session in all aspects of poor-relief policy. The General Session response was unexpectedly swift. On 7 October, it voted 42 to 34 to abolish itself, rather than acknowledge subordination to the civic governmment. In one respect, of course, this was what Chalmers had desired.[108] The 'artificial' restraint on the emergence of independent parish communities in Glasgow was removed, and each parish left solely responsible for its church-door collections and sessional relief. At the same time, however, the dissolution vote reflected considerable resentment in the Church directed against himself. He had, many believed, betrayed his clerical brethren, and proved willing to subordinate the Church to State authority in order to achieve his ends. The General Session was defeated, but the clergy were defiant.

Chalmers, meanwhile, endeavoured to repair his damaged public image. In mid-September he wrote to Andrew Thomson from Anstruther, attributing his difficulties to the machinations of his personal enemies, and asking Thomson to come to his aid by introducing him to his new congregation at the formal opening of St. John's church. Thomson, as warm-hearted to rivals in difficulties as he was ruthless in dealing with strong adversaries, agreed to his request.[109] Finally, on 23 September, after nearly six weeks in Anstruther, Chalmers returned to Glasgow. In a carefully timed move, his published defence of his conduct regarding the Edinburgh chair appeared in the Glasgow book-shops the day after his return. In this defence, he admitted that he had seriously considered the Edinburgh chair, but only because he had reason to believe the Glasgow Magistrates and Council intended to renege on their agreement regarding the St. John's exemption from the General Session. The parish experiment, he asserted, had always been his primary consideration, and he had made this clear to Thomson and Brewster. He had, he concluded, neither vacillated in his purpose, nor lied to either his Glasgow Tory supporters or Edinburgh Whig friends.[110]

In truth, however, Chalmers *had* vacillated. It had required con-siderable nerve to pursue his St. John's proposals in the face of public and clerical opposition, while his support base, consisting almost exclusively in the influence of Ewing and Finlay in the Town Council, was so narrow. By early August 1819, his nerve had begun to fail. He had been too quick to suspect the Tory politicians of duplicity, and had acted rashly in rushing off to Edinburgh. In all probability, Chalmers would have accepted the Edinburgh Chair of Natural Philosophy if Thomson could have secured it for him. The chair would have allowed him to pursue the speculations on the relationship of revealed religion and science, which had already gained him such public approbation through his *Astronomical Discourses*. An Edinburgh chair, moreover, would have represented the fulfilment of his youthful ambition for academic status. He was weary of Glasgow, where he experienced neither stability nor peace, and of the Glasgow clergy, with whom he felt no fellowship. In Glasgow he had become once again an outsider. He now questioned whether he could possibly succeed in St. John's, in view of the public obloquy already directed against the experiment.

Nevertheless, he was now committed to begin the experiment. On 26 September, three days after his return to Glasgow, the St. John's church was formally opened, with an introductory sermon by Thomson 'in the presence of the Magistrates and a most crowded congregation'. Later, in the evening, Chalmers demonstrated his commitment to the labouring orders, by preaching his first sermon in St. John's to an evening congregation, consisting exclusively of working-class par-ishioners who could not afford the high seat-rents set by the Magistrates and Town Council for the day service. This evening congregation, he announced, was to be a permanent part of his parish experiment. 'It was', the Tory *Glasgow Courier*, one of his few supporters during the recent weeks, observed on 28 September, 'felt as a novel and affecting singularity to witness such a multitude from the labouring classes of our city so respectably provided with sabbath accommodation in one of the churches of the establishment.'[111]

'I have been much turmoiled and agitated of late,' Chalmers confided to Wilberforce a few months later, on 21 December 1819, 'by certain unhappy controversies about the management of my parish; but these I have now got over, and breathe a far freer and more peaceful atmosphere.'[112] In recent months, Chalmers had been responsible for disrupting the poor-relief system which had functioned for over ninety years in Glasgow. He had alienated the Glasgow clergy, and much of the Glasgow public. His reputation now rested upon his ability to achieve significant results in St. John's

IV

The autumn and winter of 1819-20 were an unpropitious time to begin the experiment.[113] The post-war depression had reached its bleakest period, and social suffering in Glasgow was acute. Thousands were unemployed. The harvests had been poor for the last several years, and the threat of starvation was real. The city put hundreds to work digging ditches on the Glasgow green; many churches opened charity soup-kitchens and distributed free fuel. Yet the distress continued. Mob violence and political radicalism remained a constant threat to social order. Among the weavers, secret societies continued to administer illegal oaths, but now they also began to collect pikes and other weapons. 'The population', Chalmers observed to Wilberforce on 15 December 1819, 'are overawed for the present by the large military force in town. But you know that this is not the most pleasant, neither is it the most permanent means of tranquillity. It were greatly more desirable to sweeten the spirits of the disaffected than to subdue them.'[114] Social tensions, he believed, made the need for success in his communal experiment more pressing.

The new parish of St. John's was composed mainly of the western portion of the Tron parish, with sections of the neighbouring College and Barony parishes. It did not include the most destitute districts of the Tron, such as the Saltmarket, nor did it exhibit the overcrowded conditions found in parishes nearer the old city centre. In October 1819, according to a survey conducted by Chalmers's elders, the parish population was 10,513. Approximately 54 per cent of the laburing population was engaged in the fluctuating textile industry. The remainder were scattered among service occupations (10 per cent), metal working (4.3 per cent), construction trades (2.6 per cent), or simply general labour. Although the parish population was almost exclusively working class, St. John's suffered less from the general economic distress than did other working-class parishes. In September 1819, for instance, before Chalmers had begun his programmes, St. John's ranked only sixth among Glasgow's ten parishes in number of sessional paupers. At the same time, the number of St. John's residents receiving assessment relief represented only about 3 per cent of the city's 1,524 assessment paupers. In short, although Chalmers would later describe St. John's as the poorest parish in Glasgow, it was in fact a parish of substantial labouring families, who were managing to weather the post-war distress. Many owned single-family homes, and their geographical mobility, a characteristic of the extremely poor, was low, as Chalmers later admitted. Of those families who attended church, most were Dissenters. In October 1819, 21.1 per cent of the population held seats in a Dissenting church, while only 7.6 per cent held seats in the Church of Scotland. This reflected the fact that seat-rents in Dissenting churches were generally lower, and labouring families more welcome than in the Establishment.[115]

Chalmers based his St. John's experiment on the programmes described in his 1817 *Edinburgh Review* article on pauperism and church extension, whereby pauperism, including both assessment and sessional relief, was to be gradually eliminated. This was not to be accomplished, however, by depriving paupers already dependent upon the assessment or sessional rolls of their accustomed relief. 'Old' paupers would continue to receive their usual relief until they either died of natural causes (most, Chalmers observed, were either very old or terminally ill), or voluntarily chose to regain independence. The abolition of pauperism would be achieved through a combination of limiting the number of 'new' paupers accepted for relief and of educating the parish population in the values of industry, 'moral restraint', and communal benevolence.

First, Chalmers promised, no St. John's poor would be referred to the Town Hospital for assessment relief after September 1819, and only the most needy would be granted sessional relief from the parish. With the 'old' paupers gradually dying or regaining independence, and with the ever-decreasing rate of acceptance of 'new' paupers for sessional relief after September 1819, there would be an increasing surplus in the sessional fund based on church-door collections. Secondly, with this surplus, augmented by private subscriptions, he proposed to build and endow both parish schools and an additional parish church in St. John's. The schools and churches, in turn, would educate the labouring poor to spurn the 'moral degradation' of pauperism. Thirdly, Chalmers promised to pursue a vigorous Evangelical ministry in St. John's, combining Evangelical preaching, 'aggressive' lay visitations in territorial proportions, and support for overseas missions.[116] These three programmes—poor-law abolition, parish schools, and Evangelical ministry—would, he argued, gradually restore the urban parish of St. John's to the communal ideal of the traditional rural parish. The working-class parishioners would embrace the old communal values, preserving themselves from the evils of pauperism, ignorance, and irreligion. Success in St. John's, further-more, would demonstrate that any urban parish could 'retrace' its path back to the rural communal ideal.

Chalmers's programmes for eliminating legal poor relief formed the core of his St. John's community-building operation. These pro-grammes were complicated. In essence, however, they involved the separation of 'old' and 'new' paupers, by creating two separate poor-relief funds and managing agencies in the parish. In September 1819, he established two congregations in the parish church—one meeting for Sunday worship during the day, and another in the evening. The 'day' congregation, like other Glasgow congregations, was non-parochial, consisting of wealthy families from throughout the city who were able to pay the high seat-rents required by the Magistrates and Town Council. Chalmers's preaching attracted a sizeable day congregation, and the church-door collection was extremely large, averaging over £400 per annum. With this collection, he provided relief to all 'old' sessional paupers, those St. John's residents who had been receiving General Session relief when he began his experiment. The annual expense of the 125 'old' sessional paupers was only about £225 in 1819, which left an annual surplus in the day collection of about £175.[117] The distribution of relief to the 'old' sessional paupers was administered by twenty-five elders. The parish was subdivided into twenty-five propor-tions, and each elder was assigned to supervise one proportion.

The evening congregation was Chalmers's special provision for his parishioners. With the permission of the Magistrates and Council, he rented the evening seats at a much reduced rate—just sufficient to cover the expenses of heating and lighting the church on Sunday even-ings and to pay a modest stipend for an assistant minister. The volun-tary church-door collections of the working-class evening congregation averaged only about £80 per annum: with this collection he provided relief to all 'new' paupers. Once the 'old' paupers, who were receiving either assessment relief from the Town Hospital, or sessional relief from the day congregation, died or regained independence, all St. John's poor relief would be provided from the strictly parochial working-class evening collection. When this occurred, he maintained, it would be possible to eliminate gradually even the sessional relief based on the parochial evening collection and to replace it with a spontaneous com-munal benevolence.[118] The day and evening collections would then be used to support the building of additional church and school accom-modation in the parish.

His plan depended upon limiting the number of new paupers ac-cepted for relief after September 1819. Because no new paupers would be granted relief from either the assessment or the day congregation

collection, they had to be restricted to a number which could be provided for from the evening collection alone. To help achieve this purpose, Chalmers revived a lay office long neglected in the Church of
Scotland—that of parish deacon. Each deacon was assigned to supervise
relief to the new paupers in one of the twenty-five parish proportions.
The deacons were, Chalmers emphasized, the main defence against the
increase of pauperism, and he devoted care to their selection and
training. They were to reduce institutional relief by discouraging the
poor from applying for sessional relief, and by endeavouring to inspire
a communal benevolence among the inhabitants. In response to any
application for parish relief in his proportion, the deacon was first to
appeal to the applicant's sense of social responsibility, encouraging him
to increased industry and sacrifice in order to avoid his becoming a
burden to the parish. If the applicant was truly without resources, the
deacon was then to appeal to the applicant's family or neighbours for
private charity, or, if the applicant was a Dissenter, to his Dissenting
congregation. If this failed, the deacon was to provide the applicant
with small donations from his own private resources, or to employ his
influence to find the applicant employment. Only if none of these efforts
proved sufficient, and if investigation revealed the applicant to be a
legal resident of Glasgow and eligible for relief, would he be considered
for regular sessional relief. At this stage, the deacon was to ask the
opinion of another deacon. If both deacons concurred, the case would
be submitted to the monthly meeting of the deacons' court, which
would review the case and determine the amount of relief to be granted
from the evening collection.[119]

The most important feature of the St. John's poor-relief system was
this trained order of deacons, with each deacon assigned to a specific
territorial district, and all deacons meeting together monthly for discussion of methods and problems. Chalmers instructed his deacons to
visit the homes in their proportions regularly, and familiarize themselves with all aspects of neighbourhood life. They were to discover
the character of each inhabitant, and investigate the relationships of
kinship, friendship, and prior obligations that existed among their
people. They were not simply to wait for the destitute to apply for help,
but were to act on rumours, or their own instincts, to seek out the
poor who might be too proud or too weak to request assistance. Further,
they were to endeavour to close public houses, remove health hazards,
strengthen families, and encourage education. In short, they were to be
friends and advisers to their proportions, but with good intentions firmly
rooted in awareness of social realities. The alcoholic or immoral,
although not eligible for parish relief, were not to be ignored. 'Even
with them', Chalmers instructed one of his new deacons in December
1819, 'show good-will, maintain calmness, take every way of promoting

the interest of their families, and gain, if possible, their confidence and regard by your friendly advice and the cordial interest you take in all that belongs to them.'[120] All this was innovative; indeed, as one later scholar has observed, Chalmers's deacons anticipated the development of the late twentieth-century social worker.[121] One weakness in both his deacons and his elders, however, was their excessively paternalistic relationship to their proportions. Chalmers felt obliged to recruit exclusively upper- and middle-class non-parish residents for these offices, because, as he later explained, he did not believe that any of his parishioners were sufficiently educated to be entrusted with poor-relief management. But he realized that this was a dilemma: his lay-visitors, although educated, were also outsiders, with no intention of becoming members of the parish community.[122]

Despite this problem, the St. John's poor-relief programmes began to achieve results. During the first year, owing to the dismal winter of 1819-20, progress was slow. By July 1823, however, less than four years after beginning the experiment, the programmes had significantly decreased the number of sessional paupers. Between September 1819 and July 1823, the total number of St. John's sessional paupers, both 'old' and 'new', had decreased from 125 to 91, or by 27.2 per cent. Of this decrease, a total of 5 paupers, or 4 per cent, can be accounted for by administrative transfers of paupers to other parishes; the remaining 23.2 per cent, however, resulted from the deacons' success in limiting the number of 'new' paupers accepted for sessional relief, combined with the 'natural' decline, through deaths and other causes, in the number of 'old' sessional paupers.[123]

Even more significant results were achieved in decreasing the assessment-supported pauperism. As Chalmers had promised, no new cases from St. John's were referred to the Town Hospital for assessment relief after September 1819. At the same time, the number of St. John's residents on the assessment relief rolls from before September 1819 declined, through deaths and other causes. In September 1819, 49 St. John's residents had been receiving assessment relief, at an annual cost to the Glasgow rate payers of £152. By March 1823, this number had decreased to 34, and the annual expense to £90.[124] In February 1822, meanwhile, encouraged by their progress, the deacons and elders pressed Chalmers for more decisive action to dramatize the success of their programmes. Chalmers's original plan had called for all 'old' St. John's paupers on the assessment rolls in September 1819 to continue to draw assessment relief from the Town Hospital until they died or voluntarily regained independence. The deacons and elders, however, now advocated that the parish church take over the full expense of the remaining assessment paupers. Chalmers initially opposed this departure from his plan, fearing that it might over-extend the sessional fund. However, rather than dampen his agents' enthusiasm, he finally acceded to their wishes. In March 1823, St. John's took over the full expense of its Town Hospital paupers, thus abolishing assessment relief in the parish.[125] Initially, St. John's continued to board its former assessment paupers in the Town Hospital, where there were facilities for care of the sick and aged. But in mid-1825, the paupers were removed from the Town Hospital and boarded in homes within the parish, with medical care provided by private physicians.[126] According to the 1823 agreement with the civic authorities, a portion of the £140 in rates paid annually by assessed St. John's residents was to be returned each year to the St. John's session to help defray expenses of the former assessment paupers. But in fact the Magistrates and Council reneged on this agreement, and no portion was ever returned.[127]

Chalmers called public attention to the St. John's achievement with a pamphlet published in 1823.[128] For the first time in Scotland, an urban parish, in a city dependent upon a legal assessment for poor relief for over ninety years, had 'voluntarily' abolished the assessment and 'retraced' its path back to the traditional rural parish system of relief based upon church-door collections. Most observers, he noted, had believed the abolition of assessment relief to be impractical in a large city, with a labouring population dependent upon a fluctuating capitalist economy, and with paternalism replaced by urban anonymity. But now he had accomplished the feat—and in an almost exclusively working-class parish in the major industrial city of Scotland. He claimed to have succeeded, moreover, without increasing social misery. On the contrary, between 1819 and 1823, more paupers from other Glasgow parishes voluntarily moved into St. John's than left the parish, indicating, he argued, that the poor were better cared for in St. John's than in other parishes.[129] His St. John's experiment, he insisted, had proved a 'perfect' system of poor-relief management, vindicating him in his struggle with the Glasgow General Session. His main anxiety was that the public would find his success too rapid to be believable.

Chalmers's success had indeed been substantial. To be sure, he had been aided, as critics observed, by the general improvement in economic conditions in Glasgow after 1820. None the less, the end of the post-war distress was not the determining factor. Despite the improving economic conditions between September 1819 and November 1822, the total number of sessional paupers in the other nine Glasgow parishes had increased slightly, from 1,134 to 1,155. During this same period, however, the number of St. John's sessional paupers had decreased from 125 to 94 (not including the total of five paupers shifted to other parishes as a result of administrative transfers). Between September 1820 and August 1823, moreover, the other nine Glasgow parishes had sent a total of 353 paupers to the Town Hospital for permanent assessment relief, while St. John's had sent none.[130]

While most critics acknowledged Chalmers's real achievement in decreasing St. John's pauperism, many questioned the means. In particular, they focused upon the callousness of some of Chalmers's deacons. Alexander Ranken, a Glasgow magistrate, later observed in a published letter to Chalmers in 1830: 'I may mention having, on one occasion, been under the necessity of sending, in my Magisterial capacity, from the Police Office to the Town's Hospital, a miserable object belonging to your parish, who had been found in the street in a perishing condition, from mere want of sustenance.'[131] In truth, most St. John's deacons, although zealous about decreasing pauperism, neglected the other, more demanding responsibility Chalmers had assigned to them—that of serving as friend and adviser to the community. In their responses to a questionnaire Chalmers circulated among them in July 1823, most deacons boasted that they spent less than four hours a year in their proportions, and had so discouraged pauperism that they had virtually no applicants for relief. Far from seeking out victims of poverty, many evidently ignored suffering in the interest of decreasing relief rolls.

Rather than discourage such callousness, however, Chalmers published these responses in his 1823 pamphlet as evidence of the ease with which his deacons discouraged pauperism.[132] He was convinced that it was not callousness on the part of his deacons, but rather a revival of a spirit of self-help among his parishioners that accounted for the ease of his deacons' task, and he failed to see the suffering among some of the poor. Chalmers had, to be sure, organized a middle-class order of deacons enthusiastic about decreasing the expense of pauperism, and, as demonstrated in the 1823 abolition of assessment relief in the parish, eager to take an active role in decision-making. But he must be faulted for failing to emphasize their communal responsibilities, and for allowing his deacons to evolve into an impersonal and perhaps callous group of poor-relief managers.

He achieved, meanwhile, more genuine progress towards his communal ideal with his parish education programmes—including the continuation of his system of district sabbath schools and the establishment of the first parish schools in Glasgow. First, importing to St. John's the successful system of local sabbath schools which he had established three years before in the Tron parish, he integrated this system into the general design of his experiment. In the Tron, it will be recalled, sabbath-school instruction had been conducted by a voluntary parish society, which had operated independently of the parish kirk-session, and defined its own sabbath-school districts. In St. John's, however, each sabbath-school teacher was assigned one of the twenty-five proportions as the district for his school. These teachers, moreover, were united with the elders and deacons to form the St. John's Agency, a parochial administrative body which met four times a year under

Chalmers's chairmanship for discussion of parish affairs and programmes. Sabbath-school instruction prospered under this arrangement. Shortly after the operation was begun, 35 sabbath-school teachers
were teaching 1,039 pupils—480 boys and 559 girls—representing over
half the parish children between the ages of six and fifteen.[133]

Secondly, he established day-schools, which he modelled after those
of the Scottish rural parish. There were, it will be recalled, no parish
schools in Glasgow in 1819, and a large portion of Glasgow's children
lacked any opportunity for education. In late September 1819, immediately after beginning the St. John's experiment, Chalmers privately
printed a pamphlet describing a plan to establish a model parish school
in St. John's. Three principles, he asserted, would be adhered to in the
school. First, attendance would be restricted to residents of the parish.
Secondly, the quality of instruction would be equal, if not superior, to
the best private schools in the city. Thirdly, the school would be financed
according to the same 'mixed system' of support that existed for rural
schools; that is, in part by a permanent endowment and in part by
modest fees required from the pupils. This last principle, he maintained, was particularly important. Only by requiring contributions from
families, he believed, would the labouring poor be taught to value
education. At the same time, however, the fees at his parish school
would be considerably lower than those of private schools. In order to
provide the partial endowment, meanwhile, he requested private subscriptions from wealthy citizens. Eventually, he argued, his model
school would convince the Magistrates and Town Council to redirect
part of the poor-relief assessment towards the partial endowment of
parish schools in all Glasgow parishes, so that in the future such private
subscriptions would become unnecessary.[134]

On 27 September 1819, the day after opening the St. John's church,
he convened the first meeting of a St. John's Committee of Education.
At this meeting, he and five others subscribed £100 each. Smaller subscriptions soon followed,and by early October £1,200 had been raised.
The Committee selected property on MacFarlane Street as the best site
for the school. As this property belonged to Glasgow University,
Chalmers had to negotiate with William Taylor, Principal of the
University, and a leader of the clerical opposition to St. John's, for its
purchase. Taylor initially opposed the sale. 'We have', he informed
Chalmers in reference to the Glasgow clergy, 'been talking for twenty
years of establishing parochial schools in Glasgow,' implying that
Chalmers would not succeed in what the body of clergy had determined
was impractical. 'Yes,' countered Chalmers, 'but how many years
more do you intend to talk about it? Now we are going to do the thing.'
Indeed, he suggested with a smile, Taylor should get him the lowest
possible price, 'seeing we are going to take the labour of talking and

projecting entirely off your hands'. Taylor finally acquiesced, and Chalmers obtained the property on favourable terms.

The MacFarlane Street schoolhouse was opened on 16 July 1820. It comprised two separate schools, each with its own schoolmaster—an English school, with a curriculum of reading and grammar, and a commercial school, with instruction in writing, arithmetic, and book-keeping. The fees, as Chalmers had promised, were low enough to enable boys from labouring families to attend; indeed, at 2s. per quarter for the English school, and 3s. per quarter for the commercial school, they were only about one-quarter of the fees charged by comparable private schools in Glasgow. Chalmers and the Educational Committee devoted care to the selection of talented and innovative schoolmasters. Emphasis in teaching was placed upon rewards for achievement, such as the loan of books from the school library, rather than upon physical punishment for failure. Chalmers insisted, moreover, upon restricting attendance to boys living within the parish. The parents of disappointed applicants from other parishes, he argued, would thus be obliged to press for similar schools in their own parishes.

The demand for education in St. John's exceeded all expectations. On 7 August 1820, less than a month after their opening, Chalmers reported to the Educational Committee that the MacFarlane Street parish schools were already overcrowded. Both schoolmasters were obliged to teach two day classes instead of one, and a large number of parish boys had been refused admittance because of lack of space. Additional sums were subscribed, and in September 1821 a second parish schoolhouse was opened, also comprising both an English and commercial school. The four St. John's parish schools now provided education to 419 boys, or 42 per cent of the male children in the parish between the ages of 6 and 15.[135]

The St. John's parish schools were an immense success, and a showpiece for the entire experiment. The costs, however, had also been considerable. Including building costs and endowments, at least £3,500 had been invested in the parish schools between 1819 and 1823—belying the often repeated criticism that Chalmers was concerned mainly to save money for the wealthy by depriving the poor of legal relief. He, meanwhile, found great personal satisfaction in the schools. 'His visits to my school', James Aitken, the first master of the MacFarlane Street English school, later recalled of Chalmers, 'were almost daily. In all states of weather, and in every frame of mind he was there; depositing himself in the usual chair, his countenance relaxing into its wonted smile as he recognized the children of the working classes.' Time and again, said Aitken, Chalmers would turn to him, 'his eye beaming with peculiar tenderness, [and exclaim] 'I cannot tell you how my heart warms to these barefooted children.'[136]

This represented more than simply sentimental attachment to ragged children. Amid the controversy which continued to surround his St. John's experiment, he found consolation in the belief that these children, as they matured to adulthood, would vindicate his communal ideal and elevate society, from its very base, to a new moral order. After about 1820, Chalmers increasingly employed millennarian language regarding the progress of mankind towards a new reign of Christian principle in his sermons and discourses. Education assumed a central position in his vision. In July 1820, in a discourse delivered to his parishioners shortly before the opening of his first parish schools, he proclaimed that education would lead to the 'millennium of light and love, of which it is prophesied. ... If the world is to stand, there will be a great amelioration of the life of general humanity. The labouring classes are destined to attain a far more secure place of comfort and independence in the commonwealth than they have ever yet occupied.' Education, he continued, was not only important for such utilitarian purposes as job training, or teaching Malthusian 'moral restraint'. At its highest level, it would enrich communal life by extending participation in literature and science to all social orders:

I trust the time is coming when humble life will be dignified both by leisure and by literature, when the work of the day will be succeeded by the reading and improving conversations of the evening, when many a lettered sage as well as many an enlightened Christian will be met with even in the very lowest walks of society, when the elements of science and philanthropy and high scholarship will so ripen throughout the general mind of the country as to exalt it prodigiously above the level of its present character and accomplishments.

The main purpose of his parish schools was not to encourage poor children to pursue entrance into the learned professions (although he hoped that some would find positions), but rather to create a learned order of labourers—'not to furnish them with the means of abandoning their status, but to furnish them with the means of morally and intellectually exalting it.'[137]

The new moral order was to be erected upon Christian foundations. As Chalmers had assured his former St. Andrews mentor James Brown on 30 January 1819: 'I should count the Salvation of a single soul of more value than the deliverance of a whole empire from pauperism.'[138] In St. John's, he remained the fervent Evangelical. Besides the two services in his church each Sunday, morning and evening, for as long as his health permitted he devoted two or three afternoons each week to visiting, and completed a visitation through every parish household during his first two years at St. John's. He continued his regular weeknight services, which he conducted in a local cotton mill, mechanic's workshop, or large dwelling. Between 1819 and 1821, moreover, his ministry benefited from the assistance of a young clergyman destined to greatness in his own right. In October 1819, on the recommendation of Andrew Thomson, Chalmers appointed as his assistant minister the twenty-seven-year-old Edward Irving, a village schoolmaster and probationer for the ministry. Emerging from a Dumfriesshire peasant community, and loyal to the Church of Scotland as 'a free plebeian Church·which never pined till she began to be patronized', Irving embraced Chalmers's communal objects, and was an enthusiastic visitor among the poor.[139] Irving venerated Chalmers, and the two men developed an affectionate conpanionship that continued after Irving left St. John's in December 1821 to begin his extraordinary, and ultimately tragic, career as minister of a Scottish congregation in London.

Chalmers's spiritual ministry in St. John's continued to emphasize lay visitations and an outward-reaching missionary impulse. The role of spiritual guides to the people belonged primarily to the elders, the highest lay office in the Church of Scotland. Elders were instructed to visit regularly in their assigned proportions and to encourage family prayer and Bible study. They were, moreover, to impose moral discipline, admonishing offenders according to biblical standards with the spiritual authority of their office. The missionary impulse also remained an essential part of Chalmers's parish ministry. His ideal parish community required a purpose, which transcended the material self-interest of its members, and encouraged the community to unite in sacrifice. Despite the financial demands of the poor-relief and educational programmes, he continued to call for special collections for the British and Foreign Bible Society, the Moravian overseas missions, the Hibernian Society, and other missionary causes. During his St. John's ministry, his day and evening congregations contributed an average of £200 per annum to missions and outside charities.[140]

In March 1822 Chalmers began efforts towards building a chapel in his parish, to provide church accommodation with low seat-rents for his working-class parochial congregation which worshipped Sunday evenings in the St. John's parish church. He first approached the Magistrates and Town Council for financial support. When they refused his request, he adopted the church-extension plan introduced to him in 1817 by John Gladstone of Liverpool, and raised the money for construction by the sale of £100 shares in the chapel, with each share bearing an annual interest of 5 per cent, to be paid from the seat-rents.[141] There were, however, serious difficulties involved. To begin with, the chapel was legally a 'chapel-of-ease'. This meant, among other things, that St. John's parish had no legal right to retain the chapel collections for poor relief. As soon as they learned of his chapel plans, Chalmers's opponents, led by Principal Taylor and including the majority of the Glasgow presbytery, demanded that the civic authorities seize all future collections at the proposed chapel for support of the Town Hospital. Chalmers was forced to plead his case before the May 1822 General Assembly. He managed to convince the Assembly to grant him dispensation to retain the chapel collections for poor relief,[142] but it was a bitter blow to learn how strongly his fellow Glasgow clergy continued to oppose his work in St. John's, despite his achievements in the past two-and-a-half years. Furthermore, he proved unable to find enough purchasers of shares to meet the £2,400 construction costs for the chapel; indeed, he was only able to complete the chapel by selling £1,000 in shares to James Douglas of Cavers, a wealthy landed gentleman who resided outside Glasgow.[143] His upper- and middle-class supporters in Glasgow were evidently losing interest in the St. John's experiment. When finally opened on 29 June 1823, the chapel was heavily burdened with debts. In order to service the debts and pay the stipend of the chapel minister, seat-rents had to be set above what most parishioners could afford.[144]

Perhaps it was the chapel difficulties that finally convinced him it was time to leave. In January 1823, his supporters were stunned by the news that Chalmers had accepted an appointment to the St. Andrews Chair of Moral Philosophy, and would leave St. John's in the autumn of that year. He was not only leaving Glasgow, but also relinquishing the parish ministry—and that, for a purely academic position in St. Andrews, the centre of Scottish Moderatism. In a letter to the St. John's Agency on 20 January, Chalmers presented two reasons for his decision. First, he explained, his health was no longer strong enough for a vigorous parish ministry. He had suffered a severe illness as a result of visiting during the previous spring, which had incapacitated him for several weeks, and obliged him to relinquish household visitations. He could no longer meet the physical strains of regular preaching and continual meetings with his agents. After over three years of incessant activity in supervising every aspect of his parish experiment, he was exhausted. Secondly, he had become so active in the work of disseminating his communal ideal through his publications, correspondence, and speaking and fact-finding tours outside Glasgow, that he was no longer able to give enough attention to his parish. In order to remain in the parish ministry he would have to become in effect a clerical pluralist. It was, he believed, more important that he devote his 'remaining years' to building public support for the parish community ideal and helping to educate the next generation of clergy. The St. John's experiment, he maintained, was now almost complete. The poor-relief, educational, and Evangelical programmes were functioning smoothly; the new chapel, once completed, would add the capstone to the edifice. He expressed confidence that he had created a system for a communal parish ministry that transcended his own personality, and would function under the supervision of any reasonably motivated minister. Indeed, he argued, his departure would free the St. John's parish community ideal from its excessive association with his name.[145]

He failed, however, to confide to the Agency perhaps the most important reason for his decision. He was, in fact, weary of the continuing attacks upon his poor-relief programmes from the Glasgow press. More importantly, he was hurt and disappointed by his continuing conflict with the Glasgow clergy over his reform ideal, a conflict which after 1819 assumed an increasingly personal nature. After 1819, he dreaded meetings of the Glasgow presbytery, which were for him painful affairs. 'Find nought but misery in the field of my earthly contemplations,' he noted in his diary on 16 January 1822, a year before his resignation. 'An ordinary meeting of Presbytery,' he wrote in his diary on 6 February 1822. 'Dislike its atmosphere though it is my duty to enter it.' 'Begin to feel again the fatigue and sore vexation of Glasgow,' he wrote on 18 February 1822. 'O my God, may I be still and do my work as thy servant.' For a man of his sensitive temperament, nurtured in the communal environment of rural Fife and needing the approbation of others, the pain of rejection and isolation was acute. This had been evidenced in his suffering over the clerical attacks upon the orthodoxy of his preaching in 1818 and over the conflicts surrounding the beginning of the St. John's experiment in 1819. Now, with the attempt by the Glasgow clergy to wreck this experiment by seizing the chapel collections, despite his sustained labour and achievements of the past four years, the cup of bitterness was filled to overflowing. In his diary during the spring of 1822, he repeatedly referred to being tormented by the 'great anxiety' of the chapel affair and the fate of the experiment. 'I'm still very much touched and engrossed by the great anxiety,' he noted after a meeting of his chapel subscribers on 12 March 1822, 'and I feel how difficult a thing it is to live a life of Faith.' 'Vexed with the treatment of me by one whom I applied to [for a subscription] for the chapel,' he wrote a few days later, on 20 March. 'Depressed a little, and the great anxiety still weighs upon me... Find that nothing but a firm hold of the judicial righteousness can do me good.'[146]

Further, the tensions of his position were affecting his relations with his family. He now had three daughters, and his wife was expecting their fourth child. It was time, he believed, to take his family home. There, near his Anstruther birthplace, surrounded by stable rural communities and the memories of his youth, he hoped to rediscover a sense of communal belonging. His conflict with the Glasgow clergy, to be sure, had been of his making. He had endeavoured on his own to change long-established procedures and had, in 1819, employed his influence with Ewing and Finlay to impose his will upon the civic authorities against the expressed desire of the majority of his brethren, undermining the General Session. To the clergy, his ambition recognized no limits, and he had placed himself outside the bounds of their fellowship.

The news of Chalmers's impending departure raised a cry of exaltation among his enemies, who circulated rumours about the 'untold' reasons for his precipitate departure. 'Few individuals', an anonymous pamphleteer observed in 1823, in a defence of Chalmers's decision to leave St. John's, 'have been so much assailed as the immortal person whom we are now attempting to defend. … What unheard-of stories were not circulated, with busy and most incorrigible malignity? The purest actions of his life, were they not turned over, that perhaps something might be got out of them, wherewith they might brand and throw ridicule upon his name?' Chalmers's enemies, his friend and elder William Collins informed him on 20 January 1823, were 'triumphant', and predicted 'that your Parochial arrangements will go to wreck when you are withdrawn'.[147]

On 9 November 1823, Chalmers preached his farewell sermon in St. John's church. Whatever the opinions of him, his departure from the parish ministry was regarded as a major event in Scotland. The crowd, consisting largely of 'strangers' from outside Glasgow, was immense. A minor riot occurred at the church door, 'such as we hope will never again be witnessed in Glasgow', the *Glasgow Courier* noted two days later. Three days after the farewell sermon, on 12 November, he was fêted at a farewell dinner sponsored by Ewing and Glasgow's Tory élite. As toast after toast echoed through the banquet hall, however, and the company grew more raucous, it grew apparent that even these Tory friends were not greatly sorry over his departure. The post-war years had been a period of social misery and bitter conflict in Glasgow, and Chalmers's social reform activity had reflected the tension.[148] But now, coinciding with the return of relative prosperity, Chalmers was leaving, and the Glasgow élites could return to the business of producing goods and pursuing their self-interest in peace.

The St. John's experiment, the culmination of Chalmers's Glasgow ministry, had been an impressive demonstration of his Evangelical social ideal in action. In little over three years, assessment-based poor relief had been eliminated, four parish schools established, a chapel built, and an agency of visiting elders, deacons, and sabbath-school teachers organized and trained. The success was a tribute, not only to Chalmers, but to the generosity and tenacity of his upper- and middle-class supporters. Despite the predictions of his opponents, his St. John's experiment was continued for a number of years following his departure, mainly through the zeal of his Agency. Not until 1837, eighteen years after its inception, was the Agency forced, as a result of steadily mounting debts and declining church-door collections after 1826, to relinquish its poor-relief experiment and begin referring paupers for assessment relief on the same terms as the other city parishes. With this decision, the St. John's experiment was brought to a close.

Chalmers attributed the final collapse of the experiment to two main causes. First, the Magistrates and Town Council had refused to refund a portion of the assessment paid by the St. John's residents back to the parish, despite the fact that after 1823, the parish had undertaken the full support of its assessment paupers. Secondly, the Magistrates and Council had done nothing to stop the inflow of 'old' sessional paupers from other Glasgow parishes into St. John's. With greater co-operation from the civic authorities, he argued, the experiment would have succeeded. But in fact, as two scholars have recently demonstrated, these causes were relatively minor in their effect, and the weaknesses of the St. John's system more deeply rooted than Chalmers would admit to, or even recognize.[149] In truth, the programmes never succeeded in achieving his main object—the formation of a closely-knit working-class community, united by Evangelical ideals, and centred upon the parish church. In his Tron ministry, between 1815 and 1818, he had converted a significant body of upper- and middle-class supporters to his parish community ideal. They, in turn, had provided the financial support and effort required for the experiment. In St. John's, however, neither Chalmers nor his Agency succeeded in inspiring the working-class parishioners with similar enthusiasm. The parishioners never achieved, and apparently never even sought, independence from the paternalism of the non-parochial higher classes.

In March 1834, according to an article in the Evangelical *Church of Scotland Magazine*, 108 upper- and middle-class parish labourers were employed among 11,513 St. John's parishioners. These included 96 elders, deacons, and sabbath-school teachers, and 12 salaried ministers, parochial missionaries, and schoolmasters, paid from the contributions of the mainly non-parochial church and chapel congregations. Among the parishioners, however, only 22.9 per cent held seats in either a Dissenting or Establishment church, a decrease of 5.8 per cent from September 1819, the date when the experiment was begun. The article did not specify how many parishioners held seats in the Establishment, but from this silence, and from the high seat-rents required in both the church and chapel, it may be inferred that the number was very low.[150] Although in many respects a model parish for an aggressive Evangelical philanthropy, no working-class Christian community such as that envisaged by Chalmers was ever created in St. John's. His communal

ideal never penetrated beyond his upper- and middle-class supporters
to the Glasgow labouring orders. If Chalmers had remained longer
in St. John's, he might have recognized the weakness of a class-
oriented Agency, and realized that excessive concern for the reduction
of legal pauperism was compromising the effectiveness of the St. John's
programmes. As it was, he began a campaign for national reform
based upon a parochial system which had achieved only questionable
results.

V

Chalmers's parochial experiment might have passed into obscurity
after he departed from Glasgow, little known outside a narrow circle
of supporters. But in fact it inspired considerable enthusiasm outside
Glasgow, and prompted a number of additional parochial operations
based upon the 'Chalmerian' system. His real achievements in St.
John's were exaggerated, and his experiment became widely perceived
as an immense success. This perception was created in large part by
his three-volume treatise, *The Christian and Civic Economy of Large Towns*,
published between 1819 and 1826. In these volumes he transformed his
St. John's experiment into a 'proved' plan, not simply for the restoration of the traditional parish community ideal in Scotland, but for
comprehensive reform which would serve to organize the entire British
nation into a godly commonwealth of stable Christian communities.

Chalmers had first decided upon publishing a lengthy work describing his parish ideal in the summer of 1819, while opposition to his
proposed experiment was mounting in Glasgow. In 1817, it will be
recalled, Francis Jeffrey, the editor of the Whig *Edinburgh Review*, had
offered Chalmers the *Edinburgh* as a vehicle for disseminating his social
theory through quarterly or biannual articles. After he had published
two articles in the *Edinburgh* in 1817 and 1818, however, his new Tory
supporters had convinced him to relinquish this arrangement.[151]
Instead, he decided to issue independently a lengthy treatise in quarterly
numbers, enabling him both to reveal his communal reform plans
gradually, and to keep his St. John's experiment constantly in the public
eye. By publishing independently, moreover, he was able to assume
the status of a Christian social reformer, above political party identifi-
cation.

To publish his *Christian and Civic Economy*, Chalmers embarked upon
one of the more important ventures of his career—the establishment of
a new publishing house. The story behind this venture is a complicated
one. Since 1808, following the failure of his *Enquiry into the Extent and
Stability of National Resources*, he had harboured a distrust of publishers;
yet as a social reformer, his influence depended mainly upon his publi-

cations. He felt uneasy about placing his reform proposals in the hands of publishers, whose main object was profit, and who, he also suspected, might be swayed by political bribes or threats to undermine his influence through insufficient distribution and advertising of his works. By 1817, however, Chalmers believed that in the Glasgow firm of John Smith he had at last found a publisher he could trust. Smith was a member of the Tron congregation. His eldest son and business manager, John Smith junior, was a Tron elder. Chalmers, moreover, had developed a warm friendship with Smith's youngest son, Thomas, in the final months before his tragic death from consumption in May 1816. Smith had further gained Chalmers's confidence with his effective advertising of the *Astronomical Discourses*. None the less, Chalmers's distrust of the publishing industry revived, and in the summer of 1819 it culminated in a bitter dispute with Smith.

The occasion was the indifferent public reception of Chalmers's second volume of sermons, the *Tron Church Sermons*, published in March 1819. Unable to understand the poor sales of this volume after the success of the *Astronomical Discourses* two years earlier, Chalmers became convinced that Smith was engaged in an intrigue to undermine his influence. His allegations were probably baseless. Smith had incurred serious financial loss—if he is to be believed, as much as £2,530— in purchasing, publishing and advertising Chalmers's work. In truth, Chalmers' *Tron Sermons*, an attempt to vindicate his Calvinist orthodoxy through a straightforward treatment of the doctrine of salvation by grace alone, had simply failed to capture the public interest. The experience of being personally insulted by Chalmers, on top of his financial losses, was too much for Smith: following a series of bitter exchanges, their arrangement was terminated in the late summer of 1819.[152] Chalmers's ill-treatment of Smith was unjust. The pressures of mounting opposition to his Calvinist orthodoxy and social reform ideal had revived the insecurities of his youth, and he reacted with childish malice.

Following the termination of his arrangement with Smith, Chalmers employed his personal resources to help finance the formation of a new publishing house. To head the enterprise he selected William Collins, a successful Glasgow schoolmaster, and the most trusted of his St. John's parish elders. He also used the opportunity to provide a position for his younger brother Charles, a bright but unstable young man, who had left St. Andrews Divinity Hall without standing for his divinity trials. Accordingly, the publishing house of Chalmers and Collins was opened in September 1819. Almost immediately, they issued their first work— the initial quarterly number of the *Christian and Civic Economy*. Chalmers now had command over his own publisher, and could publish his works and determine levels of distribution and advertising virtually at will.

Under Collins's capable management the enterprise thrived, paying Chalmers richly for his initial investment. Charles Chalmers soon grew bored with the business and left, but Collins continued, building the House of Collins into one of Britain's great publishing concerns.[153]

Throughout Chalmers's year at St. John's, the numbers of the *Christian and Civic Economy* appeared quarterly. In mid-1821, Collins republished the first eight numbers as volume one. The following eight numbers were republished as volume two in mid-1823, and after a brief hiatus when Chalmers left St. John's, the final eight numbers were republished as volume three in 1826.[154] Each of the three volumes was well advertised and distributed to booksellers throughout Britain.[155] Indeed, the three volumes of the *Christian and Civic Economy* constituted a definitive statement of his social ideal, and became perhaps the most influential work of his career. In the first eight numbers, he introduced his parish community ideal, focusing in particular upon his plan to restore the new urban districts to the traditional rural parish community ideal through an aggressive territorial ministry, embodying extensive lay participation. He outlined his St. John's programmes, including household visitations, the subdivision of the parish into proportions, the reduction of seat-rents, and the establishment of parish schools and sabbath schools. He pressed for church extension, or the building of new parish churches, to ensure that no parish would exceed 2,000 inhabitants, which he regarded as the maximum size for a viable parish community. Further, he invited Protestant Dissenters to participate in this effort, by building additional churches of their own denomination in irreligious urban districts, and by mapping out districts around these churches as ground for their own aggressive territorial ministry.[156]

In the next eight numbers, he focused upon pauperism, and especially the role of parish communities in eliminating the need for legal poor relief. He described his St. John's poor-relief programmes, which, he argued, would educate men for a spontaneous communal benevolence, and elevate the condition of the labouring poor by promoting their industry and responsibility. The most significant portions of this volume were numbers fourteen to sixteen, in which he advocated poor-law reform in England based on what he termed the 'permissive process'. This will be discussed in greater depth at the beginning of chapter 4.

In the final eight numbers, written after his departure from Glasgow, Chalmers turned to the broader questions of political economy, as they related to the elevation of the labouring orders. He based his hope for these orders upon strict Malthusian doctrine, agreeing with Malthus that wages were a direct function of the supply and demand for labour, and that therefore even a slight decrease in the labour supply would effect considerable improvement in wage-levels. He focused upon the capacity of an educated working class to improve its own condition, through 'preventative action' designed to reduce the labour supply, and thus drive up wages. For this, he proposed two measures. First, they should reduce their numbers through 'moral restraint'. Secondly, they should voluntarily reduce the hours they would work. This, he argued, could be accomplished through the relatively new institution of working-class savings banks, which were becoming widespread in Britain at this time. Savings banks, he maintained, by encouraging labourers to accumulate a small capital when times were good, would enable them to refuse to work when wages were too low. In general, Chalmers approved of the legalization of trade unions. He supported the repeal, in 1824, of the Combination Acts of 1799 and 1800, which had outlawed strikes and the formation of trade unions. At the same time, however, he believed the real value of the repeal of the Combination Acts was that it would demonstrate to labourers that their best hopes lay not in union-directed strikes (which he argued were easily broken up by employers), but rather in individual 'moral restraint' and the use of savings banks.

Finally, he reiterated the central argument of his 1808 essay in political economy, that Britain's national wealth was a function not of foreign trade, but of home consumption. For this reason, he maintained, Britain's economic development did not depend, as some economists argued, upon limiting or reducing wages in order to compete with foreign producers for overseas markets. Rather, it depended upon increasing home consumption by the elevation of the hitherto oppressed labouring orders. Thus, he concluded, the religious and moral education of the labouring orders in small parish communities was not only a Christian imperative: by transforming the oppressed labouring orders into an industrious class of mass consumers, his parish communities would also contribute to the steady economic development of the nation. The Christian communal ideal would liberate the nation from periodical economic depressions, which, he argued, resulted from excessive dependence upon overseas markets.[157]

Chalmers's *Christian and Civic Economy* revealed considerable development of his social ideal from the Spartan, militaristic community of his 1808 *Enquiry*, or the arcadian community of his later Kilmany writings. Eight years in Glasgow had given him awareness of the problems of urbanization and greater appreciation for the industrial dynamic. He now accepted orderly industrial growth as a social good, and he demonstrated better understanding of Classical Liberal economic theory. Even among those who did not accept his Malthusian beliefs, his *Christian and Civic Economy* was respected as an expression of 'rational philanthropy', based upon a sincere attempt to comprehend the changing social structures and to help the labouring orders achieve a more fulfilling life.[158] His social idea remained communitarian; his purpose was ultimately to subsume economic individualism in a parish communal ideal, and to control industrial development for the elevation of the labouring orders.

A transcendent Christian purpose, moreover, continued to form the value system around which his ideal parish community would be organized. Since 1808, he had consistently maintained that community members had to unite for a common purpose that transcended individual self-interest, before they would practise benevolence towards one another. In the 1808 *Enquiry*, the vision of national glory, reflected in national independence and national intellectual achievements, had represented his transcendent ideal. With his Evangelical conversion, he had elevated the ideal of an active overseas Christian mission. Now, in his *Christian and Civic Economy*, he defined a third ideal—the pursuit of social justice, particularly through the spiritual, moral, and material elevation of the oppressed labouring poor of industrializing cities. These three ideals were not mutually exclusive. On the contrary, together they formed a triple goal for a covenanted Christian commonwealth.

It is, finally, important to contrast his commonwealth ideal to two related movements in early nineteenth-century Britain—first, the rise of religious Dissent, and secondly, the communitarian movement of the celebrated Utopian socialist Robert Owen. Chalmers had little real sympathy for Dissent. His communal purpose was to be interpreted and disseminated to the national community by an Established national Church, either the Church of Scotland, Church of England, or Church of Ireland. The national Establishments assumed special significance, as the builders of the national consensus. In the *Christian and Civic Economy,* to be sure, Chalmers affirmed his desire for Christian fellowship with Protestant Dissenters, and even encouraged them to begin territorial Christian community-building operations on the St. John's model in districts where the Establishment remained weak. His real object, however, was not to encourage Dissent but to overcome it. The value of Dissenting church-extension efforts, he believed, would be to stimulate the Established Churches to increased activity. 'I am glad', he confided to Malthus on 12 December 1821, in reference to the first volume of the *Christian and Civic Economy*,

that you have caught my real wish and disposition with regard to Establishments. ... When I urge Methodists and other sectarians to do their utter most, it is because I honestly believe that the ultimate effect of a movement amongst Dissenters would be a similar movement on the part of the Church, which in the strength of its own inherent powers, would soon outstrip all the other Denominations in our Land, and leave them far behind in the career of real usefulness.[159]

Once the Establishments, he maintained, had been infused with a liberal Evangelical theology and an active social mission, it would be perverse for Dissenters to remain outside. They would, he trusted, embrace the new sense of national purpose, and assume their proper place within the Christian commonwealth.

'Either you are right and I am in error,' Robert Owen, the Utopian socialist, wrote to Chalmers from New Lanark on 24 April 1820,

or I am right and you are in error, or we both misunderstand each other. ... Now as we are both conscientious in our opinions, with the impression also that the opinions which we hold true are the best calculated to improve society, and as with such conviction are both likely to promulgate these opposing sentiments, I am really anxious to enter upon the great discussion as proposed at our last meeting with a desire on my part to detect the error whereever it may lie.

Owen had just returned from a visit to Chalmers at St. John's. Now, prior to their 'great discussion', he invited Chalmers to visit him at New Lanark. 'Come and see what *is* done here as a preliminary step toward the more important improvements which with your aid and help a remedy may be immediately assured for our suffering fellow creatures.' In a word, Owen was suggesting that they might co-operate in a campaign for a communitarian reorganization of society. Chalmers, however, refused to pursue this possibility for an alliance. Although he despatched William Collins to survey Owen's New Lanark community, he himself did not visit New Lanark until four years later. The 'great discussion' proposed by Owen as a preliminary to their co-operation never occurred.[160] None the less, the two great communitarian thinkers of early nineteenth-century Scotland had met and discussed their positions at some length.

There were important similarities in their respective social ideals. Both proposed small communities characterized by close personal relationships among members, as an alternative to eighteenth-century interest politics and Classical Liberal economic individualism. Both sought to control and limit large-scale industrialization and foreign commerce, and looked to a traditional rural communal organization. Both believed that in a properly engineered communal environment individuals would be educated to assume a place within a new moral order which they were certain was approaching. Both represented significant movements of reaction against the worst effects of rapid urbanization and industrialization in early nineteenth-century Britain. But there were also significant differences between their communal ideals. Owen placed greater emphasis upon the role of production in his communal organization, while Chalmers emphasized the needs of the consumer. More important, Owen was less attached to the concept of private ownership of property than Chalmers, who for all his emphasis upon communal benevolence refused to countenance the idea of communal ownership of land or capital.

Their basic difference, however, and that which precluded any possibility of their co-operation, lay in their respective views of the spiritual dimension of the new moral order. Both were millennarians, but in 1817 Owen had publicly rejected traditional Christianity at his celebrated London Tavern meeting, and he now embraced a millennarian faith with focus upon a moral order embodying imperatives of social harmony in this world, without transcendental content.[161] 'After forty years deep consideration,' he confessed candidly to Chalmers in his letter of 24 April 1820, '[of Christianity and] of also the other religions which have been taught ... my conviction is that they are directly calculated to destroy the first feeling of human nature and pervert the best faculties which belong to it and that while they should be taught men cannot become either good wise or happy.' Chalmers, on the other hand, embraced a Christian millennarian tradition, with faith that through the extension of vital Christianity, represented by the Evangelical revival, the world would pass through its present suffering, and enter a thousand-year reign of 'light and love' preliminary to the second coming of Christ. The communal structures were to be a school, teaching men to rise above material self-interest. Through benevolence towards others, they would learn to love God, and open themselves to the saving influence of his Spirit—as preparation for Christ's reign on earth.

This difference was important. It meant that, unlike Owen, Chalmers was able to draw upon the rich traditions of the Bible and the Church in forming his social message. It meant that this message appealed to a wider public in Christian Britain, and particularly Scotland, than did that of Owen and his followers. But above all, Chalmers's Christianity represented a fundamental difference with Owen in their respective views of the individual in society. Lacking a transcendental vision, Owen viewed man primarily as a physical being, whose highest achievement would be social happiness in this world. In order to achieve communal harmony, Owen was concerned to diminish individual differences among men through non-sectarian education, communal ownership of property, and co-operative labour. Owen believed that as an essentially physical being, man's character was moulded by his material and social environment. Thus, by forming ideal socialistic communities, Owen felt that he would create a new order of social beings.

For Chalmers, however, the individual was a being with an immortal soul. His highest destiny was not only to achieve happiness in this world, but also to transcend the world—to find eternal salvation through the acceptance of divine grace. Man possessed a conscience, or inner light, which was something holy. For Chalmers, then, individual differences were divinely ordained and were to be reverenced as expressions of the uniqueness of each eternal soul. He wished, to be sure, to subordinate economic individualism to his ideal of a traditional rural community infused with benevolence. His starting-point, however, was not an emphasis upon shaping a perfect social environment, but rather an emphasis upon reforming individual character through appeals to the individual conscience—by means of Evangelical preaching, parish visitations, and parish schools. Individual conscience, representing man's relationship with God, was more fundamental for him than social relations; the eternal fate of a single soul was of more value than even the total abolition of pauperism throughout Britain. The greatest value of a Christian community was to help prepare individuals for acceptance of grace and eternal life. This Evangelical individualism, this emphasis upon reforming individual character as the first step towards social reform, set Chalmers's communal message apart from that of Owen and indeed all later nineteenth-century movements of materialistic socialism.

Chalmers's eight years in Glasgow had ultimately elevated him to a new height of influence. Despite the conflicts and the failures, his achievements had been significant. He had assimilated his rural parish community ideal to new urban conditions, gained the participation of a considerable body of the Glasgow upper and middle classes in his parish ideal, established himself as one of the foremost preachers of liberal Evangelical theology in Britain, and finally, through the *Christian and Civic Economy,* transformed his St. John's failure into success, and begun to extend his influence as a communitarian social reformer throughout Britain. Encouraged by the success of the early numbers of the *Christian and Civic Economy*, he also began, in co-operation with several leading Scottish Whigs, an effort for national poor-law reform, intended to abolish legal assessments, and restore the nation to independent parochial poor-relief management, based upon his ideal of communal benevolence.

LIBERAL REFORM AND
THE NATIONAL ESTABLISHMENT

I

In the first two decades of the nineteenth century, legal assessments for poor relief increased dramatically in England. Many observers attributed the rising expenditures to the rapid expansion of the Speen-hamland system, a policy first adopted in Berkshire in 1796, by which the poor rates were used to subsidize deficient wages in order to ensure that families could afford enough bread. Others attributed it to the fact that many English parishes employed paupers for road repair or as labourers on local farms, and paid them from the assessment. In fact, local practices under the old English poor law varied immensely. One thing, however, is clear: among the English propertied classes, many feared that the rising assessments would eventually swallow the profits of property, disrupt the economy, and tear asunder the social fabric. In Scotland, assessments were much lower than in England; in 1820, moreover, they were legally established in only about 100 of the nearly 1,000 Scottish parishes. None the less, there was widespread anxiety in Scotland that its assessments were increasing and would soon reach the English levels. This anxiety was aggravated by the fact that most of Scotland's assessed parishes lay in the border districts. The English contagion, it was feared, was spreading northwards. This, in turn, contributed to a growing belief in Scotland that its assessments could not be diminished or eliminated until something was done to arrest rising assessments in the southern nation.[1]

Late in August 1822, over a year before his departure from Glasgow, Chalmers embarked upon a tour of England, in order to investigate English poor relief at first hand, and to determine how his St. John's system might be introduced into that country. His six-week tour was carefully planned. At nearly every stop, he had prearranged that one of his English supporters would gather local clergy, magistrates, and poor-law overseers, to whom he presented a list of questions. His tour was as extensive as his time would permit, encompassing the industrial Midlands, the agricultural southern and eastern counties, and much of London.[2] He was encouraged by what he encountered. 'I shall only at present assure your Lordship', Chalmers wrote his friend, the Tory Earl of Elgin, on 16 September, from Gloucestershire, 'that all I have seen, has not at all shaken, but rather strengthened my confidence in the reducible and remediable state of English Pauperism. I am quite in spirits about it, and there are men of great practical sense and sagacity whom I have got to harmonize with me on this topic at various places.'

Elgin had already corresponded with Robert Peel, the Home Secretary, regarding Chalmers's St. John's experiment; and he now pressed Chalmers to approach Peel with the suggestion of a Government-sponsored poor-law bill based upon his principles.'Chalmers, however, was hesitant to meet Peel just yet. 'My only reluctance', he told Elgin in his letter of 16 September, 'in visiting Mr. Peel and other official or parliamentary men, is founded on the circumstance of their being so often exposed to the crudities and speculations of sanguine philanthropists that for a time at least I must lay my account with the incredulity and perhaps even pity of my auditors.'[3]

Instead of immediately proposing new legislation, Chalmers decided to employ the results of his English tour to educate the 'enlightened public' of England. In particular, the English would have to be convinced that it would be possible for their parishes to adopt his St. John's system. This became a focal point for his activity during his final months in Glasgow. Late in January 1823 he had announced his decision to leave St. John's. One of his reasons for this decision, he told the English MP and philanthropist, Joseph Butterworth, on 12 February 1823, was the fact that the St. Andrews professorship would allow him, 'the full command of the six summer months, which I can devote to general objects, and more particularly to London, the great theatre of philanthropy'.[4] During the next several months, he organized the evidence gathered on his English tour into concrete proposals, and in the late summer of 1823, several weeks before he left Glasgow, he published three tracts entitled 'The Likeliest Means for the Abolition of Pauperism in England', which represented numbers fourteen to sixteen of his *Christian and Civic Economy*.[5]

It would, Chalmers argued, be a relatively simple administrative procedure to adapt the St. John's poor-relief system to the different institutional structure of a Church of England parish. The Anglican parish vestry, he explained, could be made to function in the same manner as the St. John's parish Agency. For this purpose, the vestry would be divided into two categories of lay-visitors—one approximating to the Scottish office of elder, to supervise relief to 'old' paupers, and one to the Scottish office of deacon, to supervise relief to 'new' paupers. In the same manner as in St. John's, then, 'old' paupers would continue to receive assessment relief until they died or regained independence, while 'new' paupers would receive relief only from parish church-door collections or private charity. The English parish would also be divided into districts, or proportions, to facilitate regular household visitations; and in time it would 'retrace' its path back to the system of purely communal benevolence.

The greatest barrier to the extension of his St. John's system to England, Chalmers argued, involved not the institutional differences between the Churches of Scotland and England, but rather the different habits of thought in the two nations. In England, virtually all parishes had been assessed since the sixteenth century; in Scotland, however, he maintained that assessments had not been introduced on a permanent legal basis until the eighteenth century, and even then they had been adopted in only a minority of Scottish parishes. Thus, the English were more accustomed to legal concepts of charity than the Scots, and less open to his communal alternative. During his English tour, he had discovered that while most English observers were anxious about the effects of assessment relief upon the character of the labouring orders, few perceived any possibility of abolishing legal relief. In order to overcome this long-established habit of thought, therefore, Chalmers proposed what he termed a 'permissive process'. According to his process Parliament would pass a law enabling any parish in England, on the vote of four-fifths of the parish householders who were not paupers, to abolish its assessment relief and adopt the St. John's system. He admitted that initially only a few English parishes would choose to exercise this option. None the less, he argued, success in these few parishes would encourage other English parishes, and their success would encourage still more—until gradually all 10,000 parishes in England would abolish assessments and embrace the communal ideal.[6] He realized the English would be wary of returning to traditions of communal benevolence that they had discarded centuries before. 'We do not want', he asserted, 'the whole of England to be thrown adrift, at the bidding of a yet untried hypothesis. But we want England to put herself to school. We think she needs to go to school; and when looking to those trial parishes, she is, in fact, learning the first lessons, and acquiring the sound rudiments of a sound education. Those parishes will be to her the alphabet, whence she may venture forward to achievements still more arduous.'[7]

The English, meanwhile, demonstrated no inclination to become Chalmers's pupils. His tracts on English pauperism were on the whole badly received south of the Tweed. They did, however, capture the interest of the Scottish Whig, Thomas Francis Kennedy (1788-1879), member of a wealthy Ayrshire landed family, and, since 1818, the MP for the county of Ayrshire. Kennedy was acutely concerned about the increasing assessments in Scotland. In 1815, he had undertaken an independent enquiry into Scottish poor relief, 'to ascertain whether there be not a burthen gradually coming upon the country which will progressively increase, and to consider whether it be possible that a Parliamentary Enquiry might be followed by some measure to arrest the rapid progress of oppressive poor rates.'[8] In 1819, shortly after his election to Parliament, he introduced a bill to abolish the right of the Scottish poor to appeal to any higher civil law court against a poor-relief decision made by the local parish heritors and kirk-session. Such appeals were increasing in frequency after about 1810, and Kennedy suspected they not only encouraged the spread of assessments, but also threatened the sanctity of private property and the proper deference of the poor towards their social superiors. Kennedy's bill was read twice in the Commons, but dropped when his friend and supporter, the Whig Earl of Minto, proved unable to mobilize sufficient interest in the Lords.[9] Yet Kennedy and most Scottish Whigs remained convinced that something had to be done to protect property from the encroachments of legal poor relief. He was advised, however, to concentrate upon educating the public to the dangers of assessment relief before introducing another bill in Parliament.[10] Then, four years later, Chalmers published his tracts summoning England to the St. John's 'school', and Kennedy seized the opportunity for an alliance.

Early in September 1823, a few weeks after the publication of Chalmers's English pauperism tracts, Kennedy visited him in Glasgow, and shortly after this meeting, on 17 September, sent Chalmers 'a hasty sketch of a Bill framed as an attempt to embody the views, which when I had the pleasure to see you, you thought might form a useful enactment respecting the Poor in Scotland'.[11] Kennedy's draft bill was a complicated document, but in essence its proposals were twofold. First, it would give the heritors in rural parishes, and the magistrates in burghs, the power to abolish a legal assessment and relinquish all poor-relief responsibility, provided only that they continued to give the usual assessment relief to 'old' assessment paupers until they died. According to existing Scottish law, assessments were imposed and administered by the joint action of the kirk-session and heritors in rural parishes, and by the joint action of the kirk-session and magistrates in burghs. Kennedy's bill, then, would enable the heritors and magistrates to end the assessment and to throw the whole responsibility for poor relief upon the kirk-sessions, who would have to provide all relief solely from the voluntary church-door collections and other private donations to the parish church. Secondly, the bill would abolish the right of the poor to appeal against a kirk-session's relief decision in any civil law court. In a word, Kennedy's bill would relieve the propertied classes of all legal obligation for poor relief and deprive the civil courts of any supervisory authority over Scottish relief. All responsibility would then fall upon the parish kirk-sessions of the Church of Scotland. In order to meet this responsibility from their voluntary church-door collections, Kennedy reasoned, kirk-sessions would have to adopt Chalmers's St. John's system.[12]

Chalmers was initially hesitant about the bill. Although it 'perfectly embodied' their mutual views, he informed Kennedy on 20 September 1823 that he feared the Scottish people were not yet sufficiently educated regarding the evils of pauperism to accept such a radical remedy. In particular, the clergy of the border parishes, where assessments were widespread, were likely to object to being suddenly saddled with the full responsibility of poor relief. 'I fear from that quarter a shout of most vehement clamour and opposition.' Why not, he therefore asked, attach a 'permissive process' clause, such as that described in his tracts on English pauperism? The bill, he explained, could be made to apply immediately in all unassessed parishes, to halt any further spread of assessments. But in those parishes already assessed, where the inhabitants had developed habits of thought favouring assessments, the heritors or magistrates would be allowed to abolish assessments only with the permission of the parish kirk-session. In short, no kirk-session would be forced to undertake the St. John's system against its will. Initially only a few assessed parishes would adopt Kennedy's act. Chalmers, however, was confident that their success would encourage other assessed parishes to do the same, until the approximately 100 assessed parishes of Scotland would 'work back their way to a right state in that piecemeal way that would create no alarm or disturbance'. He asked Kennedy's permission to circulate copies of the draft bill among his acquaintances for further opinions.[13]

Two months later, however, on 21 November 1823, he wrote to Kennedy from his new home in St. Andrews, expressing his complete approbation for the bill, which he now termed 'excellent and unexceptionable'. All doubts had apparently vanished, and he made no mention of the need for a 'permissive process'. His change of heart, he explained, had resulted from favourable reports from several clergymen and landowners from the border districts, to whom he had sent copies of the bill. In short, he now believed Kennedy's Scottish bill would receive widespread support in precisely that region of Scotland where he had most expected resistance, and he advised Kennedy to introduce it in Parliament.[14]

Encouraged by his discussions with Kennedy, Chalmers had also begun to draft a separate poor-law bill for England. When he had broached this subject with Kennedy in early September, Kennedy had suggested that he approach Henry Brougham, a Scottish Whig who represented an English constituency in Parliament, and who was at that time investigating abuses in English philanthropic foundations. Accordingly, Chalmers met Brougham in late September 1823, and early in October attended a dinner in honour of Brougham given by the Glasgow Whigs.[15] Chalmers's friend, the Tory Earl of Elgin, who had previously suggested that Robert Peel sponsor a Government poor-law bill based upon the St. John's system, was appalled by

Chalmers's new relationship with Brougham. 'I cannot pass unnoticed', Elgin wrote on 15 October, 'the risk you have run in being taken to Mr. Brougham's public dinner—It really makes me shudder when I think of it. You are well aware of my extreme anxiety that you should keep clear of all approximation to opposition politicks.... I anxiously confess, that I should consider the good-will of a leading member of the Government-side far more valuable for you, than that of a member of opposition.' Chalmers, however, now blamed his difficulties in Glasgow on his alliance with the Glasgow Tories, and he decided to try the Whig connection.[16] Late in December 1823, therefore, when Brougham recommended W. Woolriche Whitmore, a moderate English Whig connected with the Russell family, as a sponsor for the English poor-law bill, Chalmers immediately sent Whitmore his draft of a bill for English poor-law reform, representing the 'permissive process' he had described in his three tracts on English poor relief.[17] At the same time, he also wrote to the English Evangelical Whigs, Thomas Babington and Zachary Macaulay, informing them of his intention to have Whitmore introduce this English poor-law bill during the next Parliamentary session, at the same time as Kennedy introduced the Scottish bill.[18]

Chalmers's plans, however, soon went awry. In early January 1824, Whitmore informed him that he would not sponsor his English bill. Chalmers immediately wrote to Babington, asking him to press Whitmore further, but either Whitmore would not be pressed, or Babington did not press very hard. Brougham now disassociated himself entirely from the matter, and in late February 1824, Chalmers was forced to abandon his English bill for the present Parliamentary session. The decision, Babington assured him on 16 March, was 'discreet and judicious'.[19] In truth, although his English friends appreciated many aspects of Chalmers's St. John's system, including district visitations and local sabbath schools, few advocated adopting his communal ideal in its entirety.[20]

With the failure of his English plans, Chalmers grew nervous about Kennedy's bill for Scotland. His unease increased when in mid-February the influential Earl of Elgin informed him that he would oppose the bill.[21] Late in February, Chalmers wrote Kennedy that he now feared extensive opposition to their bill in Scotland. For this reason, he requested Kennedy to add the 'permissive' clause to the bill before introducing it in Parliament, in order to quiet the alarm.[22] Kennedy, however, refused. He had no confidence in Chalmers's 'permissive' process, and preferred defeat to what he considered emasculation of the bill. 'If the clamour be raised,' he wrote to Chalmers from London on 18 March, 'we must endeavour to quell it, but if Scotland does not express any strong opinion, I have a great idea that it will be allowed quietly through the Commons.' What they needed now was political nerve. 'It is no doubt an attempt of some hazard,' he admitted, 'but that it must be at any time, and my belief is that the longer it is delayed, the greater the difficulties will be to be encountered.'[23] At midnight on 6 April, Kennedy finally introduced the Scottish bill in the House of Commons, in an obvious attempt to slip the bill through its first reading in a thin house. William Rae, the Tory Lord Advocate for Scotland, protested the timing of its introduction, but declined to begin a debate at such an hour, and a second reading was scheduled. 'The people of Scotland', Rae observed, 'would appreciate the manner in which the bill was brought in.'[24]

Rae proved correct. The cry raised against Kennedy's bill in Scotland was overwhelming. The Church of Scotland protested against being saddled with the full responsibility of poor relief in Scotland. Dissenters claimed that their paupers would be discriminated against. Responsible property owners protested that the abolition of assessments would oblige them to provide a disproportionate share of the expense of poor relief through private donations, while irresponsible property owners would be rewarded for their indifference towards the poor. This would be true not only in assessed parishes, but also in unassessed parishes, where the threat of imposing assessments was all that stirred many property owners to donate anything to the kirk-session fund. Virtually everyone agreed that the Church of Scotland alone could not bear the whole burden of poor relief, and that the resulting social misery would threaten social order. 'The streets', the Moderate clergyman John Inglis warned in the Edinburgh presbytery on 28 April, 'would be crowded, not only with real objects of distress, but with sturdy beggars, sorners, and blackguards of every description, to the disgrace of the country, and injury of the morals of the people.'[25]

Many, like Rae, were enraged at the manner of its introduction, believing that Kennedy was attempting to manœuvre the bill quietly through Parliament without allowing the Scottish people to express themselves on a matter so vital to the national interest. The Evangelical Stevenson Macgill, for example, exclaimed in the Glasgow presbytery on 7 May that he was 'indignant, not only at the bill itself, but at the mode of procedure which had been pursued with respect to it'. Public meetings were held throughout Scotland to protest against it, and by early May Parliament was flooded with petitions from parishes, presbyteries, synods, burgh councils, and counties.[26] 'The late Edinburgh papers', Henry Cockburn informed Kennedy, who had remained in London, on 7 May, 'will show you that [all] the ... fools in the kingdom are up against the Poor Bill.' Cockburn advised Kennedy to withdraw the bill for the present, then collect all relevant statistics and documents, 'put them into Chalmers's hands, and insist on his expounding the system which he had recommended, and which he sees thus attacked'.[27] But Kennedy decided upon a different tactic. On 14 May, he announced in the Commons that he would neither respond to the petitions now pouring in from Scotland, nor make any further statement, until the second reading of the bill, scheduled for 27 May.[28] The General Assembly of the Church of Scotland would convene on 20 May, and Chalmers, Kennedy knew, would be a member. As there would be a motion against the bill in the Assembly, Chalmers would be obliged publicly to defend the plan he had recommended.

Chalmers, meanwhile, was remaining silent, hoping only that the 'engrossing annoyance' of the Kennedy bill would soon pass over.[29] He realized now that the bill would not be enacted by Parliament, and that nothing would be gained by prolonging the affair. His reputation, moreover, was suffering. His name was vilified with Kennedy's at public meetings and in the Scottish press. In the House of Commons on 11 May, the Scottish Tory MP, Sir George Clerk, had virtually named him as the real author of the bill, a remark widely reported in Scotland.[30] For Chalmers, the affair was especially distressing for its effect upon his relations with his fellow Evangelical clergy. By leaving Glasgow, he had hoped to end the bitter controversies surrounding St. John's, and then to resume his former position of influence within the Evangelical party. But the *furor* over the Kennedy bill had revived and enlarged the debate over St. John's and threatened his future in the Evangelical movement. His position was delicate. He could not denounce the Kennedy bill, which was too obviously based upon St. John's, yet to support it would place him in opposition to the expressed opinion of Scotland.

His way was made somewhat more easy in the General Assembly, however, by the strategy adopted by his supporters among the Evangelical party. On 20 May, the first day of the Assembly, the Evangelicals managed to thwart a motion for immediate discussion of the Kennedy bill, and to postpone debate for almost a week, in order to allow tempers to cool. Then on 26 May, the day before Kennedy was to speak on the bill in the Commons, Chalmers's close friend Henry Duncan, the Whig Evangelical minister of the border parish of Ruthwell, moved that the General Assembly petition Parliament to drop the Kennedy bill. Duncan's speech was flattering to Chalmers. He applauded the elevated view of human nature that had inspired him to pursue his St. John's experiment, but he confessed that in his view, man was too selfish for a system of purely communal benevolence to work effectively.[31] Then, following Duncan's brief speech, Chalmers rose to address the Assembly.

He began by expressing his confidence that, had it passed, Kennedy's bill would have proved effective for eliminating assessment relief in any parish, without sacrifice of the poor. His St. John's experiment had demonstrated just that. However, he continued, the problem now before them involved not the viability of the St. John's system, but rather the scepticism and hostility of the Scottish people towards the system. He reviewed for the benefit of the Assembly his 'weary struggle' with the Glasgow clergy, magistrates, and public over St. John's—a struggle 'so perpetual and seemingly endless ... that I was well nigh worn out in attempting to maintain it. ... I found it far easier practically to do the thing than to spread the belief that the thing was practicable.' Even now, he admitted, most inhabitants of Glasgow considered St. John's to have been a failure. Human nature resisted change, even change designed to restore traditional communal values. For this reason, he maintained, any national plan for the abolition of assessments on the St. John's model must be 'permissive', allowing parishes which so desired to begin the experiment, but not imposing the St. John's model upon those which lacked confidence in the system. Kennedy's bill, however, lacked such a 'permissive' clause. Therefore, Chalmers seconded Duncan's motion that the General Assembly petition against the bill.

Indeed, he now proclaimed his opposition to any attempt to effect his St. John's ideal through Parliament. Instead, he requested his supporters throughout Scotland to begin a few parochial experiments on the St. John's model. He wanted no legislation, but asked only that the civil and ecclesiastical courts allow the parishes to begin the experiments without legal interference. Gradually, he maintained, these isolated experiments would reawaken the country to the communal ideal of 'the old Parochial system'. He did not expect ignorance and prejudice to be overcome quickly, and he imagined that Glasgow would hold out against his system to the very last. 'It is ... not perhaps till we and our children and mouldering in the dust, that I could ever expect ... the metropolis of the West to open their gates to [the] system.' None the less, once fairly begun, his 'permissive process' would eventually triumph. Following Chalmers's seconding speech, Duncan's motion to petition Parliament against Kennedy's bill was adopted without a vote.[32]

Chalmers's turn-about in the Assembly earned the approbation of at least one of Kennedy's Whig friends. 'I yesterday heard Chalmers make a most admirable exposition of the leading principle of your Poor Bill in the Venerable Assembly,' Henry Cockburn wrote to Kennedy on 27 May,

accompanied by a powerful eulogium on its excellence, and a half ludicrous and half eloquent account of what he called the 'impregnability' of the intellects of Conveners of Counties, Provosts of Burghs, and Moderators of Synods. Notwithstanding all this he seconded, and was wise in seconding, Duncan of Ruthwell's motion *against* the bill; his ground being, that the country was not prepared, from ignorance, to receive it heartily, and it would not do to force. ... Hearing that he had mistaken the stare of delight with which I listened to him for a frown of disapprobation, I went and called on him, and consoled him, and had a long talk with him. The report in the newspapers looks so adverse to you, that he was afraid of your being surprised at him; but I told him I should write to you to explain how matters stood.[33]

On 27 May, as promised, Kennedy delivered a lengthy defence of the bill in the House of Commons, praising Chalmers's St. John's efforts as the inspiration for the bill. He then withdrew the bill for the present, but promised to reintroduce it in three months, after tempers had cooled.[34] When Kennedy learned a day or two later of Chalmers's speech in the General Assembly, he was both 'surprised' and not much pleased. What apparently upset him most was not just that Chalmers had openly opposed the bill, but that he had made no mention of his having assisted in the drafting of it. Despite Cockburn's attempted explanation, Kennedy ceased corresponding with Chalmers, and did not reintroduce his bill. Although Kennedy probably never learned of it, Chalmers had, in fact, explicitly denied that he had helped draft the bill, assuring Lord Elgin on 27 May that he had not helped Kennedy formulate it, and giving Elgin a letter to this effect which, with his permission, Elgin forwarded 'very privately' to both Robert Peel, the Home Secretary, and Lord Liverpool, the Prime Minister.[35]

Chalmers does not emerge from the Kennedy bill fiasco in a very attractive light. He had not been honest about his role in advising Kennedy: in fairness he should have explained the extent of his involvement to the Assembly. As it was, his speech left the impression that Kennedy had borrowed some of his ideas, but had otherwise acted alone. Worse still, Chalmers had lied to Peel and Liverpool about his co-operation with Kennedy, and had done so, moreover, knowing that his lie would probably never be detected. Men of honour and integrity such as Peel and Liverpool were highly unlikely to expose letters marked 'very private' under any circumstances at all.

Although not very laudable, however, Chalmers's behaviour had been shrewd. The Kennedy bill affair had threatened his future within the Scottish Evangelical movement, and rather than further jeopardize his career he had chosen to desert Kennedy, recognizing that the latter did not carry much political weight. Further, their relationship had never been a warm one. Kennedy was an aristocratic Whig, with little appreciation for Chalmers's communal ideal. His main concern had been to protect property owners from the encroachments of legal assessments, and not to improve the condition of the poor. Chalmers felt no loyalty towards either the man or the propertied interest he claimed to represent. In short, Kennedy's friendship was expendable. It is significant, too, that the Edinburgh Whigs bore Chalmers no ill will for his behaviour towards Kennedy. Indeed, on 1 June 1824, a few days after the close of the General Assembly, Chalmers shared the speakers' platform with three of them, Henry Cockburn, Francis Jeffrey, and Leonard Horner, at the annual meeting of the subscribers to the Edinburgh School of Arts, a 'mechanics institute' offering inexpensive evening courses for labouring men.[36] And in October 1824 Cockburn published a flattering essay on the St. John's experiment and communal ideal in the Whig *Edinburgh Review* which was intended to help restore Chalmers's reputation as a social reformer.[37]

Chalmers's General Assembly speech of May 1824 was important in another respect. Although he did not renounce his St. John's communal ideal, he extended his hopes for its implementation on a national level into the distant future—'not till we and our children are mouldering into dust'. His opponents could now have little reason for alarm that his plans would cause social dislocation. All he asked of his supporters was to protect his St. John's experiment from his Glasgow opponents, and to begin a few additional 'retracing' experiments in different parts of the country. In response to his request, four such parochial experiments were begun—three in the border districts (Ancrum, Langholm, and Ruthwell), and one in the village of Dirleton, about fifteen miles west of Edinburgh. Of these, only the experiment in Dirleton, under the direction of the Church of Scotland clergyman William Stark, proved successful. Stark later published a short volume describing his Dirleton success, and his experiment captured the interest of the English Poor Law Commission formed in 1832.[38] The other three experiments foundered because of lack of interest among the local heritors. Chalmers did not totally relinquish his campaign for the abolition of legal poor relief after 1824, however. He corresponded with supporters in Britain, the United States, and on the European Continent regarding his St. John's programmes, and he pressed for further experiments modelled after St. John's. Nevertheless, throughout the remainder of the 1820s, Chalmers shifted his social reform focus from poor relief to the two other supports of his godly commonwealth ideal—education, and the dissemination of Evangelical Christianity.

The Kennedy poor-law-bill affair had also given Chalmers a certain distrust of Parliament. It had demonstrated that this was a forum beyond his power to manipulate, at least without better advice and stronger support than Kennedy had been able to provide. He now concentrated his talents upon strengthening his position within the national religious Establishment of Scotland. For Chalmers, the national Establishment encompassed not only the Church of Scotland with its parish churches and schools, but also the five universities of Scotland. These he regarded primarily as seminaries for the Christian education of parish clergy and schoolmasters, and for the application of Christian doctrine to a changing society. Thus he perceived his move from the parish ministry to the Chair of Moral Philosophy of St. Andrews University not as a departure from the national religious Establishment, but as an elevation to a more responsible position within it.

II

St. Andrews had been a decaying university when Chalmers had been a student there in the 1790s. Now, thirty years later, its decline was even more apparent. The buildings had fallen into such disrepair that it resembled, as Chalmers remarked in 1827, more 'an old cottonmill' than a college. The faculty, since the death of George Hill in 1819, was undistinguished. William Ferrie, the Professor of Civil History, whose plural appointment to the parish of Kilconquhar Chalmers had opposed in 1813, had not lectured since 1808, although he continued to draw his salary. Other professors lectured during the brief five-month academic term, but remained in repose for the rest of the year. The self-interest of the faculty, meanwhile, prevented significant university expansion. Most appointments continued to be made on the basis of family connection or friendship. At the end of each year, moreover, the professors divided all surplus university revenues among themselves to augment their salaries, in an appropriation known as the 'Candlemass Dividend'. Some of this surplus revenue was obtained through the sale of medical degrees, although there was no medical faculty. Overall university revenues, meanwhile, were declining, largely as a result of the general economic decay of northern Fife, which diminished the value of the university-owned properties.

The St. Andrews student population remained the smallest of Scotland's five universities, with an average of 220 resident students. There were no entrance requirements, and most students matriculated directly from a rural parish school at the age of fourteen or fifteen, ill-prepared for college study. Expenses were modest. A student was expected to find his own lodgings in town, but by sharing a room and having provisions sent him from home, he might, with some sacrifice in health and comfort, complete an academic term for less than £10, including fees. There were, moreover, a number of bursaries (scholarships), most of them small, but sufficient to encourage poor students to undertake university study.[39] For all its failings, then, St. Andrews University did provide at least some opportunity for the poor rural 'lad o' pairts' to pursue a career in the learned professions. The sacrifice made by so many poor youths, however, only rendered its declining academic standards more disturbing. 'Poor St. Andrews', the Scottish missionary Alexander Duff later recalled of his student days there in the mid-1820s,

> lay ... isolated and apart, in a region so cold that the thaw and the breeze, so relaxing and vivifying elsewhere, scarcely touched its hardened soil. The great stream of national progress flowed past, leaving it undisturbed in its sluggishness. The breezes of healthful change blew over it, as over the unruffled surface of a land-locked bay. From all external influences, even of an ordinary kind, it seemed entirely shut out. No steamer ever entered its deserted harbour ... No mail coach, or even common stage-coach ever disturbed the silence of its grass-grown streets.[40]

It was, in many respects, surprising that Viscount Melville, the Crown's patronage manager in Scotland, should have offered Chalmers the vacant St. Andrews Moral Philosophy chair. As mathematics lecturer at St. Andrews in 1801-2, Chalmers had outraged most of the university community by his attacks upon Professor Vilant. In Glasgow, he had disrupted established institutions and antagonized his colleagues. Further, he was an Evangelical, with Whig sympathies, while St. Andrews was solidly Moderate and Tory. Offering him the chair seemed only to invite trouble. In fact, the responsibility for bringing Chalmers back to St. Andrews belonged primarily to Francis Nicoll, Principal of the United College. Nicoll was concerned over the declining state of the university, and believed that new talent was needed. Learning of Chalmers's unhappiness in Glasgow and his 'longing for a Literary retirement', and believing that maturity had mellowed him, Nicoll recommended Chalmers to Melville for the vacancy. 'To show your Lordship that my ideas are not illiberal,' he wrote to Melville on 25 October 1822, 'I beg leave respectfully to state to you the name of a clergyman whose fame cannot be unknown to your Lordship—Dr. Chalmers of Glasgow. ... [T]ho high in his Religious opinions, [he] is by no means a violent Party man—if he be a party man at all. He is a man of unobtrusive and amiable manners, a Gentleman, and an honest man, so that he would make an excellent member of our Society whilst his transcendent abilities, and his great fame would in all probability give new lustre to our University.' Melville agreed that the university needed talent. 'My only doubt,' he replied on 29 October to Nicoll's recommendation of Chalmers, 'would be as to his fitness for the situation, which requires not only talent, but solidity, and I should be afraid that he might sometimes be eccentric.' None the less, 'taking into consideration his great reputation', Melville agreed an offer should be made.[41] Nicoll did so, and on 18 January 1823 he was able to inform Melville that Chalmers had accepted. 'This event', Nicoll added, 'will create a considerable sensation in this country and will even be of some interest to many in London, where his fame is high.'[42] Indeed, the entire town was excited. Unpleasant memories of Chalmers's previous connection with the university were forgotten, while shopkeepers and landlords anticipated the benefits to flow from the revival of the university.[43]

Chalmers arrived in St. Andrews in mid-November 1823, immediately prior to the beginning of the term. He enjoyed the sense of triumphant homecoming, and looked forward to a long and peaceful association, amid the communal attachments of his childhood. The passage of time had apparently softened the memory of his past disputes and humiliations at the university. 'I never thought', he observed in his inaugural address,

> that on this side of time I should have been permitted to wander in arbours so desirable, and that thus embowered among my most delicious recollections, I should have realized in living and actual history the imagery of other days; that the playfellows of my youth should thus become the associates of my manhood; and that the light-hearted companions of a season that has long passed away should, by the movements of a mysterious but, I trust, kind Providence, stand side by side as colleagues in the work of presiding over the studies of another generation.[44]

Chalmers's teaching responsibilities at St. Andrews involved essentially one course in moral philosophy. Fresh from an active pastoral ministry amid the Glasgow slums, he had not had time to prepare his lectures prior to his arrival. Nor did he have any real taste for the usual approach to the subject in Scotland. For a generation, Scottish moral philosophy had been dominated by the 'common sense' school. The 'common sense' philosophers concentrated upon detailed analysis of the functions of the human mind, in order to demonstrate that the mind possessed an internal moral regulator, a common sense which reflected the existence of divinely-ordained moral dimension in the world. For Chalmers, however, this process of analysis had continued long enough, and was yielding diminishing returns for the intellectual effort being invested.[45] He accepted, to be sure, the concept of a common moral sense, which he termed 'conscience'. Through his conscience, or inner light, each man was enabled to perceive, intuitively, his social duty.[46] Further, man possessed the power of attention, by which he might direct his senses away from objects which excited anger or jealousy, and concentrate them upon objects which stimulated the conscience.[47] The greatest force for social duty, however, was created when man directed his conscience, or inner light, towards the direct revelation of God in Scripture. The biblical concept of salvation by grace alone liberated man from the terrors of death and supernatural powers, and inspired him to follow the dictates of his conscience, not from 'slavish' fear, but as a free autonomous individual. The life of Christ provided a positive example of moral social action. Chalmers argued that the stirrings of conscience found their fulfillment in the gospels.[48] For him, the focus of moral philosophy was not upon epistemology, but upon practical Christian ethics, as comprehended through conscience and embraced by a conscious act of will.[49] Through conscience, he argued, the ethical imperatives became obvious to all men. 'It is well', he observed, 'that, amid all the difficulties attendent on the physiological inquiry, there should be such a degree of clearness and uniformity in the moral judgements of men—insomuch that the peasant can with a just and prompt discernment, equal to that of the philosopher, seize on the real moral characteristics of any action submitted to his notice, and pronounce on the merit or demerit of him who has performed it.'[50]

The most crucial problems of moral philosophy, he maintained, involved not epistemology, but rather the application of the ethical imperatives of Scripture and conscience to current social problems. This, in turn, led him to lengthy explication of his views on poor relief and communal benevolence. Encouraged by his students' interest in these topics he offered during his second academic year at St. Andrews an additional course in political economy. He employed Adam Smith's *Wealth of Nations* as the basic text, but criticized Smith's doctrine of economic progress with reference to Malthus's theory of population.[51] This was the first political economy course taught at the university. It was not part of the regular Arts curriculum, and enrolment was voluntary. None the less, 35 students, or nearly 16 per cent of the resident student body, attended the course during the first year it was offered.

In the classroom, Chalmers combined the impassioned oratory of his preaching with the sincere personal involvement which had characterized his pastoral visitations. He excited his students with eloquence until he was often hard pressed to silence their cheers. At the same time, he made an effort to become personally acquainted with each student. He required periodic essays from his students, and devoted considerable care to criticizing their work. He could be overbearing in the classroom, particularly when students challenged his most deeply held social views. George Lewis, later editor of the Evangelical *Scottish Guardian*, minister of Dundee, and active educational reformer, recalled vividly the day that a student in the political economy class characterized Chalmers's arguments in favour of the crucial role of moral education to social happiness as 'Quixotic' and 'fantastic'. The student refused to acknowledge that a teacher or clergyman was as important to society as a producer of even insignificant material goods. 'This', Lewis related, 'was too much. The Doctor felt it, and coloured deeply; replied by a profusion of argument and illustration, and after thrice slaying the slain, he returned next day with an elaborate written defence, until we roared out our conviction in unmistakable sounds; and the champion of squibs, and crackers, and puff-paste, was fain to hide his head amid the general uproar.'[52] It is difficult not to sympathize with the champion of puff-paste. None the less, it is evident that, to a degree, Chalmers encouraged student responses, and that if he overbore them, it was with arguments, not authority. He endeavoured, moreover, to preserve an atmosphere of equality of opportunity within his classroom. 'When academic proprieties are infringed upon,' he admonished two young men of gentle birth who regularly disturbed the class by arriving late, 'and the respect due to academic station is violated, no rank and no fortune shall shield it from the chastisement of my scorn. These distinctions are proper in general society, but within the walls of the university they should ever be unknown.'[53]

His activity was not confined to the classroom. A major function of the university was to prepare candidates for the ministry, and Chalmers endeavoured to inspire the Moderate St. Andrews University community with Evangelical fervour. Early in 1824, a few months after his arrival, he accepted election as president of the St. Andrews Missionary Society. Formed during the brief outbreak of missionary enthusiasm in 1812, the society had been largely lifeless for nearly a decade. Now, revived by Chalmers's vivid descriptions of overseas missions, it soon grew too large for its meeting-place in the Mason's lodge, and moved to the town hall.[54] Impressed by his orations before the town missionary society, several students in the Divinity Hall organized themselves into a separate student missionary society in the spring of 1824. Their example was soon followed by students in Chalmers's moral philosophy class, and in December 1824 the two groups united to form the St. Andrews University Missionary Society, which held monthly meetings, collected penny subscriptions for overseas missions, and formed a small library of mission publications. By 1825, nearly a third of the student body were members.[55]

He also worked to impress St. Andrews with his parish ideal. A few weeks after his arrival, he began a local sabbath school. He selected a district in the poorest section of town, visited the families, and by this means collected children for regular Sunday instruction in his home. Further, he encouraged his students to begin similar sabbath schools under the supervision of a local parish or Dissenting clergyman. The students responded with enthusiasm. 'Sabbath schools', young Alexander Duff later informed Chalmers on 20 January 1829, 'have now overtaken almost the whole population. I have personally visited all the lower classes in the town, and did not find twenty children who were not attending some school or other.'[56] During Chalmers's second year at St. Andrews, several students began applying his 'local principle' to Sunday Bible classes for adults. St. Andrews was divided into districts. A few students would then visit among the inhabitants of one of the districts, collect a group for meetings in one of the district homes, and explicate a selection of Scripture or read from a pious tract. In the spring of 1825, several of Chalmers's students asked his permission to establish a mechanics institute in St. Andrews during the summer, with free lectures in history, moral philosophy, political economy, mathematics, and natural philosophy. He evidently discouraged this effort as too ambitious for undergraduates, but he was no doubt pleased with the spirit it demonstrated.[57]

Within his first two years at St. Andrews, Chalmers had effected considerable change in student life. Prior to his arrival, there had been few student societies and little sense of student community. Now, the students not only demonstrated Evangelical enthusiasm in the missionary society, local sabbath schools, and district visitations; they also began meeting together regularly at Chalmers's home on Sunday evenings and at their own lodgings on week-nights for prayer and religious discussion. 'Such a change', John Urquhart, one of Chalmers's students, wrote to his father on 15 December 1824, 'I did not certainly expect to see in my day. On the whole, our college seems at present to present an aspect something similar to that of the University of Oxford in the days of Hervey and Wesley.' For young men bored with Enlightenment rationalism and Moderate theology, Chalmers's Evangelical idealism offered exciting new possibilities. Many had already been stimulated by the Romantic movement in literature and the arts, and thus responded fervently to his pastoral rhapsodies on traditional peasant communities and to his stirring descriptions of the sacrifices and heroism of overseas missionaries. Chalmers's fame also attracted students of different denominations from throughout Britain and Ireland. 'Dr. Chalmers', Urquhart informed a friend on 18 February 1825, 'has effected a good deal by his own example and his own exertions; but he has even been more useful in drawing to this place a number of pious young men of various denominations, who have been the instruments of bringing about a great change in the externals, at least, of our University.'[58]

Not everyone was pleased with Chalmers's influence upon the university. Many professors felt that his emphasis upon emotional religion and practical ethics prompted both disrespect for the Enlightenment's intellectual traditions and overconfidence among the young. One of those displeased with Chalmers's influence was Robert Haldane, Principal of the St. Andrews Divinity Hall. In 1825, he later related to the Edinburgh Moderate clergyman John Lee, several of his students asked Haldane's permission to catechize among the labouring poor. At first, Haldane 'refused to give any sanction to the plan, because I conceived it to be one of Chalmers' vagaries with which he was turning the heads of our students'. Later, however, he reconsidered, and allowed his students to participate in the movement, but only in order that he might establish some authority over it. None the less, as he confided to Lee, 'I found the field occupied by persons over whom I had no such controul as I had over my own Students—Independents, Baptists, and a set of trash whom Chalmers had collected from England and Ireland.'[59]

Chalmers was not content merely to exercise influence over his students. He had, to be sure, brought an Evangelical style to his teaching at St. Andrews, and begun to inspire a group of future clergymen with Evangelical fervour. One of his students, Alexander Duff, later became the first overseas missionary representing the Church of Scotland; four other students also became overseas missionaries, and several more emerged as pastoral workers among the urban poor.[60] But Chalmers soon became convinced that St. Andrews University required more substantial reform. The university, he believed, had degenerated into a privileged corporation of professors, more concerned with their self-interest than with the educational needs of the nation. His experience in Glasgow had convinced him that Christianity was on the decline in Scotland, and that committed Christian clergymen and laity were desperately needed if the Christian commonwealth were to revive. In quiet St. Andrews, however, the professors seemed to have little concept of the pressing challenges of industrialization and urbanization. Shortly after his arrival, Chalmers began to advocate reforms designed to restore the university to the position of a truly national institution. His reform proposals involved, first, university patronage, and secondly, the administration of university revenues.

In 1817, it will be recalled, the General Assembly had abolished all pluralities in the Church of Scotland, except the union of a parish living and university chair when both offices were located within the same town. Chalmers, however, had refused to regard the issue as settled and had continued to agitate against this last remaining plurality. Shortly after his arrival in St. Andrews, his anti-plurality fervour brought him into conflict with Francis Nicoll, the man largely responsible for his appointment there. In the summer of 1824, Nicoll, who was overburdened by his plural office as both Principal of the United College at St. Andrews and minister of St. Leonards, the college chapel, requested the Crown to appoint James Hunter, St. Andrews Professor of Logic and Rhetoric, as Nicoll's assistant minister in the chapel. It seemed an innocent request. Hunter was the son of a highly respected St. Andrews professor of the George Hill era, and was himself popular among the faculty.

Hunter, however, intended to hold both his Logic professorship and chapel assistantship together as a plural appointment. Chalmers immediately protested against this proposed plurality, and began to organize opposition to Hunter's chapel assistantship in the St. Andrews presbytery. Further, he demanded that Nicoll also resign from the chapel living, and devote himself exclusively to his Principalship.[61] Nicoll was astonished and hurt. On 30 August 1824, he requested Chalmers, as a favour between friends, not to pursue his case against himself and Hunter in the Church courts, where both their reputations and that of the university might be damaged. He could not, he confided to Chalmers, resign the chapel without losing face. Chalmers, for his part, had proved his willingness to act upon his convictions, and might now discreetly allow the matter to drop. Besides, Nicoll added, university incomes were so small that pluralities were necessary.[62] Lord Elgin, whom Chalmers had asked to employ his influence with Melville against Nicoll's plurality, also advised him to forbear; on 4 September he warned Chalmers that Nicoll was popular with both Evangelicals and Moderates in the Church, as well as with the ascendant Tory party. If Chalmers insisted upon pursuing his case against Nicoll, Elgin added, he must 'not go beyond the boundaries of public and open warfare, or allow a suspicion to arise as if you were personally hostile to him'. After his conflicts in Glasgow, Chalmers could ill afford 'any overstepping the limits of the strictest propriety'.[63]

But Chalmers would not forbear. On 15 September, therefore, rather than submit to further pressure from Chalmers, Nicoll resigned from the chapel living. He did, however, also specifically request the Crown to appoint Hunter to the vacant chapel living in conjunction with his Logic professorship. Chalmers, in turn, continued his case against Hunter alone. He now insisted that Elgin transmit to Melville a letter he had composed condemning Hunter's candidature for the chapel, and lecturing Melville, who had administered St. Andrews University patronage for over twenty years, on the need to improve patronage by abolishing pluralities. 'Such is the declining state of our funds and buildings', Chalmers informed Melville in this letter, 'that there remains positively nothing to uphold our College but the superior style of its education and discipline.' Melville was not impressed, and returned the letter to Elgin. 'I cannot persuade myself', he informed Elgin on 24 October, 'that the presentation of Dr. Hunter to the parish of St. Leonard's (which I have recommended to Mr. Peel) is likely to be attended with the slightest detriment to the interests of the University of St. Andrews.' Further, he warned, if Chalmers and the St. Andrews presbytery attempted to block Hunter's appointment, 'it would be on their part a direct and manifest violation of the law'.[64] Chalmers now lost support in the presbytery, and on 12 May 1825 Hunter was admitted to the chapel living in conjunction with his university chair. But Chalmers still refused to relinquish his opposition to Hunter's plurality. It was mandatory at St. Andrews for all students belonging to the Church of Scotland to attend services at the college chapel. Following

Hunter's appointment to the chapel, however, a number of students protested against this rule and demanded the right to attend more Evangelical services elsewhere in town. Chalmers disclaimed any role in organizing this movement, but once it was under way he gave it his support. The affair was highly embarrassing for Hunter. The movement was eventually suppressed by the university authorities, though not without bitterness.[65]

In pursuing his anti-plurality principles, Chalmers's actions had been consistent with his long-standing resentment of privileged academic élites; but, although his behaviour had been honourable, he had also demonstrated disregard for the feelings of his colleagues. His behaviour towards Nicoll, whom Henry Cockburn later described as 'a plain, good-natured man, with the appearance and manner of a jolly Farmer, and an attractive air of candour and simplicity', was especially injudicious.[66] Chalmers had cause to focus attention upon patronage policies at St. Andrews. But in this provincial university, fellowship among the professors was also important, and Chalmers had now begun to place himself outside the pale. His relations with his colleagues grew still more strained when he began to demand reforms in the administration of university finances. Upon arriving in St. Andrews, he had become 'painfully' concerned over the 'Candlemass Dividend'.[67] This had first been instituted at St. Andrews in 1784, as a means of augmenting professorial salaries which had not been formally increased since 1779. Chalmers's portion of the Dividend would have averaged about £100 per annum, as compared to his regular annual income from his chair of about £270. But he refused to accept his portion. After requesting legal advice from the Whig lawyer James Moncrieff, son of the Evangelical leader Sir Henry Moncrieff Wellwood, Chalmers concluded that the professors had no right to the Candlemas appropriation. He was not personally entitled to a portion of the Dividend until the end of his first complete fiscal year at St. Andrews, in late December 1825.[68] On 4 December 1825, then, Chalmers announced at a faculty meeting that he would reject his portion of the Dividend, and that he might refer the whole matter to the Court of Session, or highest civil court in Scotland. His colleagues were furious. If the Court of Session decided in his favour, most professors would be deprived of nearly a third of their income, not to mention the humiliation of being declared to have illegally appropriated public funds. The professors united against him, and in late December Chalmers decided against immediate legal action, which Moncrieff had assured him would prove long and expensive. None the less, he continued to protest against the Candlemass Dividend', and to refuse to accept his share. His colleagues therefore allowed his portion to accumulate in a separate bank account.[69]

The 'Candlemass Dividend' affair furthered his estrangement from his colleagues. His desire to improve the university had been sincere, and his behaviour principled, particularly his refusal of his portion of the Dividend. A university, he argued, was a public institution, not a private business conducted by the professors for personal profit. Any surplus revenues should be invested in repairing the decaying buildings, or for the endowment of new university chairs. But from the professors' point of view, Chalmers was now threatening their standard of living as well as their reputations. Chalmers's diary conveys his increasing sense of alienation. 'Thronged with college and university meetings,' he noted on 14 January 1826; 'Can imagine a rising storm. O my God, may I quit myself like a man, and yet do all my things with charity.' 'College and university meetings,' he wrote on 11 February, 'Suffer not the triumph of wrong to disturb me away from the triumph of the gospel.' 'Two college meetings,' he recorded on 21 February; 'The whole previous time spent by me in great anxiety, and yet, as far as it has gone, I never felt so much the power of truth over a body unanimously against me.' 'In a state of depression all day,' he observed on 8 March, 'arising partly from fatigue, and partly from the feeling of the un-congenial atmosphere by which I am surrounded.'[70]

Throughout the spring, his relations with his colleagues grew more strained. Then, in the summer of 1826, he learned that the Govern-ment in London, alarmed by a bitter patronage dispute at Edinburgh University and by reports of questionable practices at other Scottish universities, had decided to appoint a Royal Commission of Inquiry to investigate the five Scottish universities, and to recommend improve-ments. Chalmers was elated over this development.[71] First, he believed, the Commission would serve as an arbitrator over his disputes with his colleagues, and spare him recourse to a prolonged legal conflict in the Court of Session. Secondly, he anticipated that the investigation would lead to proposals for comprehensive university reform in Scotland. His controversies in St. Andrews, he believed, reflected radical weaknesses in the entire Scottish university system, which for too long had been masked by the brilliant achievements of the eighteenth-century Scottish Enlightenment.

The formation of the Royal Commission did not ease tensions between Chalmers and the St. Andrews professors. On the contrary, as soon as the Commission was appointed, both Chalmers and his colleagues began assailing it with memorials, each side accusing the other of dishonesty or corruption. With the exception of one professor, his boyhood friend Thomas Duncan, Chalmers's alienation from his colleagues was complete. He was, he confided to Sir Henry Moncrieff Wellwood, a member of the Commission, on 13 October 1826, 'dis-gusted' with his colleagues, and 'resolved to give up all further co-operation [with them.]' None the less, he continued, their corruption was now so blatant, that 'there has devolved upon me a constant attendance at all their meetings, and I am more convinced every day of the need of looking after them'. Indeed, he added, he feared to leave St. Andrews, even for a short visit to Moncrieff's home, because he suspected the professors would use his absence as an opportunity for some new treachery.[72] The Commission, meanwhile, progressed slowly in its inquiry. Not until the summer of 1827 did it arrive at St. Andrews to receive oral evidence from the individual professors on the state of the university.

Chalmers was examined before the Commission for nearly five hours on 2 August 1827. The examiners attempted to direct the discussion away from his controversies with his colleagues, but Chalmers refused to be deprived of a 'constitutional vent' for his grievances, and he devoted most of his testimony to the 'Candlemass Dividend' and Hunter's plurality. 'When one is so thwarted as I have been,' he explained to the Commissioners, 'and with violence, too, to the first principles of equity, it is most disquieting.' The Dividend, he maintained, was depriving the university of capacity for expansion. Further, he had discovered that the university had on several instances borrowed from the principle of the endowment in order to meet extraordinary expenses, while at the same time the professors continued to appropriate 'surplus' revenue—so that in reality, he argued, the professors were appropriating from the endowment and slowly bleeding the university to death. But the Hunter plurality, he asserted, was even more dangerous. Injudicious patronage had awarded Hunter the income of both a church and chair, thus depriving the public of the full benefit of the two offices. Even worse, the university authorities had then forced students to attend Hunter's church services. This combination of unwise patronage and intolerance, he predicted, would create public contempt for the national religious Establishment. 'I think,' he maintained of the Hunter affair,

that what has happened these two years in the College of St. Andrews, exemplifies, in miniature, what happens in the country at large. When the policy is adopted of following up a high-handed patronage by a high-handed intolerance, I think that those two things united put us upon the high-road of bringing down that Establishment which we profess to idolize.[73]

He did not neglect other matters of university reform in his testimony. He proposed that additional courses be established at St. Andrews, especially in such practical fields as modern languages and pastoral care. In the teaching of moral philosophy, he suggested a shift in emphasis from epistemology to practical ethics. Most important, he advocated the establishment of mandatory entrance examinations at all Scottish universities, to ensure that matriculating students were

qualified for university study. In order to prepare students for these
entrance examinations, he proposed the creation of preparatory high
schools, or '*Gymnasiums*', in each university town, on the model of the
Prussian educational system. The *Gymnasium* would provide two years
of instruction in Latin, Greek, and mathematics. He admitted that
Gymnasium preparation might discourage some poor students from
university study, and thus act counter to Scotland's tradition of the
'democratic intellect'. However, he maintained, there were already
five times more divinity students in Scottish universities than there
were vacancies in the Church, and therefore concluded: 'We might
elevate the style of education, even though it should add very materially
to the length and to the expense of the Course.'[74]

Following his appearance before the Commission, Chalmers hurried
to completion a treatise on the national Establishments. Published in
late 1827, *On the Use and Abuse of Literary and Ecclesiastical Endowments*
represented further development of his oral testimony to the Commission.[75] The Establishment, he argued, possessed authority over the
moral education of the nation. The State might secure the nation from
foreign enemies, protect property, and collect taxes. But it was the
national religious Establishments of Scotland, England, and Ireland,
with their parish churches, their parish schools, and their universities,
which formed the national character, provided men with aspirations
worthy of sacrifice, and ensured that the ideal of the Christian commonwealth would be transmitted from generation to generation. Individuals, he maintained, had no natural inclination to sacrifice for the
ideals of Christian civilization, and would not adequately support
churches and universities if they were placed on a purely voluntary
basis. Thus, it was incumbent upon the State to protect the endowments
of the Establishments. It was, moreover, the responsibility of the
Establishments to ensure that their endowments were effectively
administered, and that their patronage ensured the appointment of
qualified and committed spiritual and moral instructors. This, he
asserted, was crucial in the present 'age of reform', when many in
Britain were beginning to challenge the sanctity of national Establishments, and to advocate appropriating portions of their endowments for
secular purposes. Were the Establishments to fall, he warned, either
as the result of internal corruption or external attacks from radical
reformers, the highest national aspirations would be lost. Higher learning
would wither, 'and in all the prouder and nobler walks of discovery, we
must consent to be outrun in glory by other nations'. Vital Christianity,
while it might survive in small isolated sects, would no longer reach the
'vast majority' who would 'be left in a state of practical heathenism'.[76]
He concluded by expressing confidence that the Scottish University
Commission would make effective recommendations for reform.[77]

The Commission continued to progress slowly through its enquiries, and not until 1831 did it publish its report. It was a thorough and judicious document, with proposals for significant reforms in university patronage, teaching, and administration. Although the Commission declined to recommend Chalmers's proposals for entrance examinations and *Gymnasiums*, it did agree with him on the two major themes of his St. Andrews controversies—first, that all pluralities should be abolished, and secondly, that the 'Candlemass Dividend' was an illegal appropriation. In spite of this, Chalmers was enraged by the report. For although it condemned pluralities and the 'Candlemass Dividend' at St. Andrews, the Commission's report had neglected to mention Chalmers's active opposition to these practices; rather, it made it appear as though he had participated equally with his colleagues. In 1829, to be sure, he had accepted his portion of the Dividend, but only after the Commission had assured him, in a preliminary judgement, that the practice was legal. Now he became convinced that the Commission had tricked him into complicity with the St. Andrews professors. Early in 1832, he assailed the Commission with a pamphlet of bitter invective, providing the public with the details of his conflicts in St. Andrews and accusing the Commission of dishonesty.[78] It was a violent release of years of anger and frustration.

On the whole, Chalmers's return to St. Andrews had proved a bitter disappointment. He had hoped to rediscover a sense of belonging in the 'much loved' university community, rich in memories of his youth. It was to have been his homecoming, a quiet 'Literary retirement' for his final years. Instead, he found himself in prolonged conflict with the professors, alienated from their community, an unwelcome outsider. His return, moreover, was associated with other unhappy experiences, which crystallized his sense of alienation from northern Fife. Old friends had been altered by the years, or had died. The beautiful Anne Rankine, whom he had loved passionately in the days before his Evangelical conversion, now lay buried, her infant child at her side, in quiet Kilrenny churchyard, a few miles outside St. Andrews. He made repeated visits to her grave.[79] On 14 February 1827 his mother died at the age of seventy-seven. He and his wife had tried to convince her for the last few years to move in with them at St. Andrews, but without success. 'She cleaves to Anster [Anstruther],' he had written his sister Jane in despair the previous year, 'and will not leave it.' With her death, family ties to Anstruther were severed. 'The ·Chalmerses', he wrote Jane on 14 February 1827, 'have ... been ninety years in Anstruther, and after the death of my aunt Jane [who died a few months later] there is no further prospect of our being connected with the place.'

The remaining family property in Anstruther had been inherited by

James, the eldest brother, who lived in London and who had no intention of travelling north to oversee the disposal of the remnants of his grandfather's fortune.[80] The final arrangements, then, were left to Thomas. Rummaging through his mother's papers after her death, Chalmers discovered her charity book, in which she kept a detailed account of her distributions to the Anstruther poor. He was moved to discover that, despite her own poverty, she had continued her distributions until shortly before her death. 'I prize it', he confided to Jane of the book on 24 February, 'as the best of legacies, and should like to prosecute her Anster benefactions. There is one half of the book blank, and I mean to begin where she ended. I feel a tender and melancholy pleasure in doing so.' A few weeks later, he made a round among the eighteen families in her book, and 'left with each of them a trifle for her sake.' The family house, meanwhile, still stood. 'I like to recall,' he wrote Jane on 17 April 1827, 'the associations of former years by taking an occasional night in it.' Nonetheless, he informed James, it was 'going fast to wreck'.[81] James elected to sell the house, and it was later demolished. After distributing his 'trifle' to the Anstruther poor, moreover, Thomas took no further account of Elizabeth Chalmers's charity book. The Chalmers family had passed from Anstruther.

By early 1827, Chalmers's conflict with the St. Andrews professors and his unhappiness at St. Andrews had become known throughout Britain. On 26 February 1827, less than two weeks after his mother's death, Chalmers received a letter from F. A. Coxe, Secretary to the Council of the University of London, exploring the possibility of his accepting their Chair of Moral Philosophy. Founded in 1825 by an alliance of Whigs, Dissenters, and Benthamite radicals, London University was intended to provide inexpensive, utilitarian, and nonsectarian higher education. Although actual construction of the buildings had not yet begun, and classes were not scheduled to commence until 1828, the Council had begun to seek professors who would bring prestige to the new institution. Surprisingly, Chalmers expressed interest in the position, which would not only require his departure from Scotland, but would also terminate his role as an educator in the Church of Scotland. His alienation from Scotland, it seemed, was now almost complete. On 28 February, he replied to Coxe with a lengthy letter, describing the themes of his Moral Philosophy lectures, and asking specific questions regarding the length of the London term, the nature of instruction, the size of the salary, and the possibility of his offering extramural lectures in theology. His final decision, he explained to Coxe, would depend upon the judgement of the Scottish University Commission regarding his St. Andrews controversies, which he incorrectly expected would be made shortly. 'They may', he observed, in reference to the Commission's impending report on the Scottish

Establishment, 'place it on a footing so good that very few situations indeed could tempt me from the office of a Scotch professor; or they may place it on a footing so bad that I should be glad to make my escape into another situation.'[82]

A few months later, in early May 1827, Chalmers travelled to London, in part to deliver a sermon at the opening of a new church built for his former Glasgow assistant, Edward Irving, but more importantly to investigate further the London University offer. On 8 May, he had a long interview with Coxe, who pressed him for immediate acceptance of the chair. Henry Brougham and Zachary Macaulay, both actively involved in the founding of London University, also met him. The Whig Evangelical Macaulay was especially zealous, believing that Chalmers's appointment would add a Christian dimension to the new university. But, understanding from Coxe that classes would not begin until the autumn of 1828, Chalmers demurred, requesting additional time to consider. He left London on 19 May, without having made a formal decision, although it was widely rumoured that he had accepted the London chair.[83]

Throughout the summer, his London friends pressed him for a formal declaration. Brougham, moreover, exercised his influence to secure a position as London University librarian for Chalmers's brother Charles, who in the previous April had relinquished his partnership with Collins in Glasgow, and now wished to accompany Thomas to London.[84] On 25 August 1827, following the University Commission's visitation in St. Andrews, Macaulay again wrote to him, urgently requesting a declaration of acceptance—first, because of 'the positive and extensive good I should anticipate under the divine blessing from your appointment', secondly, to ensure against the appointment of a 'latitudinarian' to the chair, and thirdly, to increase civic support for the university. 'Your name', Macaulay added, 'would I think put an end to competition and unite all taxpayers.' Chalmers, however, continued to hesitate. In early September, he asked Macaulay to convey to the Council his request that he now be given until December to make up his mind. Macaulay, growing impatient, informed him on 13 September that they would keep the position open until December, but reminded him that there were other candidates, including the Whig MP, Sir James Mackintosh, and the celebrated Evangelical preacher, Robert Hall.[85]

In fact, Chalmers had turned his attention towards another position. For several years, William Ritchie, the seventy-nine-year-old Professor of Divinity at Edinburgh University, had been too infirm to fulfil his teaching responsibilities. However, Ritchie could not be deprived of his income as long as he lived, and the Edinburgh Town Council was loath to appoint another professor to fulfil his duties, as this would mean paying a double salary for the same office. So instead, several Edinburgh clergy took turns reading Ritchie's lectures to his classes. Since 1824, Chalmers's friends had entertained the hope that when Ritchie finally died, he would receive the Edinburgh Divinity chair.[86] He made no secret of his interest in the chair. But Ritchie showed no sign of accommodating Chalmers's friends. Now, with Chalmers apparently soon to accept the London chair, his friends began placing additional pressure upon the Edinburgh Town Council. 'We have been told', the Edinburgh Whig, Lachlan Maclaurin, wrote to Chalmers on 8 August 1827, in reference to the London Whigs, 'that they count you in the London University. ... We are also told they want you here. The provost elect and his council will be glad if an opportunity offers to effect that.'[87] In order to understand the Edinburgh Town Council's desire to acquire Chalmers's services for Edinburgh University, despite his bitter controversies in St. Andrews, it must be noted that Chalmers had not been exclusively engaged in his St. Andrews duties between 1824 and 1827. Throughout these years, he continued to preach occasional sermons in Edinburgh. He remained the unrivalled master of Scottish pulpit oratory, inspiring the Edinburgh professional classes with his impassioned Evangelicalism. Perhaps more important, he had also managed to reassert a position of leadership within the General Assembly of the Church of Scotland.

III

Chalmers's renewed influence within the General Assembly resulted largely from the revival of the plurality issue. Between 1813 and 1817, it will be recalled, he had first established his reputation in the Church courts by his role in the plurality controversy which had followed William Ferrie's plural appointment to the St. Andrews Chair of Civil History and the rural parish of Kilconquhar. This controversy had culminated in the plurality act of 1817, the first major defeat of the Moderate party in the Church courts in over thirty years, and a sign of the rising power of Evangelicalism. For several years after their 1817 defeat, the Moderates did not attempt another plural presentation, even within the legal guidelines of the 1817 act.

Then in mid-1823, encouraged by the division among the Glasgow Evangelicals over Chalmers's St. John's programmes, the Glasgow Moderates, assisted by the Tory civic government, finally exercised their right. On 11 June 1823, the Moderate Duncan Macfarlane, the recently appointed Principal of Glasgow College, was also presented by the Town Council to the Inner High Church of Glasgow, despite his avowed intention to hold both offices as a plural appointment. The Moderates, however, had overestimated the extent of the Evangelical divisions. Despite their differences over poor relief, Chalmers, who had at this time not yet left Glasgow, immediately joined with Stevenson Macgill, the Glasgow Professor of Divinity, to oppose Macfarlane's plural appointment. In the autumn of 1823, the Evangelicals managed to convince both the presbytery of Glasgow and the synod of Glasgow and Ayr that, regardless of the 1817 act, no individual was capable of fulfilling the duties of both a university principalship and an urban parish, and that therefore Principal Macfarlane was unqualified for the presentation to the parish church.[88] The Moderates appealed the case to the 1824 General Assembly. There, despite Chalmers's eloquence in defending the Evangelical position, the Evangelicals were defeated by a vote of 185 to 80, and Macfarlane received the plural appointment.[89] None the less, Chalmers had impressed the Assembly with his power in debate. 'I was delighted', the Evangelical Henry Duncan informed Chalmers on 31 May 1824, at the close of the Assembly, 'to see you take so active a share in its deliberations. Much good may be done by you in this department ... and I hope you will not shrink from taking a lead.'[90]

Chalmers had attended the 1824 Assembly as a ruling elder representing the royal burgh of Anstruther Easter. This was a 'safe' seat, which he held each year from 1824 to 1828, or until the Chalmers family connection with Anstruther was finally terminated.[91] During these years, he combined his reform efforts at St. Andrews University with a vigorous campaign in the General Assembly to abolish all remaining pluralities within the Scottish Establishment. In the Assembly of 1825, he introduced an 'overture' (a motion for a new act of Church law) to end all plural appointments. After a lengthy debate, however, the Moderates defeated his overture by a vote of 144 to 118. The following year, Chalmers reintroduced it. Again, he was defeated, this time by a more substantial vote of 159 to 105. Undaunted, he introduced his overture yet a third time in the 1827 Assembly. By a previous agreement between the parties, however, debate was limited, and a compromise motion was adopted, which postponed further discussion on the question until the Royal Commission on Scottish Universities had made a decision on pluralities.[92] In early 1828, a few years before the publication of its final report, the Commission made a preliminary decision against pluralities. This effectively ended the practice in the Scottish Establishment.[93]

Notwithstanding his repeated disappointments over the Assembly votes, the plurality debates had revived Chalmers's influence within the Church courts. Largely through his efforts, pluralities had become the central issue in the Church in the mid-1820s. He had taken up the battle where it had been left off in 1817, before he had immersed himself in the poor-law question, and made it a cause around which to rally the Evangelical party. The plurality issue, he maintained, was fundamental to the mission of the national religious Establishment. Both the parish ministry and the university chair were vocations demanding the full commitment of the incumbents. Pluralists compromised the integrity of their offices, deprived individual souls of the vehicles of divine grace, and encouraged public contempt for the national Establishment. Only when ministers and teachers overcame their self-interest and ambition would the ideal of the godly commonwealth be realized.[94]

Chalmers reached new heights of oratorical power during the plurality debates of the 1820s. The issue touched a fundamental tension in his life—that between individual ambition and communal service. In condemning the pluralist's sin, it was difficult to avoid reviewing his own continuing struggle to subordinate ambition to social responsibility. Raw nerves were touched, old wounds reopened. Perhaps the most dramatic moment in the Assembly's plurality debates occurred on 25 May 1825. Late that evening, after nearly twelve hours of debate on Chalmers's anti-plurality overture, an opponent rose and read to the Assembly selections from Chalmers's early pamphlet, *Observations on a Passage in Mr. Playfair's Letter*, published in 1805. In this work, it will be recalled, the young Chalmers had passionately defended pluralities as vital to the intellectual development of the nation, while he had denigrated the duties of the parish ministry. Ambition for academic fame as a mathematician, he had argued, did not interfere with a clergyman's responsibility to the Church. This was, the opponent now exclaimed, indeed an illuminating document. Obviously, he explained, Chalmers had experienced no difficulties with pluralities when he thought he might derive personal benefit from the practice. But although Chalmers now opposed pluralities, had his basic motivations in fact changed? Was he not still pursuing personal benefit, in the form of influence within the Assembly? Was he not using the plurality issue for his own personal ends?

Chalmers immediately demanded the right to respond. He had, however, already spoken twice in the debate, the maximum allowed by the Assembly rules, and the Moderates declared him out of order. By now the hall was in an uproar. Chalmers remained on his feet and amid cries to silence him, he began to reveal the circumstances which had led him to compose the pamphlet. With deep feeling, he confessed his youthful arrogance and ambition for fame as a mathematician. Soon the hall grew silent; the Assembly listened 'with breathless attention'. 'Alas Sir,' he concluded his confession,

so I thought in my ignorance and pride. I have now no reserve in saying that the sentiment was wrong, and that, in the utterance of it, I penned what was most outrageously wrong. Strangely blinded that I was! What, Sir, is the object of mathematical science?

Magnitude and the proportions of magnitude. But then, Sir, I had forgotten two
magnitudes—I thought not of the littleness of time—I recklessly thought not of the
greatness of eternity!

The Assembly broke into long and enthusiastic applause; the challenge
to his integrity was disarmed by eloquence. In truth, he had not only
preserved his reputation, but had actually enhanced it. Whatever his
personal weaknesses, Chalmers retained the power to move audiences
with his oratory.[95] At the same time, his anti-plurality speeches also
helped to focus increased public attention upon the Assembly debates.
'Our little world of Scotland', the Whig *Scotsman* observed on 27 May
1826, in reference to Chalmers's anti-plurality campaign in the following year, '... is almost exclusively occupied with the proceedings of
our General Assembly; and much of the interest of those proceedings
has resulted from the genius and eloquence of one individual.'[96]

Chalmers's influence within the General Assembly, then, ensured
that serious attempts would be made to thwart his threatened move to
London University, and keep him in Scotland. On 9 August 1827, Sir
Henry Moncrieff Wellwood, the leader of the Evangelical party for
over twenty years, died at the age of seventy-seven. The patronage of
his now vacant St. Cuthbert's church in Edinburgh belonged to the
Crown, and on 25 September 1827, after consulting with leaders of
Scottish public opinion, the Home Secretary, Lord Lansdowne,
offered Chalmers the presentation. This was one of the most important
church livings in Scotland, and it would have represented a high
honour to succeed Moncrieff Wellwood. Chalmers, however, declined
the presentation, informing Lansdowne that he had no intention of
ever returning to the parish ministry.[97] In short, if he were not offered
a university appointment in Edinburgh, he would accept the London
chair. Then on 17 October, the Edinburgh Town Council finally
decided to pay a second salary for the Edinburgh Divinity chair. Ritchie
now resigned the chair (retaining his full salary), and the Town Council
began the search for his replacement. '*Of course*,' Robert Paul, a
prominent Edinburgh banker, informed Chalmers on 18 October,
'*with the public*, you are to be the new Professor!'[98]

Following Moncrieff Wellwood's death, the leadership of the Evangelical party had passed to Andrew Thomson. On 22 October, Thomson
wrote to Chalmers to invite his candidature for the chair. None the
less, Thomson added, there would be difficulties involved in his candidature, of which he should be aware. First, the endowment of the
chair was small, yielding only £196 per annum. Previously this had
not mattered too much, because the chair had been combined with
an Edinburgh church living. Ritchie, for example, combined his
university income with the Edinburgh parish of St. Giles. But in
Chalmers's case a plural appointment was clearly out of the question.

Because the Edinburgh Town Council, moreover, was now committed to pay a double salary for the chair, it was difficult to say when, if ever, the income would be augmented. Secondly, there was considerable opposition to Chalmers's candidature among the Edinburgh clergy. Although no one doubted his talent, some did question his Calvinist orthodoxy. 'I find', Thomson explained, 'that your notions about *systematic* divinity are brought forward.' As a preacher, Chalmers had never demonstrated much deference to scholastic Calvinism. His efforts on behalf of Catholic emancipation, particularly his 1818 Hibernian Society sermon, raised additional questions. Even Thomson confessed to having some doubts. Chalmers's chances for the appointment, Thomson concluded, would be improved if he could provide Thomson with a written statement of his faith in the Calvinist system, 'which I can show to others'.[99]

Chalmers was annoyed by Thomson's request and almost resolved not to respond. 'I am far from questioning the friendship of Dr. Thomson,' he confided to Robert Paul on 23 October, immediately upon receiving Thomson's letter, 'but between ourselves I do not feel great confidence in his delicacy.' None the less, recognizing Thomson's leadership within the party, Chalmers wrote to him on 24 October, declining to provide a written confession of faith, but assuring him that he would teach theology 'systematically'.[100] On 31 October, the Town Council unanimously elected Chalmers to the Edinburgh Divinity chair. The same day, the Edinburgh clergy signified their approval. 'The thing', Paul informed him immediately after the election, 'has been well done, and is one of the most popular acts that ever passed the Town Council.' Much of the credit for this, in fact, belonged to Thomson. Despite his own uncertainty about Chalmers's Calvinism, Thomson had laboured to overcome the doubts of the Edinburgh clergy and to secure their approval for his appointment.[101]

Chalmers accepted the appointment in early November. The Edinburgh University term had already begun, and he was therefore allowed another year in which to prepare his lectures. During this time he remained in his position at St. Andrews, while Ritchie's friend, the Moderate Edinburgh clergyman John Lee, conducted the Edinburgh divinity class. For Chalmers, a pressing problem remained the meagre salary of the Edinburgh chair, which was over £80 less than that of his St. Andrews chair. His private income, he complained to Paul, amounted to only £200 per annum, and he was concerned about whether he could afford the higher cost of living in Edinburgh. He now had quite a large family, with six daughters, and he feared he would be hard pressed to maintain a style of life corresponding to his national prominence. Thomson wrote to his friend Henry Brougham, attempting to interest the Parliamentary Whigs in Chalmers's plight.

Chalmers and the Town Council also considered instituting special fees for the divinity lectures, though such fees had never been required for such lectures at any Scottish university, and would no doubt be opposed by the clergy.[102]

The question of the income had not been resolved when, in late October 1828, Chalmers and his family moved to Edinburgh. On 10 November, he delivered his inaugural lecture at the university. Despite showers of snow and sleet, a large crowd began gathering at nine in the morning in the Old College courtyard for his eleven o'clock lecture. Admission was by ticket only, and a body of police had to be summoned to guard the entrance. 'It was a day,' the young divinity student William Bruce Cunningham later recalled, 'as you will easily believe, of no common expectation and excitement. ... If I may judge of other minds from the state of my own, I may safely state, that at no time, either before or since, has a tumult of emotions so peculiar and intense, agitated the hearts of the many who waited for his first appearance in the chair of theology.'[103] Chalmers's move to Edinburgh was a significant event. He had declined the London University Chair of Moral Philosophy and committed himself to a career in the Scottish Establishment. He had moved to the ecclesiastical and political centre of the Scottish nation, where the Chair of Divinity at Edinburgh University promised him a base of influence within both the Scottish universities and Established Church. For many years, the Edinburgh Divinity chair had been a neglected office, held by an infirm incumbent: Chalmers, however, recognized its potential importance; it would be a 'fulcrum' upon which he would move the Christian nation.

He soon exercised this influence in the campaign for Roman Catholic emancipation in Britain, which was renewed in early 1827 following the resignation of Lord Liverpool, a committed anti-emancipationist, from the leadership of the Government. The office of prime minister now went to the liberal Tory George Canning, long a proponent of emancipation. The campaign for Catholic emancipation in Ireland, led by the great Irish national agitator, Daniel O'Connell, combined with more liberal attitudes among the educated public in England, encouraged Whigs and liberal Tories to press the new Canning Government for the final removal of all remaining legal disabilities under which Catholics had for so long suffered. Chalmers, it will be recalled, had long been committed to emancipation. Now, with the renewed public agitation for emancipation, he delivered two sermons supporting the cause, both of which he subsequently published.

In the first of these, delivered at the opening of Edward Irving's new church in London on 11 May 1827, he asserted that the Protestant faith had nothing to fear from Catholic emancipation.[104] On the contrary, Protestantism would actually benefit from a more liberal climate of opinion in Britain. The great achievement of the Protestant Reformation, he maintained, had been to elevate the concept of individual freedom of conscience above the authoritative structures of the medieval Church. Protestantism's great failure, however, had come after it had defeated Roman bigotry—for it had then turned upon Catholics with equal bigotry. 'After having wrested from Popery its armour of intolerance,' he asked, 'was it right to wield that very armour against the enemy that had fallen? After having laid it prostrate by the use alone of a spiritual weapon, was it right or necessary, in order to keep it prostrate, to make use of a carnal one?' British Protestantism, he concluded, now had the opportunity to correct its historic error.[105]

A few months later, during his first visit to Ireland in late September 1827, Chalmers delivered his second pro-emancipation sermon at the opening of a Presbyterian church in Belfast.[106] In this sermon, he directed his remarks to the political unrest in Ireland. Roman Catholicism, he assured his Irish Protestant listeners, was a grievous error. None the less, the penal laws directed against Catholics had served not to suppress this error, but only to antagonize Irish Catholics; Protestant intolerance was creating a distinct Irish Catholic nation, which was becoming impervious to Protestant influence. 'The glories of martyrdom', he exclaimed,

have been transferred from the right to the wrong side of the question; and superstition, which, in a land of perfect light and perfect liberty, would hide her head as ashamed, gathers a title to respect, and stands forth in a character of moral heroism, because of the injustice which has been brought to bear upon her. ... [W]e must recall the impolicy by which we have turned a whole people into a nation of outcasts.[107]

Early in May 1828, Parliament repealed the Test and Corporation Acts, penal statutes which had been directed against Protestant Dissenters in England and Wales. Although these acts had not been enforced for years, their existence in the statute books had represented a grievance for Dissenters and a symbol of religious intolerance. More important, the repeal served as a precedent for Catholic emancipation. For if Dissenters could be granted full political rights, it meant that the British State might also admit Catholics into the political constitution without further sacrifice of principle.

In the eighteenth century, the Test and Corporation Acts had also constituted a grievance for members of the Church of Scotland, who were subject to penal restrictions when they travelled south of the border. None the less, during the early months of 1828, leaders of both parties in the Church of Scotland had avoided making any statement concerning these acts, not because they did not sympathize with the demands of Protestant Dissenters, but rather because they did not wish to embarrass the Church of England or encourage the cause of Catholic emancipation. Chalmers, however, would not allow the General Assembly to ignore the subject, despite pleas from other Church leaders that he remain silent. On 24 May, the first day of the 1828 General Assembly, he moved that the Assembly express to the Crown its 'high-satisfaction' over the recent repeal of the Test and Corporation Acts. These acts, he asserted, had been a 'stigma' upon the Church of England—an 'unnecessary security' which had only reduced her in the public estimation. Full toleration of all religious persuasions, he maintained, would strengthen the national religious Establishments, placing them once more upon the side of individual freedom of conscience, which had represented the true achievement of the Reformation.

Despite his eloquent appeal, his motion was defeated by a vote of 123 to 77;[108] nevertheless, his Assembly speech, combined with his two earlier published sermons on toleration, established Chalmers as perhaps the leading champion of liberal Evangelicalism in Scotland. The Scottish Whigs were especially pleased by his efforts. Many leading Evangelicals strongly opposed Catholic emancipation, and this, in turn, was creating tensions in the long-standing Whig-Evangelical alliance in Scotland. Chalmers, however, was Evangelical without the intolerance which too often flawed the devout. The Whig *Scotsman* newspaper, though long one of his severest critics, now praised his 'liberal and truly Christian spirit'. His efforts, the *Scotsman* observed on 28 May 1828, in reference to his motion on the Test and Corporation Acts, promised to recover the 'mental integrity' of Scottish Protestantism, and to revive the Reformation as a movement for freedom of conscience and human dignity.[109]

Following the repeal of the Test and Corporation Acts, the agitation for Catholic emancipation increased. Canning had died in August 1827, and a few months later a more conservative Tory Government had been formed under the leadership of the Duke of Wellington, a committed anti-emancipationist. However, even Wellington eventually became convinced that emancipation was a practical necessity for peace in Ireland, and on 5 February 1829 the Government announced that it would shortly introduce a motion for the abolition of the penal laws.

But in the weeks that followed, it grew apparent that, despite the agitation for toleration, Catholic emancipation was in fact still opposed by the majority of the British population. Long-standing anti-Catholic prejudice was combined with more rational arguments that Catholics, as subjects of the temporal power of the Papacy, could not be trusted with full British citizenship. In Scotland, the Government's announcement inspired intense popular opposition, especially in the South-west and north, where covenanting traditions remained strong.[110] There was a minor anti-Catholic riot in Glasgow, and public meetings and demonstrations occurred in most districts in the country. 'The extraordinary sensation', the anti-emancipationist Tory *Glasgow Courier* observed on 12 February, in reference to the national reaction to the Government's announcement, 'increases with every passing hour. Doubt increases. Fear spreads.' Within three weeks of the announcement, dozens of anti-emancipation petitions had been sent to London from Scottish parishes, towns, counties, and Church presbyteries and synods.[111]

Popular opposition to emancipation now threatened to pressure the Government into dropping the proposed bill. Recognizing this danger, Parliamentary Whigs began to organize counter-demonstrations in support of emancipation throughout the country. On 27 February, the influential Whig MP Sir James Mackintosh requested Chalmers's assistance. 'I have,' Mackintosh wrote,

always understood your opinion to be favourable to the abolition of all civil disabilities for religion. If you retain that opinion, it now stands in utmost need of your patronage. Popular frenzy, which may, perhaps, revive court intrigue, is at work to dispel a union of all statesmen, certainly produced only by a sense of public necessity. One of the unfortunate circumstances of this clamour is, that it professes to arise from religion, and, I am very sorry to say, does often arise from men who are truly religious.

'Of the mode of making your weighty opinion known', Mackintosh added, 'you are best qualified to decide; I can only say, that delay may lessen its efficacy.' On 2 March, Chalmers promised Mackintosh his support. Until now, he observed, there had been no agitation on the question in Edinburgh. 'All the emancipationists ... whom I have met with, think it better to remain quiet, unless provoked to bestir themselves by any demonstrations of principle on the other side of the question'. None the less, he added, 'should there be a public meeting [in Edinburgh] on the side of emancipation, I shall hold it my duty to attend and give my testimony in its favour.'[112] In fact, Chalmers and the Edinburgh Whigs were already contemplating such a meeting, in response to an anti-emancipation meeting proposed by what Henry Cockburn termed a 'Holy Alliance' of several Evangelical clergymen and Tory politicians. 'If they call it,' Cockburn informed T. F. Kennedy on 2 March, in reference to the possible anti-emancipation meeting, 'there will be a counter one, where Chalmers has engaged to speak, and for which he has already prepared a petition.' A few days later, the 'Holy Alliance' held their meeting, and began collecting signatures for an anti-emancipation petition.[113] Thus 'provoked', the Edinburgh Whigs held their public meeting on 14 March.

Despite inclement weather and a shilling admission fee, the Whig affair was, to that date, the largest indoor meeting ever held in Scotland, with an estimated crowd of 2,000 packed into the Edinburgh Assembly Hall. More than simply an expression of pro-emancipation sentiment, the meeting was a demonstration of the increasing influence of Scottish Liberalism. The meeting began at noon, and for the next four hours, the crowd was addressed by the great talents of the Scottish Whig party, including Henry Cockburn, James Moncrieff, and Francis Jeffrey. The afternoon progressed, and the hall darkened. The crowd, pressed closely together in the poorly ventilated hall, grew restless. James Dodds, a seventeen-year-old university student, squeezed uncomfortably in the crowd in the rear of a gallery, unable to sit down or even see the speakers platform, felt a growing numbness in his limbs, and wondered only when the meeting would finally close. Suddenly, he later recalled, he felt a surge of excitement pass through the crowd: 'First, there was a hush, as if breath and movement had suddenly stopped; then people started to their feet; then there was a shout, a long piercing shout, as of passionate triumph; which made my young temples throb, and—''Chalmers! Chalmers!'' was on every tongue.'[114]

Many would later recall this speech as Chalmers's greatest oratorical moment. With intense passion, he described his position of religious toleration. The policy of depriving Catholics of their political rights, he again asserted, served only to consolidate the Irish Catholic nation and render it hostile to the British State. 'It has', he observed of the penal policy, '... been met by the unyielding defiance of a people irritated but not crushed, under a sense of indignity; and this notable expedient for keeping down the Popery of Ireland has only compressed it into a firmness, and closed it into phalanx, which, till opened up by emancipation, we shall find to be impenetrable.' The penal laws, moreover, had weakened Protestantism, encouraging it to rely upon political force, rather than spiritual truth, and thus thwarting its Evangelical mission. 'It is since the admission of intolerance, that unseemly associate, within our camp, that the cause of the Reformation has come down from its vantage ground; and ... from that moment it has been at a dead stand.' The moment had arrived, he concluded, for the Protestant faith to throw off the shackles of intolerance. The time had come to recognize that its power lay, not in political force, but in the Word of God. Only this, he assured his listeners, would revive the Reformation as a vital spiritual force; the Bible alone would penetrate the Irish Catholic nation. 'Give the Catholics of Ireland', he exclaimed,

their emancipation; give them a seat in the Parliament of their country; give them a free and equal participation in the politics of the realm; give them a place at the right ear of majesty, and a voice in his counsels; and give me the circulation of the Bible, and with this mighty engine I will overthrow the tyranny of Antichrist, and establish the fair and original form of Christianity on its ruins.[115]

His oratory moved his audience as perhaps never before in his career. For those present, the effect transcended words. 'I felt,' young James Dodds later recalled,

as I never felt before, and never again under any man. It was not mere argument that swayed me; it was not mere eloquence that roused me; it was something indescribable. I felt as if carried away, not by any human power, but by some great force of nature. It was not the youthful bosom only that was agitated.... the whole assembly were catching the inspiration of the master; a strange afflatus filled the hall. Peal after peal, becoming almost ceaseless, not of applause—the word is too cold, but where is the word sufficiently glowing?[116]

'No more powerful emotion was ever produced by words', Cockburn later observed, 'than the close of Chalmers's address. Brilliant and glowing as his written pages are, they are cold and dull compared with his spoken intensity. The rough broken voice,—the ungainly form—the awkward gesture,—the broad dingy face,—gave little indication of what was beneath. But the capacious brow!—and the soul!—*mens agitat molem*!'[117]

Two weeks later, at a meeting of the Edinburgh presbytery on 1 April, Chalmers delivered a less emotional speech advocating emancipation. To the presbytery, he emphasized political theory, as he developed it from Scripture. Christ, he argued, had not ordained the State as a spiritual institution, nor had he given it authority to enforce religious beliefs. On the contrary, he had established temporal government long before he had entered the world to found the Church, and then had instructed his Church to obey the laws even of the irreligious ruler. Thus, Chalmers argued, there was no theological justification for penal laws directed against Catholics, nor any reason why the State should not extend constitutional rights to all citizens regardless of religious persuasion, so long as it did not directly threaten the endowments and mission of the national religious Establishment. The Establishment, he further argued, was independent of the State. The Church of Scotland had been created and endowed by the Scottish nation, to provide the commonwealth with a Christian purpose. The combination of these two separate institutions—a tolerant State to protect property and administer impartial secular justice, and an aggressive national Establishment to inspire the nation with a common Christian purpose—formed what Chalmers regarded as 'the perfection of an ecclesiastical system in every land'.[118]

On 10 April the Catholic emancipation bill passed its third reading in the House of Lords, and on 13 April, it received the king's signature. Roman Catholics were now eligible for election to Parliament, and for any administrative or judicial appointment. In Scotland, the new act was associated closely with Chalmers; he emerged as a symbol of the spirit of religious toleration. This new role was a controversial one. For many Evangelicals, especially in the west and north, his advocacy of Catholic emancipation had been a great betrayal. Peter Stuart, one of the Highland Evangelical 'Men', or lay catechists, bitterly mocked Chalmers's role at the great Edinburgh Assembly Hall meeting:

> And there with Chalmers as their mouth
> They set on foot a court,
> A man of rotten savour, worse
> Than any of his sort
> Beneath the sun, whose belly burst
> With pride and self within;
> He led the boobies to believe
> He'd heal the Man of Sin.

For many others in Scotland, however, Chalmers had emerged as 'the most redoubted Champion of Evangelical Liberalism'.[119] He had, it seemed, assumed a leading role in the two great movements of early nineteenth-century Britain—the Evangelical revival and the rise of political liberalism. His connection with the Scottish Whigs had never appeared closer; indeed, his appearance on the speakers platform at the Edinburgh Assembly Hall meeting seemed to signify his entrance into the inner circle of the Scottish Whig party.

In truth, however, Chalmers's Whig connection was more tenuous than these appearances suggest. Despite their co-operation on such specific issues as Catholic emancipation, there was a radical difference between their larger social views. His ideal of the godly commonwealth was in fact fundamentally opposed to Whig faith in economic individualism and industrial expansion. As the Whigs advanced along the path to political power in the British State, these differences soon became increasingly evident, and Chalmers's dual role in the Evangelical revival and Scottish Whiggism more and more difficult to maintain.

IV

The passing of the Catholic Emancipation Act marked the beginning of nearly a decade of liberal reform in Britain. Wellington's Tory Government experienced increasing pressure from a loose coalition of Whigs, Radicals, independents, and ultra-Tories. One urgent matter, which received renewed attention following the debate over Catholic emancipation, was the poverty and social unrest in Ireland. Late in the winter of 1830, several months after the passing of Catholic emancipation, Thomas Spring Rice (1790-1866), the Whig MP for the Irish borough of Limerick and the leading Whig expert on Irish affairs, obtained the appointment of a select committee of the House of Commons to investigate the condition of the Irish poor and to consider remedies for their distress.[120] Ireland had no system of poor laws, and this was to be a main subject of the enquiry. On 26 March 1830, Spring Rice, who had also been appointed chairman of the select committee, requested Chalmers to testify before the committee in London. 'Many members of Parliament', he informed him, 'recommend the introduction into Ireland of the English system of Poor-Laws; others suggest a modification of that system; the practice of Scotland is referred to by a third class. On all these points, but more particularly with respect to your experience in North Britain, your evidence would be of the most extreme value and importance.' Pleased by the renewed legislative attention to the poor-relief question, and anxious to thwart the extension of the 'English' system of assessment-based poor relief into Ireland, Chalmers accepted the committee's invitation. After hurriedly collecting information on social conditions in both Scotland and Ireland, he travelled to London in mid-May 1830.[121]

In his oral evidence before the committee, Chalmers emphasized his ideal of the Christian community, organized around the parochial institutions of a national religious Establishment.[122] His testimony consisted in three parts. First, he described the traditional Scottish system of parish poor relief, the deterioration of that system through the influence of the 'English' system of legal assessments, and his own efforts in St. John's to restore an assessed urban parish to the traditional Scottish ideal. Secondly, he argued against the extension of legal assessments into Ireland. However great the present distress in Ireland, he asserted, conditions would grow far worse if legal assessments were adopted. From an economic viewpoint, he maintained, Ireland's problems were two-fold—over-population and inefficient use of natural resources. Assessment relief would only aggravate both these social ills. It would encourage the poor to multiply beyond their means, until nothing could spare Ireland from the Malthusian horror of over-population. It would, moreover, discourage industry among the labouring orders and thwart the free movement of labour, resulting in further economic stagnation. Thirdly, Chalmers maintained that the only real hope for Irish social improvement lay in strengthening the national Established Protestant Church of Ireland as a force for the religious and moral education of the Irish people. The economic imperatives for national prosperity, as described by Adam Smith and the Classical Liberal economists, had to be combined with the social imperatives of communal responsibility, as revealed in the Bible. Poor relief, he continued, must be based upon private charity among relatives and neighbours, inspired and directed by parish visitors. Parish schools must educate individuals to practise 'moral restraint', to seek independence for their families, and to help care for disabled neighbours. In a word, Ireland would be saved only by an Evangelical Protestant Establishment. Now that the State had granted full political toleration to Catholics, it was time the Irish Establishment assumed greater responsibility for the Evangelical mission. For this, he advocated internal reforms for the Church of Ireland, including more efficient use of its endowed revenues and more effective Church patronage.[123]

His fundamental disagreement with advocates of legal assessments for poor relief, Chalmers explained to the committee, involved the relationship 'between a high state of character and a high state of economic comfort'. Both he and his opponents, he observed, recognized that a connection existed between character and comfort—that men of 'moral character' generally enjoyed a decent material standard of living. They differed, however, in their views of the reason for this connection. Advocates of assessments, he had found, believed that most individuals required material security before they could concern themselves with improving their character. For this reason, assessment relief, guaranteeing the basic necessities of life to all men, was considered the necessary first step in the moral and spiritual elevation of the lower social orders. But for Chalmers, the opposite was true. An individual, he argued, required a sound moral character before he could achieve or sustain material security. Education, not material relief, was the necessary first step. Simply to grant the poor a legal right to assessment relief would not contribute to the improvement of character; on the contrary, the uneducated poor would dissipate the money through improvidence and vice, to their further moral degradation. They would then only require further relief, becoming permanent burdens upon society. 'It does not appear,' he observed,

that if you lay hold of a man thirty or forty years old, with his inveterate habits, and improve his economic condition, by giving him, through a poor rate or otherwise, £3 or £4 a-year more, it does not appear to me that this man will be translated thereby into other habits, or higher tastes, but he will dissipate it generally in the same reckless and sordid kind of indulgence to which he had been previously accustomed: whereas, if instead of taking hold of the man, and attempting to elevate him by the improvement of his economic condition, you take hold of the boy, and attempt to infuse into him the other element, which I conceive to be the causal one, by means of education, then you will, through the medium of character, work out an improvement in his economic condition.

What, then, was to become of the adult poor, with their 'inveterate habits', while the next generation was receiving a Christian education? His answer was uncomprising. Ireland, he asserted, must remain firm against legal assessments, even though this should mean continued social distress for another generation.

What I should advise is, that education be made universal in Ireland, and that you should weather for a season the annoyance of Ireland's mendicity, and the annoyance of that pressure which I conceive to be altogether temporary. This appears to me the only principle upon which Ireland can be securely and effectually brought to a higher standard of enjoyment, and into the state of a well-habited and well-conditioned peasantry. I think that if patiently waited for, very great results might be looked for ere another generation pass away; but then the establishment of a poor law would throw a very heavy obstruction indeed on that educational process, to which alone I look for a permanent improvement in the state of Ireland.[124]

Chalmers's actual influence upon the committee's report, which was published on 16 July 1830, was minor. On the question of an Irish poor law, the committee declined to make any substantial recommendations, and simply advised the House of Commons to consider the matter further during the next session. Moreover, although the committee advocated a comprehensive system of national education for Ireland, it did not recommend placing the proposed school system under the authority of the Protestant Church of Ireland as Chalmers had advised. Instead, it proposed that the schools be non-denominational and be administered by the secular government.[125] Setting aside the question of his influence upon the committee's report, however, his evidence had been significant. After an interval of six years since the failure of the 1824 Kennedy poor-law bill, he once again began endeavouring to influence Parliament on the subject of poor relief. His evidence, which was published in the committee report, revived his reputation as perhaps Britain's leading opponent of legal poor relief. It also made a profound impression upon at least two leading politicians. One of these was Nassau Senior (1790-1864), an influential Whig political economist and administrative reformer, who was beginning to direct his attention to the question of comprehensive poor-law reform in England. Senior, who shared Chalmers's sentiments on assessment relief, was delighted with his evidence, and later pressed him to republish it as a separate volume. This evidence, Senior observed in a pamphlet on Irish poor relief which he published in 1831, was 'the most instructive, perhaps, that ever was given before a Committee of the House of Commons'.[126]

The other politician was Daniel O'Connell (1775-1847), the celebrated Irish Catholic champion of national autonomy. Although he did not appreciate Chalmers's hopes for a revived Protestant Establishment, O'Connell did share his communitarian views and his antipathy to legal poor relief. On 1 July 1833, three years after the initial publication of his evidence, while Chalmers was visiting in London, O'Connell approached him in the House of Commons. '[He] shook me most cordially by the hands,' Chalmers informed his eldest daughter Anne, 'complimenting me on my evidence about the Irish Poor-Laws, saying he was a disciple of mine upon that subject, and not of his own priest, Dr. Doyle. ... I am sure it would have done your heart much good to have seen how closely and cordially Mr. Daniel O'Connell and your papa hugged and greeted each other.' It is significant that despite their religious differences the two great national leaders on Britain's Celtic fringe were in agreement on the subjects of communal benevolence and legal poor relief.[127]

Chalmers remained in London for nearly a month following his appearance before the committee on the Irish distress, meeting leading politicians and Anglican churchmen to discuss the poor laws and religious Establishments. In late July 1830, shortly after his return to Edinburgh, the news of revolution in France reached Scotland. Once again, the Bourbon monarchy was toppled, and the contagion of revolution spread to neighbouring states. Chalmers's reaction was mixed. On the one hand, he approved of the French people's struggle for civil liberty and responsible government. But on the other hand, he also believed that man could be truly free only by accepting God's sovereign will, and that attempts to achieve social happiness without reference to the divine purpose revealed in Scripture would end in failure. 'Look at the new French Revolution,' he observed to the Quaker John Joseph Gurney during a private conversation in Edinburgh in mid-August 1830. 'There is much that one approves *at present* both in its tendency and its results.' 'But you see', he went on,

it has been effected by the growth of merely human intelligence—by the working of the unregenerate mind without a particle of Christian principle. It is just the striving of natural wisdom and pride of man after [what] we are apt to conceive to be the consummation of our happiness—a *condition of independence*. I am not one of those who underrate the value of civil and political liberty; but I am well assured that it is only the principles of Christianity which can impart true security, prosperity, and happiness, either to individuals, or to nations. I am prepared to expect, that on the efforts which are now making in the world to regenerate our species, without religion, *God will impress the stamp of solemn and expressive mockery.*

He suspected the new French revolution, like the old, would culminate only in terror and bloodshed. Further, he feared the revolutionary seed would be communicated to the British population, among whom, because of the increasing insufficiency of the national religious Establishments, it would find fertile ground. 'The population in England and Scotland', he continued to Gurney, 'has immensely outgrown the provisions of the two Establishments—and what becomes of the surplus? They do not provide *themselves* with religious privileges, but are more than content to continue without them.' As a result, the

British nation was losing its Christian foundation, and becoming vulnerable to the delusion that man alone could structure a just society.[128]

His fears increased when three months later, on 15 November 1830, the loose coalition of Whigs, Radicals, independents, and ultra-Tories in Parliament brought down Wellington's Tory Government. The king now summoned Earl Grey, leader of the Whig party, to form a Government. For the Whigs, this meant a return to power after nearly twenty-five years in opposition (and in substance, much longer). They were no longer a coherent political party, nor could they count upon a clear majority in the Commons. None the less, they assumed responsibility with a single-minded commitment to introduce a bill for Parliamentary reform. In Scotland, the Whigs were triumphant; after twenty-five years in the wilderness, they at last tasted power. 'In the beginning of December', Henry Cockburn wrote later that same month, 'the Whigs came into power; avowedly on the great principle, and for the great object of Parliamentary Reform. ... We have come upon the public stage in a splendid, but perilous scene. I trust we shall do our duty.'[129]

The Whig Government introduced its Parliamentary reform bill in March 1831. It proposed to disenfranchise a number of smaller burghs, to create additional seats for larger burgh and county constituencies, and to extend the franchise to all £10 householders (renters or owners of buildings of an annual value of £10) in Parliamentary burghs. Chalmers, however, opposed the bill. He admitted the need for limited Parliamentary reform, including the suppression of some small burgh constituencies; none the less, he was intensely dissatisfied with the Whig plan. First, he believed that extending the franchise to £10 householders was too great a step towards democracy. The £10 householder, he argued, did not possess a sufficient stake in the country to respect or to support adequately the national institutions.[130] He particularly feared that the enlarged electorate would soon encroach upon the privileges and endowments of the national religious Establishments.

Secondly, and more importantly, he believed that the reform bill would encourage the British population to view the secular State, rather than the Established Churches, as the focus for national aspirations and the hope for national prosperity and happiness. The reform bill agitation threatened to destroy the godly commonwealth ideal; like the revolutionaries in France, the Whig reformers encouraged the popular delusion that man alone could master his world, and create, through political means, the perfect society. In April 1831, a month after the Whigs introduced their reform bill, Chalmers began to organize the lectures on political economy, which he had delivered occasionally to his divinity class at Edinburgh University during the 1830-1 academic session, into a treatise intended to demonstrate the limits of man's power to control nature and society. Published by

William Collins in January 1832, in a volume of 566 octavo pages, Chalmers's *On Political Economy, in Connexion with the Moral State and Moral Prospects of Society* challenged the concepts of social progress dominant in Britain since the Enlightenment.

The work opened on a note of urgency. Despite industrial and commercial progress in Britain, he argued, the condition of the lower social orders was growing worse. The economy was unsettled by recurring crises brought on by over-production. There was widespread political and social violence, and a growing threat of revolution. The fundamental cause of this increasing social dislocation, he continued, was to be found in the Malthusian doctrine of population. Industrial and commercial expansion were gradually undermining the traditional Christian parish communities; parish instruction in 'moral restraint' and communal responsibility was waning. As a result, population growth in Britain was beginning to press beyond the limits of its natural resources for food production. These natural resources, he argued, could not be expanded, and therefore the continued population increase would eventually bring disaster. 'Our endeavour is to prove that in every direction, there is a limit to the augmentation of our physical resources; and that, in virtue of this, there must, especially in old countries, be a felt pressure and discomfort throughout every community, which has either outgrown the means for its Christian instruction, or in any other way, renounced the habits and decencies of a Christian land.'[131]

The book was carefully structured. After describing the increasing social distress in Britain, Chalmers proceeded, with a reductionist approach, to dismiss most of the solutions proposed by those economists, mainly followers of Adam Smith, who would later be referred to as the Classical Liberal school, as well as the proposals of the Whig (and liberal Tory) reformist politicians. He began by assailing the optimism of the Classical Liberal economists. Their major solutions to the Malthusian spectre of over-population, he observed, were threefold. First, many Liberal economists advocated the extension of agriculture to hitherto uncultivated land in Britain, through various schemes of 'home colonization'. Chalmers responded by arguing that most uncultivated land in Britain was too infertile to support the labourers who would be needed to cultivate it; therefore, the 'home colonies' could survive only by permanent government subsidies obtained by taxing the surplus wealth of the more productive land already under cultivation. This, in turn, would diminish the amount of national wealth available to support the religious and educational Establishments, the arts and sciences, and the military. Further population growth, meanwhile, would soon overtake the modest increases in food production created by the home colonies, so that Britain would have sacrificed the higher benefits of its civilization only to create an enlarged, but impoverished population.[132] Secondly, Liberal economists placed great confidence in industrial development as a panacea for social misery. But, argued Chalmers, industrial development depended upon surplus agricultural wealth, not only for capital investment in industrial concerns, but also for the purchase of industrial products. The increasing population, meanwhile, diminished this surplus wealth. Thus, though some large landowners continued to invest in industrial concerns, there were too few home consumers able to purchase the industrial products. The result was economic instability.[133]

Thirdly, many Liberal economists advocated the abolition of the Corn Laws, the tariffs on imported grain which protected the British agricultural interest. This, they argued, would allow Britain to exchange industrial products for foreign foodstuffs on a large scale, and to support in comfort a vastly enlarged industrial population. Chalmers was in fact an advocate of free trade. He had long believed, with the physiocrats, that just as all wealth emanated from the cultivation and mining of the land, so all taxation, in the final analysis, involved the taxing of surplus agricultural and mineral wealth. The most efficient policy of taxation, then, would be to abolish all tariffs in favour of an increased land tax. Unlike most Classical Liberal economists, Chalmers was confident that improvements in agricultural methods on the land already under cultivation would enable the landed interest to bear all the taxation needed to support the national institutions, provided that the population size could be kept under control.

Although in favour of free trade, however, Chalmers did not believe that it would result in real improvement for the labouring poor. The increased exchange of industrial products for foreign food would also encourage population growth, and very soon the population would expand beyond the limits of even the imported food supply. The only result would be a larger, but no more prosperous industrial population, permanently dependent upon foreign food and therefore vulnerable to any interruptions of Britain's trade.[134] Perhaps the greatest benefit to be achieved through the adoption of free trade, he argued, would be that it would convince the labouring orders that even one of the most enlightened policies proposed by the Classical Liberal economists would prove no panacea for their continued suffering.

Having thus dismissed the Classical Liberal economics of Adam Smith and his followers, Chalmers then considered the solutions to the problem of increasing social misery proposed by Whig (and liberal Tory) political reformers. Again, he focused upon three solutions, each of which he dismissed in turn. First, reformist politicians advocated reducing taxes through reforms directed towards greater economy in government. Chalmers, however, perceived no benefit for the labouring

orders from tax reduction. All real wealth, he believed, derived ultimately from the soil, and therefore all taxation ultimately fell upon
landowners, who would be the sole real beneficiaries of tax cuts. The
landowners, meanwhile, would use the additional private wealth
gained through the tax cuts either to increase their luxury consumption,
or else to invest in industry (thus encouraging over-production). In
neither event would the labouring poor experience much improvement.[135] Secondly, many reformers recommended that the State
subsidize working-class emigration to the colonies. This, Chalmers
admitted, would benefit a limited number of labouring families, and
emigration schemes should certainly be encouraged. None the less, he
further maintained that the disinclination of most people to leave their
homeland, combined with the magnitude of the numbers who would
have to be transported in order to have a significant impact upon social
conditions, rendered emigration no real remedy for over-population.
The existence of emigration schemes, moreover, would discourage
'moral restraint' among the poor.[136] Finally, many reformers argued
that the extension of legal assessments for poor relief would both
mitigate the worst effects of poverty and encourage an improvement in
moral character among the poor. For Chalmers, however, assessments
were the worst possible expedient, which would only discourage
industry and personal responsibility, destroy existing communal
bonds, and encourage further population growth.[137]

Thus, Chalmers concluded, neither the doctrines of Classical Liberal
economics, nor the social legislation of a liberal State, could elevate the
condition of the labouring poor or preserve social order. 'We have
laboured', he asserted, 'to demonstrate the futility of every expedient,
which a mere political economy can suggest for the permanent well-
being of a community. At best, they but tend to enlarge the absolute
wealth of a country, without enlarging the relative comfort of the people
who live in it.' The grim Malthusian spectre haunted man's every
effort for social progress. 'All round, and in every direction,' he continued,

there is a besetting limit, which the mighty tide of an advancing population tends to
overpass, and which, being impassable, throws the tide back again upon general
society; charged, as it were, with a distress and a disorder that are extensively felt
throughout the old countries of the civilized world. The only question remains then, Is
there no way by which the tide can be arrested, before it comes into contact and collison
with the barrier that repels it?

There was, he concluded, only one hope for Britain: 'The high road ...
to a stable sufficiency and comfort among the people, is through the
medium of their character; and this is effectuated by other lessons
altogether than those of political economy.'[138] Individuals had to learn

to respect the limits of their natural environment, and the importance of 'moral restraint'. They had to become more industrious, and develop habits of foresight and saving. Above all, they had to embrace a communal benevolence, through which each individual would recognize a responsibility for his neighbour's needs. This reformation of national character, he maintained, could only be achieved through universal Evangelical Christian education, disseminated by the parish churches and schools of a national religious Establishment. Only Evangelical Christianity, he argued, could intrude upon the natural man with sufficient emotional force to reform moral character. And only an endowed territorial Establishment could reach all men with Christian teachings, including the irreligious who were not attracted by any inner spiritual impulse to attend a voluntary Dissenting church.[139] The great lesson of political economy was the incapacity of society, independently of Christianity, to achieve either stability or progress. There was no 'invisible hand', such as that suggested by Adam Smith and his disciples, acting in society to harmonize competing economic interests for the general welfare. Nor was there any possibility that the secular State could control the economy or direct social progress through legislation. Nations, like individuals, were absolutely dependent upon God for their stability and prosperity; they had to relinquish their arrogant pursuit of mastery over the world and submit, with humility, to God's will.

The social ideal which Chalmers presented in his *Political Economy* of 1832 was similar to that of his 1808 *Enquiry into the Extent and Stability of National Resources*. In both works, he advocated a social organization of small, stable, largely self-sufficient communities, which respected the limits of the country's natural resources and endeavoured to maintain independence from foreign trade. In both works, moreover, he challenged the concept of unlimited material progress through unrestricted industrial and commercial development, which was fundamental to the Classical Liberal economic theory of Adam Smith and his disciples. The two essays differed, however, regarding the manner in which their social ideal was to be achieved. In Chalmers's 1808 *Enquiry*, the great threat to the nation had been an external one—the military power of Napoleonic France. In response to this threat, the British State was to have served as the principal agent for social reform. The Spartan national-community ideal of the *Enquiry* was to have been achieved by increased taxation of surplus agricultural wealth and by the military conscription of the 'redundant' population, thus strengthening the military establishment, while at the same time depriving the economy of both the investment capital and labour supply necessary for large-scale industrial development. In his 1832 *Political Economy*, however, the threat to the nation was an internal one—that of over-population.

In the face of this threat to the social fabric, he now maintained, the secular State was not only powerless, but its actions usually caused only more harm. In the last twenty-five years, for instance, the State had been gradually expanding legal poor relief. This expansion, Chalmers argued, had only increased social instability and over-population. Now, he argued, fundamental social authority had to be shifted from the secular State to the national Church Establishments. The Christian communal ideal alone would save the nation.

'Your political economy', Nassau Senior informed Chalmers from London on 8 July 1832, 'is creating a great sensation here.'[140] Chalmers's reputation ensured that the work received public attention and was widely reviewed. None the less, upon the whole, reviewers were not much more favourable to the new work than they had been to its earlier version nearly twenty-five years before. Its three main themes— the dismissal of the promise of Classical Liberal economics, the dismissal of the hopes of political reform, and the elevation of the religious Establishment—found little support in the major national reviews. It was, the Tory *Quarterly Review* maintained, absurd to dismiss the benefits of industrial and commercial growth because of concern over the Malthusian horror of over-population, when in fact Britain possessed an empire with vast expanses of uncultivated fertile land and vast potential markets for manufactured goods. Britain's home population, it argued, need not fear dependence upon its colonies for food, any more than London's population need fear its dependence upon the farms of Kent or Middlesex. 'Whether in time', the *Quarterly Review* continued,

Dr. Chalmers's eloquence will persuade us to realize his Utopia of a 'self-contained' nation,—producing all it consumes within its own limits, shutting itself out from all communication with the rest of the world, and sedulously keeping down its population by 'virtuous efforts,' considerably within the number which its internal resources are calculated to maintain in plenty,—we know not. This, however, we know, that if our first parents had acted on these principles, their descendants would never have spread beyond the boundaries of Mesopotamia.[141]

The Benthamite *Westminster Review,* under the proprietorship of Chalmers's friend, Thomas Perronet Thomson, agreed with much of Chalmers's Malthusian critique of *laissez-faire* capitalism, but not with his dismissal of all social legislation. No single political expedient, it admitted, would prove a panacea for Britain's social distress. Never-the less, 'though one expedient ... may be ineffectual to permanent good, a succession may form a chain, of which very different things may be predicated.'[142] The *Eclectic Review*, a vehicle of Protestant Dissent, recognized Chalmers's eloquence on behalf of religious Establishments as a plea for a commonwealth based upon strict religious

consensus. It recalled for the benefit of its readers his 1808 *Enquiry*, and
asserted that despite his new reputation as a champion of religious
toleration, his social views had really not changed, but still constituted
a threat to liberty. The increasingly liberal spirit of the times had
scarcely touched him; he still resided mentally in the stagnant backwaters of 1808 northern Fife. 'Dr. Chalmers dwells not in the low region
of facts, and he soars above all argument. His speculative opinions,
then, once moulded, are fixed and unimpressible.'[143]

The most bitter blow, in Chalmers's mind, came from the *Edinburgh
Review*. Under the editorship of his friend, Francis Jeffrey, the Whig
Edinburgh had both defended the Malthusian doctrine of population
and advocated Chalmers's social views. In 1817, it will be recalled,
Jeffrey had placed the *Edinburgh* at his disposal, publishing four articles
by him on social questions between 1817 and 1820. In October 1824, in
the wake of the Kennedy bill *furor*, the *Edinburgh* had published the
flattering account of Chalmers's St. John's experiment by his friend,
Henry Cockburn, which had been intended to help restore his damaged
reputation as a social reformer. In 1829, when Jeffrey had resigned
from the editorship, he was replaced by Chalmers's close friend, the
Whig lawyer and author, Macvey Napier. One of Napier's first acts as
editor had been to invite Chalmers's assistance in editing and writing
for the review (which he had politely declined because of the pressing
duties of his chair).[144] For all these reasons, Chalmers had expected
strong support from the *Edinburgh* for his *Political Economy*.

Upon receiving the work, Napier had sent it for review to J. R.
McCulloch, the celebrated Scottish Whig political economist, with
special instructions that McCulloch treat it with the highest respect.
McCulloch, however, was an anti-Malthusian and an ardent disciple
of Adam Smith.[145] Needless to say, he found a favourable review impossible. 'The book', he wrote to Napier on 3 August 1832, 'is really
a tissue of abominable absurdities. It would extenuate every Gov't
abuse; or rather it would show that there can be no abuse: a more
thorough piece of quackery never came into my hands and but for
the relation in which you stand to him he ought to be effectually
showed up.' Napier, McCulloch added, might not wish to publish
his review. 'Should you reject it altogether,' he observed, 'it will
be no great matter, as I daresay I will be able to get it inserted some-
place else.'[146] Napier was placed in a quandary. McCulloch was one
of the foremost contributors to the *Edinburgh*. By rejecting his review
in order to shield his friend, Napier would risk losing McCulloch's
future services, not to mention damaging his own reputation. In truth,
Chalmers's social views had now so diverged from the Whig principles
of the *Edinburgh Review* that it would have been difficult for even Napier
himself to review the work favourably. In the end, he decided to publish

McCulloch's review. 'I had nearly resolved', Napier confided 'very privately' to Chalmers on 29 September 1832, 'at one time, not to notice your book, from an apprehension that you might think less favourably of my friendship than before, if I should publish an adverse critique; but on second, and I think better thoughts, I came to the conclusion, that silence in regard to such a work would, by the world generally, be thought more disrespectful than opposition.'[147]

McCulloch's review appeared in October 1832.[148] He focused first upon Chalmers's critique of Classical Liberal economics, challenging his contention that in spite of industrial and commercial expansion, the condition of the labouring orders had declined in Britain during the last fifty years. On the contrary, McCulloch maintained, the evidence demonstrated that their standard of living had improved immensely. He cited accounts of social conditions published between 1780 and 1830, in order to illustrate improvements in working-class housing, clothing, and diet. Even more important, McCulloch asserted, recent studies in both England and France had demonstrated that contrary to Chalmers's Malthusian speculations, population did not continually press upon the limits of food production; in fact, the birth-rate declined as material conditions improved. Basic economic security encouraged families to consider the future, and to adopt family planning. The Malthusian spectre of over-population, McCulloch argued, was a bugbear which would vanish with further economic progress. Secondly, he maintained, far from being ineffectual for social good, liberal government was essential for creating a stable social environment in which the economy could continue to flourish. Such effective government included poor laws for the unemployed, tax reduction, and emigration schemes.

McCulloch's discussion of government led him to the problems of Ireland, which Chalmers had described at some length. The great problem in Ireland, he asserted, was not, as Chalmers maintained, the weakness of its Protestant Establishment, but rather the years of misgovernment, which had created an insecure social climate. McCulloch recognized that the crux of Chalmer's whole argument was his belief that reform of individual character necessarily had to precede the reform of society, and that the reform of individual character could only be achieved through Christian and moral education. But, McCulloch responded, Chalmers failed to see that character formation and social climate were, in fact, inseparable; indeed, he argued, the fundamental weakness of Chalmers's entire reform system lay in its failure to recognize the crucial role that social climate played in character formation. 'Dr. Chalmers', he observed,

appears to have formed too limited an idea of education. As far as we can discover, he seems to consider it as confined to instruction derived from books or masters; but so

sagacious an observer should not have shut his eyes to the education of circumstances—an education that is, if possible, still more important than the other, and has
the most powerful influence over the character.[149]

For McCulloch, economic expansion and political development steadily
improved social circumstances in Britain, and created a superior
national character. The hope for national happiness lay not in Chalmers's static agrarian communities, focusing narrowly on the Bible,
but rather in the dynamic of industrial and political progress.

   In December 1832, two months after the appearance of McCulloch's
review, Chalmers responded with a lengthy pamphlet, *The Supreme Importance of a Right Moral to a Right Economical State of the Community:
With Observations on a Recent Criticism in the Edinburgh Review*, in which he
challenged McCulloch's assertion that industrialization was creating a
social climate that improved the character and condition of the labouring
poor.[150] There had, Chalmers now admitted, been a general improvement in material living standards since 1780. But along with this, there
had been a radical increase in hours worked, and a decline in working
conditions. Industrial growth was not creating an environment which
improved moral character. On the contrary, increased hours of labour,
dehumanizing factory conditions, and increased child labour were
destroying family, community, and religious life. Children were growing
up without parental guidance, formal education, or religious instruction;
the labouring poor were being degraded into beasts of burden by a
society which valued only their brute strength and endurance. If they
were better fed and clothed, it was only to maintain their value as
beasts of burden during their brief season of usefulness. The tone of the
work was one of moral outrage. Industrial society was transforming the
labouring man 'into an animal, or rather, into a mere piece of living
enginery, where the vital principle may be regarded as but the moving
force … of a peculiar mechanism.' 'No wage,' he continued, 'however
liberal, for repairing the expenditure of human strength, can reconcile
us to the forfeiture of all human comfort and dignity that must be
incurred by those wretched victims of modern industry.' The factory
conditions were especially tragic in their effect upon the children
'doomed to fourteen hours every day of confinement and hard labour,
amid the dust, and the steam, and the dizzying sounds. … It is a
melancholy outlook for the next generation, that, with so large a portion
of England's boyhood, the first openings of moral and intellectual
nature should thus be subjected to the killing influences of a base and
brutalizing servitude.' He sympathized with the Tory paternalist sentiment which motivated the English factory reformers Richard Oastler
and Michael Sadler to advocate legislation for reducing the number of
hours children could labour in the factories, and for raising the minimum
age at which they could begin to work. None the less, he believed, mere

factory legislation would prove to no avail, but would rather hurt the labouring classes by prompting factory owners to curtail production and lay off adult as well as child labourers.[151] More radical social change, he maintained, was necessary. Only a revived communal ideal, emphasizing reformation of individual moral character through an Evangelical national religious Establishment, would restore social stability and happiness in Britain.

The exchange between Chalmers and McCulloch foreshadowed the future long-standing debate between the 'pessimistic' and the 'optimistic' views of the social effects of the industrial revolution. For McCulloch and the 'optimists', industrial society promised vast improvements in material standards of living—a material Utopia offering decent diet, clothing, housing, and the opportunity of happiness for the labouring orders. For the few human victims of the industrial process, emigration and an improved system of legal poor relief would prove sufficient for their needs. For Chalmers and the 'pessimists', however, the material improvements were more than offset by the weakening of traditional institutions, including the family, the community, and the Church. Long hours of labour and brutal factory conditions were depriving labouring men, from their earliest years, of every spiritual and intellectual influence which defined their humanity.

Chalmers regarded his controversy with McCulloch and the Whig *Edinburgh Review* as more than simply a 'philosophical disagreement', as Napier had tried to characterize it. The *Edinburgh Review*, he believed, had assumed an immoral position in defending the existing industrial society as beneficial to the labouring poor. The Whig offence was heightened, in Chalmers's mind, by the high tone they had assumed during their campaign for the Parliamentary reform bill. Throughout 1831 and early 1832, Whigs had mobilized popular demonstrations in favour of the bill, in part by promising the labouring orders that Parliamentary reform would lead to necessary social reforms. On 7 June 1832, the reform bill received the royal assent, and the middle classes were granted the vote. Now, in late 1832, the Whigs had evidently reversed their pre-reform-bill position, and had begun to defend the existing social structure. Chalmers began to suspect them of political opportunism, of exposing concern over the distress of industrial labourers when working-class political demonstrations suited their purposes in Parliament, while in fact caring only for the liberties and prosperity of the middle and upper classes, the landowners and mill-owners who constituted the reformed Parliamentary electorate.

His dissatisfaction with the Whig Government increased when it introduced its plan for poor-law reform in England. In February 1832, shortly after the publication of his *Political Economy*, the Whig Government appointed a Royal Commission of Inquiry to investigate English

poor relief. Chalmers hoped that the Commission might be persuaded
to recommend legislation embodying his 'permissive process', by
which English parishes would be enabled to abolish assessments and to
adopt the communal ideal of his St. John's system. Accordingly, he
sent copies of his *Political Economy* to several influential members of the
Commission. On 28 July 1832, Nassau Senior, a prominent Commissioner, informed him that although the Commission's inquiry was
formally confined to England and Wales, they had decided to send an
assistant commissioner, the talented young barrister E. Carleton
Tuffnell, to investigate poor relief in Scotland, and they requested that
Chalmers assist Tuffnell in his enquiries.[152]

Tuffnell arrived in Scotland in late August 1832. According to his
instructions, he called upon Chalmers before beginning his investigative
tour. Chalmers helped plan Tuffnell's route, and supplied him with
letters of introduction to Scottish clergymen who shared Chalmers's
views on poor relief.[153] Tuffnell's main interest was to visit the celebrated St. John's parish in Glasgow. There he was astonished at the
unpopularity of the St. John's system. 'Your system in St. John's
still flourishes,' he wrote to Chalmers on 2 October, '... but it is extraordinary to what an extent hostility to it prevails in other parishes, in
spite of the success with which it has been carried on; its enemies are
never tired out of finding some extraordinary reasons for its existence
for 13 years, and predicting its speedy extinction.'[154] Upon completing
his report in late October 1832, Tuffnell sent it to Chalmers, requesting
him 'to correct, expunge or express disapprobation of any part', before
Tuffnell submitted it to the Commission. When finally printed, his
report included a flattering description of St. John's and a defence of
Chalmers's poor relief principles against what Tuffnell referred to as
'McCulloch's doctrine'.[155]

Despite Tuffnell's evidence and Chalmers's own efforts to influence
the Commission, its poor-law report, published in early 1834, fundamentally opposed Chalmers's Christian communal principles. The
report contained two major recommendations for poor-law reform in
England and Wales. First, it proposed the elimination of outdoor
distribution of relief and the confinement of paupers within regimented
workhouses, where conditions would be made harsher, or 'less eligible'
than those for the poorest labourers outside. Secondly, it advocated the
establishment of secular poor-law districts, with poor-law guardians
elected by local ratepayers. The Commission nevertheless expected
Chalmers's support for their recommendations, which promised to
reduce poor-relief expenditures. 'I should like', Tuffnell wrote to
Chalmers on 10 March 1834, 'to bring under your notice a subject that
has been several times mentioned by members of the Central Board
of P. L. Commissioners, vizt that it would be of greatest service if you

would write a pamphlet or preach a sermon giving a review of the Report.'[156] But Chalmers did not approve of the report. Workhouses, he believed, were dehumanizing, separating the poor from their communities, rather than educating them to communal responsibility through active participation in the community's goals and ideals. Poor-law districts and guardians, moreover, would diminish the Church's role in social services and further the secularization of society.[157] The new Poor Law Act for England and Wales, based on the Commission's report, however, received the royal assent on 14 August 1834. Chalmers now directed his efforts towards ensuring that the principles of the new act would not be extended to Scotland.

In 1829, Chalmers had been widely regarded as the champion of Evangelical liberalism. He had entered the inner circle of leadership in the Scottish Whig party, helping to plan and sharing the speakers platform at the great Edinburgh Catholic emancipation meeting. Immediately after that meeting, he had been invited to assume an active role in the Whig *Edinburgh Review*. Among many Whigs, he had begun to rival the influence of Andrew Thomson, the leader of the Evangelical party in the Church of Scotland. In November 1830, the Whigs had at last come to head the government. Now, it seemed, the Evangelicals would benefit from their long-standing alliance with the Scottish Whig opposition, while Chalmers's influence would be enhanced as a leading fugure in both the Evangelical and Whig parties. But shortly after the Whigs came to power, Chalmers began to oppose their Government—first, on Parliamentary reform, then on the larger questions of social theory and the needs of the labouring classes. In truth, Chalmers's communitarian ideal of the godly commonwealth, and the emerging Whig ideal of the Liberal nation-state, bore little resemblance to each other. Despite their agreement concerning religious toleration and the dangers of legal poor relief, conflict between Chalmers and the Whig Government was inevitable. Another event, meanwhile, ensured that this conflict would threaten the long-standing Whig-Evangelical alliance, at precisely the moment when the Evangelical party in the Church of Scotland seemed about to reap the benefits of its connection with the ruling party in Government.

V

On 9 February 1831, over a month before the Whigs introduced their Parliamentary reform bill, Andrew Thomson collapsed at his doorstep while returning from the monthly meeting of the Edinburgh presbytery. Chalmers, learning of the event almost immediately, hurried to Thomson's home. But Thomson died moments before Chalmers arrived, victim of heart failure. Thomson was fifty-two years of age (a year and a half older than Chalmers)—an active man, with no history of previous illness. His sudden death was a profound shock to the Church of Scotland. He was buried on Tuesday, 15 February, with an estimated 10,000 lining the streets to watch in silence as the cavalcade rumbled past. On the following Sunday, Chalmers preached the formal funeral sermon to Thomson's St. George's congregation, which was subsequently published for the benefit of Thomson's widow and children.[158]

The friendship between the two men had always been an uneasy one, never free of rivalry.[159] The source of Chalmers's influence lay principally in the pulpit and lecture hall; Thomson, on the other hand, was not an inspiring preacher, but he was unrivalled in debate in the Church courts, and was a first-rate journalist, establishing the *Edinburgh Christian Instructor* as the leading voice of Scottish Evangelicalism. Thomson was a more cultivated man than Chalmers: he loved music, and composed hymns. He mixed well with the wealthy congregation of St. George's, situated at the prestigious west end of New Town, and he enjoyed close friendships with leading Scottish Whigs among the Edinburgh professional classes. In theology, Thomson was a dogmatic Calvinist, and while this involved him in some bitter disputes with liberal Evangelicals in his party, it also ensured that his orthodoxy was unquestioned. The most important difference between the two men, however, had involved social theory. Thomson had never agreed with Chalmers regarding the evils of legal assessments for poor relief, nor did he subscribe to Chalmers's communitarian ideal of the godly commonwealth. Thomson had supported the Whig campaigns for Catholic emancipation and Parliamentary reform, and had acknowledged liberal representative government as a force for the moral improvement of the nation. His relations with the Whig leadership had remained cordial until his death.[160]

When that occurred, Chalmers appeared the probable successor to leadership of the Evangelical party.[161] His influence as a preacher, lecturer, and author was unrivalled in the Church of Scotland. His Chair of Divinity at Edinburgh University represented a position of authority in both the Church and universities of Scotland. None the less, two factors worked against his assumption of party leadership. The first was his reputation as an unstable character who loved controversy. He was still hated in Glasgow for disrupting long-established poor-relief procedures, in St. Andrews for impugning the integrity of the professors, and in much of the west and north of Scotland for his 'betrayal' over Catholic emancipation. With his temperament, could he be trusted to exercise the restraint and sound judgement necessary to establish trust, and unite all elements of the Evangelical movement in the Church of Scotland? The second factor involved his worsening

1. Thomas Chalmers, DD, LL D (D. O. Hill, 1843)

2. Andrew M. Thomson, DD, minister of St. George's parish, Edinburgh, 1814–31 (artist unknown)

3. Three leading Evangelical Church Extensionists of the 1830s: William Cunningham (1805–61), James Begg (1808–83), Thomas Guthrie (1803–73) (D. O. Hill, 1843)

relations with the now ruling Whig party. Would he be able to work with the Whig leadership, so that the Evangelical party might at last begin to benefit from its long-standing alliance with the Whigs? The affair involving the Edinburgh Chair of Ecclesiastical History, which developed shortly after Thomson's death, focused attention upon both these factors, and cast serious doubts upon Chalmers's capacity for leadership.

On 11 June 1831, Hugh Meiklejohn, minister of rural Abercorn and Professor of Ecclesiastical History at Edinburgh University, died at the age of sixty-six. Meiklejohn's apparent successor was the Moderate clergyman John Lee (1779-1859), minister of Lady Yester's parish in Edinburgh and Principal Clerk of the General Assembly. Lee had been Professor of Ecclesiastical History at St. Andrews University from 1812 to 1820, and upon assuming an Edinburgh parish, had lectured regularly in divinity at Edinburgh University for the infirm William Ritchie. He was the foremost expert in ecclesiastical history within the Church of Scotland, and he desired the appointment.[162] The Edinburgh Chair of Ecclesiastical History was in the gift of the Crown, rather than the Edinburgh Town Council. By mid-June, Francis Jeffrey, writing on behalf of the Edinburgh Whigs, had recommended Lee for the chair to Viscount Melbourne, the Whig Home Secretary. The matter seemed resolved.

Jeffrey, however, had not asked Chalmers's advice before making the recommendation. Chalmers now raised a protest, requesting both Cockburn and Jeffrey to block Lee's appointment. Once again, the anti-plurality cause was at issue. Lee, Chalmers explained, had stated that he would not resign his Edinburgh parish living if appointed to the chair, but would insist upon holding both offices as a plural appointment. Chalmers reminded the Whigs that in 1828 the Royal Commission on Scottish Universities had determined, in a preliminary judgement to their still unpublished report, that pluralities were detrimental to both the Church and universities. The Government, then, would have to act according to the principles established by the Commission.[163] Jeffrey and the Edinburgh Whigs were placed in an embarrassing position. They had already pledged their support to Lee. None the less, in the past they had supported the Evangelical anti-plurality campaign as a means for challenging the Tory-Moderate ascendancy in Scotland, and they could not easily ignore the anti-plurality principles now that they held power. 'I never myself', a disgruntled Jeffrey confided to Cockburn on 19 June, in reference to Chalmers's protest, 'went very warmly into the anti-plurality rage,—in so far as [it] related to proper Theological Chairs and to Professors having livings in the same town with the university.' 'But it is', he added facetiously, 'a virtuous rage no doubt.'[164] On 26 June, Jeffrey informed Chalmers that he had convinced Melbourne to delay Lee's appointment, in order to allow Chalmers the opportunity to locate a suitable non-pluralist candidate. But he added that there was no possibility of the Crown increasing the endowment of the chair, so Chalmers would have to find a candidate willing to live upon the existing £200 per annum. Further, Chalmers would have to locate a candidate before the beginning of the next academic term in October, or the appointment would go to Lee by default.[165]

The entire affair, meanwhile, was complicated by the well-known personal enmity which existed between Chalmers and Lee. Temperamentally, the two men were incompatible. Lee was cool and formal, a careful scholar who based his arguments solidly upon facts and was disdainful of impassioned rhetoric or eloquence without substance. A weaver's son, Lee had known poverty in his youth, but he shared none of Chalmers's sentimental attachment to peasant communal traditions, and he questioned the sincerity of his professed desire to help the labouring poor by abolishing legal poor relief. For Lee, who had ministered for six years in one of Edinburgh's poorest parishes, assessment relief was a social necessity. Chalmers and Lee had been rivals for the Edinburgh Chair of Divinity in 1827, and had opposed one another on most issues in the Church courts, including pluralities and Catholic emancipation. Their most bitter dispute, however, had occurred several months before the Ecclesiastical History chair fell vacant. At the beginning of the 1830-1 academic term, Chalmers, hard pressed to support his family on the £196 per annum endowment of his chair and angry with the Whig-dominated Edinburgh Town Council for not increasing his endowment, had decided to exercise his legal right to exact fees from students in his divinity class. No Scottish Divinity Professor had ever before exercised this right, and in May 1831, Lee submitted a formal protest against Chalmers's action to the General Assembly. Chalmers's fees, Lee argued, would discourage the poor student, who might have a special calling from God for the ministry; it would introduce the influence of 'privilege' into training for the clerical profession. Chalmers managed to retain his right to require fees, but Lee had succeeded in raising doubts about the degree of his commitment to the Church.[166] Now, it seemed to many, Chalmers was avenging his bruised reputation by thwarting Lee's well-deserved appointment to the Ecclesiastical History chair.

In any event, he had little time to locate an alternate candidate before the beginning of the term. In late June, he settled upon David Aitken, minister of rural Minto, a bachelor and a scholar of Church history, who had studied briefly on the Continent. Aitken expressed interest in the chair, but was concerned over the low income. Chalmers assured him that the income would be increased, as soon as the Royal

Commission on Scottish Universities published its report.[167] But Aitken took the liberty of writing to Melbourne, who informed him that the Government had no intention, under any circumstance, of raising the endowment. On 20 July, then, Aitken informed Chalmers that he declined to become a candidate.[168] Chalmers, however, not knowing of Aitken's correspondence with Melbourne, believed that he was simply being coy, and only wanted a little pressure, which he applied generously through Aitken's friends. Aitken instead grew angry over Chalmers's heavy-handed methods, ceased all contact with him, and circulated complaints that he was being used as a pawn in Chalmers's vindictive personal campaign against Lee.[169] Chalmers, in turn, was enraged by Aitken's 'ingratitude'. He publicly claimed that Aitken had given him private assurances that he would accept the chair if Chalmers could locate additional revenues. Then, with the term soon to begin, Aitken had turned upon him. In a word, Chalmers maintained, Aitken had betrayed him into Lee's hands. 'Chalmers' wrath', the Edinburgh Whig lawyer James Abercromby told Aitken's friend and patron, the Whig Earl of Minto, on 17 August, 'is not surpising. It is annoying and painful to find that you have been unconsciously engaged in the support of an undesirous person.'[170]

Chalmers soon had reason to regret his attack upon Aitken. For this unobtrusive rural clergyman had the ear of the powerful Minto, first Lord of the Admiralty in the Whig Government, who replied to Abercromby on 20 August that he had no sympathy with Chalmers's wrath. Chalmers had attempted to use Aitken as a pawn against Lee, and Aitken had been right to refuse to play his game. 'I will not pretend to deny', Minto continued,

that I have been a good deal disturbed by the tone that Chalmers has assumed on this occasion. It is the second time in my life in which I have had to do with him on public business. The first was on the occasion of Kennedy's Poor Laws bill which Chalmers vehemently urged forward and assisted to prepare; and afterwards voted against in the General Assembly. And my conclusion from this double experience is that he is a man with whom it will be safer for me not to act again. In this instance there must have been much passionate misrepresentation to produce the outcry which he has raised against Aitken's conduct.

Chalmers, Minto added, would have to learn that the Scottish Establishment was not his personal domain, but that authority lay in the Government. 'However,' he concluded, in a bitter humour,

I am a bad judge of Edinburgh notions in such matters, for so far from imagining that there was anything in the nature of a contest where one man was supported by Chalmers against another, my impression was that nothing farther was required of him, or of other literary or ecclesiastical authorities who might be applied to, than a fair opinion with regard to the qualifications of the different candidates, upon whom the Government might act for itself.[171]

Chalmers's attacks upon Aitken had a similar impact upon other observers, until soon opinion began to favour Aitken in the dispute. In September, shortly before the beginning of the term, Chalmers at last found a candidate. David Welsh, the unmarried minister of St. David's parish, Glasgow, and author of a biography of the Whig moral philosopher Thomas Brown, was willing to accept the chair despite the low income. Welsh, accordingly, received the appointment.[172] None the less, Welsh was aware that he had not been Chalmers's first choice for the chair, and he did not regard himself as owing any debt of gratitude to Chalmers for the appointment.

The affair of the Ecclesiastical History chair had contributed to Chalmers's estrangement from the Whig Government, and had made him a powerful enemy in the person of the Whig Earl of Minto. He had also used up much of the remaining 'political capital' he had derived from his friendships with the Whigs, Jeffrey and Cockburn. They had withdrawn their recommendation of Lee for the chair in respect for Chalmers's anti-plurality fervour. But it had caused them considerable embarrassment, and it was doubtful whether they would again go to such lengths either for Chalmers, or against Lee. Above all, it raised serious doubts about Chalmers's capacity to take up Thomson's fallen mantle. In thwarting Lee's appointment and in applying pressure upon Aitken, he had shown a domineering manner, devoid of consideration. When Aitken had declined to become a candidate, Chalmers had been too quick to regard it a personal betrayal and to fly into a rage. Such behaviour had been bad enough when Chalmers had possessed little real authority in the Church. Then, his friends could overlook his outbreaks as simply the eccentricities of genius. Now, with Thomson gone, and no serious rivals to Chalmers for the leadership of the Evangelical party, his flaws of character suddenly became more serious. He was unquestionably the greatest orator in the Church of Scotland. His social views were intelligent and comprehensive; for many in Scotland, his communitarian ideal of the godly commonwealth was the only viable alternative to the continued social dislocations of industrialization and urbanization. In his lecture halls, first at St. Andrews and now at Edinburgh, he was inculcating a new generation of clergymen with his Christian social ideal. But influence was not authority. The requirements for an effective ecclesiastical politician continued to elude him.

THE CHURCH MILITANT

I

The decade from 1820 to 1830 had witnessed a phenomenal growth of Evangelical influence in Scotland. The religious pulse of the nation had quickened. Aided by the Romantic movement in literature and the arts, with emphasis upon the sentimental, the unsophisticated, and the aspiring, Evangelical piety captured the imagination of the educated public. Vast crowds flocked to hear fashionable Evangelical preachers. There was an increase in family worship, and a marked decrease in swearing and drunkenness among the upper and middle classes. Strict religious observances became a sign of respectability. Bible study and prayer groups proliferated. Young men and women cemented friendships with earnest religious discussion and prayer. The novels of Sir Walter Scott, John Galt, and James Hogg rekindled interest in Scotland's religious heritage. Along with the Romantic revival of Highland culture, of the kilt and the bagpipe (which received dramatic expression in the pageantry surrounding George IV's royal visit to Edinburgh in 1822), there was a renascence of strict Calvinist piety. The 'Old Theology' of the seventeenth-century Covenanters, scorned by the eighteenth-century Moderates, now became venerated by many as the faith of the fathers, which had inspired acts of national heroism.[1]

The Church of Scotland was revitalized. The best and the brightest young men crowded into the divinity halls. As Chalmers observed before the Royal Commission on Scottish Universities in 1827, there were five times more divinity students enrolled in Scotland's universities than there were vacancies in the Church to accommodate them. More and more patrons presented Evangelicals to vacant churches within their influence, often inviting Chalmers and other Evangelical leaders to furnish them with lists of candidates. The differences between the two parties diminished, as many Moderates began to share in the new religious vitality. In 1796, it will be recalled, the Moderate-dominated General Assembly had rejected an Evangelical motion that it instruct all parishes to hold collections for the overseas mission societies. In 1824, however, Moderates and Evangelicals united to support the formation of a permanent General Assembly Committee on Foreign Missions. The Committee was chaired by the Moderate party leader John Inglis (1762-1834), minister of the Edinburgh parish of Old Greyfriars, who embraced the cause of overseas missions with enthusiasm. Five years later, in 1829, the young Evangelical Alexander

Duff, one of Chalmers's former St. Andrews students, was ordained in Edinburgh for service in India as the first overseas missionary of the Church of Scotland. Previously, advocacy of overseas missions in Scotland had been left to voluntary missionary societies, such as the British and Foreign Bible Society—co-operative ventures supported by both Churchmen and Dissenters. Now, the Established Church entered the field itself.[2]

The new vitality of the Church of Scotland was not only expressed in overseas missions. After 1825, Churchmen also increasingly spoke of the need to strengthen the 'home mission'. Twenty years earlier, such a phrase would have had little meaning: Then Scotland regarded itself as a Christian nation, with an effective parochial establishment for nurturing the faith and morals of the entire population. But now, influenced by Chalmers's activities in Glasgow, the Church was awakening to the fact that a large and growing portion of the population, particularly in industrializing urban areas, had little exposure to Christianity. It was awesome to discover that eternal souls were perishing for want of pastoral care, not only in India or China, but in the slums of Edinburgh, Glasgow, or Dundee, often within sight of a church. During the 1820s, a growing number of young Evangelicals dedicated themselves to serve the urban poor, as sabbath-school teachers, lay-visitors, or 'home missionaries'. Some home missionaries received financial support from voluntary societies, such as the Glasgow City Mission, founded in 1826, or the Edinburgh City Mission, founded in 1832. Others were supported by local parish churches or by wealthy individuals.[3]

Within the Church, there was also new awareness that the number of parish churches was no longer sufficient for the needs of the population. The number of parish churches in Scotland, about 990, had scarcely changed from the sixteenth century. The population, however, had increased dramatically, particularly during the first three decades of the nineteenth century. In 1755, according to the census by the Moderate clergyman Alexander Webster, the population of Scotland was 1,265,380. By 1801, according to the Government census, it had increased to 1,608,420, and by 1831, to 2,364,386. The increase was more dramatic in urban areas. In 1755, the population of the county of Midlothian (including Edinburgh) was 90,412; in 1831, 219,345. In 1755, the county of Lanark (including Glasgow) numbered 81,726; in 1831, 316,819.[4] In response to this growing population, the Church began attempting to increase the number of its churches. In 1818, encouraged by a recent Parliamentary grant to the Church of England for building new churches, the General Assembly began requesting a similar grant for the Scottish Establishment. In 1824, Parliament finally approved a grant of £50,000 for building churches in the Highlands and

Islands, and by 1834, forty-three 'government churches' had been built in these regions.

Between 1790 and 1834, moreover, with the approval of the General Assembly, sixty-six chapels had been erected by private contributions to ease the pressure upon overcrowded parish churches. Most of these 'chapels-of-ease' and all the government churches were unendowed. The congregations, therefore, were obliged to support their ministers from the proceeds of their seat-rents and church-door collections. For this reason, the Government and the chapel-of-ease proprietors tended to appoint popular Evangelical preachers, who attracted large congregations. The Church of Scotland, however, regarded these additional churches as only the beginning of its response to the increasing population. In 1828, the General Assembly appointed a standing Church Accommodation Committee to press Parliament for an additional grant to support church-building in the Lowlands, and particularly in the growing cities.[5]

Another reflection of the new vitality of the Church was the mounting theological debate regarding the Westminster Confession of Faith, which culminated in the celebrated heresy trials of the early 1830s. The rising Evangelical fervour in the Church had, by the 1820s, begun to create tensions within Scottish Calvinism. Many Evangelicals in the Church of Scotland began to strain against what they regarded as excessive legalism and formalism. They questioned the harsh doctrines of double predestination and limited atonement, and the emphasis upon God's wrath towards those he had predestined to eternal damnation. The Westminster Confession, perhaps more than any other Christian doctrinal statement, conveyed God's awesome power and man's absolute dependence upon divine law. But many now longed for a more personal relationship to God, with emphasis upon love rather than law, and assurance rather than fear. There was also a growing mood of millennarian expectation, a hope that the Evangelical revival was a harbinger of still greater spiritual manifestations. Associated with the new theological temper were three individuals who would later be ranked among Scotland's greatest theologians, Thomas Erskine, John Macleod Campbell, and Edward Irving.

Thomas Erskine of Linlathen (1788-1870), a landed gentleman residing in the neighbourhood of Dundee, was by birth and upbringing a Scottish episcopalian, although he personally regarded himself as attached to no institutional church. He published his first theological treatise, *Remarks on the Internal Evidence for the Truth of Revealed Religion* in 1820. This was followed by several more works during the 1820s, concluding with *The Brazen Serpent* in 1831, which marked the end of his creative theological writing. Erskine emphasized the paternal love of

God for his children—God, Erskine maintained, offered his grace not only to the elect, but freely to all men. Hell was not a realm of punitive punishment, but rather signified man's alienation from God. In his love for mankind, God sought to overcome this alienation, and draw all men back into the heavenly family.[6]

In about 1827, in the parish of Row on the edge of the western Highlands about thirty miles north-west of Glasgow, the young Church of Scotland clergyman John Macleod Campbell (1800-72) began to preach similar doctrines. Macleod Campbell's divergence from scholastic Calvinism was essentially twofold. First, he proclaimed universal atonement, or the doctrine that Christ had died for the sins of all men, not simply for those of the predestined elect. Secondly, he preached that assurance of salvation through Christ's atonement was essential to the Christian faith. Men need not live in terror of God's wrath. Christ had fulfilled the requirement of God's law for all mankind, and man had only to recognize the new covenant in Christ to experience assurance of salvation.[7]

Edward Irving (1792-1834), Chalmers's former assistant at St. John's, had experienced a meteoric rise to national fame following his arrival in London as minister of the small Caledonian Church in 1822. Tall and handsome, with a powerful gift for oratory, and an intense Evangelical passion, Irving's ministry soon attracted large crowds. In 1827, a new church was completed on Regent Square to accommodate his growing congregation. Then, in mid-1827, Irving published a volume on the millennium, which raised doubts in Scotland about his orthodoxy; for he had begun to express certain charismatic views, proclaiming the imminent return of the miraculous gifts of the Holy Spirit.

Shortly after the publication of this volume, in May 1828, Irving visited Edinburgh, where his preaching, including a series of weekday lectures on prophecy delivered at 6 a.m., attracted vast numbers.[8] Macleod Campbell travelled to Edinburgh at this time and sought to convince Irving of his views on the atonement. In June, Irving visited Row, where he continued conversing with Macleod Campbell and became convinced of the truth of the latter's position on universal atonement. Irving's sermons on the approaching millenium and the gifts of the Holy Spirit also created new expectations in Row. Some months after his visit, strange events began occurring around the parish. Individuals began exercising the gift of faith-healing. They fell into trances and spoke in 'tongues'. Erskine of Linlathen travelled to Row, witnessed these occurrences, and became convinced that they were indeed the work of the Holy Spirit. By 1830, large numbers of devout Evangelicals and curious spectators flocked to Row, transforming the quiet village into a focus of national interest. Macleod Campbell

informed Irving of these miraculous events and soon similar manifestations of the Holy Spirit, including the gifts of healing and 'tongues',
appeared among Irving's congregation in London.[9]

Then the Calvinist reaction began. In early 1830, Irving's theological positions were assailed as heretical by the Evangelical and
Calvinist *Edinburgh Christian Instructor*.[10] In mid-1830, Macleod Campbell was convicted of heresy by the presbytery of Dumbarton. The
case was referred to the General Assembly of 1831, where on 24 May
Macleod Campbell was deposed from the ministry by a vote of 119 to
6, with 185 members abstaining. The next day, the Assembly deposed
Irving's intimate friend Hugh Baillie Maclean, minister of an Ayrshire
parish church; two days later, it deposed A. J. Scott of Paisley, a
young probationary minister who admitted that he could no longer
accept the Westminster Confession. During the next two years, the
Church deposed several more ministers for participation in the 'Rowite
heresies.'[11]

In 1832, the proprietors of the Regent Square church in London,
concerned that Irving was allowing members of the congregation to
disrupt worship with their moanings and speaking in 'tongues', finally
dismissed him from the charge. The General Assembly then instructed
him to appear before the presbytery of Annan, where had had first
been licensed to preach. He obeyed, and was deposed by the presbytery
on 13 March 1833. A little more than a year later, he died in Glasgow,
a broken man at the age of forty-two.[12] Erskine of Linlathen, it will be
recalled, was not a member of the Church of Scotland. His views, however, were repeatedly condemned, and he ceased theological writing
after 1831. The heresy trials were a traumatic experience for the Church
of Scotland. The ministers deposed were men of sincere conviction,
leading blameless Christian lives. None the less, they had reneged in
their vows to uphold the Westminster Confession, which remained the
Church's standard of faith, subordinate only to Scripture.

Chalmers's behaviour during the heresy trials was ambiguous. He
was not unsympathetic to the new views. He had met Erskine of
Linlathen in 1818, and the two men had later become close friends
during Chalmers's years at St. Andrews. He shared many of Erskine's
views regarding the free and unconditional nature of the gospel offer,
and God's universal love for all mankind.[13] Chalmers's relationship
with Irving was also close, almost paternal, during their years together
in St. John's, although by 1827 he began to fear that Irving was growing
too close to Samuel Taylor Coleridge, the Romantic poet and theologian,
whose mind Chalmers suspected was unsound. None the less, Chalmers
was favourably impressed with Irving's 1827 work on prophecy, and
after reading the book confessed that he too was 'very much inclined'
to millennarian views.[14] In May 1828, Macleod Campbell met Chalmers

to discuss his views on universal atonement, later recalling that Chalmers listened sympathetically, and promised to weigh his words.
When the outbreak of speaking in 'tongues' occurred in Row, Chalmers
asked Macleod Campbell to send him written samples of the utterances,
which he carried with him during his trip to London in May 1830, in
order to submit them to leading oriental scholars for analysis.[15] In
truth, Chalmers himself had never strictly adhered to the scholastic
Calvinism of the Westminster Confession. His Evangelical faith was
warmly personal; his sermons emphasized God's passion for all souls,
not only the elect. He longed to believe that the millennium was
nigh, and for several months he entertained the hope that the strange
occurrences at Row might indeed be the harbingers of a new world.

Nevertheless, when the reaction to the heterodox doctrines began,
Chalmers remained silent. In mid-1830, when the *Edinburgh Christian
Instructor* began assailing Irving's views, Irving appealed to Chalmers,
as a Doctor of the Church and Professor of Divinity, to intervene in the
conflict. Chalmers, however, refused to become involved. He had not
been a member of the 1831 General Assembly, and so had not voted for
deposing Macleod Campbell, Maclean, and Scott. Nor had he played
an active role in the Church's deposition of Irving. However, neither
did he make any public pronouncement against the proceedings. For
this silence he was later accused of cowardice. 'He was not bold enough',
Margaret Oliphant asserted in her biography of Irving in 1872, 'at that
crisis, to put that "largeness of comprehension and charity of heart,"
in which Irving trusted, into competition with the vulgar fervour which
swept the popular Assembly into anathema and deposition.'[16] 'If he
had been a man', John Tulloch, Principal of St. Andrews University,
observed in 1885, 'of more independent, courageous, and clear-sighted
vision than he was, he might have done something to stay these proceedings, or guide them to a more lenient result.'[17]

For such later observers, the theological views of Erskine, Macleod
Campbell, and Irving represented a progressive force in Scottish
theology. They overlooked, however, what was for Chalmers and his
contemporaries probably the most important consideration. Whatever
the merit of the theological contributions of Erskine, Macleod Campbell, and Irving, the excesses of many of their followers fundamentally
threatened the institutional Church of Scotland. The Rowite movement
attracted not only sincere Christians, but also a number of disturbed
individuals. Many of those who claimed the gifts of healing and tongues
were merely vain or hungry for power. With the Holy Spirit in them,
they recognized no other authority or discipline, including that of the
Church. Soon after he carried specimens of the 'tongues' to London in
May 1830 (and was assured by experts in languages that it was simply

gibberish), Chalmers grew concerned about the cult that was developing in Row.[18]

His concern increased as a result of an experience in early 1831, a few months before the Assembly deposed Macleod Campbell. Helen S. Mowbray, the highly-strung daughter of a respectable Edinburgh family, ran away from home to join the group at Row. There she became engaged to R. H. Herschell, a converted Jew with a shady past, including several romantic liaisons, who had also joined the Row cult. Her parents refused their consent for the marriage, and sought to bring her home, appealing to Chalmers to employ his influence with Irving and Macleod Campbell. But Irving refused to intervene, informing Chalmers that the dictates of the Holy Spirit assumed precedence over parental authority. In March 1831, moreover, Macleod Campbell informed Chalmers that he had no knowledge of either Miss Mowbray or Herschell, and could exercise no influence with them.[19] Chalmers believed Macleod Campbell was lying, and his subsequent anger helps to explain his silence when, two months later, Macleod Campbell was tried in the Assembly. The Herschell affair also ended his friendship with Irving. 'I have in the course of my doings about Herschell's marriage', Chalmers confided to Fergus Jardine, a chaplain and tutor employed by the Earl of Elgin, on 11 October 1831, 'seen much of the weakness and much of the disingenuity among the members of the [Macleod] Campbell coterie, and I grieve that the last letters of Mr. Irving which I have seen upon this subject have completely broken up all my confidence and moral comfort in thinking of him.'[20]

For Chalmers, the Rowite movement was far more dangerous to the Evangelical revival in the Church of Scotland than the legalism of scholastic Calvinism. For 'Rowitism' represented antinomianism, the doctrine that the sanctified Christian, possessed by the Holy Spirit, stood above Scriptural law and ecclesiastical authority. Chalmers had long regarded antinomianism as the greatest threat to the Evangelical movement: the very intensity of Evangelical faith, if allowed to assume an antinomian expression, might disintegrate the organized Church of Scotland. The Rowite excesses now confirmed his fears. While he did not join in the orthodox zeal to purge the Church of the heretics, neither would he publicly challenge the authority of the Westminster Confession. It is worth noting that both Erskine and Macleod Campbell also eventually separated themselves from some of their more extreme followers.[21]

It was well for his influence in the Church of Scotland that Chalmers had not challenged the Westminster Standards. Probably the most significant effect of the heresy trials of the early 1830s was a revival of dogmatic Calvinism in the Church of Scotland. After 1831, the slightest charge of 'Rowitism' was sufficient to preclude a candidate for the ministry from receiving a living within the Church.[22] The young clergymen who rose to influence within the Evangelical party after 1830— including Robert Candlish (1806-73), William Cunningham (1805-61), and Robert Buchanan (1802-75)—were strict Calvinists, committed in heart and mind to the Westminster Standards, and intolerant of other religious persuasions.[23] Chalmers probably could not have driven back the rising tide of dogmatic Calvinism within the Evangelical party even had he tried. His own theological views, it will be recalled, were not above suspicion. He had received the Edinburgh Divinity chair in 1827 against formidable clerical opposition. Had he actively defended Erskine's views on free grace, Macleod Campbell on universal atonement, or Irving on the gifts of the Holy Spirit and the human nature of Christ, he might well have forfeited his chair. As it was, the excesses of the 'Rowites' had convinced him that the new theological views might be more the fruits of human speculation than of divine inspiration. Despite the harsh legalism of the Calvinist Westminster Confession, it was not to be dismissed lightly. It had passed the test of nearly two centuries, and had sustained the Church of Scotland through periods of revolution, civil war, and social turmoil. Now, with the Scottish nation facing the social dislocations of massive industrialization and urbanization, he had become convincd that it was not the time to throw out the creed which had provided the national Church's strength in the past.

In the midst of the *furor* surrounding the Rowite heresy trials, Chalmers was occupied with the composition of his own theological statement, in the form of a contribution to the *Bridgewater Treatises.* In 1829, the Earl of Bridgewater, an eccentric clergyman in the Church of England, died leaving £8,000 in trust to subsidize the publication of a work *On the Power, Wisdom and Goodness of God, as manifested in the Creation.* The trustees decided that the work should be divided into eight separate treatises, and on 1 October 1830, C. J. Blomfield, the Bishop of London, invited Chalmers, on behalf of the trustees, to submit the first treatise, on the subject of moral philosophy.[24] Chalmers completed his contribution, *On the Power, Wisdom and Goodness of God as Manifested in the Adaptation of External Nature to the Moral and Intellectual Constitution of Man,* in May 1833, and it was published a month later in London.

The work consisted of two parts. In the first, Chalmers examined the principle of design in the world, as evidenced in man's moral nature. God, he argued, had created man as a social creature, with an internal moral regulator, or conscience, which directed him towards acts of benevolence. Emotional frictions, to be sure, such as anger, often obscured the promptings of conscience. None the less, in his natural condition, man experienced his greatest happiness in fulfilling his familial and communal responsibilities.[25] Chalmers then proceeded to survey his communal ideal at length, emphasizing the organic character of communal organization, and the dangers of artificial governmental interference in the natural moral order through such expedients as legal poor relief.[26] In the second part, Chalmers analyzed the evidence of God's design in man's intellectual nature. God, he maintained, had created man with a rational enquiring mind, which continually extended mankind's knowledge of the physical universe. Yet each new discovery merely presented new, ever greater mysteries; natural science carried man's enquiring mind, by an independent force of its own, towards ever more awesome demonstrations of the sublime majesty of God. Of science he asserted: 'It emits, and audibly emits, a note of terror; but in vain do we listen for one authentic word of comfort from any of its oracles. It is able to see the danger, but not the deliverance.'[27] In the final analysis, the 'march of intellect', in which the spirit of the age placed so much confidence, created in man increasing uncertainty, anxiety, and alienation, until he was driven to embrace with still greater passion the offer of saving grace in revealed Christianity. Intellectual progress, man's apparent drive towards mastery of his world, in fact increased his sense of absolute dependence upon God's grace. In short, the Evangelical revival was not a reaction to, but rather a consequence of the eighteenth-century Enlightenment, part of a continuum in the development of mankind.[28]

It was an effective performance, and one which contrasted sharply with the Rowite movement. Where the Rowites had emphasized the miraculous gifts of the Holy Spirit, Chalmers emphasized the constancy of natural law. Where the Rowites had emphasized the spiritual dimension, Chalmers stressed the evidences of divine design in the moral and intellectual realms. God, he argued, had intended that the world should be a scene of social happiness. Along with the moral philosophers of the eighteenth-century Scottish Enlightenment, Chalmers maintained that man was created as a social creature, who would experience pleasure in co-operation and benevolence. Much of Chalmers's essay was devoted to political and economic theory. He discussed, for example, the importance of limiting governmental involvement in poor relief, and of allowing human relationships to be ordered by 'the superior wisdom of nature'. Finally, he defended the power of individual human reason, not as something to be overcome by spiritual impulses, but as necessary for Christian growth and the acceptance of saving grace. It was a reassertion of Wilberforce's rational Evangelicalism, which Chalmers had embraced at his conversion over twenty years earlier—a world-affirming faith, emphasizing man's social nature and respecting man's intellectual achievements.

He did not mention the Westminster Confession, or God's plan for man's salvation, which he described as outside the limits of his present enquiry. None the less, in his descriptions of a law-bound universe and man's absolute dependence upon God, there was nothing that offended scholastic Calvinism.

His *Bridgewater Treatise* was on the whole well received, and reached a second edition before the end of the year.[29] In the wake of this success, his rising literary fame was recognized with three major distinctions. In January 1834, he was elected both a member of the Royal Society of Edinburgh and a corresponding member of the Royal Institute of France. In July 1835, he was awarded the degree of Doctor of Divinity from Oxford University.[30] In short, he was emerging as an author of international reputation, and perhaps the brightest ornament of the Church of Scotland.

II

In 1829, the Church of Scotland confronted the new challenge of radical Voluntaryism, that is, the sustained agitation by a group of Scottish Dissenters for the disestablishment of the national Church. For a number of years, voices had occasionally been raised in Scotland against the principle of a religious Establishment. There was, however, no organized movement until after the repeal of the Test and Corporation Acts (and the recognition of the political power of Dissent) in 1828. Credit for beginning the Voluntary campaign in Scotland is generally given to Andrew Marshall, a United Secession Church minister. In a celebrated sermon delivered in Glasgow on 9 April 1829, and published a few weeks later, Marshall sounded a call for disestablishment. The Catholic emancipation bill was then being debated in Parliament. The prospect of the bill being passed, argued Marshall, demanded a reconsideration of the State's connection with organized religion. If the Irish Catholics, he explained, who constituted the majority of the Irish population, were to be granted full political rights, then how could they be denied the right to disestablish the Protestant Church of Ireland, and to endow the Roman Catholic Church as the new Irish Established Church? The British Government would then be obliged to grant State protection and tax support to a religious system regarded by most British people as a grievous error. The only alternative to this evil, Marshall continued, was to abolish all religious Establishments. Total disestablishment would not only spare the nation a revival of Roman political influence; it would also ensure the most efficient dissemination of Protestant truth. All churches in Britain, he explained, would compete fairly and openly. Such an environment of 'free trade' would ensure maximum evangelical effort.

Those churches without the Holy Spirit would wither; those preaching the true Word would prosper.[31]

Marshall's seed fell upon fertile ground, and soon his sentiments were echoed in dozens of pamphlets. The barrage of pamphlets was followed by public meetings and political organization. A series of large public meetings in Edinburgh began in January 1832, and culminated in the formation of the Edinburgh Voluntary Church Association on 13 September 1832. A few weeks later, on 12 November, the Glasgow Voluntary Church Association was formed. By the end of 1833, Voluntary associations had been formed in dozens of Scottish towns and villages. In March 1833, the Glasgow Voluntary Church Association began publishing the monthly *Voluntary Church Magazine,* which directed violent abuse against the Church of Scotland, and became the major organ of the Voluntary movement. Early in 1835, the Edinburgh Young Men's Voluntary Church Association began the monthly *Edinburgh Voluntary Churchman*. Several newspapers, most notably the Whig *Scotsman*, also advocated the Voluntary position. The associations organized Voluntary lectures and sent agitators throughout the country to stir popular resentment against the Church. Voluntaries joined political Radicals in condemning the Church as a Tory institution which functioned to justify the oppression of the labouring poor. In December 1834, the Scottish Central Board for Extending the Voluntary Principle and Vindicating the Rights of Dissenters was formed in Edinburgh to oversee the movement as a whole.[32]

Three causes might be suggested for this eruption of aggressive Voluntaryism. First, religious Dissent in Scotland had increased dramatically since the mid-eighteenth century. By 1830, perhaps one third of the Scottish church-going population were Dissenters.[33] Most of these Scottish Dissenters were both presbyterian and Calvinist, members of denominations which had seceded from the Moderate-dominated Church of Scotland during the eighteenth century in protest against patronage. Until about 1800, the presbyterian secession churches had remained loyal to the principle of a national Establishment, professing their willingness to return to the Church once it had been purified of patronage. After 1800, however, encouraged by their own increasing numbers and organizational strength, presbyterian seceders began experiencing 'New Light': any state connection, they began arguing, corrupted a Church.[34] Secondly, the Voluntary movement was encouraged by the triumphs of liberal political reform in the late 1820s and early 1830s, and by the increasing influence of *laissez-faire* economic theory. Voluntaryism, its supporters believed, represented the extension of liberal principles into the religious world—

promising to revive Christianity through the 'free trade' dynamic. Finally, many Dissenters were concerned about the Evangelical achievements in revitalizing the Church of Scotland. Prior to 1820, the Moderate-dominated Establishment had represented little threat to the growth of Dissent. The Church had been waning in national influence, and its opponents could confidently predict that internal corruption and an indifferent ministry would soon bring about its destruction. By the end of the 1820s, however, this trend had reversed. Through the influence of Evangelicalism, the Church demonstrated new vigour. By requesting Parliamentary grants for church-building, moreover, the Church demonstrated its intention to employ its State connection to advantage. In a word, it had become a force which Dissent could no longer ignore.[35]

The Church of Scotland was initially slow to respond to Voluntary challenge. But gradually, Churchmen awakened to the seriousness of the threat. On 31 January 1833, the Glasgow Society for Promoting the Interests of the Church of Scotland was formed, and in March 1834, it began publishing the monthly *Church of Scotland Magazine,* the major anti-Voluntary review, matching in abusive language its rival *Voluntary Church Magazine.* Soon Church defence associations were formed throughout Scotland.[36] The conflict grew increasingly bitter. Friendships were ended. Missionary and philanthropic societies, previously composed of both Churchmen and Dissenters, were torn apart. Scottish society grew more and more polarized, as two conflicting social ideals began to emerge. The Voluntaries, as has been noted, embraced the liberal ideal of a pluralistic society of competing religious, social, and economic interests. They espoused the principles of Classical Liberal *laissez-faire* economic theory and looked favourably upon Whig and Radical efforts to secularize the State. Defenders of the Established Church, however, tended to embrace the ideal of the Christian commonwealth. The nation, they argued, would find unity and strength in religious consensus. In this time of social unrest, Scotland must renew its commitment to the Calvinist faith of its fathers. Secularization, and the division of society into competing social and economic interests, were evils to be resisted. The two social ideals were thus described in the pro-Church *Presbyterian Review* in January 1833:

We have first,... the old religious theory, coeval with the origin of civil society, and based on the principle, that the powers that be are ordained of God, are sanctioned by his authority, amenable to his jurisdiction, and subject to the guidance of his revealed word.

We have next, what may be termed, the new, the Sectarian or Infidel, the Liberal or Atheistic theory; according as we refer to its modern date, the parties by whom it has been introduced and advocated, its maintenance of the absolute liberty of human thought, or its systematic exclusion of all recognition of the Deity, and his communications to his creatures, as subjects on which men may differ, and which it is necessary to dismiss, in order to escape disagreeable controversies.[37]

Perhaps the most influential organ of the Church militant was the *Scottish Guardian* newspaper, which began publication in Glasgow in January 1833, under the editorship of Chalmers's former St. Andrews student, George Lewis. The *Scottish Guardian* opposed both religious Voluntaryism and *laissez-faire* capitalism. It advocated factory legislation and increased State support for the Church of Scotland's efforts to provide Christian and moral instruction to the labouring poor. It represented, in short, Christian paternalism. Active participants in the Voluntary controversy, like Lewis, tended to be younger men, with uncomprising idealism.

One significant effect of the Voluntary challenge was renewed agitation in the Established Church for the abolition of patronage. After about 1785, it will be recalled, the patronage issue, the fundamental controversy of the eighteenth-century Church of Scotland, had been allowed to lapse by the old Popular party leaders, who had concluded that they could not secure its abolition and that continued anti-patronage agitation would only encourage further secessions from the Church. In 1820, Sir Henry Moncrieff Wellwood, the leader of the Scottish Evangelical party, observed with satisfaction that the patronage issue was moribund. The mob violence once directed against the intrusion of unpopular patron's candidates upon parishes, Moncrieff Wellwood believed, had represented a less civilized, more fanatic era of Scottish history, beyond which both Church and society had happily advanced.[38] However, with the increasing strength of Evangelicalism after 1820, a group of Evangelicals revived the patronage issue. In 1825, largely through the efforts of Andrew Thomson, a 'Society for the Improvement of Church Patronage' was founded in Edinburgh. Its original purpose was to raise money to purchase church patronages and hand them over to the male heads of families in the parish, who would then have the right to elect their own minister. The response, however, was disappointing. Moncrieff Wellwood opposed any effort to revive the patronage issue, and the Evangelical public demonstrated little enthusiasm. Only one parish patronage was secured. The Society soon relinquished its effort to purchase patronages, and concentrated instead upon educating public opinion. It also encouraged the formation of auxiliary societies in towns and villages outside Edinburgh, though with little initial success.

Then in about 1831 the anti-patronage campaign began to receive widespread public support. Auxiliaries to the Society for the Improvement of Church Patronage were formed throughout Scotland. In 1827, there were only four auxiliaries outside Edinburgh; by 1833, there were thirty-seven. Anti-patronage petitions began to flood Parliament. In

1833, 152 anti-patronage petitions were presented in the House of Commons, representing 142 Scottish parishes and burghs. In 1834, 271 petitions were presented in the Commons, representing an additional 131 parishes and burghs. Nearly a third of Scotland's parishes petitioned Parliament against patronage during these two years.[39] Patronage became the focus of debate in presbyteries and synods, as well as in the public press.

One cause for this revival of anti-patronage agitation was the Whig political campaign for Parliamentary reform which had culminated in the reform bill of 1832. As an Evangelical historian of the period later observed, many Scots were traditionally more concerned with their ecclesiastical affairs than their political rights. It was, therefore, not surprising that in Scotland the Parliamentary reform movement should also focus attention upon the mode of clerical appointment.[40] But perhaps a more significant cause was the Voluntary offensive. In their attacks upon the Establishment, Voluntaries claimed that patronage demonstrated the compromised nature of the Church of Scotland. Patronage, they alleged, ensured that the Church remained the instrument of landowners and the Crown (who owned the vast majority of patronages). Voluntaries emphasized that in their congregations, ministers were elected by the male heads of families, rather than appointed by a local landlord or a Crown official. In response, an increasing number of Churchmen, Moderates as well as Evangelicals, became convinced that some measure of reform had to be adopted by the Establishment to ensure a greater popular voice in the selection of ministers. The Moderate Whig clergyman David Aitken, for instance, had little sympathy for the godly commonwealth ideal held by Evangelical Church defenders. None the less, he agreed that patronage reform had become necessary for the preservation of the Establishment. If this were neglected, he warned the Earl of Minto on 8 October 1832, 'we shall soon be in a rather puzzling predicament in Scotland, in consequence of something like an Irish system of [anti-Establishment] agitation, projected and begun by our Dissenters.'[41]

An additional effect of the Voluntary controversy was to augment the influence of Chalmers's social views within the Church. From the beginning of their offensive, Voluntaries had focused attacks upon his ideal of the godly commonwealth. His pastoral rhapsodies on covenanted parish communities, Andrew Marshall observed in a pamphlet in 1830, sounded delightful. 'But upon inquiry you will find', Marshall added, 'that out of the mind of Dr. Chalmers, the thing does not exist.'[42] Within the Church defence associations, however, Chalmers's social views found new adherents. For many, his Christian communal ideal represented the most convincing justification for a national religious Establishment. For years, his social views had received at best polite forbearance from the Evangelical party leadership. Now, he found a constituency. For many young Evangelical Church defenders, he became an oracle—a social prophet, who had early recognized the dangerous tendencies of Classical Liberal economic theory and had been willing to struggle in isolation for the godly commonwealth ideal which alone would save the nation. 'He has insisted,' the *Scottish Guardian* asserted on 1 February 1833, 'in season and out of season, that the labouring population can only be saved by their own foresight and self-denial; and that the best aid Government can bestow, is to grant them the schoolmaster and the teacher of Christianity in every district.' At last, the *Scottish Guardian* maintained, aggressive Voluntaryism and increasing working-class suffering were awakening the Church to his message.[43]

In May 1832, Chalmers's rising influence was recognized with election to the Moderatorship of the 1832 General Assembly, one of the highest honours in the Scottish Establishment. The 1832 Assembly was significant mainly for its debate on patronage. As a result of the increasing anti-patronage agitation, eleven presbyteries and synods submitted overtures for patronage reform to the Assembly. The overtures varied in content, from demands for the immediate abolition of patronage and its replacement by a form of popular election of ministers, to more moderate suggestions that the Assembly simply consider means to provide parishioners with greater influence over the patron's presentation. Following a long debate, the Assembly decided, by a vote of 127 to 85, that it was 'unnecessary and inexpedient to adopt the measures recommended in the overtures now before it'. However, it was significant that popular agitation had brought patronage to a major debate in the General Assembly for the first time in nearly fifty years. The vote had been sufficiently close, moreover, to encourage further efforts. During the debate, at least one speaker had commented that a mere eleven overtures were not sufficient indication of strong anti-patronage sentiment in the Church as a whole. Taking the hint, patronage reformers stepped up their campaign to agitate the patronage issue in the lower Church courts and among the public.[44]

As Moderator of the 1832 General Assembly, Chalmers had not participated in its debates. His behaviour had been circumspect; he had adhered to the conventions of impartiality attached to the Moderatorship. He was not, however, unconcerned about the patronage issue, and during the following year, as popular anti-patronage agitation increased, he sought a solution that would both satisfy the popular demands and preserve the unity of the Church. He did not favour the abolition of patronage. First, patronage was a property right recognized by the civil law, and it was improbable that even the reformed Parliament would allow the Church to expropriate private property.

Secondly, the landowners and Crown, who possessed the majority of church patronages, were among the strongest supporters of the Church in its struggle against Voluntaryism; most patrons, moreover, were careful to consult the preference of the parishioners before making a presentation. Thirdly, Chalmers did not believe that popular election of ministers would constitute any improvement over patronage. He was not a democrat; popular elections of clergy, he suspected, would too often be won by those who inflamed the prejudices of parishioners, rather than by candidates representing rational Scriptural Christianity. In the past, the system of patronage had provided the Church of Scotland with a wide variety of different talents—men of subtle and refined intellect as well as impassioned preachers. Under a system of popular election, however, he feared the clergy of the Establishment might degenerate to the level of the despised Voluntary clerical agitators.

By early 1833, anti-patronage agitation had grown so intense that the Whig Government finally instructed the Church to reform its patronage system. On 7 May 1833, Francis Jeffrey, now Lord Advocate for Scotland, drafted a letter from London on behalf of the Government, which he asked Cockburn to circulate among leaders in the Church. The Government, Jeffrey wrote, had decided 'that no presentee should be forced upon a parish against the serious and earnest reclamation of a decided majority of the people; and that when this is evinced, the settlement ought not to be proceeded with, but the patron set to present anew'. Further, Jeffrey added, if the approaching 1833 General Assembly neglected patronage reform, the Government would have to take action of its own: 'I am not only convinced that [the Government] will feel great disappointment, but fear that they will find it impossible to avoid (or long delay) bringing in a legislative enactment, without the light and encouragement they would receive from the example and opinion of the Venerable Body.'[45] In a word, the Government directed the Assembly either to provide parishioners with the right to veto an unpopular presentation, or be prepared to have the State impose this reform upon the Church. The lower Church courts, meanwhile, also demanded that the Assembly take action. While only eleven overtures for patronage reform had been submitted by the synods and presbyteries to the 1832 Assembly, no fewer than forty-two were sent to the 1833 Assembly.

In mid-May, a few days before the opening of the 1833 Assembly, the Evangelical party leadership met privately to draft their proposal for patronage reform. Chalmers initially suggested a policy of gradual reform, aimed at reviving the 'Call'. According to the 1712 Patronage Act, parishioners were supposed to have the right to hear a patron's presentee preach. If they considered the presentee acceptable, they would issue a 'Call' for his ministry, signed by the majority of heads of families. Only after receiving this 'Call' would the local presbytery be authorized to ordain the patron's candidate to the charge. During their eighteenth-century ascendancy, the Moderates had relegated the 'Call' to a mere formality, often ignoring it altogether. None the less, Chalmers observed, the 'Call' still remained on the statute books. Therefore, by instructing presbyteries to demand a proper 'Call' before admitting any minister to a vacant parish, the Assembly could, through a series of test cases, gradually restore authority to the opinion of parishioners. To ensure against possible legal complications, moreover, Chalmers recommended that the Assembly petition Parliament for an act acknowledging the Church's authority to enforce the existing ecclesiastical law respecting 'Calls'.

The Evangelical Whig lawyer James Moncrieff, however, now a judge on the Court of Session and a member of the inner circle of the Scottish Whig party, disagreed with Chalmers. The series of test cases suggested by Chalmers, Moncrieff argued, would take too much time to effect significant change, while the wording of the 1712 Patronage Act was so vague that any attempt to enforce it would only create further difficulties. The best course for the Assembly would be that recommended in Jeffrey's letter—simply to pass a new act of Church law giving the majority of male heads of family in a parish, who were in communion with the Church, the right to veto an unpopular presentation. There would, Moncrieff argued, be no need to request Parliament to legislate on this matter; the authority of the Church alone would be sufficient. Chalmers deferred to Moncrieff's legal and political expertise, and agreed to introduce the veto act overture in the 1833 Assembly.[46]

Chalmers's speech before the Assembly in May 1833 was another of his great oratorical performances. In it he attempted to chart a middle course for the Church, challenging the liberal and democratic spirit of many anti-patronage agitators, while at the same time asserting the need to give more weight to popular opinion in the selection of ministers.[47] He began by opposing any proposal to abolish patronage and replace it with popular election. A more democratic constitution, he asserted, would not improve the Church. What was democracy, he asked, but the transference of patronage from the few to the many? If, as Christians believed, all men were by nature sinful, then how would such a transference guarantee the selection of a higher quality of clergy?—'How are you to get quit of the evils incidental, I fear, to all sorts of human patronage, merely by multiplying the number of human patrons?' Under the existing patronage system, he argued, there was at least an individual or small group of individuals who could be held accountable for an ill-considered presentation. Indeed, precisely because they stood openly in view of the public, patrons were under pressure to improve the quality of their presentations.[48] But who, he asked, would be held accountable under a democratic system?

The best means for recognizing the popular voice in clerical appointments, he argued, was the veto. The veto would ensure that no presentee would be intruded upon parishioners against their will; at the same time, it would also ensure that responsibility for presenting candidates remained grounded in a visible authority. Thus, the veto would represent a compromise between the new spirit of democracy and the old spirit of aristocratic paternalism. Some individuals, he observed, feared that the veto was too democratic; as a safeguard, they demanded that parishioners be required to submit reasons for their disapproval of a candidate, which would be judged by the local presbytery. This type of scrutiny, he asserted, must not be imposed. If the majority of heads of families opposed the presentee, for whatever reason, then that presentee would not make an effective minister for their community. Uneducated peasants, he argued, might not be able to articulate their deep-felt objections before a presbytery. 'In very proportion to my sympathy and my depth of admiration for the Christian appetency of such cottage patriots', he exclaimed,

would be the painfulness I should feel when the cross-questionings of a court of review were brought to bear upon them; and the men, bamboozled and bereft of utterance by the reasonings which they could not answer, or perhaps, the ridicule which they could not withstand, were left to the untold agony of their own hearts.... To overbear such men is the high way to put an extinguisher on the Christianity of our land,...the Christianity of our ploughmen, our artisans, our men of handicraft and of hard labour.

'In the olden time', he added, such Christian peasants had demonstrated heroic valour in defence of the Reformed faith against religious persecution. Now, 'it is their remnant which acts as a preserving salt among our people, and which constitutes the real strength and glory of the Scottish nation.' To alienate them would be to destroy the Christian commonwealth by undermining its foundation at the local community level.[49] 'Chalmers', Cockburn remarked in his journal, 'in proposing the veto, raised himself above most modern orators by a great speech.' Again, it was his 'intensity of manner', rather than his arguments, which moved the Assembly. 'How he burns', Cockburn added. In the event, notwithstanding his impassioned appeal, his veto motion was defeated by a vote of 149 to 137.[50] None the less, the Evangelicals were encouraged by his eloquence and now grew confident that they could carry the veto in next year's General Assembly.

While the courts of the Established Church were wrestling with patronage reform, the Voluntaries had begun a major battle in Edinburgh over the Annuity tax, or Edinburgh church tax. In virtually all Scottish burghs, the stipends of the burgh clergy were paid from the income derived by the seat-rents, augmented, if necessary, by a tax, or teind, upon the heritable property in the burgh. In Edinburgh, however, as a result of several early seventeenth-century enactments, the clergy were paid from the income of the Annuity tax, a 6 per cent impost on the annual rental of the buildings in the burgh, payable by the occupiers, and collected by the Magistrates.[51] In mid-1832, the Edinburgh Voluntaries began what Cockburn termed an 'Irish Anti-Tythe' campaign, refusing to pay the Annuity tax. Their consciences, they claimed, would not allow them to support an oppresssive Establishment. Even non-Dissenting Edinburgh citizens joined this Voluntary-inspired taxpayers' revolt, protesting against injustices in the incidence of the tax, particularly the immunity of the lawyers and judges of the College of Justice, and of residents outside the burgh limits who attended city churches. The matter soon became serious. During the past six months, Cockburn informed Chalmers on 22 April 1833, the Magistrates had managed to collect only £173 of the Annuity tax, leaving an estimated £11,000 unpaid, 'a great part of which must inevitably be lost'.[52]

In April 1833, Jeffrey, the Lord Advocate, drafted a Government bill to reform the Annuity tax, which would have abolished the exemption of the College of Justice and transformed the Annuity tax into a part of the city revenues, with the city clergy to be paid directly from the general city funds. The Voluntaries, however, demanded nothing less than total abolition of all public financial support for the clergy, and in June 1833 Jeffrey dropped the bill. The city clergy, meanwhile, could not be paid, and the Magistrates were obliged to begin prosecuting delinquent taxpayers in the civil courts. This, in turn, created Voluntary martyrs. At a series of public meetings in Edinburgh during the summer of 1833, Voluntaries vowed to fill the gaols rather than pay an unjust tax. In 1833, 846 persons submitted to prosecution for refusing to pay the Annuity, and several allowed themselves to be incarcerated for a few days in the old Calton gaol. Upon their release, these prisoners were often paraded through the city by triumphant processions numbering as many as 10,000, with music and banners.[53] 'The process of imprisoning and of parading', Cockburn noted in his journal on 28 August 1833, 'is still going on, [though] ... it is odious in the eyes of all fair or rational men.'[54]

Early in January 1834, the Town Council decided that the Annuity tax could no longer be collected, and they submitted a series of proposals to the presbytery of Edinburgh. First, the Annuity tax would be abolished, and the clergy's salaries paid from the general city revenues. Secondly, in order to pay the salaries from the city revenues without the Annuity, the number of city clergy would be reduced from eighteen to thirteen, and the Edinburgh ministers' stipends would be lowered from £600 to £550. The number of clergy in the decaying Old Town of Edinburgh, the Council argued, could be reduced without harm to the religious interest of the people. Most of the Old Town parish churches were collegiate charges—that is, with two or more clergymen attached to the same church. The Council's plan, then, was to remove one clergyman each from five of these collegiate charges.

The Town Council's proposals were regarded by many as an unprovoked attack upon the Church. 'The clamour against the Church,' Cockburn noted in his journal on 29 January 1834,

which has been raging here for above a year has been taken up and fomented by the Radicals and Dissenters of the town-council, who have come to open war with the presbytery. Their object is to suppress some of the Edinburgh clergy, and to do various other foolish things, merely to diminish taxation; and in the prosecution of this object they have taken a tone of accusation and abuse which is quite new in this country, even among Dissenters, as applied to the Established clergy. It is very painful and very dangerous.[55]

In April 1833, at an early stage in the Voluntary revolt against the Annuity tax, the presbytery had appointed Chalmers convener of a committee for the preservation of its income and endowments, in large part because, as Professor of Divinity, he did not receive his income from the Annuity, and therefore might be considered disinterested. Chalmers made no secret of his contempt for the Voluntary civil disobedience. 'The general desire', he exclaimed before the presbytery in September 1833, 'for a change or rectification of the system by means of a new law—that I can understand; but anything like a general refusal of the old law, and that by a simple and spontaneous cessation of the wonted payments, with no other account of the matter than they they so choose it, and no other authority than the bidding of their own will—*this* is what I do not understand.'[56] He was enraged when, in January 1834, the Town Council announced that it would defer to the Voluntary law-breakers, abolish the Annuity, and reduce the strength of the Edinburgh Established Church.

A series of angry meetings were held in January between Chalmers's committee and the Town Council, in an attempt to reach a compromise. The Edinburgh lawyer and Whig Evangelical Alexander Dunlop advised Chalmers to be moderate: the majority of the Reformed Edinburgh Town Council, Dunlop pointed out, were Dissenters, and Chalmers must not press them too hard.[57] But Chalmers refused to be moderate. The Church was threatened by the new alliance of middle-class Whigs and Dissenters now gaining control of the nation's political institutions, and he would resist them. On 20 January, the Town Council requested a final response to its proposals from the presbytery.

Three days later, Chalmers presented to the presbytery his committee's report on its negotiations with the Town Council. The presbytery court was crowded with a delegation from the Town Council and a large number of spectators and newspaper reporters.

His committee, Chalmers asserted, had after careful deliberation decided to reject the Town Council's main recommendations. First, it refused to accept the abolition of the Annuity tax and the payment of the clergy from the general city revenues. A large portion of these city revenues, he observed, were derived from the seat-rents, and his committee suspected that in order to meet financial losses resulting from the abolition of the Annuity, the Town Council would begin presenting new ministers to city churches solely according to their ability to satisfy the popular taste for preaching, or in other words, to attract large seat-rents for the city treasury. One of the benefits of the Annuity tax, Chalmers maintained, was that it enabled the Edinburgh Church to comprise diverse clerical talents and abilities, including men of high scholarly achievements, who were, none the less, unpopular preachers. By 'putting the ministers up to auction' through a seat-rent test, however, the Town Council would restrict the Edinburgh clergy to one type—the popular preacher. Further, Chalmers argued, the Annuity tax was a property right belonging to the Church. In the past, the city had taken over large tracts of land belonging to the Church, in exchange for granting the Annuity tax. If the Council now insisted upon abolishing the Annuity, the Church would have to consider legal measures to repossess its former properties in the city.

Chalmers's committee adamantly refused, moreover, to accept the suppression of any clerical livings in the city. The 'sordid and un-generous' attacks of the Voluntaries, the 'vulgar economic spirit' of the Whig Town Council, would not intimidate the Edinburgh Church into relinquishing its commitment to the Christian commonwealth. In the final analysis, Chalmers asserted, the issue at hand involved the conflict between the 'luxury' of the rich, and the religious rights of the poor. The Voluntary system of church maintenance, he argued, served the interest of the upper and middle classes. The rich could afford higher seat-rents to maintain their clergy and churches, and they cared not how many Establishment churches and clerical positions were suppressed, so long as they were spared having to pay the Annuity tax. The Establishment, however, was the poor man's Church. It placed parish churches and ministers in destitute districts of the city, where the inhabitants could not support these institutions themselves, in order to reach the poor with Christian and moral teachings. 'Our cause,' he declared,

in spite of all the obloquy which has been upon it, is emphatically the cause of the unprovided—it is the cause of the poor against the rich—of the men who should reap the benefits of the Establishment in the lessons of Christian instruction, against the relatively few would retain what was not legally theirs ... who would stop, for their own private uses, that which ought to be expended on the best and highest objects of patriotism.

Some, he observed, equated Voluntaryism with political Radicalism. But if by Radicalism they meant the cause of the common man, then it was the Church, and not the Voluntaries, who deserved the title. With rising passion he exclaimed:

I have already professed myself, and will profess myself again an unflinching—an out-and-out—and I maintain it—the only consistent radical. The dearest object of my earthly existence is the elevation of the common people—humanized by Christianity and raised by the strength of their moral habits to a higher platform of human nature, and by which they may attain and enjoy the rank and consideration due to enlightened and companionable men. I trust the day is coming when the people will find out who are their best friends, and when the mock patriotism of the present day shall be unmasked as an act of robbery and spoilation on the part of those who would deprive the poor of their best and highest patrimony. The imperishable soul of the poor man is of as much price in the sight of heaven as the soul of the rich, and I will resist to the uttermost—I will resist even to the death—that alienation, which goes but to swell the luxury of the higher ranks at the expense of the lower orders.

The meeting was swept with enthusiasm by Chalmers's oratory. The presbytery adopted his report with a unanimous vote of appreciation.[58] It was a significant moment. Rather than simply defend its position against Voluntary attacks, Chalmers now proclaimed that the Church would press forward aggressively in its mission. In the face of opposition from a middle- and upper-class Voluntary-Whig alliance, the Church would appeal to the working classes. It was, he exclaimed, the poor man's Church; it would accept battle with the *laissez-faire* doctrines of the new élite, in the name of the old godly commonwealth ideal. A militant mood was emerging in the Church, for which Chalmers provided a voice. A few years earlier, after the death of Andrew Thomson, many had doubted whether Chalmers, with his combative temperament, would be a fit leader for the Evangelical party, especially now that it was beginning to gain control over the Church as a whole. But confronted by the increasing influence of the Voluntary offensive, many began to view him as the only man who could save the Establishment, and the Christian commonwealth it represented.

But then, with the leadership, not only of the Evangelical party, but of the entire Church of Scotland before him, Chalmers was suddenly struck down. Leaving the presbytery after his speech, he began walking home alone. Professor Macdougal of Edinburgh University met him on the way, and Chalmers began excitedly relating the events of the presbytery meeting, while leaning on Macdougal for support. 'We had', Macdougal later recalled, 'not gone many yards when he suddenly stopped short, and said, in a subdued, but agitated voice, that ''he felt very strangely.'' I asked instantly, *how*? He said he felt giddy—a numbness down one side, and a tendency to fall in that direction.' Alarmed, Macdougal called for a carriage and took him home. When Chalmers's physician, James Begbie, reached Chalmers's home shortly thereafter, he found him 'calm, but with the conviction that he was struck down with a formidable disease'. His mind, Begbie later related, seemed unaffected. But his speech was slurred, the right side of his face partially paralysed, his right arm and leg almost fully paralysed. He continued to beat his right leg with his left hand, Begbie added, 'in the hope, as he said, of recalling the banished sensation'. Visiting Chalmers a few days later, on 29 January, Cockburn found him still partially paralysed on the right side. 'His face', Cockburn recalled, 'was more cadaverous, his eye more dead, his voice more gutteral than usual.'[59]

For a time, it seemed that his paralysis might prove permanent. By mid-February 1834, he was able to return to the duties of his chair— but his health remained poor, and he suffered a series of relapses, probably minor strokes. The memory of his father, who had been deprived of hearing, sight, and mental capacity by the series of strokes beginning in 1804, apparently troubled him, and perhaps more than death, he began to fear that he might be losing his mental clarity. In early June 1834, he retired for the summer to a cottage in the village of Penicuik, a few miles south of Edinburgh. 'A long intermission,' he wrote in his diary on 9 June 1834, 'an arrest laid on me on the 23[d] of January last, fears of an apoplectic tendency; see things I imagine through a medium of haze and twilight more than I wont. It is my desire to prepare for eternity; and if imagination and sensibility decay I desire that intellect, and still more that principle, should have the entire possession and ascendancy over me.' Even in the retirement of Penicuik, the relapses continued. 'Considerable and constant noise in my head,' he noted in his diary on 13 June. 'A second suspicious visitation,' he wrote on 20 June: 'Sent for Dr. Begbie, who orders an entire cessation of study.'[60]

Because of his illness, Chalmers was only a passive observer to the momentous events in the General Assembly of May 1834, when the Evangelical party finally wrested control of the Church from the Moderates, and passed the three acts which would shape Church policy during the next troubled decade. First, on the motion of James Moncrieff, the Veto Act was passed, by a vote of 180 to 131. The Church now recognized the authority of the majority of male heads of family in a parish, who were in communion with the Church, to veto a patron's presentation, provided there was no evidence of personal ill will or libel involved in the rejection. Secondly, the Assembly passed the Chapels Act. According to this act, all chapels-of-ease, which had previously been unrepresented in the Church courts, were now to be considered parish churches in the Scottish Establishment. They were to have kirk-sessions, with disciplinary authority, and their clergy and elders were granted full membership on the presbytery, synod, and General Assembly courts. Further, the new churches received territorial parish boundaries recognized by the Church. The new parishes were termed, *quoad sacra*, to distinguish them from the existing *quoad civilia* parishes, which were defined by the civil law, over which the Church of Scotland had no authority. The laws respecting poor relief and parish schools continued to apply only to *quoad civilia* parishes; but in all matters of ecclesiastical discipline and legislation, the Church recognized the new *quoad sacra* parishes as legal jurisdictions.

There was, meanwhile, a serious question about whether the British State would permit the Church of Scotland to form the proposed new parishes. For parishes were a civil as well as an ecclesiastical jurisdiction, with considerable importance in local poor-law and educational administration. According to a 1707 act of the Scottish Parliament, a parish could be subdivided only with the consent of the heritors who possessed three-quarters of the heritable property in the parish. In February 1834, therefore, the Scottish Evangelical Tory MP for the county of Lanarkshire, J. C. Colquhoun, introduced a bill in Parliament to enable the Church of Scotland to create the new parishes. The bill was passed in July 1834, shortly after the General Assembly had passed its Chapels Act. Colquhoun's act was vaguely worded: it permitted the Church of Scotland to create the *quoad sacra* parishes, but only so long as they did not interfere with the existing legal arrangements respecting the *quoad civilia* parishes. In a word, it left the State with the option to suppress the *quoad sacra* parishes if they were perceived to be infringing upon the rights of heritors, paupers, or other individuals with a vested interest in the old parish arrangements. Colquhoun's act, as will be seen, would later cause the Church serious damage and bitter disappointment. However, in 1834, it was viewed as a Parliamentary mandate, not only for the Chapels Act, but for a new Assembly campaign to increase the number of *quoad sacra* parishes.[61]

Thirdly, the General Assembly of 1834 reformed and issued new instructions to its Church Accommodation Committee. This standing committee, it will be recalled, had been appointed in 1828, under the convenership of the Moderate clergyman Alexander Brunton. In its report on 28 May 1834, however, Brunton's committee announced that it foresaw little likelihood of a grant from the present Government, and advised the Assembly to begin collecting funds and erecting new churches on its own to meet the nation's need for additional church accommodation. Accordingly, the Assembly enlarged the Church

Accommodation Committee and instructed it to organize a new church-building campaign within the Church. Further, it formed a second committee, the Church Endowments Committee, under the convener-ship of the Evangelical lay-elder Charles Fergusson, which was to continue negotiations with the Government for a Parliamentary grant— not for building new churches, but rather for endowing those which the Assembly hoped to erect.[62]

Brunton, meanwhile, resigned his convenership of the enlarged Church Accommodation Committee and despite his delicate health, Chalmers accepted the Assembly's request that he take Brunton's place. There was doubt about his physical capacity for leadership, but he had become the symbol of Evangelicalism in the Church, particularly among young activists in the Church defence associations. For his part, he was convinced that his appointment was providential: God had spared him from death for the task of saving and extending the Church of Scotland. His moment for great service had arrived. 'Nor can I regard it as otherwise than a gracious Providence,' he asserted at the first meeting of the enlarged Church Accommodation Committee, in early June 1834,

that after having been unhinged, enfeebled, and well-nigh overborne in an arduous conflict with those who would despoil our beloved Church of her endowments, and abridge the number of her ministers, I should now be called upon, in the hour of my returning strength ... to enlarge her means and multiply her labourers, instead of maintaining as heretofore, a weary struggle with the men whose unhallowed hands are lifted up against our Zion, to mutilate and destroy her.[63]

The Church, he proclaimed, had now shifted its stance from the defence to the offence, and he was ready to lead it against its enemies. The Voluntaries threatened to destroy the ideals of Christian community and covenanted national commonwealth—ideals to which he had dedicated his life. They had, he believed, nearly killed him; his stroke in late January had been their doing. But God had called him back to life for a purpose. Filled with a sense of divine mission, seeking personal revenge against his Voluntary enemies, surrounded by young Evan-gelical idealists in the Church, troubled by delicate health and a 'hissing' noise in his head, Chalmers began the greatest campaign of his life—to realize the godly commonwealth in Scotland. For this crusade, it seemed, he now had a unified Evangelical Church behind him. The Moderate party was in disarray: John Inglis, the Moderate party leader, had died in January 1834, and the party now lacked both leadership and a defined cause. Many Moderates supported Chalmers's committee, which now represented the main mission of the Church. Instead of the old Evangelical-Moderate conflict, the religious life of the Scottish nation was now dominated by the conflict between aggressive Voluntaryism and an equally aggressive Evangelical Establishment. The Voluntary challenge had united the Church.

III

The campaign to increase church accommodation in the Scottish Establishment had in fact begun, on a local level, a few months before the General Assembly of 1834. In January 1834, largely through the initiative of Chalmers's publisher, the St. John's parish elder William Collins, the Glasgow Association for Promoting the Interests of the Church of Scotland began a five-year plan to build and endow, through private subscriptions, twenty additional churches in Glasgow, with 1,000 seats in each. This would more than double existing church accommodation in the Glasgow Establishment. Each new church would be built at a cost of £2,000, and would receive an endowment of an additional £2,000. The endowment was expected to yield £80 per annum through investment. This would be applied to the minister's annual stipend of £200, in order to allow the new churches to require only minimal seat-rents. Low seat-rents, in turn, would enable the labouring poor to attend church as families. Indeed, a major purpose of the plan was to place new churches in impoverished working-class neighbourhoods, where Collins hoped that eventually each new church would be surrounded by a model parish community of 3,000 inhabitants, with poor relief and education programmes based upon Chalmers's St. John's experiment. By March 1834, a fair start had been made, and £6,800 of the £80,000 required for the project had been subscribed.[64] In February 1834, meanwhile, inspired by reports of the Glasgow church-building plan, a second local church accommodation society was begun in Aberdeen.[65] These two local societies represented a new departure in the Church. For several years, the Church Accommodation Committee under Brunton's direction had negotiated in vain with the Government for a Parliamentary church-building grant. Now, stirred by the Voluntary challenge, and disillusioned with the Whig Government, Church members began to organize local church-building societies, independent of Government support. The irony is that Churchmen were being obliged to adopt Voluntary methods in order to to find the funding necessary to enlarge the Establishment.

The General Assembly's instructions to Chalmers's Church Accommodation Committee were threefold. First, the committee was to gather statistics demonstrating Scotland's need for additional churches. Secondly, it was to use these statistics to determine where new churches should be built. Thirdly, it was to formulate a plan for collecting funds to support the building campaign.[66] In laying the foundation for the new campaign, Chalmers also borrowed heavily from Voluntary principles. Impressed by the example of Collins's Glasgow association, he decided that the best means for collecting information and funds was to encourage the formation of local church accommodation societies, over which he would exercise only a loose general supervision from his Edinburgh headquarters. Local societies, he believed, could better ascertain local statistics and determine local need for more churches. Individuals, moreover, were more likely to contribute to the building of a local church, than to send funds to a General Assembly committee centred in Edinburgh. 'What I particularly wish', Chalmers informed Collins from Penicuik on 9 June 1834,

is to combine a wise general superintendence on the one hand, with an entire and intense local feeling in each separate town and district for its own local necessities on the other. I do hope you will prosecute your own separate object as energetically as if we did not exist.... I foresee that however influential one Committee may prove for the whole of Scotland, a tenfold revenue may be gained for the cause, by each distinct association being made to feel its own individuality; and to concentrate its efforts on the object of providing for its own wants wherever these wants exist.[67]

He advocated the formation of a loose hierarchy of local associations, from 'sectional' societies directing church-building operations in a city or county, such as those already formed in Glasgow and Aberdeen, to parochial societies in each parish, and finally to sub-parochial societies in a particular neighbourhood within a parish. As the societies became smaller and the goals more immediate, he believed, the emotional commitment would become greater. 'You deepen the culture of the soil on which we are all operating,' he explained to the Aberdeen Evangelical clergyman Abercromby Gordon, while recommending to him the formation of sub-parochial associations on 28 June 1834, 'and in proportion as you descend [to smaller neighbourhood societies], you have the advantage of a far more intense local feeling, and greatly more numerous contributions.'[68]

The British and Foreign Bible Society, he informed the young Glasgow Evangelical clergyman Robert Buchanan on 30 June 1834, 'with its Parent Institution, its countless auxiliaries, and above all its Parochial Associations,' should form the model for the national church accommodation operation. He advocated that new local societies adopt a 'penny-a-week' scheme, by which labouring families would be encouraged to subscribe a small sum each week. Twenty years before, in 1814, it will be recalled, he had advocated 'penny-a-week' parish Bible societies as a means for uniting communities in support of the overseas mission. Now, penny-a-week local societies would increase support for the Establishment among the lower social orders. 'Every man whom you suceed in gaining as a penny-a-week contributor to our cause,' Chalmers explained to John Cook, the Moderate minister of the Fifeshire parish of Lawrencekirk, on 9 July 1834, 'you will succeed in reforming as a friend to the Church of Scotland.... I know not a wiser policy than that by which you interest the great bulk of our families in behalf of the venerable Establishment.' A major function of the local societies was to combat Voluntaryism, by encouraging the poor to feel that they held a personal stake in the national Establishment.[69] In mid-July 1834, Chalmers sent the first of a series of printed circulars to all presbyteries, urging the formation of parochial and sub-parochial societies. 'This is', he asserted, 'an age of hostility to Endowments by the State; and our great dependence, under heaven, for the fuller equipment of our Church is on the endowments of Christian charity. The spoilators of our Establishment are on the wing, and their unhallowed hands are already lifted up to mutilate and to destroy.'[70] In response to his initial plea, dozens of local societies were formed in towns, parishes, and districts throughout Scotland.

Under Chalmers's guidance, then, the Church began to form local voluntary societies, based upon private philanthropy, 'the endowments of Christian charity'. He termed this voluntary effort on behalf of the Establishment 'internal Voluntaryism', in order to distinguish it from the 'external Voluntaryism' of the Dissenters. 'Internal Voluntaryism', he declared, was private effort dedicated to the communal purpose of the godly commonwealth, and was opposed to any concept of 'free trade' in religion. 'Internal Voluntaryism' emphasized the elevation of the labouring poor within Christian communities, which would be created by voluntary sacrifices made by all social orders. 'External Voluntaryism', on the contrary, functioned only to further the interests of the middle and upper classes who could afford to provide churches for themselves.

At the same time as he was encouraging the formation of local societies, Chalmers began organizing a general Church Accommodation Committee fund. The purpose of the general fund was threefold. First, it would defray the committee's administrative costs, including printing and mailing expenses. Secondly, it would supplement the collections of local societies in poorer districts, encouraging local church-building operations in neighbourhoods otherwise unable to collect sufficient funds. Thirdly, and most important, by paying administrative costs and subsidizing local operations, the general fund would help to preserve a sense of unity among the many local societies—and thus ensure that the 'internal Voluntaryism' of the local societies was directed to the higher national purpose of the godly commonwealth.[71] Unlike contributions to the local societies, which were motivated in part by 'intense local feeling', Chalmers expected that contributions to the general fund would represent broader concern for the nation as a whole. In July 1834, he began personally soliciting wealthy acquaint-

4. George Cook, DD, Professor of Moral Philosophy, St. Andrews University, 1829–45 (D. O. Hill, 1843)

5. David Welsh, DD, Professor of Ecclesiastical History, University of Edinburgh, 1831–43; Moderator of the Disruption Assembly, 1842–3; Professor of Church History, New College, Edinburgh, 1843–5 (D. O. Hill, 1843)

6. Robert S. Candlish, DD, minister of St. George's parish, Edinburgh, 1834–43; minister of Free St. George's, Edinburgh, 1843–73 (D. O. Hill, 1843)

7. Thomas Chalmers in the year of the Disruption (D. O. Hill, 1843).

ances for general-fund contributions. 'I feel more emboldened to address your Grace upon this subject,' he informed the Duke of Buccleuch on 9 July 1834,

from the conviction that a generous sacrifice on the part of the affluent, not for the temporal necessities but for the moral culture and moral well-being of the poor, beside yielding a substantial repayment in the arrest that would thus be laid both on pauperism and crime, would serve more effectually than any other expedient, in these days of distemper and menace, to reunite the various orders of the state into a harmonious and pacific understanding with each other.

In December 1834, he sent a printed circular to members of the Scottish landed aristocracy and gentry, and to wealthy urban merchants and professionals.[72] If a major purpose of the local societies was to interest the 'common people' in the Church Accommodation campaign, a major purpose of the general fund was to attract support from among the social élites, the 'enlightened public' who Chalmers believed possessed broader and more comprehensive social views. Their support would help ensure that the local 'internal Voluntaryism' of the common people was elevated to serve the higher purpose of the godly commonwealth.

While he was thus organizing the local societies and the general fund, Chalmers also began a model church-building operation in Edinburgh, intended to serve as an example for local operations in the rest of the country. He had actually conceived such an operation a few months before his appointment as convener of the Church Accommodation Committee. On 1 March 1834, little more than a month after his stroke, Chalmers had presented the Edinburgh Town Council with a proposal to build a new church in the Cowgate, one of the most impoverished districts of the city. He had collected thirty subscribers for the building costs, and intended to erect the church according to the plan introduced to him by John Gladstone of Liverpool in 1817—by which subscribers would be paid 4 per cent per annum on their shares from the seat-rents. He asked only that the Town Council agree to transfer a clergyman to the proposed Cowgate church from one of the Old Town collegiate churches, and to continue to pay his stipend as an Edinburgh parish minister from the Annuity tax. The new church could thus require only minimal seat-rents, allowing it to attract a working-class congregation from the Cowgate.

The Dissenter-dominated Town Council, however, had refused his request.[73] Now, with the beginning of the General Assembly's new Church Accommodation campaign, Chalmers decided to revive his local church-building plan in the Water of Leith, a working-class district immediately outside the Edinburgh burgh limits (and therefore beyond the Town Council's jurisdiction). 'I have long contemplated', he informed a wealthy Edinburgh philanthropist, John Leermouth, on 25 August 1834, 'that on the failure of the Cowgate proposition, there should be an attempt made in a locality where the City Corporation cannot interfere with us.' His plan was to build, through private subscriptions, a *quoad sacra* parish church. Two-thirds of the seats would be rented at moderate prices to working-class families, while one-third would be rented at the usual Edinburgh prices to upper- and middle-class families—'thus constituting a Church occupied by such a gradation of wealth and rank as is exhibited in our agricultural parishes'.[74]

Erecting an unendowed *quoad sacra* parish church in an urban working-class district, Chalmers realized, required careful preliminary proceedings. Merely to concentrate upon the 'stone and lime' of church-building would not suffice. The new church might not be attended, in which case it would add fuel to Voluntary arguments that the Establishment was declining and no longer warranted State support. It might be partially attended, but still not provide enough income from its seat-rents to support its minister. Or, like other urban churches, it might attract only an upper- and middle-class congregation, leaving the poor outside. ('The system of exclusively aristocratic congregations', Chalmers informed Leermouth in his letter of 25 August, 'has been the curse of Edinburgh, and the discredit of our establishment in all large cities.') In pursuing his Water of Leith plans, then, Chalmers determined first to explore the territory.

Late in August 1834, he established a Water of Leith local society. With the assistance of this society, statistics were collected from the district. Out of a population of 1,287, it was discovered, less than 150 individuals held seats in any church, either Establishment or Dissenting, despite the fact that several churches with unlet seats existed in the vicinity. Indeed, a chapel-of-ease (now a *quoad sacra* parish church), recently built in nearby Stockbridge, attracted only seven seat-holders from the Water of Leith district. The real cause for the low church attendance in the Water of Leith, then, was not simply insufficient church accommodation. Rather, it was the lack of any sense of Christian community in the neighbourhood. The habit of regular church attendance, which Chalmers had observed in rural Anstruther and Kilmany, had ceased to exist among the Water of Leith poor. Thus, before proceeding to the 'stone and lime', Christian sentiments would have to be disseminated and a new congregation created through an active territorial missionary operation, including regular household visitations, week-night Bible and prayer meetings, and informal Sunday services in the district. In short, the moral foundation for a Christian community would have to be created before any building was begun. This, he maintained, was crucial.

Since November 1833 a young urban missionary, James Keith Hay, had been employed by several wealthy patrons to evangelize in the Water of Leith. In the late summer of 1834, Chalmers began working closely with Hay, encouraging his household visitations and attending his Sunday services, which were held in an abandoned malt granary. By the end of 1834, nearly 400 Water of Leith inhabitants regularly attended Hay's services, despite the cold and damp of the unheated building. With this sizeable congregation, Chalmers and the local society finally determined to risk building the new church. Property in the district was purchased, the structure completed, and on 15 May 1836, Chalmers preached the opening sermon. A few days later, the General Assembly declared the new Dean church a *quoad sacra* parish church, with Hay appointed as the minister.[75]

By early 1835, Chalmers had created the administrative framework for the new church-building campaign—a combination of local initiative, represented by the local societies, and general supervision and financial support, represented by his Church Accommodation Committee and general fund. Chalmers's framework was intended to comprehend all social orders, from the poor labourer subscribing his penny a week to a neighbourhood sub-parochial society, to the wealthy businessman or professional contributing £50 or £100 to a sectional society, and finally to the landed magnates contributing £200 or more to the general fund. In the Water of Leith, meanwhile, Chalmers was pursuing a model for local church-building which demonstrated the communal goals of the campaign. The Church Accommodation effort, he maintained, should not focus merely upon 'stone and lime'. Rather, the object was to create viable Christian parish communities in neighbourhoods where such communities did not exist, and especially among the labouring orders, who were rapidly slipping away from any religious affiliation. Local church-building operations were to be preceded by statistical surveys to determine the extent of genuine need for additional accommodation. Local societies were instructed to begin aggressive territorial missionary operations, in order to create a parochial congregation, before beginning a new church structure. Above all, a large portion of the seats were to be rented at the low 2*s.*-per-quarter rate, to encourage working-class attendance.

In a pamphlet published in February 1835, Chalmers endeavoured to calm the violent Voluntary response to the new Church Accommodation campaign, by maintaining that the Church's object was 'not to supplant the Dissenters, but to supply the outfield population whom neither they nor we have overtaken'. 'External Voluntaryism', he asserted, had proved beneficial in attracting upper- and middle-class Dissenting congregations, but only 'internal Voluntaryism' and an aggressive territorial ministry aimed at the creation of a viable parish community, with regular household visitations by a local minister and agency of elders and deacons, could reach the great part of the Scottish population, and especially the labouring poor. 'It is on this,' he maintained, 'and this alone, in fact, that our plea for an Establishment, and a sufficiently extended one, is founded—on the moral and spiritual desolation of all remoter hamlets and villages in large country parishes, on the outcast thousands and tens of thousands in large towns—only to be assailed by the territorial methods of an Establishment, and by the aggressive forces which belong to it.'[76]

The key to his Church Accommodation campaign, Chalmers believed, was the Parliamentary grant, which the Scottish Establishment had pursued, without success, since 1828. 'Internal Voluntaryism' had to be matched by State assistance to ensure an effective Establishment. Only a Parliamentary grant, he argued, providing an endowment for paying part of the minister's stipend, would allow the new *quoad sacra* parish churches to set their seat-rents low enough to enable the lower social orders to attend church regularly as families. Without such an endowment, the labouring poor would continue to be excluded from the national Establishment. Religion in Scotland would become an exclusively middle- and upper-class affair, while the poor would be relegated to ignorance and depravity, endangering both their eternal souls and the social stability of the commonwealth.[77] Chalmers was convinced that renewed negotiations with the Government would now prove fruitful. Three things encouraged him in this belief. First, in June 1834, Henry Brougham, the Lord Chancellor, had advocated the extension of the Church of Scotland, in a speech in the House of Lords.[78] Secondly, the local societies were beginning to collect statistical evidence which demonstrated low church attendance in many areas of the country, resulting from insufficient church accommodation. Thirdly, and most important, the Scottish public was beginning to contribute considerable time and money to local church building. This demonstrated, Chalmers believed, a changing mood in Scotland, which a representative Parliament, and particularly a Whig Government which emphasized the role of public opinion, would have to respect.[79] In truth, the case for a Parliamentary grant was a strong one. So long as Scotland retained a national Establishment, it was Parliament's responsibility to ensure that it was sufficient for the nation's needs. If non-attendance at church, particularly among the labouring orders, could be demonstrated to have resulted from an insufficient number of parish churches and from high seat-rents, then it was incumbent upon Parliament to supply the requested endowments.

So in July 1834, a month after the close of the General Assembly, a deputation from the Assembly's Church Endowments Committee travelled to London to renew negotiations with the Whig Government. Because of his delicate health, Chalmers did not accompany the deputation. On 2 July, however, he provided written instructions to Charles Fergusson, the convener of the Endowments Committee, describing the type of grant he desired. First, the purpose of the grant would be to endow all new *quoad sacra* churches, not in order to benefit the clergy, but to enable the new churches to reduce their seat-rents. 'It ought to be given on the part of government, in return for such a regulation of the seat rents as shall make the means of Christian instruction accessible to the great mass of the community.' Secondly, in providing the endowments, the Government should demand that preference in renting the inexpensive seats be given to residents of the *quoad sacra* parish. It should insist that the new churches emphasize a territorial parish ministry, intended to create a Christian community. 'In this way, altogether new ground will be entered upon. A real movement or advance will be made among a here-to-fore neglected population. Christian instruction will be let down to the poorest of our families, and our Establishment if extended in this way, will become, at a very cheap rate, an effective home mission.' In order to ensure effective parochial supervision, moreover, he suggested that the Government impose a maximum limit of 3,000 inhabitants for each new *quoad sacra* parish.

Finally, Government endowments should only be awarded to those churches already erected by 'internal Voluntaryism'. The sacrifice and efforts of the local societies in building the church would serve as the Government's 'security' for the fact that the new church was indeed needed by that community. He requested an endowment of £100 per annum for each new *quoad sacra* parish church. An initial annual grant of £6,600 would suffice to provide the £100 endowment for the sixty-six chapels-of-ease made into *quoad sacra* churches by the 1834 General Assembly. But his annual grant would then gradually increase, as the Church Accommodation campaign erected new churches. Eventually, Chalmers expected that the annual Parliamentary grant to the Scottish Establishment would reach £50,000, representing an endowment of £100 to each of 500 new churches he believed were required in Scotland.[80]

Fergusson's Church Endowment deputation received encouragement from leading Whig Government ministers in London, including Lord Melbourne, who in June 1834 had assumed the office of Prime Minister. None the less, the Whig ministers requested the Church of Scotland to postpone its formal application for the grant for several months. The recent shake-up in the Cabinet, including the resignation of the former Prime Minister, Lord Grey, and several other leading ministers, had placed the Government in a precarious position. Further, July was too late in the Parliamentary session to introduce a new financial appropriations bill.[81] Before it left London in late July, however, Fergusson's deputation was assured that the Government would try to introduce a measure at the opening of the next Parliamentary session. 'As yet,' Fergusson reported to Chalmers on 11 August 1834, 'we have no reason to complain.' Nevertheless, Fergusson also feared that the Whig Government's increasing dependence upon the support of organized Dissent would make it difficult for Melbourne to fulfil the Whig promises.[82]

Encouraged by the Government's promised support, however, Chalmers proceeded, in September 1834, to draft a formal Parliamentary bill 'by which the deficiences of our Establishment might be repaired; and the Church of Scotland be made commensurate to the wants of her population'. In addition to the three conditions which he had described to Fergusson in July, he now added a fourth: 'that every new church so endowed should undertake to supply the ordinary Sessional management for the pauperism of its own parish, and that the produce of its ordinary collections should be given up for this object.' In short, he now also sought Government support for the extension of the traditional system of parish poor relief, based upon voluntary church-door collections, to all new *quoad sacra* parishes. Thus, the Church Accommodation movement would not only provide additional churches, but would also reduce assessment relief by obliging new churches to adopt the St. John's model. 'Could this new direction be given to [all new *quoad sacra* parish churches],' he noted in his draft bill, 'it might at length rid our towns and populous parishes of their compulsory provision for the poor altogether.'[83]

Chalmers sent copies of his proposed bill to several MPs. Among them was William Ewart Gladstone, the twenty-four-year-old son of Chalmers's Liverpool friend and supporter, John Gladstone.[84] The elder Gladstone had been born in Leith, near Edinburgh, where the Gladstones continued to own property and exercise local influence.[85] In the late 1820s, William had made several extended winter visits to Edinburgh, frequently breakfasting with Chalmers. Indeed, the elder Scottish ecclesiastical politician and the future Prime Minister had developed a close relationship, based upon mutual veneration for the national religious Establishments, as well as the friendship between Chalmers and William's father. In December 1833, young Gladstone had been returned to Parliament and had soon established himself as a protégé of Sir Robert Peel. Chalmers was delighted. He greatly admired Peel, regarding him the strongest advocate of religious Establishments in Parliament. Yet he was intimidated by Peel's haughty manner, and hesitated to communicate with him directly. Since the retirement of the ailing Earl of Elgin from public life, he had lost his channel of communication with the Tory leader. Now, in young Gladstone, Chalmers perceived the means of introducing his Church Accommodation campaign to Peel's attention.[86]

In November 1834, before it had the opportunity to present the Church's grant proposals before the next Parliamentary session, Melbourne's Whig Ministry was dismissed from office, and the Tory Peel was summoned to form a Government. It was a weak Government, with the Tories in a minority in the Commons, facing an assortment of Whigs, Radicals, Dissenters, and Irish. A general election was held in December-January, which strengthened the Tory position slightly, but left it still a minority Government. On 30 December 1834, Gladstone advised Chalmers to press to have his Church bill introduced early in the 1835 Parliamentary session, as the future of Peel's Government was uncertain. If Peel fell, Gladstone warned, Melbourne and the Whigs would be more dependent upon organized Dissent than before, and therefore less disposed to assist the Scottish Establishment.[87] Chalmers, meanwhile, was already consulting with William Rae, the Tory Lord Advocate of Scotland, and a strong friend of the Church.[88] By this point, Chalmers regarded the Parliamentary grant negotiations as too important to be left to Fergusson's Endowment Committee, and he had undertaken them himself. In late January, on Gladstone's advice, he communicated his proposed endowment bill directly to Peel, who promised his Government's assistance. 'I do assure you', Peel informed Chalmers on 28 January 1835, 'that the Church of Scotland has few more attached friends among its own immediate members, than myself ... Your proposals are therefore addressed to one favourably disposed to them, and who will take them into very early consideration.'[89] On 2 February, in the King's Speech opening the new session of Parliament, the Government announced that it would consider means to meet the need for more church accommodation in the Scottish Establishment. Chalmers and his supporters were overjoyed. The endowment grant, it appeared, was theirs.

The Scottish Central Board of Dissenters, however, had not been inactive. In the previous autumn, they had mounted a campaign against any Parliamentary grant for the Church of Scotland. This campaign grew more intense after January 1835. Numerous petitions were sent to Parliament, protesting the proposed enlargement of the Church, and in some cases urging disestablishment. The Voluntaries denounced the Church Accommodation movement as a Tory scheme, intended to increase Tory patronage and introduce a clerical tyranny into Scotland.[90] The Church responded in kind. On 19 January 1835, a pro-grant petitioning drive was begun with a circular sent to all presbyteries and local church accommodation societies, signed by Chalmers, Fergusson, and Patrick MacFarlan, Moderator of the General Assembly. Pro-grant petitions soon began to flow into Parliament.

The Church of Scotland appeared united behind Chalmers's Church Accommodation plan.[91] In April and May, moreover, Chalmers published two major pamphlets in support of his parish community ideal, one focusing upon the need for a territorial parish ministry in the new urban slums, and the second replying to the Voluntary arguments in a recent statement issued by the Scottish Central Board of Dissenters.[92]

In late April, Chalmers renewed his conflict with the Dissenter-dominated Whig Edinburgh Town Council. The Town Council had not dropped its proposal of January 1834, to reduce the number of Establishment clergy in Edinburgh. On the contrary, a society had been formed in Edinburgh to promote the reduction of ministers, and a Whig bill for this purpose was introduced in Parliament in the autumn of 1834. In March 1835, the Town Council issued a statement in support of the Parliamentary bill, pointing out that there were hundreds of unlet seats in the Edinburgh Established Church, including a large number of vacant charity seats. Clearly, the Council maintained, the existing church accommodation was more than sufficient for the city's needs.[93]

Chalmers replied to the Council's statement with a bitter eighty-eight page pamphlet, *On the Evils which the Established Church in Edinburgh Has Already Suffered, and Suffers Still, in Virtue of the Seat-Letting Being in the Hands of the Magistrates.*[94] Unlet seats, he asserted, were not an acceptable criterion for determining the need for churches and ministers, when it was obvious that thousands in the city, particularly among the labouring poor, attended no church. Rather, concerned citizens had to look for the reasons why the poor did not rent seats; and these reasons would demonstrate that the Town Council was largely to blame. First, he maintained, the Council set the seat-rents too high for working-class families. They were more concerned with making money for the city corporation, by charging what the wealthy upper and middle classes would pay, than with providing religious instruction to the poor. The few charity seats provided by the Council, he continued, were considered demeaning by the poor. Such seats were located in the least desirable places in the church—behind pillars, in the upper corners of the galleries, or beside draughty windows—and were publicly advertised as charity sittings. What self-respecting labouring man or woman, he asked, would wish to attend church under such conditions?

Secondly, and more important, the Town Council failed to recognize the purpose of a territorial Establishment. Voluntary churches, he observed, might function upon a 'supply and demand' basis, and be satisfied when unlet seats indicated apparent excess of church accommodation over existing demand. But a territorial Establishment was responsible for providing religious instruction to every inhabitant in the country. It could not be content to minister only to those with the money to rent seats or the inclination to attend church. Rather, it had to pursue an aggressive mission among the irreligious, the profligate, and the poor. For this mission, it required a large number of inexpensive sittings, which the poor might occupy without sacrifice to their self-respect. Above all, it required smaller parishes, in which the minister and his agency of lay-visitors could regularly visit each family, to introduce them to the gospel and encourage their church attendance. Such small parishes, even in the most irreligious slum districts, would, if properly cultivated with an aggressive territorial ministry, be gradually transformed into closely-knit Christian communities, in which the inhabitants would be elevated through improved industry, morals, and communal benevolence. He had hoped to demonstrate just such a community-building operation in the Cowgate. But the Town Council had refused to provide the proposed church with one of the city clergyman—because, he implied, it feared he would succeed. The only means for vindicating the religious rights of the Edinburgh poor, Chalmers concluded, was to retain, and if necessary to increase the Annuity tax, and to transfer the authority for determining seat-rents from the callous Town Council to the presbytery of Edinburgh. The religious instruction of the Established Church was not to be treated as a scarce resource, distributed according to mechanisms of a free market economy. Nor should it be left to the authority of a Dissenter-dominated Town Council, concerned primarily to represent the interests of their middle- and upper-class reform-bill constituency—those who counted in society as opposed to the working classes who did not.

The prominent Edinburgh publisher, Whig member of the Town Council, and Dissenter, Adam Black, replied to this attack upon the Town Council with an equally caustic pamphlet, *The Church Its Own Enemy, Being an Answer to the Pamphlets of the Rev. Dr. Chalmers,* in which he reiterated the Voluntary arguments, adding that Chalmers's ill-conceived Church Accommodation campaign, and particularly his attacks upon civic authorities, only hastened the Establishment's fall. Black dismissed Chalmers's communitarian ideal for the territorial Establishment as Utopian, and compared his social ideal to that of the other great communitarian idealist, Robert Owen. 'That benevolent but absurd enthusiast, Owen,' Black asserted, 'by means of his co-operative societies, all working under a regulated plan, in certain districts which he called parallelograms, promised to banish vice, and spread universal happiness through the world; but his system was in the political what Dr. Chalmers' is in the religious world, at utter variance with the constitution of our nature, and could only end in the mortification and distress of the unhappy schemer and his followers.'

Chalmers's concept of a covenanted commonwealth of small parish communities, under the authority of a national Establishment, had no place in liberal Britain. 'If it were possible,' Black asked, 'would it be desirable that the Presbytery or Town-Council should have the power of causing the inhabitants to form themselves into parishes, as the King of Prussia orders his troops to form themselves into squares?' In order to realize his ideal of a society organized into parish communities of 2,000 inhabitants each, Edinburgh, with its population of 136,000, would need to maintain sixty-eight parish churches, instead of the existing thirteen. The cost for his parish system in Edinburgh would be £40,800 per annum in stipends alone.[95] The public had no wish to embark upon Chalmers's national experiment at such a cost— knowing that it would only rediscover the lesson of the seventeenth-century Civil Wars: that religion was a matter of individual conscience, and could not be imposed by an authoritative national Church. Despite Black's rejoinder to Chalmers, however, the Parliamentary bill for the reduction in the number of Edinburgh clergy had to be dropped in the face of massive resistance from the Church.

By April 1835, the Scottish nation was convulsed by the endowments question. Mass meetings were held by both sides. Petitions flowed into Parliament, with each side accusing the other of fraudulent methods in obtaining signatures. Newspapers and magazines vented violent emotion on the question. The Glasgow publisher, William Collins, with Chalmers's assistance, had previously begun issuing a series of 'Tracts on Religious Establishments'. By the Spring of 1835, Collins was printing 50,000 such tracts each month, directed mainly towards the working-class reader.[96] In Parliament, meanwhile, the Peel Government was moving slowly on the Scottish endowments question. The Government, Gladstone had previously explained to Chalmers on 18 February 1835, hesitated to introduce Chalmers's proposals until it had consolidated its own position in Parliament and could be assured of the support of at least a majority of Scottish MPs. It had to proceed with careful deliberation. For the defeat of a Government Scottish Church endowment bill at this time, Gladstone explained, 'would be one of the severest blows which the principle of a Church Establishment has yet received in this country'.[97] Chalmers now undertook the task of writing to the Scottish MPs, and by early March, he assured Gladstone that of the fifty-three Scottish members in the Commons, twelve had promised Chalmers their support, and another fifteen appeared 'hopeful'—constituting a probable slight majority of Scottish MPs for the endowment.[98]

Chalmers was again suffering from excessive fatigue. None the less, on Gladstone's advice, he decided to travel to London with a Church deputation in April, after the Easter holiday, to assist the Government with the introduction of the endowments bill.[99] Events, however, obliged them to postpone their journey. On 7 April, the Peel Government was brought down on the question of Irish Church reform. 'The best friends of the Church', Chalmers informed Peel on 22 April, 'felt the deepest disappointment and sorrow at the suspension (for I trust it is no more) of your administration.'[100] As the weeks passed, however, it became clear that Peel was indeed out, and that the Church of Scotland would again have to deal with Melbourne and the Whigs, who had assumed office on 18 April.

On 28 May 1835, Chalmers delivered the first annual report of his Church Accommodation Committee to the General Assembly. If the Church had been rendered despondent by the fall of the Peel Government, its hopes now revived. Chalmers's committee had produced wonders during its first twelve months. Subscriptions to the general fund, he announced, now totalled £15,168, while subscriptions to the local societies were £50,458—representing total Church Accommodation subscriptions of £65,626. Local societies throughout the country had either completed, or were in the process of erecting, sixty-four new churches. The fall of the Peel Government was certainly a disappointment. Nevertheless, Chalmers asserted, in view of such sacrifice and effort on behalf of the Establishment by the Scottish public, he was confident that the new Whig Government would perform its duty and endow the new churches.[101] The Assembly was swept with enthusiasm. Chalmers's report was unanimously adopted. The intensity of emotion was also expressed in a striking incident. As he concluded reading his report, a member of the Assembly moved a vote of thanks to him for the achievements of his committee. Another member, believing this was not sufficient, moved that they should first return thanks to God. Heated discussion followed, until finally the Moderator, in a mechanical voice, put the question before the house: thanks to Chalmers or thanks to God. 'On this', Cockburn noted in his journal, 'there was a general and confused cry of "Dr. Chalmers! Dr. Chalmers!" and "prayer! prayer!"' In the event, Chalmers was declared the victor, and the Moderator proceeded to eulogize him accordingly. 'On the whole,' Cockburn added, 'calm men have a painful anticipation of the course, as evinced by this Assembly, which the pilotage of the Wild party [Evangelicals] is putting the Church into. I wish they would change their tack, or at least lay to; but it is plainly an evangelical race between them and the Dissenters, and I do not expect either of the runners to be soon spent.'[102]

Among the most significant acts of the 1835 Assembly was the unanimous decision to combine the former Church Accommodation and Church Endowment committees into a single committee, the Church Extension Committee, under Chalmers's convenership. Chalmers thus became head of the most powerful permanent committee ever formed by the Church, including over 130 individual members, with authority over dozens of local societies throughout the country. He now assumed full authority not only over the church-building campaign, but also over the negotiations with the Government. The new name of the combined committee, moreover, was important. The Church signified that it was not content simply to increase church accommodation, or 'stone and lime'; rather, its purpose was to 'extend' Christian communal sentiment throughout the nation with an aggressive parochial ministry.

With the formation of the Church Extension Committee, Chalmers emerged to leadership, not only of the Evangelical party, but of the Evangelical-dominated Church of Scotland. He had created a power base in the Church—a vast permanent Committee, with a national hierarchy of sectional, parochial, and sub-parochial societies, and control over a large financial apparatus. Indeed, in power and influence, his Church Extension Committee rivalled the Church Courts. The Voluntary controversy had forged a new consensus in the Church, an Evangelical drive to extend the Church to the undecided portion of the Scottish population. The Moderate party was in disarray—there were, it seemed, no rivals to Chalmers's ascendancy. After years of struggle for his Christian communal ideal, he now had the backing of the Church for an immense national effort, intended to realize the ideal of the godly commonwealth in Scotland. Although his health remained poor, and he tired easily, he pursued his vision to the limits of his strength.

IV

Early in July 1835, Chalmers and a Church Extension deputation travelled to London to begin negotiations with Melbourne's Whig Government for the Parliamentary endowment grant. But they soon discovered that the Whigs were no longer as encouraging to the Church as they had been in the summer of 1834. As Gladstone had predicted in the previous December, the Whig Government was now more dependent upon the support of organized Dissent. In the face of contradictory Church and Voluntary claims, moreover, the situation in Scotland had become increasingly unclear in London. The Government, accordingly, announced that it would appoint a Royal Commission of Inquiry to investigate the extent of 'religious destitution' in Scotland. The Commission, Chalmers was assured, would be an impartial one, and if it discerned genuine need for additional churches, the Government would perform its duty to ensure an efficient Establishment.[103]

Chalmers left London on 20 July, disposed to accept the inquiry without complaint. He was confident that an inquiry, focusing upon the statistical evidence already compiled by his local societies, would quickly convince even the Whigs of the need for the endowment. But he was greatly distressed when, shortly after leaving London, he learned the names of the Commissioners. First, the Commission was headed by the Earl of Minto, with whom Chalmers had clashed over both the Kennedy poor-law bill of 1824 and the Ecclesiastical History chair controversy of 1831, and with whom he could hardly expect cordial relations. Secondly, of the other Commissioners named, the majority were either active Voluntaries, Dissenters, or Churchmen opposed to Church Extension. The Secretary of the Commission, George Logan, was an active Voluntary, and three of the six active Commissioners were also known to be hostile to the Church. Chalmers now became convinced that he had been the victim of Whig duplicity while in London. 'It were a great want of frankness', he wrote to the pro-extension Tory MP Patrick Maxwell Stewart from Leamington on 21 July 1835, '... not to confess the sad and sore humiliation of my own feelings when I read certain of the names [of Commissioners]—names I fear which will excite the utmost dissatisfaction and even disgust throughout Scotland. I no longer wonder at the reserve which has been practiced towards us and at the full revelation being postponed till we were fairly out of London.' The Church, he decided, should still co-operate with the Commission. None the less, he warned, if the Commission proved unfair, he would appeal beyond it to the nation as a whole. 'We must', he further informed Stewart, 'comfort ourselves with such being the strength of our cause that even its deadliest enemies will not be able to injure it without our being able to convince an indignant public that both they and the Government who have ap-pointed them are most palpably in the wrong.'[104]

In Scotland, meanwhile, the announcement of the Commission elicited angry protests from both the Church and the Tories. Church-men protested that the Government's instructions to the Commission were too broad in scope, amounting to a State inquisition into the value of the Establishment. Despite Lord John Russell's claims to the contrary, many suspected that the Commission, with its strong Voluntary membership, was in fact the first stage of a Whig-Dissenter plan to disestablish the Church of Scotland. The Tories, moreover, were infuriated by the almost exclusive Whig membership of the Commission. They suspected that the Whigs had no intention of alienating Dissent by introducing a Church grant, and that if their Commission recom-mended anything for the Church, it would be the expropriation of unclaimed teinds (income from medieval Church lands still in possession of private landowners)—thus obliging the landed interest to bear the full burden of endowing the new churches.[105] Chalmers, for his part, continued to recommend co-operation with the new Commission.

'Chalmers', the Tory Dean of the Faculty of Advocates, John Hope, informed the Earl of Aberdeen on 20 August 1835,

is eloquently and pathetically indignant at the selection of the Com^{rs} and speaks of the conduct of the Gov't with 'moral loathing'. But, absorbed (as usual) with the *one* idea of building a Church at the Village of the Water of Leith, for which he hopes to get the *first* of any grant of money, sanguine as to his Powers, and full of belief that the *evidence* will compel even the Com^{rs} to report all he wishes, he [is] keen to be examined,... and will not join in opposing the Inquiry.[106]

Chalmers's Tory friends in London, however, soon convinced him that nothing good could be expected from the Whig Commission. 'Since I last wrote you,' Chalmers informed Hope on 25 August, 'I have received letters from London teeming with fresh proofs of the hollow and insincere policy of Government and of their wretched vacillations. I have now ceased to look for truth or justice or consistency at their hands, and now participate in all your apprehensions of the abuses to which this Commission might be turned.' Hope was surprised, and not a little contemptuous, of Chalmers's sudden change of position. 'What a strange man he is,' he confided to Aberdeen on 26 August. 'He did not look to the *principle* till he saw that he had no hope of making his own use of the Comm. Now that he finds the Comm. will not work, I sh^d not be surprised if he wishes again to proclaim ... the Solemn League and to upraise the Standard of the Covenant.'[107]

Chalmers now proceeded, in three lengthy letters, to lecture Melbourne on the evils of the Commission as currently constituted, and on the resolve of the Church of Scotland to defend its independence.[108] A special meeting of the Commission of the General Assembly, moreover, was summoned on 30 September for the purpose of condemning the Royal Commission. A few days before the meeting of the General Assembly Commission, however, Lord John Russell repeated his assurances that the Government intended a fair and impartial inquiry, and had every intention of providing additional funds to the Church if it discerned a genuine need for additional accommodation. Russell's statement dampened the anti-Government fervour. The General Assembly Commission condemned the membership of the Whig Commission of Inquiry, but otherwise decided to co-operate.[109] In many respects, the vacillation of the Church of Scotland was understandable. This was the first Royal Commission of Inquiry into ecclesiastical affairs in Scotland, and while the Church was confident of the justice of its demand for additional church accommodation, it also demanded assurances that the inquiry would focus upon the religious condition of the population, and not upon the effectiveness of the Church of Scotland. The existence of the Establishment was to be above question.

It is difficult to decipher the original Whig intentions in appointing the Royal Commission—whether, as Russell asserted, they genuinely wished to discern the extent of 'religious destitution' in Scotland, or whether, as many Churchmen suspected, they intended only to bury the endowments question. Whatever the original plan, however, it became apparent after September 1835 that the Whigs meant to prolong the Commission's inquiry, as a means to defuse the high emotions of ecclesiastical conflict in Scotland. In view of the violent language directed against their Government by the Church, the Whigs were particularly anxious that the influence of Chalmers and his Church Extension Committee be reduced. The urbane Melbourne and his Government had no desire to negotiate with Chalmers and the Evangelicals—enthusiasts who viewed the Whigs with 'moral loathing'. The Whigs apparently hoped that by prolonging the Commission's inquiry, the excitement would burn itself out, and frictions would develop within the Church Extension movement. The Whigs, moreover, did not believe the Church Extensionists had much real support among the public. Therefore, they had little fear of Chalmers's threat to inspire popular anti-Government fervour if thwarted by the Royal Commission. On 27 September 1835, the Scottish Whig James Abercromby, Speaker of the House of Commons, assured the Earl of Minto, head of the Royal Commission, that a slow and steady course by the Commission was the best response to the Church Extension zealots. 'If you give them rope enough,' Abercromby explained, 'and take all things quietly, they will destroy themselves. The country is in no temper to listen to such parties as they will probably set up.'[110] Few suspected that Chalmers would be able to consolidate his ascendancy in the Church. With his volatile and vacillating character, his many enemies, and his poor health, his fall from power seemed probable. Once he was gone, and cooler heads prevailed, the Government would decide what, if anything, should be done about insufficient accommodation in the Establishment.

The Religious Instruction Commission, then, proceeded slowly. It was January 1836 before it finally began visiting localities to gather statistical and oral evidence. The first place it visited was Edinburgh. There it became clear that the Commission had determined to accept evidence from the Central Board of Dissenters, as well as from the Church. This enraged Chalmers and the Church Extensionists, who believed the Commission should investigate only those communities where the Church of Scotland had built, and proposed to build new *quoad sacra* parish churches.[111] None the less, Chalmers contained his anger, and appeared before the Commission on 13 February and 20 February 1836, describing with eloquence his parish community ideal and the goals of the Church Extension movement.[112]

The Commission completed its Edinburgh inquiry in late February, and drew up a preliminary report. To the frustration of the Church Extensionists, however, it refused to release the report. In April 1836, it finally moved to Glasgow for the second visit in its investigation. At this rate of progress, Churchmen complained, it would require years for the Commission to visit every locality on its itinerary. Tempers grew hot. The young Glasgow Evangelical clergyman Robert Buchanan complained to Chalmers on 7 April that 'The Voluntaries [on the Commission] are wasting the time of the Commission here to a great extent with their tedious, irrelevant, and often most unmannerly cross examinations.' The Commission, Buchanan further complained to the Evangelical lawyer Alexander Dunlop on 10 May, was accepting Dissenter statistics without 'testing the accuracy of their statements. ... My notion is, that the whole proceeding ... is disgraceful, and that if it is not exposed it may become the means of furnishing Lord J. Russell with the pretext he wishes to have for throwing the whole subject over the table.'[113]

By early 1836, tensions began to appear within the Church Extension movement. First, a conflict developed regarding the stipends of ministers in the new *quoad sacra* parish churches. Convinced that the Government endowment was now a dead issue, many Churchmen argued that the Church courts should require a 'bond' signed by all subscribers to a new church, promising to ensure the minimum stipend of £150 per annum required by Church law for a parish minister. If seat-rents did not provide this sum, the subscribers, or their heirs, would be obliged to pay the difference. Chalmers realized that the 'bond' requirement would halt church-building in impoverished districts, where subscribers would avoid committing themselves and their heirs to permanent expense. By the spring of 1836, he managed to thwart the bond requirement, but he was unable to suggest any alternative plan for ensuring the minimum stipend should there be no Government endowment.[114] As a result, the Whig *Scotsman* observed on 3 February 1836, Chalmers was placing church extension on 'ultra-voluntary' principles.[115] Secondly, contributions to the Church Extension campaign declined dramatically after the summer of 1835. In marked contrast to his 1835 report, Chalmers's Church Extension report to the General Assembly of 1836 was grim. Subscriptions to the general fund during the past twelve months were only £1,547, about 10 per cent of the subscriptions of £15,168 during the first year. As a result, the general fund was nearly bankrupt. Local society subscriptions were also down—from £50,458 in 1834-5, to £30,812 in 1835-6. Only twenty-six new churches were begun in 1835-6, as compared to sixty-four in 1834-5. Chalmers had expected subscriptions to decline slightly after the initial surge of enthusiasm, but, he asserted, a decline of this magnitude was intolerable, and if not reversed would mean the end of the Church Extension campaign. He blamed the decline upon the slow progress of the Royal Commission of Inquiry which, he implied, reflected deliberate policy by the Whig Government to thwart Church Extension.[116]

His response was twofold. First, he began tightening the movement's internal discipline and organization. In the first year of operation, it will be recalled, he had encouraged local societies to form on an *ad hoc* basis, while he exercised only loose general supervision from the central Church Accommodation Committee. Now he instructed every synod, presbytery, and parish to form Church Extension committees, for disseminating information concerning the movement and for ensuring that every parish church held at least one annual Church Extension collection for the general fund. Gradually, he organized a hierarchy of Church Extension committees, which paralleled the structure of the Church courts, and which recognized his personal authority.[117]

Secondly, in the spring of 1836, he decided to begin sending agents from the central Church Extension Committee into the country, to agitate for the endowment grant. The Scottish Central Board of Dissenters had already been sending Voluntary orators from Edinburgh into the country to organize resistance to the grant. Now the Church would respond. In his May 1836 report to the General Assembly, Chalmers requested approval for a national agitation. As a precedent, he pointed to the recent national tour of Alexander Duff, the India missionary, who had inspired considerable public enthusiasm for the overseas mission movement by his mass meetings. What the printing press was in the Reformation era, Chalmers asserted, the public speakers' platform had become for the present, and it was the Church's duty to employ this new vehicle of influence. 'In fighting the battles of the faith,' he maintained,

the men of former generations did not leave the mighty engine of the press to be monopolized by infidelity; and if now, in this age, so impatient for reading or the sustained exercise of thought, yet with a certain impetuous demand for mental excitement on all topics of great and national concern,—if, in such an age, the press have in any measure been superseded by the platform, let it be recollected, that ours is that cause which can be maintained under all modes of warfare, and on every arena.[118]

The Assembly granted approval, and Chalmers created a sub-committee on agents, under the convenership of Alexander Lockhart Simpson, the Evangelical minister of Kirknewton. In July 1836, local committees were instructed to prepare for the arrival of the agents by locating suitable meeting-places and providing advertisement. In early September, approximately twenty agents, mainly young Evangelical ministers, began their first lecture 'circuits'. They quickly achieved

results, increasing both subscriptions and public support. Chalmers
instructed the agents to refrain from allusions to secular politics.[119] He
was not ready to begin an anti-Whig, anti-Government agitation in the
nation, despite his continued expressions of 'moral loathing' for the
Whigs: nevertheless, he was demonstrating to the Government his
capability.

By late 1836, he had created an effective political organization for
influencing mass public opinion. He had established a national hierarchy
of Church Extension committees, reaching in many areas to the sub-
parochial level. There was an effective Church Extension press,
including pamphlets published by Chalmers and other Church Extensionists, the widely-distributed 'Tracts on Religious Establishments'
published by Collins of Glasgow, and several pro-Extension newspapers and journals, such as the *Scottish Guardian,* the *Church of Scotland Magazine,* and the *Presbyterian Review.* Finally, there were the
twenty agents, travelling on circuit to address public meetings and to
encourage local contributions to the general fund. It was an effective
propaganda organization, anticipating the great mass organizations—
the anti-Corn Law League and the Chartist movement—which began
a few years later. In setting up his organization, Chalmers had been
inspired largely by the overseas mission movement, and particularly
the British and Foreign Bible Society, in which he had participated in
his youth.

One effect of his organization was to increase Chalmers's personal
influence in the Church of Scotland. He was creating a hierarchy of
committees, which paralleled and rivalled the authority of the presbyterian system of Church courts. But unlike the Church courts, which
recognized a parity of ministers, with authority flowing upwards from
the parish level, Chalmers's Church Extension organization was
virtually a personal domain. At the same time, his growing influence,
combined with his movement's increasing hostility towards the Royal
Commission and Whig government, finally culminated in a major
split within the Evangelical party leadership. This was the celebrated
Moderatorship controversy, a serious expression of intense dissatisfaction with Chalmers's leadership by the older generation of Whig
Evangelicals—men who had reached maturity during the era of Sir
Henry Moncrieff Wellwood, Andrew Thomson, and the Whig-
Evangelical alliance. The central figure in this controversy was Chal-
mers's old rival, the Whig Moderate clergyman, John Lee.

The Moderatorship controversy had its origins in 1835. According to
the practice of the Church, each year, usually in the summer, the old
Moderators, those who had previously held the office, met to nominate
a candidate for the Moderatorship of the next General Assembly. The
nomination of the old Moderators would then be confirmed by a vote of

the Assembly at the opening session in the following May. This system had been evolved to eliminate the often bitter struggles between two parties for the Moderatorship, which had plagued the eighteenth-century General Assemblies. In the summer of 1835, Chalmers, who, it will be recalled, had been Moderator in 1832, was requested to attend the meeting of the old Moderators, to be held in Glasgow. He was unable to attend this meeting, but he sent the name of John Lee as his recommendation for Moderator of the 1836 Assembly. Despite their personal differences, Chalmers respected Lee's abilities and eminence in the Church. Nothing, however, was decided at the Glasgow meeting, and another meeting was scheduled for November 1835. Then, before this meeting was held, Chalmers reversed his position on Lee, withdrawing his recommendation and insisting that Lee could not be trusted with the Moderatorship.[120]

The reason for this reversal, Chalmers later explained, was the 'singular part' Lee had played in the special Commission of the General Assembly held on 30 September 1835, to express the Church's dissatisfaction with the Royal Commission of Inquiry. Lee had been the only clerical member of the Assembly's Commission to dissent from its resolution against the membership of the Royal Commission. His dissent, Chalmers believed, had encouraged the Whigs to proceed with the Royal Commission and their policy of 'indefinite postponement' of the endowment grant. 'The truth is', he later observed, 'that, whether intended by him or not, he achieved for [the Whig] party a great service. He broke the clerical unanimity, that would else have stood forth, in one entire and unbroken array against them.'[121]

Lee's dissent became still more serious in February 1836, when the Royal Commission was collecting evidence in Edinburgh. Chalmers, it will be recalled, had first been examined by the Commission on 13 February, and had delivered an eloquent defence of his parish community ideal, emphasizing the need to revive the parish system in the urban environment. His testimony had apparently made a considerable impact upon the examining Commissioners. Then, five days later, on 18 February, Lee appeared before the Commission, in a closed session, and challenged Chalmers's evidence. From his experience of nearly thirteen years as a minister in three of Edinburgh's poorest parishes, Lee assured the Commissioners that Chalmers's ideal parish system was 'visionary and impractical' in the urban slums. First, geographical mobility among the urban poor was too great for a minister to succeed in organizing them into a viable parish community. 'Many of them are changing [their residence] not only every month, but every week; almost all of them are weekly tenants.' Further, a large portion of the slum population were Roman Catholic, and no amount of ministerial visiting would convince them to participate in a Protestant parish community. Lee graphically described the often hideous living conditions of the poor in the Edinburgh Old Town (some of his remarks were lated cited by Friedrich Engels in his celebrated critique of capitalism, *The Condition of the Working Class in England*). Such conditions, Lee argued, would not be improved by embracing Chalmers's rural parish ideal. Lee supported the building of additional churches in the countryside, and advocated an endowment grant to ensure the independence of *quoad sacra* parish minister. But in the towns and cities, he maintained, there were already enough churches. What the urban poor really needed, he concluded, were more schools, to provide moral and vocational instruction.

This was essentially the position of the Whig Government regarding urban poverty, and Lee's evidence was therefore welcomed by the Commission. The fact that Lee had been an urban parish minister for the last thirteen years, while Chalmers had been occupying a university chair, made Lee's evidence seem all the more credible. One of the Commissioners, meanwhile, betrayed the confidentiality of Lee's testimony, informing Chalmers of Lee's evidence.[122] Chalmers immediately instructed his local societies to collect evidence demonstrating relatively low levels of geographical mobility, and at his own request he reappeared before the Commission on 20 February to reply to Lee. His new evidence, however, proved inconclusive, and Chalmers had to admit that Lee might be correct about the mobility of the poor. He later endeavoured to circumvent Lee's evidence by arguing that although geographical mobility among the poor might now be high, the formation of viable parish communities would reduce it.[123] This, however, did not reduce the impact of Lee's testimony.

It has been suggested that Lee's dissent from Chalmers's Church Extension ideal was motivated in part by his desire to cultivate favour with the Whig Town Council of Edinburgh, which advocated reducing the number of Edinburgh parish ministers. It was well known that Lee hoped to succeed George Baird, the seventy-five-year-old Principal of Edinburgh University, when Baird died. As the Principalship was in the gift of the Town Council, it is not surprising that Lee should have seized this opportunity to assist the Whigs, as well as to deal a blow to his rival, Chalmers.[124] At the same time, however, Lee's objections to Chalmers's parish community ideal were sincere. He had long regarded Chalmers's Church Extension campaign a 'revolutionary movement'. 'I do not hold the views of Dr. Chalmers', he had told John Hope on 25 August 1835,

with regard to the chief advantages of our Establishment. He seems to think it to be its primary or almost its sole recommendation that it issues to the poor a supply of spiritual instruction. My notion is that its principal recommendation is, that a Minister of the establishment, (according to the system now vanishing away under auspices of a democratic character) is as independent of the great as of the small, and that in all his Ministrations he feels himself in a condition to speak with as much authority to the rich as to the poor.[125]

Lee's principal loyalty, then, was to the clerical profession, as an independent body with recognized spiritual and moral authority. He distrusted the tendency toward laicization—that is, the 'democratic character' which Chalmers's Church Extension campaign was giving to the Establishment, with its emphasis upon lay Church Extension societies, lay parochial visitors, and the needs of the poor.

Chalmers succeeded in thwarting Lee's nomination to the Moderatorship of the 1836 General Assembly, and Dr Macleod, the 'violent Tory' minister of rural Campsie, was elected. Immediately after the 1836 Assembly, however, the venerable Whig Evangelical, Stevenson Macgill, Professor of Divinity at Glasgow University and a former Moderator, began to canvass for Lee's election as Moderator of the 1837 Assembly.[126] Macgill, it will be recalled, had opposed Chalmers's parish ideal in Glasgow as early as 1819. He was soon joined by the most eminent names in the old Whig-Evangelical party. Among them were the Edinburgh clergymen, Dr David Dickson and Dr Robert Gordon, protégés of Sir Henry Moncrieff Wellwood, and probably the second and third most influential ministers in the Church; Lord Moncrieff, son of Sir Henry Moncrieff Wellwood, Judge on the Court of Session, and the formulator of the Veto Act; Robert Bell, Procurator of the Church of Scotland, and member of the Royal Commission on Religious Instruction; Robert S. Candlish, minister of the prestigious St. George's church in Edinburgh and the most talented of the younger Evangelical clergy; David Welsh, Professor of Ecclesiastical History at Edinburgh University; and the leading Whig Evangelical lawyers, Alexander Dunlop, John Cowan, and Alexander Earle Monteith.

Together, these men represented virtually the entire remaining leadership of the old Whig-Evangelical party of Moncrieff Wellwood and Andrew Thomson. Their sponsorship of Lee's candidature for the Moderatorship, after Chalmers had declared Lee unfit for the position, was an open challenge to Chalmers's authority. In joining the revolt, some were influenced by the violence of his attacks upon the Whig Government, some by disagreement with his parish community ideal, and virtually all by the growing influence of his Church Extension Committee organization. 'The intemperate language used by Dr. Chalmers in your late meeting,' the Evangelical clergyman James Thomson informed Lee on 19 December 1836, referring to a recent meeting of the General Assembly Commission, 'against Lords Melbourne and John Russell ought not to be passed over without notice. It is disgraceful, and may be very injurious. ... I am dissatisfied with the conduct of the Church Extension Committee. They never consult the

presbytery about the new erections.' 'The causes of the strife', the
Whig clergyman David Aitken informed Minto on 19 December 1836,
'are to be sought in the various heartburnings arising out of the
manner in which church-extension has been forced on [the Church],
and mixed up with politics.'[127] It was, in short, a movement from
within the Evangelical party to overthrow Chalmers, and re-establish
the old order.

Chalmers and Patrick McFarlan, minister of Greenock—a former
Moderator, and one of the few older Evangelical leaders to remain
loyal to Chalmers—were hard pressed to find a candidate to stand
against Lee and his formidable supporters. Finally, they managed to
convince Matthew Gardner, a relatively unknown rural clergyman, to
become their candidate.[128] A hurried meeting of old Moderators was
summoned in early August 1836, and Gardner was nominated. On
29 August, Chalmers sent a circular letter to all the presbyteries,
announcing Gardner as the nominee of the old Moderators, and
warning of the danger 'at the present juncture' to have a Moderator
'not possessed of the right zeal or the right intelligence ... and more
especially if cold or disaffected ... to the extension of the Church.'[129]
Lee's supporters were incensed. The August meeting of old Moderators, they maintained, was not a proper meeting, but rather a secretive
affair managed by Chalmers and McFarlan. (Stevenson Macgill complained that, although a former Moderator, he had not even been
notified of the meeting.)[130] Further, they argued that Chalmers's
circular letter amounted to a libel against Lee, implying that Lee could
not be trusted with a position of authority in the Church. On 2 December 1836, his supporters held a large meeting in Edinburgh, to condemn Chalmers's behaviour towards him, and to nominate Lee for the
Moderatorship of the 1837 Assembly.[131] Chalmers's position became
precarious. Much of the Evangelical party seemed ready to join the
2 December memorialists against him. The Evangelical *Presbyterian
Review* supported the Lee party. Even the Glasgow *Scottish Guardian*
newspaper, previously Chalmers's strong supporter, now declared
itself neutral.[132] The Whigs' strategy of postponing the endowment
grant, it seemed, was now bearing fruit. Chalmers was being destroyed
by his own party.

His back against the wall, Chalmers now turned, and with disregard
for all the conventions of polite society, he demonstrated his instinct for
political warfare. In early January 1837, he published a pamphlet
entitled *A Conference with Certain Ministers of the Church of Scotland, on the
Subject of the Moderatorship of the Next General Assembly*, in which he discredited his leading opponents by name. Lee, he asserted, had attacked
the Church Extension movement in order to gain favour with the
Whigs and to revenge himself on Chalmers for having thwarted his

appointment to the Edinburgh Chairs of Divinity and Ecclesiastical History. He had deliberately damaged the Church, in order to gain Whig patronage for his personal preferment.[133] Lee's supporter, Robert Bell, he continued, was playing a more devious game. Chalmers now named Bell as the member of the Royal Commission who had betrayed the confidentiality of Lee's testimony before the Commission, by privately confiding to Chalmers what Lee had said. At the same time, however, Bell had apparently not provided Dickson, Gordon, and the other pro-Lee Evangelical clergy with similar information. Evidently, Bell was engaged in a plot to split the Evangelical party.[134] Dickson, Gordon, and the other clergy, 'perfect children in understanding', had all too easily fallen prey to the machinations of Lee and Bell. As for Welsh, Chalmers reminded him that he owed his professorship to Chalmers's support of his candidature over that of Lee, and that if this matter had been left to Welsh's Whig friends, Welsh would still be a parish minister. Further, Chalmers had struggled against the Whig administration to ensure Welsh an adequate stipend; indeed, he had regarded Welsh as one of his closest friends—only to be betrayed by him. Lord Moncrieff, he implied, had sacrificed his Evangelical principles for the fellowship of his Whig friends. He was somewhat softer in his rebuke of Candlish, trusting that he would perceive the error into which he had been led by more devious minds.

Chalmers realized that many in the Church would judge him harshly for exposing personal weaknesses of his opponents. None the less, he had struggled tooth and nail through most of his life for his godly commonwealth ideal, and he would not weaken now that its realization seemed near. 'It has been,' he averred of his parish community ideal,

the fondest theme of my speculations, and indeed of my authorship, for more than twenty years; and is all the more endeared to me by the incredulity and the ridicule which overhung its outset—and since, by all the resistance and rough handling through which it has had to fight its way. The greatest step in advance ever made by it, was when the General Assembly set it forth over the land, with the crown upon its head of their high approbation; and the consequence has been, that, in the glorious awakening of less than three years, a hundred and fifty new churches for the use of the working classes are starting into existence.[135]

Lee's supporters were surprised and stung by Chalmers's personal attacks. 'The tone of Dr. Chalmers' production', James Thomson wrote to Lee on 18 February 1837, '... is considered as most disgusting, and altogether unworthy of a man of religious principle and feeling. ... If the Dr's Power was equal to his Will, he would annihilate you all.'[136] Lee had previously consulted legal opinion about whether to bring libel charges against Chalmers in the civil courts, but John Hope, the Dean of Faculty, advised him not to pursue the case.[137] Lee and his

supporters then adopted the unfortunate policy of answering Chalmers with similar invective. Lee, Robert Bell, James Moncrieff (Lord
Moncrieff's son and Bell's son-in-law), and several other 'Leeites'
published pamphlets personally abusing Chalmers.[138] Late in February
1837, moreover, the Royal Commission suddenly published its Edinburgh evidence, in an apparent attempt to vindicate Lee by demonstrating that Chalmers had misrepresented Lee's testimony.[139] The
Leeite attacks, however, began to swing public sympathy to Chalmers,
while the publication of Lee's evidence actually strengthened Chalmers's position by demonstrating that a large portion of Edinburgh's
working-class population were indeed without church accommodation.[140] Chalmers left the task of answering his opponents' personal
attacks to William Cunningham, a belligerent young Edinburgh
Evangelical clergyman, and a loyal Chalmers supporter.[141] Then, in
late April, a few weeks before the opening of the 1837 Assembly,
Chalmers published a supplement to his *Conference* pamphlet. He now
adopted the gentle tone of one hurt and disappointed by his former
friends. He declined to answer the 'hideous' charges brought against
him, but consoled himself with the knowledge that he had suffered for
a just cause, and looked to the approaching Assembly for justice.[142]

The General Assembly of 1837 was a triumph for Chalmers. On
18 May, the opening day of the Assembly, Gardner was elected Moderator, obtaining 262 votes to Lee's 59.[143] The Leeite rebellion had
been broken. Chalmers followed up this victory by announcing, in his
annual Church Extension report on 25 May, very substantial achievements over the past year. His efforts towards reforming the national
Church Extension organization with a rigid hierarchy of synod and
presbytery committees, and towards revitalizing the movement with
travelling agitators, had borne fruit; the dangerous downward trend of
1835-6 had been reversed. Subscriptions to the general fund had
increased from £1,547 in 1835-6 to £6,318 in 1836-7, and subscriptions
to the local societies from £30,812 in 1835-6 to £52,992 in 1836-7. An
additional sixty-seven new churches had been begun in 1836-7 as
compared to the twenty-six in 1835-6. In the three years since Chalmers
had been appointed head of the Church Extension movement, a total of
157 new churches had been built, or begun, by private contributions.
Further, Chalmers asserted, the Royal Commission on Religious
Instruction, in its recently published Interim Report on Edinburgh
church accommodation, had admitted that between 40,000 to 50,000
Edinburgh inhabitants capable of attending church did not do so;
further, this non-church attendance was 'almost exclusively confined to
the poor and working classes, and chiefly the very lowest'. In short,
nearly a third of the city population neglected public worship. Clearly,
Chalmers maintained, the Whig Government could now have little
choice but to endow the new *quoad sacra* parish churches.[144]

'The Church of Scotland', the young Glasgow Evangelical, Robert Buchanan, had informed Chalmers on 6 January 1837, when the Leeite party had seemed on the verge of triumph, 'whatever may be the conduct of a few individuals, cannot, and will not, and does not forget what she owes to the Convener of the Church extension schemes. If she did, the stones of a hundred and fifty new churches would cry out shame upon her.'[145] In the 1837 Assembly, then, the Church of Scotland chose Chalmers and Church Extension over Lee and the Whig connection. In part, this resulted from Chalmers's gift for adversary politics. His victory, however, also owed a great deal to his organizational skills. He controlled a vast national organization with local societies, agents, and a general fund. The influence of the old Whig-Evangelical alliance, on the other hand, was limited mainly to Edinburgh clerics and lawyers. Chalmers, moreover, could point to the positive achievement by his Church Extension campaign of over 150 new churches. Despite some dissatisfaction with his methods, there could be no question that he got results.

Following his overwhelming defeat, Lee's support rapidly melted away. Most of his supporters eventually made their separate peace with Chalmers. Isolated and humiliated, Lee exhibited signs of mental distraction. Francis Nicoll, Principal of the United College of St. Andrews University, had recently died, and on 12 June 1837, two weeks after the close of the General Assembly, Lee accepted the Whig Government's offer of the vacancy, apparently to escape from Edinburgh. But he did not resign his Edinburgh parish living, nor did he demonstrate any intention of travelling to St. Andrews to assume his new duties. Months passed, while Lee continued to draw both salaries. Finally, Chalmers's young supporter, William Cunningham, threatened to bring charges against Lee in the Church courts for breaking the 1817 law respecting pluralities, and on 30 November 1837, Lee resigned the St. Andrews Principalship.[146]

Lee now began to complain of persecution at the hands of Chalmers's dominant Evangelical party. '[They] hate me with a perfect hatred,' he confided to Professor Thomas Gillespie of St. Andrews on 30 November. 'Little do you know the extent of the rancour with which they have been watching every occasion to find me halting or tripping.'[147] He further complained of lack of support from the Moderates, and berated the Moderate St. Andrews professors for cowardice in the face of their common enemy, Chalmers. 'I am perfectly in earnest in saying', Lee informed Robert Haldane, the Principal of St. Mary's College of St. Andrews University on 2 December, 'that if I am to be annoyed and insulted by one party and coldly deserted by another I will not remain any longer in communion with the Church of Scotland. I will rather become Episcopalian.' The Moderates, however, did not take up Lee's fight. On 11 January 1838, James Hunter, the St. Andrews Professor of Logic whose plural appointment Chalmers had bitterly opposed in 1824-5, simply advised Lee to think twice before he continued venting his rage.[148] In January, Chalmers persuaded Cunningham to withdraw his libel proceedings against Lee's six-month long illegal plurality. Lee had been humiliated enough.

With the breakup of the old Whig-Evangelical leadership in the Church, Chalmers and his Church Extensionists now dominated the Church courts as well as the hierarchy of Church Extension committees. In the months following the 1837 General Assembly, Chalmers took steps to impose discipline upon the older Whig Evangelicals. This included increasing the number of travelling Church Extension agents and enlarging their supervisory authority over local societies. On 7 August 1837, he instructed his lieutenant, A. L. Simpson, to remove James Esdaile, the sixty-two-year-old Whig Evangelical minister of the East Church in Perth, and former close friend of the late Andrew Thomson, from his leadership of the synod's Church Extension committee on charges of being 'inert and indifferent' towards the cause. Simpson, accordingly, directed their more 'zealous and efficient' supporters in the Perth area to reconstitute the synod committee, and promised to 'make further efforts to get a more systematic course introduced' in all the local societies.[149] On 15 August, Chalmers informed Simpson that such efforts should include disciplinary action by the Church courts against all clergy not supporting Church Extension. 'I should like it better', he informed Simpson, 'that Presbyteries and higher Church-courts take it in hand to convert and control all our hostile and reluctant Clergy, than that we, the Committee, should come into conflict with them.' At the same time that the Church courts were wielding the 'stick' of threatened disciplinary action, he continued, the Church Extension Committee should reward the zealous clergy with the 'carrots' of influential positions on local committees and societies, and with generous subsidies from the general fund to their local church-building operations. In this way, he maintained, 'we should at length get quiet possession of the whole land'.[150]

Indeed, one young clergyman discovered Chalmers's 'loathing' for Whig Evangelicals the hard way. In September 1837, Thomas Guthrie, a young clergyman from rural Arbirlot, near Arbroath, and the future advocate of 'ragged schools' for slum children, was appointed the second collegiate minister of Old Greyfriar's Church in Edinburgh. The appointment was largely a reward for his effective services as a speaker on behalf of Church Extension at meetings in the Arbroath region. Indeed, after June 1837, success as a speaker for Church Extension became one of the surest routes to preferment in the Church. Guthrie's main task was to begin what Chalmers termed an 'excavation' in the Cowgate district of the large Old Greyfriar's parish: that is, to conduct regular household visitations among this impoverished and irreligious lower-class population as an initial step towards creating the nucleus of a parish congregation. He entered into the work with enthusiasm, eager to win Chalmers's approval. But in February 1838, he discovered that a zealous parish ministry alone was not sufficient to gain that favour. Chalmers had recently named a deputation of the Church Extension Committee to travel to London to renew negotiations with Melbourne's Whig Government; this proposed deputation, however, was exclusively Tory. The Whig Evangelicals on the Edinburgh presbytery Church Extension committee realized that the deputation would require some Whig members if it were to negotiate effectively with Melbourne, yet they were afraid to suggest this to Chalmers. 'In consequence of the personal quarrels and antipathies engendered by what was called the "Moderatorship Controversy,"' Guthrie later recalled in his autobiography, '... Dr. Candlish, [Alexander] Dunlop, [Sheriff Graham] Spiers, and others felt that it might appear like a personal attack on Dr. Chalmers were they to propose a counter-motion to his.' So they gave the task to Guthrie, who made the suggestion at the next meeting. Chalmers was enraged, and rejected the suggestion. As he angrily stormed out of the meeting, someone asked him, within earshot of Guthrie, what had happened. 'It had gone well, sir,' Chalmers snapped back, 'but for a raw lad from the country!' Guthrie learned from his error, and did not again openly question Chalmers's authority. 'This "raw lad from the country"', Guthrie later recalled, 'soon proved himself as zealous for Church Extension as Dr. Chalmers himself could be, and I was gratified to find that the Doctor soon afterwards changed his opinion of the "lad," saying to some one who happened to mention my opinion on a certain matter of policy, "Mr. Guthrie, sir, is a man of sound mind."'[151] A few years later, Guthrie was rewarded for his active parish ministry and 'sound mind'. In 1841, Chalmers at last fulfilled his dream of building a parish church in the destitute Cowgate. The new church was named, appropriately, St. John's, and Guthrie received the charge.

Guthrie's anecdote reveals, however, another aspect of Chalmers's victory over the Leeites. In breaking up the old Whig-Evangelical party, Chalmers had also, at a crucial juncture in Church-State relations, silenced all dissent within the Church Extension movement. Such central figures as Robert Candlish and Alexander Dunlop had feared to recommend to Chalmers even so sensible an expedient as adding a few Whig members to a deputation assigned the task of consulting with a Whig Government. Guthrie, too, had quickly learned the virtue of silent acquiescence. Chalmers had suffered in the past from a failure to distinguish self-interest from the communal welfare, personal ambition from communal service. Now in late 1837 and early 1838, with dissenting voices silenced, and even his errors receiving apparent approval from those surrounding him, his flaws grew more pronounced. His hatred of the Whigs became a consuming passion. He was blind to the fact that while his power within the Church was un-rivalled, his dictatorial behaviour was in fact weakening his influence, as well as that of the Church, in the nation as a whole.[152] He continued to believe that he possessed the support of the Scottish nation, and that in a test of strength with the Whig Government, his Church Exten-sionists would triumph. 'The evidences', he had stated to A. L. Simpson on 18 May 1837, the day of Lee's defeat in the Moderator-ship contest, 'are multiplying on every side of me that attempts, I fear insincere and hypocritical, are making by the agents of government to nullify the Church Extensionists.... Believe me, my dear Sir, that such is our strength in the country as might well enable us to maintain a firm and honest attitude on the present occasion.' The Church Extensionists would now have to overcome their 'extreme simplicity and good natures' and prepare for struggle against the 'insidious Whigs'.[153]

V

On 19 June 1837, William IV died, and young Victoria succeeded to the throne. The accession of the monarch was followed, in July 1837, by a general election. It was a quiet election, with few seats contested, although in Scotland Church affairs had some effect upon the election. Chalmers, however, made no real attempt to influence the voting. This was not the result of any improvement in his relations with the Whigs. While it was true that the Whigs endeavoured to keep the Church Extensionists quiet by communicating to them private assurances that something would be done for the Church in the 1838 Parliamentary session, Chalmers received their promises with contempt. 'I am pain-fully disgusted', he informed A. L. Simpson on 11 July 1837, 'by the *confidential* intimations which I and others have received of the friendly dispositions of the Ministry, accompanied in the mean time with the expression of a hope that nothing ... would be done by us to embarrass them—the plain English of which is that we should be quiet till they have got over their General Election, after which they will exhibit the same perfidious heartlessness as before.'[154] The real reason for Chalmers's forbearance was a convention peculiarly sacred to the Evangelical party in the Church of Scotland—that is, the strict separ-ation of Church and State in their internal government. According to this convention, while the Church as a body might petition Parliament, or even resist an unchristian monarch, it was not to interfere directly in the internal affairs of government. The lines separating legitimate from illegitimate uses of the Church's political influence were hazy; none the less, Church interference in a Parliamentary election was considered an unacceptable breach of convention. In the previous year, Chalmers had made the error of printing a letter in the Tory *Edinburgh Advertiser* supporting the candidature of his friend, the Tory Church Extensionist Alexander Campbell of Monzie, in a Parliamentary by-election in Ayrshire. This elicited a *furor* of public protest, which weakened Campbell's position, and may have been the deciding factor in his electoral defeat.[155]

Although Chalmers did not interfere in the 1837 election, however, he was not disappointed by the result. The Whigs, to be sure, remained in office. But their Parliamentary majority had been reduced to less than thirty, and their position was vulnerable. Chalmers's relationship with Sir Robert Peel, meanwhile, grew more and more cordial. In January 1837, Chalmers had travelled to Glasgow to attend the great banquet held in Peel's honour, and had spent two days with him at the country estate of Henry Monteith. On 1 December 1837, Chalmers was sufficiently confident of his relationship with Peel to write him a personal letter introducing two Church Extensionists who had been returned to Parliament at the 1837 election. Peel replied with a warm affirmation of regard. 'I had long learned to honour and respect you,' he informed Chalmers on 21 December 1837, 'long before I had the opportunity of making your acquaintance, and I can truly say that I should be raised higher in my own esteem could I think myself really entitled to the friendship and warm attachment of so good a man.'[156]

By early 1838, the Royal Commission on Religious Instruction in Scotland had completed its investigation and published several interim reports on various localities. Its reports were impressionistic, reflecting the contradictory evidence provided by the Church and Dissenters. None the less, the Whig Commission acknowledged that, even including the Dissenting churches, church accommodation in Scotland was insufficient for the needs of its population. In Glasgow, for example, the Commission found that total church accommodation, both Church and Dissent, was sufficient for only 48.2 per cent of the city population. Chalmers now decided to increase pressure on Melbourne's Government for the endowment grant, and he requested assistance from leading Tory politicians, including Lord Aberdeen.[157] Early in March 1838, Chalmers dispatched a deputation of Tory Church Extensionists to London, to press the Church's claims. Because of his poor health, he did not accompany the deputation.

Members of the Church deputation began arriving in London late on the night of 9 March, only to discover that a few hours before their arrival, Melbourne, in response to a question from Lord Aberdeen in the House of Lords, had defined the Government's proposals regarding

insufficient church accommodation in Scotland. The deputation was
mortified when they learned of Melbourne's plan. There would be no
Parliamentary endowment grant. Instead, Melbourne offered three
measures, amounting to only a small fraction of what the Church
requested. First, unclaimed Crown teinds (income from lands once
belonging to the medieval Church but now in the possession of the
Crown) would be used to build additional churches in the Highlands.
Secondly, unclaimed teinds in the possession of private landowners
would be appropriated to build churches in rural parishes requiring
additional church accommodation. Thirdly, nothing would be done for
the towns and cities. The proposals were a total victory for Dissent.
The Dissenters had few if any churches in the Highlands, where poverty
and low population density rendered it almost impossible to support a
church and clergyman on Voluntary principles. They did not, therefore, object strongly to additional government churches in the Highlands, especially as they would be built with Crown teinds, and not
through a Parliamentary grant. By the second proposal, Melbourne
would create discord between Chalmers's Church Extensionists and
the largely Tory Scottish landed interest. The landowners would oppose
the appropriation of the teinds in their possession for church-building,
and would thereby be brought to resist the continuation of Chalmers's
Church Extension campaign. Finally, by providing no endowment
grant for the new urban churches, the Whigs ensured that the Establishment would be unable to pursue its plan of reducing city seat-rents
to encourage working-class attendance.[158] 'It is unnecessary to say',
Robert Buchanan, a member of the deputation, wrote to the Church
Extension Committee on 10 March, 'that to leave out the towns, is to
leave out 9/10ths of the whole case of Scotland's destitution.' 'The
Government', Buchanan further informed Chalmers in a letter that
same day marked *'private and confidential'*, 'have evidently made up their
minds to play off upon us the most discreditable manœuvre ever practiced by men in office.'[159]

For the next three weeks, Buchanan and the Church deputation
remained in London, meeting leading politicians in both parties. Peel
and Aberdeen were sympathetic. However, they made it clear that
there was little they could do, and that the deputation's only hope lay
in a personal appeal to Melbourne. The Prime Minister received them
civilly, and admitted his ignorance of the content of the Royal Commission's reports on Scottish religious instruction. Nevertheless, he
assured them that he had no intention of changing his Government's
three proposals of 9 March. A few days later, as the deputation prepared to accept Melbourne's proposals as at least better than nothing,
the old Duke of Wellington, feeling sympathy for their *naïveté*, finally
opened their eyes to the harsh realities. Melbourne, Wellington in-

formed them in an interview on 21 March, had no real intention of giving the Church of Scotland even the pittance he had proposed on 9 March. 'Gentlemen,' he stated emphatically, 'you will get nothing.... I am sorry for it; but so you will find it. You have two parties against you—the Radicals, with Lord Brougham at their head; and the Government, who are really as much opposed to you as the Radicals.' The Whigs and Radicals, Wellington continued, would ensure that Melbourne's first proposal, the use of Crown teinds for Highland church building, would not pass in the Commons. The Scottish landed interest, moreover, both Whig and Tory, would oppose the second proposal, the appropriation of unclaimed teinds in possession of landowners for rural church building.[160] In truth, Melbourne's proposals were only a ruse intended to placate those who argued that something should be recommended after the expense and effort of the Royal Commission, while at the same time not alienating the support of the Radicals and Dissenters by actually doing anything.

It has been suggested that Melbourne's harsh treatment of the Church resulted in part from Chalmers's public attacks upon the Whigs, particularly during the Moderatorship Controversy. This is dubious. Melbourne, it was true, had no love for Chalmers. Yet political considerations alone were sufficient to account for his decision. By giving the Church of Scotland all it asked, he would, to be sure, have pleased the Scottish Church Extensionists. The majority of Scottish Church Extensionist MPs, however, were Tories, and they would not have changed their political allegiances and supported the Ministry simply because it provided a grant which they believed had been owed to the Church for years. To give the Church the endowment grant, then, would only have risked losing Radical and Dissenter support in Parliament, for no real political benefit. In late March, the deputation left London, frustrated and indignant. There was, it seemed, nothing more to be done.

Chalmers was disappointed, but hardly surprised by Melbourne's actions. He had long suspected that the Government would only endow the new Scottish churches if forced to do so by an overwhelming display of public indignation. He had long threatened that if the Whig Government rejected the Church's request for the endowment grant after the completion of the Royal Commissions's inquiry, he would mobilize the country against the Government. Now, he determined to act upon this threat. In April, he travelled to London, where between 25 April and 12 May he delivered before the English Church Influence Society his celebrated *Lectures on the Establishment and Extension of National Churches*.[161]

His main purpose was to introduce the Church of Scotland's case to the English people. He began by presenting his definition of an Establishment

—an endowed institution which provided 'ducts of conveyance' for irrigating the nation with divine grace through the reading and the preaching of Scripture. He described again his parish community ideal, and emphasized the importance of reviving the Christian communal ideal in the growing cities. He repeated his argument that a religious Establishment of territorial churches and schools represented the highest aspirations of a nation, elevating it above the politics of self-interest and the shallow vision of utilitarianism. He reiterated, moreover, his arguments against Voluntaryism, the 'supply and demand' system of religion, which functioned only to meet the demand of those with prior religious impulse and the means to afford high seat-rents, while neglecting the irreligious, the ignorant, and the poor. He compared this Voluntary system with an endowed territorial Establishment, which functioned despite man's natural depravity, and aggressively pursued the moral and spiritual elevation of all. There was nothing new in his lectures. He simply repeated the ideal of the godly commonwealth to which he had dedicated his life—but with an intensity and eloquence that spellbound his London audiences.

His most fervent language was directed against the Government's rejection of the Church of Scotland's request for an endowment of its new *quoad sacra* parish churches. In its endowment campaign, he asserted, the Church had the support 'of the great mass of the commonality in Scotland'. The working classes of Scotland recognized that the object of the endowment was to reduce the seat-rents in the new churches, in order to transform them into institutions for the moral, spiritual, and ultimately economic elevation of the lower social orders. 'Yet this, we are told, is but the cry of the unfranchised population, of men who have no suffrages, and are therefore of no weight in the senate-house.' In post-reform-bill politics, Parliament protected the interests only of the 'ten-pounders', the middle and upper classes who possessed the vote. But the Church would not relinquish its advocacy of the rights of 'the unprotected and the poor'. The Government would 'soon hear a fresh representation on the subject, of the growing strength and popularity of our cause'. There would, he asserted, be more new churches built, more public meetings, more petitions, more agitation. The Church would raise such a cry in Scotland that 'the British Legislature will at length give way'. 'We are', he exclaimed of the clergy of the Scottish Establishment, 'the tribunes of the people, the representatives of that class to whom the law has given no other representatives of their own,—of the unfranchised multitude, who are without a vote, and without a voice in the House of Commons.' Time, he warned, was running out. The masses, too long neglected by a Parliament concerned only with a narrow conception of the interests of the propertied classes, were every day growing more disaffected. He warned ominously that

Unless the emollients of Christian kindness and Christian instruction be brought to bear on the turbulence of the popular mind, a smouldering fire, which now lies at the bottom of the social and political edifice, will at length burst forth, and explode it into fragments. And a day of fearful recompense for the moral wrongs of a long-neglected population will be the sure result or re-action of that process, by which our rulers shall have conducted us onwards, step by step, in the path of deterioration, till we have landed in the veriest dregs and degeneration of an iron age.[162]

Many supporters of the Establishments in England and Ireland shared Chalmers's concern about the Government's treatment of the national Churches. The rooms in Hanover Street where Chalmers delivered the lectures were 'crowded to suffocation' with members of England's governing élite, including royal princes, prelates of the Church of England, great nobles, leading statesmen, and MPs from both parties. When Chalmers had entered the room to deliver the first lecture, the English clergyman, J. A. Clark, later recalled that '[he] was welcomed with clappings and shouts of applause, that grew more and more intense till the noise became almost deafening'. The six lectures were published in both London and Glasgow almost immediately after their delivery; within the year, eight thousand copies had been printed.[163]

Of course, not everyone was pleased. The English United Committee [of Congregationalists, Baptists, and Unitarians] immediately offered a prize for the best published essay in response to Chalmers's *Lectures*, and several replies soon appeared in print. Voluntary journals also reviewed the *Lectures* harshly.[164] Many High Church sympathizers, moreover, were disturbed by the enthusiasm for Chalmers's *Lectures* within the Church of England. Among them was William Gladstone, who was then writing his own essay on Church-State relations. 'Such a jumble of church, un-church, and anti-church principles,' Gladstone wrote to Henry Edward Manning on 14 May 1838, 'as that excellent and eloquent man Dr. Chalmers has given us in his recent lectures, no human being ever heard. ... I do not believe he has ever looked in the face the real doctrine of the visible church and the apostolic succession, or has any idea what is the matter at issue.'[165] Gladstone was correct about the lack of any real theological doctrine of the Church in Chalmers's lectures. Like most Scottish Evangelicals, he neglected ecclesiology. His focus was not exclusively upon the Church, but upon the godly commonwealth, over which the Church shared authority with the State. He endeavoured to demonstrate that Church and State were two separate but equal authorities in the Christian nation, and that the State had no right to withhold from the Church public funds necessary for its efficient operation.

Following his London lectures, Chalmers hurried by steamboat back to Edinburgh for the convening of the General Assembly. In his Church Extension report, delivered on 22 May 1838, he announced that thirty-two additional churches had been completed or begun during the past year, raising the total of new churches built or begun since June 1834 to 187. It was an impressive achievement. None the less, he asserted, the Church Extension campaign was only beginning to provide church sittings for the lowest social orders through 'internal Voluntaryism'. The Establishment had reached a limit in the descent of its mission down the social scale, beyond which it could not pass without State endowment of the new *quoad sacra* parish churches. Thus, the Church could not afford to relax its efforts. The recent rebuff from the Government must serve to rekindle the Church's fervour. There must be more church-building and more agitation, to force Parliament to fulfil its obligation to the Church. Above all, the Church must appeal to the common people. 'At the glorious era of the Church's Reformation,' he exclaimed, 'it was the unwearied support of the people which, under God, finally brought her efforts to a triumphant issue: in this the era of her Extension,—an era as broadly marked, and as emphatically presented to the notice of the ecclesiastical historian, as any which the Church is wont to consider as instances of signal revival and divine interposition, the support of the people will not be wanting.'[166]

Early in June, following the close of the General Assembly, Chalmers travelled to Paris, in order to read a paper before the Royal Institute of France, to which, it will be recalled, he had been elected a corresponding member in 1834. It was his first visit to the Continent, and he was accompanied by his wife and two of his daughters. Chalmers was highly respected among the literate public of Paris as both a Christian author and political economist. Several of his works, including his *Tron Church Sermons* and *Christian and Civic Economy* had been translated and published in Paris. The celebrated mathematician, Pierre-Simon Laplace, had drawn consolation from Chalmers's *Evidences of Christianity* at his death in 1827; the political economist Jean-Baptiste Say had been highly impressed with his *Political Economy*. Upon his arrival, he had an interview with Francoise Guizot, the leading Crown minister and a French Protestant, in which they discussed Chalmers's social theories. Later, he spent a few days at the Normandy estate of Guizot's friend and political collaborator, the Duc de Broglie. Guizot and the Duc de Broglie, moreover, personally arranged for Chalmers to be introduced in both the Chamber of Peers and the Chamber of Deputies. In a word, he was received as a distinguished State visitor. On 16 June, he read his paper before the Academy of Moral and Political Science of the Royal Institute. An epidemic of typhus was, at this time, sweeping through western Europe; Chalmers directed his paper to this problem, advocating legal assessments upon property for support of medical facilities, while at the same time repeating his arguments against legal pauperism.[167]

It is unclear whether Guizot was aware of Chalmers's conflict with Melbourne's Government over the endowment question, and whether his warm welcome to Chalmers was intended to embarrass Melbourne. To be sure, relations between Britain and France were cool at this time. But Chalmers did not openly call attention to his difficulties with his Government while in France. He treated the tour as a pleasant respite from the tensions and effort of the spring. None the less, his Paris trip did have symbolic importance for his endowment campaign. First, it served to direct public attention in Britain to his international reputation. He was not simply a provincial clergyman whom the Whig Government might slight or insult with impunity. His writings on Christian social theory, which formed the basis of his Church Extension campaign, were in fact widely respected throughout Europe and America. Secondly, his reception in Paris symbolized his position as a leader of the Scottish nation. The 'auld alliance' between Scotland and France still survived in the public imagination. Chalmers's Paris visit served to remind both his own countrymen and London that Scotland possessed a separate national identity. The Scots were not merely North Britons, and the Union of 1707 was not licence for the London Government to treat their most sacred national institution with indifference or contempt.

Chalmers returned to Scotland in late July. At a series of Church Extension Committee meetings in Edinburgh in early August, he revived the campaign in Scotland, which had lanquished during his months in London and Paris.[168] Agents were once again sent on circuits through the country, to hold meetings, collect funds, and encourage local petitions to Parliament for the endowment grant. There must not, he asserted, by any diminution of effort. The time had finally arrived to mobilize the working classes and to overwhelm the Government with a demonstration of national solidarity. Then, on 15 August 1838, Chalmers announced that despite his weak health he would personally tour south-west Scotland and carry his case to the labouring classes.

On 18 August, he left Edinburgh for the six-week circuit that one critic termed a 'tour of spiritual O'Connellism'. Chalmers did not object to the phrase. For like the celebrated Irish nationalist, he intended to hold mass meetings that would force the Government to recognize the seriousness of the Church Extension campaign. The area selected for his tour was significant. The south-west of Scotland had been the stronghold of late seventeenth-century Covenanter resistance to the Government of Charles II, and popular memories of the tenacity of the resistance and the brutality of the military suppression still survived.

During the tour, Chalmers visited ten presbyteries, and delivered Church Extension addresses at Stranraer, Wigton, Greenock, Dunoon, Kilmarnock, Ayr, Paisley, Dumbarton, Hamilton, Lanark, and Biggar. It was his first time on the platform before largely working-class audiences. He spoke passionately of his parish community ideal and of his lifelong desire to elevate the working classes through the dissemination of Christian communal sentiment. Church Extension, he proclaimed, was the cause of the people; it represented radical social change intended to restore to the working classes their communal traditions. With the support of the masses, the movement would overwhelm the existing political and economic system based upon the narrow self-interest of the propertied classes, and create a new moral order. 'We are labouring', he exclaimed before a large public meeting at Ayr on 13 September, 'for the unenfranchised population, and therefore, do I say, ecclesiastically speaking, that more resolute, more determined, more out-and-out radicals, than the Church Extensionists of Scotland, are not to be found in the empire.'[169]

For a time, it seemed that Chalmers's appeal would achieve the desired result. The agricultural population of southern Wigtonshire, where Chalmers began his tour, was sympathetic. 'It is quite manifest', the *Dumfries Herald* observed in its report of his meeting at the village of Minnigaff on 29 August, 'that the men of the Stewartry of Wigtonshire are fast arriving at the conclusion that the cause of Church Extension is the cause of the common people of Scotland, and we have no doubt that the rejected petition of the last General Assembly will be borne back to the Legislature in the arms of a roused and thoroughly awakened nation.'[170] But as Chalmers proceeded to the industrial districts around Glasgow, the enthusiasm waned. The crowds grew sullen or hostile. Voluntaries and genuine Radicals hounded his meetings and challenged his statements. Collections declined; few signed the petitions. When Chalmers finally returned, exhausted, to Edinburgh in early October, it was clear that his appeal for a national working-class demonstration of solidarity behind Church Extension had come to grief. For the first time, his power of oratory had failed him.

Chalmers later attributed this failure to his being tempermentally unsuited for the political platform. He was, he confided to William Hanna, uncomfortable in addressing working-class meetings, and he regretted the necessity of having to appeal in such a way for working-class support.[171] In truth, Chalmers's western campaign collapsed because he failed to gain the confidence of the working classes. They knew him to be a Tory, the friend of Peel, as well as of many Scottish Tory aristocrats and gentry. His claim to be a radical seemed insincere and opportunist. It was easily portrayed as contemptible by his Voluntary opponents. 'Let him be consistent in his toryism,' the Voluntary clergyman, David King, asserted in Glasgow on 23 October, in response to Chalmers's recent western tour, 'and we shall respect his convictions: but to hold conservative principles, and display radical and revolutionary colours, in the hope of thereby gaining the populace to his cause, is, I cannot refrain from saying, a pandering to prejudice, a bidding for popularity altogether unworthy of his honoured name.'[172]

Further, along with distrust of Chalmers's motives, most labouring men apparently did not believe that his parish communities would either represent their interests or improve their condition. Many had experienced his ideal of a parochial home mission as practised by middle-class Evangelical enthusiasts—visiting working-class neighbourhoods, distributing pious tracts, exhorting the poor on the evils of pauperism and the importance of moral improvement and self-help. If Chalmers's Church Extension campaign succeeded, and the working classes were placed under the parochial authority of such Evangelical ministers, elders, deacons, and sabbath-school teachers, possessing power over poor relief and education, would their condition improve? Voluntary orators, like the Stirling Congregational minister, Dr Hugh Heugh, assured them that it would not. In Chalmers's godly commonwealth, they would simply receive another set of masters, and be 'compelled by civil force to submit [to parochial ecclesiastical authority], like the serfs of Muscovy ... or the bestial [tenants] of a Highland laird.'[173] In short, argued Voluntaries, to revive the social structures of the past was also to strengthen the propertied orders. The working classes of western Scotland apparently agreed. They focused their concern upon the practical realities of factory conditions, wages, and hours. Few embraced Chalmers's pastoral vision of a revived Christian commonwealth. After October 1838, and the failure of his bid to mobilize mass popular support for Church Extension, public confidence in the campaign rapidly diminished. For years, he had claimed to possess the overwhelming support of all social orders in Scotland. But now he had been proved wrong, and there seemed to be no possibility of State endowment for the new churches. 'The secret reason', William Collins informed Chalmers on 10 December 1838, 'why the original scheme is not making more progress,... is, that the intense feeling, and intense interest which formerly existed in the public mind on the subject of Chu. Ext. *is now gone*. Every where there is a sickening apathy and indifference to it. ... A great and desperate effort must be made to keep it alive.'[174]

Chalmers was not yet defeated. He still possessed considerable support among the middle and upper classes, and in the late autumn of 1838 he decided to make a final appeal to their 'internal Voluntaryism'. First, he established a new subscription scheme, which he termed the supplementary fund. According to this scheme, individuals were requested to subscribe £1 or more for each of 100 additional churches to be built after 1838. The supplementary fund would then provide 25 per cent of the building costs for the 100 new churches. Secondly, he continued to apply pressure upon local societies to begin new churches. Thirdly, he declared that the general fund, which had previously been used to subsidize local church building, would now be employed to pay part of the salaries of the ministers in new churches. In a word, the general fund would provide the partial endowment which the Whig Government had refused the Church. This would only be a temporary measure. The 100 new churches, he believed, would provide London with overwhelming evidence that the Church of Scotland had not relinquished the Extension campaign.[175] Further, Melbourne's Government was growing steadily weaker, and it could not be long before Peel and the Tories were in office. The important thing was to keep the campaign alive until Melbourne fell. Then Peel would provide the endowment grant, and encourage another surge of church building.

The campaign began well. In May 1839, about six months after the initial subscription lists had been circulated, Chalmers reported to the General Assembly that £27,000 had been pledged to the supplementary fund. The general fund reserves, moreover, were sufficient to provide partial stipendiary support to ministers in poorer parishes for a few years. The major problem involved the local societies. Most had apparently dissolved in the spring and summer of 1838, following the Government's refusal to provide the endowments. Between May 1838 and May 1839, only fourteen new churches had been built or begun, as compared to thirty-two in 1837-8, and sixty-seven in 1836-7.[176] None the less, Chalmers was confident that he could revive the local efforts. For this purpose, he conducted lengthy speaking tours, visiting Dundee, Perth, Stirling, and Dumfermline in the early spring of 1839, and Brechin, Montrose, Arbroath, and Aberdeen in the early summer. Late in the summer of 1839, following yet another trip to London, he devoted nearly five weeks to a speaking tour of the Highlands. It was an impressive, and exhausting display of energy and perseverance.[177]

Then disaster struck. In 1834, it will be recalled, the General Assembly had declared that all former chapels-of-ease, and all new churches to be erected through the Church Extension campaign, would be *quoad sacra* parish churches, with the same ecclesiastical authority as the existing *quoad civilia*, or State-defined parishes. An act had been passed in Parliament, moreover, confirming the Church's right to create these *quoad sacra* parishes. In the summer of 1839, however, the Scottish Court of Session delivered two decisions which effectively invalidated the *quoad sacra* parishes, and dealt the death-blow to Church Extension.

First, in a case involving a new *quoad sacra* parish church in rural Brechin, near Montrose, the Court of Session awarded the heritors of the local *quoad civilia* parish with the right to seize the church-door collections at the *quoad sacra* church for poor relief. Secondly, in a dispute involving a new church at rural Stewarton, the Court of Session held that the heritors of the local *quoad civilia* parish not only had the right to all church collections, including collections made for the Church Extension General Fund; but that they also had the right to forbid the local presbytery to declare the new church a *quoad sacra* parish church. Heritors throughout the country now began seizing the collection boxes at the new Church Extension churches. When elders at the new churches refused to co-operate, the heritors sent agents to supervise the collections.[178]

The Court of Session decisions were devastating. First, because the State had refused to provide the endowment grant, most new *quoad sacra* parish churches were dependent upon the income from *both* their seat-rents and their regular church-door collections. New churches were now forced to raise seat-rents above what the poor could afford, thus negating a basic purpose of Church Extension. Secondly, and perhaps more important, the Court of Session decisions effectively killed all hope for the realization of Chalmers's parish community ideal in the new churches. He had long argued that, once the endowment grant was received, the new churches would use their church-door collections for their own parish poor relief; indeed, the *quoad sacra* parishes would become self-contained communities, with independent poor-relief and educational programmes, modelled upon his Glasgow St. John's experiment. He had collected money for Church Extension on the basis of this promise. But now the Court of Session had determined that the *quoad sacra* parishes had no legal existence. They were simply 'preaching stations', subject to the authority of local heritors, most of whom had contributed nothing to their erection. The new churches were in fact placed in worse circumstances than the Dissenting congregations, which, although not endowed by the State, were at least able to retain their collections. The situation for the Church Extension churches was soon made even more intolerable. Three years later, early in 1843, the Court of Session decided that *quoad sacra* parishes had no ecclesiastical existence and could not be represented in the Church courts.

Chalmers was deeply distressed by the 1839 Brechin and Stewarton decisions. The dream of nearly a lifetime had been cruelly mocked; the effort and sacrifice of the Church Extension campaign had been rendered meaningless. It was as though he were watching his children being martyred. He felt an awesome responsibility to those he had convinced to contribute to the cause—from the wealthy supporters, with their individual donations of hundreds of pounds, to the poor labourers, participating in a local 'penny-a-week' subscription plan. 'It grieves me', he wrote in his *Remarks on the Present Position of the Church of Scotland*, published in October 1839, 'that I should have to tell the noble-hearted contributors to our great cause, that all the money, which they meant for the Christian instruction of the poor in Scotland, passes into the pockets of the Heritors.' It would have been more merciful, he lamented, had the Court of Session delivered these decisions in 1834, and 'strangled our enterprise in its infancy'. He raged against the authorities of the secular State, whose vindictiveness against the Establishment seemed unbounded. 'We are placed between two hostile forces. The [Government] has refused to give; but, worse than this, the [Court of Session] has taken away.'[179]

At the General Assembly of 1840, Chalmers announced his retirement as convener of the Church Extension Committee. 'I must', he confided to A. L. Simpson on 29 May, the day before the formal announcement, 'be pre-emptory on the Convenorship. The thought of it in any form is downright agony.' To the Assembly, he cited the Court of Session decisions as the major reason for the collapse of the campaign.[180] At the urgent request of the Assembly, he agreed to occupy the position for one more year, to allow time to find a successor. But he did not take an active part in the committee, and indeed did not even appear before the Assembly of 1841 to deliver his final report.[181] By May 1841, the Church Extension campaign was virtually dead.

The achievements had been considerable. During the seven years of Chalmers's convenership, from May 1834 to May 1841, 222 new churches had been built, increasing the total number of churches in the Scottish Establishment by over 20 per cent.[182] It was an impressive exhibition of middle- and upper-class philanthropy. For in truth, despite Chalmers's emphasis upon the sacrifice of working-class 'penny-a-week' subscribers, and despite his attacks upon the politics of interest and the utilitarian philosophy of the middle- and upper-class post-reform-bill electorate, the vast amount of contributions to his scheme had come from those middle and upper classes. These philanthropists had formed the local societies and conducted the initial social 'excavations' in impoverished and irreligious neighbourhoods—visiting homes, collecting statistics on church attendance, hiring and supporting missionaries, and eventually supervising the building of the *quoad sacra* parish church. Once the new churches were completed, it was these same middle- and upper-class philanthropists who became the elders and sabbath-school teachers in the new parishes. Their sacrifice and tenacity were often impressive. Stirred by a combination of Evangelical passion for the souls of the poor and concern to preserve social peace and order, they had embraced Chalmers's communitarian godly commonwealth ideal as the only alternative to class conflict and the secularization of society. Chalmers had provided an eloquent voice, a coherent social philosophy, and considerable organizational abilities. He had given the Evangelical revival in Scotland a new social direction and dynamic. He had moved the Church away from the preoccupation with strict theological formulations exhibited in the heresy trials of the early 1830s, towards a rational Scriptural Christianity expressed through an aggressive and laicized pastoral ministry. In response to the Voluntary challenge, he had demonstrated dramatically that the Church of Scotland had not relinquished its claim to be the institution responsible for the religious instruction of the nation.

None the less, the Church Extension campaign had failed to achieve the ideal of the godly commonwealth. The movement had not built enough churches to accommodate Scotland's increasing population. Nor had the movement, despite its emphasis upon the needs of the labouring poor, succeeded in achieving significant working-class church attendance or in creating viable working-class Christian communities based upon parochial religious, educational, and social welfare institutions. In the autumn of 1838, while Chalmers was pursuing his western 'tour of spiritual O'Connellism', the Voluntary agitator, David King, had visited and studied several Church Extension churches which Chalmers frequently described as examples of effective working-class churches. Among them was Chalmers's Dean church in the Water of Leith. King discovered that these churches in fact had only a small working-class attendance. Out of 1,000 seats at the Dean church, for instance, less than 300 were rented by inhabitants of the working-class *quoad sacra* parish. Further, King maintained, he found the new churches to be unpopular among the working lcasses, who were often antagonized by the visitations, and objected to being told what church they should attend.[183] King, to be sure, was hardly an objective observer. However, even Chalmers admitted that the new churches were not reaching the poorer order of labourers.

He blamed this on the Government, which had refused to support a Parliamentary endowment grant to enable the new churches to reduce seat-rents. Indeed, the most significant effect of the Church Extension movement was the endowment controversy and the resulting deterioration in relations between the Church of Scotland and the British State. By 1838, a large number in the Church of Scotland had become convinced that the State was no longer concerned to ensure its effectiveness. With the Brechin and Stewarton decisions of 1839, it seemed that the Church of Scotland's connection with the State had become a positive liability, and that the Courts were actively working to destroy Church Extension and render the Church less effective and less able to expand than its Dissenting rivals.

In truth, Melbourne and the Whigs had treated the Church badly. So long as the Church of Scotland remained a national Establishment, it was the State's responsibility to provide funds to enable it to expand with the increasing national population. The Government's contemptuous rejection of the Church's legitimate claims, when viewed in conjunction with the large number of unendowed churches in the Scottish Establishment (nearly 290, including the 67 unendowed chapels-of-ease built before 1834), caused many to scrutinize critically the value of a continued connection of the Church of Scotland with the British State. Indeed, by its actions, especially in the years 1838-9, the Government seemed to be encouraging the Church either to disestablish itself, or to throw over its Evangelical leadership and the aggressive home mission which Evangelicalism represented, and accept a declining social influence. For unless it expanded the number of its parish churches and schools along with the rapidly increasing population, and unless it extended its influence beyond its mainly middle- and upper-class membership to the working classes, the Church of Scotland would stagnate. Chalmers may be faulted for his expressions of 'moral loathing' for the Whigs, which did nothing to ease the growing tension. Yet it is not clear that such expressions did much harm. The real problem was that Melbourne, a political opportunist, survived for too long as head of a minority Whig Government, dependent upon the support of organized Dissent, Irish Catholics, and Radicals—who were opposed to any expansion of the national religious establishments. If Peel and the Tories had survived in office in 1835, or if they had returned to office in 1837, they probably would have at least introduced a Government endowment bill in Parliament. Even if the bill had not passed, the attempt would have diffused much of the ill-feeling growing in the Church. But Peel and the Tories did not return to office until August 1841. Before they returned, the resentments first stirred by the endowments question had, as will be seen in the next chapter, flared into a major conflict between Church and State involving patronage and the Church's Veto Act of 1834.

There was, meanwhile, still another effect of the failure of Church Extension to achieve Chalmers's godly commonwealth ideal. By 1839, a growing number of Churchmen, both outside and inside the Evangelical party, were beginning to question the value of Church involvement in social welfare. There was now little likelihood that the Establishment would be able to organize the Scottish population into closely-knit parish communities of 2,000 inhabitants, as Chalmers had hoped. More important, in those working-class neighbourhoods where churches had been built, there was no evidence that religious instruction was improving the inhabitants' material standard of living. One result of the increase in Evangelical household visitations during the

Church Extension campaign was to awaken Churchmen to just how bleak conditions were for the poor, particularly in the deteriorating urban slums. Visitors found families crowded into rat-infested tenements, without bedding, fuel, or food, and began to question whether Chalmers's proposed cure through religious and moral instruction alone could prove effective amid such conditions. Many of those who had, at his urgent request, gone into the urban slums with an idealistic faith in the power of moral persuasion, had emerged with quite different social views. By 1839, many began to suspect that the only hope for both the nation and the Church was not only perhaps the separation of Chuch and State, but also the separation of religion and social welfare. Only poor relief based upon legal assessments, they believed, would prove effective in preserving the lives of the destitute; the reform of moral character alone was not enough. Moreover, in the wake of the Court of Session's Brechin and Stewarton decisions, which enabled heritors to seize collections at new churches for poor relief, many believed the Church should devote its resources solely to religious instruction, and leave poor relief to the State. Chalmers's Church Extension campaign of the 1830s had represented an impressive, indeed heroic, effort to transform the nation in accordance with the Christian communal ideal. After the failure of his campaign, however, fissures began appearing within his Evangelical ascendancy in the Church of Scotland.

THE CHURCH DIVIDED

I

By the late 1830s, Chalmers's hair had turned grey, and he allowed it to grow long over his clerical collar. He had always been a heavy-set man, with a large head and large bones, and he remained so, standing five feet nine inches, and weighing over fourteen stone. Despite his weak heart, contemporaries were impressed with his aura of physical strength—the brisk walk, barrel chest, and long walking staff, which he flourished formidably as he moved. He had never been a handsome man. Yet, as he aged, he almost became so, his face assuming a rugged character, with square-set jaw and high forehead. They had at least this advantage over 'folks with finer faces', he observed with humour to an old Anstruther friend: 'Theirs have been aye getting the waur [worse], but ours have been getting aye the better of the wear.'[1] His eyes remained his most distinctive feature. They appeared drowsy, even vacant much of the time. But when stirred by emotion, they became singularly expressive, beaming with merriment in the midst of a joke, softening with kindness as he recognized an old acquaintance or was introduced to a new, narrowing with anger when he perceived an injustice, or bulging with frenzy at the height of a sermon or speech. There was an unmistakable presence about the man, a solidity and weight which commanded respect. The Evangelical clergyman, John Brown, a student under Chalmers in the 1830s, later recalled vividly:

his great look, large chest, large head, his amplitude everywhere; his broad, simple, childlike, inturned feet; his short hurried, impatient step; his erect, royal air, his look of general good-will; his kindling up into a warm but still vague benignity when one he did not recognize spoke to him; the addition, for it was not a change, of keen speciality to his hearty recognition; the twinkle of his eyes; the immediately saying something very personal to set all to rights, and then the sending you off with some thought, some feeling, some remembrance, making your heart burn within you; his voice indescribable; his eye—that most peculiar feature—not vacant, but *asleep*—innocent, mild, large; and his soul, the great inhabitant, not always at his window, but then, when he did awake, how close to you was that burning vehement soul![2]

'He was a man', Thomas Carlyle later observed, 'essentially of little culture, of narrow sphere, all his life; such an intellect, professing to be educated, and yet so ill-*read*, so ignorant in all that lay beyond the horizon in place or in time, I have almost nowhere met with. A man capable of much soaking indolence, lazy brooding, and do-nothingism, as the first stage of his life indicated; a man thought to be timid, almost to the verge of cowardice: yet capable of impetuous activity and blazing audacity...'.[3] Chalmers was not a profound scholar. He venerated, to be sure, the 'republic of letters' and especially its symbols. His friend Lord Elgin recalled him romping like a child about Oxford University during a visit there in 1833, rousing Elgin from bed early one morning to inform him of a sequestered courtyard he had 'discovered', as though no one before could have set eyes upon it. He regarded his Oxford DD and his election to the Royal Institute of France as among the most important events of his life.[4] Yet he was essentially a man of action, a politician, with little time for literature, and visitors who expected a refined academic mind were usually disappointed. Carlyle, for example, was probably surprised at Chalmers's ignorance of German philosophy and theology, which he dismissed contemptuously as 'mental gymnastics'. 'Germany!' he once exclaimed to a group of breakfast guests, 'a country where system after system was springing up, none of them lasting a day; every man, as it were, holding up his cheeks, crying, "Look at me, too!" I tell you I'll have none of you;— your Skillers [Schillers], and your Skagels [Schlegels].'

He was also a poor listener, and in social situations, tended either to withdraw into his own private reveries, or to launch into some lengthy monologue on one of his favourite and well-worn themes.[5] One result of his relatively narrow sphere of reading and conversation was that throughout his life he remained wedded to the intellectual capital of the Scottish Enlightenment, with its emphasis upon the moral foundations of society. A notable exception to this tendency was his appreciation for the works of Thomas Carlyle. He had become acquainted with Carlyle's future wife, Jane Welsh, during a summer excursion to Loch Lomond in 1821, and with Carlyle himself through their mutual friendship with Edward Irving. Chalmers was impressed with Carlyle's 1839 essay on *Chartism*, with its attacks upon utilitarianism, the middle-class reform-bill electorate, and the 'mammon' of profit and self-interest which inspired the new business élites, as well as with its longing for an idealized past of communal responsibility and benevolence. He was still more impressed with Carlyle's four-volume biography of Cromwell, which appeared a few years later. Chalmers had long venerated Cromwell and his Puritan commonwealth.[6] Carlyle's portrait was of Cromwell as hero, imposing God's order upon a rebellious and selfish nation, and elevating that nation, if only briefly, to moral greatness. This combination of force and sacrifice, in the name of God's will, resonated with Chalmers's own perceptions of the heroic.

Chalmers continued to exhibit inner tension between his personal ambition for power and authority, which had carried him out of rural Fife to national leadership, and his longing for a sense of communal belonging. Observers were often struck by his two natures—the one hard, dictatorial, logical, unscrupulous; the other warm, sentimental, romantic, eager to be loved. He was, on the one hand, an instinctive, and not overly scrupulous politician, who could go for the jugular vein of those who stood in his way. He lied to Elgin, Peel, and Liverpool regarding his co-operation with Kennedy in drafting the poor-law bill of 1824, and deserted Kennedy by his speech in the General Assembly. He directed personal abuse against Lee and his supporters in the Church, betrayed Robert Bell's confidential information regarding Lee's testimony before the Royal Commission, and continued to harass Lee and the Whig Evangelicals after their rebellion had been broken. He was not above seeking personal revenge. He employed the parallel hierarchies of Church Extension committees and Church courts to impose his personal will upon the Church and nation. In his personal life, he was often domineering and dictatorial. He was cruel, for example, to his Glasgow publisher and friend, William Collins, often repaying Collins's loyalty with accusations and suspicion, and finally provoking a quarrel with him which ended their professional association and friendship. He could be a tyrant at home with his family. He had an explosive temper, and was quick to perceive a personal affront, often when none was intended. In most of his relationships, he demanded absolute loyalty.[7]

There was, however, another Chalmers—warm, benevolent, and sentimental, a gentle man who could set a stranger at ease with a simple remark or kind look. He was playful with children, and during his frequent absences would write long and affectionate letters to his daughters, with a touching, childlike prose. Despite his quick temper at home, his daughters were genuinely fond of him, smothering 'papa' with their embraces and competing for his attention. The completion of his regular morning task of written composition was often marked by a resounding 'hurra, hurra', as he summoned his children for a romp in the garden. As they grew older, he would fool with them, displaying a mock chivalry, and quoting heroic lines of Sir Walter Scott at inopportune moments. His love for children was proverbial.[8] One memorialist recalled an excursion of several families in the Pentlands in the 1830s, when Chalmers gathered all the children together, instructed each to find a round stone, then trudged with them up a nearby hill in order to roll them down and trace their paths.[9] He loved the countryside, and shortly after his move to Edinburgh he began renting a rural cottage for the summer, first in the village of Penicuik; and then, between 1835 and 1839, in the village of Burntisland, on the Firth of Forth. Here he discovered again, for brief periods, the peace of rural Anstruther and Kilmany. He found solace in nature, whether the sublime beauty of a mountain or waterfall, or the quiet of a seaside cove or forest. He loved a rural walk, and would usually entertain his

summer visitors with a tour of the local scenic spots. It was his habit to
sink into silent meditation on such walks, which often disconcerted his
urban guests. Or, surrounded by pastoral beauty, he might abruptly
open up with personal revelations, confiding inner feelings regarding
his childhood, the passage of time and the loss of friends. David Cooper,
the minister of Burntisland, later recalled how such a mood came over
him while resting upon a wall during a rural walk in the late 1830s.
Suddenly, he launched into 'a very curious and racy train of observation', recalling his Anstruther childhood and how, despite the
passage of years, he often felt as though he were still that Anstruther
child, owing obedience to adults many years younger than he. Such
events were apt to be followed quite suddenly by another withdrawal
into silence.[10]

'He was a man', according to Carlyle again,

of much natural dignity, ingenuity, honesty, and kind affection, as well as sound
intellect and imagination. A very eminent vivacity lay in him, which could rise to
complete impetuosity (glowing conviction, passionate eloquence, fiery play of heart
and head),—all in a kind of *rustic* type, one might say, though wonderfully true and
tender. He had a burst of genuine fun too, I have heard; of the same honest, but most
plebeian, broadly natural character: his laugh was a hearty, low guffaw,[11]

Despite his rise to national, and international, reputation, Chalmers
never lost his attachment to the rural communities of northern Fife. He
remained a 'rustic' figure, who spoke English in a broad Fifeshire
accent, who often reverted in speech to his native Scots, who loved a
humorous country story, who had a keen sense of the ridiculous, and
could on occasion laugh at himself.[12] He respected refinement of
manners; but, although he possessed a natural grace, he remained out-
of-place in genteel society: he had too many rough edges. He maintained
the close friendships from his youth in Anstruther and Kilmany.
Among them were the Kilmany ploughman, Alexander Patterson, for
whom Chalmers secured a position as an Edinburgh city missionary;
the Evangelical widow, Janet Coutts, who had moved from northern
Fife to Edinburgh in the 1820s; the eccentric land-reform advocate,
Robert Gourlay, a fellow St. Andrews student who in 1824 was confined
to the Bridewell prison in London for several months for flogging
Henry Brougham in the lobby of the House of Commons; his brother
James, who had no taste for Evangelical enthusiasm; his sister Jane,
who married a factor of a Somerset landed estate; and above all,
Thomas Duncan, a boyhood companion and later St. Andrews Pro-
fessor of Mathematics. This last relationship was especially interesting.
Duncan was a staunch Whig, an anti-Malthusian, and a religious
Moderate. None the less, Chalmers allowed Duncan liberty to poke
gentle fun even at his bitter conflicts of the 1830s. The two, Chalmers

observed in 1841, had been young 'callants' together fifty years before; now, although old 'carls', they still enjoyed the same boyish playfulness. Their lifelong affection transcended political and even religious convictions.

Chalmers's social views, nurtured during his youth in the tradition-bound rural society of northern Fife, were paternalistic. He believed in an organic, hierarchical social structure, with emphasis upon each individual's divinely-ordained social duties and obligations. In the 1830s, moreover, he relinquished his Whig sympathies, as that party moved in the direction of political democracy and the secularization of British society, and turned to the Tory party, which he believed would work to preserve traditional social and religious values. He differed, however, from other leading Tory paternalists—such as Lord Ashley or Lord Aberdeen—being neither by birth nor wealth a member of the propertied élite. In language, manners, and outlook, he remained part of the rural communal Scotland of his birth.

Chalmers's family was growing up. His six daughters all survived to maturity; in 1840, they ranged in age from Anne, twenty-seven, to Frances, thirteen. His two eldest daughters had married. In 1836, the bright and vivacious Anne, perhaps his favourite, had married the Irish presbyterian clergyman and Chalmers's future biographer, William Hanna, son of the eminent clergyman Dr Samuel Hanna of Belfast. The younger Hanna was licensed as a clergyman of the Church of Scotland, and in 1837 was admitted to the ministry of rural Skirling, about thirty miles south of Edinburgh. In 1837, Anne gave birth to Chalmers's first grandchild, Thomas Chalmers Hanna. In 1839, Chalmers's second daughter Elizabeth married John Mackenzie, the Church of Scotland minister of the rural parish of Dunkeld, in Perthshire.

Chalmers's wife, Grace, was forty-eight years old in 1840, and was already frail with age. Because of her weak health and her aversion to crowds, she seldom accompanied her husband on his frequent excursions around the country. Nevertheless, she was deeply devoted to Thomas, ever anxious about his health and well-being. In the later 1830s, as their daughters grew older, she assumed an increased role in his work, reading and answering some of his letters, and handling many of the details of his business affairs with his publisher and their mutual friend, William Collins. A kind woman, she was a gracious hostess to the endless stream of callers and guests, from Europe and America as well as Britain. In truth, however, she probably would have preferred a quieter life, with her husband more often at home. Chalmers was fortunate in his marriage and in his daughters; yet he was also haunted by a certain guilt, or regret, that he had given so little time to his family. While he had been intent upon the struggle to achieve the godly commonwealth, his daughters had grown and two had left his household. Their childhood had slipped away from him, and he was anxious over whether he had fulfilled his responsibility to them. 'I have often felt', he wrote his daughter Elizabeth on 28 August 1839, during one of his Church Extension tours,

it is a great evil of too public a life, that it dissevered one from his family; and when I think how highly furnished I have been in that though 27 years a family man, I have never yet been exposed in my household to the visitation of death, I deeply feel that such a lengthened opportunity should have been connected more to the culture and preparation of those immortal spirits over whom I am appointed to watch.[13]

Had he not, perhaps, sacrificed too much of his own family's interest in striving for his vision of the Christian commonwealth?

In the mid-1830s, Chalmers seemed to have made substantial progress towards realizing his vision of a godly commonwealth in Scotland—towards organizing the nation into small parish communities, covenanted in the service of God, and for the subordination of private interests to the communal welfare. But, with the disappointments of 1838-9, and the virtual collapse of the Church Extension campaign, the fabric of his life-work began to unravel. It had long been his intention, that, with his sixtieth birthday in March 1840, he would retire from active leadership in the Church and nation, and devote his remaining years to his professorship, to the spiritual interests of his family, and to preparation for death and eternity. He would watch peacefully as his younger supporters carried the Church Extension campaign to its fulfilment. But this would not be. Instead, he became immersed in a dogged struggle to preserve the remnants of the Christian commonwealth against the encroachments of an expanding secular State, committed to exerting its authority over social functions once reserved to Church direction.

The years between 1832 and 1836 had been a period of plentiful employment and good harvests. There was relative prosperity in the country and peace among the social classes. In 1836, however, this situation changed dramatically. The series of good harvests ended. A financial crisis broke the trade boom of the early 1830s, and developed into a severe recession in 1837. Merchants and manufacturers were hard hit, and in the major cities, thousands of labourers became unemployed or forced on short hours. There was slight improvement in the economy between 1838 and 1840. But harvests remained poor, unemployment high, and business prospects bleak. In 1841, the economy sank into a serious and prolonged depression; in 1842, the British people experienced perhaps the darkest year of the nineteenth century. Four years of bad harvests had forced bread prices to famine levels. The optimism of the 1830s, the 'decade of reform', had ended; the 'hungry forties' had begun.

Working-class suffering and despair in the late 1830s found expression in the Chartist movement. The Charter, first published in May 1838, demanded radical reform of Parliament, including universal manhood suffrage, annual elections, payment of members, and representative districts proportionate to population. Only when the working classes were directly represented in Parliament, Chartists argued, would their condition improve. By 1839, agitation for the Charter had extended throughout Britain. Mass meetings were held, Chartist newspapers published, and a national Convention established.

The propertied classes of Britain were alarmed. Along with upper-class fear, however, Chartism also awakened concern about social conditions. In 1839, Thomas Carlyle published his celebrated essay, *Chartism*. The Chartist agitation, he affirmed, was misguided; the labouring classes would achieve salvation only through their individual moral improvement. None the less, Carlyle continued, their desperate efforts must serve as the occasion for a new national focus upon the 'condition of England question'. For decades, the propertied élite had embraced the doctrine that their pursuit of self-interest would contribute to the social welfare. They had relinquished the paternalistic duties of their fathers, for the 'mammon' of profit and material wealth. Was it any wonder that the lower social orders had been driven to desperate acts? Only a revival of moral and spiritual leadership among the propertied orders, Carlyle maintained, and a renewed respect for their paternalistic responsibilities, would save the social fabric.

Social conditions became a focus of public interest and debate in the 1840s. New attention was paid to experiences of Evangelical and philanthropic visitors, and to the reports of Parliamentary Committees of Inquiry and Royal Commissions. Social conditions, many discovered to their surprise, were cruel and intolerable. In urban slums throughout Britain, families were crowded into decrepit tenements, without bedding, fuel, or proper clothing. Trash and sewage collected in the courtyards and closes. John Lee had testified of his Edinburgh parish before the Commission on Religious Instruction in 1836 that

He had never before seen such misery as in his parish, where the people were without furniture, without everything, two married couples often sharing one room. In a single day he had visited seven houses in which there was not a bed, in some of them not even a heap of straw. Old people of eighty years sleep on the board floor, nearly all slept in day-clothes. In one cellar room he found two families from a Scotch country district; soon after their removal to the city two of the children had died, and a third was dying at the time of his visit. Each family had a filthy pile of straw in a corner; the cellar ... was, moreover so dark that it was impossible to distinguish one person from another by day.

'It was enough,' Lee added, 'to make a heart bleed to see such misery in a country like Scotland.'[14]

Special attention was given to the reports of physicians who visited among the poor. Urban slums, argued such physicians as James Phillip Kay [later Kay Shuttleworth] of Manchester, Neil Arnott of London, Alexander Cowan of Glasgow, and William Pulteney Alison of Edinburgh, were seed-beds of contagious disease. Not only did thousands of slum dwellers die of typhoid each year; but slum conditions, physicians maintained, had also contributed to the devastating cholera epidemic of 1832, which had spread out of the slums and claimed lives from all social classes. Clearly, they argued, the general interest required an end to slum conditions.[15] Many now looked to the State as the only authority capable of significant social action. None the less, the English Poor Law Act of 1834, with its 'less eligibility' principle and its workhouses, was proving extremely unpopular—so much so that in 1839, Parliament began renewing the Act for periods of one year only, to ensure against any appearance of permanence.[16] In short, combined with the sense that something had to be done, there was uncertainty among the propertied classes about the proper course of action. This was particularly true in Scotland, as a growing debate over the old Scottish poor law revealed.

In 1838, Parliament passed a poor law act for Ireland, extending the principles of the 1834 English Poor Law Act to that country. It was now widely believed that the Whig Government, through the influence of such Benthamite administrative reformers as Edwin Chadwick, was aiming for uniformity in poor law administration throughout Britain, and that the principles of the 1834 English act would soon be extended to Scotland. These suspicions were confirmed when, in 1838, the Government requested the General Assembly to report on Scottish poor-law administration. The General Assembly report, submitted in 1839, revealed a substantial increase in the number of persons living under a system of legal assessment in Scotland. In 1818, 340,000 of Scotland's approximately 2,000,000 inhabitants, or 17 per cent, lived in assessed parishes. In 1839, however, this had increased to 1,138,000 of Scotland's approximately 2,500,000 inhabitants, or 45 per cent.[17] The General Assembly reaffirmed its commitment to the traditional system of Church-directed poor relief. None the less, with nearly half the population now living under a system of legal relief, the transition to the principles of the 1834 English Act might be accomplished easily. In 1839, the Government instructed Chadwick and the poor-law guardians to conduct an enquiry into sanitary conditions among the labouring classes of England and Ireland, as a preliminary to public health legislation. The implication of Scotland's exclusion was clear: Scotland would be included in the public health legislation only when its poor laws were reformed in conformity with the rest of the kingdom.[18]

In January 1840, William Pulteney Alison (1790-1859), an Edinburgh

Professor of Medicine and a philanthropist involved for twenty-five years
in medical visitations among the poor, published a 198-page pamphlet
entitled *Observations on the Management of the Poor in Scotland, and its Effects
on the Health of the Great Towns*. It was a devastating indictment of the old
Scottish poor law. Social conditions in Scotland, Alison argued, were far
worse than in England and Wales. Infectious disease was more pre-
valent, and life expectancy shorter. In 1837-8, the mortality rate in
England and Wales as a whole was 1 in 45, and in London 1 in 32. No
similar statistics existed in Scotland as a whole for that year. In the city
of Edinburgh, however, the rate was 1 in 21.8 and in Glasgow 1 in 24.[19]
A cycle of despair, Alison maintained, had developed among the
Scottish urban poor. They were mistreated, abandoned, or orphaned
in childhood. They reached adulthood without moral instruction or
vocational skills. In despair, many turned to crime and alchoholism.
They mistreated their own children, and passed on their vicious habits
and despair to the next generation. High birth rates in the urban
slums, meanwhile, more than compensated for high mortality rates.
Sexual morals were loose, and prostitution was rampant. Indeed, the
evidence demonstrated that, contrary to the assertions of Malthusian
social reformers, it was not high poor-relief allowances, but rather
extreme destitution, that most discouraged 'moral restraint'. The
poor were multiplying at a faster rate than the rest of the population,
and it was becoming increasingly difficult to contain their crime and
disease within the urban slums.

The root of social evil in Scotland, Alison maintained, was the
Scottish poor law. It was, he argued, the most inefficient system of relief
in Europe. Its failures were twofold. First, the system relied too much
upon voluntary charity. Even in legally-assessed parishes, the allowances were insufficient to support an individual or family; they were
intended only to supplement what paupers were expected to receive
from private benevolence. But, asserted Alison, in an advanced and
complex state of social development, where rich and poor seldom came
into direct contact, voluntary charity was no longer sufficient, and the
poor were forced either to starve on meagre parish allowances, or to
supplement them by crime.[20] Secondly, poor relief in Scotland was
legally reserved only for individuals of sound moral character, who
were physically or mentally disabled. This, Alison maintained, doomed
innocent children of dissolute parents to misery, and perpetuated the
cycle of despair. It submitted the neighbours of immoral poor, and
indeed the whole society, to the effects of slum conditions, including
crime, public begging, and especially epidemic disease. Moreover,
he maintained, slum environments thwarted the development of moral
character. Who, he asked, could sit in judgement and condemn
individuals whose character only reflected the harsh circumstances

society had created for them? 'If we reserve our charity until we meet with human beings exempt from sinful propensities or indulgences ... we may reserve it for the next world, for we assuredly shall not find fit objects for it in this.'[21]

The only way to break the cycle of despair, Alison concluded, was to provide every individual, the dissolute as well as the moral, with a regular, uniform, and sufficient subsistence. For this, the old Scottish poor law would have to be reformed in accordance with the principles of the 1834 English Poor Law Act. Poor-relief authority would have to be removed from the Church of Scotland, and lodged in the State, which would create a secular system of administration, including a uniform national legal assessment, the introduction of workhouses and the principle of 'less eligibility,' and a vast increase in annual poor-relief expenditure, from the present £140,000 to at least £800,000. Above all, poor relief had to be divorced from the morality test. 'We must', he asserted, 'learn to regard pauperism, in so far as it is an evil at all, as a necessary evil in every country in an advanced state of civilization.'[22]

Alison's pamphlet excited considerable public concern. On 23 March 1840, at a public meeting in Edinburgh, an association was formed to agitate for Alison's reform proposals. Among the committee of forty managers appointed to head the new society were John Lee and several Whig Evangelicals, including the former 'Leeites' Robert Gordon, R. S. Candlish, David Welsh, and Graham Spiers.[23] In late April, Chalmers's friend, the retired Senator of the College of Justice, David Monypenny of Pitmilly, published a rejoinder to Alison's *Observations,* in which he defended Chalmers's parish community ideal and recalled the success of the St. John's experiment. The present weakness of the old Scottish poor law, Monypenny argued, had resulted from rapid population growth. Parishes had grown overcrowded, and the system was breaking down under the weight of numbers. But if the Government would provide the endowments and requisite legal status for the new *quoad sacra* Church Extension parishes, the old Scottish poor law, with its emphasis upon communal values, would prove effective for diminishing poverty.[24]

Alison immediately demolished Monypenny with a second pamphlet. The supporters of the old Scottish poor law, he argued, were deluded by the absurd belief that pauperism was synonymous with poverty—that if parish deacons kept poor-relief expenses low (as in St. John's), this meant that poverty had been diminished. But in fact, small allowances only contributed to social misery and despair, discouraging any 'moral restraint' or 'self-help'. Alison challenged Chalmers's parish community ideal, and the alleged success of his St. John's experiment: the traditional communal ideal, he proclaimed, was dead. Relatives and neighbours did not in fact assist the destitute. Chalmers's St. John's experiment, moreover, had been a failure. By his own admission, Chalmers had not carefully scrutinized the poor-relief activities of his individual elders and deacons. If he had, Alison maintained, he would have found that they had reduced legal pauperism only by neglecting the genuine needs of the poor and thus increasing destitution and misery. It was, he added, significant that Chalmers's supposed success had not been duplicated elsewhere.[25] In 1840, moreover, Alison's brother, Archibald Alison (1792-1867), the Tory Sheriff of Lanarkshire, and later a celebrated historian, published a massive two-volume work, *The Principles of Population,* in which he also characterized Chalmers's St. John's experiment as a failure, and debunked his Malthusian views.[26] It appeared that W. P. Alison's proposal for extending the 1834 English Poor Law Act to Scotland might eventually gain national approval. Chalmers's parish community ideal was rapidly losing public support. Church Extension had been thwarted, and now his St. John's experiment, the foundation of his parish community ideal, was also being discredited. He therefore determined to accept Alison's challenge to his communal ideal, and in September 1840, he travelled to Glasgow to debate with Alison at the annual meeting of the British Association for the Advancement of Science.

The crowd which gathered for the great debate was immense, and the meeting had to be moved from a Glasgow College lecture hall to the College church. The debate continued for four days, and was extensively reported in the newspaper press. Public interest fastened upon this contest between Scotland's two greatest philanthropists. For his part, Chalmers reviewed at length his communal ideal, and discussed his two social experiments—his St. John's experiment and his recent community-building operation in the Water of Leith. Contrary to the statements of his critics, he asserted, these social experiments had achieved significant results. They had diminished poverty and crime, and elevated parish inhabitants with Christian and moral education. If the results had not been overwhelmingly convincing, it was because he had not received the necessary co-operation from the civil authorities.

His dispute with Alison, he continued, involved essentially the conflict between the environmentalist and the moral approaches to social theory. This was the crux of the argument—as it had been earlier in his dispute with McCulloch. Reform the social environment, Alison maintained, and individual moral reform would follow. But Chalmers believed the opposite. The first step was to reform individual moral character through Christian instruction, and then improvement in social conditions would 'necessarily follow'. He expressed faith in the inherent strength of the human spirit; even in the most brutal social surroundings and at his most degraded moral condition, man possessed a conscience which could be reached by Scripture and human kindness. Religious and moral instruction alone would break the cycle of despair so eloquently described by Alison. Of this he was certain—so much so, that he offered, in the presence of several Glasgow magistrates, to return to the parish ministry and begin another communal experiment in the most impoverished urban district that could be found, provided he were given the civil co-operation denied him in St. John's.

Finally, he reviewed the disappointments of his Church Extension campaign, and insisted that if only the Government would provide the endowment grant, pauperism would be eradicated through the moral elevation of the people. There would then be no need for the £800,000 per annum poor-relief expenditures recommended by Alison. 'The question here', he asserted, 'was were they willing to pay £800,000 a-year to provide for the poor, or £200,000 for an endowment.' Archibald Alison, he observed, had discovered that £1,200,000 was spent each year for intoxicating liquor in Glasgow alone, chiefly by the working classes. Religious and moral instruction, Chalmers added, would convince the poor to devote that money to self-help and communal benevolence, eliminating the need for legal pauperism.[27]

Alison, on his side, repeated his positions, backed by weighty statistical data. He was, however, no match for Chalmers on the speakers' platform. Chalmers was on his best oratorical form, playing upon his audience's emotions, entertaining them with anecdotes, gaining their confidence with a combination of earnest appeals and homely wit. He dominated the debate and carried the crowd. Alison and his supporters, however, did not relinquish their campaign. They acknowledged Chalmers's eloquence, but argued that it was without substance. Statistical evidence and medical reports, they maintained, documented conclusively the need to extend the 1834 English Poor Law Act to Scotland.[28]

In 1841, the severe depression increased the agitation in Scotland for the new poor law. In the summer of that year, Chalmers responded with a new treatise on his communal ideal, based largely upon lectures previously delivered in his divinity class. *The Sufficiency of a Parochial System, without a Poor Rate, for the Right Management of the Poor* was published by Collins of Glasgow in September 1841. It was a definitive statement of his social ideal. He described once again his ideal parish system, with visiting elders and deacons, sabbath schools and parish schools—elevating the parish inhabitants to communal self-sufficiency through moral instruction. He reaffirmed his commitment to legal assessments for the support of medical hospitals, asylums for the mentally and physically disabled, and measures of public health. His aim, he asserted, was not to spare the propertied classes expense for social welfare, but rather to ensure that this money was expended in

the true interest of the poor.²⁹ He denounced the 1834 English Poor
Law Act as 'a moral gangrene'. Workhouses were 'pauper bastiles'; if
a man required relief, 'he must be put into confinement, separated
from his home, subjected to the irksome and galling restraints of a prison
discipline'. 'The truth is, they have been made as repulsive as possible
for the very purpose of scaring applicants away.' The 1834 act was in
fact based on a lie—'the principle being that every human creature in
want has a right to relief; and the practice being [that] it were a very
wrong thing in either man or woman to assert it.' 'Meanwhile,' he
added, in reference to Chartism, 'a vehement, but most natural outcry,
has arisen in many parts of England—provoked we have no doubt, in
the contemplation of this new system.... a system of harshness, in the
guise or at least with the title of a system of charity.'³⁰

Perhaps most interesting was his appeal to Scottish national
sentiment. Under the influence of Benthamite administrative reformers,
he maintained, the London Government was increasing in power and
authority, and destroying local traditional institutions in the name of
administrative uniformity. It was extending its influence into Scotland,
Ireland, and Wales, intent upon replacing their communal traditions
with London-based legal and contractual institutions. A Behemoth was
developing in London, which threatened to demolish all that was *sui
generis* in Scotland's national heritage. '[Of all the principles] in the
science of government,' he observed,

perhaps the one most frequently quoted is centralization, which aims at the establishment
of a uniform regime for the whole empire, and has all the greater charms to an
administration which seeks to strengthen and perpetuate its own power, that it so often
makes room for the multiplication of offices, and for the consequent increase of patronage in its own hands. That is what we have most to dread in the projected changes which
are said to be now in contemplation on the pauperism of Scotland, and that for the
purpose of harmonizing it with the system of pauperism in England.

A poor-law commission for Scotland, he warned, such as that advocated
by Alison and the Edinburgh association, would be dominated by
English commissioners. 'They will come in among a people who have a
different standard or rather a different style of enjoyment from their
own, each deviation from which will in their eyes appear to be a
deficiency.' In truth, Chalmers asserted, Scotland had a rich national
tradition, different from that of England, but no less viable. Scotland
was, to be sure, a poorer nation that its southern neighbour, but this
had resulted from less abundant natural resources, and not from
inferior national institutions. Despite their poorer resource base,
moreover, the Scots were rapidly catching up with England in material
civilization. They could, he asserted, continue their development
without forsaking their native institutions. In St. John's and the Water

of Leith, he had demonstrated that Scotland's Christian communal ideal could be made to work in modern urban conditions. Let the English, he added, look at the failings of their 1834 Poor Law Act among their own people, 'ere they offer to palm it upon us'.[31]

Following the publication of his *Parochial System*, Chalmers began to agitate for the introduction of a 'permissive clause' into the 1834 English Poor Law Act, which would enable English parishes to withdraw from the act, and adopt a 'retracing process' towards a system of Church-directed parish charity. The unpopularity of the 1834 act among the working-classes, and among such authors as Thomas Carlyle and the English lawyer and Anglican social theorist, S. R. Bosanquet, had convinced Chalmers that England might be prepared to adopt his communal ideal. He sent nearly 100 copies of his *Parochial System* to leading politicians, clergymen, and literary figures, and requested William Gladstone to introduce the 'permissive clause' in Parliament. Gladstone, however, politely declined Chalmers's request, and as no one else expressed support, he was soon obliged to abandon the effort.[32]

In truth, by late 1841, public opinion even in Scotland was shifting decisively towards Alison's position. In part, this resulted from the success of Alison and his supporters in influencing public opinion. During 1841, the pro-Alison Edinburgh association published a series of reports, emphasizing the brutal social conditions in Scotland.[33] Immediately after the appearance of Chalmers's *Parochial System,* Alison published a *Reply to Dr. Chalmers' Objections to an Improvement of the Legal Provision for the Poor in Scotland*. Alison the author was far more effective than Alison the public speaker, and his pamphlet proved a sharp and convincing rejoinder—focusing upon Chalmers's inconsistency in denying relief to the 'undeserving' poor and thus condemning their innocent children, dependents, and neighbours to suffer. Chalmers's ideal communities, based upon a simplistic morality, were 'utopian' in complex urban-industrial society.[34] The London Benthamite *Westminster Review* also joined the rising anti-Chalmers chorus, further flogging the 'myth' of his St. John's success by arguing that it was based upon deceptions and mistreatment of the poor.[35] Contributing to the success of the Alison party, moreover, was the worsening economic depression. By late 1841, the old poor law was tottering under the pressure of massive unemployment. According to the old law, kirk-sessions and burgh councils were not obliged to grant any relief to these able-bodied unemployed. The sources for relief of even the disabled, however, were proving insufficient. The result was appalling suffering in the large towns. The most dramatic conditions occurred in Paisley, a town of 48,416 inhabitants, almost all of whom were engaged in the manufacture of shawls. The collapse of the shawl trade in the early 1840s caused massive unemployment. The poor-relief system in Paisley, based upon church-door collections and a modest assessment, broke down, and the propertied classes were requested voluntarily to contribute an additional 15 per cent of their normal assessment to meet the emergency. But the vast majority of ratepayers refused. In consequence, urgent appeals had to be made throughout the kingdom for collections to avoid starvation.[36] It was a dramatic illustration of the bankruptcy of the old poor law and traditional communal ideal in the face of industrial and urban realities. Thomas Carlyle probably reflected the opinion of many when he declined to support Chalmers's anti-poor-law campaign. He sympathized with Chalmers's communal ideal, but regarded it as Quixotic in a society so degraded by selfish and utilitarian values. 'That you, with your generous hopeful heart,' he wrote to Chalmers on 11 October 1841,

believe there may still exist in our actual Churches enough of divine fire to awaken the supine rich and the degraded poor, and act victoriously against such a mass of pressing and ever-accumulated evils—alas! what worse could be said of this by the bitterest opponent of it, than that it is a noble hoping against hope, a noble strenuous determination to gather from the dry deciduous tree what the green alone could yield?... With a Chalmers in every British parish much might be possible! But, alas! what assurance is there that in any one British parish there will ever be another?[37]

By 1842, the majority of even Chalmers's Evangelical party in the Church of Scotland evidently favoured a new poor law for Scotland. Many leading Evangelical clergy had joined the pro-Alison Edinburgh Association. In April 1842, even the Evangelical *Presbyterian Review* admitted the need for a new act.[38] A consensus was developing among Churchmen that the Church should withdraw from such 'economic' concerns as poor relief, and concentrate upon 'spiritual' matters. In January 1843, the Tory Government appointed a Royal Commission of Inquiry to investigate poor relief in Scotland and to suggest suitable legislation.[39] Chalmers's parish community ideal was fading from the public imagination.

II

In 1834, it will be recalled, the Church had passed the Veto Act, in an effort to achieve a compromise between patronage and popular rights. On the whole, the Veto Act had functioned smoothly during its first five years of operation. Most patrons and parishioners were disposed to give the new measure a fair trial. In general, patrons consulted the opinion of parishioners before making a presentation to a vacant church. Most parishioners, or rather male heads of families in communion with the Church, acted with restraint in exercising their new right. In nearly 150 settlements of new ministers between 1834 and 1839, only 10 presentations had been vetoed.[40] None the less, slowly at first, a conflict developed, involving fundamental principles of political and social organization, and ultimately the nature and location of sovereignty in the British State.

In October 1834, four months after the passing of the Veto Act, Robert Young, a recently-licensed probationary minister, was presented to the Perthshire parish of Auchterarder by the patron, the Earl of Kinnoull. Young's intellectual and moral qualifications were unquestionable. He was not, however, an inspiring preacher, and he was slightly crippled. Auchterarder, moreover, had a history of anti-patronage fervour. In the event, Young's presentation was vetoed. Of the 330 heads of family on the parish communicants' roll, 287 expressed disapproval of Young, while only 2 signed the 'Call' in his favour. Young appealed against the veto to the higher Church courts, and the case was eventually referred to the General Assembly. But on 30 May 1835, the Assembly confirmed that Young's presentation was invalid by the terms of the 1834 Veto Act. The local presbytery, accordingly, rejected Young's presentation. Young again appealed the case to the synod of Perthshire and Stirling. But he did not continue to pursue this second appeal in the Church courts. Instead, he privately met John Hope, the Tory Dean of Faculty, and son of Charles Hope, Lord President of the Court of Session. Hope had dissented against the Veto Act in the 1834 General Assembly, arguing that the Church had over-extended its authority in interfering with the civil rights of patrons and their candidates. He now decided to make Young's a test case in the civil courts. On his advice, Young dropped his appeal in the Church courts, and took his case to the Court of Session, the highest civil court in Scotland.[41] In short, he appealed from ecclesiastical to civil authority. The Court of Session accepted the case, and this ensured the development of a fundamental conflict of jurisdiction.

Nearly three years later, on 8 March 1838, the Court of Session delivered its verdict. By a vote of eight judges to five, the Court decided that in rejecting Young on the basis of the Veto, the presbytery had infringed upon the civil rights of patrons and presentees. The court instructed the presbytery to provide Young with the customary trials, and if found qualified in doctrine, education, and morals, to induct him to the Auchterarder parish living. In a word, the Veto Act was declared illegal, and the presbytery was ordered to disregard both ecclesiastical law and the instruction of its superior ecclesiastical courts.[42] The Church was stunned by the decision. In the Church of Scotland, inducting a probationary minister into a parish also involved his ordination to the ministry, so in effect the Court of Session had dictated to the Church conditions by which it must ordain its ministers. It had implied that the civil courts possessed authority over the ecclesiastical courts in all matters, including internal Church discipline. The decision was regarded as an open challenge to the spiritual integrity of the Church of Scotland.

The Church was in no mood to submit to such humiliation. The year 1838 was the bicentenary of the Solemn League and Covenant, by which the Scots had asserted the spiritual independence of the Kirk against the encroachments of Charles I, and commemorations were stirring public zeal. Further, the Church was smouldering under the humiliation of the Government's recent rejection of the proposed endowment grant. At its annual meeting in May 1838, the General Assembly responded to the Court of Session decision with two measures. First, by a vote of 183 to 142, it passed a resolution affirming its spiritual independence. Quoting from both the Westminster Confession of Faith and the Second Book of Discipline, the Assembly solemnly proclaimed its belief 'that "the Lord Jesus Christ as King and Head of the Church, hath therein appointed a government in the hands of Church officers distinct from the civil magistrates."' The Church courts 'possess an exclusive jurisdiction founded on the Word of God, which "power Ecclesiastical … flows from God and the Mediator, Jesus Christ, and is spiritual, not having a temporal head on earth."' Secondly, the Assembly determined to appeal against the Court of Session's Auchterarder decision to the House of Lords, the highest civil court in the kingdom. This second measure was probably the Church's first major mistake. For an appeal to the Lords was a tacit admission that the Church's spiritual independence was subject to review by the very civil courts whose authority it had disavowed in its first resolution. The Assembly was aware of the inconsistency. None the less, it wished to take every step possible to reach an agreement with the State, and it evidently felt certain that the House of Lords would decide in its favour.[43]

On 4 May 1839, however, the House of Lords upheld the decision of the Court of Session. The appeal in the Lords was heard before Lords Brougham and Cottenham, the past and present Lord Chancellors. The eccentric Brougham was the nephew of the celebrated eighteenth-century Scottish Moderate ecclesiastic, William Robertson, and was himself an opponent of both Evangelical enthusiasm and Church Extension. Although in 1834 he had approved of the Assembly's Veto Act, he now reversed his opinion. The right of the 'Call', he asserted, which the Veto Act had revived, was in fact an obsolete formality, with no real legal status. Indeed, the opinion of the 'assembled people' of a parish regarding a presentee had 'no more weight than the recalcitration of the champion's horse in Westminster Hall during the festival attending the [coronation] solemnity'. Cottenham, an Englishman, agreed. The Church was shocked, not only by the judgement, but by the frivolous manner in which the Lords had dis-

missed its claims.[44] Cockburn, one of the minority of judges on the
Court of Session in the Auchterarder decision, reflected this anger and
frustration in his journal on 6 May 1839. 'There never was', he wrote,
'a greater cause adjudged in the House of Lords on reasons more
utterly unworthy of both. A case about a horse, or a £20 bill of exchange, would have got more thought. The ignorance and contemptuous slightness of the judgement did great mischief. It irritated and
justified the people of Scotland in believing that their Church was
sacrificed to English prejudices.'[45]

Chalmers had not been a member of the General Assembly of 1838,
nor had he seemed overly distressed by the Court of Session's Auchterarder decision in March 1838. His attention was focused upon
Church Extension, and particularly his campaign to stir popular resentment against the Government's decision regarding endowments. The
dispute over the veto was for him simply an unfortunate diversion from
the more fundamental endowments issue. If necessary, he believed the
Church should simply repeal the Veto Act in order to end the dispute.
He felt, at this time, no commitment to the veto. Was it not essentially
a Whig measure, forced upon the Church by the Whig Government?
At the Evangelical leaders' meeting in early May 1833, it will be recalled, Chalmers had initially recommended against the veto, arguing
that the Church should concentrate upon reviving the popular 'Call'
through a series of test cases. He had only relinquished his opposition
on the advice of the Whig Lord Moncrieff, a Court of Session judge.
Now that the Court of Session had decided against the veto, he believed,
the Church should not press the matter to a major conflict that would
further jeopardize Church Extension.

The House of Lords' Auchterarder decision of 4 May 1839, however,
changed the situation. The Lords had not only declared the veto illegal,
they had also ruled against the popular 'Call' in any form. Parishioners,
they declared, had no voice in the selection of their minister, and the
civil courts had full authority to 'intrude' unpopular patron's presentees
into parish livings. More important, the Lords had upheld the Court of
Session's position that the Church courts were subordinate to the
civil courts in matters of internal spiritual discipline. The simple repeal
of the Veto Act, Chalmers realized, would no longer suffice; the conflict
had gone beyond that point. The Church, he believed, was now constrained by events to respond forcefully to the challenge to its prerogatives.[46] He had, meanwhile, secured his election to the General
Assembly of 1839, and on 22 May, he introduced a motion in response
to the Lords' Auchterarder decision. His motion consisted in three
parts. First, the Church should acquiesce in the loss of the church,
manse, and endowed living of Auchterarder, 'the civil rights and
emoluments secured by law', which, he maintained, the civil courts

were competent to dispose of as they wished. In short, there should be
no further resistance to Young's claim to the 'temporalities' of the
living. Secondly, the Church should reaffirm its commitment to the
principle of 'non-intrusion', that is, that no presentee should be intruded into a parish living against the expressed will of the parishioners.
'The principle of Non-intrusion', he asserted, 'is one coeval with the
Reformed Kirk of Scotland, and forms an integral part of its constitution,
embodied in its standards, and declared in various Acts of Assembly.'
Thirdly, the Assembly should appoint a standing committee to consider
how best to preserve the spiritual independence of the Church, and to
confer with the Government about measures to end the 'collision
between the civil and ecclesiastical authorities'.[47]

   Chalmers introduced his motion with a speech of three hours, in
which he focused upon the theory of a compact between Church and
State in Scotland. Church and State, he maintained, were independent
polities, 'two kingdoms', the one under the sovereignty of God through
his revealed Word, the other under the sovereignty of the Crown. The
compact, he argued, had been initiated by the State. In return for the
social benefits of the spiritual instruction provided by the Church, the
State had promised to provide civil protection, church buildings, and
endowments. But in accepting these 'temporalities', the Church had
not relinquished the sovereignty of Christ. The State, he continued,
might abuse its part in the compact, and order the Church to induct
certain candidates into the livings it had provided. That had been the
judgement of the House of Lords. But in the Church of Scotland,
induction and ordination occurred together, and ordination was a
spiritual act. The Church, he argued, could not allow the State to dictate
conditions for ordination, and still maintain its integrity as a Christian
Church. If it accepted the sovereignty of the State in spiritual matters,
it would become nothing more than a department of State. The Church
of England, he asserted, would never have accepted such a humiliation;
nor, he implied, would the House of Lords ever presume to treat it with
such contempt. 'Ask any English ecclesiastic whether the Bishop would
receive an order from any civil court whatever on the matter of ordination; and the instant, the universal reply is, that he would not. In
other words, we should be degraded far beneath the level of the sister
Church if we remain in connexion with the State, and submit to this
new ordinance, or if you will, to this new interpretation of their old
ordinances.'

   This, then, would be the message in the Church's decision to relinquish the Auchterarder living: that while it recognized the State's
authority over the church buildings and endowments, the Church
would not recognize State authority over ordination and spiritual
discipline. Before it submitted to such authority, it would dissolve its

compact with the State, even though this meant the loss of all its buildings and endowments. It would turn for support to the Scottish nation, which, he asserted with an appeal to national pride, would not forsake the Church in time of crisis. The English were not the only people with a history of defending their national Church. 'Let us not be mistaken,' he exclaimed. 'Should the emancipation of our Church require it, there is the same strength of high and holy determination in this our land. There are materials here too for upholding the contest between principle and power; and enough of the blood and spirit of the olden time for sustaining that holy warfare.' In short, he raised the prospect of a disruption of the Church of Scotland.[48]

Chalmers was exhausted by the effort. Immediately after the conclusion of his speech, he retired to the vestry of the church to lie down. Throughout the evening, his friends were anxious about his condition, fearing another stroke. He was not present when at 2 a.m., after twelve hours of debate, the Assembly adopted his motion by a vote of 204 to 155. In response to the challenge from the civil courts, the Church had chosen to stand with Chalmers on the principles of non-intrusion and spiritual independence. A few days later, the Assembly named Chalmers convener of the Non-intrusion Committee appointed to negotiate with the Whig Government.[49]

By June 1839, the Auchterarder affair, which had begun as a minor patronage dispute, had developed into a major conflict between Church and State. There were two fundamental issues involved in the dispute. The first was the matter of non-intrusion, or the Church's refusal to allow patrons and the civil courts to force ministers upon parishes in the face of sincere opposition from the majority of parishioners. The second was the matter of the Church's spiritual independence, or its exclusive authority to govern its own internal spiritual affairs, including ordination and the disciplining of its clergy. Non-intrusion, Chalmers believed, was vital for an Evangelical and popular national Church. It was a grievous evil to force ministers upon parishioners against their will, at the bidding of a Crown patronage adviser or individual member of the social élite. A policy of 'intrusion', or unrestricted patronage, would only encourage popular contempt for the Establishment and diminish its usefulness, particularly in the present 'age of reform' when the State was granting an increased popular influence in the important social and political institutions. But far more important than even non-intrusion, Chalmers maintained, was the principle of spiritual independence. Intrusion of patron's candidates would diminish the Church's usefulness. But to deprive the Church of Scotland of its spiritual independence was to destroy its nature as a true Church of God. There might be some room for the Church to compromise on the matter of non-intrusion, and particularly the Veto Act; indeed, in the following years, as will be seen, Chalmers did repeatedly attempt to negotiate a compromise settlement on this question. But he believed there could never, never be any compromise over the fundamental point of the Church's spiritual independence. This was the bottom line, on which there could be no negotiation.

Chalmers's unbending stand on spiritual independence was by no means an innovative position in the Church of Scotland. Since the sixteenth-century Reformation, doctrinaire Calvinists had asserted the spiritual independence of the Church of Scotland, and the concept of the 'two kingdoms'. For probably the majority of the Church in 1839, the aggressor in the present conflict was the expanding British State, the new Behemoth, which now asserted an all-encompassing sovereignty that was, they argued, unknown to the British constitution. The fact that the sovereign power in Britain was now lodged in a Parliament which included Dissenters and Roman Catholics did not encourage the Church's confidence in the State's competency to determine internal Church policy; but the doctrines of non-intrusion and spiritual independence pre-dated both the repeal of the Test and Corporation Acts in 1828, and the Catholic Emancipation Act of 1829. The Church regarded its position as conservative, defending traditional privileges against encroachments by an expanding secular State.

The Auchterarder affair had introduced three additional factors into Church affairs, which would assume increasing importance. First, it had helped to revive the Moderate party in the Church of Scotland. In the mid-1830s the Moderates were in disarray: Chalmers's Church Extension campaign had all but rendered the Moderate party irrelevant in Church politics, an obsolete survivor of the eighteenth century. The conflict over patronage, however, gave the Moderates new significance. Under the leadership of George Cook, nephew of the celebrated Moderate leader, George Hill, and Chalmers's successor as Professor of Moral Philosophy at St. Andrews, the revived Moderate party advocated a return to both the patronage policies and the more cordial Church-State relations of the late eighteenth century. They agreed with the civil courts that the Veto Act was illegal and the 'Call' a mere formality. At this stage in the conflict, most Moderates supported the doctrine of spiritual independence, but argued that a return to eighteenth-century patronage practices was the best means to preserve that independence. There were, however, some Moderates, led by the talented James Bryce, minister of rural Strachan, who rejected even the doctrine of spiritual independence. There was, Bryce and the extreme Moderates argued, no historical compact between two sovereign kingdoms of Church and State. Rather, the State, the sole sovereign authority, had created the Established Church, and the Church owed the State absolute obedience.[50] As the conflict deepened, these extreme Moderates increased in influence.

Secondly, the Auchterarder affair augmented the power of the group of younger Evangelical zealots, who had risen to influence within the Church during the battles over Voluntaryism and Church Extension. They were often referred to as the 'Wild party', a term once used to denigrate the eighteenth-century Popular party. They were masters of adversary politics, well organized and quick in debate. Like the eighteenth-century Popular party, they were doctrinaire Calvinists and opponents of patronage. They were also advocates of popular rights. Probably the most talented of this group was Robert Smith Candlish, minister of the prestigious St. George's church in Edinburgh whose support for Lee in the Moderatorship Controversy had demonstrated that he was by no means a blind follower of Chalmers, and indeed might become a rival. He was a small, thin, energetic man, and a dangerous adversary. Other 'Wild' men included William Cunningham, a large, powerfully-built Edinburgh clergyman, often criticized for a 'bullying' manner, Robert Buchanan, a Glasgow clergyman and a fiery and imaginative orator, and Thomas Guthrie, a tall, ruggedly handsome man, with a country wit and winning manner—and a sincere belief in the rights of the common man. By May 1839, these militant Evangelicals spoke openly of breaking the Church's State connection.

Finally, by his speech in the Assembly of 1839, Chalmers had demonstrated a disposition to side with the young extremists in the Evangelical party, assuming a high view of the Church's prerogatives and insisting upon a firm stand against State encroachments. Prior to this, it had been widely believed that Chalmers would act to restrain the 'Wild party'. But his speech had proved more violent than any had anticipated. On the day before, for instance, the Earl of Dalhousie, a Tory lay-elder and a supporter of Church Extension, had agreed to second Chalmers's motion. But after hearing his speech, Dalhousie stormed angrily out of the Assembly hall without delivering his seconding remarks. A few days later, he announced before the Assembly that Chalmers had deceived him, and that he would have no part in his plan to raise rebellion in the Church.[51]

In truth, Chalmers had vacillated in the weeks before his Assembly speech—on the one hand not wishing to jeopardize a possible revival of his Church Extension campaign by extending the Auchterarder conflict, but on the other hand enraged by the House of Lords decision. In the end, as so often before in his life, his rage triumphed. In the failure of his Church Extension movement, he was witnessing the death of his life's dream. He was, therefore, in no mood for compromise on the veto question with State authorities who seemed intent upon depriving the Church of all its remaining dignity. With his 1839 Assembly speech, he committed himself to a hard line on both non-intrusion and spiritual independence. Above all, he introduced the threat of a disruption

of the Church of Scotland if the State did not cease encroaching upon
the Church's spiritual independence. If this threat was not clear
enough in his speech of 22 May, he soon made it still more explicit,
'Rather than be placed at the feet of an absolute and uncontrolled
patronage,' he informed the influential English Tory MP, Sir James
Graham, on 6 June 1839, 'there are ... very many of our Clergy, and
these the most devoted and influential in Scotland, who are resolved to
quit the Establishment and who, if they do so, will by stripping it of all
moral weight, leave it an easy prey for the Radicals and Voluntaries
and Demi-infidels both in and out of Parliament who are bent upon
destroying it.'[52]

Chalmers's Non-intrusion Committee, meanwhile, continued to
prepare for negotiations with the Government. In the atmosphere of
mutual distrust engendered by the Voluntary and endowments controversies, however, compromise would be difficult. Cockburn, for
instance, sympathized with the Church's plight, but entertained little
hope. 'I cannot blame them', he observed in his journal on 29 May
1839, 'for trying to assert what until lately no man doubted was their
right, and what seems essential to their existence as a Church.'

But they will fail. They have appointed a committee to confer with Government ...
If it be a Whig Government, the answer must be—'You boast of your hatred to us, and
wish us to renew the persecution of Dissenters; we won't run our heads against an
English and Irish post to please you.' If it be a Tory one, the answer will be...'You are
against patronage and the law; get you gone.' If it be a Radical—'We hate the
Church; your ruin rejoices us.'[53]

In the summer of 1839, another patronage dispute reached a climax,
making a negotiated settlement still more dubious. This involved a
festering dispute in the rural Perthshire parish of Lethendy, in the
presbytery of Dunkeld. In 1835, Thomas Clark, a probationary
minister, was presented as the assistant and successor to the infirm
minister of Lethendy by the Crown, the legal patron of the parish. After
hearing Clark preach, however, fifty-three of the eighty-nine male
heads of family on the communicants' roll dissented from the presentation. The presbytery of Dunkeld accordingly rejected Clark according
to the Veto Act. Clark appealed against his rejection to the higher
Church courts, but in June 1836, the General Assembly upheld the
presbytery's decision. The Crown, therefore, withdrew Clark's presentation. In January 1837, the old minister of Lethendy died, and the
Crown now presented another probationer, Andrew Kessen, to the
Lethendy vacancy. The male heads of family approved of Kessen, and
the presbytery conducted Kessen's final trials, which proved satisfactory.

But Clark, although disappointed in the Church courts, had not
relinquished his claim to the living. Encouraged by the Auchterarder

case, Clark carried his case to the Court of Session. He obtained a Court of Session interdict, ordering the presbytery of Dunkeld not to proceed with Kessen's induction to Lethendy. The presbytery referred the matter to the General Assembly of 1838, which in June decided that 'admission to the pastoral charge of a parish and congregation is entirely an ecclesiastical act', and ordered the presbytery to ordain Kessen without further delay. The Court of Session now issued a second interdict forbidding Kessen's induction. The presbytery again turned to its superior ecclesiastical court, referring the matter to the Commission of the General Assembly meeting in August 1838. The Commission again ordered it to ordain Kessen. The rural clergymen of Dunkeld presbytery were placed in a cruel dilemma: obey the Court of Session, the highest civil court in Scotland, or obey the General Assembly, the highest ecclesiastical court? In late August, John Hope, the Dean of Faculty, warned the presbytery that their ecclesiastical office would not afford them immunity from civil punishment. If they defied the Court of Session interdict, 'the members of Presbytery will most infallibly be committed to prison'. Several members of the presbytery were intimidated by Hope's threat. None the less, by the narrow majority of one, the presbytery (which included Chalmers's son-in-law John MacKenzie) decided to obey the General Assembly. On 13 September 1838, they ordained Kessen to Lethendy.[54]

Two months later, Clark initiated civil action against the presbytery of Dunkeld for breach of interdict. He did not appeal to have Kessen's ordination annulled, so the case focused solely upon the breach of interdict, which the Court of Session subsequently found proven. In June 1839, it summoned the presbytery of Dunkeld to Edinburgh. The final stages of the trial occurred between 12 and 14 June, a few days after the close of the 1839 General Assembly. By a narrow majority, the judges decided against imprisoning the delinquent presbytery. Instead, the Court censured the presbytery, imposed court costs upon them, and warned that any similar act of disobedience by a Church court would in the future be punished by imprisonment. In delivering the censure, Lord President Charles Hope responded decisively to Chalmers's recent warning in the General Assembly of a possible disruption of the Church: 'As for those ministers of the Church whose conscience cannot submit to the law so long as it remains the law, I am afraid nothing remains for those ministers but to retire from the Established Church. It is impossible that they should remain ministers of the Established Church, and yet reject the law by which they have become an Established Church.'[55] The fact that Chalmers's own son-in-law had narrowly escaped imprisonment with the Dunkeld presbytery no doubt gave the affair a particularly personal dimension for him.

A few months after the Lethendy judgement, John Hope published in London a 290-page *Letter to the Lord Chancellor*, asserting the Moderate position. It was a rambling effort, 'over-lengthy, ill-arranged, repetitious, and obscure'. None the less, due to Hope's central position in the controversy, it received considerable attention, particularly in England. The Church, Hope declared, was a creature of the State, fully subordinate to the civil courts in all matters. Now that it had chosen to rebel against the State, there was no alternative but to proceed against it with the full rigour of the law—to subdue the rank and file of the clergy, and if necessary to force the leaders of the rebellion out of the Establishment. He portrayed Chalmers as perhaps the most dangerous of the rebels, a man whose radical schemes in the areas of poor relief, political economy, and Church Extension, if not curtailed, would ruin the State.[56] In December 1839, Chalmers published his reply, *Remarks on the Present Position of the Church of Scotland, Occasioned by the Publication of a Letter from the Dean of Faculty to the Lord Chancellor.*

Chalmers began by reasserting the principles of non-intrusion and spiritual independence. With regard to non-intrusion, he now expressed full and unqualified support for the Church's Veto Act of 1834. Any doubts he may have had about the veto prior to the 1839 General Assembly were for the moment relinquished. His support for the veto, he asserted, was not based upon considerations of abstract right or historical precedents. (The best legal minds of the country had determined that no such right or historical precedents existed.) Rather, he argued that the veto had, in its five years of operation, proved beneficial in its effects. It had increased support for the Established Church among the people of Scotland, improved the quality of patronage, and produced a more zealous and committed body of probationary ministers. In view of such effects, the arguments against it based on historical precedent were irrelevant. No court, for instance, had declared the Parliamentary reform bill of 1832 illegal for lack of historical precedent. The Church, he maintained, possessed full authority to reform its laws and ecclesiastical constitution in order to improve its spiritual ministry. In short, it was independent in spiritual matters, a 'sanctuary' from State powers, which acknowledged only the sovereignty of Christ. The Evangelical revival had in recent years awakened the Church of Scotland to its true nature as an independent spiritual kingdom. Having experienced this truth, it would not again be reduced to its servile and compromised position of the late eighteenth century. If, as John Hope and the Court of Session judges maintained, the law demanded the Church be reduced to a mere department of State, then the law must be changed. He asked, therefore, that the Court of Session observe a 'truce', while the Church pursued negotiations with Parliament.[57]

Most important, he presented a lively defence of his Church Extension campaign and Christian communal ideal. There was, he argued, a firm connection between the Court of Session's Auchterarder and Lethendy decisions, impugning the spiritual independence of the Church, and its recent Brechin and Stewarton decisions, halting the extension of the Church. The Church, he maintained, was effecting substantial improvements in Scottish national life. These very achievements, however, had aroused jealousy among those who felt their privileges threatened, or who lacked the vision to appreciate the possibilities now opening for Scotland. Chalmers condemned the 'old Toryism of Scotland', which opposed social progress and the elevation of the common people, from a self-interested concern for such social privileges as unrestricted patronage.[58] Further, he condemned lawyers, such as John Hope, who lacked a larger social vision—who with a narrow and static concept of the law, scrutinized the Church's legal constitution, 'while the great moral and practical design of such an institute, appears to be scarcely, if indeed ever, in [their] thoughts'.[59] The eighteenth-century constitution, Chalmers proclaimed, which 'old Tories' and lawyers now sought to reimpose, had in fact collapsed: 'Men have broken loose from all those ancient holds which kept the community together; and there is now a waywardness in almost all spirits, which nothing, nothing, but the education of principle can stem.'[60] The eighteenth-century system of interest politics was dying; society was feeling its way towards a new social organization. The new order, he asserted, would be based upon principle rather than interest, moral force rather than privilege. In this approaching era, the Church was destined to exercise a primary influence over social structure and purpose. It must not relinquish its spiritual claims at this crucial juncture.

With the Lethendy decision, then, Scotland, had grown still more polarized. The Court of Session had determined to impose civil law upon the Church, while leading lawyers, including John Hope, had declared the Church in rebellion. Chalmers, however, as leader of the dominant Evangelical party in the Church, declared that the Church would neither return to its eighteenth-century position, nor obey an unjust law based upon narrow interest politics or mere historical precedent. Society, he claimed, was in the midst of revolutionary changes, a new era was dawning, and only a popular, Evangelical, and spiritually independent church could direct those changes towards a beneficial result.

As Chalmers and Hope were conducting their pamphlet duel, a third patronage dispute was approaching its climax. This was the celebrated dispute involving the Banffshire parish of Marnoch, in the presbytery of Strathbogie. In 1837, William Stronach, the minister of Marnoch, died after a ministry of nearly thirty years. A firm of lawyers representing the trustees of the Earl of Fife, the patron of the parish, presented John Edwards, a forty-four-year-old schoolmaster from a neighbouring parish, to the vacant living. Edwards, however, had previously served as the assistant minister of Marnoch, and had proved so unpopular with the parishioners that he had been dismissed at their request a year before Stronach's death. His presentation, then, was not well received. Of the 300 male heads of families, only one, a local innkeeper, signed the 'Call', while 261 vetoed it. The presbytery of Strathbogie, on instructions from the 1838 General Assembly, rejected Edwards's presentation. The firm of lawyers acting for the patron issued a second presentation in favour of David Henry, an Evangelical preacher who had succeeded Edwards as assistant minister and who was popular among the parishioners. The issue appeared settled.

Edwards, however, carried his case to the Court of Session, which issued an interdict forbidding the presbytery to proceed with Henry's induction. The presbytery referred the case to the General Assembly of 1839. The Assembly, in accordance with the Church's desire for a truce between the civil and ecclesiastical courts while the Church negotiated with the Government, instructed the presbytery to obey the inderdict and to suspend proceedings. This instruction was given early in June 1839. But a month later, in early July, the Court of Session made it clear that it would honour no truce. It now issued a decision in favour of Edwards, ordering the presbytery to take him on trials, and if found qualified, to proceed to his induction. In the Lethendy case, it will be recalled, the presbytery of Dunkeld had ignored the Court of Session's interdict, and obeyed the General Assembly. In the Marnoch case, however, the presbytery of Strathbogie took the opposite course. Without consulting the higher Church courts, seven of the twelve ministers in the presbytery took it upon themselves to give Edwards his trials and proceed towards his induction. In doing so, they ignored the General Assembly's 1838 instruction that Edwards's presentation be rejected, as well as the second presentation and 'Call' in favour of Henry.[61]

Now it was the Church's turn to discipline an insubordinate presbytery. In December 1839, the Commission of the General Assembly suspended the seven offending Strathbogie ministers from office. The Commission, moreover, appointed a committee of ministers to provide regular sabbath services in the parishes of the suspended ministers. The Court of Session immediately responded with an interdict forbidding any minister from entering the 'churches, churchyards, or schoolhouses' in the seven parishes either to announce the suspension, or to conduct religious services. The Church respected the Court of Sessions's authority over the buildings and property, and its committee therefore issued the suspension notices, and held religious services in the open air. By now, considerable public interest had been excited and the open-air gatherings were well attended. Frustrated, the Court of Session responded on 14 February 1840 with the notorious 'extended' interdict, forbidding any minister of the Church of Scotland from entering the parishes of the Strathbogie seven without their consent to conduct religious service. In short, it placed an interdict upon open-air preaching in the seven parishes.[62]

The response of Chalmers and the Evangelicals was swift. On 24 February 1840, they held a public meeting to protest the Court of Session's action. Until now, Chalmers observed, the Scottish public had been confused by the legal intricacies of the conflict. But suddenly the Court of Session had made its position clear. By forbidding the Church of Scotland to preach the Word of God within part of the country, the Court had revealed its intention to degrade the Church into a mere servant of civil authority. This, Chalmers added, was only the beginning. Once the Church had submitted to civil authority over where it could preach, the Court would soon begin dictating what it must preach and even the conditions under which it must administer the sacraments. Some now argued that the only solution to the crisis was for the Church to retract the Strathbogie suspensions and apologize to the Court of Session. But Chalmers would have no retraction, no apology, from the Church. 'Why, this', he exclaimed, 'would be lording it over us with a vengeance! It would be making us swallow the whole principle; and the Church of Scotland, bereft of all moral weight, might henceforth be cast a useless and degraded thing into the bottom of the sea.' 'Be it known, then, unto all men,' he continued, 'that we shall not retreat one single footstep,—we shall make no submission to the Court of Session ... They may force the ejection of us from our places: they shall never, never force us to the surrender of our principles.'[63] A few weeks later, the March Commission of the General Assembly resolved to defy the Court of Session's 'extended' interdict. The ministers assigned by the Church to conduct services in the seven Strathbogie parishes were instructed to continue. The Strathbogie seven did not press charges against these ministers and so the open-air preaching continued. For the participating preachers it was exhilarating, recalling the days of the seventeenth-century Covenanters.

Despite Chalmers's claim to public support, however, the public was in fact divided in its sentiments regarding the bizarre 'reel of Bogie', as the Strathbogie affair had become known. The Voluntaries were delighted by the Church's troubles—on the one hand, declaring the Establishment compromised because of its subordination to civil authority, but on the other hand, condemning the Church's attempts to assert the principles of non-intrusion and spiritual independence as a 'rebellion' warranting the severest punishments of the law. Many Whigs, as Cockburn had predicted in 1839, were only too pleased to take their vengeance upon the Church for its insulting behaviour towards them during the endowment controversy. Many Tories condemned the non-intrusionists as 'apostles of Socialism or radicalism', intent upon bringing 'the agitation measures of the Irish priests' to Scotland.[64] The Church's attempt to raise the standard of the seventeenth-century Solemn League and Covenant inspired only limited support in a nineteenth-century nation that was increasingly secular and pluralistic in character. In late March, for instance, the presbytery of Edinburgh, 'in accordance with an ancient practice', appointed a weekday prayer service in all its churches in response to the Church's troubles. The churches, however, were sparsely attended, the Magistrates and Town Council refused to recognize the proceeding, and the shops remained open. 'Two centuries ago, in the controversies of that period,' David Aitken informed the Earl of Minto on 30 March 1840, in reference to the Covenanters, 'such week-day meetings were common, and formed one great instrument by which the public mind then was governed. I trust that this [recent failure] will prove [that] our agitators make a false step, when they would fall back on the usages and opinions of a very different period.'[65] Nor was this indifferent response to the Church's appeal reserved to the cities. Rural clergymen, too, often faced strong opposition from landowners and tenants when they endeavoured to hold non-intrusion meetings.[66]

By April, Chalmers began to suspect that he might have gone too far in his speech of 24 February. Accordingly, between 4 April and 2 May, he published a series of five 'Letters on the Church Question' in the *Witness*, an Edinburgh non-intrusionist newspaper, in which he sought to define a less uncompromising position, while at the same time affirming the Church's commitment to its spiritual independence. The result was an inconsistent and confusing presentation. In the first three letters, he expressed his opposition to any direct interference by the Church in secular party politics, while at the same time he encouraged popular agitation to pressure Parliament into recognizing the Church's claims. The Church, he insisted, was now trapped between an alliance of 'Liberalism and Popery' on the one hand, and the 'inveterate old Tories' on the other, and its only hope lay in organizing a national campaign. Perhaps most interesting, however, were the final two letters. In these, he now argued that the principles of spiritual independence and non-intrusion were in fact distinct and separate. There could, he asserted, be no compromise on the principle of spiritual independence. However, the Church might make concessions on the principle of non-intrusion, in order to preserve both its spiritual independence and State connection. In particular, it might repeal the Veto Act of 1834 and return to the practice embodied in an act of 1690, by which the heritors and elders in a parish would nominate candidates for a parish living, and male heads of family, although having no right of veto, would be allowed to present reasons of dissent against a nominee to the local presbytery. This, he asserted, would eliminate both the veto and the 'Call', which the civil courts had determined to be illegal, while at the same time preserving the Church from the evils of unrestricted patronage. It would be 'the short and complete way to rid us of all our embarrassments', enabling the Church to return to the more crucial business of Church Extension.[67]

Once again, then, Chalmers had reversed his position on the veto. After having vigorously defended it in 1839, he now suggested its repeal. Observers were perplexed by his vacillations. 'Chalmers is writing letters in [an Edinburgh] paper,' Aitken informed Minto on 20 April, 'alternately blowing hot and cold, sometimes asserting high pretensions, then taking a more temperate tone; it is conjectured, however, that now a much more reasonable enactment would satisfy him personally, than he would have been disposed to accept a short while ago.' Aitken attributed Chalmers's vacillations in part to his impulsive temperament, but there was also, in his view, an added complication: that Chalmers was falling increasingly under the influence of Candlish, Cunningham, and the 'Wild party'. They apparently played upon his insecurities and rashness, goading him into violent statements which it was difficult for him to retract. 'The Dr.,' Aitken explained to Minto, 'is a nervous and anxious man,... rash and impetuous from impulse, but in his calmer moments by no means sanguine; yet at the same time he is led by men far more resolute than himself, who will not fail to goad him on as they have done.'[68]

Aitken was largely correct in his judgement. Throughout his life, Chalmers had demonstrated, even at his best times, a rash and impulsive temperament. This was aggravated by the bitter frustrations of the recent years, as he witnessed the rapid desturction of his social ideal. Church Extension had been thwarted. There was a growing movement to abolish the existing system of Church-directed poor relief in Scotland. The Voluntaries were anticipating with delight the impending ruin of the Church. Now the Court of Session was challenging even the Church's spiritual independence. Chalmers had no wish to witness the final defeat of his godly commonwealth ideal—the disruption of the Established Church. None the less, as Aitken observed, he was losing the initiative to younger Evangelicals, who were less concerned to avoid disruption.

There was, however, another reason for Chalmers's vacillations, apart from his personality. The conflicts of recent years had created bitter divisions within the Church, as well as between the Church and State. As leader of the Evangelical party, Chalmers needed not only to find a compromise that would appease Parliament and the Court of

Session; he also had to find a solution satisfactory to the young zealots in his own party. If he failed in the latter endeavour, the 'Wild party' might well secede from the Church on their own, carrying much of the young talent of the Evangelical party into the Voluntary camp. A large number of the *quoad sacra* parish ministers and congregations, moreover, recently deprived of their church collections by the Court of Session's Brechin and Stewarton decisions, might join the secession. In a word, his waverings reflected his struggle to preserve some unity in a divided Church. As the conflict between Church and State intensified, Chalmers and the Non-intrusion Committee were also pursuing negotiations with the Whig Government and the Tory opposition, in the hope of reaching a settlement before events had carried all the parties beyond hope of reconciliation.

III

Early in July 1839, two months after the establishment of the General Assembly's Non-intrusion Committee, with Chalmers as its convener, he and a deputation from the Committee travelled to London, where they began negotiations with Melbourne's Whig Ministry. Their goal was a Parliamentary act legalizing the Church's Veto Act, and thus terminating the conflict between Church and civil courts. The reception of the deputation was cool. Chalmers now paid the price of his attacks upon the Whig Government during the endowments controversy. Melbourne received the deputation on 8 July, but openly snubbed Chalmers, refusing to shake his hand or acknowledge his presence. Consequently, when the deputation held a second interview with Melbourne on 15 July, Chalmers felt obliged to remain behind. 'It was not politic for me to go', he complained angrily to his wife that same day, 'me who am in disgrace at Court—me who am the hapless object of the chief of the Cabinet's frowns—me who must retire in chagrin from public life, and spend in obscurity and pining neglect the remainder of my days.' Yet despite Melbourne's disdain for Chalmers, the Whigs promised to assist the Church. Although his vanity had been wounded, Chalmers returned to Edinburgh confident that a solution was within reach. The Whig Government, he informed the Commission of the General Assembly on 14 August 1839, had promised to introduce a bill early in the 1840 Parliamentary session that would terminate the conflict in a manner satisfactory to the Church. In the mean time, the Government had also promised to conduct all crown patronage, which represented about a third of the church patronages in Scotland, as though the Church's Veto Act were already legal.[69]

Then in late December 1839, a few weeks before the opening of the 1840 Parliamentary session, the Earl of Aberdeen, a leading Tory, decided to attempt to arrange a solution. Aberdeen was both a member of the Church of Scotland and the owner of several church patronages. A humane and kindly man, with a sincere concern for the Church and considerable influence in Parliament, he felt confident that he could communicate with all parties and frame a satisfactory measure. His close friend and adviser in Scottish ecclesiastical affairs, John Hope, warned him against attempting to negotiate with Chalmers and the Evangelical leaders, whose motives, Hope suggested, were suspect.[70] None the less, Aberdeen persevered. On 31 December, he wrote to Chalmers saying that, according to his information, Melbourne's Government had changed its position and no longer planned to introduce legislation favouring the Church. Aberdeen, therefore, might on his own initiative introduce a bill, but only if he could be assured of the Church's support. Chalmers received Aberdeen's offer warmly. He was quick to believe that the Whigs had determined to betray the Church. He would, moreover, greatly prefer that a Tory should assist the Church, than that he should again have to submit himself to humiliation by approaching Melbourne's Government.[71] Early in January 1840, Chalmers and a deputation from the Non-intrusion Committee met Aberdeen in Edinburgh. Chalmers emphasized the importance of securing the independent judicial powers of the Church courts in spiritual matters. Aberdeen evidently agreed, and although he expressed doubts about the expediency of the Veto Act of 1834, both Chalmers and he emerged from the meeting confident that a compromise could be arranged.[72]

On 16 January 1840, Chalmers sent Aberdeen a draft bill that would have affirmed the Church's sovereign power over its spiritual doctrine and discipline, including the authority to administer the Veto Act. Aberdeen, however, now decided that the Veto Act was totally unacceptable. To enable a majority of heads of families to veto a presentation without requiring valid reasons, was, for him, simply to grant authority to popular prejudice. Instead, he suggested an alternative— that the popular veto be abolished, and be replaced by a presbytery veto. In the event of a disputed settlement, parishioners would present their objections to the local presbytery court, which would judge their reasons of dissent, and if it found them valid, might veto the presentation. 'If the Presbytery,' he explained to Chalmers on 22 January 1840, 'in every case, shall be at liberty to give the weight they may think proper to the reasons of dissent, without reference to the number of persons dissenting, I should be perfectly satisfied; but I cannot support a measure which shall compel Presbyteries blindly to give effect to the arbitrary and capricious dissent of any proportion of parishioners, however large.'[73]

Chalmers, it will be recalled, had long opposed any law that would oblige the majority of heads of family to present reasons for their dissent to the presbytery. Honest but uneducated peasants, he had argued, might prove unable to express adequately their deeply felt conviction that something was wrong with a presentee. They might be overpowered in argument by a presbytery dominated by educated clerics, whose sympathies would usually favour the probationary minister, as one of their own professional order. None the less, he now professed himself willing to relinquish the popular veto and accept Aberdeen's presbytery veto. He asked only one condition: the presbytery must have the power to veto a presentation if it discovered that the majority of parishioners, even though unable to formulate substantial reasons of dissent, strongly and sincerely opposed a candidate, with no evidence of personal rancour or prejudice. He did not ask that the presbytery be obliged to veto a candidate under such conditions; only that it have the power to do so if it believed that the settlement might result in the disaffection of the community from the Established Church. 'We are willing', Chalmers explained on 27 January, 'that reasons should be dealt with and canvassed to the uttermost; but we are not willing that we should be bound to admit the presentee if the people do not make good their reasons. On the contrary, we hold ourselves free, though not obliged, to exclude a presentee because of the strength of the popular dislike, though not substantiated by express reasons, a case which may occur, though not once in a hundred,—I believe not once in a thousand times.' If a presbytery was to have the judicial power of veto, it must have authority to consider all the circumstances of a case, not simply the stated reasons of dissent. It must have what he termed a *'liberum arbitrium'*.[74]

By rejecting Chalmers's proposal, Aberdeen revealed that there was, in fact, a radical difference between their respective positions. Presbyteries, he asserted to Chalmers on 22 February, could not be allowed to reject a presentee without stated reasons, because they might reject a candidate for 'reasons which are not only groundless and bad, but absolutely illegal'. Indeed, from the recent extravagant conduct of the Church courts, he suspected that such illegal rejections would be common. The purpose of requiring a presbytery to base its veto of a presentation on stated reasons was to ensure that the civil courts would be able to review the veto decisions of the presbyteries, and if necessary to override them. 'After the spirit we have seen in the [General] Assembly, and the opinions of those [Evangelicals] who have obtained an ascendancy,' he further asserted, 'I am not much disposed by legislative enactment totally to deprive the Civil Courts of the power, which they now possess under the law, of doing right and justice to the Queen's subjects in case of necessity.' In short, the Church courts could not be trusted to administer Church affairs.[75] Chalmers was surprised and distressed. He reminded Aberdeen that at their January meeting, Aberdeen had signified his approval of the principle of spiritual independence, and had encouraged Chalmers to believe he also desired to free the Church courts from the encroachments of the civil courts in matters of internal discipline. By Aberdeen's proposed bill, however, the Church would simply relinquish the popular veto, and receive nothing in return. The presbyteries would have no more judicial power than they had before 1834, and the civil courts would continue to overrule the veto decisions of presbyteries at will.[76] Aberdeen recognized this, but refused to be swayed. 'The monstrous pretensions of the [General] Assembly', he informed Chalmers curtly on 10 March, 'leave us no security that any measure we may adopt will prove satisfactory.'[77]

Aberdeen had, in fact, shifted his position between early January and late February 1840. He had moved from a disposition to compromise with Chalmers and the Non-intrusion Committee, to one of demanding that the Church must both relinquish the popular veto and its pretensions to spiritual independence. There were apparently two reasons for his change. First, he was disturbed by the violent language employed by many Evangelicals in response to the Court of Session's Strathbogie 'extended' interdict of 14 February. Secondly, John Hope, with whom he was in constant communication, had convinced him that Chalmers's Evangelical ascendancy in the Church was breaking up under the firm pressure from the Court of Session.[78]

Whatever the reasons for Aberdeen's shift in position, it placed Chalmers in an awkward and vulnerable position. The Whigs had learned of his correspondence with Aberdeen, and they now employed it as a means to extricate themselves from their previous promises to the Church, as well as to attack Chalmers's leadership. On 10 March 1840, Andrew Rutherford, the Whig Lord Advocate of Scotland, informed a deputation from the Non-intrusion Committee that the Melbourne Government had planned to introduce legislation to assist the Church, but was now so annoyed by the Church's 'double negotiations' with both the Whig and Tory parties that it had given up its plans. In particular, the Whig leaders had learned that Chalmers had employed violent anti-Government language in his private correspondence with Aberdeen. If Chalmers had so much faith in Aberdeen and the Tories, Rutherford implied, then let the Tories rescue the Church from its quandary.[79]

It is difficult to understand how the Whigs had discovered the content of Chalmers's private letters to Aberdeen, unless perhaps Aberdeen's confidant, John Hope, had informed them. In fact, on 10 March, the same day Rutherford had condemned Chalmers's conduct to the Church deputation, Chalmers complained to Aberdeen that rumours of their correspondence were being publicly circulated by Hope, who implied that Chalmers had given up the popular veto and betrayed the rights of the people, in exchange for a measure that would give the veto power exclusively to the clergy. 'I beg,' Chalmers wrote,

that your Lordship will be pleased to observe the difficulty which [Hope's] report placed us in. It just enabled the Dean [Hope] and his friends to reiterate the ambi-dextrous charges which he ever and anon prefers against us ... telling us at one time that we had laid ourselves at the feet of the people, and at another that it was all a movement for powers to ourselves;—we were ready to give up the people if we could but secure that object.

In view of Hope's allegations, Chalmers maintained, it was all the more important that Aberdeen's proposed bill enable presbyteries to consider all aspects of a disputed settlement, including the strength of popular dissatisfaction, before making a judgement.[80] After 10 March, however, Aberdeen declined for several weeks to respond to Chalmers's repeated letters. Aberdeen's mind was made up, and with Hope's assistance he now drafted a bill based upon his concept of a limited presbytery veto.[81]

On 5 May 1840, Aberdeen introduced his bill in the House of Lords. 'In framing this measure,' he informed Chalmers that evening, 'I can truly say that I have been solely animated by a desire to confirm and promote the stability and prosperity of our national Establishment. ... The question is not now so much, what is the best and most desirable measure, but what is practicable.' But Chalmers could not approve. 'I have now examined the Bill,' he informed Aberdeen on 12 May, 'and it is with inexpressible grief and concern that I am forced to confess myself dissatisfied.' His opposition to the bill focused on three points:

First, the obligation laid on the Presbytery to give its judgement exclusively on the reasons [of dissent], instead of leaving a *liberum arbitrium* in all circumstances of the case ... Second, because the Bill, in its whole tone and structure, subordinates the Church to the Civil power in things spiritual, and that by a directory so minute and authoritative as to lay us open at every turn to the hazard of Civil coercion ... Thirdly, it is substantially the same measure which was [previously] moved by Dr. [George] Cook and rejected by the Church.

He complained to Aberdeen of the difficult position in which the bill had placed him. After his 'incessant attempts' to convince Church leaders to adopt those principles which Aberdeen had seemed to express at their January meeting, Aberdeen had now introduced a bill embracing entirely different principles, which challenged the Church's spiritual independence.[82]

Chalmers's correspondence with Aberdeen degenerated into mutual recrimination. 'The most pious ministers, and most enlightened and respectable of the laity in Scotland,' Aberdeen assured Chalmers on 18 May, '[expressed] entire satisfaction with the Bill.' The only criticism of the bill among members of Parliament, Aberdeen added, was that it gave too much judicial authority to the Church. This was not so, Chalmers replied on 20 May. Not only did the majority in the Church oppose the bill, but he had also received the 'entire concurrence' of the Tory leaders, Sir James Graham, Sir George Clerk, and Sir William Rae, for his principles. Not true, Aberdeen responded on 23 May. Whatever the present mood of the Church, not a single member of the Commons, and only one member of the Lords would support Chalmers's plan for unlimited judicial power for the Church courts. He had, moreover, recently consulted Graham, Clerk, and Rae, and they assured him they had never given Chalmers any such assurances of support. He had not lied, Chalmers replied curtly on 25 May. 'In terms as explicit as human language can make it, I have the assent of the three members named to my own principle of the Presbyterial Veto. I ... can only now express my regret that your Lordship's last letters do not warrant the hopes which I had founded on all our previous correspondence.'[83]

On 27 May, in delivering the first annual report of the Non-intrusion Committee before the General Assembly, Chalmers condemned Aberdeen's bill, and advised the General Assembly to use every means to ensure its defeat. He admitted to his correspondence with Aberdeen. None the less, he asserted, the actual content of Aberdeen's bill had come as a complete surprise to him. Aberdeen, he explained, had ceased communicating with him several weeks before he introduced the bill in Parliament; however, before breaking off the correspondence, Aberdeen had led him to believe that the bill would embody an unfettered *liberum arbitrium* for presbyteries. 'I was led to expect it, and I think I have right and reason to be disappointed.' In a word, Aberdeen had deceived him. He was, however, willing to assume responsibility for having trusted Aberdeen, and he therefore resigned his convenership of the Non-intrusion Committee. By a vote of 221 to 134, the General Assembly determined to oppose Aberdeen's bill.[84]

Chalmers had been placed in a precarious position by Aberdeen's refusal to give presbyteries an unlimited veto power. It was widely believed, and it was perhaps true, that his flirtation with Aberdeen and the Tories had prompted the Whig Government to relinquish any legislation to legalize the popular veto. The stakes in his negotiations with Aberdeen had been extremely high, involving not only his personal reputation, but also the unity of the Scottish Establishment. Perhaps this heavy burden of responsibility had caused Chalmers to misinterpret Aberdeen's intentions, and to believe that Aberdeen's silence in response to his repeated letters between 10 March and 5 May signified that he had been convinced by his arguments in favour of the *liberum arbitrium*. But whatever the reasons, Chalmers had been wrong when he stated to the General Assembly that up until 5 May, Aberdeen had deliberately led him to believe his bill would embody an unrestricted presbytery veto. Aberdeen's confidant John Hope, who had access to the private Chalmers-Aberdeen correspondence, would not allow the attack upon Aberdeen's honesty to pass unanswered. Shortly after Chalmers's Assembly speech, Hope published an anonymous letter in the *Edinburgh Advertiser,* which accused him of having made unfounded charges against Aberdeen. Hope denied that Aberdeen had led Chalmers to expect that his bill would incorporate his idea of an unfettered *liberum arbitrium* for presbyteries. Further, Hope cited selections from the Chalmers-Aberdeen correspondence which proved Chalmers's accusations to be false.[85]

Aberdeen, too, was enraged by Chalmers's false charges. On 16 June, he moved the second reading of his bill in the House of Lords. There was, in the wake of the General Assembly's rejection, no hope that his bill would be passed. None the less, Aberdeen desired an opportunity in Parliament both to condemn the 'monstrous and extravagant pretensions' of the General Assembly and to impugn Chalmers's integrity. On 10 July, he finally abandoned the bill.[86] A few days later, he published the whole of his private correspondence with Chalmers in both London and Edinburgh.[87] Such an action violated the conventions of the day regarding the use of private correspondence: Aberdeen, however, was now convinced that Chalmers was not an honourable man and therefore did not warrant the respect due a gentleman. Even Chalmers's resignation from the convenership of the Non-intrusion Committee, Aberdeen maintained, was not a sign of honour, but of cowardice. 'Having brought the Church into a state of jeopardy and peril,' Aberdeen wrote to Robert Gordon in late June 1840, in reference to Chalmers's resignation, '[Chalmers] had left it to find its way out of the difficulty as well as it could.'[88]

'What do you think of Lord Aberdeen's charge of dishonesty,' Chalmers raged to A. L. Simpson on 19 June 1840. 'I shan't probably reach upon it for some little time: but his Peerage will be no protection to him— when he thus dares to attack a higher privilege, even that of character and reputation, than all which rank or power can bestow.'[89] In July 1840, Chalmers published his statement on the Aberdeen bill affair, a pamphlet entitled *What Ought the Church and the People of Scotland to do Now?* The traditional political parties in Scotland, he asserted, based as they were upon the eighteenth-century system of interest politics, were waning in influence as a result of the Church question. The old party divisions were being replaced by the more fundamental conflict between self-interest and religious principle. Both major political parties represented the 'singularly perverse and infatuated policy on the part of the upper classes' to destroy the Church, at precisely the moment when it was reasserting its influence over the national community. At this juncture, therefore, Church supporters must relinquish loyalty to both political parties. The Aberdeen affair, he confessed, had opened his eyes to the vanity of his 'old affection' for the Tory party. He now renounced his 'idolatrous and over weening partiality' for Toryism, in favour of his higher commitment to the Church. The Tories had proved no better than the Whigs. 'If on the question of Church Endowments', he asserted, 'I have been grievously disappointed by the [Whigs], on the question of Church Independence, I have been as grievously disappointed by the [Tories].'[90] The Church must now stand firm against both parties, and the civil power they represented. 'It is impossible for the Church to give in, without the abandonment of her most sacred prerogatives as a Christian Church.' The Church's spiritual independence, he warned, was 'conducive in the highest degree to the peace and good of society, but ... nevertheless might prove an occasion of violence when the civil power attempts to overbear it.'[91] As in the case of his disillusionment with the Whig Government over the endowment question in 1838, Chalmers responded to his disappointment with Aberdeen and the Tories with an impassioned appeal to the Scottish nation, and with threats of popular violence. Unable to admit his errors of judgement in his negotiations with Aberdeen, he covered them with a torrent of eloquent, and impetuous, language. Both he and the Church had been betrayed by the politicians. The Church now had to stand with him against the politicians and privileged social élites.

Chalmers's prestige outside the Church, meanwhile, was waning. In January 1840, George H. Baird, Principal of Edinburgh University, had died, and Chalmers had become a candidate for the position. He had received, however, only two votes in the Town Council, and was easily defeated by his rival, John Lee. In September of that year, the venerable Evangelical, Stevenson Macgill, Professor of Divinity at Glasgow University, also died, aged seventy-five. In the wake of the Aberdeen bill affair, Chalmers now decided to leave Edinburgh; believing he would find more support and fellowship among the Evangelicals in Glasgow, he became a candidate for the chair. The Moderate candidate was Alexander Hill, a son of the celebrated eighteenth-century Moderate, George Hill, but otherwise an undistinguished rural clergyman whose abilities did not approach those of Chalmers. Nevertheless, the competition became a political issue, with the Tories in particular seeking to ensure Chalmers's rejection. Sir James Graham, a leading Tory politician and the Lord Rector of Glasgow University, whose support Chalmers had earlier sought to gain for the Church's cause, made a special trip from London to Glasgow to cast his influential vote against Chalmers. On 19 October 1840, Hill was elected to the position.[92]

It was a painful humilitation for Chalmers, and even the Edinburgh *Scotsman* newspaper, one of his strongest opponents, was moved to express sympathy. There was, the *Scotsman* admitted on 24 October, no comparison between the respective talents of Chalmers and Hill, and it could only hope that 'Dr. Chalmers may see in the event which has just occurred, how the influence of his genius is paralyzed by his crotchets, and the intemperance of his language.' 'Prudent men,' the *Scotsman* added, 'are afraid to co-operate in any scheme or undertaking with one who is so restless, so precipitate, and so apt to turn short and abuse those who will not go all lengths with him.'[93] The Tory hostility towards Chalmers in the wake of the Aberdeen bill affair, meanwhile, did not improve Chalmers's relations with the Whig leadership. Melbourne continued to hate him with uncharacteristic passion. 'I particularly dislike Chalmers,' he informed the Scottish Whig, Fox Maule, on 28 October 1840; 'I think him a madman, and all madman are also rogues.'[94]

The open hostility of both the Whig and Tory leadership drove Chalmers still further into association with Candlish, Cunningham, and the militant non-intrusionists. The Aberdeen affair, he asserted, had blasted 'all my fondest hopes for the good and peace of our Church, in my correspondence with public and parliamentary men'.[95] There was nothing more for the Church to do but to persevere in its policies according to its standards of faith, and if necessary to suffer martyrdom. In May 1840, it will be recalled, the General Assembly had suspended seven ministers of the Strathbogie presbytery for giving trials to John Edwards in defiance of the instructions from the General Assembly. The Court of Session, however, declared the suspension invalid, and instructed the presbytery of Strathbogie to ordain Edwards minister of Marnoch. On 21 January 1841, the seven ministers met at Marnoch and performed the ordination ceremony. The scene was dramatic. The parishioners occupied their customary places in the church as the suspended seven entered the church to perform the rite. Then, immediately before the ceremony, the congregation rose as a body, and solemnly left the church through the snow. 'It was', William Hanna later observed, 'an ordination altogether unparalleled in the history of the Church, performed by a Presbytery of suspended clergymen, on a 'Call' by a single communicant, against the desire of the Patron, in face of the strenuous opposition of a united Christian congregation, in opposition to the express injunction of the General Assembly, at the sole bidding,and under the sole authority, of the Court of Session.'[96] A call for subscriptions was immediately made on behalf of the Marnoch parishioners, and over £8,000 was collected for building a new church in Marnoch. It was opened for worship in March 1842, with David Henry as minister.[97] In March 1841, meanwhile, the Commission of the General Assembly found libel charges proven against the Strath-bogie seven, and referred the matter to the General Assembly of May 1841.

Chalmers secured his election to this Assembly, and on 27 May, he moved that the action of the Strathbogie seven, in performing the spiritual act of ordination while under sentence of suspension, required their deposition from the ministry. Their 'solemn mockery of the Church's most venerable forms' could not be ignored. Were the Assembly to shrink from action before this open contempt for its authority, 'the Church would be left without a government, both doctrine and discipline would be given to the winds, and our National Church were bereft of all her virtue to uphold the Christianity of the nation.' 'The Church of Scotland,' he exclaimed, 'can never give way, and will sooner give up her existence as a national establishment, than give up her power as a self-acting and self-regulating body, to do what in her judgement is best for the honour of the Redeemer and the interest of His Kingdom on earth.' The seven should be given a final opportunity to 'humble themselves' before the authority of the Church. If they refused, 'their deposition is inevitable'.

After a debate of nearly twelve hours, Chalmers's motion was carried by a vote of 222 to 125. One of the Strathbogie seven now appeared before the Assembly and read a statement on behalf of the seven, in which they refused to recognize the Church's authority over that of the State, asserting: 'We cannot consent ... to assist in violating the law, or to abandon the duty which we owe to the State, merely because a majority of office-bearers in the Church have arbitrarily resolved to require it.' The Assembly had little choice but to proceed to its sentence. It was now past midnight, and Chalmers, no longer physically strong enough for extended debates, had long since retired from the hall. After the statement of the seven had been read, however, he made a dramatic reappearance from a dark corner of the hall, advanced to the Moderator's table, and 'amid the profound silence of the vast as-semblage', moved that the seven be deposed. The motion was carried without a vote. Immediately, George Cook, the leader of the Moderate party, read a protest, insisting that it was 'binding upon every member of a Church as established by law to be subject to the civil power in all matters declared by the supreme civil authorities of the country to affect temporal rights'. Cook, therefore, declined to recognize the depositions, and at his invitation, a large number of Assembly members rushed forward to sign the protest. The majority of the Assembly, however, refused to accept the protest, on the ground that it would create a total schism between the two parties. Cook then agreed, in the interest of preserving the remaining unity of the Church, not to submit the protest, despite pressure from James Bryce and the other Moderate extremists.[98]

Two days later, on the evening of Saturday, 29 May, the proceedings of the Assembly were interrupted by a messenger-at-arms, waiting to serve an interdict from the Court of Session, which ordered the Assembly not to proceed with the depositions. When the Assembly refused to admit him, he left the interdict at the Assembly door. The interdict was not obeyed, and the depositions stood. On Monday, 31 May, moreover, Candlish moved that the Assembly protest against the interdict directly to the Queen, in order 'to make her majesty aware of this act so derogatory to her royal prerogative and disrespectful to her royal dignity'. After a short debate, the motion was carried by a vote of 189 to 90. Two weeks later, on 15 June, Aberdeen presented a petition from the deposed Strathbogie ministers to the House of Lords, and he demanded that the Whig Government take punitive action against the General Assembly. 'The presumption manifested by the general assembly in these proceedings', he asserted, 'was never equalled by the church of Rome—tyranny such as was exhibited in this case would annihilate the liberties of the people of this country.' Melbourne could not resist commenting with droll humour upon Aberdeen's new-found rage against the Church of Scotland. He refused, however, to involve his Government in punitive measures, preferring that the dispute should 'work itself out by the efforts of the conflicting parties'.[99]

With the deposing of the Strathbogie seven, a disruption of the Church of Scotland became inevitable. The Evangelical majority had demonstrated its resolve to depose any minister who acknowledged a superior authority of the civil courts in matters of internal spiritual discipline. The Assembly, moreover, manifested no inclination to limit its depositions to the Strathbogie seven. Late in July 1841, several Moderate leaders demonstrated solidarity with the deposed ministers by assisting them in serving the communion sacrament. In response, the General Assembly Commission of August 1841 instructed the presbyteries to begin libel proceedings against the Moderate offenders. For many Moderates, this seemed the first step towards deposing all who dissented from the actions of the Evangelical majority. George Cook now reminded the August Commission that in the previous May he had chosen not to protest formally against the Assembly's deposition of the Strathbogie seven, in order to avoid schism. But if the Assembly persisted in punitive action against those who dissented from the deposition decision, the Moderates would be compelled to ask the State authorities whether they, or their non-intrusionist opponents 'are to be held by the legislature as constituting the Established Church'.[100] The Evangelical majority, however, refused to back down. 'The Church', Candlish exclaimed at a public meeting in late August, in response to Cook's threat, 'ought to be established on the principles which we are contending for, or there should be no establishment in the land at all.' 'It is our bounden duty', he continued in reference to the Moderates, 'to use every effort [to ensure] that, if we be driven out, they shall be driven out too.'[101]

To the rising tension between the two parties in the Church was now added another event which ensured the inevitability of disruption—the return of the Tory party to office. In late June 1841, Melbourne's Whig Government dissolved Parliament, and a general election was held in July and early August. It was a quiet election, especially in Scotland, where only twenty-three of the fifty-three seats were contested. The question of non-intrusion was raised in a number of Scottish contests, but the Evangelicals did not agitate the question in organized fashion, and the issue was important in only a few constituencies.[102] What was decisive for the Church was the fact that in the country as a whole the Tories were returned with a majority, and Peel was summoned to form a Government.

Peel was decidely hostile to the non-intrusion cause. Not only was he a strong Erastian, with little sympathy for the history and standards of the Church of Scotland; he was also personally offended by the non-intrusionists' behaviour towards his friend Aberdeen, who now received a major Cabinet appointment (Foreign Secretary). Before the election, Peel had defined his position regarding what he termed privately 'the Popish-Presbyterian party'. Early in May 1841, the Tory Duke of Argyll had introduced a bill in the House of Lords which would have legalized the popular veto, provided it was proved not to have resulted from irrational prejudice. The bill had passed its first reading, but was postponed with the dissolution of Parliament. In late June, Argyll and a deputation from the Church met Peel in London to discuss the fate of the bill, and Peel made it clear that his party would not support Argyll's bill, or any similar measure, unless the Assembly first repealed the depositions of the Strathbogie seven.[103] The Assembly was in no mood for such a submission, so with Peel's return to office, Argyll dropped his bill. There was now little hope for a legislative solution.

Chalmers had viewed the general election with indifference. He expected nothing from either the Whigs or the Tories, and he was largely resigned to the inevitability of a disruption. He was now turning his attention to the mission of the post-disruption Evangelical Church. 'Be assured,' he wrote his old friend, Janet Coutts, on 9 July 1841, 'that I feel very calm and confident on the Church Question—not on the ground of the Parliamentary returns, or in the assured prospect of anything being done in our favour by the present or any future Government; but on the ground that our way of duty is clear.' 'Should the Establishment be broken up,' he continued' 'I think that, if true to our principles, there is a very great field of usefulness before us; and that we need be at no loss for turning ourselves to such openings for the

Christian good of the people as will amply compensate for all the hard-
ships to which we might in consequence be exposed.'[104]

After the general election of 1841, Chalmers and the Evangelical
party began to organize popular support for the impending disruption.
'Be it known unto all men,' Chalmers exclaimed before a special meeting
of the General Assembly Commission on 25 August 1841, 'that we
have no wish for a disruption, but neither stand we in the overwhelming
dread of it. We have no ambition, as has been pleasantly said of us, for
martyrdoms of any sort, but neither will we shrink from the hour or
day of trial.'[105] In the final months of 1841, Church defence organizations were formed throughout the country, their members pledged to
non-intrusion.[106] By 1842, the question was not so much whether there
would be a disruption, but rather how many would follow Chalmers
out of the Establishment when it came.

                                  IV

Beginning in 1839, the rising tension of the controversies regarding
both Church Extension and the spiritual independence of the Church,
combined with the economic depression and a darkening social environment, contributed to a series of religious revivals within the Church of
Scotland. The occasion for these events was in large part the *Lectures on
the Revivals of Religion*, by the American evangelist, Charles Finney.
These appeared in Scotland in 1838 and were widely read among
Scottish Evangelicals. Reviewing Finney's work in October 1838, the
Edinburgh *Presbyterian Review* was struck by the present lack of revivalist
fervour in Scotland.[107] There had, it asserted, been no significant
revivals since the celebrated events at Cambuslang and Kilsyth in
1742. The Holy Spirit had withdrawn from the land, or rather, 'we
have grieved him away—we have provoked him to withdraw'. In its
overemphasis upon the structures of its territorial Establishment, upon
Church extension schemes, poor-relief reform, and ecclesiastical-
judicial forms, the Church of Scotland had 'lost sight of the Holy
Spirit's work ... 'The perpetual play and din of the machinery so
delight and engross us, that all else is forgotten.'[108] The present
difficulties of the Church revealed the cost of its overemphasis upon
external forms. The Church must now relinquish vainglory in its
structures and procedures, and devote itself to prayer for the return of
the Spirit and to constant vigilance for the symptoms of revival. It
must transform its Church courts from institutions for debate and
adversary politics, into forums for prayer. Each kirk-session, presbytery,
and synod must become a prayer meeting. 'And our General Assembly
would be a mighty prayer-meeting, from which would ascend the
united voice of our gathered church, crying mightily for a revival over

all the land.' The signs, the *Presbyterian Review* concluded, indicated that a new era of the Holy Spirit was imminent: 'We are now almost arrived at the centenary of the last great revivals, and in this fact, there is much to interest and much to arouse.'[109] Further works on the subject of revivals appeared in Scotland during the next year, including James Douglas's *The Revival of Religion*, W. B. Sprague's *Lectures on Revivals of Religion*, and the republication, by William Collins of Glasgow, of Jonathon Edward's *Narrative of the Revival of Religion in New England*.

Then, in the summer of 1839, the first great revival occurred, appropriately, in Kilsyth—the scene of a celebrated revival in 1742. 'Kilsyth', the *Presbyterian Review* proclaimed in October 1839, 'has at length received the plenteous rain!... In that parish the scenes of a former century have all been renewed.' For years, William Burns (1779-1859), the Evangelical minister of Kilsyth, had pursued a rather undistinguished parish ministry. But in July 1839, his preaching suddenly began to attract vast crowds. There were tent meetings, attended by over 10,000 'deeply attentive hearers', from throughout the country. The parish community was transformed. Dancing parties and Chartist meetings were suppressed. 'Infidel' books were publicly burned under Burns's supervision. Some sixty separate prayer-meeting groups were formed among the village population of about 2,600. 'It has', the *Presbyterian Review* reported, 'changed the whole parish. Drunkards have been reformed. Licentious have become chaste. The moral aspect of the village and parish is altered. Politics have been swept away, and political clubs converted into prayer-meetings. ... Formerly, it is said, that in the evening as you walked the town, you heard the sound of riot and drunkenness; now you hear the melody of psalms and the voice of prayer.'[110]

In the autumn of 1839, Burns's son visited Dundee, where his message inspired a similar revival in the parish of Robert Murray M'Cheyne, who was then on leave of absence investigating the overseas mission in Palestine. Upon his return in November 1839, the twenty-six-year-old M'Cheyne was profoundly affected by the spiritual changes in his parish. He not only continued the revivalist work in his own parish, but also communicated the revivalist spirit to neighbouring districts.[111] In 1840, there were clusters of revivals in the counties of Angus, Aberdeenshire, and Ross-shire, and scattered revivals throughout much of the country. Even in parishes where no revival occurred there was often a group of inhabitants who took a keen interest in revivals elsewhere, travelling to revival meetings in neighbouring districts and organizing prayer meetings at home.[112]

The revivalist spirit in the country served to strengthen the Evangelical non-intrusionist party as it prepared for an impending disruption of the Church. With their emphasis upon the spontaneous workings of the

Holy Spirit, revivalists were not strongly committed to the principle of a State Established Church. On the contrary, many welcomed the Church-State conflict as a means for liberating the Church from its legal and social welfare obligations. A post-disruption Evangelical Church, they believed, would be a purely spiritual Church, a gathered Church of true believers, which would institutionalize the revivalist impulse, without threatening its spontaneity or 'grieving away' the Holy Spirit with excessive legal-ecclesiastical structures. Many revivalists looked upon the national crises—the economic depression, the breakdown of social welfare institutions, Chartism and working-class violence, the conflict between Church and State—as the preparation for a new outpouring of the Holy Spirit, and the beginning of the millennium. 'It seems', the *Presbyterian Review* observed in January 1840, 'as if some universal convulsion were on the point of bursting forth, to wrench and shake assunder the entire fabric of society.... No principles or laws, civil or political, seem to have any power to avert the dire convulsion.'[113]

In March 1842, anxious over the uncompromising positions assumed by both sides in the Church controversy, a group of leading Evangelical ministers met to form a 'middle party'. Among them were Matthew Leishman of Govan, Alexander Lockhart Simpson of Kirknewton, William Muir of St. Stephen's parish in Edinburgh, and several other prominent figures in the anti-Voluntary and Church Extension campaigns of the 1830s. Eventually attracting about forty adherents, the middle party professed commitment to non-intrusion, but opposed the style of adversary politics pursued by the Evangelical party. Instead, they advocated more conciliatory attitudes from both Church parties, and a renewal of negotiations with the Peel Government based upon a slightly modified version of Aberdeen's bill of 1840.[114] Peel placed considerable hope upon this middle party. Their intervention, however, came too late. Hugh Miller, the militant editor of the non-intrusionist *Witness* newspaper, quickly dubbed them the 'forty thieves', and most Evangelicals evidently regarded them as cowards or opportunists who sought an excuse for not relinquishing their State stipends and manses. Their major effect was to stiffen Peel and the Tories in their resolve not to negotiate with the Church until the deposition of the Strathbogie seven was rescinded. For the Government, the emergence of the 'middle party' indicated that despite the violent language of a few militant leaders, the vast majority of Evangelical clergy were seeking for a 'middle' course and had no wish to secede.[115]

The middle party challenge was a source of concern to Chalmers and the Evangelical leadership in the weeks preceding the May 1842 meeting of the General Assembly. It was rumoured that in order to assist the middle party, the Government would offer a more liberal version of Aberdeen's bill, or even legalize the popular veto—while at the same time refusing to concede the Church's pretensions to spiritual independence. It would, in short, offer concessions on the principle of non-intrusion, in return for the Church's submission to civil authority. The middle party could then argue that the Church had achieved its goals and should desist from further confrontation. The middle party evidently held some hope that Chalmers might join them, bringing with him most of the Evangelical party, and leaving Candlish, Cunningham, and the more militant Evangelicals in an isolated minority. But Chalmers would not accommodate. He had consistently placed his primary emphasis upon the Church's spiritual independence, while expressing some willingness to compromise on non-intrusion. He would not now reverse his priorities. On 10 April 1842, he circulated a lengthy letter among leading Evangelical clergy, in which he advocated that the approaching General Assembly focus upon the principle of spiritual independence, and treat non-intrusion as a subordinate issue. This would offset any Government attempts to divide the Evangelical majority with an offer of compromise on patronage. Further, it would help inspire support for the Church of Scotland among Christians of other nations, who might not understand the legal complexities of patronage and non-intrusion, but who could sympathize with the Church's struggle to defend the sovereignty of Christ against an Erastian government. There must not, he insisted, be any wavering regarding the deposition of the Strathbogie seven, nor should the Church shrink from deposing any Moderates who persisted in treating the seven as ministers.

'On this matter there must be no shrinkings, nor do I know aught of more imperious obligation, both in wisdom and principle, than that the Church, in dealing with the refractory and the Erastian members of her own body, should proceed against them with a firm and unfaltering hand. I know they are boasting of their numbers, and triumphantly ask if we can depose sixty. What a noble reply should we be prepared to make, if we can say yes, or you must drive off six hundred. Let the Government take their choice.[116]

Chalmers, in short, was in no mood for compromise.

Nor, it proved, was the General Assembly. The Strathbogie depositions were again brought to the forefront on the first day of the Assembly. Two deputations arrived at the Assembly, each claiming to represent the presbytery of Strathbogie—one appointed by the ministers who had obeyed the Assembly's instructions regarding the Marnoch settlement, and the other by the seven deposed ministers. The Assembly, George Cook argued, should reject both sets of representatives. A significant portion of the Church refused to acknowledge the deposition of the seven, and the matter, therefore, should be held in abeyance until a final decision was made. This was absurd, countered Chalmers. If the Moderate minority refused to acknowledge the authority of the majority, they must either secede, or face disciplinary action. The Assembly agreed with Chalmers and rejected the represent-atives of the deposed seven. The Court of Session responded with an interdict, forbidding the representatives of the Church-recognized Strathbogie presbytery to attend the Assembly. The Assembly im-mediately broke the interdict and instructed the representatives to attend. With this episode, the tone of the Assembly was fixed and a message conveyed to Peel that the new Assembly would not negotiate on his terms.

The Assembly then proceeded to pass two major acts. First, despite Chalmers's request that the Evangelicals ignore the subject of non-intrusion, the young Evangelical, William Cunningham, introduced a motion calling for the total abolition of patronage. Chalmers gave Cunningham's motion qualified support, thus preserving solidarity in the Evangelical ranks. The motion was carried by a vote of 216 to 147, and petitions were sent to both houses of Parliament, requesting legis-lation to remove this source of evil. One intention of the anti-patronage motion may have been to guard against any possible deal between the Tories and the middle party that could split the Evangelical party. While the Government might have offered to legalize a popular veto in exchange for the Church's submission to the civil courts, there was little possibility of its abolishing patronage.

Secondly, by a vote of 241 to 110, the Assembly adopted the cele-brated Claim of Right.[117] This was a document of some 5,000 words, prepared by the Evangelical lawyer, Alexander Murray Dunlop, in which the Church asserted its claim to spiritual independence. The document consisted in three parts. First, civil statutes and legal deci-sions were cited to prove that, prior to 1834, the State had recognized the Church's independence in matters of internal spiritual discipline. Secondly, the recent decisions of the civil courts were portrayed as a revolutionary and unconstitutional assertion of State authority over the Church. Finally, the Church pledged to resist the 'illegal' encroach-ments of the courts.[118] The Claim of Right, Chalmers asserted in moving its adoption on 24 May, was an ultimatum to the English-dominated legislature. Either the Church of Scotland's spiritual independence must be recognized, or there would be a disruption. 'We are', he asserted,

not dealing in threats, but in remonstrances. We are not making an experiment on English courage; that we know would be in vain. We are making an appeal to English justice; and that we hope will not be in vain. We are letting the Capital of the empire know a case of gross, and grievous, and multiplied oppression, which is now going on in one of the provinces—an oppression which, if not remedied, will have the effect of trampling down the Church of Scotland into utter insignificance; will despoil her of all moral weight, or better greatly than this, though itself a great and sore calamity, will dissever her from the State altogether.

This, he asserted, was the Church's final appeal. The Church would not allow itself to be broken up by order of the Court of Session. But if Parliament 'by an act of the greatest national injustice', chose to reject the Church's historic privileges, the Evangelical majority would be forced to relinquish the temporal benefits of the State connection.[119]

The Government's response was not long in coming. In mid-June 1842, Peel announced in the House of Commons that after careful deliberation upon the Church conflict, 'Her Majesty's Government had abandoned all hope of settling the question in a satisfactory manner, or of effecting any good by introducing a measure relative to it.'[120] Peel's hopes for the middle party had been thwarted. Chalmers remained in command of a united Evangelical party, committed to the principle of spiritual independence, which Peel vehemently rejected. In August 1842 the House of Lords increased the pressure upon the Church with its decision in the second Auchterarder Case. Lord Kinnoull, the patron of Auchterarder, and Robert Young, the presentee who had secured his claim to the benefice against the veto of the parishioners in the first Auchterarder Case, had subsequently raised a second legal action against the presbytery of Auchterarder, suing them for £16,000 as compensation for the injury they sustained as a result of Young's initial rejection. The Court of Session decided against the presbytery, and the case was appealed to the House of Lords. On 9 August 1842, the House of Lords confirmed the Court of Session's decision, and held the presbytery liable for the damages. In a word, the individual members of a presbytery were subject to civil penalty, including payment of damages and imprisonment, if they rejected a presentee according to the ecclesiastical law to which they had vowed obedience at their ordination.[121] By this date, there were thirty-nine lawsuits against the Church pending in the civil courts regarding veto decisions and breaches of interdict, so the House of Lord's decision affected far more than the £16,000 damages at stake in the second Auchterarder Case.[122] In effect, the decision made it virtually impossible for ministers who believed in the principle of spiritual independence to remain in the Established Church.

Early in July 1842, Chalmers travelled with his family to northern Ireland, where he remained for two months in a rented cottage in the village of Rostrevor, near Newry. The tensions of the Church conflict were affecting both his health and family life, and a rest outside Scotland was crucial. He later described his two months in the quiet rural community, among the Irish whom he loved, as 'the sunniest recollection of my life'. None the less, the storm clouds were ever visible

across the narrow Irish Sea. Following the House of Lords' second
Auchterarder decision, many Evangelical non-intrusionists advocated
immediate secession. Chalmers, however, refused to give the word.
'To go out now', he explained in a letter to his son-in-law, John Mackenzie, minister of rural Dunkeld, on 22 August 1842,

> would be receiving our doom as an Establishment from the Civil Court, or at the
> bidding of a mere fellow and co-ordinate with ourselves—for the House of Lords, in its
> judicial capacity, is nothing more. When we do go out, it must be at the bidding of that
> party in virtue of whose ordination it was that we became an Establishment ... In
> other words, we should not quit the Establishment till we have obtained from Parliament
> a deliverance [on the Claim of Right], whether by an adverse proposition, or a
> refusal to entertain our cause.[123]

There was, however, another reason to postpone the disruption. Despite repeated threats, the Evangelical non-intrusionist party was in fact
unprepared for the final act. The break, they continually asserted, would
be more than merely another secession; it would represent a disruption
of the bond between the State and the true Church of Scotland. But in
fact, there was no clear idea of how many clergymen would leave the
Establishment. Nor was there any defined plan for the maintenance of
those clergy who relinquished their State stipends and manses. The
Government, meanwhile, was delaying its response to the Church's
Claim of Right, in the belief that as the clergy considered their fate
without the Establishment, they would re-examine the course defined
by their leaders. In order to overcome clerical anxieties regarding the
impending event, Chalmers and several Edinburgh Evangelical leaders
organized a special Convocation in November 1842.

Only ministers believed to support the principle of spiritual independence were invited to attend, and on 17 November, following an
opening sermon by Chalmers in the prestigious St. George's church,
465 ministers crowded into the small Roxburgh church on an obscure
Edinburgh street. The public was forbidden entry, and no minutes
were kept. Chalmers, who had been invited to take the chair, introduced a plan for financing the creation and maintenance of the proposed
Free Church. Money would be collected by local congregations, and
redistributed, according to need, by a central committee. In a short
time, new churches and manses would be erected for all the seceding
ministers. No minister, he further promised, no matter how poor his
local community, would receive less than £200 per annum. But this
would be only the beginning. There would be new Free Church schools
and universities. There would be a vigorous Church Extension campaign; new churches, with an aggressive territorial ministry, would be
placed in urban slums and remote hamlets. Combined with this home
mission would be an active overseas mission. None of the great missionary
schemes of the period of Evangelical ascendancy in the Church would

be relinquished. In short, the Free Church would continue to pursue the creation of the godly commonwealth in Scotland—only with more vigour and vitality, because it would be free from the constraints imposed by an Erastian and utilitarian State. There were, Chalmers asserted, ample resources among the Scottish public for the support of the great venture, and his plan for local collection and central administration would prove effective. Near the close of the six-day meeting, two sets of resolutions were put before the gathering. The first was a statement of the Church's grievances at the hands of the civil courts. It received the assent of 423 ministers. The second was a pledge that if Parliament refused to take steps to redress these grievances, and to recognize the Claim of Right, the signatories would resign their office and endowments, and enter the Free Church. Only 354 of the 465 present signed this pledge, indicating a reluctance among even Evangelical loyalists to take the final step.[124]

Every effort was made to portray the resolutions of the Convocation before the public as a consensus, achieved through a general unanimity of purpose. 'Still, it has oozed out, through themselves,' the Moderate clergyman, David Aitken, informed Lord Minto on 13 December 1842, 'that everything was not so decorous, nor the harmony altogether entire.' Aitken had not been invited to attend. From some of those who did attend, however, he had learned of tensions. A number of rural clergymen complained that they had not been summoned to deliberate policy, but merely to ratify what Chalmers and a small group of Edinburgh clergy had already determined. Expressions of dissent from the policies of the Edinburgh leadership were evidently either shouted down by the younger enthusiasts, or interrupted by sudden calls for prayer and spiritual reflection. 'Chalmers, it seems', Aitken continued, was as vehement as the youngest; his appeals frequently brought them on their legs in loud shouts and cheering. And no wonder he was received with such acclamation, for among other things he told them that he would undertake to raise for the good cause £100,000 per annum.'[125] Despite the enthusiasm engendered by Chalmers's promises, however, Aitken suspected that few, even among the 354 who signed the second resolution, would actually secede. They were intimidated for the moment by Chalmers, but would shrink from the final act. That opinion was shared by Peel, who was enraged by the Convocation proceedings. 'I believe', Peel informed the Scottish Tory MP, Sir George Sinclair, on 2 December 1842, 'the main cause of the present embarrassment is the subjection of very many Ministers of the Church of Scotland, through fear and against their own conscientious convictions, to the violence and menaces of their leaders.'[126]

'If the Parliament grant us no redress,' Chalmers informed an American correspondent on 31 December 1842, 'I have no doubt that the decision of our Convocation in November will be the decision of our General Assembly in May. It lies therefore with our statesmen whether there shall not be an utter disruption of our Church.'[127] The Government's response was not long in arriving. On 4 January 1843, in a 'Queen's Letter' to the Church, the Government announced its refusal to consider the Church's Claim of Right. Two weeks later, on 20 January, the Court of Session 'again maimed the Church by another most effective slash'. In its final decision regarding the Stewarton Case, the Court declared the General Assembly's Chapels Act of 1834 to be illegal. With this decision, all *quoad sacra* parishes were legally abolished, and the ministers and kirk-sessions of all churches erected through Chalmers's Church Extension campaign of the 1830s were deprived of representation in the Church courts. Most *quoad sacra* ministers were Evangelical non-intrusionists, and thus a major effect of the decision was to remove the prospect of another strong non-intrusionist majority in the next General Assembly.[128]

Chalmers, meanwhile, was laying the foundation for the Free Church. As early as December 1842, he had formed a model local society near his home in the parish of Morningside, for the purpose of organizing a Free Church congregation and collecting funds. A few additional societies were formed in other localities in January. Then, after the final Stewarton decision, the tempo increased substantially. On 1 February a provisional committee was created in Edinburgh to supervise preparations. There were three sub-committees—finance, architecture, and statistics; Chalmers assumed the convenership of the finance subcommittee. On 16 February, at a public meeting in Edinburgh, he announced that in response to the first circular letter, sent out only a few days before, £18,550 had already been subscribed, and subscriptions were arriving at a rate of £1,000 a day. At this rate of increase, he asserted, it would not be long before churches and stipends were provided for all the outgoing ministers, and the proposed Free Church could begin building additional churches for a home mission committed to the thorough Christianization of Scotland. 'When we come to that—and I think it may be soon—I shall feel myself in my old element, at my old work of Church Extension.' He felt exhilaration at the prospect of being freed from dependence upon the British State. 'For Church Extension', he exclaimed,

I knocked at the door of a Whig ministry, and they refused to endow. I then knocked at the door of a Tory ministry, but they offered to enslave. I now therefore turn aside from both, and knock at the door of the general population. ... To make Ireland what he wanted it to be, O'Connell gave forth his watchword—'Agitate, agitate, agitate;' and the consequence was, that Ireland for a few years was lord of the ascendent.... Scotland seeks no ascendency, and she neither hopes for, nor is ambitious of power. She seeks the Christian freedom of her Church and the Christian good of her people, and to make out this, let her watchword be—'Organize, organize, organize.'

Chalmers revived the organizational methods of his Church Extension campaign. Travelling agents were sent on circuits through the country to organize Free Church local societies. In many districts, they needed only to revive the dormant local societies of the recent Church Extension movement—associations with considerable experience at raising funds, collecting statistics, and building churches. The pre-existence of this organizational structure and experience accounted in part for the amazing rapidity with which Chalmers created a Free Church financial foundation. His efforts were also assisted by the revivalist fervour in the country, and such revivalists as William Burns and Robert M'Cheyne became leaders in the organizational campaign. By 19 April 1843, 405 local associations had been formed.[129] It was now clear to the Government that the disruption would be a substantial one. None the less, Peel's Ministry would not accept the principle of spiritual independence, and so, despite a few efforts by Scottish politicians to thwart disruption through an eleventh-hour compromise, events hastened to the final scene.

Between four and five o'clock on the morning of 18 May 1843, the public galleries of St. Andrews church in Edinburgh were filled to capacity with spectators willing to wait for over ten hours to witness the opening of the 1843 General Assembly. As the morning progressed, the crowd outside the church steadily increased, until by about half past two in the afternoon, when the Royal Commissioner arrived, thousands had gathered. Inside, David Welsh, the retiring Moderator of the 1842 General Assembly, led the Assembly in opening prayer. Then, at the point where it was customary to read the roll of the new commissioners, Welsh suddenly broke from the routine. 'Amid the breathless stillness', he read a long statement, protesting the new conditions which the State now demanded from the Church in order for it to remain a State Establishment. Upon concluding the statement, he 'laid it upon the table, turned and bowed respectfully to the Royal Commissioner, left the chair, and proceeded along the aisle to the door of the Church'. Chalmers had been standing to Welsh's left. He appeared 'vacant and abstracted' while Welsh read the statement. Perceiving Welsh's movement, however, he awakened from his reverie, and hurried after him. Several leading Evangelicals standing near the platform followed. A cheer burst forth from the galleries, but it was instantly restrained as unsuited to the occasion. Then, row after row, ministers and elders began filing out of the church, until the left, or Evangelical side of the church, was nearly vacant.

Outside, there was a cry of 'They come! they come!' as Chalmers and Welsh appeared at the door. There had been no plan to form a procession as they departed the Assembly hall, but the pressure of the crowd was so great that the outgoing ministers and elders were forced to walk in column, three or four abreast, with Chalmers, Welsh and Gordon at the head. Henry Cockburn counted only 123 ministers and 70 elders who actually filed out of St. Andrews church. Once outside, however, the procession was joined by hundreds of ministers who were pledged to join the Free Church, but who had not been elected members of the General Assembly, or who, as *quoad sacra* ministers, had been deprived of the right to attend. A procession of black gowns a quarter of a mile long moved solemnly through the New Town of Edinburgh toward Tanfield Hall, which had been prepared as the new Assembly hall. On the whole, the crowd which lined the streets along the entire course of the procession was quietly respectful. Hats were raised, heads bowed, and tears shed, particularly as the crowd discerned some venerable minister in the procession, who they knew was relinquishing the peace and security of his final years. Upon reaching Tanfield Hall, the procession organized themselves into the First General Assembly of the Free Church of Scotland. Chalmers was appointed Moderator, and in the presence of nearly 3,000 spectators, 470 ministers signed the 'Act of Separation and Deed of Demission', by which they did 'separate from and abandon the present subsisting ecclesiastical Establishment in Scotland, and renounce all rights and emoluments pertaining to them in virtue thereof'.[130]

Francis Jeffrey, a judge on the Court of Session, was reading quietly in his home, when a friend burst in with the news. 'Well, what do you think of it?' he was asked. 'More than four hundred of them are actually out.' 'I'm proud of my country,' Jeffrey replied. 'There is not another country upon earth where such a deed could have been done.' It was indeed a great act. More than 450 ministers had voluntarily renounced their stipends, manses, and churches, in exchange for an uncertain future for themselves and their families. They had sacrificed personal interest for their principles. 'I know no parallel to it,' Cockburn observed a few days after the event.

Whatever may be thought of their cause, there can be no doubt or coldness in the admiration with which all candid men must applaud their heroism. They have abandoned that public station which was the ambition of their lives, and have descended from certainty to precariousness, and most of them from comfort to destitution, solely for their principles. And the loss of the stipend is the least of it. The dismantling of the manse, the breaking up of all the objects to which the hearts and the habits of the family were attached, the shutting the gate for the last time of the little garden, the termination of all their interest in the humble but respectable kirk—even all these desolations, though they may excite the most immediate pangs, are not the calamities which the head of the house finds it hardest to sustain. It is the loss of station that is the deep and lasting sacrifice, the ceasing to be the most important man in the parish, the closing of the doors of the gentry against him and his family, the altered prospects of his children, the extinction of everything that the State had provided for the decent dignity of the manse and its inmates.[131]

Some of those swept by the initial tide of enthusiasm to sign the Deed of Demission in Tanfield Hall later retracted their adherence. None the less, most stood firm. Of 1,195 clergymen in the Church of Scotland in May 1843, 454, or 38.1 per cent, entered the Free Church. A detailed analysis of those who went out and those who remained, published by the Evangelical clergyman (and later President of Princeton University in the United States), James M'Cosh, in late 1843, revealed something of the character of those who joined the Free Church. First, younger men, ordained to the ministry during the years of Evangelical ascendancy, had a greater tendency to go out. Of the 399 ministers ordained before 1820, only 98, or 24.6 per cent went out, while of the 796 ordained after 1820, 356 or 44.7 per cent went out. The greatest percentage going out were among those ordained during the height of the Evangelical ascendancy, 1830-40—208 out of 389, or 53.5 per cent.

Secondly, although most districts reflected the national average, there were some regional diversities. The lowest percentages of outgoing ministers occurred in the southern counties, where parishes were generally well-endowed, and where English attitudes regarding the nature of Church-State relations probably had greater influence. In the synod of Dumfries, only 19 per cent went out, in the synod of Merse and Teviotdale, 25 per cent, and in the synod of Galloway, 22.5 per cent. The highest percentages occurred in the northern synod of Ross (75.8 per cent), which had experienced a series of revivals beginning in 1840, and in the synod of Sutherland and Caithness (65.5 per cent), which reflected both anti-Government sentiment caused by the Highland land clearances, and the strength of strict Highland Calvinist piety as a bond holding the suffering Highland communities together. Percentages of outgoing ministers tended to be higher in urban districts. In the presbytery of Edinburgh, 34 out of 56 ministers, or 59.1 per cent joined the Free Church; in the presbytery of Dundee (influenced, perhaps, by the revivalist activity of Robert M'Cheyne), 15 out of 29, or 53.6 per cent; in the presbytery of Glasgow, 31 out of 58, or 53.4 per cent; and in the presbytery of Aberdeen, 19 out of 36, or 52.8 per cent.

Thirdly, and perhaps most significant, was the behaviour of the ministers in the unendowed, *quoad sacra* churches. Of 233 *quoad sacra* parish ministers in 1843, the vast majority of whom had been ordained to churches built as a result of the Church Extension campaign of the 1830s, 162, or 69.5 per cent, joined the Free Church. Indeed, 35.7 per cent of all outgoing ministers were *quoad sacra* ministers. In part, this reflected the recent decisions of the Court of Session, which deprived *quoad sacra* parish churches of their church-door collections and representation in the Church courts. However, it also represented the effect of Chalmers's Church Extension campaign in strengthening the Evangelical position within the Church.[132]

In addition to the 454 ordained ministers who went out, 192 probationary ministers also joined the Free Church. Considering the financial precariousness of the Free Church, and the many well-endowed charges in the Establishment made available by the Disruption, this was a remarkable demonstration. Of the fourteen overseas missionaries supported by the Church of Scotland in 1843, moreover, all joined the Free Church. No account exists of the percentage of lay membership which left the Establishment. From the subsequent difficulties of the Free Church in supplying ministers to all the new congregations, it may be assumed that about 40 per cent of the lay membership went out.[133] It is difficult to imagine a split of such magnitude without Chalmers's leadership. There might, to be sure, have been a minor secession of a few militant Evangelicals in response to the Government's uncompromising position regarding spiritual independence. But it was Chalmers's organizational genius, his oratory, and his fame which had ensured that the Church of Scotland should suffer disruption. His political abilities and influence had not proved sufficient to ease tensions and ward off the final clash between Church and State. He had, however, succeeded in preserving unity in the Evangelical ranks during the final stages of the crisis. 'Let us follow', the leading Evangelical clergyman, Robert Gordon, had written in reference to Chalmers to a fellow Edinburgh clergyman in April 1842, 'the course so plainly and powerfully laid out for us by our venerable and beloved father. If it come to [disruption], I trust that his setting sun will exhibit him to Christendom in a brighter blaze than in all his other works— leading his brethren in one of the noblest testimonies that have ever been borne to the glorious headship of our adorable Redeemer.'[134] The majority of the party did follow Chalmers out of the Church. Of 714 clergymen described by James M'Cosh as Evangelical in 1843, only 260, or 36.4 per cent, declined to renounce their endowments and manses.[135] Considering the sacrifices involved, and the complexities of the issues, this was a remarkable achievement. In the final event, each clergyman was left to wrestle with his own conscience on whether to remain with the 'auld Kirk'. But the presence of Chalmers at the head of the procession out, a man who, for all his weaknesses, remained the greatest Scottish Churchman of his day, was sufficient guarantee for many that it was indeed the true Church that was abandoning the State connection.

The great challenge now confronting those who had left the Establishment was the financial one. The Free Church had a desperate and immediate need for money. At the Convocation in November 1842, it will be recalled, Chalmers had promised not only to raise sufficient funds for building new churches and manses, but also to provide at least £100,000 per annum for the support of the outgoing clergy. This was an extraordinary claim. Chalmers, to be sure, had produced financial marvels during his Church Extension campaign of the 1830s, but opponents of the Free Church predicted that he would fail to meet this far greater financial challenge. A few days before the Disruption, Hope had assured Aberdeen that while two or three hundred ministers might go out, the Government and Establishment had nothing to fear. In a short time, he predicted, poverty would undermine the new venture. 'People will wonder at the anxiety they at first felt and will laugh at the secession and its wooden churches.'[136] Chalmers was acutely aware of this danger. The Free Church required not only high principles, but also brick, mortar, and above all money. The consolidation of the Disruption would in the final analysis be a financial achievement.

V

The Disruption, Chalmers maintained, was not a secession. Rather it was a tragic severing of the relationship between the true Church of Scotland and a British State which had broken its pledge to preserve the Church's integrity. He did not relinquish either his godly commonwealth ideal, or his commitment to the principle of a religious Establishment. For him, it was the Free Church that now represented the national Establishment and Christian commonwealth. Before the first Free Church General Assembly in May 1843 he exclaimed:

> We hold that every part and every function of a commonwealth should be leavened with Christianity, and that every functionary, from the highest to the lowest, should, in their respective spheres, do all that in them lies to countenance and uphold it. That is to say, though we quit the Establishment, we go out on the Establishment principle; we quit a vitiated Establishment, but would rejoice in returning to a pure one. To express it otherwise—we are the advocates for a national recognition and national support of religion—and we are not Voluntaries.[137]

Implicit in this statement is the promise that if the State should relinquish its Erastian opposition to the doctrine of spiritual independence, the Free Church might return to the State connection. Until this occurred, however, Chalmers asserted that the Free Church would not only represent the spiritual independence of the Church of Scotland, but also the spiritual and moral independence of the Scottish nation from British rule. It would not become simply a gathered Church of true believers; rather, it would assume responsibility for the religious and moral education of the entire nation.

This was a great undertaking. In all previous secessions from the Church of Scotland, the seceders had functioned upon the Voluntary principle. Congregations had been required to provide their own churches and support their own ministers. New churches had been established only where sufficient interest and wealth existed in the local community. The secession churches had, in consequence, scarcely penetrated the Highlands and Islands, where communities were generally too poor and sparsely populated to support a church and minister. The Free Church, however, proclaimed that it would duplicate the national Establishment. It would establish churches throughout the country, and organize a hierarchy of territorial parishes, presbyteries, and synods. It also undertook to create parish schools, found colleges, and maintain a vigorous overseas mission. Further, it sought to create this national territorial 'establishment' without delay, so that outgoing ministers, schoolteachers, and lay-adherents would not suffer deprivation as a result of their Free Church loyalties. This was especially important if the Free Church wished to retain its substantial numbers. The degree, meanwhile, to which the Free Church fulfilled its goals in the initial years was phenomenal. For it must be remembered that in addition to difficulties arising from the hostility of the State and much of the population, the Free Church was also obliged to finance the building of churches, manses, and schools, and the support of ministers and teachers, in the midst of perhaps the worst economic depression of the nineteenth century.

The work of creating the new national Church had begun several months before the Disruption. By 18 May 1843, the day of the Disruption, there were already 687 local associations in existence throughout Scotland.[138] Within several weeks, that number had grown to over 750. Each association represented a potential Free Church congregation and thus required a church and minister. 'Our greatest pressure', Chalmers informed the English industrialist, Michael Longridge, on 5 July 1843, 'arises from the vast amount of adherence that we enjoy. Congregations are springing up in all quarters more than we can supply. There are at least 756 places to be preached in, and what with ministers and probationers we have as yet only about 600 who are available.'[139] A few of these potential congregations broke up, or consolidated with neighbouring groups. None the less, the number of districts to be provided with ministers and churches was staggering.

The building of new churches proceeded rapidly. The Assembly conducted the building campaign according to Chalmers's plan in the 1830s Church Extension campaign. First, there was a general building fund, made up of donations collected both in Scotland and overseas. By the date of the Disruption, the general building fund had reached £76,253.[140] The fund was employed to stimulate local action by providing a portion of the church-building expenses (generally about 20 per cent, but often more, depending on the need) for poorer congregations. Secondly, the main responsibility for church-building was placed upon the local congregation. Before the Disruption, Evangelical leaders had consulted with several architects, who had submitted plans for inexpensive but serviceable churches, constructed of brick, with wood frames and felt roofs—instead of the usual stone and slate. In some localities, sympathetic tradesmen or merchants supplied labour and materials without charge, while members of the congregation assisted as unskilled labour. In others, one or two wealthy individuals bore the major expense for the new church. The church-building effort was in fact assisted by the economic depression, which had virtually halted new construction in Scotland. Skilled labour and materials, therefore, were phenomenally inexpensive—a sign, many believed, of providential favour. The greatest problem involved obtaining sites for churches. Hostility towards the Free Church was strong among the landed gentry and aristocracy, and many refused to sell property for Free Church sites. None the less, new churches were erected at a rate that made the achievements of Church Extension in the 1830s appear pale in comparison. In May 1844, a year after the Disruption, 470 churches were reported as completed, or nearly finished. In addition, through litigation, the Free Church had managed to wrest fifty of the Church Extension campaign churches built during the 1830s from control of the Established Church. In 1844-5, sixty additional churches were reported completed, in 1845-6, ninety-five churches, and in 1846-7, fifty-five churches. After four years of existence, then, the Free Church claimed to have 730 churches.[141] Most of these were unpretentious brick and wood structures, usually later replaced by more substantial stone buildings. None the less, the success of the building campaign was astonishing, and demonstrated the deep commitment of the Free Church adherents.

Chalmers had not been worried about the building campaign, and had not assumed an active role in its management. It was, he maintained, relatively easy to encourage local congregations to erect churches. To be sure, considerable work and financial sacrifice were required for church-building; however, the amount of sacrifice involved was of limited duration and quantity, and once it was completed, the community possessed a palpable symbol of its commitment, as well as a meeting-place which all might enjoy. The initial excitement of the Disruption, he believed, would prove sufficient to ensure most of the necessary church-building. His greatest concern involved the permanent support of the clergy. He would not have the clergy supported solely on Voluntary principles, with each individual congregation supporting its own minister with seat-rents and collections. This would ensure support only for the popular preacher in a wealthy neighbourhood, while leaving the poor and the irreligious outside the Free Church's purview. The great failure of his Church Extension campaign, he believed, had been the Church's inability, as a result of the Government's refusal to sponsor an endowment grant, to support ministers in the poorest districts where need for religious instruction was most desperate. He was determined that the Free Church would reach these districts with a territorial parish ministry, modelled upon his St. John's communal experiment—a goal which, without endowments, appeared hopelessly Utopian.

To achieve the goal of a national territorial 'establishment', based upon voluntary contributions, Chalmers devised his celebrated Sustentation Fund scheme. The scheme consisted in three parts. First, each local congregation was to collect all it could each year for the general support of all the Free Church clergy. This money would then be sent to Edinburgh in quarterly payments, where it would accumulate in the central Sustentation fund. At the close of the year, an equal dividend would be paid from the Sustentation Fund to every minister in the Church, no matter how great or small the contribution from the minister's local congregation. This would ensure a basic stipend to each minister, including those in remote Highland hamlets or urban slum districts. Secondly, not all of the Sustentation Fund would be divided up among the existing clergy each year. Rather, a portion would be invested in Church Extension—that is, for employing new 'territorial missionaries' to organize congregations in districts not already provided with a local Free Church. Thirdly, once a congregation had contributed its fair share to the central Sustentation Fund, it might then reward its minister with additional local collections, thus raising his salary above the minimum stipend provided by the annual dividend.

In devising the Sustentation Fund scheme, Chalmers avoided defining what a local congregation's fair share to the central fund should be, or what portion of the central fund should be divided among the existing clergy and what portion should be invested in Church Extension. The Free Church, he believed, comprised the most dedicated and idealistic clergy and laity of the old Kirk. They would act as a perfect community, with each local congregation contributing to the whole Church according to their ability, and receiving according to their needs. Their communal spirit, in turn, would inspire the entire commonwealth. His scheme, Chalmers admitted before the first Free Church Assembly on 20 May 1843, was widely criticized as 'utopian', even among Free Church adherents. None the less, he promised that it would both provide a sufficient income for the clergy, and finance a Church Extension campaign for creating a complete national territorial Free Church 'establishment'.[142]

Chalmers devoted considerable effort to the Sustentation Fund scheme. It had to be made to work, if the Free Church were to avoid a Voluntary form of organization that would deprive much of the country of Free Church ministry. Many leaders pressed him to embark upon fund-raising tours in England or even the United States, where his international reputation would have ensured large contributions. But while other Free Church leaders conducted such tours, Chalmers would not. The Free Church, he argued, would only succeed when it became financially self-sufficient within Scotland. In August and September 1843, he made a Sustentation Fund tour throughout north-eastern Scotland, in order to introduce the scheme to ministers, elders, and deacons of the new congregations. In Aberdeen, he addressed an assembly of 1,400 clergy and lay office-bearers. He preferred, however, to meet smaller groups, among whom he could discuss practical local problems, and exercise a more personal persuasion. In May 1844, a year after the formation of the Free Church, over £68,700 had been contributed to the central Sustentation Fund, and each of the approximately 600 ministers received an annual dividend of £100. In 1844-5, £67,641 was contributed to the Sustentation Fund, and the individual dividend paid to each minister was £122. In 1845-6, Sustentation Fund receipts totalled £76,003, with the individual dividend remaining at £122. In most parishes, the dividend was augmented by local contributions, and indeed in many wealthy urban parishes, popular preachers evidently received from £300 to £500 per annum, equal to or even greater than their incomes before the Disruption.[143]

In view of the sums also being invested in church-building, the success of Chalmers's Sustentation Fund was impressive. It ensured an extensive distribution of ministers throughout the nation, and especially in the impoverished and sparcely-populated Highlands and Islands, where it had long been believed that only a State-endowed Church could penetrate. Further it ensured an adequate stipend to every minister in the Free Church. It must be recalled that the minimum stipend in the Church of Scotland at the Disruption was only £150 per annum, so that after a mere two years of existence, the Free Church minimum was only £28 less than that of the endowed Church of Scotland. There was, to be sure, some acute suffering, particularly among rural clergy with large families who had renounced well-endowed parish livings. There was also some criticism levelled against those clergy in wealthy upper- and middle-class parishes who received stipends far above the minimum. None the less, Chalmers's Sustentation Fund provided the cement which held the Free Church clergy together during the initial years of trial, and it formed the foundation for the permanent Free Church financial constitution.

The Free Church did not neglect education. Most of those who left the Church of Scotland were deeply committed to the Reformation ideal of Church-directed universal education, and were apprehensive about leaving national education in the control of the 'residuary

Establishment'. Most new members agreed with Chalmers that the Free
Church should provide parish schools. There was, moreover, another
reason for directing immediate attention to education. A large number of
teachers, as Chalmers informed the first Free Church Assembly on
20 May 1843, had already been dismissed from their positions for
expressing approval of Free Church principles, and they must not be
forsaken. 'Such cases, I think, fairly come within our cognisance, and
it is our duty to provide for them. We can get teaching for schoolmasters.' As in the case of the outgoing ministers, however, a great
challenge involved the large number of teachers who were dismissed.
Within about a year of the Disruption, 212 Church of Scotland teachers
and 196 private school teachers, or a total of 408 teachers, had been
dismissed for holding Free Church principles. This number included
the entire staffs of the Normal Schools, or teacher-training academies,
in both Edinburgh and Glasgow.[144] With the Free Church struggling to
collect funds for church-building and ministers' stipends, it appeared
that the teachers would have to wait for financial assistance. At the
special meeting of the Free Church General Assembly in Glasgow in
October 1843, however, John MacDonald, a young minister from
rural Blairgowrie, introduced a plan for collecting £50,000 in voluntary
subscriptions in one year, for use in founding 500 Free Church schools.
The Assembly listened with incredulity, but encouraged his attempt.
Within six months, MacDonald had collected £52,000. The Assembly
now made the Educational Fund a permanent part of the financial
constitution. By May 1847, 513 teachers were receiving stipendiary
support from the Educational Fund, while another 130 private teachers
were connected to the Free Church. According to returns submitted to
the General Assembly of 1847, over 44,000 children attended Free
Church schools, nearly equal to the number in Church of Scotland
schools. The schools were a source of pride to the Free Church, which
regarded itself the repository of the best in Scotland's national heritage.
'Where you have men of a firm principle,' Candlish had exclaimed
before the Free Church Assembly in May 1847, 'you will invariably
find that these are not the men of the least intellectual energy.' 'We
have got,' he added, 'the flower of our Scottish teachers.'[145]

The educational thrust was also reflected in the founding of the Free
Church College. In late May 1843, a few days after the Disruption, the
Assembly appointed a committee headed by David Welsh to plan a
College. The pressing need for clergy to supply the hundreds of local
congregations clamouring for ministers, combined with the large
number of divinity students who had joined the Free Church, prompted
immediate action. The New College in Edinburgh was opened on 1
November 1843. Chalmers served as primary Professor of Divinity and
Principal, Welsh as Professor of Divinity and Church History, and

John 'Rabbi' Duncan, a former missionary in Jerusalem, as Professor of Hebrew and Oriental literature. Classes were held in rented rooms on George Street, in Edinburgh's New Town. There were seventy-six students in the first year, including twenty or thirty more mature men, who, in the excitement of the Disruption, had relinquished positions in business or law to enter the Free Church ministry.[146]

Chalmers, Welsh, and the Free Church leadership were not content that the New College should offer only classes in divinity. Their College plans included a complete arts curriculum, with chairs in moral philosophy, logic, and natural science. Chalmers was confident that, unburdened as it was with irrational historic traditions and narrow professorial interests, New College would emerge as one of the foremost centres of scholarship in Europe. In May 1844, the General Assembly authorized Welsh's committee to begin planning for erection of new college buildings. Within six months, the committee had collected £32,000. In January 1845, the committee approved the plans of the celebrated Edinburgh architect, William Henry Playfair, for the erection of the college building upon the commanding heights of the Old Town Mound, adjacent to the Castle Rock.[147] In the early spring of 1845, Welsh died suddenly, and Chalmers assumed the convenership of the College Committee. He laid the foundation stone for the college building on 3 June 1846, delivering an eloquent speech which summarized his views on the role of Church and College in the commonwealth. Despite the accusations of some Tory and even Whig opponents, Chalmers emphatically denied that the Free Church was a radical institution, dedicated to social and political revolution. But at the same time, he affirmed that a major mission of the Free Church was the elevation of the labouring poor, through the dissemination of a Christian social ideal. 'We leave to others,' he exclaimed,

the passions and politics of this world; and nothing will ever be taught, I trust, in any of our halls, which shall have the remotest tendency to disturb the existing order of things, or to confound the ranks and distinctions which at present obtain in society. But there is one equality between man and man which will strenuously be taught,— the essential equality of human souls; and that in the high count and reckoning of eternity, the soul of the poorest of nature's children, the raggedest boy that runs along the pavement, is of like estimation in the eyes of heaven with that of the greatest and the noblest of our land ... Heaven grant that the platform of humble life may be raised immeasurably higher than at present, and through the whole extent of it—that the mighty host who swarm upon its surface, brought under the elevating power of the gospel of Jesus Christ, and so rescued from grovelling ignorance and loathsome dissipation, may rise to a full equality with ourselves in all that is characteristic of humanity ...[148]

The faculty and staff occupied the completed structure in 1850. For a short period, New College offered both an arts and a divinity course.

By the 1850s, however, it had relinquished instruction in the arts, and concentrated upon organizing what developed into one of the world's foremost centres of Reformed theological scholarship.

The building of the Free Church was one of the great achievements of Victorian Britain. In four years, 730 churches had been built throughout Scotland, and supplied with ministers. Each minister received an adequate stipend, regardless of the poverty of the local community. An entire presbyterian hierarchy of Church courts with territorial juris-dictions—kirk-sessions, presbyteries, synods, and General Assembly— had been formed. Over 500 new elementary schools had been created, staffed by nearly 650 teachers. Two Normal Schools, or teacher-training academies, were established. A college was created. In addition to these achievements, the Free Church pursued an active overseas mission, actually spending more on foreign missions during its difficult initial years than had the united Church of Scotland before the Dis-ruption. Most impressive, the Free Church 'establishment' had been created entirely with voluntary contributions. These contributions were substantial. In the fiscal year 1844-5, total contributions were listed as £334,483; in 1845-6, £301,067.[149] Behind these achievements, stood Chalmers's organizational and financial genius. With the methods for mobilizing private charity developed during the Church Extension campaign of the 1830s, he had created the financial constitution which ensured rapid Free Church growth and consolidation.

The rapid growth, however, had not been achieved without cost to the original principles and ideals of the Evangelical leadership in 1843. Along with the monumental achievements of the initial years, there was also a narrowing of focus and a hardening of attitudes within the Free Church. The achievements demanded sacrifice and discipline, and very soon divisions began appearing between those who accepted the sacrifice and those who did not. At the same time, the bitterness of the Disruption, combined with obstacles confronting the Free Church in its early expansion, created defensive attitudes in the Free Church towards other Christians. The ideal of the godly commonwealth and the national Church was rapidly replaced by a sectarian ideal, with members regarding themselves a bastion of true believers standing against a sinful world.

The financial consolidation of the Free Church was only achieved through considerable pressure upon the membership, and especially the labouring poor, who could ill afford any contributions amid the economic depression of the early 1840s. In his fund-raising schemes, Chalmers placed special emphasis upon the penny-a-week plan. Every poor family, he argued, could afford to contribute at least a penny each week to the Free Church. Their accumulated weekly contributions, he calculated, would represent a vast annual sum, so that in addition to making every family feel it had a stake in the Free Church, penny-a-week contributions promised to provide a large portion of its financial needs. He instructed every new congregation to appoint deacons, one of whose tasks would be to make weekly rounds among each family in the congregation to collect at least a penny, and ideally more. If it zealously pursued penny-a-week collections, he argued, each congregation, no matter how poor, would be able to make substantial contributions to the Sustentation Fund and other fund-raising schemes of the Church. The support of the Free Church would thus be a communal effort, with the munificient gifts of the wealthy matched by equally impressive sacrifices from the poor. 'To neglect or underrate the mites of our artizans and labourers,' Chalmers later wrote in defence of his penny-a-week scheme, 'because of their insignificance, is to rate the moral value of a sacrifice at nothing, and to make the moneyed value of it all in all.' 'We are not,' he continued, 'for bearing hard upon the humbler classes; but we deem it no kindness to spare them the expense of what they might, and what they ought, to contribute for the precious blessing of a gospel ministration for their families.'[150]

As the number of fund-raising schemes in the Free Church—church-building, manse-building, elementary education, Sustentation Fund, College Fund, overseas missions—multiplied, the Church placed increasing pressure upon each congregation for contributions. As a result, the deacons did 'bear hard' upon the poor for more and more money during their weekly collecting rounds. When families protested their poverty, the deacons were often swift to point out a daily pipe of tobacco, pint of beer, or some other 'luxury' which might be sacrificed for the Free Church. The fact that most deacons were members of the middle classes gave the weekly collecting rounds an odour of middle-class arrogance towards the poor. 'Your money,' an anti-Free Church pamphleteer observed in 1844, 'if you belong to the "Free Church" must be forthcoming. Money! money! with the "F.C." is everything.'[151] Chalmers complained of the attacks directed against Free Church collection methods—'as if we proposed to grind the faces of the poor, and, for the support of our ecclesiastical system, ravenously ... seize on a portion of their hard-won earnings.' He denied that the Free Church acted in any such way.[152] None the less, as in his St. John's experiment, Chalmers the social theorist had all too little idea of how his schemes were actually being implemented at the local level. In truth, local congregations often competed with one another for status as generous supporters of the numerous Free Church schemes, and financial pressures upon the membership were onerous. Many Free Church members, meanwhile, and particularly working-class families, wearied of the incessant demands for contributions and began leaving the Free Church. Some returned to the Established Church; many more probably left organized religion altogether. The Free Church became an increasingly middle-class body, with a membership proud of their strict work ethic and social status.[153]

Along with this middle-class orientation, there was also a narrowing theological focus and diminishing commitment to the national Church ideal. Following the heresy trials of 1831-4, it will be recalled, there had been an increase in dogmatic Calvinism among younger Evangelicals. The Church-State conflict of the late 1830s and the early 1840s, with the consequent revival among Evangelicals of the language of the seventeenth-century Covenants, had further encouraged strict Calvinist beliefs. The outgoing ministers at the Disruption had brought with them an intense commitment to scholastic Calvinism, including the doctrines of election, limited atonement, and man's total depravity. The Free Church became one of the more theologically conservative denominations. There was a turning away from the broader Evangelical tradition of liberal Calvinism represented by Chalmers—a shift in emphasis from the universal gospel message to the preservation of the true Church of the elect. Combined with strict Calvinism was a growth of anti-Catholicism in the Free Church, with anti-Irish undertones.

Revivalism emerged as a powerful influence in the Free Church. The series of revivals beginning at Kilsyth in 1839 had been important in strengthening Evangelical fervour prior to the Disruption. After 1843, revivalism helped to inspire the sacrifice demanded by the Free Church building operations. It also exerted influence over many members' perception of the nature and mission of the Free Church. The revivalists advocated a gathered-church principle of organization, rather than Chalmers's ideal of a national territorial establishment. While he conceived of the Free Church as an institution for the spiritual and moral nurture of all inhabitants of Scotland, many revivalists wished to limit local Church membership to those converted by the Holy Spirit. They emphasized the Church's nature as a gathering of elect saints, rather than as an institution for universal religious and moral instruction. They focused upon the congregation of true believers, rather than upon the commonwealth. From the beginning, there was tension within the Free Church between the revivalists' gathered-church principle and Chalmers's national territorial establishment ideal. This tension surfaced in a debate between the two groups in the Free Church General Assembly on 21 May 1844. A significant portion of the Assembly rejected Chalmers's concept of the Free Church as a national territorial establishment, and the revivalists managed to have an act passed, by which the Assembly instructed every Free Church congregation to maintain constant prayer for a revival in its district. The Free Church, many believed, could not, and should not, assume responsibility for providing church and school accommodation for every inhabitant. If the Free Church prayed for divine grace, they argued, the Holy Spirit would ensure that God's elect saints were attracted to its existing congregations.[154]

Along with the revivalist impulse, moreover, there was a growing tendency towards Voluntaryism, particularly among younger Free Church members who had not participated in the Voluntary controversy of the previous decade. The Free Church was being created with considerable sacrifice; should not, Free Church Voluntaries argued, its services be reserved for those faithful who were willing to participate fully in the effort? By the summer of 1844, many Free Church members maintained that the Church should no longer subsidize congregations that were unable to support themselves.[155] In short, Chalmers's Sustentation Fund should be abolished. Many could not understand his aversion to Voluntaryism. Had not the Free Church achieved impressive results through Voluntary means?

Amid the triumph of rapid Free Church growth and consolidation, then, Chalmers's vision of the godly commonwealth, which had been revived at the Disruption, was again fading. The Free Church, he had believed, was to have been the means through which the godly commonwealth would finally be achieved. If only the Church of Scotland were freed from its connection with a secular State which represented only self-interested social élites and narrow utilitarian values, it would fulfil his social vision. It would become an ideal territorial establishment, committed to elevating the nation, and especially the working classes, through the creation of closely-knit parish communities. But now the increasing influence of the revivalists and Voluntaries in the Free Church was destroying his comprehensive plan. He inveighed against the narrow vision of these Free Church revivalists and Voluntaries; their principles, he insisted, would limit the Free Church ministry to those with previously-held religious convictions, to the neglect of the irreligious and immoral. 'It were in truth', he protested in a letter to the Free Church *Monthly Statement* on 27 July 1844, 'a glaring cross-purpose, a practical absurdity ... thus to keep back from the men who are deficient in righteousness that gospel which has been expressly brought into the world not to call the righteous, but sinners to repentance.'[156]

Chalmers's influence in the Free Church, however, was waning. By mid-1844, he was no longer able to dominate committee meetings, and he was being forced from power by younger, more vigorous men. The talented Robert Smith Candlish now successfully asserted his claim to leadership of the Free Church, and although he shared Chalmers's preference for the national territorial establishment ideal, he was more flexible and willing to accommodate the changing mood. Chalmers continued

to be revered as the father of the Free Church, the man whose international reputation had helped to secure for the Disruption the admiration of most of Protestant Christendom. Yet his unflinching advocacy
of his godly commonwealth ideal now appeared impractical, and even
stubborn, to many Free Church leaders, including some who had been
excited by his social ideal during the 1830s. For many, his obstinacy
on this matter was a sign that he was now too old to maintain an active
leadership role. In May 1845, Chalmers finally bowed to growing
pressure, and resigned both his convenership and membership in the
Sustentation Committee, thus relinquishing his direction of the general
financial management of the Free Church. Publicly, he attributed his
resignation to poor health.[157] Privately, however, he complained that
he had been forced out by opposition to his national Church ideal. 'The
torture I have had to endure,' he confided of his resignation to William
King Tweedie, his successor as head of the Sustentation Committee,
on 14 May 1845, 'in the want of a common intelligence and adequate
sympathy on matters which I deem essential to the vital good of my
Church and country will not be known till the day when the secrets of
all hearts shall be opened. Even if I had had the strength which I have
not, it would have been indispensable for me to have made my escape
from a misery I find to be intolerable.'[158]

The Disruption, then, ultimately proved to be a tragic chapter in
Chalmers's life. Throughout his career, he had argued that only a
national territorial established Church could succeed in elevating the
nation above the unbridled competition between individual interests,
the selfishness of social élites, and the narrow utilitarian values, which,
he believed, accounted for most social misery in early industrial
Britain. In small parish communities, organized around the religious
and moral teachings of church and school, men would learn to subordinate self-interest to the communal welfare, and to redirect social energies
from unrestrained commercial and industrial expansion to the cultivation of higher spiritual, moral, and intellectual values. The British
State, however, had rejected his godly commonwealth ideal. It had
refused to share ultimate social authority with the Church of Scotland,
or to recognize the Church as an equal partner. An aggressive, expanding Evangelical national Church had clashed with a nineteenth-
century State which was also concerned to enlarge its sphere of control
over British social life, and which was, moreover, committed (after
1829) to protect the liberties of Dissenters and Roman Catholics who
did not accept the teachings of the Established Church. In the end, the
State had taken action against the Church's 'rebellious' challenge to its
exclusive sovereignty. It had thwarted Church Extension, rejected the
Church's pretensions to spiritual independence, and ultimately threatened the Evangelical clergy with fines and imprisonment unless they

accepted unrestrained patronage and absolute civil authority over the Church.

But Chalmers had not accepted the Disruption as the end of his Christian commonwealth ideal. With characteristic tenacity, he had insisted that the Free Church cause possessed the support of the vast majority of the Scottish nation. Inspired by the example of sacrifice provided by the outgoing ministers and schoolteachers, the nation would rally to the Free Church cause, and build and support a new national 'establishment'. The Disruption would be essentially a second Scottish Reformation. Chalmers's vision, however, was not fulfilled. The achievements of the Free Church were, to be sure, substantial. None the less, very soon after the Disruption, the Free Church had indicated disenchantment with his national 'establishment' ideal. Despite his pleading, the Free Church began to perceive itself as a gathered Church of true believers. It relinquished ambition to act as a national Church for the Christian nurture of all inhabitants of Scotland, or for the universal dissemination of Christian communal teachings. Chalmers's godly commonwealth ideal now appeared moribund. The Disruption in 1843 had ultimately rendered his vision for Church and nation hopeless, and paved the way for the increase of secular and State authority over Scottish society.

THE VISION FADES

I

With the breakup of the Established Church of Scotland, the State moved rapidly to assert increased authority over poor relief. The Royal Commission of Inquiry into Scottish poor relief, appointed by the Government in 1843, had proceeded with its investigation throughout the final months of the Church-State conflict. On 23 March 1843, several weeks before the Disruption, Chalmers had appeared before the Commission, and delivered a poignant defence of his parish community ideal for Church-directed poor relief.[1] After the Disruption, however, his parish community ideal seemed only more Utopian, and the testimony of William Pulteney Alison and his supporters proved more convincing to the Commission. Late in May 1844, the Royal Commission finally published its report, recommending that the principles of the English poor law be extended to Scotland.[2] Accordingly, the Government proceeded to draft a new Scottish poor law bill. The Scottish public, meanwhile, had been profoundly shocked by the Commission's report, with its revelations of appalling social conditions, particularly in the urban slums. The report stirred an immediate public outcry. In early June 1844, Adam Black, Lord Provost of Edinburgh, issued an urgent appeal to all the city churches for a united effort to combat urban poverty and degradation.[3] Soon another voice was also heard. Disappointed by the failure of the Free Church to embrace his vision of the godly commonwealth, and deeply disturbed by the Commission's report, Chalmers had determined upon a final campaign for his Christian communal ideal.

In June and July 1844, he delivered a series of public lectures in Edinburgh, in which he announced the beginning of a new Church Extension campaign to create no fewer than sixty additional working-class territorial churches in the city. The Royal Commission on Scottish poor relief, he asserted, had opened the nation's eyes to the suffering and human degradation in the urban slums. There was a growing and just rage among the working classes directed toward a social élite which for too long had ignored their needs. The Royal Commission had recommended that increased State action, particularly a new poor law based upon the English act of 1834, was necessary to preserve the social fabric. But Chalmers could not accept this judgement. Legal poor relief and 'bastille' workhouses, he argued, would in fact increase social devisiveness and further degrade the poor. Only the dissemination of Christian and moral principles among all social classes would restore the bonds of communal benevolence and educate the poor to communal responsibility. For thirty years, he had struggled to implant his Christian communal ideal in the nation. But looking about himself now, he perceived only the triumph of the Voluntary principle. Everywhere, there were only gathered churches, competing with one another to attract the financial support of middle- and upper-class Christians, while ignoring the poor and the irreligious, who, it was argued, demonstrated no 'demand' for religion. The churches had withdrawn from their social welfare responsibilities. This evil could not be allowed to continue. Despite his poor health, he decided to make one final attempt to realize his parish community ideal. He would begin in Edinburgh. But eventually, he maintained, the sixty proposed working-class territorial churches in Edinburgh would serve as an inspiration to the entire nation.

To create the new churches, he appealed to Christian philanthropists in Edinburgh to form societies of about twenty members. Each society would select a destitute district of the city as its field of operation, and begin a territorial operation consisting in three distinct programmes. First, the society would divide the district into twenty sub-districts, or 'proportions', with a society member assigned to each proportion to conduct regular household visitations, collect information regarding neighbourhood needs, encourage church and school attendance, and organize a neighbourhood sabbath school for children and a prayer meeting for adults. Secondly, the society would organize a district school, with a salaried schoolmaster, supported by modest fees from the students. Thirdly, the society would employ a salaried missionary to conduct regular sabbath services for the district inhabitants. The cost of the entire operation, Chalmers maintained, would be modest (perhaps £100 per annum), and would be met by contributions from society members. In a few years, the combined action of the three programmes would create a viable working-class Christian community in the district. The new working-class community would then undertake, through its own efforts, the expense of erecting a church and school building. Working-class community leaders would assume the responsibility for visitations, sabbath schools, and prayer meetings. Its task complete, the original voluntary society of philanthropists would be disbanded, and a new working-class territorial church would assume an equal place among the existing churches in the city. This emphasis upon creating working-class lay leadership represented a significant shift in Chalmers's social thought. In St. John's, he had placed permanent authority in the hands of middle- and upper-class people. His later home mission experiments at St. Andrews and the Water of Leith had also emphasized middle- and upper-class paternalism. As a result, he had inspired considerable effort and sacrifice from wealthy Evangelicals, but little or no working-class enthusiasm. Now, he made full working-class participation the clear and definite goal. If the working-classes were to be redeeemed by self-reliance and communal benevolence, they would have to assume responsibility for their communities. While the initial effort for cultivating the impoverished irreligious neighbourhoods would be made by outside upper-class philanthropists, their primary purpose would be to prepare the working-class community for self-sustained growth.[4]

The key to Chalmers's new campaign lay in the concept of interdenominational effort. He had now relinquished all hope for a Free Church territorial 'establishment'. He appealed, therefore, to philanthropists from all Protestant denominations—Baptists, Episcopalians, Methodists, Congregationalists, Presbyterian seceders, Free Churchmen—to join him by forming local community-building societies. On the surface, the interdenominational effort would assume the form of competition. Each of the sixty proposed working-class territorial churches would have to be affiliated with an existing denomination. Affiliation, in turn, would depend upon which denomination's members assumed the greater part of the financial and visitation effort in the initial organization of the distict. 'Woe betide the hin'most!' he exclaimed. 'Let us all set forth,—let us strive to outrun each other in this good work,—see who will get congregations formed soonest, and who will form most.'[5]

Chalmers had failed to reach the poorest working-class neighbourhoods with his Church Extension campaign of the 1830s, because, he believed, the Government had refused to provide the endowment grant. He had also failed to reach them through the Free Church. Now, he based his hope upon a vigorous interdenominational competition. There was, meanwhile, another goal to be achieved through interdenominational effort. Ultimately, he argued, competition between the denominations would lead to co-operation in a shared social ideal. The participating denominations would gradually realize that their doctrinal differences were subordinate to the practical Christian duty of benevolence. He confessed to having little appreciation for the theological differences separating the denominations—'for those people, who ... speak of standing up for every "pin in the tabernacle."' If the denominations could co-operate to restore the Christian communal ideal, 'there is no saying what the effect may be'. 'The most blessed result', he observed, 'would follow from such a plan of intermingling co-operation, not only to the district toward which their labours would be directed, but also to themselves. The line of demarcation which separates the various denominations would in that way be trodden and retrodden, so soon to be altogether effaced and invisible.'[6] Eventually, his godly commonwealth of parish communities would be created, not, as he had previously anticipated, by either the Established Church or the Free Church, but by a union of the Protestant denominations.

It was an ambitious programme, and a token of Chalmers's tenacity. Despite the failure of Church Extension, the trauma of the Disruption, and his disappointment with the Free Church, he refused to relinquish his ideal of the godly commonwealth. At the public meeting in February 1842, it will be recalled, Chalmers had promised that once the existing outgoing congregations had been provided with ministers and churches, he would return to his 'old work of Church Extension'. He now resolved to fulfil this promise. With sincere concern for the suffering of the working class, he refused to relent in what he believed was their only hope for a better life—their moral and spiritual regeneration. Weary of the incessant denominational strife of the last decade, he now appealed for Church union, which would be achieved through interdenominational co-operation in a territorial home mission. The campaign represented his final appeal for unity of Christian purpose. He refused to be deterred by those who dismissed his vision as unrealistic. 'Utopianism!' he exclaimed defiantly. 'Who are the Utopians?' Surely not those who believed with him that human nature was essentially the same the world over, and that those 'brought up in the smoke of factories, and amid the ringing din of our mills', nevertheless possessed a soul and conscience, which could be stirred by Christian teaching and human kindness.[7] From the experience of a long career, he assured his audiences that his proposed community-building operation was practical in any district of the country. To prove his point, he announced that he was beginning a model operation in the West Port, one of the most impoverished and crime-ridden districts in Edinburgh. If his operation succeeded in the West Port, he argued, it could be emulated anywhere.

The selection of the West Port demonstrated Chalmers's flair for the dramatic. Sixteen years earlier, the district had achieved national notoriety as the scene of the nefarious deeds of Burke and Hare, two Irish immigrants who made their living smothering drunks, prostitutes, and aged derelicts in the lodging houses for sale as cadavers to the Edinburgh University medical faculty. Their celebrated trial had first awakened the public to the sordid underworld of urban Scotland.[8] While critics had questioned the extent of real poverty in the St. John's parish of Glasgow, there was no doubt that the West Port population was as poor, ignorant, and irreligious as could be found anywhere in Britain. The West Port district was in the south-west portion of Edinburgh's Old Town, under the shadow of the Castle rock. The main road through the district wound down a gradual slope from the edge of the city to the Grassmarket—the traditional site for public hangings in Edinburgh. Immediately to the north of the district was a cattle-market and slaughterhouse. A number of closes, or narrow alleys, branched off from the main road, each forming a separate neighbourhood. At the north-eastern end of the West Port, near the Grassmarket, stood a number of large, ramshackle tenements, like that at 'number one West Port', which according to the 1841 census schedule housed 180 lodgers, mainly unmarried labourers, journeymen, and female servants. To the south-west, there were smaller family dwellings, housing more substantial master masons, butchers, blacksmiths, and shoemakers. No map of the exact district of 2,000 inhabitants selected by Chalmers has survived. While it included the main West Port road, it evidently did not include all the adjoining closes.[9]

Some idea of the district's social composition was revealed by the 1841 census schedules for the main West Port road, and three closes, Killie Brae, Stevenson's Close, and St. Cuthbert's Close, which most certainly were included. The population of this area was 836, of whom 348, or 42 per cent, were born outside Edinburgh, and 110, or 13 per cent, were described as Irish. Occupations were listed for 353 individuals. The largest occupational category was that of general field or farm labourer (70), many of whom had probably recently arrived in the city in search of work. Other major occupations listed were female servants (29), shoemakers and apprentices (25), street-hawkers and pawnbrokers (21), smiths, nailers, and apprentices (21), and carters (10). Virtually all were independent tradesmen or labourers in small manufacturing shops, reflecting the fact that Edinburgh was not an industrial city.[10] Geographical mobility among West Port inhabitants was high. Of a random sample of thirty families with children under five years of age taken from the 1841 census, only six families remained in the area in 1851. Mobility among single lodgers in the overcrowded tenements was even higher: most inhabitants left the district at the first opportunity.[11] A survey conducted by Chalmers and his associates in September 1844 revealed that of 411 families surveyed only 45 families belonged to a Protestant church and 70 families were practising Roman Catholics. Of over 400 school-age children, only 122 attended school.[12] The challenge confronting Chalmers, then, was twofold. First, he had to create a sense of community among the impoverished and fluid population. Secondly, he had to convince them of the value of religious and moral instruction. The West Port exhibited the collapse of the traditional Christian communal ideal in urban Scotland.

Chalmers had, in fact, proposed a territorial church-building operation in the West Port as far back as Januay 1839, when he had delivered a public lecture on the subject, and requested subscriptions and volunteers.[13] The collapse of the Church Extension movement, however, had delayed the project until May 1844, when he began communicating with James Ewan, a young salaried agent of the Edinburgh City Mission, a Dissenter-dominated voluntary society. Ewan was conducting sabbath services on behalf of the City Mission in the old Portsburgh court-house for the West Port and Grassmarket districts. After receiving permission from the City Mission directors, Ewan agreed to assist in Chalmers's West Port territorial operation. Chalmers, meanwhile, gathered a group of supporters, and on 27 July 1844, the first meeting of the West Port Local Society was held in the Portsburgh court-house. By this date, he had recruited ten voluntary visitors—seven middle-class professional men from Edinburgh's wealthy New Town and three respectable West Port inhabitants, selected by Ewan from his congregation. With Ewan's help, Chalmers had also divided the West Port district into twenty proportions of about 100 inhabitants each. At the initial meeting, each of the ten visitors was assigned a proportion and requested to begin regular household visitations immediately. The Society, meanwhile, agreed to meet on a weekly basis, in order to allow the visitors to share with one another reports of their progress and problems. Chalmers experienced difficulty in recruiting the additional ten visitors needed to fill all twenty proportions. The prospect of walking alone through the dangerous West Port closes and stairs was enough to intimidate all but the most intrepid. None the less, by early January, he had managed to recruit at least one, and in some cases two visitors for each proportion.[14]

The visitors formed the vanguard of the West Port community-building operation, with responsibility for permeating the district with religious and moral principles, creating a demand for a church and school, and encouraging communal cohesion and responsibility. Each visitor was to become closely acquainted with the inhabitants of his proportion. He was to introduce them to the gospel and encourage their attendance at Ewan's City Mission sabbath services at the Portsburgh court-house. Above all, he was to encourage working-class participation in the operation, informing the inhabitants of the Society's plan to establish a church, school, and other programmes in the district, but assuring them that their assistance was crucial.[15] Chalmers avoided giving strict directions to his visitors, preferring that they should use their initiative to respond creatively to the unique conditions in each neighbourhood. He was also concerned to dispel the myth that a territorial operation could not succeed without his personal supervision. 'Be assured', he informed the Society on 6 September 1844, 'that our doings will be regarded as far more imitable [by philanthropists elsewhere in the country] if, instead of being stimulated by the personal influence of any one individual, they are quietly and perseveringly performed by each man doing his duty.'[16] He was confident that, in a short time, each visitor would develop a warm, sympathetic relationship with the inhabitants of his proportion.

In marked contrast to his St. John's experiment of 1819-24, Chalmers did not involve his West Port visitors in the distribution of poor relief. The Society maintained no poor-relief fund, and visitors were discouraged from distributing private gifts from their own resources. He would not have his West Port Local Society become simply another voluntary charity society, distributing money on behalf of the upper and middle classes. Nor did he wish to create a competition among the inhabitants for material charity, which would subvert the basic communal purpose of the operation. The only means for the long-term improvement of West Port social conditions, he believed, was to encourage self-help and communal responsibility among the working-class inhabitants themselves. Indeed, a fundamental purpose of the operation was to emancipate the working-classes from any need for middle- and upper-class charity. He later explained to the Countess of Effingham on 10 January 1846: 'I have raised no fund and recommended no method for providing for the temporal wants of the inhabitants of the West Port—convinced that if this formed any ostensible part of our proceedings, it would vitiate and distemper our whole system and raise an insuperable barrier in the way of achieving a pure Christian and moral good among the families of our district.'[17]

Although he refrained from distributing material charity, Chalmers did instruct his visitors to be sensitive to social conditions. They were to seek jobs or apprenticeships for the unemployed, petition the Edinburgh Town Council to close local taverns and remove public health nuisances, and bring cases of extreme destitution or illness to the attention of the city poor-relief authorities.[18] Above all, they were to encourage the poor to develop habits of regular saving. Chalmers placed great hope upon a plan for a West Port district savings bank, open exclusively to West Port inhabitants and operated with the assistance of the visitors. Through participation in a district savings bank, he believed, the inhabitants would learn self-reliance and foresight, while at the same time accumulating enough capital to carry them through periods of unemployment in reasonable comfort. On 9 May 1845, following an address to a meeting of West Port inhabitants, Chalmers formally opened the new bank. According to the plan, the visitors solicited 'penny-a-week' deposits during their visitation rounds. An individual's savings then accumulated in a West Port district bank office until they reached one shilling. At this point, an interest-bearing account was opened for the individual in the National Security Savings Bank of Edinburgh. Money could be withdrawn from this account only with the written permission of the West Port savings bank treasurer. By January 1846, over sixty separate accounts had been established. Although the deposits were small, Chalmers was satisfied that a fair beginning had been made.[19]

Chalmers, it will be noted, placed heavy burdens of responsibility upon his voluntary visitors. Armed with moral and religious principles, they provided the operation's primary thrust into the district. They did not bring with them material charity. Rather, they endeavoured to organize the West Port into a self-respecting and self-sustaining working-class community. At their weekly Society meetings, the visitors discussed their experiences, while Chalmers provided them with occasional instruction in what he regarded as the latest innovations in philanthropic activity—emphasizing public sanitation, temperance, and savings banks. None the less, the burdens placed upon the voluntary visitors were onerous, and their progress was slow. Some visitors demonstrated initiative, organizing weekly neighbourhood prayer meetings and achieving some noticeable improvement in their proportions during the initial months.[20] But for most, as will be seen, the personal dangers of household visiting, the horrors they often discovered in the overcrowded tenements, and their inability to communicate with the inhabitants, proved disheartening.

Once the visitation effort was begun, Chalmers turned his attention to the establishment of a West Port territorial school, and requested William Gibson, superintendent of schools for the Free Church, to help locate a suitable schoolmaster. Gibson recommended Alexander Sinclair, a young teacher who had achieved notable success with working-class youth in Greenock. Late in October 1844, Chalmers invited Sinclair to join his operation, promising him national exposure for an experiment in 'plebian education'. He made no attempt to conceal the grim reality of West Port conditions, but he reaffirmed his belief that intellect was not a function of social class or environment. 'Be assured', he informed Sinclair, 'that you will meet with a full average of talent among the ragged children of this outlandish population. Our great object in fact is to reclaim them from their present outlandishness and raise them to a higher platform.'[21] Sinclair accepted the challenge, and on 11 November 1844 the West Port school was opened. Classes were held in large furnished rooms above a deserted tannery, only a few feet from the tenement where Burke and Hare had dispatched their victims. There were in fact three separate sets of classes under Sinclair's superintendence. First, young boys attended a day school, taught by Sinclair. Secondly, young girls attended Sinclair's day school with the boys in the morning, and in the afternoon received instruction in domestic skills from a Miss Rodgers. Thirdly, adolescents and young adults, of both sexes, attended an evening school for two hours each week-night, taught by a Mr Thomson. The teachers were assisted by several 'monitors', advanced students from the nearby Free Church Normal Academy for teacher training.[22]

The basic curriculum at the school consisted in reading, writing, natural science, geography, and Bible study. There was also additional instruction in English grammar, mathematics, and Latin available to the 'lad o'pairts' who demonstrated special promise or interest.[23] School fees were a modest 2*s*. per quarter for day school pupils, and 1/6*d*. for evening students—about a quarter of the fees required at other Edinburgh schools. Publicly, Chalmers insisted that the fees were mandatory, and he instructed the visitors to collect the fees during their visitation rounds. The fees, he argued, were necessary to impress the families with the value of education. Privately, however, he and Sinclair agreed that no child should be excluded for non-payment, as this would punish children for parental irresponsibility. At no point between November 1844 and March 1846 (the only period for which information on fee payments exists), did more than half the pupils pay their fees, and consequently the schools remained dependent upon funding by the Society.[24] School attendance, meanwhile, increased steadily. In November 1844, 64 attended the day school, and 57 the evening classes. By November 1845, attendance had grown to 250 and 70 respectively.[25]

The success of the schools encourged additional welfare and educational programmes. In December 1844, a laundry room and public bath were constructed in rooms adjoining the school, and a 'bleaching field' for drying clothing was set up on property behind the tannery. All school children were regularly bathed, and boys received periodic haircuts at the Society's expense. In April 1845, Chalmers established a district lending-library in the deserted tannery, with an adult reading-room offering several newspapers and journals. In May 1845, a nursery school was begun, with a divinity student hired as the teacher.[26] Nor did Chalmers neglect his old plan for district sabbath schools. Initially, he requested each visitor to establish a sabbath school in his proportion. The visitors, however, were already overburdened with other responsibilities, and by September 1845 only three sabbath schools had been formed. In October, Chalmers made a fresh start—organizing a separate West Port Sabbath School Society of twenty-two voluntary teachers, mainly women. The sabbath-school movement now progressed rapidly, and by March 1846, about 150 pupils were receiving regular sabbath instruction.[27]

On 6th August 1845, Chalmers held a public exhibition of the West Port schools, inviting a number of influential Edinburgh citizens to the old tannery to view the classrooms and other facilities, and to observe an oral examination of the children. The day went beautifully. The children performed well, and afterwards Chalmers joined them for strawberries and cream—a look of benign contentment upon his face as he sat amid the noise and confusion of the excited youngsters. 'Smile as one might,' Hugh Miller, editor of the *Witness* newspaper, observed of the exhibition in his paper a few days later, 'there is no mistaking the fact, that the minds of these children, which save for this school, would in all probability have slept on for life, were fully awakened.'[28]

While the schools were being organized, Chalmers was also working to create a West Port Free Church congregation. Before the beginning of his operation, it will be recalled, James Ewan was conducting services for the City Mission in the Portsburgh court-house, with an average attendance of 50 at the morning service and 100 at the evening. Although Ewan was not a Free Church member, Chalmers decided that he would make an excellent minister for the proposed West Port Free Church. In November 1844, Ewan's services were moved from the court-house to the schoolrooms above the tannery, and Ewan was enrolled in the Free Church College, in preparation for Free Church ordination.[29] Chalmers's plan went awry, however, when in January 1845 Ewan was discovered to have augmented his meagre £40 per annum City Mission salary by accepting a bribe while arbitrating a financial dispute between two West Port inhabitants. The City Mission requested Ewan's resignation. Although Chalmers's Society retained Ewan's services and now took on the payment of his £40 per annum salary, Chalmers decided he could not risk appointing Ewan minister.[30]

In early February 1845, Chalmers decided upon William Tasker for the West Port ministry. Tasker, a former school teacher and home missionary in Port Glasgow, had entered the Free Church College in late 1843. He was a superior student, and had a bright future ahead of him. Nevertheless, at Chalmers's invitation, he relinquished his considerable prospects elsewhere and committed himself to the West Port.[31] Free Church leaders in Scotland had intended Tasker for the pleasant rural parish of Kilmalcolm, and were enraged when they learned that Chalmers had enlisted him. 'Edinburgh has the command of more than one half of our preachers', Chalmers's long-time supporter, Patrick MacFarlan, complained to another Free Church leader on 6 March 1845. 'If Dr. C. cannot find one so well-fitted as Mr. Tasker for the district in which he takes so deep an interest, he is at least in a better situation than we are who can find none at all for Kilmalcolm.' Chalmers's visionary interdenominational campaign, MacFarlan argued, should not be allowed to deprive real Free Church congregations of needed ministers. But his remonstrances were in vain, and in April 1845, Tasker began work as the West Port missionary, with a salary of £100 per annum (later raised to £150) paid by the West Port Local Society.[32]

Tasker pursued his duties with dogged determination, visiting families, assisting in the schools, and conducting three services each Sunday. Chalmers gave Tasker valuable assistance, accompanying

him on visitation rounds, and occasionally preaching for him (which
attracted vast crowds and large collections). The two men became close
comrades, with shared enthusiasm for the practical details of West Port
progress. Chalmers found this return to the parish ministry exhilarating,
redolent with the memories of younger days. He felt a satisfaction in
immediate, personal relationships with the West Port poor, which he
had missed in his national campaigns. There was again a sense of
communal belonging, and of performing manifest service. Chalmers
and Tasker soon created a regular congregation of over 200 West Port
inhabitants.[33]

It had been Chalmers's original plan that the working-class congregation itself would gradually accumulate the capital needed to build a
church. But he now grew impatient to provide the nation with a more
substantial symbol of West Port progress. In the summer of 1845, he
purchased property in the district for £330, supplied by the West Port
Local Society, and in January 1846 he began soliciting public contributions for a new building to replace the now overcrowded tannery.
Plans for a simple but dignified brick structure, large enough to
accommodate church, schoolrooms, meeting-hall, library, laundry,
and other facilities, were drawn up by a noted Edinburgh architect.
The building was completed in early 1847, at a cost of £2,007.[34]
Chalmers dedicated the church on 19 February 1847. Tasker was
ordained to the ministry, and the West Port Territorial Church was
admitted into the Free Church. The completion of the new church, 'the
child of Dr. Chalmers' old age', marked for him the fulfilment of the
communal vision for urban society, which he had first introduced in
Glasgow over three decades before. 'I wish', he wrote to an American
correspondent on 27 March 1847, 'to communicate what to me is the
most joyful event of my life. I have been intent for 30 years on the
completion of a territorial experiment, and I have now to bless God for
the consummation of it.'[35]

His achievements were impressive. In less than three years, he had
organized well-attended schools and a substantial Free Church congregation in perhaps the most destitute and crime-ridden district in the
city. Hundreds, hitherto untouched by organized philanthropy and
religion, had been provided with opportunities for education, better
hygiene, and neighbourhood worship. None the less, some questions
remain. Had Chalmers in fact fulfilled his promises in his lectures in
the summer of 1844? Had his visitors succeeded in creating a viable,
self-sustaining working-class community? Had he emancipated the
West Port working-classes from the need for middle- and upper-class
charity, or produced significant improvements in social conditions? In
truth, despite the very considerable achievements, his West Port

territorial experiment had proved less than successful in three central purposes of the operation.

First, the visitation effort, intended to permeate the West Port with Christian communal purpose, had in fact collapsed. Many visitors, as mentioned earlier, had rapidly grown disheartened in confronting conditions of poverty and human degradation which were alien to their whole experience. Despite their good intentions, they found themselves unable to communicate with many inhabitants, such as the mother Tasker had discovered pawning a loaf of bread in front of her hungry children for drink, or the participants in a funeral whom he found collapsed in drunken stupor around the corpse.[36] They distributed religious tracts (indeed, by June 1846, the visitors reported having distributed over 4,000 tracts), but to what purpose in a district where most inhabitants were illiterate?[37] They introduced Bible teachings, and gave moral advice, but to what effect? In truth, they would have required more training and stricter direction in order to penetrate the barrier of social class and recognize the real needs of the district. But as Chalmers had become increasingly enthusiastic about the church, schools, and other programmes, he had neglected attending the weekly meetings of the visitors. Gradually, visitors began quitting the Society, while even those who remained ceased regular household visiting. By September 1846, the Society had been forced, because of lack of visitors, to reduce the number of proportions from twenty to fourteen. Of these, two were unoccupied, two had been assigned visitors only within the last three weeks, and one had received no attention from its visitor for several months. Only six visitors reported having even entered their assigned proportions during the previous month. Of the ten original visitors of July 1844, only two remained.

At the 6 September meeting, William Wilson, the most active of the original visitors, confessed 'his district to be sinking into a worse condition than ever'. He had given up his weekly prayer meeting, 'owing to the bad attendance'. At the same time, the Society expressed its despondency over 'the increasing immorality and destitution which prevails in the West Port'. This was, in fact, the last meeting of the West Port Local Society. Chalmers attempted to revive the vistitations with a letter to the Society on 26 September, in which he apologized for his frequent absences and promised to exercise more leadership in the future.[38] His letter, however, was too late. The Society had dissolved and the visitations ceased. The West Port visitors had been among the most dedicated and determined Christian philanthropists in Edinburgh. Their failure demonstrated more than simply Chalmers's flagging power to inspire sustained voluntary philanthropic activity. Rather, it raised serious questions about the effectiveness of purely voluntary effort in the urban slums of the 1840s.

Secondly, the operation had not served to emancipate the West Port working-class community from dependence upon outside middle- and upper-class charity. On 7 March 1845, Chalmers had asserted in a public meeting at Glasgow that a territorial operation for a population of 2,000, such as that in the West Port, could be successfully pursued at a cost of £100 per annum. Several months later, in a public lecture at Edinburgh on 27 December 1845, he raised this estimate slightly to £150 per annum. He had also argued that within a few years, the working-class community would become self-sustaining and assume the responsibility for building and supporting its own church and schools.[39] But in fact, the West Port expenses were far greater than Chalmers claimed. The initial costs for constructing the schoolrooms and other facilities in the deserted tannery, and for providing books, paper, soap, haircuts, heating, etc. had been high. Further, in part because of the ineffectiveness of his voluntary workers, Chalmers had been forced to rely to a greater degree than anticipated upon salaried agents. By 1846, the West Port Society was supporting two missionaries (Tasker and Ewan) at a cost of £190 per annum, and four schoolteachers at £150 per annum. It also employed eight part-time monitors and a part-time librarian.

During the first sixteen months, Chalmers received and spent at least £1,137 in outside donations for his West Port operation.[40] He may, in fact, have received and disbursed far more than this amount, for it is difficult to ascertain precisely the financial arrangements. In marked contrast to his St. John's experiment and Church Extension campaign, in which he had been very forward in publicizing the financial details, he was secretive about West Port finances. The funds were originally kept in a bank account under the authority of several Society business managers. In May 1845, however, Chalmers cleared this account, and deposited the funds in two personal accounts. On 11 October 1845, moreover, he informed the Society that he would no longer regard himself obliged to reveal the amounts he received or disbursed.[41] He evidently intended to conceal the growing costs of the operation. If these costs had become public knowledge, critics might have argued that a West Port operation could succeed only where there was a Chalmers to mobilize donations from wealthy admirers.

Nor would such criticism have been unjustified. Between September 1844 and January 1846, for instance, James Lenox, a wealthy New York lawyer of Scottish descent, donated £1,000 to Chalmers for his West Port operation, on the condition that the gifts remained anonymous.[42] Lenox had never visited Scotland, and his donations were largely an expression of personal admiration for Chalmers. According to William Hanna, £5,500 in outside donations were spent on the West Port operation between 1844 and 1852.[43] Even after 1852, moreover, the West Port church continued to draw large subsidies from the Free Church Sustentation Fund. Chalmers should not be faulted for the amounts spent. There was almost certainly no financial mismanagement. None the less, the fact remains that the West Port operation had consumed nearly ten times the amount of outside financial assistance he had claimed it would require, and that the operation had not become financially self-sustaining. At a similar rate of expenditure for other operations, it would have required over £300,000 for the sixty territorial operations he had requested for the Edinburgh slums alone in his 1844 lectures—nearly three times the sum that had been collected for the general fund during the entire Church Extension campaign of the 1830s.

Finally, Chalmers's operation did not effect significant improvement in West Port social conditions. By 1851, to be sure, Tasker's congregation included more than 400 communicants, while the system of day, evening, and sabbath schools provided instruction to 470 children and young adults.[44] The church and schools attracted a group of upwardly mobile working-class families, prepared to pursue opportunities for social advancement and respectability. Most of these people, however, eventually left the West Port district, only travelling back from other neighbourhoods to attend Tasker's services or the West Port school. The church and school, in fact, functioned largely upon a 'gathered church' principle, attracting the new working-class élite which began to take shape with improving economic conditions in the 1850s. The great mass of West Port inhabitants, however, remained rootless, impoverished, and often lawless. As late as 1869, Tasker complained to the Edinburgh Lord Provost that the overcrowded tenements remained the same 'sink of social and moral pollution' that they had been when 'Dr. Chalmers and I set up our Church and Schools in 1844'.[45] The West Port, in fact, remained one of the worst slum districts in Edinburgh throughout the nineteenth century. Religious and moral instruction alone had not proved sufficient to transform it into the closely-knit community Chalmers had envisaged.

II

At the same time as he was pursuing his West Port model operation, Chalmers had worked vigorously to create public enthusiasm for his interdenominational community-building campaign. In 1844 and 1845, he published three articles in the *North British Review*, in which he again repeated the arguments in favour of his parish community ideal. Only a vigorous territorial ministry, he argued, would preserve the nation from the growing evils of pauperism and working-class political disaffection. A new Scottish poor law, such as that recommended by the Royal Commission, would only aggravate social divisiveness and class conflict.[46] In March 1845, he delivered a public lecture in Glasgow, describing the West Port operation as the culmination of his earlier St. John's experiment and urging Glasgow philanthropists, particularly those who had participated with him in the St. John's experiment and the Church Extension campaign, to join him by beginning similar territorial operations.[47] In Many 1845, it will be recalled, he resigned his convenership of the Free Church Sustentation Fund. He now pledged to devote his remaining strength to his interdenominational campaign. In 1845, moreover, he assumed an active role in organizing Scottish participation in the 'Evangelical Alliance' of Reformed Protestant denominations in Britain, Europe, and America, which was being organized by his friend, the English Dissenter, Edward Bickersteth. He endeavoured in particular to direct the attention of the Alliance to his territorial plan. In the introductory essay to a volume of *Essays on Christian Union*, published in London by supporters of the Alliance in late 1845, he developed his argument that an interdenominational urban mission enterprise would provide the catalyst for Church union. Urban poverty, he argued, was a pressing problem in the entire Western world, and demanded a co-operative territorial mission among all Protestant denominations.[48]

On 27 December 1845, Chalmers invited a group of Edinburgh civic leaders to the Royal Hotel, in the city's New Town. The purpose of the meeting, he explained to his guests, was to report that the Edinburgh campaign which he had announced in his public lectures in the summer of 1844 was now under way. First, he asserted, his West Port model territorial operation was making substantial progress. Indeed, he argued, the West Port model had already demonstrated conclusively that a successful territorial operation could be pursued in any district of the country for the modest cost of £150 per annum. Secondly, and most important, he announced that his West Port model was beginning to inspire additional territorial efforts in the Edinburgh slums. No fewer than five districts for territorial operations, he claimed, had been mapped out by new local visiting societies in the city's destitute Old Town, which promised to establish 'a chain of forts all the way from the South Bridge to the Main Point'. In addition to these five 'forts', he understood that the Duchess of Gordon had promised to pay the expenses for an operation at the lower end of the Canongate, and that members of the Revd James Robertson's United Secession congregation in the Vennel might undertake an operation in the Grassmarket. In a word, it appeared that Chalmers's plan for organizing Edinburgh into Christian communities would soon be fulfilled.[49]

He now appealed for still more effort and financial donations. He described again the elements of his plan, emphasizing the need to enlist the active participation of the working-class inhabitants of a district in the community-building operation. 'I don't think', he observed, 'that you will achieve any permanent good for the population, unless you list them as fellow-workers in, or at least fellow contributors to the cause. I think that a great and radical error in the management of our population has just proceeded from the idea that they are utterly helpless and unable to do anything for themselves ... Unless you enlist their co-operation, you will never achieve anything like permanent good for them.'[50] The entire campaign must be interdenominational. He bristled at accusations by critics that his campaign was in fact an underhanded manoeuvre to secure interdenominational contributions for extending his Free Church. 'Who cares about the Free Church,' he exclaimed, 'compared with the Christian good of the people of Scotland? Who cares for any Church, but as an instrument of Christian good? For, be assured that the moral and religious well-being of the population is infinitely of higher importance than the advancement of any sect.'[51] (Little did his critics realize the extent of his disappointment with the Free Church.)

Impressed by Chalmers's apparent progress, the Edinburgh City Mission now attempted to establish an institutional structure for his campaign. At a public meeting on 30 January 1846, chaired by the Whig Lord Provost, Adam Black, the City Mission directors announced a plan by which each territorial operation established by Chalmers's West Port model would send one delegate to a City Mission general committee. This committee, headed by a salaried, full-time super-intendent, would advertise the campaign, collect subscriptions, and supervise the operations on city-wide level. Because of ill-health, Chalmers was unable to attend the meeting, but he sent a letter of encouragement which was read aloud and published in the report of the proceedings.[52] On 28 February 1846, moreover, he sent further recommendations to Charles Spence, the City Mission secretary. He opposed too much central direction over the individual operations, which he feared might discourage local initiative. But he agreed that a general committee would be valuable for collecting and administering a central mission fund, from which local operations could draw according to their needs.[53] In short, the effort should be pursued along the lines of his former Church Extension campaign, with a balance of local initiative and central direction. It was interesting that the Dissenter, Adam Black, who ten years before had caustically compared Chalmers's territorial communities to Robert Owen's Utopian 'parallelograms', should now assume a leading role in organizing Chalmers's teritorial campaign. With the Established Church broken up, Black had evident-ly reconsidered his former objections to a territorial ministry, at least among the urban working classes.

Despite initial progress and City Mission support, Chalmers's campaign soon lost momentum. Most of the proposed territorial operations which he had described in his address of December 1845 collapsed during the next few months. The 'chain of forts', in Edinburgh's Old Town never materialized. Only three operations modelled upon his West Port experiment were actually pursued—two in Edinburgh, and one in Glasgow. These apparently had some success in extending church accommodation and educational opportunities, but like the West Port operation, they required considerable financial contributions and did not radically transform their working-class districts.[54] After several months of effort, the City Mission relinquished its plan for the general committee, and by late 1846 Chalmers's campaign was effectively finished.

His concept of a territorial urban mission for the revival of Christian communal sentiment had failed to capture the imagination of Scottish philanthropists. Despite his new emphasis upon working-class participation and interdenominational co-operation, Chalmers's West Port operation had represented essentially the same social position that he had advocated in Kilmany over three decades before—that only religious and moral instruction, directed towards restoring traditional Christian values, would secure the welfare of the working classes. But by the mid-1840s, public interest in his godly commonwealth ideal had waned, hastened by the failure of Church Extension and the Disruption. In August 1845, the new Scottish poor law received the Royal assent, and secular poor-law districts and workhouses began to replace the traditional system of parish poor relief. The secular State also began to extend its influence in the areas of public health and education,[55] and the Scottish churches increasingly withdrew from social welfare. Chalmers's West Port operation had represented an impressive effort to revive the social ideal to which he had devoted most of his life's work; but he now lacked the energy and tenacity of his younger days. With the failure of his territorial mission in 1846, he began to realize that Scotland had changed radically since his youth in rural Anstruther and Kilmany, and that these changes perhaps could not be reversed.

In December 1846, shortly after the collapse of Chalmers's final church extension effort, Richard Oastler, the celebrated Tory factory reformer, travelled to Scotland to agitate for the Ten Hours Bill, a proposed Parliamentary measure to limit the working day for factory labour. Oastler placed particular emphasis upon gaining Chalmers's support. For a significant portion of Scotland's middle and upper classes, Chalmers remained the most dedicated 'friend of the working classes'; yet he had consistently opposed factory legislation. Through Chalmers's friend and former student, George Lewis, Oastler managed to obtain an interview with him.[56] So important did Oastler regard the conversation, that he later wrote a full account of it from memory.

At first, Chalmers expressed his total opposition to Oastler's campaign. He was, he claimed, an advocate of free trade, who had long opposed State intervention in industry and commerce, as well as in social welfare. Only the Christian and moral education of the working classes would rescue them from their present misery. But Oastler refused to accept Chalmers's objections. Throughout his career, Oastler insisted, Chalmers had in fact opposed Classical Liberal economics, especially the Liberal economists' emphasis upon self-interest and the 'invisible hand'. 'The Christian', Oastler asserted, in paraphrase of Chalmers's often-expressed sentiments, 'knows that Society is one compact body, each individual member being dependent on the rest, each requiring the protection of all. The Free-Trader, on the contrary, persuades himself that each member is a separate piece of independence, an isolated self.' Oastler reviewed at length the horrors of factory conditions, horrors that Chalmers himself had vividly described in his 1832 debate with J. R. McCulloch. Only Parliamentary legislation, Oastler maintained, could now preserve the Christian commonwealth against the growing evils of unrestrained industrial capitalism. Chalmers suddenly relented. He did not relinquish his lifelong support for free trade. But he did now pledge his full support to Oastler's Ten Hours Bill, and gave him a letter of introduction to several influential friends. At a public meeting in Edinburgh on 24 December 1846, Oastler was able to announce that Chalmers was now a participant in the Ten Hours movement, an endorsement of no small consequence for the movement in Scotland.[57] It was, for Chalmers, a significant conversion. With the collapse of his territorial church and community-building campaign, he began to acknowledge that the State was perhaps the only available regulator of social relations with sufficient power to preserve the weak from the strong.

In the autumn of 1845, the potato crop in Ireland, and in the Highlands and Islands of Scotland, had failed, leaving literally hundreds of thousands facing starvation. This was followed by an even worse failure in the autumn of 1846. The famine was the great tragedy of nineteenth-century British history, and a tragedy peculiarly localized on the Celtic fringe. In November 1846, Chalmers assumed an active role in organizing the famine-relief effort, and issued urgent appeals for subscriptions. Largely through his efforts, the Free Church collected over £15,000, assuming the leading role among Scottish churches in the relief effort.[58] In the early months of 1847 the situation grew more urgent. Typhus and other epidemic diseases swept through the famine-stricken populations, and numerous cases of death by starvation began to be reported.

Private philanthropy, meanwhile, was proving insufficient. Many, in fact, refused to contribute to relief efforts, on the grounds that it would only encourage the 'notorious' lack of foresight and 'moral restraint' among the Gaelic poor of Ireland and the Scottish Highlands. The poor had brought their misery upon themselves; to support them through the famine would only be to attempt to circumvent Malthus's iron law of population—an attempt doomed to failure. Better to let nature take its course and remove by starvation the redundant population, than to attempt to keep it alive by artificial means. The Whigs, moreover, were now back in office. In their commitment to the doctrine of *laissez-faire*, their Government was hesitant to provide State relief in any significant amounts, and indeed was attempting to close the public-works projects, soup-kitchens, and other relief facilities currently in operation.

Chalmers was appalled by such attitudes. It was, he asserted in a letter published in the Edinburgh *Witness* on 6 March 1847, 'presumptuous and unwarrantable in the highest degree' to attribute the famine to the faults of the suffering poor themselves. It was not the Christian's place to condemn his fellow man; rather, he should do all in his power to relieve suffering, according to the simple Scriptural law of compassion. 'If the agonies and cries of those dying creatures', he warned, ''do not reach our ears to the awakening of an effectual compassion, it may be that they shall reach the ears of Him who sitteth above, to the effect of a fearful retribution upon ourselves.' Above all, he demanded more substantial Government relief grants to supplement private philanthropy. 'It would have been wrong, certainly, in the public to have abstained from their subscriptions in the hope that Government would do all. But is it right in the Government to abstain from their grants in the hope that we, the public, will do all?'[59]

Chalmers developed these ideas further in a long article, 'The Political Economy of a Famine,' published in the *North British Review* in May 1847. Only a massive redistribution of national wealth, he argued, would save the British nation from the horror and guilt of mass starvation within its shores. He agreed with Daniel O'Connell that at least £30,000,000 was now needed. Private philanthropy would not be sufficient to raise such a sum. Rather, the Government must raise most of the money through massive direct taxation upon the luxuries of the wealthy. The nation must finally transcend the doctrines of *laissez-faire* economics, forsaking its 'deification' of commercial and industrial expansion in favour of the higher glory of compassion. Nor, he insisted, would mere grants of State relief assistance be enough. There must be a Parliamentary Commission to supervise the distribution of relief, and to halt profiteering by grain merchants. Further, this

Commission must broaden its inquiry to include a large-scale survey of social conditions in Ireland, in preparation for major land reform and poor-law reform once the crisis was over. In describing his plan for massive State intervention in the economy, he cited his first major work of political economy, the 1808 *Enquiry into the Extent and Stability of National Resources*. He reaffirmed his adherence to the basic principles of this work—that massive Governmental taxation and management of the economy were necessary to preserve the common welfare against self-interested commercial and industrial élites. In 1808, the occasion for his appeal for increased State intervention had been the Napoleonic threat to Britain's independence; now it was the threat of starvation to a significiant portion of Britain's population. In his conclusion, Chalmers promised to publish several more articles in the *North British Review* detailing his plans for reform of the Irish land tenures and poor law.[60]

His social thought had finally run full circle. With the collapse of his church extension effort in 1846, and the prospect of mass starvation in Ireland and the Highlands and Islands of Scotland, he returned to many of his 1808 views. His Evangelical Christian faith remained unshaken, but he now accepted that the power of the Church and private Christian philanthropy to preserve the general social welfare against the self-interest of the few was declining. He began to relinquish his ideal of the godly commonwealth directed by a territorial national Church, and to regard the State as the only institution capable of enforcing social justice. It was ironic that his attempts to inspire a private relief effort in Scotland should have been shadowed by the very Malthusian doctrines which he had helped to disseminate. In fairness, however, it must be observed that Chalmers had never allowed his Malthusian views to supersede Christian compassion, nor suggested that the 'redundant' population should be allowed to starve. It is interesting to speculate on what views he might have expressed in his proposed *North British Review* articles—whether he would have retreated still further from his opposition to legal poor relief and the secularization of social welfare in the wake of the famine. But although the proposed articles were never written, one thing is fairly certain: like so many other dreams, Chalmers's godly commonwealth ideal succumbed to the grim realities of the great famine of 1846-7, which both devastated the Celtic population and destroyed his confidence in the sufficiency of purely voluntary benevolence.

Early in May 1847, Chalmers travelled to London in the company of his son-in-law, John Mackenzie. His primary purpose in the journey was to deliver oral testimony before a Select Committee of the House of Commons, appointed to investigate Free Church complaints of difficulties in obtaining sites for new churches. A number of landed proprietors, including the powerful Duke of Sutherland, had persisted in refusing to sell property to the Free Church. In some districts, particularly in the Highlands where individual landholdings were vast, this made it impossible for congregations to build churches. Chalmers appeared before the Committee on 12 May. Sir James Graham, evidently hearing of Chalmers's dissatisfaction with some of the positions taken by the Free Church, pressed him hard during the examination about the entire Disruption controversy, hoping for a partial recantation that might open the way for eventual reconciliation. But Chalmers refused to back down from his position that it was the State's refusal to recognize the Church's spiritual independence which had forced the Disruption. Frustrated, Graham grew increasingly caustic in his questioning, and the examination degenerated into a cruel but unsuccessful attempt to catch Chalmers in inconsistencies. Chalmers held his ground remarkably well, until finally the other Committee members were obliged to silence Graham and end the testimony.[61] There had been no recantation.

While in London, Chalmers took the opportunity to call upon old acquaintances. He visited and prayed with the widow of his brother James, who had died a few years before. 'It was a serious interview,' he wrote his wife, 'and my brother's faithful and vivid picture has haunted me ever since.' On 14 May, he called upon Thomas Carlyle and his wife at Chelsea.[62] Carlyle raised the subject of the Disruption and the 'Free Kirk War', but Chalmers had no desire to speak of this, and 'softly let it drop'. Instead, they spoke of Chalmers's territorial community ideal, and of his boyhood friend from the Anstruther district, the painter, Sir David Wilkie, who had died a few years before. Chalmers had just been viewing Wilkie's work in the National Gallery, and he now related how Wilkie had often struggled 'long and to no purpose' before he could capture precisely the right symbol to convey the moral message in one of his romantic pastoral paintings. The conversation circled around the communal virtues of rural Scotland in which Chalmers and Carlyle had been raised, and which both had struggled to convey to a rapidly changing nation. 'Chalmers', Carlyle later recalled, 'was very beautiful to us during that hour; grave, not too grave, earnest, cordial; face and figure very little altered, only the head had grown white, and in the eyes and features you could read something of a serene sadness, as if evening and silent star-crowned night were coming on, and the hot noises of the day were growing unexpectedly insignificant to one.'[63]

Chalmers arrived back in Edinburgh on the evening of 28 May, after an overland journey that included a visit to his sister in Gloucestershire. He was weary from the trip, and rested in bed most of the following day. Friends and family were concerned about his health, but he waved off their anxieties. 'I do not by any means feel unwell,' he informed a caller whom he received at his bedside, 'I only require a little rest.' On Sunday, 30 May, he attended worship, and called upon his old friend from the Kilmany district, Janet Coutts. He was too weary to conduct family worship that evening, but promised to lead family prayer in the morning. He retired early, 'bidding his family remember that they must be early tomorrow' for prayer, and wishing all 'a general good-night'. But the next morning, he was not up as promised. At eight, the housekeeper entered the room to wake him. She found him sitting half-erect in bed, leaning against the headboard. He had been dead for hours. Apparently he had succumbed to a sudden heart failure shortly after leaving his family the night before.[64]

Chalmers was buried in Edinburgh on 4 June 1847. The funeral service was held in Free St. Andrew's church, in the presence of the Free Church General Assembly and deputations from the Presbyterian Churches of England and Ireland. Following the service, a procession of over 2,000 mourners, headed by the Magistrates and Town Council, began a slow, winding march of three miles through the city to the Grange cemetery. Most of the shops and businesses were closed for the solemn event, and the route was lined with an estimated 100,000 silent spectators. As the procession moved through the Old Town, it was joined by the congregation of the West Port church. It was a gloomy day, with a heavy mist and a raw east wind. Nevertheless, as the funeral procession reached the Grange cemetery, it found the surrounding fields already filled with thousands of mourners. 'The appearance', recalled one observer, 'was that of an army.' 'Never before, in at least the memory of man,' the *Witness* reported the following day, 'did Scotland witness such a funeral.... It was the dust of a Presbyterian clergyman that the coffin contained; and yet they were burying him amid the tears of a nation, and with more than kingly honours.'[65]

III

Chalmers had been a man of one seminal vision—the elevation of the nation through a communal social ideal, based upon a shared Christian purpose. The social dislocations of early industrialization had convinced him that social happiness would not be achieved by the iron laws of the market economy. While he acknowledged the role of self-interest in the economy, he argued that it alone was not enough to preserve the larger social fabric. Rather, individuals had to subordinate self-interest to the general welfare and embrace the values of communal responsibility and benevolence. True freedom for the individual would be achieved only through conscious subordination of self-interest to a Divine purpose. His godly commonwealth ideal offered a communal alternative to the social anxieties and suffering of early industrialization—a turning backward to an idealized past, when, he assured the nation, the social orders had lived in communal harmony, and sacrificed together for common ideals represented by a national covenant with God. Chalmers was a communitarian, part of a rich early nineteenth-century communitarian movement that included such varied figures as William Godwin and Robert Owen. His considerable influence in Britain indicated that a large portion of the population was profoundly disturbed by the rate of social change in the early industrial era, and longed to return to a stable social organization characterized by close, personal interrelationships.

With his communal vision, Chalmers provided a social direction to the early nineteenth-century Evangelical revival. His Evangelical piety embraced not only an intense passion for men's souls, but also a genuine concern for their temporal happiness, which for him meant not only a degree of material comfort, but also human companionship, and faith in a loving and forgiving God. He was an inspiring preacher, who motivated the educated middle and upper classes with a combination of Evangelical piety and communal benevolence. Some of his specific remedies for the social suffering in early nineteenth-century Britain, to be sure, were misguided—for instance, his demand for the total abolition of assessment-based legal poor relief, and his insistence that religious and moral instruction alone would greatly improve the condition of the working classes. None the less, his demand that Christians express their faith through social service, and his support for the extension of popular education and church accommodation, constituted significant steps towards improving social conditions. By encouraging middle- and upper-class Evangelicals to enter the urban slums on visitation programmes, moreover, he helped to increase public awareness of social conditions and to foster debate over the causes and cures of industrial poverty, which had considerable impact upon later developments in social policy.

Chalmers's influence was limited mainly to the educated upper and middle classes, and especially to the young. He managed to inspire impressive voluntary efforts from lay-visitors and sabbath-school teachers, who embraced his Christian communal vision with enthusiasm. He never succeeded, however, in inspiring the same enthusiasm among the working classes. Despite his concern for their moral and material welfare, he neither gained their full confidence, nor convinced them that their condition would improve within his ideal parish communities. The new industrial working classes were being lost to organized religion during the nineteenth century, and Chalmers proved unable to reverse this trend. None the less, he was a great theorist of an Evangelical pastoral ministry, whose influence upon the clergy and laity of the Church helped to alleviate some of the worst suffering of the early industrial revolution—until the secular State began to realize that neither the Church nor private philanthropy was sufficient to meet the social challenges, and that new systems of social service adminis-tration had to be developed under State authority.

Chalmers was also a considerable ecclesiastical politician, who extended the social influence of the Scottish Establishment. In the late 1830s, he created a personal ascendancy within the Church of Scotland unlike any since the era of John Knox. With his Church Extension Committee, and (after 1837) his dominance of the hierarchy of Church courts, he managed to consolidate his power at virtually every level of Church activity. The Church Extension campaign of 1834-41 was the climax of his career. Through this campaign, he thwarted the Volun-tary threat of disestablishment, formed a solid Evangelical majority around his godly commonwealth ideal, and created over 220 parish churches, most of them in the new urban centres. He convinced a considerable portion of the Scottish nation (although not the British Government) that the Establishment had to be made sufficient to provide religious and moral instruction to every inhabitant, not simply the wealthy or those with previous Christian conviction. For a time, it appeared that he would realize his vision; but in the final event, the State refused to provide the endowments that were necessary to enable the Church to expand to the urban slums, and the movement collapsed. In truth, the British State ultimately had no intention of allowing the Church of Scotland to reassert the authority it had once held over Scottish society. It was committed to defending the rights of Dissenters, which would have been threatened within Chalmers's ideal Evangelical commonwealth. Perhaps more important, the State was beginning to expand its own administrative authority, and in particular was en-deavouring to create administrative uniformity in such matters as poor relief throughout every part of Britain and Ireland. Some kind of con-flict between the militant Evangelical Church of Scotland and the expanding British State had become almost inevitable by the late 1830s. This conflict finally surfaced in the non-intrusion controversy, and later developed into the more fundamental controversy over the Church's spiritual independence. Once the conflict had begun, the State's condition for peace was the Church's acknowledgement of the State's sole and absolute sovereignty. There could be, both the civil courts and Parliament declared, no 'two kingdoms'—spiritual and temporal—with shared authority over Scottish society; there could be no 'spiritual independence' for the Established Church. But Chalmers would not acquiesce. He chose to lead the Disruption, rather than passively witness the humiliation of his Church.

The Disruption represented the final failure of his godly commonwealth ideal. His attempts to revive it through the Free Church, and later through his interdenominational church-building campaign, proved unsuccessful. Indeed, the Disruption was not only the greatest failure of Chalmers's career, but also a tragedy for organized religion in Scotland. It broke up the Establishment, ensuring that the Church would never again exercise the same influence over Scottish society as it had before 1843. For the remainder of the nineteenth century, Scottish religious life was characterized by competition between the residual Establishment, the Free Church, and the Dissenters, which thwarted the revival of any national feeling of Christian community. Chalmers has been blamed for the Disruption, and characterized as the 'evil genius' behind the decline of religious influence in Scottish society.[66] In many respects, to be sure, he did contribute to the growing tension between Church and State in the years prior to the Disruption. One of the great ironies of his career was that although a superb ecclesiastical politician, he was never able to function effectively in secular politics.

In part, this resulted from his failure to understand either the conventions or the dominant personalities of political life. Further, he was an idealist, and once firmly convinced of the righteousness of his cause—once he believed he was representing God's will for mankind—he found it difficult to retreat from his principles. He tended to regard his opponents as enemies of God's cause and to indulge in expressions of 'moral loathing' for Voluntaries, Whigs, Tories, or any group or individual who thwarted his purpose. The same stubborn tenacity which had characterized him as a young man, struggling for a church living or university chair, remained with him after his Evangelical conversion and his discovery of a larger social vision. He looked for truth in the Bible, in Church traditions, and in his own reason, rather than in the political Constitution, or the debates between adversary groups in the political forums of Parliament and the public press. In many respects, the very characteristics which had enabled him to rise to leadership within the militant Evangelical Church of the 1830s—his tenacity, single-mindedness, and certainty in his principles—made it difficult for him to lead the Church in retreat before the civil courts and Government in the 1840s. Adding to these difficulties, moreover, was his opposition to privileged élites—an opposition which remained a powerful motivating force throughout his life. The British State was dominated by such élites—the landed interest, rising commercial and industrial interests, and professional politicians. He found it difficult to understand or respect these holders of real power.

However, Chalmers should not be held entirely responsible for the bitter controversies which led to the Disruption. Leading politicians, including Melbourne, Peel, and Aberdeen, demonstrated lack of understanding for the conventions of the Church of Scotland, and a tendency to dismiss Chalmers as a 'madman' or 'scoundrel' when he refused to accept their demands. If he hated their 'privilege', they, in turn, often treated him with contempt, and evidently sought to discredit him personally, as a means of breaking up the Evangelical ascendancy and restoring the Church to quiescence. They failed in this attempt, for in the final analysis the issues at stake in the Church-State controversy—endowments for new churches, the need for an increased popular voice in the administration of church patronage, the 'spiritual independence' of an Established Church—transcended the personalities involved. Despite all the bitter consequences of the Disruption, Chalmers had surely been right in the stand he had taken. Although it had meant sacrificing his godly commonwealth vision, he and the Evangelicals had delivered a powerful message to the modernizing British State—that a Christian Church, whether Established or not, must be independent from State authority in matters of internal spiritual discipline, and must be free to pursue its spiritual mission to the whole of society.

As an ecclesiastical politician, Chalmers had also advanced the laicization of the Church. The Moderate party of the early years of the nineteenth century, with its social ideal of 'enlightened elitism', had discouraged any popular voice in the appointment of parish clergy, and neglected the traditional lay offices of elder and deacon. Chalmers's Evangelical ministry, however—in particular his organization of sabbath-school teachers into what amounted to a third lay office, his Church Extension campaign, and his advocacy of the right of heads of families in a parish to veto an unacceptable presentation—represented a major attempt to increase the role of the laity in Church affairs.

In all these efforts, to be sure, his emphasis had been upon middle- and upper-class lay participation. In the West Port operation of the 1840s, however, he also began to perceive the need for increased working-class lay participation in Church affairs. Although not a political democrat, Chalmers's policies which extended lay authority helped to ensure that Church life reflected the movement towards democracy in nineteenth-century Britain. Here again, his lifelong opposition to privilege had been translated into positive action. It was this aspect of Chalmers's work that most impressed many American observers, among them Charles Richmond Henderson, the late nineteenth-century advocate of the 'social gospel' and Professor of Sociology at the University of Chicago. 'The lofty and noble figure of Dr. Chalmers', Henderson observed in the *American Journal of Theology* in January 1900, 'characterizes the transition from clerical and aristocratic dominance to modern democracy in church and state.'[67]

Along with his impact upon ecclesiastical life, Chalmers also made significant contributions to the development of method and theory in the administration of charity, particularly in the urban environment. In his work in St. John's, the Water of Leith, and the West Port, he provided a model of Christian philanthropy, which influenced the development of social work as an independent discipline. Three themes of his social ideal exercised particular influence. First, there was the principle of 'locality', or the idea that social activists should focus upon improving conditions in a small and well-defined territorial district. Secondly, there was his principle of 'aggression', or the concept that activists should regularly visit the households of a district, seeking out the 'invisible' victims of poverty, convincing the ignorant of the value of education, and reaching to the immoral with kindness, concern, and advice. Thirdly, there was his emphasis upon moral and religious intruction as the most effective response to poverty, and his opposition to legal 'pauperism' as a degrading influence upon the poor. Every effort, he argued, had to be made to preserve the self-respect and independence of the poor. Only when there was no other recourse should an individual be granted material charity; and then that charity should be combined with careful investigations by visitors, and be given discreetly, in order to avoid public stigma upon the recipient.

From the early 1820s, voluntary charity societies throughout Britain had begun adopting Chalmers's principles, particularly as they were described in his *Christian and Civic Economy,* published between 1819 and 1826. Chalmers's writings also apparently had some influence upon the development of the Elberfeld system of poor-relief visitations in Rhenish Prussia, which was established in its mature form in 1853, and which inspired similar operations in towns and villages throughout Germany. It was, however, upon the Charity Organization Society of London, founded in 1869, over twenty years after his death, that Chalmers's teachings exercised their most direct influence. The COS assumed a major role in rationalizing and refining the techniques of charitable administration and visiting; within twenty-five years, it had disseminated its principles to over eighty-five corresponding organizations in British cities and towns. The founders of the COS, and especially its first secretary, Charles Loch, had regarded Chalmers as their 'patron saint'. Their movement borrowed heavily from his ideas, including the principles of local territorial administration, household visitations, thorough investigation of all applicants for relief, and the use of educational methods to encourage independence and social responsibility among the poor. The COS, to be sure, made some departures from Chalmers's teachings, advocating, for instance, State involvement in social welfare, and regarding assessment-based legal poor-relief as an absolute necessity in industrial society.[68]

In the United States, advocates of the 'social gospel' in the late nineteenth-century urban centres also discovered Chalmers's writings, in part through the publications of the London COS. In 1900, Charles Richmond Henderson of the University of Chicago published an abridged edition of Chalmers's *Christian and Civic Economy,* with a lengthy commentary recommending the work as a model for rational Christian philanthropy in industrial society. Chalmers's pragmatic and comprehensive approach to social problems, Henderson argued, had established him as one of the pioneers in the development of the science of sociology.[69] In her highly influential text on social work, *Social Diagnosis,* first published in 1917, the American reformer, Mary Richmond, credited Chalmers for being one of the founders of case work in social welfare administration, citing his emphasis upon systematic visitations and investigation of relief recipients.[70]

Chalmers also made significant contributions to educational reform, and particularly to the extension of popular education. He was, indeed, primarily an educator, spending most of his career as a university professor. His Christian communal ideal rested largely upon the education of all men in a set of shared Christian and moral ideals. As a university professor, he contributed to reforms in patronage and financial administration. He helped to broaden the study of moral philosophy in Scotland, rejecting the obsessive concern with epistemology that had characterized the eighteenth-century 'common sense' school, and giving fresh emphasis to questions of practical ethics. He was not an original theologian, and his posthumously published Edinburgh lectures in theology, the two-volume *Institutes of Theology,* has been a disappointment to many of his supporters. The most original aspect of the *Institutes* is the organization of the work, which in many respects is in the form of an extended Evangelical sermon. Beginning with the 'disease' of mankind—man's innate sinfulness and alienation from God—he demonstrates how only the doctrines of salvation in Scripture can penetrate beyond the mere symptoms of man's alienation and reach to the actual disease. In truth, the *Institutes* reveals a mind struggling against doubts about some of the harsher doctrines of scholastic Calvinism and seeking a more personal form of Christianity—while at the same time concerned not to challenge openly the Calvinist orthodoxy of the Westminster Confession which he was bound by his professorial office to uphold. The experience of Erskine of Linlathen and Macleod Campbell had evidently made a profound impact on Chalmers, and his concern for the ecclesiastical organization and Evangelical mission of the Church discouraged him from experimenting in his lectures or in print with new theological ideas. In another, more peaceful time, Chalmers might have been a first-rate theologian, but he did not perceive the turbulent 1830s and 1840s to have been such a time.

His real impact as a Professor of Divinity lay in his regular lecture-hall discussion of such subjects as pastoral visiting and counselling, administration of charity, and political economy—which until his professorship were not regarded as proper subjects in the Divinity Hall. He also encouraged his students to gain practical experience through missionary work in the Edinburgh slums. If the Church, he believed, were to assume a more decisive social role, its candidates for the ministry would require a broad exposure to the social, economic, and political challenges confronting society. He succeeded in training a generation of dedicated parish ministers sensitive to the challenges of rapid urbanization and industrialization. His influence helped to broaden the scope of education in divinity throughout Scotland.

But probably more important were his contributions to the development and expansion of popular education. In Glasgow and Edinburgh, his parish day-schools and sabbath-schools became models for similar efforts throughout Scotland. He had demonstrated not only that it was possible to establish inexpensive territorial schools in urban working-class districts, but also that there was a tremendous demand for educational opportunity among the urban working classes. Even in the grim West Port of Edinburgh, the inhabitants embraced education as affording hope for their children to enjoy a decent life. Chalmers argued with eloquence and power that society owned every individual the opportunity to receive a good education, in order to fulfil his human potential. Indeed, society could only neglect this obligation at the peril of profound upheaval. Chalmers's Church Extension campaign created dozens of parish schools as well as parish churches, while the Free Church later continued his emphasis upon the extension of popular education. His efforts helped to preserve Scotland's Reformation heritage of the 'democratic intellect' into the industrial era.

Chalmers failed to realize his vision of the godly commonwealth. His life was, in one sense, a tragic disappointment. He lived long enought to witness the collapse of the Church Extension campaign of 1838, the breakup of the Establishment in 1843, the rejection of his social ideal by the majority of the Free Church by 1845, and the failure of his final interdenominational Church Extension campaign by 1846. After his death in 1847, his godly commonwealth vision faded rapidly from the public imagination, lost amid the sectarian controversies of the later nineteenth century, and overshadowed by the new materialistic visions of capitalism and State socialism. None the less, in striving for his ideal, he had also made substantial and lasting contributions to ecclesiastical, social, and educational reform. In the final analysis, perhaps the greatest contribution of Chalmers and his godly commonwealth ideal was an inspirational one—encouraging others to strive for social improvement with a sustained and unselfish commitment to God and the future good of mankind. 'We never met with an individual', one of his students later recalled, 'who had the power Dr. Chalmers possessed of lifting the mind above earthly views.'[71] He was, in many respects, an emphatically practical social reformer, with well-defined programmes for the reorganization of the nation. But he was also a visionary, who touched the conscience of his age.

NOTES

Abbreviations Used in References

BL	British Library
EUL	Edinburgh University Library
NCL	New College Library, Edinburgh University
NLS	National Library of Scotland
NRA (Scot.)	National Register of Archives (Scotland)
OPR	Old Parish Records
SCHS	*Records of the Scottish Church History Society*
SHR	*Scottish Historical Review*
SRO	Scottish Records Office
TCP	Thomas Chalmers Papers, New College Library

Chapter One: Ambition and Community

1. J. Forrester, 'Parish of Anstruther Wester', *The Statistical Account of Scotland*, ed. Sir John Sinclair (21 vols., Edinburgh, 1791-9), iii. 77-88; anon., 'Parish of Anstruther Easter', ibid. xvi. 244.

2. L. Namier and J. Brooke, *The History of Parliament: The House of Commons, 1754-1790* (3 vols., HMSO, 1964), ii. 24; W. Wood, *The East Neuk of Fife* (Edinburgh, 1887), 227-30.

3. Namier and Brooke, *The History of Parliament*, i. 498-500; D. Cook, *Annals of Pittenweem* (Anstruther, 1867), 148; H. Furber, *Henry Dundas* (London, 1931), 245; H. Dundas to Lady Anstruther, 11 April 1789 (SRO, Melville Muniments, GD 51/1/198/10/11). For an account of political life in a similar grouping of Scottish royal burghs, see W. Ferguson, 'Dingwall Burgh Politics and the Parliamentary Franchise in the Eighteenth Century', *SHR*, xxxviii (October 1959), 89-108.

4. G. Gourlay, *Anstruther* (Anstruther, 1888), 141-2; Anne Simson Chalmers Hanna, 'Short Account of her Family', unpubl. MS, (TCP, CHA 6, 'Family Records' box).

5. Correspondence between John Chalmers and George Hall, 1780-5, and documents relating to the sloop, *Friendship*, 1785-6 (TCP, CHA 1); James Chalmers to John Chalmers, 27 September 1800 (TCP, CHA 1, 'Family Letters 1'); John Chalmers to James Chalmers, 30 October 1804 (CHA 1, 'Family Letters 3'); Anne Simson Chalmers Hanna, 'Short Account of her Family' (TCP, CHA 6). The total loss of one of John Chalmers's sloops with its cargo in a storm in the autumn of 1802 was also a serious blow. See, T. Chalmers to Mrs Kedie, 12 October 1802, in W. Hanna, ed., *A Selection from the Correspondence of the Late Thomas Chalmers* (Edinburgh, 1853), 49-50.

6. Gourlay, *Anstruther*, 142-3.

7. John Chalmers to James Chalmers, 24 April 1805 (TCP, CHA 1, 'Family Letters 3').

8. John Chalmers to James Chalmers, 18 May 1807 (TCP, CHA 1, 'Family Letters 3').

9. Anne Simson Chalmers Hanna, 'Short Account of her Family'; Elizabeth Hall Chalmers's account book, containing records of her disbursements to the

Anstruther poor (TCP, CHA 1); E. Chalmers to James Chalmers, 23 July, 17 October 1812, 2 December 1813 (TCP, CHA 1, 'Family Letters 3').

10. W. Hanna, *Memoirs of Dr. Chalmers* [hereafter, *Memoirs*] (4 vols., Edinburgh, 1849-52), i. 36-7, 98-100.

11. *Parliamentary Papers,* Reports from Commissioners, Universities (Scotland): 3. St. Andrews, 1837 (94) xxxvii, 252.

12. Ibid. 292-3.

13. R. G. Cant, *The University of St. Andrews: A Short History* (Edinburgh, 1970), 99-100; J. B. Morrell, 'The Leslie Affair: careers, kirk and politics in Edinburgh in 1805', *SHR,* liv (April 1975), 63-82; G. Cook, *The Life of George Hill* (Edinburgh, 1820), 211-15, 235-47.

14. Thomas Duncan to W. Hanna, 21 January 1848 (TCP, CHA 2, Hanna Letters).

15. Ibid.; James Miller to John MacKenzie, 6 July 1847; Robert F. Gourlay to W. Hanna, 19 November 1847 (TCP, CHA 2, Hanna Letters).

16. Hanna, *Memoirs,* i. 465-7; Morrell, 'The Leslie Affair', 70-1; 'Letters chiefly addressed to James Brown' (EUL, Dc. 2. 57).

17. J. Miller to W. Hanna, 21 January 1848 (TCP, CHA 2, Hanna Letters).

18. T. Chalmers to William Chalmers, 4 January 1794 (TCP, CHA 3.1.10); T. Chalmers, 'That the miser is more pernicious to society', unpubl. MS, (TCP, CHA 6).

19. T. Duncan to W. Hanna, 21 January 1848 (TCP, CHA 2, Hanna Letters); Hanna, *Memoirs,* i. 15.

20. G. Hill, *Lectures in Divinity,* ed. A. Hill (Philadelphia, 1842), 541-86; Cook, *Life of George Hill,* 219-35, 397-401.

21. William Burns to W. Hanna, 9 June 1847 (TCP, CHA 2, Hanna Letters).

22. T. Chalmers to John Chalmers, 24 November 1796 (TCP, CHA 3.1.17); T. Duncan to W. Hanna, 21 January 1848 (TCP, CHA 2, Hanna Letters).

23. W. Burns to W. Hanna, 9 June 1847 (TCP, CHA 2, Hanna Letters).

24. H. W. Meikle, *Scotland and the French Revolution* (Glasgow, 1912), 158-60; H. Cockburn, *Life of Lord Jeffrey* (2 vols., Edinburgh, 1852), i. 91-5.

25. W. Ferguson, *Scotland 1689 to the Present* (New York, 1968), 261-3; Meikle, *Scotland and the French Revolution,* 178-85.

26. W. Burns to W. Hanna, 9 June 1847 (TCP, CHA 2, Hanna Letters).

27. T. Chalmers, 'Blessed are the poor in spirit', unpubl. student sermon, 12 November 1796 (TCP, CHA 6).

28. T. Chalmers to John Chalmers, 23 May-12 December 1798 (TCP, CHA 3.1. 22-41); Hanna, *Memoirs,* i. 25-32.

29. T. Chalmers to John Chalmers, 19 July 1798 (TCP, CHA 3.1.25).

30. T. Chalmers, 'That a minister is more beneficial to society than a schoolmaster', unpubl. student discourse, 25 May 1796 (TCP, CHA 6).

31. T. Chalmers, 'Blessed are the poor in spirit'.

32. T. Chalmers to John Chalmers, 29 October 1798 (TCP, CHA 3.1.36).

33. T. Chalmers to the Lodge of St. Vigeans (Free Masons), 30 November 1798 (TCP, CHA 3.1.40); Patrick Wilson to W. Hanna, 26 October 1847 (TCP, CHA 2, Hanna Letters).

34. T. Chalmers, 'Divine Summary of Human Duty', in *Sermons by Thomas Chalmers ... 1798-1847,* ed. W. Hanna (Edinburgh, 1849), 6; Chalmers, 'Blessed are the poor in spirit'; Chalmers, 'Leaven of the Pharisees', unpubl. student sermon, 29 September 1797 (TCP, CHA 6).

35. H. Perkin, *The Origins of Modern English Society 1780-1880,* (London, 1969), 17-38.

36. Wood, *The East Neuk of Fife,* 227-30.

37. D. Craig, *Scottish Literature and the Scottish People, 1680-1830,* (London, 1961), 19-71.
38. Gourlay, *Anstruther,* 109-11.
39. J. Miller to J. MacKenzie, 6 July 1847 (TCP, CHA 2, Hanna Letters); D. MacKinnon, 'Reminiscences of Dr. Chalmers', unpubl. MS, 24 March 1852 (TCP, CHA 2, Hanna Letters).
40. T. Chalmers to John Chalmers, 11, 17 January, 8 February 1799 (TCP, CHA 3.1.43-6); T. Duncan to W. Hanna, 21 January 1848 (TCP, CHA 2, Hanna Letters); Hanna, *Memoirs,* i. 32-3.
41. T. Chalmers to John Chalmers, 6 November 1798 (TCP, CHA 3.1.38).
42. T. Chalmers to John Chalmers, 26 October, [?] November 1799 (TCP, CHA 3.1.57-60).
43. T. Chalmers to John Chalmers, [?], 7 January 1800 (TCP, CHA 3.1.64, CHA 3.2.1).
44. Hanna, *Memoirs,* i. 473.
45. Ibid. 43-8.
46. Ibid. 42, 469-74; T. Chalmers to James Brown, 2 January, 25 February 1801 (EUL, Dc. 2.57., fols. 43-4, 50-1).
47. J. Miller to W. Hanna, 6 July 1847 (TCP, CHA 2, Hanna Letters).
48. H. Scott, *Fasti Ecclesiae Scoticanae: The Succession of Ministers in the Church of Scotland from the Reformation,* 2nd edn. (8 vols., Edinburgh , 1915), v. 181, 184, 189, 199, 214, 228.
49. T. Chalmers to John Chalmers, 8 March 1798 (TCP, CHA 3.1.20); Scott, *Fasti,* v. 184, 214.
50. This was evidently the parish living of Forgan, in the Synod of Fife; Scott, *Fasti,* v. 204.
51. T. Chalmers to John Chalmers, 18 July 1800 (TCP, CHA 3.2.3).
52. T. Chalmers to John Chalmers, 10, 12, 19, 25 November 1800 (TCP, CHA 3.2.5-10); Scott, *Fasti.* v. 121.
53. James Chalmers to John Chalmers, 22 September 1801 (TCP, CHA 1, 'Family Letters 1'); see also, James Chalmers to John Chalmers, 18 January 1800 (TCP, CHA 1, 'Family Letters 1'); T. Chalmers to John Chalmers, 24 July, 23 December 1801 (TCP, CHA 3.2.18, CHA 3.2.28).
54. T. Chalmers to W. B. Shaw, July 1801, in Hanna, *Memoirs,* i. 51-2; T. Chalmers to John Chalmers, 23 December 1801 (TCP, CHA 3.2.28).
55. T. Chalmers to John Chalmers, 21 September 1801 (TCP, CHA 3.2.20); Hanna, *Memoirs,* i. 53-4. The presentation to Kilmany was determined by a majority vote of the professors and masters of the United College; see, *Parliamentary Papers,* Reports from Commissioners,Universities (Scotland): 3. St. Andrews, 1837, (94) xxxvii, 349.
56. T. Chalmers to John Chalmers, 21 September, 23 December 1801 (TCP, CHA 3.2.20, CHA 3.2.28); T. Duncan to W. Hanna, 21 January 1848 (TCP, CHA 2, Hanna Letters).
57. T. Chalmers to Samuel Somerville, 15 January, 27 April 1811 (TCP, CHA 3.6.11, CHA 3.6.26).
58. Hanna, *Memoirs,* i. 48-51, 53-8; T. Elliot, 'Parish of Cavers', *Statistical Account of Scotland,* xvii. 89-92; T. Chalmers to John Chalmers, 23 December 1801 (TCP, CHA 3.2.28).
59. T. Chalmers to James Brown, 25 February 1801 (EUL, Dc. 2. 57., fols. 50-1); Hanna, *Memoirs,* i. 472-4.
60. T. Chalmers to James Brown, 8 December 1801 (EUL, Dc. 2. 57., fol. 47); T. Chalmers to John Chalmers, 13 January 1802 (TCP, CHA 3.2.30).

61. Hanna, *Memoirs*, i. 58-66; David Duff to T. Duncan, 29 September 1847 (TCP, CHA 2, Hanna Letters).
62. T. Chalmers to John Chalmers, 18 October 1803 (TCP, CHA 3.3.2).
63. Kilmany Parish Records, 1706-1819 (SRO, OPR 437/1).
64. Hanna, *Memoirs*, i. 75.
65. T. Chalmers, 'Diary, 1803-1804', 7-23 November, 24 December 1803 (TCP, CHA 6).
66. Ibid., 20 November, 7 December 1803, 24 February, 12 March 1804; James Brown, who had resigned the Glasgow Chair of Natural Philosophy in 1797 because of poor health, and who now lived in St. Andrews, was influential in maintaining cordial relations between Chalmers and the St. Andrews Whigs (see, e.g., 10, 24 November, 18 December 1803, 20, 30 January, 6 February 1804).
67. Ibid., 7 November, 6, 19, 21 December 1803, 19 February 1804; Hanna, *Memoirs*, i. 78-81, 474-83.
68. Chalmers, 'Diary, 1803-1804', 20 January and 13 February 1804.
69. George Hill to Alexander Carlyle, 12 April 1796, 4 November 1800 (EUL, Dc. 4.41. fols. 80-1, 83-4).
70. Hanna, *Memoirs*, i. 82-5, 484-8.
71. T. Chalmers to J. Brown, 8 May 1804 (EUL, Dc. 2.57. fol. 49).
72. Minutes of the Presbytery of Cupar, 1789-1807 (SRO, CH2/82/12); Hanna, *Memoirs*, i. 87-9.
73. G. Hill to Viscount Melville, 26 November 1804 (St. Andrews Univ. Library, Melville Papers, fol. 4802).
74. After lengthy litigation resulting from the close election, MacDonald was deprived of his chair by a House of Lords decision on 26 May 1809, and his closest competitor, Thomas Jackson, received the position. Morrell, 'The Leslie Affair', 74-5.
75. T. Chalmers to John Chalmers, 1 December 1801 (TCP, CHA 3.3.17).
76. John Chalmers to James Chalmers, 28 February 1805 (TCP, CHA 1, 'Family Letters 3'); John Chalmers to Adam Brooks, 2 February 1805; John Chalmers to James Bell, 16 February 1805 (TCP, CHA 1, 'Legal and Business Documents of John Chalmers, letter-book 1802-1810').
77. I. D. L. Clark, 'The Leslie Controversy, 1805', *SCHS*, xiv (1962), 179-97; Morrell, 'The Leslie Affair', 63-82; G. Grub, *An Ecclesiastical History of Scotland* (4 vols., Edinburgh, 1861), iv. 154-5; J. Cunningham, *The Church History of Scotland* (2 vols., Edinburgh, 1859), ii. 600-5; W. L. Mathieson, *Church and Reform in Scotland 1797-1843* (Glasgow, 1916) 90-100.
78. John Chalmers to James Chalmers, 24 April 1805 (TCP, CHA 1, 'Family Letters 3').
79. T. Chalmers, *Observation on a Passage in Mr. Playfair's Letter* (Cupar-Fife, 1805), 10-12.
80. Ibid. 15, 46-7.
81. Ibid. 39-40.
82. J. Clive, *Scotch Reviewers: The Edinburgh Review 1802-1815* (London, 1957), 17-41; Cockburn, *Life of Lord Jeffrey*, i. 124-45; H. Brougham, *Life and Times of Henry, Lord Brougham* (3 vols., Edinburgh, 1871), i. 251-64.
83. T. Chalmers to Archibald Constable, 1 October 1803 (NLS, MS 669, fols. 139-40).
84. Cockburn, *Life of Lord Jeffrey*, i. 83-4.
85. John Chalmers's enthusiasm for the volunteer movement was encouraged by the fact that, as a merchant in woollen goods, he profited from the sale of uniforms to three companies of volunteers in eastern Fife; Gourlay, *Anstruther*, 143; John

Chalmers to Messrs Prest, Brown, and Prest, 1803 (TCP, CHA 1, 'Legal and Business Documents of John Chalmers, letter-book 1802-10'); Hanna, *Memoirs,* i. 51-2.

86. Cockburn, *Life of Lord Jeffrey,* i. 153-4, ii. 73-5; H. Cockburn, *Memorials of his Time* (Edinburgh, 1856), 186-97; Brougham, *Life of Henry, Lord Brougham,* i. 309-13.

87. Cockburn, *Memorials of his Time,* 186-7.

88. T. Chalmers, Fast-Day Sermon, 20 October 1803', in *Sermons by Thomas Chalmers 1798-1847,* 40-9.

89. Hanna, *Memoirs,* i. 95-6; J. Anderson, *Reminiscences of Thomas Chalmers* (Edinburgh, 1851), 9-11.

90. T. Chalmers, 'Journal of visit to London', 21, 24, 29 April 1807 (TCP, CHA 6).

91. In 1802, while a merchant in Liverpool, James had become bankrupt as a result of injudicious speculations in the West Indies trade. After eighteen months of 'house-arrest' in Liverpool, he was allowed to leave the city.

92. Chalmers, 'Journal of visit to London', 4, 5, 12, 16, 17 May 1807.

93. Ibid., 4, 8, 9, 11, 18, 23 May 1807.

94. James Chalmers to John Chalmers, 14 May 1807 (TCP, CHA 1, 'Family Letters 1'); John Chalmers to James Chalmers, 28 April, 18 May 1807 (TCP, CHA 1, 'Family Letters 3').

95. Chalmers, 'Journal of visit to London', 30 April, 1 May 1807.

96. T. Chalmers to James Chalmers, 9 September 1807 (TCP, CHA 3.3.37).

97. T. Chalmers to James Chalmers, 5 January, 10, 24 February, 26 March 1808 (TCP, CHA 3.3.41, CHA 3.3.44, CHA 3.3.48, CHA 3.3.50).

98. T. Chalmers to James Chalmers, 29 March, 1, 6 April 1808 (TCP, CHA 3.3.51, CHA 3.3.53, CHA 3.3.57); *Cobbett's Weekly Political Register,* xiii (16 April 1808), 602-5.

99. T. Chalmers to James Chalmers, 7, 15, 20 April 1808 (TCP, CHA 3.3.59, CHA 3.3.65, CHA 3.3.70).

100. T. Chalmers, *An Enquiry into the Extent and Stability of National Resources* (Edinburgh, 1808), 1-14, 96-128, 141-66.

101. Ibid. 236-44, 271-4, 285-8.

102. Ibid. 129-30, 306, 331.

103. *Eclectic Review,* iv (July 1808), 575-89, esp. 577-80, 585.

104. *Farmers Magazine,* ix (June 1808), 221-44.

105. Hanna, *Memoirs,* i. 123-4.

106. W. Spence, *Britain Independent of Commerce* ... 3rd edn. (London, 1808), esp. 31-68.

107. J. Mill, *Commerce Defended* (London, 1808); [T. R. Malthus], 'Spence on Commerce', *Edinburgh Review,* xi (January 1808), 429-48; xiv (April 1809), 50-60; Malthus's second article in the *Edinburgh Review* was a rejoinder to W. Spence's pamphlet, *Agriculture the Source of the Wealth of Britain: A Reply to the Objections urged by Mr. Mill, the Edinburgh Reviewers and others, against the Doctrines of the Pamphlet, entitled 'Britain Independent of Commerce'* (London, 1808).

108. T. Chalmers to James Chalmers, 16 April 1808 (TCP, CHA 3.3.67).

109. T. Chalmers to James Chalmers, 3, 13 May, 28 June 1808 (TCP, CHA 3.4.1, CHA 3.4.7, CHA 3.4.13).

110. T. Chalmers to James Chalmers, 25 May, 28 June 1808 (TCP, CHA 3.4.11, CHA 3.4.13).

111. T. Chalmers to James Chalmers, 23 July 1808 (TCP, CHA 3.4.16).

Chapter Two: Conversion at Kilmany

1. Much of the best work on eighteenth-century Scottish Moderatism remains un-published. See I. D. L. Clark, 'Moderatism and the Moderate Party in the Church of Scotland, 1752-1805' (Ph.D. Thesis, Cambridge Univ., 1963), 190-318; R. B. Sher, 'Church, University and Enlightenment: The Moderate Literati of Edinburgh, 1720-1793' (Ph.D. Thesis, Univ. of Chicago, 1979), esp. chap. 5; H. R. Sefton, 'The Early Development of Moderatism in the Church of Scotland' (Ph.D. Thesis, Glasgow Univ., 1962). See also A. C. Cheyne 'The Westminster Standards: "A Century of Reappraisal"', *SCHS*, xiv. 3 (1962), 199-214; I.D.L. Clark, 'The Leslie Controversy, 1805', *SCHS*, xiv. 3 (1962), 179-97; I.D.L. Clark, 'From Protest to Reaction', in N. T. Phillipson and R. Mitchison (eds.), *Scotland in the Age of Improvement* (Edinburgh, 1970), 200-24.
2. Clark, 'Moderatism and the Moderate Party', 46-190; Sher, 'Church, University, and Enlightenment', chap. 4.
3. A. Carlyle, *Autobiography*, ed. J. H. Burton (Edinburgh, 1860), 561.
4. Clark, 'From Protest to Reaction', 200-24; I. F. Maciver, 'The General Assembly of the Church, the State, and Society in Scotland: Some Aspects of their Relationships, 1815-1843' (M.Litt. Thesis, Edinburgh Univ., 1976), 1-23.
5. J. Lapslie, *A Foederal Union Amongst the Different Sects of Christians, and Particularly of this Kingdom, Proposed and Recommended ... April 1791* (Glasgow, 1795), 33; Clark, 'Moderatism and the Moderate Party', 114-43; Maciver, 'The General Assembly of the Church, the State, and Society in Scotland', 1-23.
6. More work is still required for a proper understanding of the eighteenth-century Popular party. The best study remains J. MacInnes, *The Evangelical Movement in the Highlands of Scotland, 1688-1800* (Aberdeen, 1951), esp. 79-196; but see also A. Fawcett, *The Cambuslang Revival: The Scottish Evangelical Revival of the Eighteenth Century* (London, 1971), 182-209; G. G. Graham, *The Social Life of Scotland in the Eighteenth Century*, 3rd edn., (Edinburgh, 1901), 267-347; Craig, *Scottish Literature and the Scottish People 1680-1830*, 166-97. Several works of Scottish fiction have focused upon the psychological tensions of eighteenth-century Calvinism. Sir Walter Scott's portrait of Davie Deans in the *Heart of Midlothian* is probably the best known, but see also J. Hogg, *Private Memoirs and Confessions of a Justified Sinner* (Edinburgh, 1824).
7. e.g. S. Miller, *Memoir of the Rev. Charles Nisbet, D.D.* (New York, 1840), 29-136; V. L. Collins, *President Witherspoon* (2 vols., Princeton, 1925), i. 26-102.
8. Clark, 'Moderatism and the Moderate Party', 114-35, 143-90; H. Moncrieff Wellwood, *The Life and Writings of John Erskine* (Edinburgh, 1818), 384-90, 460-73.
9. [J. G. Lockhart], *Peter's Letters to his Kinsfolk* (3 vols., Edinbrugh, 1819), iii. 28-86; *Scottish Guardian* (Glasgow), 10 February 1837; Maciver, 'The General Assembly of the Church, the State, and Society in Scotland', 30-55.
10. W. M. Hetherington, *Memoir and Correspondence of Mrs. Coutts* (Edinburgh, 1854), 123.
11. T. Chalmers to John Honey, 2 May 1812, in *A Selection from the Correspondence of Thomas Chalmers*, 264-6.
12. David Brewster to W. Hanna, 2 September 1854 (TCP, CHA 2, Hanna Letters); Hanna, *Memoirs*, i. 142.
13. 'List of writers in Brewster's Encyclopedia, [1808]' (NLS, Lundie Letters, MS 1676, fol. 17). Of the twenty-seven contributors listed, ten were young Evangelical clergymen.
14. Hanna, *Memoirs*, i. 142.
15. R. F. Burns, *The Life and Times of the Rev. Robert Burns, Including an Unfinished Autobiography* (Toronto, 1872), 39-40.

16. D. Brewster to T. Chalmers, 3 September 1810 (TCP, CHA 4.1.15); Hanna, *Memoirs*, i. 142.
17. T. Chalmers, *The Substance of a Speech, Delivered in the General Assembly, on Thursday, May 25, 1809, Respecting the Merits of the Late Bill for the Augmentations of Stipends to the Clergy of Scotland* (Edinburgh, 1809), 31 pp.
18. T. Chalmers to J. Chalmers, 30 May 1809 (TCP, CHA 3.4.26); Hanna, *Memoirs*, i. 140-2.
19. Hanna, *Memoirs*, i. 151-2.
20. Ibid. 158. Chalmers continued a journal regularly from 17 March 1810 to 27 June 1814. W. Hanna included extracts from this journal in his *Memoirs of Dr. Chalmers*, but omitted many pertinent items. Although the original diaries have unfortunately been slightly defaced, they can be found in TCP, CHA 6, Diaries, vols. i-iv.
21. Diaries, March-September 1810 (TCP, CHA 6).
22. T. Chalmers to E. Chalmers, 12 November 1810 (TCP, CHA 3.4.48); Diaries, November-December 1810.
23. T. Chalmers to James Chalmers, 24 December 1810 (TCP, CHA 3.4.51); Diaries, 20-30 December 1810; Hanna, *Memoirs*, i. 182-9.
24. Diaries, 10 February-18 March 1811; T. Chalmers, 'Zion Remembered by the Rivers of Babylon', in *Sermons by Thomas Chalmers 1798-1847*, 88-106.
25. Hetherington, *Memoir and Correspondence of Mrs. Coutts*, 123.
26. T. Chalmers to A. Thomson, 18 January and 5 February 1811 (TCP., CHA 3.6.12, CHA 3.6.19); A. Thomson to T. Chalmers 18 February 1811 (TCP, CHA 4.1.57).
27. [T. Chalmers], 'Review of Hints on Toleration', *Edinburgh Christian Instructor*, ii (May 1811), 311-20.
28. A. Thomson to R. Lundie, 22 July 1811 (NLS, MS 1676, fol. 30); S. Charters to T. Chalmers, 10 July 1811 (TCP, CHA 4.1.33).
29. T. Chalmers, 'Kilmany Communicants, 1810-1815' (TCP, CHA 6).
30. The income from the collections and from the interest on a small capital sum (£209) in Kilmany increased from an average of £18 per annum between 1805 and 1810, to £38 in 1811, £33 in 1812, and £45 in 1813. See Kilmany Parish Records, 1706-1819 (SRO, OPR 437/1).
31. T. Chalmers, 'Record of my preaching, March 1812-September 1816', MS (TCP, CHA 6).
32. Hanna, *Memoirs*, i. 434-6.
33. R. Simpson to T. Chalmers, 28 October 1813 (TCP, CHA 4.2.40).
34. Diaries, 13 January 1814 (TCP, CHA 6).
35. [Lockhart], *Peter's Letters to his Kinsfolk*, iii. 267-8.
36. For discussion of Chalmers's preaching, see esp. H. Watt, *Thomas Chalmers and the Disruption* (Edinburgh, 1943), 41-53, and G. D. Henderson, *The Burning Bush: Studies in Scottish Church History* (Edinburgh, 1957), 195-205.
37. Cockburn, *Memorials of his Time*, 418-19; [Lockhart], *Peter's Letters to his Kinsfolk*, iii. 266-80; *Glasgow Courier*, 23 May 1816.
38. T. Chalmers to Janet Coutts, 24 October 1811 (TCP, CHA 3.5.27); [T. Chalmers], 'Review of John Foster's Essays', *Edinburgh Christian Instructor*, iv (May 1813), 327-39.
39. Oliphant, Waugh and Innes to T. Chalmers, 14 December 1813, 4 January 1814 (TCP, CHA 4.2.37, CHA 4.3.48); T. Chalmers to William Whyte, bookseller, 10 December 1813 (TCP, CHA 3.6.57); T. Chalmers to E. Chalmers, 24 January 1814 (TCP., CHA 3.7.3).
40. *Christian Observer* xiv (April 1815), 236-48; see also, *Christian Observer*, xiv (October 1815), 685-98; *Eclectic Review*, iv (July 1815), 37-56.

41. T. Chalmers to Samuel Somerville, 15 January, 25, 27 April, 18, 21, 26 May, September 1811 (TCP, CHA 3.6.11, CHA 3.6.21, CHA 3.6.26, CHA 3.6.31-3, CHA 3.6.45; T. Chalmers to E. Chalmers, 25 February 1812 (TCP, CHA 3.5.39).

42. T. Chalmers to James Anderson, July 1812 (TCP, CHA 3.5.49); Diaries, 21 February 1814 (TCP, CHA 6).

43. E. Chalmers to J. Chalmers, 17 October 1812 (TCP, CHA 1, 'Family Letters 2').

44. G. White, '"Highly Preposterous": Origins of Scottish Missions', *SCHS*, xix. 2 (1976), 111-24.

45. J. Owen, *The History of the Origin and First Ten Years of the British and Foreign Bible Society* (2 vols., London, 1816), i. 403-16, 429-39; W. Canton, *A History of the British and Foreign Bible Society* (2 vols., London, 1904), i. 46-118.

46. Diaries, 11 September 1811, 9 January 1812 (TCP, CHA 6); T. Chalmers to J. Johnson, 11 January 1812 (TCP, CHA 3.6.50); Hanna, *Memoirs*, i. 495.

47. Diaries, 10, 11 September, 20, 23 November, 16, 27, 31 December 1811, 9-25 January, 23 February, 4, 5, 16 March 1812 (TCP, CHA 6).

48. Diaries, 9-28 March 1812; J. Anderson to T. Chalmers, 5 February [1812], 10 March 1812 (St. Andrews Univ. Library, MS 30385, fols. 18, 27); Hanna, ed., *A Selection from the Correspondence of Thomas Chalmers*, 1-3.

49. T. Duncan to T. Chalmers,, 9 March [1812] (TCP, CHA 4.1.37).

50. Hanna, *Memoirs*, i. 265, 493-4.

51. Ibid. 282-3.

52. Hanna, ed., *A Selection from the Correspondence of Thomas Chalmers*, 273-4.

53. Walter Tait to T. Chalmers, 30 March 1812; George Muirhead to T. Chalmers, 27 March 1812 (TCP, CHA 4.2.20, CHA 4.2.10); Chalmers, Diaries, 29 March, 14, 15 April 1812 (TCP, CHA 6).

54. T. Chalmers, 'On the British and Foreign Bible Society', unpubl. MS, [April 1812], (TCP, CHA 6).

55. *Edinburgh Christian Instructor,* iii (September 1812); A. Thomson to T. Chalmers, 14 September 1812 (TCP, CHA 4.2.22).

56. T. Chalmers, *The Two Great Instruments appointed for the Propagation of the Gospel; and the Duty of the Christian Public to Keep Both in Vigorous Operation* (Edinburgh, 1813), 30-42. A slightly revised version of this pamphlet is included in *The Collected Works of Thomas Chalmers* (25 vols., Glasgow, 1835-41), xi, 315-44.

57. *Edinburgh Christian Instructor*, ix (December 1813), 394-491; H. Watt, *The Published Writings of Thomas Chalmers* (Edinburgh, 1943), 14-15; Burns, *The Life and Times of the Rev. Robert Burns*, 40; George Burder to T. Chalmers, 3 March 1813 (TCP, CHA 4.2.23).

58. Hanna, ed., *A Selection from the Correspondence of Thomas Chalmers,* 273-4; Chalmers, Diaries, 18 November 1812 (TCP, CHA 6).

59. *Edinburgh Christian Instructor,* viii (February 1814), 126-9; *Eclectic Review*, 2nd ser., ii (August 1814), 168-77; James Anderson to T. Chalmers, 10 March 1812 (St. Andrews Univ. Library, MS 30385, fol. 27).

60. E. Chalmers to James Chalmers, 17 October 1812 (TCP, CHA 1, 'Family Letters 2').

61. T. Chalmers to Charles Stuart, 22 April 1813 (TCP, CHA 3.5.66); Chalmers, Diaries, 28 April 1813 (TCP, CHA 6).

62. T. Chalmers, *The Influence of Bible Societies on the Temporal Necessities of the Poor* (Edinburgh, 1814), 40 pp.; Much of Chalmers's subsequent interest in overseas missions focused upon the communitarian Moravians. See, [T. Chalmers], 'On the Efficacy of Missions, as Conducted by the Moravians', *Eclectic Review*,

2nd ser., iii (January 1815), 1-13; Christian Ignatius LaTrobe to T. Chalmers, 9 March 1818, 29 March 1819 (TCP, CHA 4.8.32, CHA 4.12.11).

63. [R. Steven], *Remarks on a Late Publication of the Rev. Dr. Chalmers, Intitled 'The Influence of Bible Societies on the Temporal Necessities of the Poor'...* (London, 1819); R. Steven to T. Chalmers, 3 February 1819 (TCP, CHA 4.13.43); more favourable reviews appeared in the *Edinburgh Christian Instructor*, viii (February 1814), 126-33; and the *Eclectic Review*, 2nd ser., ii (August 1814), 168-77.

64. J. Chalmers to T. Chalmers, 18 April 1814 (TCP, CHA 4.3.18).

65. S. Mechie, *The Church and Scottish Social Development 1780-1870* (Oxford 1960), 36-46; G. J. C. Duncan, *Memoir of the Rev. Henry Duncan* (Edinburgh, 1848), 83-148; R. Burns, *Memoir of the Rev. Stevenson Macgill, D.D.* (Edinburgh, 1842), 39-45; M. F. Connolly, 'Samuel Charters', in *Biographical Dictionary of Eminent Men of Fife* (Cupar-Fife, 1866).

66. A Haldane, *The Lives of Robert Haldane of Airthey, and of his brother, James Alexander Haldane*, 4th edn. (Edinburgh, 1855), 115-42, 193-288; J. J. Matheson, *Memoir of Greville Ewing* (London, 1843), 121-93; J. M'Kerrow, *History of the Secession Church*, 2nd edn. (Edinburgh, 1854), 578-617.

67. Andrew Thomson to Robert Lundie, 12 October 1809; [R. Lundie?], 'List of Chief Writers of the Edr. Christian Instructor', MS, n.d., (NLS, Lundie Letters, MS 1676, fols. 9, 167); *Edinburgh Christian Instructor,* ii (January 1811), v (October 1812).

68. J. Cook, 'Parish of Kilmany', in Sinclair, ed., *Statistical Account of Scotland,* xix 420-33; H. D. Cook, 'Parish of Kilmany, [1838]', in *The New Statistical Account of Scotland* (15 vols., Edinburgh, 1845), ix. 532-57; T. Chalmers, 'State of Property in the Parish of Kilmany, 1811', MS (TCP, CHA 3.6.31); T. Chalmers, 'Evidence before the Select Committee of the House of Commons on the Subject of a Poor Law for Ireland, 1831', in *Collected Works,* xvi. 302-10.

69. R. Small, *History of the Congregations of the United Presbyterian Church* (2 vols., Edinburgh, 1904), i. 177-80.

70. Cook, 'Parish of Kilmany [1838], *New Statistical Account of Scotland,* ix, 555.

71. T. Chalmers, *Considerations on the System of Parochial Schools in Scotland* (Glasgow, 1819), in *Collected Works,* xii. 191-219.

72. Diaries, 27 November 1813 (TCP, CHA 6); Hanna, *Memoirs,* i. 414-15.

73. T. Chalmers, *Scripture References; Designed for the Use of Parents, Teachers, and Private Christians* (Dundee, 1814) 15 pp.; Maurice Ogle to T. Chalmers, 16 November 1814; T. Chalmers to M. Ogle (TCP, CHA 4.3.46, CHA 3.6.62).

74. M. Gillespie to T. Chalmers, 30 November 1814 (St. Andrews Univ. Library, MS 30385, fol. 342); Hanna, *Memoirs,* i. 415.

75. Chalmers, 'Record of my preaching, March 1812-September 1816', MS (TCP, CHA 6).

76. T. Chalmers, 'Record of my spiritual intercourse with my people', MS (TCP, CHA 6); Hanna, *Memoirs,* i. 404-14.

77. T. Chalmers to J. Coutts, 27 January 1815 (TCP, CHA 3.7.17); T. Chalmers, *The Duty of Giving an Immediate Diligence to the Business of the Christian Life: Being an Address to the Inhabitants of the Parish of Kilmany* (Edinburgh, 1815), 1-31. A slightly revised version of this pamphlet is included in T. Chalmers, *Collected Works,* xii. 69-120.

78. [J. Somerville], 'Review of Chalmers' *Address to the Inhabitants of Kilmany'*, *Edinburgh Christian Instructor*, iv (December 1815), 404-12.

79. Diaries, 21 February 1814 (TCP, CHA 6).

80. T. Chalmers, *A Sermon Preached before the Society for Relief of the Destitute Sick in St. Andrews Church, Edinburgh, April 18, 1813* (Edinburgh, 1813), esp. 30-2. A revised version of this pamphlet is included in T. Chalmers, *Collected Works,* xi, 283-314.

81. [T. Chalmers], 'Review of Samuel Charters' Sermons', *Edinburgh Christian Instructor,* iii (July 1811), 43-53. A revised version of this article is included in T. Chalmers, *Collected Works,* xii. 299-322.

82. For two stimulating, though controversial, recent studies of the old Scottish poor law, see R. Mitchison, 'The Making of the Old Scottish Poor Law', *Past and Present,* no. 63 (May 1974), 58-93; and R. A. Cage, 'The Scottish Poor Law, 1745-1845', (Ph.D. Thesis, Glasgow Univ., 1974), esp. 25-80.

83. T. Chalmers, 'Kilmany Session Account Book, 1808-1810', MS (TCP, CHA 6).

84. Chalmers, 'Evidence before the Select Committee of the House of Commons on the Subject of a Poor Law for Ireland, 1831', 305.

85. Ibid. 307; for an example of a sermon on the communal theme, see T. Chalmers, 'On the Superior Blessedness of the Giver to that of the Receiver' (delivered in Kilmany on June 1814), in *Collected Works,* xi. 387-435.

86. Kilmany Parish Records, 1706-1819, 12 August 1814 (SRO, OPR 437/1).

87. Chalmers's poor-relief policies had in fact been a subject of contention in Kilmany since first introduced in March 1813; Diaries, 13, 14 March 1813 (TCP, CHA 6).

88. Kilmany Parish Records, 1706-1819, 12 August 1814 (SRO, OPR 437/1).

89. Chalmers, *The Duty of Giving an Immediate Diligence to the Business of the Christian Life: Being an Address to the Inhabitants of the Parish of Kilmany,* 40-3.

90. Hanna, *Memoirs,* i. 428-30; H. Baillie, *The Missionary of Kilmany; Being a Memoir of Alexander Paterson, with Notices of Robert Edie,* 5th edn. (Edinburgh, 1854).

91. The Fifeshire Evangelicals had long opposed pluralities, largely in reaction to the nepotism of the Hill family; see G. Hill to A. Carlyle, 12 April 1796, 4 November 1800 (EUL, Carlyle Letters, Dc. 4.41, fols. 80, 83); R. Burns, *Plurality of Offices in the Church of Scotland Examined* (Glasgow, 1824), 156-7.

92. Hanna, *Memoirs,* i. 397, 496-7.

93. Ibid. 343.

94. T. Chalmers, 'General Assembly Speech on Pluralities, 1814', unpubl. MS (TCP, CHA 6); *Edinburgh Christian Instructor,* viii (June 1814), 407-8; Hanna, *Memoirs,* i. 398-402, 497-504; Burns, *Plurality of Offices,* 157-9.

95. Cook, *Life of George Hill.*

96. Hanna, *Memoirs,* ii. 65-7, 496-9; anon., *Proceedings in the General Assembly on the 24th May, 1816, on the Overtures for the Repeal of the Enactment of Assembly, 1814, anent the Union of Offices* (Glasgow, 1816), 24 pp.

97. *Glasgow Courier,* 6 June 1816; R. Bell, *Memoir of Robert Paul* (Edinburgh, 1872), 80.

98. Hanna, *Memoirs,* ii. 69.

Chapter Three: Glasgow and the Urban Challenge

1. Hanna, *Memoirs,* i. 436-8.

2. T. Chalmers to John Wood, 30 September 1814 (TCP, CHA 3.6.58); T. Chalmers to David Pitcairn, 6 October 1814 (TCP, CHA 3.6.59).

3. Hanna, *Memoirs,* i. 436, 440-2.

4. J. Wood to T. Chalmers, 24 November 1814 (TCP, CHA 4.3.75); Robert Tennant to T. Chalmers, 25 November 1814, (TCP, CHA 4.3.60); Isabella Turpie to Grace Chalmers, 29 November 1814 (TCP, CHA 4.3.67).

5. T. S. Jones to T. Chalmers, 26 November 1814. (St. Andrews Univ. Library, MS 30385, fol. 424).

6. T. Chalmers to E. Chalmers, 30 November 1814 (TCP, CHA 3.7.10).

7. I. Turpie to G. Chalmers 29 November 1814 (TCP, CHA 4.3.67).

8. Hanna, *Memoirs,* i. 447-8, 454-6.

9. J. Chalmers to T. Chalmers, 26 November 1814 (TCP, CHA 4.3.22).

10. Hanna, *Memoirs*, ii. 9-10.
11. Hanna, *Memoirs*, ii. 19-24; T. Chalmers to E. Chalmers, 15 November 1815 (TCP, CHA 3.7.44).
12. T. Chalmers, *Speech Delivered on the 24th of May, 1822, Before the General Assembly of the Church of Scotland, Explanatory of the Measures which have been Successfully Pursued in St. John's Parish* (Glasgow, 1822), 10. A slightly revised version of this speech will be found in T. Chalmers, *Collected Works,* xvi. 141-215.
13. Hanna, *Memoirs,* ii. 18.
14. [J. G. Lockhart], *Peter's Letters to his Kinsfolk,* iii. 147-8.
15. J. Cleland, *Annals of Glasgow* (2 vols., Glasgow, 1816), ii. 372-4; J. Cleland, *The Rise and Progress of the City of Glasgow* (Glasgow, 1820), 199-200, 229-39; T. C. Smout, *A History of the Scottish People 1560-1830* (Glasgow, 1969), 355-65; G. Eyre-Todd, *History of Glasgow From the Revolution to the Passing of the Reform Acts* (Glasgow, 1934), 450; T. M. Devine, 'An eighteenth-century business élite: Glasgow-West India merchants, *c.* 1750-1815', *SHR,* lvii, (April 1978), 40-67; [Lockhart], *Peter's Letters to his Kinsfolk,* iii. 169-76; L. J. Saunders, *Scottish Democracy 1815-1840* (Edinburgh, 1950), 98-117.
16. Saunders, *Scottish Democracy 1815-1840,* 161-207.
17. W. M. Roach, 'Alexander Richmond and the Radical Reform Movements in Glasgow in 1816-17', *SHR,* li. 1 (April 1972), 1-19; Eyre-Todd, *History of Glasgow,* 449-51; W. L. Mathieson, *Church and Reform in Scotland, 1797-1843* (Glasgow, 1916), 140-50; G. W. T. Omond, *The Lord Advocates of Scotland* (2 vols., Edinburgh, 1883), ii. 232-5.
18. Cleland cited the figure of 18,656 sittings, but included in this 3,200 sittings in two *proposed* churches which had not been built. Cleland, *Annals of Glasgow,* i. 152-3.
19. Ibid. 153. Again, I have subtracted the 3,200 proposed sittings from Cleland's total figure.
20. Cleland, *Annals of Glasgow,* ii. 419. I do not include the approximately 2,370 children attending charity sabbath schools in these figures.
21. There were 144 private schools in Glasgow in 1815, with about 7,488 fee-paying pupils. Cleland, *Annals of Glasgow,* ii. 420; Saunders, *Scottish Democracy 1815-1840,* 267-71; J. Scotland, *The History of Scottish Education* (2 vols., London, 1969), i. 261-5.
22. R. A. Cage, 'The Scottish Poor Law, 1745-1845', (Ph.D. Thesis, Glasgow Univ., 1974), 81-4; Cleland, *Annals of Glasgow,* i. 225-9; ii. 428-33; T. Ferguson, *The Dawn of Scottish Social Welfare* (London, 1948), 177-81.
23. Cleland, *Annals of Glasgow,* i. 270-3. Cleland's figure of £32,942 for the total known charities of the city includes both £10,864 from the Town Hospital and £1,994 from the General Sessions of the Established Church.
24. Cage, 'The Scottish Poor Law, 1745-1845', 81-3; Cleland, *Annals of Glasgow,* i. 245-8; ii. 427-30; T. Chalmers, *Christian and Civic Economy of Large Towns,* in *Collected Works,* xv. 31-4.
25. For discussion of the major charity societies in Glasgow, see Cleland, *Annals of Glasgow,* i. 218-70.
26. Ibid. i. 151-5. Cleland gives a total of 54,255 church sittings in the city, of which 29,345 were in Dissenting churches.
27. *Witness,* 26 June 1844; Hanna, *Memoirs,* ii. 108-10.
28. *Witness,* 26 June 1844.
29. Ibid.; Hanna, *Memoirs* ii. 111-13; Cleland, *Annals of Glasgow,* i. 222.
30. Hanna, *Memoirs,* ii. 110.
31. *Witness,* 26 June 1844.
32. Hanna, *Memoirs,* ii. 67, 128-9.

33. Ibid. 121-2. See Tron Kirk Session to T. Chalmers, 26 December 1814 and Tron Kirk Session and Congregation to T. Chalmers, 12 February 1817 (TCP, CHA 5, St. John's and Tron Box) for respective lists of the Tron eldership before and after his reform. His appointees included such men as Patrick Falconer and Robert Tennent, wealthy iron merchants, and John Smith, the successful publisher.
34. Hanna, *Memoirs,* ii. 507-12.
35. Cleland, *Annals of Glasgow,* ii. 419.
36. *Witness,* 19 June 1844.
37. Ibid.; Hanna, *Memoirs,* ii. 122-7; Chalmers evidently received the idea for district sabbath schools from David Stow, a young sabbath-school teacher and later a celebrated educational reformer. W. Fraser, *Memoir of David Stow* (London, 1868), 21-33.
38. *Witness,* 19 June 1844; Cleland, *The Rise and Progress of the City of Glasgow,* 227-8 and chart; [J. Liddle], *Report of the Committee for Promoting the Establishment of Local Schools in Edinburgh and its Vicinity, June 2, 1824* (Edinburgh, 1824), 1-17; R. F. Burns, *The Life and Time of Robert Burns;* Hanna, *Memoirs,* ii. 127.
39. G. Burns to T. Chalmers, 10 December 1818 (TCP, CHA 4.7.16).
40. Hanna, *Memoirs,* ii. 113-120; *Sermons by Thomas Chalmers 1798-1847,* 330-47.
41. Hanna, *Memoirs,* ii. 131-3; T. Littlejohn, Provost of Stirling, to T. Chalmers, 12 February 1817 (TCP, CHA 4.6.29) W. Dougell to T. Chalmers, Tradeshall, Stirling, 14 February 1817 (TCP, CHA 4.6.12).
42. List of Subscribers for Assistant Minister, 12 February 1817; Petitions, 12 and 15 February 1817, (TCP, CHA 5, St. John's and Tron Box, uncatalogued).
43. T. Chalmers to W. Roger, 18 February 1817 (TCP CHA 3.8.5).
44. Hanna, *Memoirs,* ii. 62-3.
45. *Glasgow Courier,* 28 May 1816. See also 23 May, 1, 6 June 1816; *Blackwood's Edinburgh Magazine,* i. (April 1817), 74.
46. Hanna, *Memoirs,* ii. 87-8.
47. T. Chalmers, *Discourses on the Christian Revelation, Viewed in Connection with the Modern Astronomy* (Glasgow, 1817) in *Collected Works,* vii. 143.
48. Ibid. 140-1.
49. Hanna, *Memoirs,* ii. 88-91; T. Chalmers to E. Chalmers, 28 March 1817 (TCP, CHA 3.8.7); D. Keir, *The House of Collins* (London, 1952), 31-2.
50. W. Hazlitt, *The Spirit of the Age* (first pub., London, 1825), in A. R. Waller, ed., *The Collected Works of William Hazlitt* (London, 1920), iv. 228-9.
51. *Eclectic Review,* 2nd ser., viii (October 1817), 354-66, (November 1817), 466-76; See also, *Blackwood's Edinburgh Magazine,* i (April 1817), 73-5.
52. Hazlitt, *Collected Works of William Hazlitt,* iv. 230.
53. Hanna, *Memoirs,* ii. 98-102; *Blackwood's Edinburgh Magazine,* ii (May 1818), 155.
54. Hazlitt, *Collected Works of William Hazlitt,* iv. 229.
55. *Morning Chronicle,* 19, 23, 26 May 1817; *The Times,* 19, 20 May 1817; Hanna, *Memoirs,* ii. 102-4; R. I. and S. Wilberforce, *The Life of William Wilberforce* (5 vols., London, 1848), iv. 323-5.
56. Hanna, *Memoirs,* ii. 99-100.
57. Ibid. 104-7.
58. J. Gladstone to T. Chalmers, 12 August 1817 (TCP, CHA 4.6.16); J. Gladstone to T. Chalmers, 23 March, 11 April 1818 (TCP, CHA 4.8.3-4).
59. [J. G. Lockhart], 'To the Rev. Thomas Chalmers', *Blackwood's Edinburgh Magazine,* ii (May 1818), 155.
60. Watt, *Thomas Chalmers and the Disruption,* 43-4.
61. T. Chalmers, *The Application of Christianity to the Commercial and Ordinary Affairs of life, in a Series of Discourses,* (Glasgow, 1820), esp. Discourses i-iii. A revised version is included in T. Chalmers, *Collected Works,* vi. 13-81.

62. [T. Chalmers], 'Review of Hints on Toleration', *Edinburgh Christian Instructor*, ii (May 1811), 319-20.

63. T. Chalmers, 'Evidence Before the Committee of the House of Commons on the Subject of a Poor Law for Ireland, 1830', in *Collected Works,* xvi. 378, 411-13.

64. Anderson, *Reminiscences of Thomas Chalmers,* 38-40; Chalmers delivered this same sermon in Glasgow a few weeks later.

65. T. Chalmers, 'The Doctrine of Christian Charity Applied to the Case of Religious Differences', in *Collected Works*, xi. 91-115.

66. Ibid. 114.

67. T. Randall Davidson to H. Grey, February [1818] (TCP, CHA 4.6.18), [the letter is misdated in the original as February 1817]; Grey, however, approved the sermon and advised its publication. H. Grey to T. Chalmers, 24 February 1818 (TCP, CHA 4.8.16).

68. *Edinburgh Christian Instructor*, xvi (February 1818), 112-27; R. Burns, *A Letter to Dr. Chalmers, on the Distinctive Characters of the Protestant and Roman Catholic Religions...* (Glasgow, 1818); *Edinburgh Christian Instructor*, xvi (April 1818), 255-61.

69. D. Dewar to T. Chalmers, Aberdeen, 17 April 1818 (TCP CHA 4.7.34); D. Mearns, *The Principles of Christian Evidence illustrated, by an Examination of Arguments Subversive of Natural Theology, and the Internal Evidence of Christianity, Advanced by Dr. T. Chalmers ...* (Aberdeen, 1818).

70. *Scotsman,* 4 April 1818.

71. Hanna, *Memoirs,* ii. 148-60.

72. Ibid. 161.

73. Ibid. 177-83.

74. T. R. Malthus to T. Chalmers, 22 July 1822 (TCP, CHA 4.21.51).

75. K. Marx, *Capital,* ed. F. Engels (3 vols., New York, 1967), i. 617n.

76. T. R. Malthus, *An Essay on the Principle of Population ...* 4th edn. (2 vols., London, 1807), ii. 73-130, 348-87.

77. Chalmers, *An Enquiry into the Extent and Stability of National Resources,* 263-5; Chalmers, *Influence of Bible Societies on the Temporal Necessities of the Poor,* in *Collected Works,* xii. 140.

78. Cleland, *Annals of Glasgow,* i. 228-9.

79. T. R. Malthus to T. Chalmers, 23 August 1821 (TCP, CHA 4.18.21).

80. [T. Chalmers], 'Connexion between the Extension of the Church and the Extinction of Pauperism', *Edinburgh Review,* xxviii (March 1817), 1-31.

81. Ibid. 24-5.

82. T. Chalmers, 'On the Superior Blessedness of the Giver to that of the Receiver', sermon delivered in Dunfermline, Kilmany, and Edinburgh in 1814, in Glasgow in 1815, and in Surrey Chapel, London, on 22 May 1817, in *Collected Works,* xi. 401-35; Hanna, *Memoirs,* ii. 100-1; *Morning Chronicle,* 23 May 1817.

83. T. Chalmers' 'A Sermon delivered in the Tron Church, Glasgow on November 19, 1817, the Day of the Funeral of Her Royal Highness' (first pub. Glasgow, 1817), in *Collected Works,* xi. 30-53; Hanna, *Memoirs,* ii. 137-43; Anderson, *Reminiscences of Thomas Chalmers,* 37-8.

84. Cockburn, *Life of Lord Jeffrey,* ii. 173-5.

85. [T. Chalmers], 'Causes and Cures of Pauperism', *Edinburgh Review,* xxix, (February 1818), 261-302.

86. The *Glasgow Chronicle* published a series of three anonymous letters to the editor, on 21, 28 October, and 4 November 1817, directed against Chalmers's first *Edinburgh Review* article.

87. Anon., *Remarks on Two Articles in the Edinburgh Review, on the Causes and Cure of Pauperism, by the Author of 'Letters from Scotland'* (Manchester, 1818), 6.26.

88. [J. Haldane], *Two Letters to the Rev. Dr. Chalmers, on his Proposal for Increasing the Number of Churches in Glasgow, by an Observor* (Glasgow, 1818); [J. Haldane], *A Letter to the Lord Provost, Magistrates, Preceptor, and the other Directors of the Town's Hospital, Glasgow, on the Causes and Cure of Pauperism* (Glasgow, 1818); See also *Edinburgh Christian Instructor* (February 1819), 119-22.
89. [Haldane], *A Letter to the Lord Provost*, 3-13.
90. *Glasgow Chronicle*, 28 October 1817; J. G. Lockhart argued that Chalmers was demeaning his clerical status by his *Edinburgh Review* articles; *Blackwood's Edinburgh Magazine*, ii (May 1818), 155-61.
91. [J. Ewing], *Report for the Directors of the Town's Hospital of Glasgow on the Management of the City Poor ...* (Glasgow, 1818). A report by Chalmers to Ewing's committee was printed on pp. 40-51.
92. Cleland, *Annals of Glasgow*, i. 152.
93. T. Chalmers to J. Ewing, May 1818 (TCP, CHA 3.8.43); J. Ewing to T. Chalmers, 24 April, 27 May 1818 (TCP, CHA 4.7.60-2).
94. T. Chalmers to J. Reddie, 14 March 1818 (NLS, MS 3704, fols. 72-3).
95. *Glasgow Courier*, 21 March 1818; *Scotsman*, 4 April 1818.
96. *Parliamentary Papers*, House of Lords, Committee on the Poor Laws, Minutes of Evidence, 21 May 1817, 67-70; Hanna, *Memoirs*, ii. 174; Eyre-Todd, *History of Glasgow*, 433-7.
97. R. Findlay to T. Chalmers, 3 April 1818 (St. Andrew's Univ. Library, MS 30385, fol. 314).
98. J. Ewing to T. Chalmers, 9 June 1818 (TCP, CHA 4.7.63); R. Tennent to T. Chalmers, 6 June 1818 (TCP, CHA 4.9.39); T. Chalmers to W. Roger, 10 June 1818 (TCP, CHA 3.8.46); Hanna, *Memoirs*, ii. 207-8.
99. [A. Thomson], 'Review of the "Third Report from the Select Committee on the Poor Laws"', *Edinburgh Christian Instructor*, xvii (November 1818), 336-50.
100. S. Macgill, *Discourses and Essays on Subjects of Public Interest* (Edinburgh, 1819), 361-475.
101. A. Thomson to Robert Lundie, 14 June 1819 (NLS, MS 1676, fols. 172-3).
102. Hanna, *Memoirs*, ii. 211-17.
103. Ibid. 217-18; A. Thomson to T. Chalmers, 10 August 1819 (TCP, CHA 4.14.20); A. Thomson to R. Lundie, 14 August 1819 (NLS, MS 1676, fols. 114-15); Hanna, *Memoirs*, ii. 219.
104. *Scotsman*, 14 August 1819; *Glasgow Courier*, 21, 28 August 1819.
105. A. Thomson to T. Chalmers, 14 August 1819 (TCP, CHA 4.14.22). Had Chalmers pursued his candidature, his friend Thomas Duncan assured him on 15 August, 'there would have been a thousand surmises against you, and the interest of religion would have suffered' (TCP, CHA 4.11.19).
106. Hanna, *Memoirs*, ii. 219-93.
107. Cleland, *The Rise and Progress of the City of Glasgow*, 208-11.
108. Ibid. 211-17. The actual resignation was not carried into effect until over a year later, on 1 February 1821; *Glasgow Courier*, 3, 8 February 1821.
109. A. Thomson to T. Chalmers, 17 September 1819 (TCP, CHA 4.14.24).
110. Hanna, *Memoirs*, ii. 223-6; *Glasgow Courier*, 25 September 1819.
111. *Glasgow Courier*, 28 September 1819.
112. Hanna, *Memoirs*, ii. 227.
113. There have been a large number of studies of Chalmers's St. John's experiment. By far the best is R. A. Cage and E. O. A. Checkland, 'Thomas Chalmers and Urban Poverty: The St. John's Parish Experiment in Glasgow, 1819-1837', *Philosophical Journal* (Glasgow), xiii (Spring 1976), 37-56. See also, Mechie, *The Church and Scottish Social Development 1780-1870*, 47-63; A. L. Drummond and J.

Bulloch, *The Scottish Church 1688-1843* (Edinburgh, 1973), 161-79; N. Masterman, *Chalmers on Charity* (London, 1900), 288-342.

114. Hanna, *Memoirs,* ii. 249-51.

115. Cage, 'The Scottish Poor Law, 1745-1845', 202-4; Cleland, *The Rise and Progress of the City of Glasgow,* 146; T. Chalmers, *Statement in Regard to the Pauperism of Glasgow, From the Experience of the Last Eight Years* (Glasgow 1823), in *Collected Works,* xvi. 218-220, 233; Cage and Checkland, 'Thomas Chalmers and Urban Poverty', 46.

116. T. Chalmers, *Civic and Christian Economy of Large Towns,* in *Collected Works,* xv. 52-61; Chalmers, *Speech delivered on the 24th May, 1822, Before the General Assembly of the Church of Scotland,* 9-35.

117. Chalmers, *Statement in Regard to the Pauperism of Glasgow,* in *Collected Works,* xvi. 221-2.

118. Ibid. 223; T. Chalmers, *Civic and Christian Economy of Large Towns,* in *Collected Works,* xv. 49-73; xvi. 272-3.

119. Cage and Checkland, 'Thomas Chalmers and Urban Poverty', 43.

120. Hanna, *Memoirs,* ii. 298-301.

121. Mechie, *The Church and Scottish Social Development,* 61-3.

122. Chalmers, 'Evidence Before the Committee of the House of Commons', in *Collected Works,* xvi. 321.

123. Cleland, *The Rise and Progress of the City of Glasgow,* 146; Chalmers, *Statement in Regard to the Pauperism of Glasgow,* in *Collected Works,* xvi. 228-31. The transfers consisted in the following: first, 19 St. John's paupers were transferred to the new parish of St. James, when it was formed in 1821; secondly, 15 St. John's paupers voluntarily moved to other parishes; thirdly, 29 poor from other parishes moved to St. John's. Chalmers cited a figure of 77 paupers, but did not include the net total of 14 paupers who moved into his parish (i.e. 29-15 = 14). Adding these 14 paupers to Chalmers's figure of 77 gives 91. See also, A. Ranken, *A Letter Addressed to the Rev. Dr. Chalmers* (Glasgow, 1830), 12.

124. Chalmers, *Statement in Regard to the Pauperism of Glasgow,* in *Collected Works,* xvi. 232-3.

125. *Statement from the Session of St. John's Parish to the Directors of the Town's Hospital* (Glasgow, 1836), (TCP, CHA 5, St. John's and Tron Box); Cage and Checkland, 'Thomas Chalmers and Urban Poverty', 44.

126. William Collins to T. Chalmers, 1 March 1825 (TCP, CHA 4.42.34); Patrick MacFarlan to T. Chalmers, 11 February, 11 April 1825 (TCP, CHA 4.46.10-12); St. John's did, however, receive some occasional medical assistance from the Town's Hospital. Chalmers, *Collected Works,* xvi. 339.

127. T. Chalmers, *The Sufficiency of a Parochial System without a Poor Rate* (Glasgow, 1841), in *Collected Works,* xxi. 130-2; St. John's Kirk-session Minutes, 6 January 1825 (SRO, CH 2/176/1).

128. T. Chalmers, *Statement in Regard to the Pauperism of Glasgow,* in *Collected Works,* xvi. 217-84.

129. Ibid. 230-1.

130. Ranken, *A Letter Addressed to the Rev. Dr. Chalmers,* 9-12.

131. Ibid., 25; See also [John Hill Burton], 'Poor Laws and Pauperism in Scotland', *Westminster Review,* xxxvi (October 1841), 402-3; W. P. Alison, *Reply to the Pamphlet Entitled 'Proposed Alteration of the Scottish Poor Law'* (Edinburgh, 1840), 62-3; A. Alison, *Principles of Population* (2 vols., Edinburgh, 1840), ii. 86-94; *Glasgow Sentinel,* 29 May, 5 June 1822.

132. Chalmers, *Collected Works,* xvi. 241-61.

133. 'Abstract of the Survey of St. John's Parish, 1825' (TCP, CHA 5, St. John's and Tron Box); Cleland, *The Rise and Progress of the City of Glasgow,* chart opp. p. 228.

134. T. Chalmers, *Considerations on the System of Parochial Schools in Scotland* (Glasgow, 1819) in *Collected Works*, xii. 191-219; Hanna, *Memoirs*, ii. 231-3.

135. Hanna, *Memoirs*, ii. 233-6; Cage, 'The Scottish Poor Law, 1745-1845', table 23 (after p. 203).

136. Hanna, *Memoirs*, ii. 236-7.

137. Ibid. 244-6.

138. T. Chalmers to James Brown, 30 January 1819 (EUL, DC. 2.57., fol. 62).

139. J. H. S. Burleigh, *A Church History of Scotland* (London, 1960), 329.

140. Cage and Checkland, 'Thomas Chalmers and Urban Poverty', 48.

141. 'St. John's Kirk-session Minutes, 4 and 25 March 1822, including extracts from correspondence with Town Council' (SRO, CH 2/176/1); Hanna, *Memoirs*, ii. 378-80; T. Chalmers, Diaries, 22, 26, 27, 28 March, 9, 10 May 1822 (TCP, CHA 6).

142. Hanna, *Memoirs*, ii. 380, 468; *Glasgow Courier*, 23 and 28 May 1822; T. Chalmers, *Speech Delivered on the 24th of May, 1822, Before the General Assembly*.

143. Hanna, *Memoirs*, ii. 280-1; Henry Paul to T. Chalmers, 16 December 1823 (TCP, CHA 4.28.34).

144. Hanna, *Memoirs*, ii. 381-7; The chapel debts were a continual source of consternation to Chalmers. Not only were the subscribers not paid the dividend promised by him; they were on several occasions forced to pay large additional amounts to service the mounting chapel debts for which they were legally responsible. See, for example, Matthew Montgomerie to T. Chalmers, 21 October 1829, 30 September 1834 (TCP, CHA 4.125.34, CHA 4.226.41).

145. Hanna, *Memoirs*, ii. 374-7; *Edinburgh Advertiser*, 4 February 1823.

146. Hanna, *Memoirs*, ii. 466-8; T. Chalmers, Diaries, 16 January, 6, 18 February, 20, 26, 28 March, 1 April, 9, 10 May 1822 (TCP, CHA 6).

147. Anon., *Defence of the Rev. Dr. Chalmers Addressed to the Thinking and Unprejudiced Part of the Inhabitants of Glasgow* (Glasgow, 1823), 4; W. Collins to T. Chalmers, 20 January 1823 (TCP, CHA 4.24.80).

148. *Glasgow Courier*, 11 and 13 November 1823; anon., *Account of the Proceedings which Took Place in Glasgow on the Occasion of Dr. Chalmers' Leaving St. John's Parish*, 3rd edn. (Glasgow, 1823), 14-39.

149. Cage and Checkland, 'Thomas Chalmers and Urban Poverty', 45-53.

150. *Church of Scotland Magazine*, i (March 1834), 32-4; Chalmers, *Collected Works*, viii. 53; *Presbyterian Review*, vi (November 1834), 29-44.

151. Earl of Elgin to T. Chalmers, 7 November, 3 December 1818 (TCP, CHA 4.7.50-4); *Blackwood's Edinburgh Magazine*, ii (May 1818), 155-61.

152. Keir, *The House of Collins*, 30-6.

153. Ibid. 36-92.

154. H. Watt, *The Published Writings of Thomas Chalmers.* (Edinburgh, 1943), 26, 28, 35. The three volumes were later republished as volumes xiv-xvi of Chalmers's *Collected Works*.

155. See, for instance, *Eclectic Review*, 2nd ser., xv (June 1821), 560-76; xx (August 1823), 117-43; *Christian Observer*, xxii (January 1822), 39-48; xxii (February 1822), 105-17.

156. Chalmers, *Collected Works*, xiv. esp. 1-141.

157. Ibid. xv. esp. 226-65, 304-62; xvi. 7-71.

158. e.g., *Eclectic Review*, xx (August 1823), 117-19; *Christian Observer*, xxii (January 1822), 46-8.

159. T. Chalmers to T. R. Malthus, 12 December 1821 (NLS, MS 3112, fol. 228).

160. Robert Owen to T. Chalmers, New Lanark, 24 April 1820 (TCP, CHA 4.16.21); Robert Dale Owen to T. Chalmers, 27 October 1824 (TCP, CHA 4.37.30); In his final years, however, Robert Owen did claim to summon Chalmers's ghost during a seance, in order to pursue their discussion.

161. W. H. Oliver, 'Owen in 1817: The Millennialist Moment', S. Pollard and J. Salt, eds., *Robert Owen: Prophet of the Poor* (London, 1971), 166-87.

Chapter Four: Liberal Reform and the National Establishment

1. There was considerable debate in Scotland between 1815 and 1825 regarding the extension of the principle of legal assessments for poor relief. See, for example, the 'Report of the Committee of the General Assembly of the Church of Scotland, on an Inquiry into the Management of the Poor', in the 'Third Report from the Select Committee on the Poor Laws', *Parliamentary Papers*, 1819 (358), v. 23-35; R. Burns, *Historical Dissertations on the Law and Practice of Great Britain, and particularly of Scotland, with Regard to the Poor*, 2nd edn. (Glasgow, 1819), 48-80; S. Macgill, *Discourses and Essays on Subjects of Public Interest (Edinburgh, 1819)*, 361-475; R. Wilson, *A Sketch of the History of Hawick* (Hawick, 1825), 301-33; A. Dunlop, *A Treatise on the Law of Scotland relative to the Poor* (Edinburgh, 1825), 74-107; *Edinburgh Christian Instructor*, xix (October 1820), 674-82; *Edinburgh Review*, xli (October 1824), 228-58.
2. Hanna, *Memoirs*, ii. 324-67; 'Queries on English Pauperism, including shorthand notes of responses, September 1822' (TCP, CHA 6, Temp. Box 6).
3. T. Chalmers to the Earl of Elgin, 16 September 1822 (BL Peel Papers, Add. MS 40351, fol. 127 copy); Earl of Elgin to R. Peel, 25 August 1822 (Add. MS 40350, fol. 109); Earl of Elgin to R. Peel, 20 September 1822 (Add. MS 40351, fol. 125); T. Chalmers to R. Peel, 27 September 1822 (Add. MS 40351, fol. 177); Earl of Elgin to T. Chalmers, 9, 20 September, 2 November 1822 (TCP, CHA 4.2.19-25).
4. T. Chalmers to J. Butterworth, 12 February 1823 (St. Andrews Univ. Library, MS Bx. 9225, c. 4, MS 1001).
5. Chalmers, *Collected Works*, xv, 134-226.
6. Ibid. 187-205.
7. Ibid. 189.
8. T. F. Kennedy to the Earl of Minto, 18 August 1815 (NLS, Minto Papers, MS 12122).
9. Hansard, *Parliamentary Debates*, xxxix. 1264 (30 March 1819); 1469-76 (26 April 1819); 'Bill for Regulating the Relief of the Poor as respects the Jurisdiction of the Heritors and Kirk Sessions in Scotland', *Parliamentary Papers*, 1819 (180) (239) i-B. 1155, 1159; T. F. Kennedy to the Earl of Minto, 30 May 1819 (NLS, MS 12122).
10. H. Cockburn, *Letters Chiefly Connected with the Affairs of Scotland* (London, 1874), 38-40.
11. T. F. Kennedy to T. Chalmers, 17 September 1823 (TCP, CHA 4.27.6).
12. 'Heads of Scotch Poor Bill Proposed by Kennedy', 'Bill to Regulate the Relief Granted to the Poor in Scotland' (NLS, Minto Papers, MS 12122).
13. Cockburn, *Letters Chiefly Connected with the Affairs of Scotland*, 94-8.
14. T. Chalmers to T. F. Kennedy, 21 November 1823 (St. Andrews Univ. Library, MS Bx. 9225, c. 4, MS 2031); T. F. Kennedy to T. Chalmers, 23 November 1823 (TCP, CHA 4.27.8).
15. Cockburn, *Letters Chiefly Connected with the Affairs of Scotland*, 94-8; *Glasgow Courier*, 9, 13 September 1923; *Scotsman*, 13 September 1823.
16. Earl of Elgin to T. Chalmers, 15 October 1823 (TCP,, CHA 4.25.47).
17. H. Brougham to T. Chalmers, 23 December 1823 (TCP, CHA 4.24.30).
18. T. Babington to T. Chalmers, 15 January 1824 (TCP, CHA 4.31.5).

19. W. W. Whitmore to T. Chalmers, 4 January 1824 (TCP, CHA 4.40.6); T. Babington to T. Chalmers, 27 February, 16 March 1824 (TCP, CHA 4.31.7, CHA 4.31.30).

20. e.g. *Eclectic Review*, 2nd ser., xxi (January 1824), 93-4.

21. Earl of Elgin to T. Chalmers, 14 February 1824 (TCP, CHA 4.33.36); Earl of Rosslyn to T. Chalmers, 7 January 1824 (CHA 4.38.12). The Earl of Minto also expressed doubts, but later reconsidered and supported the bill. Earl of Minto to T. Chalmers, 31 January, 9 February 1824 (CHA 4.36.44-8).

22. T. Chalmers to Earl of Minto, 9 February 1824 (NLS, Minto Papers, MS 12122). Chalmers also requested the Whig Earl of Rosslyn to urge the 'permissive clause' upon Kennedy. Earl of Rosslyn to T. F. Kennedy, 22 February 1824, Cockburn, *Letters Chiefly Connected with the Affairs of Scotland*, 107-10.

23. T. F. Kennedy to T. Chalmers, 18 March 1824 (TCP, CHA 4.35.21).

24. Hansard, *Parliamentary Debates*, new ser. xi, 226-7 (6 April 1824); *Edinburgh Advertiser*, 13 April 1824.

25. *Edinburgh Advertiser*, 30 April 1824.

26. *Edinburgh Advertiser*, 30 April, 4, 7, 11, 18, 21, 25, 28 May 1824; *Scotsman*, 1, 19, May; *Glasgow Chronicle*, 6, 11, 20 May 1824; *Glasgow Herald*, 7, 10 May 1824; *Glasgow Courier*, 8, 11, 27 May 1824; R. M. W. Cowan, *The Newspaper in Scotland, 1815-1860* (Glasgow, 1946), 120-1; T. F. Kennedy to T. Chalmers, 26 April 1824 (TCP, CHA 3.35.27).

27. Cockburn, *Letters Chiefly Connected with the Affairs of Scotland*, 118-19.

28. *Edinburgh Advertiser*, 18 May 1824.

29. T. Chalmers, Diaries, 7 May 1824 (TCP,, CHA 6).

30. *Edinburgh Advertiser*, 11 May 1824; 'The mischievous measure', the *Glasgow Chronicle* observed on 11 May, 'has been imputed to a reverend person; but it seems rather the emanation of some crazy individual.'

31. *Edinburgh Christian Instructor*, xxiii (July 1824), 477-81.

32. T. Chalmers, 'Speech in General Assembly on Mr. Kennedy's Bill, 1824', corrected MS in Chalmers's hand (TCP, CHA 5, uncatalogued papers); *Edinburgh Christian Instructor*, xxiii. 481-2.

33. Cockburn, *Letters Chiefly Connected with the Affairs of Scotland*, 120-1.

34. Hansard, *Parliamentary Debates*, xi. 900-2 (27 May 1824).

35. Earl of Elgin to R. Peel, marked *'Private'*, 28 May 1824 (BL Peel Papers, Add. MS 40365, fol. 187). Chalmers's 'very private' letter to Peel and Liverpool, which Elgin enclosed with this letter, has apparently not survived.

36. *Scotsman*, 2 June 1824.

37. *Edinburgh Review*, xli (October 1824), 228-58; Cockburn *Letters Chiefly Connected with the Affairs of Scotland*, 125-7.

38. W. B. Shaw to T. Chalmers, 19 January, 25 July 1825 (TCP, CHA 4.49.14, CHA 4.49.20); H. Duncan to T. Chalmers, 31 May 1824 (TCP, CHA 4.33. 27); W. Stark, *Considerations Addressed to the Heritors and Kirk-sessions of Scotland, particularly of the Border Counties, on ... the Affairs of the Poor* (Edinburgh, 1826), 12-21; E. Carleton Tuffnell to T. Chalmers, 22 October 1832 (TCP, CHA 4.191.71).

39. Saunders, *Scottish Democracy, 1815-1840*, 307-71; Scotland, *The History of Scottish Education*, i. 163-4, 341-3; J. Kerr, *Scottish Education: School and University*, (Cambridge, 1910), 220-7.

40. G. Smith, *Life of Alexander Duff* (2 vols., New York, 1879), i. 19.

41. F. Nicoll to Viscount Melville, 25 October 1822; Viscount Melville to F. Nicoll, 29 October 1822 (St. Andrews Univ. Library, Melville Papers, MS 4644).

42. F. Nicoll to T. Chalmers, 16 November 1822, 11, 16 January 1823 (TCP, CHA 4.22.1, CHA 4.28.7-9); F. Nicoll to Viscount Melville, 18 January 1823 (St. Andrews Univ. Library, Melville Papers, MS 4648).

43. Smith, *Life of Alexander Duff*, i. 20-1.
44. Hanna, *Memoirs*, ii. 487-8.
45. Davie, *The Democratic Intellect*, 255-85, especially 266-9; Hanna, *Memoirs*, iii. 53-63.
46. T. Chalmers, *Sketches of Moral and Mental Philosophy ... and their Bearings on Doctrinal and Practical Christianity*, in *Collected Works*, v. 47-9, 405-7.
47. Ibid. 154-61.
48. Ibid. 54-9, 96-102, 396-420.
49. Ibid. 162-216.
50. Ibid. 165, 114-17.
51. 'Oral Evidence of Thomas Chalmers, August 2, 1827', *Parliamentary Papers, Reports from Commissioners, Universities (Scotland): 3. St. Andrews*, 1837 (94), xxxvii, 61-2, 79-81; 'Chief peculiarities of my course [political economy] 1824-1825', MS in Chalmers's hand (TCP, CHA 6).
52. Hanna, *Memoirs*, iii. 67-8.
53. Ibid. 68.
54. Ibid. 192-5.
55. Ibid. 195-200; Smith, *Life of Alexander Duff*, i. 24-5; W. Orme, *Memoirs of John Urquhart* (Philadelphia, 1855), 68-70.
56. Hanna, *Memoirs*, iii. 186-91; Orme, *Memoirs of John Urquhart*, 31, 76-7, 139-40. Smith, *Life of Alexander Duff*, i. 27-32.
57. Orme, *Memoirs of John Urquhart*, 85-6; Henry Craik to T. Chalmers, 15 [May?] 1825 (St. Andrews Univ. Library, MS 30385, fol. 153).
58. Orme, *Memoirs of John Urquhart*, 69-70, 85; Hanna, *Memoirs*, iii. 199-202.
59. Robert Haldane to John Lee, 6 February 1828 (NLS, Lee Papers, MS 3437, fol 17).
60. Hanna, *Memoirs*, iii. 202-3. Among Chalmers's students who remained in Scotland to pursue the home mission were George Lewis, mechanics-institute teacher, editor of the *Scottish Guardian*, Dundee parish minister, and educational and factory reformer; and John G. Lorimer, mechanics-institute teacher, Glasgow parish minister, and a noted author on the pastoral ministry.
61. Hanna, *Memoirs*, iii. 105, 494-7; Scott, *Fasti*, v, 243-4.
62. F. Nicoll to T. Chalmers, 30 August 1824 (TCP, CHA 4.37.16).
63. Earl of Elgin to T. Chalmers, 4 September 1824 (TCP, CHA 4.33.43).
64. Hanna, *Memoirs*, iii. 494-8.
65. T. Chalmers, *Letter to the Royal Commissioners for the Visitation of Colleges in Scotland* (Glasgow, 1832), 54-80; Hanna, *Memoirs*, iii. 105-9.
66. Cockburn, *Memorials of his Time*, 232.
67. 'I long for a decision', Chalmers told the Whig Evangelical lawyer, James Moncrieff, in reference to the 'Candlemass Dividend', on 15 November 1824, 'on a matter that has stirred up a very severe conflict in my heart between the love of peace and the love of principle.' (Moncrieff Papers, Private Collection, NRA (Scot), Tuliebole, Kinross).
68. Chalmers, *Letter to the Royal Commissioners*, 5, 29; J. Moncrieff to T. Chalmers, 4 December 1824, 1 January 1825 (TCP, CHA 4.36.50, CHA 4.47.21).
69. Hanna, *Memoirs*, iii. 99, 109-11; T. Chalmers to J. Moncrieff, 20 December 1824 (Moncrieff Papers, NRA, (Scot), Tuliebole, Kinross); J. Moncrieff to T. Chalmers, 21 December 1824 (TCP, CHA 4.47.26).
70. Hanna, *Memoirs*, iii. 99-103.
71. Ibid. 111; Chalmers, *Letter to the Royal Commissioners*, 35.
72. T. Chalmers to Moncrieff Wellwood, 13 October 1826 (Moncrieff Papers, NRA (Scot), Tuliebole, Kinross).

73. *Parliamentary Papers,* Reports from Commissioners, Universities (Scotland): 3. St. Andrews, 1837 (94), xxxvii, 65-75.

74. Ibid. 61-5; Hanna, *Memoirs,* iii. 168.

75. T. Chalmers, *On the Use and Abuse of Literary and Ecclesiastical Endowments* (Glasgow, 1827), in *Collected Works,* xvii. 29-184, esp. 29-70.

76. Ibid. 47, 131.

77. Ibid. 155-7.

78. Chalmers, *Letter to the Commissioners;* Hanna, *Memoirs,* iii. 111-15.

79. Hanna, ed., *A Selection from the Correspondence of Thomas Chalmers,* 201-3, 206.

80. Ibid. 204, 206-8; T. Chalmers to J. Chalmers, 24 February, 8 March 1827 (TCP, CHA 3.10-61-3).

81. Hanna, ed., *A Selection from the Correspondence of Thomas Chalmers,* 208-9; T. Chalmers to J. Chalmers, 18 March 1828 (TCP, CHA 3.11.13).

82. Hanna, *Memoirs,* iii. 155-7.

83. Ibid. 158-63; Edward Irving to T. Chalmers, 27 April 1827 (TCP, CHA 4.77.9); James Hoby to T. Chalmers, 15 June 1827 (TCP, CHA 4.76.16).

84. H. Brougham to T. Chalmers, n.d. [1827] (TCP, CHA 4.66.53).

85. Z. Macaulay to T. Chalmers, 25 August, 13 September 1827 (TCP, CHA 4.79.7-8).

86. A. Thompson to T. Chalmers, 23 October 1824 (TCP, CHA 4.39.48); Walter Tait to T. Chalmers, 25 October 1824 (TCP, CHA 4.39.39).

87. Lachlan Maclaurin to T. Chalmers, 8 August 1827 (TCP, CHA 4.79.60); W. Tait to T. Chalmers, 8 June 1827 (TCP, CHA 4.86.1).

88. Hanna, *Memoirs,* ii. 395-400; *Glasgow Courier,* 16 October 1823; T. Chalmers, *A Speech delivered in the Synod of Glasgow and Ayr on the 15th October 1823, in the Case of Principal McFarlane, on the Subject of Pluralities* (Glasgow, 1823), 11-22.

89. *Scotsman,* 26 May 1824.

90. Henry Duncan to T. Chalmers, 31 May 1824 (TCP, CHA 4.33.27).

91. The price of his return was an annual dinner, with sufficient quantities of gin to refresh the burgh council of Anstruther Easter on election evening. I. F. Maciver, 'The Evangelical Party and the Eldership in the General Assemblies, 1820-1843', *SCHS,* xx. 1 (1978), 4-5.

92. Hanna, *Memoirs,* iii. 75-6, 119, 164.

93. Anderson, *Reminiscences of Thomas Chalmers,* 104-6, 112-16, 122; Cunningham, *Church History of Scotland,* ii. 614-15.

94. *Report of the Debate in the General Assembly of the Church of Scotland on the Overtures anent the Union of Offices, May 1825* (Edinburgh, 1825), 12-23.

95. Ibid. 188-91.

96. *Scotsman,* 27 May 1826. See also *Scotsman,* 31 May 1826; Cowan, *The Newspaper in Scotland,* 108.

97. Marquess of Lansdowne to the Earl of Minto, 13 August, 25 September, 9 October 1827 (NLS, Minto Papers, MS 11805, fols. 116, 123, 126); Marquess of Lansdowne to T. Chalmers, 23 September 1827 (TCP, CHA 4.78.3); T. Chalmers to Robert Paul, 19 October 1827 (TCP, CHA 3.10.83).

98. R. Paul to T. Chalmers, 18 October 1827 (TCP, CHA 4.83.31).

99. A Thomson to T. Chalmers, 22 October 1827 (TCP, CHA 4.86.23).

100. T. Chalmers to R. Paul, 23 October 1827 (TCP, CHA 3.10.57). R. Paul to T. Chalmers, 25 October 1827 (TCP, CHA 4.83.35); Hanna, *Memoirs,* iii. 205-8.

101. R. Paul to T. Chalmers, 31 October 1827 (TCP, CHA 4.83.39).

102. T. Chalmers to R. Paul, 30 October 1827 (NLS, Paul Papers, MS 5139, fol. 129); A. Thomson to T. Chalmers, 6 November 1827 (TCP, CHA 4.86.25).

103. Hanna, *Memoirs,* iii. 224-5.

104. T. Chalmers, 'On the Respect due to Antiquity', in *Collected Works,* xi. 123-59.
105. Ibid. 152-3.
106. T. Chalmers, 'The Effect of Man's Wrath in the Agitation of Religious Controversies', in *Collected Works,* xi. 161-92.
107. Ibid. 184.
108. T. Chalmers, 'Speech on the Corporation and Test Acts', MS in Chalmers's hand (TCP, CHA 6, uncatalogued papers); Hanna, *Memoirs,* iii. 215-220.
109. *Scotsman,* 28 May 1828.
110. For an excellent study of the Catholic emancipation struggle in Scotland, see I. A. Muirhead, 'Catholic Emancipation: Scottish Reactions in 1829', *Innes Review,* xxiv. 1 (1972), 26-42, and 'Catholic Emancipation in Scotland: The Debate and Aftermath', *Innes Review,* xxiv. 2 (1973), 103-20.
111. Muirhead, 'Catholic Emancipation: Scottish Reactions in 1829', 26-33.
112. Hanna, *Memoirs,* iii. 231-4.
113. Cockburn, *Letters Chiefly Connected with the Affairs of Scotland,* 206-9.
114. J. Dodds, *Thomas Chalmers: A Biographical Study* (Edinburgh, 1879), 199-205.
115. T. Chalmers, 'Speech Against the Petition for the Continuance of the Catholic Disabilities', MS in Chalmers's hand (TCP, CHA 6, uncatalogued papers); *Report (Taken from the Caledonia Mercury) of the Speeches ... on Saturday, the 14th March 1829 ... for the Removal of the Disabilities Affecting the Roman Catholics* (Edinburgh, 1829), 17-19; Hanna, *Memoirs,* iii. 235-40; *Scotsman,* 18 March 1829.
116. Dodds, *Thomas Chalmers,* 208-9.
117. Cockburn, *Life of Lord Jeffrey,* i. 281-2.
118. Hanna, *Memoirs,* iii. 240-2, 512-19.
119. Muirhead, 'Catholic Emancipation: Scottish Reactions in 1829', 40-1; [H. Drummond], *A Letter to Dr. Chalmers, in Reply to his Speech in the Presbytery of Edinburgh* (London, 1829), 1.
120. G. Nicholls, *A History of the Irish Poor Law* (London, 1856), 95-6.
121. Hanna, *Memoirs,* iii. 249-50. Before proceeding to London, Chalmers sent requests for information to a number of individuals in both Scotland and Ireland. Responses are to be found in the Chalmers Papers. See, for example, James Carlile to T. Chalmers, Dublin, 26 April 1830 (TCP, CHA 4.134.27); Thomas Parnell to T. Chalmers, Dublin, 8, 10, 13, 17, 20, 21 May 1830 (TCP, CHA 4.145.47-60).
122. Chalmers, *Collected Works,* xvi. 285-421.
123. Ibid. 286-310, 365-82, 410-21.
124. Ibid. 367.
125. Nicholls, *A History of the Irish Poor Law,* 96-113.
126. N. Senior, *A Letter to Lord Howick on a Legal Provision for the Irish Poor* (London, 1831), 54, 85-104; N. Senior to T. Chalmers, n.d. [probably March 1832] (TCP, CHA 4, uncatalogued); T. Chalmers to N. Senior, 8 March 1832 (EUL, E 7711, AAF 47).
127. Hanna, *Memoirs,* iii. 385.
128. Ibid. 268-70.
129. Cockburn, *Memorials of his Time,* 470.
130. Hanna, *Memoirs,* iii. 299-301; John Walsh to T. Chalmers, 18 April 1831 (TCP, CHA 4.170.11).
131. T. Chalmers, *On Political Economy in Connexion with the Moral State and Moral Prospects of Society* (Glasgow, 1832), iii-iv. A revised version is included in T. Chalmers, *Collected Works,* xix and xx: the citations that follow, however, are from the first edition.
132. Ibid. 1-30, 479, 489.
133. Ibid. 31-173.

134. Ibid. 174-240.

135. Ibid. 240-331.

136. Ibid. 378-97.

137. Ibid. 398-419.

138. Ibid. 420-421.

139. Ibid. 423-49.

140. N. Senior to T. Chalmers, 28 July 1832 (TCP, CHA 4.189.57).

141. [George Paulett Scrope], 'Dr. Chalmers on Political Economy', *Quarterly Review*, xlviii (October 1832), 39-68, 52.

142. [Thomas Perronet Thompson], 'Dr. Chalmers on Political Economy', *Westminster Review*, xvii (July 1832), 1-33, 33.

143. 'Illustrations of Political Economy', *Eclectic Review*, 3rd ser., viii (July 1832), 59.

144. T. Chalmers to M. Napier, 25 July 1829 (BL, Add. MS 34,614, fol. 136).

145. J. R. McCulloch, *The Principles of Political Economy* (Edinburgh, 1825), 52-6, 354-8; Senior, *Letter to Lord Howick*, 30-7.

146. J. R. McCulloch to M. Napier, 3 August 1832 (BL, Add. MS 34, 615, fol. 382).

147. M. Napier to T. Chalmers, 29 September 1832 (TCP, CHA 4.187.8).

148. [J. R. McCulloch], 'Dr. Chalmers on Political Economy', *Edinburgh Review*, lvi (October 1832), 52-72.

149. Ibid. 55.

150. Chalmers, *Collected Works*, xx. 145-225.

151. Ibid. 184-92.

152. N. Senior to T. Chalmers, 18 July 1832 (TCP, CHA 4.189.57); S. and B. Webb, *English Poor Law History: Part II: The Last Hundred Years* (2 vols., London, 1929), i. 53n.; A. Brundage, *The Making of the New Poor Law* (New Brunswick, 1978). 85.

153. E. Carleton Tuffnell to T. Chalmers, 4, 24 August, 16 September 1832 (TCP CHA 4.191.63-6).

154. Ibid., 2 October 1832 (TCP, CHA 4.191.68).

155. Ibid., 22 October, 13 November 1832 (TCP, CHA 4.191.71-3); Tuffnell's report on the St. John's experiment and Chalmers's social ideal is reprinted in Chalmers, *Collected Works*, xvi. 437-44.

156. E. Carlton Tuffnell to T. Chalmers, 10 March 1834 (TCP, CHA 4.229.77).

157. Chalmers, *Collected Works*, xxi. 139-40, 151-5, 162.

158. Hanna, *Memoirs*, iii. 290-7.

159. See, for example, W. Collins to T. Chalmers, 22 February 1831 (TCP, CHA 4.156.9).

160. We lack an adequate biography of this very considerable figure, but see J. W. Craven, 'Andrew Thomson (1779-1831) ...' Ph.D. Thesis Edinburgh Univ. (New College), 1955; 'Memoir of Andrew Thomson', in A. Thomson, *Sermons and Sacramental Exhortations* (Edinburgh, 1831), x-lxii.

161. Henry Duncan to T. Chalmers, 29 June 1831 (TCP, CHA 4.157.42).

162. Scott, *Fasti*, i. 190-1; 73; Robert Paul to T. Chalmers, 29 November 1827 (TCP, CHA 4.83.41).

163. T. Chalmers to the Earl of Minto, 22 June, 28 July, 9, 12 August 1831 (NLS, Minto Papers, MS 12123).

164. Francis Jeffrey to H. Cockburn, 19 June 1831 (NLS, Advocates MS. 9.1.8., 51, Letter 33).

165. F. Jeffrey to T. Chalmers, 26 June 1831 (TCP, CHA 4.161.34).

166. J. Lee, 'Reasons of Dissent from the Deliverance of the General Assembly on the 23rd May 1831 ...... [Regarding] the Recently Introduced Practice of Exacting Fees from Students of Divinity' (NLS, Lee Papers, MS 3438, fol. 117-22); Patrick MacFarlan to T. Chalmers, 23 May 1831 (TCP, CHA 4.169. 50).

167. T. Chalmers to the Earl of Minto, 22 June 1831 (NLS, Minto Papers MS 12123);
      T. Chalmers to D. Aitken, 25 June 1831 (St. Andrews Univ. Library, MS Bx.
      9225, c. 4, MS 51).
168. D. Aitken to the Earl of Minto, 19, 25 July 1831 (NLS, Minto Papers, MS
      11801, fol. 23-6); D. Aitken to T. Chalmers, 20 July 1831 (TCP, CHA 4.151.
      33).
169. D. Aitken to the Earl of Minto, 15, 17 August 1831 (NLS, Minto Papers,
      MS 11801, fols. 45-7).
170. J. Abercromby to the Earl of Minto, 17 August 1831 (NLS, Minto Papers, MS
      11800, fol. 136).
171. Earl of Minto to J. Abercromby, 20 August 1831 (NLS, Minto Papers, MS
      11800, fol. 138).
172. F. Jeffrey to T. Chalmers, 27 September 1831 (TCP, CHA 4.161.36); Hanna,
      Memoirs, iii. 307-8.

Chapter Five: The Church Militant

1. T. Chalmers, 'Sermon ... on Occasion of the Death of the Rev. Dr. Andrew
    Thomson', in *Collected Works*, xi. 205-7; A. L. Drummond and J. Bulloch, *The
    Scottish Church, 1688-1843*, 180-92, 212-19; G. D. Henderson, *Heritage: A Study
    of the Disruption* (Edinburgh, 1943), 48-58.
2. Grub, *An Ecclesiastical History of Scotland*, iv. 159-60; Drummond and Bulloch,
    The Scottish Church, 1688-1843, 181-4.
3. *Church of Scotland Magazine* (Glasgow), i. (May 1834), 90-3; iii (May 1835),
    149-50; *Second Biennial Report of the Edinburgh City Mission* (Edinburgh, 1834);
    J. Baillie, *the Missionary of Kilmany: Being a Memoir of Alexander Paterson*, 40-58;
    First Report of the Royal Commission on Religious Instruction, *Parliamentary
    Papers*, 1837 (31), xxi. 9, 31-2.
4. J. G. Kyd, ed., *Scottish Population Statistics*, Publications of the Scottish History
    Society, 3rd ser., xliv (Edinburgh, 1852), 82-3; Drummond and Bulloch, *The
    Scottish Church, 1688-1843*, 184.
5. I. F. Maciver, 'The General Assembly of the Church, the State, and Society in
    Scotland: Some Aspects of their Relationships, 1815-1843', M. Litt. Thesis,
    Edinburgh Univ., 1976, 118-52; T. Chalmers, Report of the Church Extension
    Committee (Edinburgh, 1835), 9.
6. J. Tulloch, *Movements of Religious Thought in Britain During the Nineteenth Century*
    (London, 1885), 125-45; D. Finlayson, 'Aspects of the Life and Influence of
    Thomas Erskine of Linlathen, 1788-1870', *SCHS*, xx. 1 (1978), 31-45.
7. J. Tulloch, *Movements of Religious Thought*, 145-50; B. A. Gerrish, *Tradition and the
    Modern World: Reformed Theology in the Nineteenth Century* (Chicago, 1978), 71-98.
8. A. L. Drummond, *Edward Irving and his Circle* (London, 1934), 122-35; *Scotsman*,
    7 June 1828.
9. Drummond, *Edward Irving and his Circle*, 136-51; D. Campbell, ed., *Memorials of
    John Macleod Campbell* (2 vols., London, 1877), i. 51-4.
10. M. Oliphant, *The Life of Edward Irving* (New York, 1862), 370.
11. Drummond and Bulloch, *The Scottish Church, 1688-1843*, 202-5.
12. Drummond, *Edward Irving and his Circle*, 208-35.
13. Hanna, *Memoirs*, ii. 177; iii. 80, 246-7; *A Selection from the Correspondence of Thomas
    Chalmers*, 313-17; Tulloch, *Movements of Religious Thought*, 143.
14. Hanna, *Memoirs*, iii. 160-3; T. Chalmers to Mrs Henry Paul, 20 October 1827
    (TCP, CHA 3.10.85).

15. Campbell, ed., *Memorials of John Macleod Campbell,* i. 51-2; Hanna, *Memoirs,* iii. 248-9; J. Macleod Campbell to T. Chalmers, 28 April 1830. (TCP, CHA 4.134.21); Hanna, *Memoirs,* iii. 272.

16. Oliphant, *The Life of Edward Irving,* 371-3.

17. Tulloch, *Movements of Religious Thought,* 162; Gerrish, *Tradition and the Modern World,* 71.

18. Edward Craig to T. Chalmers, 29 April 1830 (TCP, CHA 4.136.50); David Rintoul to T. Chalmers, 28 August 1830 (TCP, CHA 4.147.25).

19. See the twenty-nine letters relating to the Mowbray marriage affair and Irving's involvement, 1831 (TCP, CHA 4.165.1-73); J. Macleod Campbell to T. Chalmers [18 March 1831], (TCP, CHA 4.154.46).

20. T. Chalmers to Fergus Jardine, 11 October 1831 (TCP, CHA 3.14.12).

21. Drummond and Bulloch, *The Scottish Church, 1688-1843,* 205.

22. Ibid. 205-19; F. Jardine to T. Chalmers, 7, 10 October 1831 (TCP, CHA 4, 161.22-4).

23. For a younger Evangelical's perception of this period, see R. Buchanan, *The Ten Years' Conflict,* 2nd edn. (2 vols., Glasgow, 1852), i. 172-89.

24. O. Chadwick, *The Victorian Church* (New York, 1966), Part 1, 560-1; Hanna, *Memoirs,* iii. 308-9.

25. T. Chalmers, *On the Power, Wisdom and Goodness of God as Manifested in the Adoption of External Nature to the Moral and Intellectual Constitution of Man* (2 vols., London, 1833), i. 57-132.

26. Ibid. i. 218-24; ii. 1-50.

27. Ibid. ii. 286.

28. Ibid. ii. 282-304.

29. *Presbyterian Review,* v (March 1834), 1-31; viii (March 1836), 104-43; Watt, *The Published Writings of Thomas Chalmers,* 45-6.

30. Hanna, *Memoirs,* iv. 1-7.

31. A. B. Montgomery, 'The Voluntary Controversy in the Church of Scotland, 1829-1843', Ph.D. Thesis, Edinburgh Univ. (New College) 1953, 1-16; J. M'Kerrow, *History of the Secession Church,* 724-5.

32. Montgomery, 'The Voluntary Controversy', 16-80; M'Kerrow, *History of the Secession Church,* 726-34; *Voluntary Church Magazine* i (March 1833), 1-9; *Scotsman,* 3 June 1829.

33. Precise membership statistics are not available for this period. The Royal Commission on Religious Instruction in Scotland determined that about half the Edinburgh church-going population was Dissenting, but Dissent was much stronger in the towns than in rural districts (First Report of the Commission on Religious Instruction, Scotland, *Parliamentary Papers,* 1837 (31), xxi. 9. 8-10. Some idea of relative denominational strengths in 1830 can be gained from later statistics. See R. Currie, A. Gilbert, and L. Horsley, *Churches and Churchgoers, Patterns of Church Growth in the British Isles since 1700,* (Oxford, 1977), 219-26.

34. Grub, *Ecclesiastical History of Scotland,* iv. 160-71; M'Kerrow, *History of the Secession Church,* 578-664.

35. Drummond and Bulloch, *The Scottish Church, 1688-1843,* 231-2.

36. Montgomery, 'The Voluntary Controversy', 51-80; R. Rainy and J. MacKenzie, *Life of William Cunningham* (London, 1871), 86-98; *Church of Scotland Magazine,* i (March 1834), 1-4.

37. *Presbyterian Review,* iii (January 1833), 278.

38. Moncrieff Wellwood, *Life and Writings of John Erskine,* 473.

39. Maciver, 'The General Assembly of the Church, the State, and Society in Scotland', 34-6.

40. Buchanan, *The Ten Years' Conflict,* i.193-4.

41. D. Aitken to the Earl of Minto, 8 October 1832 (NLS, Minto Papers, MS 11801, fol. 120).
42. A. Marshall, *Letter to Dr. Thomson* (Glasgow, 1830), 119-22.
43. *Scottish Guardian,* 1 February 1833; *Presbyterian Review,* ii (May 1832), 207-35.
44. Hanna, *Memoirs,* iii. 340-1; Buchanan, *The Ten Years' Conflict,* i. 209.
45. F. Jeffrey to H. Cockburn, 7 May 1833 (NLS, Advocates MS, 9.1.9., Letters 217-18, pp. 162-5).
46. Hanna, *Memoirs,* iii. 351-4; J. Moncrieff to H. Brougham, 3 March 1833 (Brougham Papers, University College, London, fols. 33,269, 33,653).
47. T. Chalmers, 'Speech delivered in the General Assembly of 1833 on a Proposed Modification of the Law of Patronage', in *Collected Works,* xii. 373-94.
48. Ibid. 376-82.
49. Ibid. 390-1.
50. H. Cockburn, *Journal* (2 vols., Edinburgh, 1874), i. 44-6; *Presbyterian Review,* iii (September 1833), 335-42.
51. J. Lee, *Letter to the Lord Provost, Relating to the Annuity Tax* (Edinburgh, 1834), 8-32.
52. H. Cockburn to T. Chalmers, 22 April 1833 (TCP, CHA 4.202.18).
53. Hanna, *Memoirs,* iii. 424-9; A. Nicolson, *Memoirs of Adam Black* (Edinburgh, 1885), 84-5; *Scotsman,* 22 June, 13, 17 July 1833.
54. Cockburn, *Journal,* i. 51-3.
55. Ibid. 56-7; *Scotsman,* 25 January 1834.
56. Hanna, *Memoirs,* iii. 426-9.
57. A. Dunlop to T. Chalmers, 16 January 1834 (TCP, CHA 4.221.62).
58. *Scotsman,* 25 January 1834.
59. Hanna, *Memoirs,* iii. 433-5; Cockburn, *Journal,* i. 57.
60. Hanna, *Memoirs,* iii. 436-44.
61. Buchanan, *The Ten Years' Conflict,* i. 237-96; Maciver, 'The General Assembly of the Church, the State, and Society in Scotland', 160-4.
62. T. Chalmers, *First Report of the Committee of the General Assembly on Church Extension* (Edinburgh, 1835), 17-22; C. Fergusson to T. Chalmers, 30 May 1834 (TCP, CHA 4.222.29).
63. Hanna, *Memoirs,* iii. 450-1.
64. [W. Collins], *Proposal for Building Twenty New Parochial Churches in the City and Suburbs of Glasgow* [Glasgow, 1834], 1-15; W. Collins, *The Church of Scotland: the Poor Man's Church,* [Glasgow, n.d.], 1-8; W. Collins to T. Chalmers, 27 February, 27 March 1834 (TCP, CHA 4.220.11-12); Keir, *The House of Collins,* 105-6; *Scottish Guardian,* 5 February 1834.
65. D. Chambers, 'The Church of Scotland's Parochial Extension Scheme and the Scottish Disruption', *Journal of Church and State,* xvi (1974), 271-2.
66. Chalmers, *First Report,* 20.
67. T. Chalmers to W. Collins, 9 June 1834 ('Church Extension Letterbook, 1834-1836', Edinburgh University, New College Library, unpubl. MS, X13b 6/3, 2).
68. T. Chalmers to Abercromby Gordon, 28 June 1834 ('Church Extension Letterbook', 13-16).
69. T. Chalmers to R. Buchanan, 30 June 1834, T. Chalmers to John Cook, 9 July 1834 ('Church Extension Letterbook', 16-18, 33-6).
70. Chalmers, *First Report,* 6-8, 26-8.
71. Ibid. 13-15.
72. T. Chalmers to the Duke of Buccleuch, 9 July 1834, T. Chalmers to the Duchess of Gordon, 9 July 1834 ('Church Extension Letterbook', 27-33); Chalmers, *First Report,* 28-9; T. Chalmers to J. A. Stuart MacKenzie, MP, 31 July 1834 (SRO, GD 46/12/68).

73. Hanna, *Memoirs,* ii. 445-7; Chalmers, *Collected Works,* xviii. 202-5; A. Black, *The Church Its Own Enemy, Being an Answer to the Pamphlets of the Rev. Dr. Chalmers,* 3rd edn. (Edinburgh, 1835), 56-60; J. Gladstone to T. Chalmers, 26 February 1834 (TCP, CHA 4.223.19).

74. T. Chalmers to John Leermouth, 25 August 1834 ('Church Extension Letterbook', 67-9).

75. *Parliamentary Papers,* First Report of the Commissioners on Religious Instruction in Scotland, 1837 (31), xxi. 19, 'Evidence of Thomas Chalmers, 13 February 1836', 264-8; Chalmers, *Collected Works,* xi. 347-53; xviii. 93-8. For Voluntary criticism of the Water of Leith operation, see *Scotsman,* 21 February 1835.

76. T. Chalmers, *The Cause of Church Extension and the Question Shortly Stated, Between Churchmen and Dissenters in Regard to it* (Glasgow, 1835), in *Collected Works,* xviii. 136-7.

77. T. Chalmers, *Churches and Chapels; or, the Necessity and Proper Object of an Endowment* (Glasgow, 1835), in *Collected Works,* xviii. 83-104; *Edinburgh Advertiser,* 17 February, 24 March 1835.

78. Maciver, 'The General Assembly of the Church, the State, and Society', 164.

79. *Edinburgh Advertiser,* 24 March 1835.

80. T. Chalmers to C. Fergusson, 2 July 1834, T. Chalmers to James Ewing, 28, 30 July 1834 ('Church Extension Letterbook', 19-23, 45-6, 50-2).

81. Hanna, *Memoirs,* ii. 461-2.

82. C. Fergusson to T. Chalmers, 11 August 1834 (TCP, CHA 4.222.32).

83. T. Chalmers, 'Outline of the Scheme by which the Deficiencies of our Establishment Might be Repaired, September 1834' ('Church Extension Letterbook', 82-3).

84. T. Chalmers to W. Gladstone, 24 September 1834 (BL, Gladstone Papers, Add. MS 44354, fol. 58); W. Gladstone to T. Chalmers, 29 September 1834 (TCP, CHA 4.223.33).

85. John Gladstone was a leading participant in both Chalmers's Cowgate and his Water of Leith church-building efforts. See J. Gladstone to T. Chalmers, 7 February, 3 September 1834, J. Gladstone to John Thomson, 26 July 1834 (TCP, CHA 4.223.17, CHA 4.223.24, CHA 4.223.19).

86. W. F. Gray, 'Chalmers and Gladstone: An Unrecorded Episode', *SCHS,* x (1948), 9-17; J. Morley, *Life of William Ewart Gladstone* (3 vols., New York, 1903), i. 169-71; W. Gladstone to T. Chalmers, 2 February 1835 (TCP, CHA 4.236.62).

87. T. Chalmers to W. Gladstone, 13, 27 December 1834 (Add. MS 44354, fols. 108, 134); W. Gladstone to T. Chalmers, 30 December 1834 (TCP, CHA 4.223.37).

88. Hanna, *Memoirs,* iii. 531-7.

89. Sir R. Peel to T. Chalmers, 24 January 1835 (BL, Peel Papers, Add. MS 40411, fol. 200); T. Chalmers to W. Gladstone, 28 January 1834 (BL, Gladstone Papers, Add. MS 44354, fol. 153).

90. G. I. T. Machin, *Politics and the Churches in Great Britain* (Oxford, 1977), 117; *Scotsman,* 21 February, 11 March, 1,4, 18 April 1835.

91. Machin, *Politics and the Churches in Great Britain,* 117; Chalmers, *First Report,* 40-5; Cockburn, *Journal,* i. 90-3.

92. T. Chalmers, *The Right Ecclesiastical Economy of a Large Town* (Glasgow, 1835), in *Collected Works,* xviii. 41-79; Chalmers, *The Cause of Church Extension,* in *Collected Works,* xviii. 107-55; Anderson, *Reminiscences of Thomas Chalmers,* 231-5.

93. *Scotsman,* 11 March 1835.

94. Chalmers, *Collected Works,* xviii. 159-234.

95. A. Black, *The Church Its Own Enemy,* 21-2; See also, *Scotsman,* 6, 20 May 1835, for further criticism of Chalmers's 'Owenite ecclesiastical parallelograms'.

96. Rainy and MacKenzie, *Life of William Cunningham,* 89.
97. W. Gladstone to T. Chalmers, 18 February 1835 (TCP, CHA 4.236.68).
98. T. Chalmers to W. Gladstone, 10, 14, 16, 21 Feburary, 7, 19 March 1835 (BL, Gladstone Papers, Add. MS 44,354, fols. 172-86).
99. W. Gladstone to T. Chalmers, 28 March, 2 April 1835 (TCP, CHA 4.236.70, CHA 4.236.74).
100. T. Chalmers to Sir R. Peel, 22 April 1835 (BL, Peel Papers, Add. MS 40,420, fol. 49).
101. Chalmers, *First Report,* 1-16.
102. Cockburn, *Journal,* i. 96-7.
103. Hanna, *Memoirs,* iii. 470-1.
104. T. Chalmers to P. M. Stewart, 21 July 1835 ('Church Extension Letterbook', 113-17).
105. Maciver, 'The General Assembly of the Church, the State, and Society', 194-211; D. Aitken to the Earl of Minto, 25 September 1835 (NLS, Minto Papers, MS 11802, fol. 16).
106. John Hope to the Earl of Aberdeen, 20 August 1835 (BL, Aberdeen Papers, Add. MS 43,202, fol. 110).
107. T. Chalmers to J. Hope, 25 August 1835; J. Hope to the Earl of Aberdeen, 26 August 1835 (BL, Aberdeen Papers, Add. MS 43, 202, fols. 126-8).
108. Hanna, *Memoirs,* iii. 472-84.
109. Ibid. 484-7, 537-9; Cockburn, *Journal,* i. 103-4; Earl of Aberdeen to J. Hope, 6 October 1835 (BL, Aberdeen Papers, Add. MS 43,202, fol. 139).
110. J. Abercromby to the Earl of Minto, 27 September 1835 (NLS, Minto Papers, MS 11800, fol. 154).
111. T. Chalmers to Mountstuart Elphinstone, 2 February 1836 ('Church Extension Letterbook', 149-53); T. Chalmers, *Second Report of the Committee of the General General Assembly on Church Extension* (Edinburgh, 1836), 22-3; *Parliamentary Papers,* First Report of the Commission on Religious Instruction in Scotland, 1837 (31), xxi. 19, 1-2, 260-3.
112. *Parliamentary Papers,* First Report of the Commission on Religious Instruction, 1837 (31), xxi. 19, 'Evidence of Thomas Chalmers, 13 February, 20 February 1836', 264-77.
113. R. Buchanan to T. Chalmers, 7 April 1836 (TCP, CHA 4.246.61); R. Buchanan to A. Dunlop, 10 May 1836, in N. L. Walker, *Robert Buchanan* (London, 1877), 58-9.
114. T. Chalmers, *An Attempt to Point Out the Duty which the Church owes to the People of Scotland ... Being an Argument on Chapel Bonds* (Glasgow, 1836), in *Collected Works,* xviii. 321-74; *Scottish Guardian,* 2 February 1836.
115. *Scotsman,* 3 February 1836; See also, R. Buchanan to T. Chalmers, 7 April 1836 (TCP, CHA 4.246.61).
116. Chalmers, *Second Report,* 3-25.
117. Ibid. 11-14; T. Chalmers to D. Dewar, 11 April 1836 (TCP, CHA 3.15.34).
118. Chalmers, *Second Report,* 14-19.
119. A. L. Simpson to T. Chalmers, 21 July, 22 September 1836; A. Dunlop to T. Chalmers, 19 July 1836; Robert Phin to T. Chalmers, 22 June 1836; T. Guthrie to T. Chalmers, 12 December 1836 (TCP, CHA 4.256.15, CHA 4.256.21; CHA 4.249.54, CHA 4.255.45, CHA 4.251.18); T. Chalmers, *Third Report of the Committee of the General Assembly on Church Extension,* 11-13.
120. D. Shaw, 'The Moderatorship Controversy in 1836 and 1837', *SCHS,* xvii, 2 (1970), 116-25; Maciver, 'The General Assembly of the Church, the State and Society', 212-34.

121. T. Chalmers, *A Conference ... on the Moderatorship of the Next General Assembly* (Glasgow, 1837), 7.

122. *Parliamentary Papers,* First Report of the Commissioners on Religious Instruction in Scotland, 1837 (31), xxi. 19, 'Evidence of John Lee, 18 February, 19 March 1835', 335-44. Once the confidentiality of his evidence had been betrayed, Lee published his entire testimony in pamphlet form. See J. Lee, *Evidence ... before the Commissioners of Religious Instruction, Scotland, in February and March 1836* (Edinburgh, 1837); F. Engels, *The Condition of the Working Class in England,* trans. and ed., W. O. Henderson and W. H. Chaloner (New York, 1958), 41.

123. *Parliamentary Papers,* First Report of the Commissioners on Religious Instruction in Scotland, 270-7; Chalmers, *A Conference,* 10-14.

124. Shaw, 'The Moderatorship Controversy in 1836 and 1837', 122.

125. J. Lee to J. Hope, 25 August 1835 (NLS, Lee Papers, MS. 3441, fol. 49).

126. Shaw, 'The Moderatorship Controversy in 1836 and 1837', 124-6.

127. J. Thomson to J. Lee, 19 December 1836 (NLS, Lee Papers, MS 3441, fol. 131); D. Aitken to the Earl of Minto, 19 December 1836 (NLS, Minto Papers, MS 11802, fol. 91).

128. P. MacFarlan to T. Chalmers, 4, 26 June, 11, 26, 28 July, 26 October 1836 (TCP, CHA 4.252.66-78).

129. T. Chalmers, 'Circular letter regarding meeting of Old Moderators, 29 August 1836' (NLS, Lee Papers, MS 3441, fol. 129).

130. S. Macgill to T. Chalmers, 13 November 1836 (TCP, CHA 4.253.6); S. Macgill to James Moncrieff, 1 December 1836 (Moncrieff Papers, File 22, NRA (Scot.), Tuliebole, Kinross).

131. *Church Review,* i (February 1837), 691.

132. *Presbyterian Review,* ix (January 1837), 282-4; P. MacFarlan to T. Chalmers, 30 November, 9, 19 December 1836 (TCP, CHA 4.252.80-6); Hanna, *Memoirs,* iii. 11-13.

133. Chalmers, *A Conference,* 6-18.

134. Ibid. 10, 19.

135. Ibid. 25-6.

136. J. Thomson to J. Lee, 18 February 1837 (NLS, Lee Papers, MS 3441, fol. 254).

137. Parine Fisher to J. Lee, 7 January 1837 (NLS, Lee Papers, MS 3441, fol. 191).

138. R. Bell, *Observations on the Conference of the Rev. Thomas Chalmers with certain Ministers and Elders of the Church of Scotland* (Edinburgh, 1837); R. Bell, *Statement in Answer to the Rev. Dr. Chalmers' Pamphlet, on the Subject of the Moderatorship* (Edinburgh, 1837); J. Lee, *Refutation of the Charges Brought against him by the Rev. Dr. Chalmers,* Part 1 (Edinburgh, 1837); [J. Moncrieff], *A Word More on the Moderatorship* (Edinburgh, 1837); *Scotsman,* 8 March, 17 May 1837; Hanna, *Memoirs,* iii. 12-13.

139. *Scotsman,* 8 March 1837.

140. *Scottish Guardian,* 31 March 1837.

141. W. Cunningham, *Reply to the Statement of Certain Ministers and Elders, published in Answer to Dr. Chalmers' 'Conference'* (Edinburgh, 1837); *Church of Scotland Magazine* [a publication founded by Cunningham and a few friends], iv (February 1837), 69-70.

142. T. Chalmers, *Supplement to his Late Pamphlet on the Subject of the Moderatorship of the Next General Assembly* (Glasgow, 1837), 37.

143. For the voting list on the Moderatorship question, see the *Church Review,* ii (August 1837), 440-5.

144. T. Chalmers, *Third Report,* 1-26.

145. R. Buchanan to T. Chalmers, 6 January 1837 (TCP, CHA 4.260.9).

146. Scott, *Fasti*, i. 73; Fox Maule to J. Lee, 24 October, 5 December 1837 (NLS, Lee Papers, MS 3442, fols. 38, 95).
147. J. Lee to T. Gillespie, 30 November 1837 (NLS, Lee Papers, MS 3442, fol. 78).
148. J. Lee to R. Haldane, 2 December 1837, J. Hunter to J. Lee, 11 January 1838 (NLS, Lee Papers, MS 3442, fols. 92, 135).
149. T. Chalmers to A. L. Simpson, 13 June, 11 July, 7 August 1837 (NCL, Simpson Letters, Assembly Library no. LSI. 6.26, Bx. 1); A. L. Simpson to T. Chalmers, 10 August 1837 (TCP., CHA 4.269.21).
150. T. Chalmers to A. L. Simpson, 15 August 1837 (NCL, Simpson Letters, Assembly Library no. LSI. 6.26, Bx. 1).
151. D. K. and C. J. Guthrie (eds.), *Autobiography of Thomas Guthrie and Memoir* (2 vols., New York, 1876) i. 214-16.
152. See, for example, the perceptive essay, 'Position of the Church in Relation to the Opinions and Feelings of Society', in the Moderate *Church Review,* ii (April 1837), 16-29, (May 1837), 80-8.
153. T. Chalmers to A. L. Simpson, 18 May 1837 (NCL, Simpson Letters, Assembly Library no. LSI. 6. 26, Bx. 1).
154. T. Chalmers to A. L. Simpson, 11 July 1837 (NCL, Simpson Letters, Assembly Library no. LSI. 6. 26, Bx. 1).
155. *Scotsman,* 13, 17 August 1836; Hanna, *Memoirs,* iv. 24-7.
156. Hanna, *Memoirs,* iv. 29-31.
157. Machin, *Politics and the Churches in Great Britain,* 117; T. Chalmers to William Muir, 13 January 1838 (BL, Aberdeen Papers, Add. MS 43,202, fol. 166).
158. Walker, *Robert Buchanan,* 60-2.
159. R. Buchanan to T. Chalmers, 10 March 1838 [two letters] (TCP, CHA 4.271. 31-3).
160. Walker, *Robert Buchanan,* 62-77.
161. Hanna, *Memoirs,* iv. 34-7; T. Chalmers, *Lectures on the Establishment and Extension of National Churches* (Glasgow, 1838), in *Collected Works,* xvii. 187-356.
162. Ibid. 277-82.
163. Hanna, *Memoirs,* iv. 37-46.
164. *Presbyterian Review,* xii (January 1840), 393-429; *Voluntary Church Magazine,* vi (October 1838), 433-41.
165. Morley, *Life of William Ewart Gladstone,* i. 171-2.
166. T. Chalmers, *Fourth Report of the General Assembly Committee on Church Extension* (Edinburgh, 1838), 3-30, 13.
167. Hanna, *Memoirs,* iv. 47-64; T. Chalmers, 'Distinction both in Principle and Effect between a Legal Charity for the Relief of Indigence, and a Legal Charity for the Relief of Disease', in *Collected Works,* xxi. 369-408.
168. R. Buchanan to T. Chalmers, 17 July 1838 (TCP, CHA 4.271.47).
169. Hanna, *Memoirs,* iv. 66; *Ayrshire Examiner,* 14 September 1838.
170. *Dumfries Herald,* 29 August 1838; *Scottish Guardian,* 23 August, 10, 13, 17 September 1838; *Paisley Advertiser,* 22 September 1838.
171. Hanna, *Memoirs,* iv. 66.
172. D. King, *Two Lectures, in Reply to the Speeches of Dr. Chalmers on Church Extension, delivered ... 18th and 23rd October 1838* (Glasgow, 1838), 42.
173. *Scottish Guardian,* 25 January 1839.
174. W. Collins to T. Chalmers, 10 December 1838 (TCP, CHA 4.272.60).
175. T. Chalmers, *Fifth Report of the Committee of the General Assembly on Church Extension* (Edinburgh, 1839), 35-8.
176. Ibid. 3-16.
177. Hanna, *Memoirs,* iv. 67-84.

178. T. Chalmers, *Sixth Report of the Committee of the General Assembly on Church Extension* (Edinburgh 1840), 19-22; T. Chalmers, *Remarks on the Present Position of the Church of Scotland* (Glasgow, 1839), 49-55.

179. Ibid. 55-7.

180. T. Chalmers to A. L. Simpson, 29 May 1840 (NCL, Simpson Letters, Assembly Library no. LSI. 6. 26, Bx. 1); Chalmers, *Sixth Report*, 19-23.

181. T. Chalmers to A. L. Simpson, 29 May, 12 June 1841 (NCL, Simpson Letters, Assembly Library no. LSI. 6. 26, Bx. 1).

182. Hanna, *Memoirs*, iv. 87.

183. King, *Two Lectures, in Reply to the Speeches of Dr. Chalmers on Church Extension*, 82-95.

Chapter Six: The Church Divided

1. Hanna, *Memoirs*, iv. 440; Dodds, *Thomas Chalmers*, 187-8.

2. [John Brown], 'Dr. Chalmers' *Posthumous Works'*, *North British Review*, viii (February 1848), 398.

3. T. Carlyle, *Reminiscences*, ed. C. E. Norton (London, 1972), 216.

4. Dodds, *Thomas Chalmers*, 388-9; Hanna, *Memoirs*, iv. 1-7.

5. Hanna, *Memoirs*, iv. 431; T. Carlyle, *Reminiscences*, 215; [L. Miller], *Passages in the Life of an English Heiress; Or, Recollections of Disruption Times in Scotland* (London, 1847), 286-95.

6. T. Chalmers to T. Carlyle, 29 September 1841 (NLS, Thomas Carlyle Papers, MS 1766, fol. 91); T. Carlyle, *Reminiscences*, 215; Hanna, *Memoirs*, iii. 263; Chalmers, *Collected Works*, xxi. 256-9.

7. Keir, *The House of Collins*, 46-52, 143-51.

8. Hanna, *Memoirs*, iv. 448, 455-6.

9. [J. Brown], *North British Reviews*, viii (February 1848), 403.

10. Hanna, *Memoirs*, iv. 457-60; E. B. Ramsay, 'Biographical Notice of Thomas Chalmers', *Transactions of the Royal Society of Edinburgh*, xvi (1849), 516-17.

11. Carlyle, *Reminiscences*, 216.

12. Ramsay, 'Biographical Notice of Thomas Chalmers', 515-16; Hanna, *Memoirs*, iv. 448-9, 451-62.

13. T. Chalmers to Elizabeth Mackenzie, 28 August 1839 (TCP, CHA 3.15.79).

14. Lee, *Evidence ... before the Commissioners of Religious Instruction, Scotland*, 15; Engels, *The Condition of the Working Class in England*, 41.

15. A. A. MacLaren, 'Bourgeois Ideology and Victorian Philanthropy: The Contradictions of Philanthropy', in MacLaren, ed., *Social Class in Scotland* (Edinburgh, 1876), 36-54.

16. G. Nicholls, *A History of the English Poor Law* (2 vols., New York, 1898), ii. 337-40.

17. *Parliamentary Papers*, 'Report by a Committee of the General Assembly on the Management of the Poor in Scotland, 1839', Reports from Commissioners, 1839, xx, 163-341.

18. *Report ... From the Poor Law Commissioners, on an Inquiry into the Sanitary Condition of the Labouring Population of Great Britain, 1842* (London, 1842), iii - xv; Chalmers, *Collected Works*, xxi. 179-81.

19. W. P. Alison, *Observations on the Management of the Poor in Scotland, and its Effects on the Health of the Great Towns* (Edinburgh, 1840), v - vii.

20. Ibid. 40-3.

21. Ibid. 139-41.

22. Ibid. 174-96.

23. *Witness,* 28 March 1840; Association for Obtaining an Official Inquiry into the Pauperism of Scotland, *First Report* (Edinburgh, 1841), 1-3.
24. D. Monypenny, *Proposed Alteration of the Scottish Poor Laws, and of the Administration Thereof, as Stated by Dr. Alison* (Edinburgh, 1840), 76-86.
25. W. P. Alison, *Reply to the Pamphlet entitled 'Proposed Alteration of the Scottish Poor Law',* 19-25, 61-7.
26. A. Alison, *Principles of Population,* ii. 86-111.
27. *Edinburgh Advertiser,* 22, 25 September 1840; *Scotsman,* 26 September 1840; T. Chalmers, 'On the Application of Statistics to Moral and Economical Questions', in *Collected Works,* xxi. 339-67.
28. *Edinburgh Advertiser,* 25 September 1840.
29. T. Chalmers, *The Sufficiency of a Parochial System, without a Poor Rate, for the Right Management of the Poor* (Glasgow, 1841), in *Collected Works,* xxi. 9-92, 176-88.
30. Ibid. 140, 151-62.
31. Ibid. 218-21.
32. T. Chalmers to W. Gladstone, 30 October 1841, 6 November 1841 (BL, Gladstone Papers, Add. MS 44,358, fols. 193, 207); W. Gladstone to T. Chalmers, 3 November 1841 (TCP, CHA 4.298.51); S. R. Bosanquet to T. Chalmers, 26 December, 4 October 1841 (TCP, CHA 4.289.1, CHA 4.296.47); Hanna, *Memoirs,* iv. 198; S. R. Bosanquet, *The Rights of the Poor and Christian Almsgiving Vindicated* (London, 1841), 222-53, 276, 381-416.
33. Association for Obtaining an Official Inquiry into the Pauperism of Scotland, *First* and *Second Reports* (Edinburgh, 1841).
34. W. P. Alison, *Reply to Dr. Chalmers' Objections to an Improvement of the Legal Provision for the Poor in Scotland* (Edinburgh, 1841), 4-18, 45-54.
35. [John Hill Burton], 'Poor Laws and Pauperism in Scotland', *Westminster Review,* xxxvi (October 1841), 381-403.
36. G. Nicholls, *A History of the Scotch Poor Law* (London, 1846), 130-4.
37. Hanna, *Memoirs,* iv. 199-201.
38. *Presbyterian Review,* xv (April 1842), 76-94.
39. Nicholls, *A History of the Scotch Poor Law,* 134.
40. Hanna, *Memoirs,* iv. 116; Cockburn, *Journal,* i. 231.
41. Watt, *Thomas Chalmers and the Disruption,* 157-60; Henderson, *Heritage: A Study of the Disruption,* 67-8; Buchanan, *The Ten Years' Conflict,* i. 340-55.
42. Watt, *Thomas Chalmers and the Disruption,* 160-9; Buchanan, *The Ten Years' Conflict,* i. 355-400.
43. Watt, *Thomas Chalmers and the Disruption,* 171-3; Hanna, *Memoirs,* iv. 95-6.
44. Watt, *Thomas Chalmers and the Disruption,* 173-6; Buchanan, *The Ten Years' Conflict,* i. 421-33.
45. Cockburn, *Journal,* i. 225-6.
46. Hanna, *Memoirs,* iv. 104-5; Watt, *Thomas Chalmers and the Disruption,* 176-7; D. Aitken to the Earl of Minto, 14 May 1839 (NLS, Minto Papers, MS 11802, fol. 114).
47. Hanna, *Memoirs,* iv. 106-7.
48. Ibid. 106-15.
49. Anderson, *Reminiscences of Thomas Chalmers,* 274; Watt, *Thomas Chalmers and the Disruption,* 181-2.
50. Buchanan, *The Ten Years' Conflict,* i. 409-13, 436-9, 464-5; J. Bryce, *Ten Years of the Church of Scotland* (2 vols., Edinburgh, 1850), 64-5; Mathieson, *Church and Reform in Scotland, 1797-1843,* 349n.
51. Cockburn, *Journal;* i. 230; Buchanan, *The Ten Years' Conflict,* i. 467-70; T. Chalmers to the Earl of Dalhousie, 29 May 1839 (SRO, *Dalhousie* Papers, GD. 45/14/566).

52. Machin, *Politics and the Churches in Great Britain,* 123.

53. Cockburn, *Journal,* i. 230-1.

54. Buchanan, *The Ten Years' Conflict,* ii. 1-13; Hanna, *Memoirs,* iv. 126-9; Watt, *Thomas Chalmers and the Disruption,* 183-7.

55. Buchanan, *The Ten Years' Conflict,* ii. 13-17; Watt, *Thomas Chalmers and the Disruption,* 187-91; Cockburn, *Journal,* i. 227-9, 233-4.

56. Hanna, *Memoirs,* iv. 135-9; Buchanan, *The Ten Years' Conflict,* ii. 56-61; Henderson, *Heritage: A Study of the Disruption,* 76-7; T. Chalmers, *Remarks on the Present Position of the Church of Scotland, Occasioned by the Publication of a Letter from the Dean of Faculty to the Lord Chancellor* (Glasgow, 1839), 34-5.

57. Chalmers, *Remarks on the Present Position of the Church of Scotland,* 17-32, 52-3.

58. Ibid. 36.

59. Ibid. 97.

60. Ibid. 99, 100-12.

61. Buchanan, *The Ten Years' Conflict,* ii. 18-21; Watt, *Thomas Chalmers and the Disruption,* 206-10.

62. Watt, *Thomas Chalmers and the Disruption,* 210-12; Hanna, *Memoirs,* iv. 143-5.

63. Hanna, *Memoirs,* iv. 145-6.

64. T. Chalmers, 'Letters on the Church Question, No. 1', *Witness,* 4 April 1840; Cockburn, *Journal,* i. 254, 270-4.

65. D. Aitken to the Earl of Minto, 30 March 1840 (NLS, Minto Papers, MS 11802, fol. 130).

66. See, for example, John Thomson to T. Chalmers, Phettleston, 2 April 1840 (TCP, CHA 4.295.48).

67. T. Chalmers, 'Letters on the Church Question, Nos. I - V', *Witness,* 4, 11, 18, 25 April, 2 May 1840.

68. D. Aitken to the Earl of Minto, 20 April 1840 (NLS, Minto Papers, MS 11802, fol. 138).

69. Hanna, *Memoirs,* iv. 116-23.

70. Frances Balfour, *The Life of George, Fourth Earl of Aberdeen* (2 vols., London, 1922), ii. 29-63, 67.

71. G. C. Wood, ed., *The Correspondence between Dr. Chalmers and the Earl of Aberdeen... 1839 and 1840* (Edinburgh, 1893), 16-23.

72. Balfour, *The Life of George, Fourth Earl of Aberdeen,* ii. 64-5; Hanna, *Memoirs,* iv. 152-3.

73. Wood, ed., *The Correspondence between Dr. Chalmers and the Earl of Aberdeen,* 24-34.

74. Ibid. 34-44.

75. Ibid. 52-6.

76. Ibid. 57-68.

77. Ibid. 73-6.

78. Balfour, *The Life of George, Fourth Earl of Aberdeen,* ii. 67, 72-3; Arthur Gordon, *The Earl of Aberdeen* (London, 1893), 129-30; See also Viscount Melville to Lord Aberdeen, 7 March 1840 (BL, Aberdeen Papers, Add. MS 43,237, fol. 126).

79. Walker, *Robert Buchanan,* 171-2.

80. Wood, ed., *The Correspondence between Dr. Chalmers and the Earl of Aberdeen,* 72-3.

81. For a copy of Aberdeen's bill, with Chalmers's comments, see ibid., 127-30; Gordon, *The Earl of Aberdeen,* 134.

82. Wood, ed., *The Correspondence between Dr. Chalmers and the Earl of Aberdeen,* 89-96.

83. Ibid. 104-21.

84. Hanna, *Memoirs,* iv. 167-8; Buchanan, *The Ten Years' Conflict,* ii. 96-115.

85. Hanna, *Memoirs,* iv. 168.

86. Machin, *Politics and the Churches in Great Britain,* 127-8; Buchanan, *The Ten Years' Conflict,* ii. 115-23; Hanna, *Memoirs,* iv. 169-70.

87. [George, Fourth Earl of Aberdeen], *The Earl of Aberdeen's Correspondence with the Rev. Dr. Chalmers and the Secretaries of the Non-intrusion Committee* ... (Edinburgh and London, 1840), 83pp.
88. Hanna, *Memoirs*, iv. 170.
89. T. Chalmers to A. L. Simpson, 19 June 1840 (NCL, Simpson Letters, Assembly Library no. LSI. 6. 26., Bx. 1).
90. T. Chalmers, *What Ought the Church and the People of Scotland to do Now? Being a Pamphlet on Principles of the Church Question* ... (Glasgow, 1840), 28, 55.
91. Ibid. 50.
92. Hanna, *Memoirs*, iv. 212-13; Watt, *Thomas Chalmers and the Disruption*, 222-3.
93. *Scotsman*, 24 October 1840.
94. Machin, *Politics and the Churches in Great Britain*, 125.
95. Chalmers, *What Ought the Church and the People of Scotland to do Now?*, 53-5.
96. Hanna, *Memoirs*, iv. 213-19; T. Brown, *Annals of the Disruption*, 2nd edn. (Edinburgh, 1893), 23-5; Buchanan, *The Ten Years' Conflict*, ii. 192-206.
97. Watt, *Thomas Chalmers and the Disruption*, 15-16; Henderson, *Heritage: A Study of the Disruption*, 83.
98. Hanna, *Memoirs*, iv. 219-25; Buchanan, *The Ten Years' Conflict*, ii. 245-79.
99. Buchanan, *The Ten Years' Conflict*, ii. 281-7; Machin, *Politics and the Churches in Great Britain*, 130.
100. Buchanan, *The Yen Years' Conflict*, ii. 298-301.
101. Ibid. 301-11; Henderson, *Heritage: A Study of the Disruption*, 85.
102. Machin, *Politics and the Churches in Great Britain*, 131-6.
103. Ibid. 129-30, 136; Buchanan, *The Ten Years' Conflict*, 287-92.
104. T. Chalmers to Janet Coutts, 9 July 1841 (TCP, CHA 3.17.10).
105. Hanna, *Memoirs*, iv. 234.
106. Watt, *Thomas Chalmers and the Disruption*, 230-2.
107. 'Finney's Lectures on Revivals of Religion', *Presbyterian Review*, xi (October 1838), 264-91.
108. Ibid. 267-9.
109. Ibid. 286-8.
110. 'Revival at Kilsyth', *Presbyterian Review*, xii (October 1839), 360-75.
111. A. A. Bonar, *Memoir and Remains of R. M. M'Cheyne* (London, 1892: repr. London, 1966), 108-33.
112. Ibid. 135-40; Brown, *Annals of the Disruption*, 7-19; *Witness*, 6 May 1840.
113. 'Doctrine of Revivals', *Presbyterian Review*, xii (January 1840), 454-71, esp. 470.
114. Watt, *Thomas Chalmers and the Disruption*, 239-42; J. F. Leishman, *Matthew Leishman of Govan and the Middle Party of 1843* (Paisley, 1921), 106-64; A. Turner, *The Scottish Secession of 1843* (Edinburgh, 1859), 266-75.
115. Hanna, *Memoirs*, iv. 279-81; Machin, *Politics and the Churches in Great Britain*, 138; Buchanan, *The Ten Years' Conflict*, ii. 344-5.
116. Hanna, *Memoirs*, iv. 281-9.
117. Ibid. 290-9; Buchanan, *The Ten Years' Conflict*, ii. 345-78.
118. Hanna, *Memoirs*, iv. 528-47.
119. Ibid. 297-8.
120. Ibid. 302.
121. Ibid. 302-4.
122. Cockburn, *Journal*, i. 334.
123. Hanna, *Memoirs*, iv. 300-2, 305-6.
124. Ibid. 307-18; Buchanan, *The Ten Years' Conflict*, ii. 385-401.
125. D. Aitken to the Earl of Minto, 13 December 1842 (NLS, Minto Papers, MS 11802, fol. 201).

126. Sir R. Peel to Sir Geoge Sinclair, 2 December 1842 (BL, Peel Papers, Add. MS 40,520, fol. 29).

127. Hanna, *Memoirs,* iv. 319-20.

128. Ibid. 320-9; Cockburn, *Journal,* i. 341-9.

129. Hanna, *Memoirs,* iv. 330-4; Watt, *Thomas Chalmers and the Disruption,* 286-7; Brown, *Annals of the Disruption,* 68-74, 81-7.

130. Hanna, *Memoirs,* iv. 335-43; Drummond and Bulloch, *The Scottish Church, 1688-1843,* 246-8; Brown, *Annals of the Disruption,* 88-96; Cockburn, *Journal,* ii. 21.

131. Hanna, *Memoirs,* iv. 339; Cockburn, *Journal,* ii. 30; Drummond and Bulloch, *The Scottish Church 1688-1843,* 248-9.

132. J. M'Cosh, *The Wheat and the Chaff Gathered into Bundles; a Statistical Contribution towards the History of the Recent Disruption* (Perth, 1843), 108-9, 17-18, 51-2, 76-7, 82.

133. Ibid. 115-17.

134. Hanna, *Memoirs,* iv. 290.

135. M'Cosh, *The Wheat and the.Chaff,* 108.

136. Machin, *Politics and the Churches in Great Britain,* 143.

137. Hanna, *Memoirs,* iv. 348-9.

138. J. Baillie, ed., *Proceedings of the General Assembly of the Free Church of Scotland, 1843* (Edinburgh, 1843), 45.

139. T. Chalmers to Michael Longridge, 5 July 1843 (TCP, CHA 3.17.62).

140. Baillie, ed., *Proceedings,* 44-9.

141. Brown, *Annals of the Disruption,* 246-90.

142. Hanna, *Memoirs,* iv. 349-51; Baillie, ed., *Proceedings,* 44-9, 146-52.

143. Hanna, *Memoirs,* iv. 357-76; *Acts of the General Assembly of the Free Church of Scotland 1844* (Edinburgh, 1844), 15-16; *Acts... 1845* (Edinburgh, 1845), 10-11, 38-9; *Acts ... 1846* (Edinburgh, 1846), 20-1, 36-7.

144. Brown, *Annals of the Disruption,* 310-13.

145. Ibid. 314-26.

146. H. Watt, *New College, Edinburgh: A Centenary History* (Edinburgh, 1946), 6-13; Brown, *Annals of the Disruption,* 327-9.

147. Watt, *New College, Edinburgh,* 13-19, 24-8; Hanna, *Memoirs,* iv. 416-23.

148. Ibid. 424-6.

149. *Acts ... 1844,* 38-9; *Acts ... 1845,* 36-7.

150. T. Chalmers, *An Earnest Appeal to the Free Church of Scotland on the subject of its Economics* (Edinburgh, 1846), 20-3.

151. A. A. MacLaren, *Religion and Social Class: The Disruption Years in Aberdeen* (London, 1974), 104.

152. Chalmers, *An Earnest Appeal,* 21-2.

153. MacLaren, *Religion and Social Class,* 100-43.

154. *Witness,* 24 May 1844; *Acts ... 1844,* 36-40.

155. Hanna, *Memoirs,* iv. 368-76; Chalmers, *An Earnest Appeal,* 31-5; 53-4; *Scottish Guardian,* 7 March 1845; *Witness,* 30 August 1845.

156. T. Chalmers to the editor of the *Monthly Statement,* 27 July 1844 (TCP, CHA 6).

157. *Witness,* 17 May 1845; Hanna, *Memoirs,* iv. 371-2.

158. T. Chalmers to W. K. Tweedie, 14 May 1845 (TCP, CHA 3.17.93).

Chapter Seven: The Vision Fades

1. *Parliamentary Papers,* Poor Law Inquiry (Scotland), Sess. 1844, Appendix, Part 1, 267-71.

2. *Scottish Herald and Weekly Advertiser,* 29 May 1844; Nicholls, *History of the Scotch Poor Law,* 134-67.

3. *Scottish Herald and Weekly Advertiser,* 15 June 1844; Edinburgh City Chambers, Edinburgh Town Council Minutes, vol. 241, pp. 254, 267, 316, 353; vol. 242, pp. 54-6.
4. *Witness,* 19, 26 June, 13, 27 July 1844.
5. Ibid., 27 July 1844.
6. Ibid.
7. *Witness,* 19 June 1844; *Scottish Herald and Weekly Advertiser,* 22, 29 June 1844; Anderson, *Reminiscences of Thomas Chalmers,* 341-6.
8. Cockburn, *Memorials of his Time,* 456-8; K. Miller, *Cockburn's Millennium* (London, 1975), 175, 196, 244-5.
9. Edinburgh census schedules for 1841, West Port and adjoining closes, parish no. 685 (St. Cuthbert's), enumerator schedule nos. 62, 70, 72, 88, 91 (SRO); William Robertson, minister of New Greyfriar's, to T. Chalmers, 2 May 1846 (TCP, CHA 4, uncatalogued).
10. Edinburgh census schedules for 1841, West Port and adjoining closes.
11. The families were traced from the 1841 census schedules cited above to those of 1851 for the same district, i.e., parish no. 705, enumerator schedule nos. 20-1; parish no. 708, 27-30; parish no. 725, 4. Virtually none of the lodgers of 1841 could be traced in the 1851 schedules.
12. Hanna, *Memoirs,* iv. 394-5.
13. *Scottish Guardian,* 25 January 1839.
14. J. Ewan to T. Chalmers, 1 June 1844 (TCP, CHA 5, West Port Box); Anderson, *Reminiscences of Thomas Chalmers,* 341-2; West Port Local Society Minutes [hereafter WPLS minutes], 27 July 1844, 11 January 1845 (Chalmers Lauriston Church Archives, Edinburgh).
15. *Wtiness,* 26 June 1844.
16. T. Chalmers to the WPLS, 6 September 1844, cited in the WPLS minutes, 7 September 1844.
17. T. Chalmers to the Countess of Effingham, 10 January 1846 (TCP, CHA 5, West Port Box).
18. *Witness,* 26 June, 13 July 1844.
19. WPLS minutes, 21, 28 December 1844, 1 February, 1 March, 28 June 1845, 24 January 1846; T. Chalmers, *Churches and Schools for the Working Classes* (Edinburgh, 1846), 12, 16.
20. WPLS minutes, 31 August, 14, 21 September 1844.
21. Ibid., 7 September, 2, 9 November 1844.
22. Finlay Macpherson (secretary, WPLS) to the Countess of Effingham, 6 January 1845 (Chalmers Lauriston Church Archives); WPLS minutes, 2 November 1844; Hanna, *Memoirs,* iv. 401-4.
23. In July 1846, 269 children attended the day school. All received instruction in English, geography, and natural science, while 80 children received additional instruction in arithmetic, 34 in English grammar, 17 in higher mathematics, and 1 in Latin. F. Macpherson to the Countess of Effingham, July 1846 (Chalmers Lauriston Church Archives).
24. *Scottish Guardian,* 11 March 1845; Chalmers, *Churches and Schools for the Working Classes,* 14-15; WPLS minutes, 22 March 1845; Extract from WPLS minutes, 21 March 1846 (TCP, CHA 5, West Port Box).
25. WPLS minutes, 16 November 1844, 8 November 1845.
26. Ibid., 5, 19, 26 April, 24 May, 12 July, 8 November, 6 December 1845; Hanna, *Memoirs,* iv. 404.
27. WPLS minutes, 13 December 1845; F. Macpherson to the Countess of Effingham, 6 March 1846 (Chalmers Lauriston Church Archives); 'Teachers in West Port Sabbath Schools, 24 June 1846' (TCP, CHA 5, West Port Box).

28. *Witness,* 9 August 1845; Anderson, *Reminiscences of Thomas Chalmers,* 358-60.

29. WPLS minutes, 24 August 1844; F. Macpherson to the Countess of Effingham, 9 April 1845 (Chalmers Lauriston Church Archives).

30. Edinburgh City Mission minutes, 5 February 1845 (NLS, Acc. 7247, 2); T. Chalmers to City Mission Directors, 27 February 1845 (TCP, CHA 5, West Port Box).

31. [J. Jolly], *Memorials of the Rev. William Tasker* (Edinburgh, 1880), 5-18; [J. Jolly], *The Story of the West Port Church* (Edinburgh, 1882), 21-8.

32. P. MacFarlan to J. Morrison, 6 March 1845 (TCP, CHA 4, uncatalogued); WPLS minutes, 29 March 1845; W. Tasker to T. Chalmers, 13 January 1846 (TCP, CHA 5, West Port Box).

33. *Witness,* 9 August 1845; E. D. Fletcher, *Autobiography* (Edinburgh, 1875), 259; Chalmers, *Churches and Schools for the Working Classes,* 15-16.

34. W. Marshall to T. Chalmers, 26 July 1845, [W. Marshall?], 'Cost of West Port Church and Schools, 3 April 1847' (TCP, CHA 5, West Port Box).

35. Hanna, *Memoirs,* iv. 411-12.

36. Ibid. 395.

37. Extract from WPLS minutes, 13 June 1846 (TCP, CHA 5, West Port Box).

38. Extract from WPLS minutes, 6 September 1846; T. Chalmers to the Secretary of the WPLS, 26 September 1846 (TCP, CHA 5, West Port Box).

39. *Scottish Guardian,* 11 March 1845; Chalmers, *Churches and Schools for the Working Classes,* 22.

40. The income was determined from three sources: first, the 'Abstract of Accounts of Treasurer of West Port Association' (TCP, CHA 5, West Port Box); secondly, letters from James Lenox of New York City to Chalmers containing contributions, of which only one of the several gifts is recorded in the treasurer's account (TCP, CHA 4, uncatalogued correspondence, 1844-5); thirdly, letters accompanying contributions from Lady Nairne of Perthshire and Miss Portal of London in April 1845, which also were not recorded in the treasurer's account (TCP, CHA 5, West Port Box). In late 1845, Chalmers began collecting subscriptions for the West Port church and school building. At this time, he and the WPLS claimed that the operation was without funds, so it may be assumed that all receipts prior to this date had already been spent.

41. Abstract of Accounts of Treasurer of West Port Association' (TCP, CHA 5, West Port Box); Chalmers Territorial Church (West Port) Kirk-session minutes, 15 July 1847 (Chalmers Lauriston Church Archives).

42. J. Lenox to T. Chalmers, 14 September 1844, 28 November 1845, 28 October 1846, 26 January 1847)TCP, CHA 4, uncatalogued).

43. Hanna, *Memoirs,* iv. 415.

44. *Christian Journal,* ii. (1851), 489-94.

45. W. Tasker to Lord Provost William Chambers, marked 'private and confidential', 11 September 1867 (Edinburgh City Chambers, Misc. Documents, vol. xxi. bundle 25a, Town Clerk's Letters, no. 14).

46. [T. Chalmers], 'The Political Economy of the Bible', *North British Review,* iii (November 1844), 1-52; [T. Chalmers], 'Report on the Poor Laws of Scotland', *North British Review,* iv (February 1845), 471-513; [T. Chalmers], 'Savings Banks', *North British Review,* vi (August 1845), 318-44.

47. *Scottish Guardian,* 11 March 1845.

48. Hanna, *Memoirs,* iv. 377-90; O. Chadwick, *The Victorian Church,* Part 1, 441-2; T. Chalmers, 'How such a Union May Begin, and to What it May Eventually Lead', in *Essays on Christian Union* (London, 1845), 1-18; T. Chalmers, *On the Evangelical Alliance* (Edinburgh, 1846), 42-58.

49. Chalmers, *Churches and Schools for the Working Classes,* 9-22.

50. Ibid. 6.
51. Ibid. 21; none the less, critics were quick to observe that of the seven proposed operations described by Chalmers, six were Free Church affiliated. James Mac-Allan, New Greyfriar's elder, to T. Chalmers, 4 March 1846 (TCP, CIIA 4, uncatalogued).
52. *Witness*, 21 January, 4 February 1846; *Seventh Biennial Report of the Edinburgh City Mission* (Edinburgh, 1846), 6-14, 44-7.
53. Hanna, ed., *A Selection from the Correspondence of Thomas Chalmers*, 453-5.
54. The three operations were the Holyrood Territorial Church (1847) and the Chalmers Territorial Church, Fountainbridge (1854) in Edinburgh, and the Wynd Church (1854) in Glasgow. All three were Free Church affiliated. R. S. Candlish, *Past Memories and Present Duties; or Chalmers' Territorial Church, Fountainbridge* (Edinburgh, 1854), 5-29; Walker, *Robert Buchanan*, 300-38; Elizabeth, Duchess of Gordon, to T. Chalmers, 9, 12 January, 14 February, 8, 17 April 1846 (TCP, CHA 4, uncatalogued).
55. Nicholls, *History of the Scotch Poor Law*, 168-97; MacLaren, ed., *Social Class in Scotland*, 36-54.
56. G. Lewis to T. Chalmers, 21 December 1846 (TCP, CHA 4, uncatalogued); J. T. Ward, 'The Factory Reform Movement in Scotland', *SHR*, xli (October 1962), 100-24.
57. C. Driver, *Tory Radical: The Life of Richard Oastler* (New York, 1946), 467-8; *Witness*, 26 December 1846.
58. Hanna, *Memoirs*, iv. 434-8.
59. *Witness*, 6 March 1847.
60. [T. Chalmers], 'Political Economy of a Famine', *North British Review*, xiii (May 1847), 247-90.
61. Hanna, *Memoirs*, iv. 497-8, 501-2, 591-607; Brown, *Annals of the Disruption*, 409-49; T. Chalmers, *Refusal of Sites: Evidence ... Extracted from the Third Report of the Parliamentary Committee* (Edinburgh, 1847), 34 pp.
62. Hanna, *Memoirs*, iv. 500-5.
63. Carlyle, *Reminiscences*, 215-16.
64. Hanna, *Memoirs*, iv. 505-16.
65. *Witness*, 5 June 1847.
66. A. L. Drummond and J. Bulloch, *The Church in Late Victorian Scotland, 1874-1900* (Edinburgh, 1978), 128.
67. C. R. Henderson, 'A Half Century After Thomas Chalmers', *American Journal of Theology*, iv (1900), 49-63, 49.
68. A. F. Young and E. T. Ashton, *British Social Work in the Nineteenth Century* (London, 1956), 67-114; K. de Schweinitz, *England's Road to Social Security* (Philadelphia, 1943), 100-13; Mechie, *The Church and Scottish Social Development*, 61-3.
69. C. R. Henderson, 'Introduction', in T. Chalmers, *The Christian and Civic Economy of Large Towns*, abr., ed. C. R. Henderson (New York, 1900), 53-75.
70. M. E. Richmond, *Social Diagnosis* (New York, 1917), 28-9.
71. Anderson, *Reminiscences of Thomas Chalmers*, 409.

BIBLIOGRAPHY

I. PUBLISHED WORKS BY THOMAS CHALMERS

The list of Chalmers's published writings comprises over 150 separate items. For a relatively complete compilation, see H. Watt, *The Published Writings of Thomas Chalmers: A Descriptive List* (Edinburgh, 1943). Most of the works by Chalmers cited in the preceding references are included in *The Collected Works of Thomas Chalmers* (25 vols., Glasgow, 1835-42). It must be noted, however, that the version given in this collection sometimes differs slightly from the original; therefore, whenever possible, I have cited from the original version. Major works cited, but either not found in the *Collected Works*, or greatly altered in that collection, include:

Chalmers, T., *The Bridgewater Treatises on the Power, Wisdom and Goodness of God as manifested in the Creation: Treatise I, On the Adaptation of External Nature to the Moral and Intellectual Constitution of Man* (2 vols., London, 1833). Portions of this work appear in volumes i to iv of the *Collected Works*, but in a fragmented form.

—, *Churches and Schools for the Working Classes* (Edinburgh, 1846).

—, *A Conference with certain Ministers and Elders of the Church of Scotland, on the subject of the Moderatorship of the next General Assembly* (Glasgow, 1837).

—, *The Correspondence between Dr. Chalmers and the Earl of Aberdeen in the years 1839 and 1840*, ed. G. C. Wood (Edinburgh, 1893).

—, *An Earnest Appeal to the Free Church of Scotland on the subject of its Economics* (Edinburgh, 1846).

—, *An Enquiry into the Extent and Stability of National Resources* (Edinburgh, 1808).

—, 'How Such a Union May Begin, and To What it May Eventually Lead', in *Essays on Christian Union* (London, 1845), 1-18.

—, *The Influence of Bible Societies on the Temporal Necessities of the Poor* (Edinburgh, 1814).

—, *Letter to the Royal Commissioners for the Visitation of Colleges in Scotland* (Glasgow, 1832).

—, *Observations on a Passage in Mr. Playfair's Letter to the Lord Provost of Edinburgh, relative to the Mathematical Pretensions of the Scottish Clergy* (Cupar-Fife, 1805).

—, *On the Economics of the Free Church of Scotland* (Glasgow, 1845).

—, *On the Evangelical Alliance; its Design, its Difficulties, its Proceedings, and its Prospects* (Edinburgh, 1846).

—, *Refusal of Sites: Evidence of the Rev. Dr. Chalmers, Extracted from the Third Report of the Parliamentary Committee* (Edinburgh, 1847).

—, *Remarks on the Present Position of the Church of Scotland, Occasioned by the Publication of a Letter from the Dean of Faculty to the Lord Chancellor* (Glasgow, 1839).

—, *Reports of the Committee of the General Assembly of the Church of Scotland on Church Extension, First to Seventh Annual Reports* (Edinburgh, 1835-41).

—, *A Selection from the Correspondence of the Late Thomas Chalmers*, ed. W. Hanna (Edinburgh, 1853).

—, *Sermons by Thomas Chalmers, Illustrative of Different Stages in his Ministry, 1798-1847*, ed. W. Hanna (Edinburgh, 1849).

—, *A Speech delivered in the Synod of Glasgow and Ayr on the 15th October 1823, in the Case of Principal McFarlane, on the Subject of Pluralities* (Glasgow, 1823).

—, *The Substance of a Speech, Delivered in the General Assembly, on Thursday, May 25, 1809,*

Respecting the Merits of the Late Bill for the Augmentations of Stipends to the Clergy of Scotland (Edinburgh, 1809).

—, *Supplement to his Late Pamphlet on the Subject of the Moderatorship of the Next General Assembly* (Glasgow, 1837).

—, *What Ought the Church and the People of Scotland to do Now? Being a Pamphlet on the Principles of the Church Question With an Appendix, On the Politics and Personalities of the Church Question* (Glasgow, 1840).

II. MANUSCRIPTS

Aberdeen Papers, BL, Add. MS 43202, 43237.

Black Letters, NLS, MS 3713.

Brougham Papers, University College, London.

Brown (James) Letters, EUL, Dc. 2.57.

Brown (John) Letters, NLS, Acc. 6134.

Buchanan Letters, Glasgow University Library, MS GEN 1036.

Carlyle (Alexander) Letters, EUL, Dc. 4.41.

Carlyle (Thomas) Papers, NLS, MS 1766.

Chalmers Correspondence, St. Andrews University Library, MS Bx. 9225; MS 30385.

Chalmers Papers, New College Library, Edinburgh University.

Church Extension Letterbook, New College Library, Edinburgh University, X13b, 6/3, 2.

Cockburn Papers, NLS, Adv. MS 9.1.8.·- 9.

Constable Letters, NLS, MS 669.

Dalhousie Papers, SRO, GD 45/14.

Dunlop Papers, New College Library, Edinburgh University.

Edinburgh Census Schedules, 1841 and 1851, SRO.

Gladstone Papers, NL, Add. MS 44354 - 8, 44527.

Lee Letters, NLS, MS 3432-44.

Lundie Letters, NLS, MS 1676.

Mackintosh Papers, BL, Add. MS 52453.

Melville Papers, St. Andrews University Library.

Minto Papers, NLS, MS 11800-8, 12122-3.

Minutes of the Edinburgh City Mission, NLS.

Minutes of the Parish of St. John's, Glasgow, 1819-37, SRO, CH2/176/1.

Minutes of the Presbytery of Cupar, 1789-1807, SRO, CH2/82/12.

Minutes of the Presbytery of Glasgow, 1808-19, SRO, CH2/171/3.

Moncrieff Papers, Tuliebole, Kinross.

Monteagle Letters, NLS, MS 2225.

Napier Papers, BL, Add. MS 34614-22.

Parochial Register, Kilmany, 1706-1819, SRO, OPR, 437/1.

Paul Papers, NLS, MS 5139.

Peel Papers, BL, Add MS 40350-598.

Reddie Papers, NLS, MS 3704.

Rutherford Papers, NLS, MS 9710.

Simpson Letters, New College Library, Edinburgh University.

Thomson of Banchory Papers, New College Library, Edinburgh University.

West Port Papers, Chalmers Lauriston Church, Edinburgh.

III. PARLIAMENTARY PAPERS

Third Report from the Select Committee on the Poor Laws, containing Returns from the General Assembly of the Church of Scotland; 1819 (358) v. 23.

Report to His Majesty by a Royal Commission of Inquiry into the State of the Universities of Scotland; 1831 (310) xii. 111.

Evidence taken before the Commissioners of the University of St. Andrews; 1837 (94), xxxvii. 1.

Report from the Select Committee of the House of Commons appointed to consider the past and present state of the Law of Church Patronage in Scotland; 1834 (512) v. 1.

First Report of the Commission on Religious Instruction in Scotland; 1837 (31) xxi. 9.

Second Report from the same; 1837-8 (109) xxxii. 1.

Report by a Committee of the General Assembly on the Management of the Poor in Scotland; 1839 (177) xx. 163.

Report from Her Majesty's Commissioners for Inquiring into the Poor Laws in Scotland; 1844 (557) xx. 1.

Appendix of the same, Part 1, containing Minutes of Evidence taken at Edinburgh, Glasgow, Greenock, Paisley, Ayr, and Kilmarnock; 1844 (563) xx. 81.

Report from the Select Committee of the House of Commons appointed to inquire whether ... large numbers of Her Majesty's Subjects have been deprived of the means of Religious Worship by the refusal of certain proprietors to grant them Sites for the erection of Churches; 1847 (237) xiii. 1.

Second Report from the same; 1847 (311) xiii. 119.

Third Report from the same; 1847 (613) xiii. 267.

IV. BOOKS AND PAMPHLETS PUBLISHED BEFORE 1880

Aberdeen, Fourth Earl of, *The Earl of Aberdeen's Correspondence with the Rev. Dr. Chalmers and the Secretaries of the Non-intrusion Committee: From 14th January to 27th May 1840* (Edinburgh and London, 1840).

Account of the Proceedings which Took Place in Glasgow on the Occasion of Dr. Chalmers' Leaving St. John's Parish, 3rd edn. (Glasgow, 1823).

Alison, A., *The Principles of Population, and their Connection with Human Happiness* (2 vols., Edinburgh, 1840).

Alison, W. P., *Observations on the Management of the Poor in Scotland, and its Effects on the Health of the Great Towns* (Edinburgh, 1840).

—, *Reply to Dr. Chalmers' Objections to an Improvement of the Legal Provision for the Poor in Scotland* (Edinburgh, 1841).

—, *Reply to the Pamphlet entitled 'Proposed Alteration of the Scottish Poor Law Considered and Commented on, by David Monypenny, Esq. of Pitmilly'* (Edinburgh, 1840).

Anderson, J., *Reminiscences of Thomas Chalmers* (Edinburgh, 1851).

Angus, J., *The Voluntary System: A Prize Essay, in reply to the Lectures of Dr. Chalmers on Church Establishments* (London, 1839).

Association for Obtaining an Official Inquiry into the Pauperism of Scotland, *First and Second Reports* (Edinburgh, 1841).

Baillie, J., *The Missionary of Kilmany: Being a Memoir of Alexander Paterson, with Notices of Robert Edie,* 5th edn. (Edinburgh, 1854).

—, ed. *Proceedings of the General Assembly of the Free Church of Scotland, 1843* (Edinburgh, 1843).

Begg, J., *Pauperism and the Poor Laws; or, Our Sinking Population and Rapidly Increasing Public Burdens Practically Considered* (Edinburgh, 1849).

—. *Seat Rents Brought to the Test of Reason, Scripture and Experience* (Edinburgh, 1838).

Bell, G., *Blackfriars' Wynd Analyzed* (Edinburgh, 1850).

—, *Day and Night in the Wynds of Edinburgh* (Edinburgh, 1849).

Bell, R., *Memoir of Robert Paul* (Edinburgh, 1872).

—, *Observations on the Conference of the Rev. Thomas Chalmers with certain Ministers and Elders of the Church of Scotland* (Edinburgh, 1837).

—, *Statement in Answer to the Rev. Dr. Chalmers' Pamphlet, on the Subject of the Moderatorship* (Edinburgh, 1837).

Black, A., *The Church Its Own Enemy, Being an Answer to the Pamphlets of the Rev. Dr. Chalmers,* 3rd edn. (Edinburgh, 1835).

Bosanquet, S. R., *The Rights of the Poor and Christian Almsgiving Vindicated* (London, 1841).

Brougham, H., *The Life and Times of Henry, Lord Brougham, Written by Himself* (3 vols., Edinburgh, 1871).

Brown, J., *On the Law of Christ respecting Civil Obedience Especially in the Payment of Tribute* (Edinburgh, 1838).

Browne, G., *The History of the British and Foreign Bible Society, 1804-1854* (2 vols., London, 1859).

Bruce, J., *A Testimony and Remonstrance regarding the Moderatorship of the next General Assembly* (Edinburgh, 1837).

Bryce, J., *Ten Years of the Church of Scotland, 1833-1843* (Edinburgh, 1850).

Buchanan, R., *The Spiritual Destitution of the Masses in Glasgow* (Glasgow, 1851).

—, *The Ten Years' Conflict,* 2nd edn. (2 vols., Glasgow, 1852).

Burns, I., *The Pastor of Kilsyth; or Memorials of the Life and Times of the Rev. W. H. Burns, D. D.* (London, 1860).

Burns, R., *Historical Dissertations on the Law and Practice of Great Britain, and particularly of Scotland, with Regard to the Poor,* 2nd edn. (Glasgow, 1819).

—, *A Letter to the Rev. Dr. Chalmers, on the Distinctive Characters of the Protestant and Roman Catholic Religions; occasioned by the Publication of his Sermon, for the Benefit of the Hibernian Society* (Glasgow, 1818).

—, *Memoir of the Rev. Stevenson Macgill, D. D.* (Edinburgh, 1842).

—, *Plurality of Offices in the Church of Scotland Examined* (Glasgow, 1824).

—, *Scottish Voluntaryism, the Atheist's Ally* (Paisley, 1836).

Burns, R. F., *The Life and Times of the Rev. Robert Burns, Including an Unfinished Autobiography* (Toronto, 1872).

Cairns, J., *Thomas Chalmers* (London, 1864).

Campbell, D., *Memorials of John Macleod Campbell* (2 vols., London, 1877).

Candlish, R. S., *Past Memories and Present Duties; or Chalmers' Territorial Church, Fountainbridge* (Edinburgh, 1854).

Carlyle, A., *Autobiography,* ed. J. H. Burton (Edinburgh, 1860).

Chadwick, E., *Report on the Sanitary Condition of the Labouring Population of Great Britain* (London, 1842).

Cleland, J., *Annals of Glasgow* (2 vols., Glasgow, 1816).

—, *The Rise and Progress of the City of Glasgow; Comprising an Account of its Ancient and Modern History* (Glasgow, 1840).

—, *The Rise and Progress of the City of Glasgow; Comprising an Account of its Public Buildings, Charities, and Other Concerns* (Glasgow, 1820).

Cobbett, W., *Cobbett's Tour in Scotland* (London, 1833).

Cockburn, H., *Journal, 1831-1854* (2 vols., Edinburgh, 1874).

—, *Letters Chiefly Connected with the Affairs of Scotland* (London, 1874).

—, *Life of Lord Jeffrey* (2 vols., Edinburgh, 1852).

—, *Memorials of his Time* (Edinburgh, 1856).

Collins, W., *The Church of Scotland the Poor Man's Church* (Glasgow, n.d.).

[—], *Proposal for Building Twenty New Parochial Churches in the City and Suburbs of Glasgow* (Glasgow, 1834).

—, *Statistics of the Church Accommodation of Glasgow, Barony, and Gorbals* (Glasgow, 1836).

Colquhoun, J. C., *Hints on the Question now Affecting the Church of Scotland* (Glasgow, 1840).

Committee Appointed in Consequence of the Establishment of an Association in Edinburgh for Obtaining an Official Inquiry into Pauperism in Scotland, *Report, with Remarks by a Member of the Committee* (Edinburgh, 1841).

Connolly, M. F., *Biographical Dictionary of Eminent Men of Fife* (Cupar-Fife, 1866).

—, *Fifiana: or, Memorials of the East of Fife* (Glasgow, 1869).

Cook, D., ed., *Annals of Pittenweem* (Anstruther, 1867).

Cook, G., *A Few Plain Observations on the Enactment of the General Assembly, 1834, relating to Patronage and Calls* (Edinburgh, 1834).

—, *The Life of George Hill* (Edinburgh, 1820).

Cox, S. H., *Interviews: Memorable and Useful* (New York, 1855).

Cunningham, J., *The Church History of Scotland* (2 vols., Edinburgh, 1859).

Cunningham, W., *Lecture on the Lawfulness of Union Between Church and State* (Edinburgh, 1835).

—, *Reply to the Statement of Certain Ministers and Elders, published in Answer to Dr. Chalmers' 'Conference' on the subject of the Moderatorship* (Edinburgh, 1837).

Defence of the Rev. Dr. Chalmers Addressed to the Thinking and Unprejudiced Part of the Inhabitants of Glasgow (Glasgow, 1823).

Dodds, J., *Thomas Chalmers: A Biographical Study* (Edinburgh, 1879).

Douglas, J., *The Revival of Religion* (Edinburgh, 1839).

[Drummond, H.], *A Letter to Dr. Chalmers, in Reply to his Speech in the Presbytery of Edinburgh* (London, 1829).

Duncan, G. J. C., *Memoir of the Rev. Henry Duncan* (Edinburgh, 1848).

Dunlop, A. M., *Treatise on the Law of Scotland relative to the Poor* (Edinburgh, 1825).

Edinburgh City Mission, *First Report* (Edinburgh, 1833).

—, *Second Biennial Report* (Edinburgh, 1835).

—, *Seventh Biennial Report* (Edinburgh, 1846).

Erskine, T., *Letters of Thomas Erskine of Linlathen*, ed. W. Hanna (2 vols., Edinburgh, 1877).

[Ewing, J.], *Report of the Directors of the Town's Hospital of Glasgow on the Management of the City Poor, the Suppression of Mendacity, and the Principles of the Plan for the New Hospital* (Glasgow, 1818).

Finney, C. G., *Lectures on Revivals of Religion* (London, 1838).

Fletcher, E. D., *Autobiography of Mrs. Fletcher* (Edinburgh, 1875).

Fraser, W., *Memoir of the Life of David Stow* (London, 1868).

Gladstone, W. E., *The State in Its Relations with the Church* (London, 1838).

Godwin, W., *Enquiry Concerning Political Justice and Its Influence on Modern Morals and Happiness* (London, 1798).

Gordon, A. L., *The System of National Education in Scotland* (Aberdeen, 1839).

Graham, J., *An Address to the Working Classes of Scotland, Containing Observations on the Scottish Poor Law* (Glasgow, 1819).

Grub, G., *An Ecclesiastical History of Scotland* (4 vols., Edinburgh, 1861).

Gurney, J. J., *Chalmeriana; or Colloquies with Dr. Chalmers* (London, 1853).

Guthrie, T., *Autobiography of Thomas Guthrie, and Memoir,* ed. D. K. and C. J. Guthrie (2 vols., New York, 1876).

—, *A Plea for Ragged Schools* (Edinburgh, 1847).

Haldane, A., *The Lives of Robert Haldane of Airthey, and of his Brother, James Alexander Haldane,* 4th edn. (Edinburgh, 1855).

[Haldane, J.], *Letter to the Lord Provost, Magistrates, Preceptor, and the other Directors of the Town's Hospital, Glasgow, on the Causes and Cure of Pauperism* (Glasgow, 1818).

[—], *Two Letters to the Rev. Dr. Chalmers, on his Proposal for Increasing the Number of Churches in Glasgow, by an Observor* (Glasgow, 1818).

Hamilton, A., *Report of the Speeches delivered at the Public Dinner to Dr. Chalmers* (Glasgow, 1823).

Hanna, W., *Memoirs of Dr. Chalmers* (4 vols., Edinburgh, 1849-52).

Hardy, T., *The Principles of Moderatism* (Edinburgh, 1782).

Hazlitt, W., *The Spirit of the Age,* in A. R. Waller, ed., *The Collected Works of William Hazlitt,* vol. IV (London, 1920).

Hetherington, W. M., *History of the Church of Scotland* (2 vols., Edinburgh, 1848).

—, *Memoir and Correspondence of Mrs. Coutts* (Edinburgh, 1854).

Hill, G., *Lectures in Divinity,* ed. A. Hill (Edinburgh, 1821).

—, *A View of the Constitution of the Church of Scotland,* ed. A. Hill, 3rd edn. (Edinburgh, 1835).

Hogg, J., *The Private Memoirs and Confessions of a Justified Sinner* (Edinburgh, 1824).

Hope, J., *A Letter to the Lord Chancellor on the Claims of the Church of Scotland* (Edinburgh, 1839).

Inglis, J., *A Vindication of Ecclesiastical Establishments* (Edinburgh, 1833).

Instruction of the Rising Generation in the Principles of the Christian Religion, Recommended, To which is added, An Account of the Edinburgh Gratis Sabbath School Society (Edinburgh, 1812).

Kay [-Shuttleworth], J. P., *The Moral and Physical Condition of the Working Classes Employed in the Cotton Manufacture in Manchester,* 2nd edn. (London, 1832).

King, D., *Two Lectures, in Reply to the Speeches of Dr. Chalmers on Church Extension, delivered in Greyfriars Church, 18th and 23rd October 1838* (Glasgow, 1838).

Kirkwood, A., *The Scottish Church Question* (Glasgow, 1843).

Lapslie, J., *A Foederal Union Amongst the Different Sects of Christians, and Particularly of this Kingdom, Proposed and Recommended: A Discourse, delivered before the Synod of Glasgow and Ayr, April 1791* (Glasgow, 1795).

Lee, J., *Dr. Lee's Refutation of the Charges brought against him by the Rev. Dr. Chalmers and Others* (Edinburgh, 1837).

—, *Evidence of Dr. Lee before the Commissioners of Religious Instruction, Scotland, in February and March 1836* (Edinburgh, 1837).

—, *A Letter to the Right Honourable, the Lord Provost, Relating to the Annuity Tax* (Edinburgh, 1834).

Lewis, G., *The Christian Duty of the Electors of Magistrates* (Edinburgh, 1833).

[—], *Scotland: A Half-educated Nation* (Glasgow, 1834).

[Liddle, J.], *Report of the Committee for Promoting the Establishment of Local Schools in Edinburgh and its Vicinity, June 2, 1824* (Edinburgh, 1824).

[Lockhart, J. G.], *Peter's Letters to his Kinsfolk* (3 vols., Edinburgh, 1819).

Lorimer, J. G., *The Deaconship* (Edinburgh, 1842).

—, *The Eldership of the Church of Scotland* (Glasgow, 1841).

M'Cosh, J., *The Wheat and the Chaff Gathered into Bundles: A Statistical Contribution towards the History of the Recent Disruption* (Perth, 1843).

M'Crie, T., *The Story of the Scottish Church* (2 vols., London, 1875).

McCulloch, J. R., *The Principles of Political Economy* (Edinburgh, 1825).

Macgill, S., *Discourses and Essays on Subjects of Public Interest* (Edinburgh, 1819).

M'Kerrow, J., *History of the Secession Church,* 2nd edn. (Edinburgh, 1854).

MacLean, A., *On the Provision for the Poor in the Parish of Dunfermline* (Dunfermline, 1815).

Macleod, D., *Memoir of Norman Macleod* (2 vols., London, 1876).

Malthus, T. R., *An Essay on the Principle of Population; or a View of its Past and Present Effects on Human Happiness,* 4th edn. (2 vols., London, 1807).

Matheson, J. J., *Memoir of Greville Ewing* (London, 1843).

Mearns, D., *The Principles of Christian Evidence illustrated, by an Examination of Arguments Subversive of Natural Theology and the Internal Evidence of Christianity, Advanced by Dr. T. Chalmers, in his 'Evidence and Authority of the Christian Revelation'* (Aberdeen, 1818).

Miller, H., *The Two Parties in the Church of Scotland* (Edinburgh, 1841).

[Miller, L.], *Passages in the Life of an English Heiress; Or, Recollections of Disruption Times in Scotland* (London, 1847).

Miller, S., *Memoir of the Rev. Charles Nisbet, D. D.* (New York, 1840).

[Moncrieff, J.], *A Word More on the Moderatorship* (Edinburgh, 1837).

Monypenny, D., *The Claims of the Established Church of Scotland on the Country to Promote its Extension in the Present Crisis* (Edinburgh, 1837).

—, *An Outline of the Scottish Ecclesiastical Establishment* (Edinburgh, 1838).

—, *Proposed Alteration of the Scottish Poor Laws, and of the Administration Thereof, as Stated by Dr. Alison* (Edinburgh, 1840).

—, *Remarks on the Poor Laws* (Edinburgh, 1836).

The New Statistical Account of Scotland (15 vols., Edinburgh, 1845).

Nicholls, G., *A History of the Irish Poor Law* (London, 1856).

—, *History of the Scotch Poor Law* (London, 1846).

Oliphant, M., *The Life of Edward Irving* (New York, 1862).

Orme, W., *Memoirs of John Urquhart* (Philadelphia, 1855).

Owen, J., *The History of the Origin and First Ten Years of the British and Foreign Bible Society* (2 vols., London, 1816).

Owen, R., *A New View of Society* (London, 1813).

—, *Report to the County of Lanark, of a Plan for Relieving Public Distress* (Glasgow, 1821).

Pitcairn, T., ed., *Acts of the General Assembly of the Church of Scotland, 1688-1842* (Edinburgh, 1843).

Presbytery of Edinburgh, *Replies to Queries Regarding the City Churches, Proposed by the Committee of the Town Council* (Edinburgh, 1834).

Proceedings in the General Assembly on the 24th May, 1816, on the Overtures for the Repeal of the Enactment of Assembly, 1814, anent the Union of Offices (Glasgow, 1816).

Rainy, R. and MacKenzie, J., *Life of William Cunningham* (London, 1871).

Ramsay, E. B., 'Biographical Notice of Thomas Chalmers', *Transactions of the Royal Society of Edinburgh,* xvi (1849), 497-518.

Ranken, A., *Letter Addressed to the Rev. Dr. Chalmers, Occasioned by his frequent allusions to the 'Impregnable Minds of Certain Conveners and Councilmen', on the Subject of Pauperism in Glasgow* (Glasgow, 1830).

Reflections on the Address of Dr. Chalmers to the Agency of St. John's, Glasgow, containing the Reasons for Relinquishing the Pastoral Care of that Parish (Glasgow, 1823).

Remarks on Two Articles in the Edinburgh Review, on the Cause and Cure of Pauperism, by the Author of 'Letters from Scotland' (Manchester, 1818).

Report of the Debate in the General Assembly of the Church of Scotland on the Overtures anent the Union of Offices, May 1825 (Edinburgh, 1825).

Scotus, *The Scottish Poor Laws* (Edinburgh, 1870).

Senior, N. W., *A Letter to Lord Howick, on a Legal Provision for the Irish Poor* (London, 1831).

Sinclair, J., *Analysis of the Statistical Account of Scotland* (2 vols., London, 1826).

—, ed., *The Statistical Account of Scotland* (21 vols., Edinburgh, 1791-9).

Skinner, J., *The Scottish Endowment Question, Ecclesiastical and Educational* (Glasgow, 1838).

Smeaton, G., *Memoir of Alexander Thomson of Banchory* (Edinburgh, 1869).

Smith, A., *An Inquiry into the Nature and Causes of the Wealth of Nations* (2 vols., London, 1775-6).

Smith, G., *Life of Alexander Duff* (2 vols., New York, 1879).

Smyth, T., *The Character of the Late Thomas Chalmers* (Charleston, South Carolina, 1848).

Society for Erecting Additional Parochial Churches in Glasgow and Suburbs, *First Annual Report* (Glasgow, 1836).

Somerville, T., *My Own Life and Times 1741-1814* (Edinburgh, 1861).

Spence, W., *Britain Independent of Commerce; or Proofs deduced from an Investigation into the True Causes of the Wealth of Nations, that our Riches, Prosperity, and Power are derived from sources inherent in ourselves, and would not be affected, even though our Commerce were annihilated,* 3rd edn. (London, 1808).

Stark, W., *Considerations Addressed to the Heritors and Kirk-sessions of Scotland, particularly of the Border Counties, on certain questions connected with the Administration of the Affairs of the Poor* (Edinburgh, 1826).

Statement in Answer to the Rev. Dr. Chalmers' Pamphlet on the Subject of the Moderatorship (Edinburgh, 1837).

[Steven, R.], *Remarks on a Late Publication of the Rev. Dr. Chalmers, Intitled 'The Influence of Bible Societies on the Temporal Necessities of the Poor' ... Showing the Dangerous Tendency of Some Clauses in that Work* (London, 1819).

Stewart, D., *Lectures on Political Economy* (2 vols., Edinburgh, 1856).

Story, R. H., *Memoir of the Life of the Rev. Robert Story* (Cambridge, 1862).

Struthers, G., *History of the Rise, Progress, and Principles of the Relief Church* (Glasgow, 1843).

Tasker, W., *Territorial Sabbath Schools* (Edinburgh, 1850).

Thomson, A., *Historical Sketch of the Origin of the Secession Church* (Edinburgh, 1848).

Thomson, A. M., *Sermons and Sacramental Exhortations* (Edinburgh, 1831).

Turner, A., *The Scottish Secession of 1843 (Edinburgh, 1859).*

Walker, N. L., *Robert Buchanan: An Ecclesiastical Biography* (London, 1877).

Wardlaw, R., *An Essay on Benevolent Associations for the Relief of the Poor* (Glasgow, 1818).

—, *National Church Establishments Examined* (London, 1839).

Wellwood, H.M., *Account of the Life and Writings of John Erskine* (Edinburgh, 1818).

Welsh, D., *Account of the Life and Writings of Thomas Brown* (Edinburgh, 1825).

—, *Sermons, with a Memoir by A. Dunlop* (Edinburgh, 1846).

Wilberforce, R. I. and S., *The Life of William Wilberforce* (5 vols., London, 1848).

Wilberforce, W., *A Practical View of the Prevailing Religious System of Professed Christians, In the Higher and Middle Classes in this Country, Contrasted with Real Christianity* (London, 1797).

Wilson, R., *A Sketch of the History of Hawick ... To which is Subjoined a Short Essay, in Reply to Dr. Chalmers, on Pauperism and the Poor-Laws* (Hawick, 1825).

V. BOOKS, ARTICLES, AND THESES APPEARING AFTER 1880

Alison, A., *Some Account of my Life and Writings: An Autobiography* (2 vols., Edinburgh, 1883).

Armytage, W. H. G., *Heavens Below: Utopian Experiments in England 1560-1950* (London, 1961).

Balfour, F., *The Life of George, Fourth Earl of Aberdeen* (2 vols., London, 1922).

Benton, W. W., 'The Ecclesiology of George Hill, 1750-1819' (Edinburgh Univ. Ph.D. Thesis, 1969).

Best, G. F. A., *Temporal Pillars* (Cambridge, 1964).

Blaug, M., 'The Myth of the Old Poor Law and the Making of the New', *Journal of Economic History,* xxiii (June 1963), 151-85.

Bonar, A. A., *Memoirs and Remains of the Rev. R. Murray M'Cheyne,* 1892 ed., (London, 1892; repr. London, 1966).

Bowley, M., *Nassau Senior and Classical Economics* (London, 1937).

Briggs, A., *The Age of Imrpovement, 1783-1867* (London, 1960).

Brotherston, J. H. F., *Observations on the Early Public Health Movement in Scotland* (London, 1952).

Brown, F. K., *Fathers of the Victorians* (Cambridge, 1961).

Brown, G. K., 'Scots Theologians and English Utilitarians', *Unitarian Historical Society Transactions,* viii (October 1943), 5-16.

Brown, S. J., 'The Disruption and Urban Poverty: Thomas Chalmers and the West Port Operation in Edinburgh, 1844-47', *SCHS,* xx. 1 (1978), 65-89.

Brown, T., *Annals of the Disruption,* 2nd edn. (Edinburgh, 1893).

Brundage, A., *The Making of the New Poor Law* (New Brunswick, 1978).

Bryson, G., *Man and Society: The Scottish Enquiry of the Eighteenth Century* (Princeton, NJ, 1945).

Burleigh, J. H. S., *A Church History of Scotland* (London, 1960).

Cage, R. A., 'The Scottish Poor Law, 1745-1845' (Glasgow Univ. Ph.D. Thesis, 1974).

—, and Checkland, E. O. A., 'Thomas Chalmers and Urban Poverty: The St. John's Parish Experiment in Glasgow, 1819-1837', *Philosophical Journal* (Glasgow), xiii (Spring 1976), 37-56.

Cairns, D., 'Thomas Chalmers' Astronomical Discourses: A Study in Natural Theology', *Scottish Journal of Theology,* ix (1956).

Campbell, A. J., *Two Centuries of the Church of Scotland* (Paisley, 1930).

Cant, R. G., *The University of St. Andrews: A Short History* (Edinburgh, 1970).

Canton, W., *History of the British and Foreign Bible Society* (2 vols., London, 1904).

Carlyle, T., *Reminiscences,* ed. C. E. Norton (London, 1972).

Chadwick, O., *The Victorian Church,* Part I (New York, 1966).

Chambers, D., 'The Church of Scotland's Parochial Extension Scheme and the Scottish Disruption', *Journal of Church and State* (Waco, Texas), xvi (1974), 263-86.

Checkland, O., *Philanthropy in Victorian Scotland* (Edinburgh, 1980).

Checkland, S. G., *The Gladstones: A Family Biography 1764-1851* (Cambridge, 1971).

Cheyne, A. C., 'The Westminster Standards: "A Century of Reappraisal"', *SCHS,* xiv (1962), 199-214.

Chitnis, A. C.,: *The Scottish Enlightenment: A Social History* (London, 1976).

Clark, I. D. L., 'The Leslie Controversy, 1805', *SCHS,* xiv (1962), 179-97.

—, 'Moderatism and Moderate Party in the Church of Scotland, 1752-1805' (Cambridge Univ. Ph.D. Thesis, 1963).

Clive, J., *Scotch Reviewers: The Edinburgh Review 1802-1815* (London, 1957).

Coats, A. W., ed., *Poverty in the Victorian Age,* iv, *Scottish Poor Laws 1815-1870* (Westmead, 1973).

Cowan, R. M. W., *The Newspaper in Scotland: A Study of its First Expansion, 1815-1860* (Glasgow, 1946).

Craig, D., *Scottish Literature and the Scottish People 1680-1830* (London, 1961).

Craik, H., *A Century of Scottish History* (2 vols., Edinburgh, 1901).

Craven, J. W., 'Andrew Thomson (1779-1831): Leader of the Evangelical Revival in Scotland' (Edinburgh Univ. Ph.D. Thesis, 1955).

Currie, R., Gilbert, A., and Horsley, L., *Churches and Churchgoers, Patterns of Church Growth in the British Isles since 1700* (Oxford, 1977).

Davie, G. E., *The Democratic Intellect: Scotland and her Universities in the Nineteenth Century* (Edinburgh, 1961).

de Schweinitz, K., *England's Road to Social Security* (Philadelphia, 1943).

Devine, T. M., 'An eighteenth-century business élite: Glasgow-West India merchants, c. 1750-1815', *SHR,* lvii (April 1978), 40-67.

Driver, C., *Tory Radical: The Life of Richard Oastler* (New York, 1946).

Drummond, A. L., *Edward Irving and his Circle* (London, 1934).

—, *The Kirk and the Continent* (Edinburgh, 1956).

—, and Bulloch, J. *The Church in Late Victorian Scotland, 1874-1900* (Edinburgh, 1978).

—— *The Church in Victorian Scotland, 1843-1874* (Edinburgh, 1975).

—— *The Scottish Church 1688-1843: The Age of the Moderates* (Edinburgh, 1973).

Elliott-Binns, L. E., *The Early Evangelicals* (London, 1953).

Engels, F., *The Condition of the Working Class in England,* trans. and ed., W. O. Henderson and W. H. Chaloner (New York, 1958).

Enright, W. G., 'Preaching and Theology in Scotland in the Nineteenth Century' (Edinburgh Univ. Ph.D. Thesis, 1968).

—, 'Urbanization and the Evangelical Pulpit in Nineteenth-Century Scotland', *Church History,* xlvii (December 1978), 400-7.

Erickson, A. B., 'The Non-Intrusion Controversy in Scotland 1832-43', *Church History,* ii (December 1942).

Escott, H., *A History of Scottish Congregationalism* (Glasgow, 1960).

Eyre-Todd, G., *History of Glasgow from the Revolution to the Passing of the Reform Acts 1832-33* (Glasgow, 1934).

Fawcett, A., *The Cambuslang Revival: The Scottish Evangelical Revival of the Eighteenth Century* (London, 1971).

Fay, C. R., *Adam Smith and the Scotland of his Day* (Cambridge, 1956).

Ferguson, T., *The Dawn of Scottish Social Welfare* (London, 1948).

Ferguson, W., 'Dingwall Burgh Politics and the Parliamentary Franchise in the Eighteenth Century', *SHR,* xxxviii (October 1959), 89-108.

—, 'The Reform Act (Scotland) of 1832: Intention and Effect', *SHR,* xlv (1966), 105-14.

—, *Scotland: 1689 to the Present* (New York, 1968).

Finer, S. E., *Life and Times of Sir Edwin Chadwick* (London, 1952).

Finlayson, D., 'Aspects of the Life and Influence of Thomas Erskine of Linlathen, 1788-1870', *SCHS,* xx. 1 (1978), 31-45.

Fleming, J. R., *History of the Church in Scotland 1843-74* (Edinburgh, 1927).

Fraser, D., ed., *The New Poor Law in the Nineteenth Century* (London, 1976).

Furber, H., *Henry Dundas, First Viscount Melville* (London, 1931).

Gerrish, B. A., *Tradition and the Modern World: Reformed Theology in the Nineteenth Century* (Chicago, 1978).

Gilbert, A. D., *Religion and Society in Industrial England* (London, 1976).

Goodwin, G., *Social Science and Utopia: Nineteenth-Century Models of Social Harmony* (Atlantic Highlands, NJ, 1978).

Gourlay, G., *Anstruther* (Anstruther, 1888).

Graham, H. G., *The Social Life of Scotland in the Eighteenth Century,* 3rd edn. (Edinburgh, 1901).

Grave, S. A., *The Scottish Philosophy of Common Sense* (Oxford, 1960).

Gray, W. F., 'Chalmers and Gladstone: An unrecorded episode', *SCHS,* x (1948), 9-17.

Hamilton, H., *The Industrial Revolution in Scotland* (Oxford, 1932).

Harrison, J. F. C., *Robert Owen and the Owenites in Britain and America* (London, 1969).

Henderson, C. R., 'A Half Century After Thomas Chalmers', *American Journal of Theology,* iv. (1900), 49-63.

Henderson, G. D., *The Burning Bush: Studies in Scottish Church History* (Edinburgh, 1957).

—, *Heritage: A Study of the Disruption* (Edinburgh, 1943).

—, *The Scottish Ruling Elder* (London, 1935).

Holl, K., 'Thomas Chalmers und die Anfange der kirklich-sozialen Bewegung', *Gesammelte Aufsatze zur Kirchengeschichte* (3 vols., Tubingen, 1928), iii. 404-36.

Horn, D. B., *A Short History of the University of Edinburgh* (Edinburgh, 1967).

Huie, W. P., 'The Theology of Thomas Chalmers' (Edinburgh Univ. Ph.D. thesis, 1949).

[Jolly, J.], *Memorials of the Rev. William Tasker* (Edinburgh, 1880).

[—], *The Story of the West Port Church* (Edinburgh, 1882).

Keir, D., *The House of Collins* (London, 1952).

Kerr, J., *Scottish Education: School and University* (Cambridge, 1910).

Kitson Clark, G., *Churchmen and the Condition of England 1832-1885* (London, 1973).

Laqueur, T. W., *Religion and Respectability: Sunday Schools and Working-Class Culture 1780-1850* (New Haven, Conn., 1976).

Laski, H. J., *Studies in the Problem of Sovereignty* (New York, 1968).

Leishman, J. F., *Matthew Leishman of Govan and the Middle Party of 1843* (Paisley, 1921).

Lovat-Fraser, J. A., *Henry Dundas, Viscount Melville* (Cambridge, 1916).

Lyall, F., *Of Presbyters and Kings: Church and State in the Law of Scotland* (Aberdeen, 1980).

Machin, G. I. T., 'The Disruption and British Politics, 1834-43', *SHR,* li (April 1972), 20-52.

—, *Politics and the Churches in Great Britain, 1832-1868* (Oxford, 1977).

MacInnes, J., *The Evangelical Movement in the Highlands of Scotland, 1688-1800* (Aberdeen, 1951).

Maciver, I. F. 'The Evangelical Party and the Eldership in the General Assemblies, 1820-1843', *SCHS,* xx. 1 (1978), 1-13.

—, 'The General Assembly of the Church, the State, and Society in Scotland: Some Aspects of their Relationships, 1815-1843' (Edinburgh Univ., M.Litt. Thesis, 1976).

MacKay, A. J. G., *History of Fife and Kinross* (Edinburgh, 1896).

MacLaren, A. A., *Religion and Social Class: The Disruption Years in Aberdeen* (London, 1974).

—, ed., *Social Class in Scotland: Past and Present* (Edinburgh, 1976).

Marwick, W. H., *Economic Developments in Victorian Scotland* (London, 1936).

Masterman, N., *Chalmers on Charity* (London, 1900).

Mathieson, W. L., *The Awakening of Scotland 1747-1843* (Glasgow, 1916).

—, *Church and Reform in Scotland 1797-1843* (Glasgow, 1916).

Mechie, S., *The Church and Scottish Social Development 1780-1870* (Oxford, 1960).

Meikle, H. W., *Scotland and the French Revolution* (Glasgow, 1912).

Miller, K., *Cockburn's Millennium* (London, 1975).

Mitchison, R., 'The Making of the Old Scottish Poor Law', *Past and Present,* no. 63 (May 1974), 58-93.

Moncrieff, H. W., *The Free Church Principle* (Edinburgh, 1884).

Montgomery, A. B., 'The Voluntary Controversy in the Church of Scotland, 1829-1843' (Edinburgh Univ. Ph.D. Thesis, 1953).

Morley, J., *Life of William Ewart Gladstone* (3 vols., New York, 1903).

Morrell, H. B., 'The Leslie Affair: careers, kirk and politics in Edinburgh in 1805', *SHR,* liv (April 1975), 63-82.

Muirhead, I. A., 'Catholic Emancipation in Scotland: The Debate and the Aftermath', *Innes Review,* xxiv. 2 (1973), 103-20.

—, 'Catholic Emancipation: Scottish Reactions in 1829', *Innes Review,* xxiv. 1 (1972), 26-42.

Namier, L. and Brooke, J., *The History of Parliament: The House of Commons 1754-1790* (London, 1964).

Nicolson, A., *Memoirs of Adam Black* (Edinburgh, 1885).

Nisbet, J. W., 'Thomas Chalmers and the Economic Order', *Scottish Journal of Political Economy,* xi (June 1964), 151-7.

Oliphant, M., *Thomas Chalmers* (London, 1893).

Omond, G. W. T., *The Lord Advocates of Scotland* (2 vols., Edinburgh, 1883).

Owen, D., *English Philanthropy 1660-1960* (Cambridge, Mass., 1965).

Parker, C. S., *Life and Letters of Sir James Graham* (2 vols., (London, 1907).

Perkin, H., *The Origins of Modern English Society 1780-1880* (London, 1969).

Pfleiderer, O., *The Development of Theology in Germany since Kant, and its Progress in Great Britain since 1825,* trans. J. F. Smith (London, 1890).

Phillipson, N. T. and Mitchison, R., eds., *Scotland in the Age of Improvement* (Edinburgh, 1970).

Pollard, S. and Salt, J., ed., *Robert Owen: Prophet of the Poor* (London, 1971).

Poynter, J. R., *Society and Pauperism: English Ideas on Poor Relief, 1795-1834* (London, 1969).

Pryde, G. S., *Scotland from 1603 to the Present Day* (London, 1962).

Rice, D. F., 'An Attempt at Systematic Reconstruction in the Theology of Thomas Chalmers', *Church History,* xlviii. 2 (June 1979), 174-88.

—, 'Natural Theology and the Scottish Philosophy in the Thought of Thomas Chalmers', *Scottish Journal of Theology,* xxiv (1971), 23-46.

—, 'The Theology of Thomas Chalmers' (Drew Univ., Ph.D. Thesis, 1966).

Richmond, M. E., *Social Diagnosis* (New York, 1917).

Roach, W. M., 'Alexander Richmond and the Radical Reform Movements in Glasgow in 1816-17', *SHR*, li. 1 (April 1972), 1-19.

—, 'Radical Reform Movements in Scotland, 1815-1822' (Glasgow Univ., Ph.D. Thesis, 1971).

Roberts, D., *Paternalism in Early Victorian England* (New Brunswick, 1979).

—, *Victorian Origins of the British Welfare State* (New Haven, Conn. 1960).

Saunders, L. J., *Scottish Democracy 1815-1840* (Edinburgh, 1950).

Scotland, J., *The History of Scottish Education* (2 vols., London, 1969).

Scott, H., *Fasti Ecclesiae Scoticanae: The Succession of Ministers in the Church of Scotland from the Reformation,* 2nd edn. (8 vols., Edinburgh, 1915).

Sefton, H. R., 'The Early Development of Moderatism in the Church of Scotland' (Glasgow Univ., Ph.D. thesis, 1962).

Shaw, D., 'The Moderatorship Controversy in 1836 and 1837', *SCHS,* xvii (1972), 115-30.

Shepperson, G., 'Thomas Chalmers, the Free Church of Scotland, and the South', *Journal of Southern History,* xvii (1951), 517-37.

Sher, R. B., 'Church, University and Enlightenment: The Moderate Literati of Edinburgh, 1720-1793' (Univ. of Chicago Ph.D. Thesis, 1979).

Small, R., *History of the Congregations of the United Presbyterian Church from 1733-1900* (2 vols., Edinburgh, 1904).

Smith, D. C., 'The Failure and Recovery of Social Criticism in the Scottish Church 1830-1950' (Edinburgh Univ. Ph.D. Thesis, 1964).

Smith, T., *Memoirs of James Begg* (2 vols., Edinburgh, 1885).

Smout, T. C., *A History of the Scottish People 1560-1830* (Glasgow, 1969).

Stevenson, G. H., 'Church and State in England and Scotland', *Theology,* xlvi (1943), 122-7, 150-5.

Tulloch, J., *Movements of Religious Thought in Britain During the Nineteenth Century* (London, 1885).

Walker, N. L., *Chapters from the History of the Free Church of Scotland* (Edinburgh, 1895).

—, *Thomas Chalmers* (London, 1880).

Ward, J. T., 'The Factory Reform Movement in Scotland', *SHR,* xli (October 1962), 100-24.

Watt, H., *New College, Edinburgh: A Centenary History* (Edinburgh, 1946).

—, *Thomas Chalmers and the Disruption* (Edinburgh, 1943).

Whetstone, A. E., 'Scottish County Government in the Eighteenth and Nineteenth Centuries' (Univ. of Minnesota Ph. D. Thesis, 1973).

White, G., '"Highly Preposterous": Origins of Scottish Missions', *SCHS,* xix (1976), 111-24.

Williams, J. C., 'Edinburgh Politics, 1832-1852' (Edinburgh Univ. Ph. D. Thesis, 1972).

Wilson, A., *The Chartist Movement in Scotland* (Manchester, 1970).

Wilson, W. and Rainy, R., *Memorials of Robert Smith Candlish* (Edinburgh, 1880).

Withrington, D., 'Non-Church-Going, c. 1750- c. 1850: A Preliminary Study', *SCHS,* xvii (1972), 99-113.

Wood, W., *The East Neuk of Fife,* 2nd edn. (Edinburgh, 1887).

Wright, L. C., *Scottish Chartism* (Edinburgh, 1953).

Wylie, J. A., *Disruption Worthies* (Edinburgh, 1881).

Young, A. F. and Ashton, E. T., *British Social Work in the Nineteenth Century* (London, 1956).

INDEX

WITHDRAWN
from
STIRLING UNIVERSITY LIBRARY